JEWS
on
TRIAL

JEWS
on
TRIAL

Judges, Juries, Prosecutors
and Defendants from the
Era of Jesus to Our Own Time

Ori Z. Soltes

Bartleby Press
Washington • Baltimore

ESHEL BOOKS
an imprint of Bartleby Press
P.O. Box 858
Savage, MD 20763
1-800-953-9929
www.eshelbooks.com

Library of Congress Cataloging-in-Publication Data

Soltes, Ori Z.
   Jews on trial : judges, juries, prosecutors and defendants from the era of Jesus to our own time / Ori Z. Soltes.
      pages cm
   Includes bibliographical references and index.
   ISBN 978-0-935437-43-0 (alk. paper)
   1. Jews--Legal status, laws, etc.--History. I. Title.
   K3242.S66 2013
   345'.07089924--dc23

                                                              2013009611

Printed in the United States of America

For Mark A. Smith:
Lawyer, scholar, but mostly, friend:
Mississippi will always burn for that microphone.

And in Loving Memory of William Levy
Consummate Federal Judge,
Inevitably Generous and non-Judgmental

Contents

Acknowledgements

This book grew out of a course that I taught several times, albeit many years ago, at the then-Cleveland College of Jewish Studies (now Siegel College) in Cleveland, Ohio. It gives me pleasure to acknowledge the suggestion and support for such a course on the part of David S. Ariel, at that time the President of the College. He started me thinking along these lines. But my thoughts on the subject were enormously aided by the excellent students who challenged, questioned, suggested and added to whatever I brought to the table of discussion. The College has always been blessed with hard-hitting, quick-thinking and deeply committed, focused students, and I was one of the beneficiaries of that blessing many times over.

I would also like to thank my former Georgetown University student, Caitlin Montgomery, who generously put her time and her sharp mind to a careful read of this manuscript, smoothing awkward edges that might otherwise have gotten by. On the other hand, this book would not have seen the light of day without the confidence and financial support offered by several generous friends: in particular Lloyd Raport, and also Beth Green Pierce, Fay and Sheldon Cohen, Ryna Cohen and Molly Witow. Finally, for a third time, my intrepid publisher and editor, Jeremy Kay, has been a friend and adviser beyond the call of duty. Thanks.

I have dedicated this book to two outstanding individuals

whose unflagging support and ongoing interest in my often idiosyncratic intellectual endeavors has made the process of thinking about this book's subject more challenging and the writing of it more interesting: Mark A. Smith, my wise and astute friend, who always offers invaluable comments—whether on this manuscript or other issues; and Judge William Levy, who always challenged me, but no time more intensely (and lovingly) than when I presumed to put legalistic lenses into my historian spectacles. *Vita nimium brevis sed amicitia aeterna.*

Preface:
History, Religion and Myth

History is a bridge between "was" and "is." As a kind of entertainment, it encompasses ideas and events that cause its audience to experience their impact as if those ideas and events were evolving now. As a form of instruction, its reshaping of the past as if it were present seeks to reinvoke the positive and teach us to excise the sort of thoughts and actions that produced the negative, for both the present and the future. We want to learn from history, to repeat its triumphs and not its mistakes.

Of course, one might say that there is no such thing as "history," if by that word we mean a progression of ideas and particularly events that share a clear causal relationship with each other. Those who purport to write history are really writing historiography: they are writing about events and ideas that they did not and could not have witnessed in an absolutely objective manner, and offer us, rather, their reconstructions and interpretations of them

When the late fifth-early fourth century BCE Greek historian Thucydides wrote about the Peloponnesian Wars, he admitted that he did not witness every event he describes and did not hear every speech he reports—that, in fact, he sometimes put in his speakers' mouths the words he imagined they would have spoken under the circumstances that he describes.[1] Did the renowned "Funeral Oration" quoted by Thucydides and supposedly delivered by Pericles in the aftermath of the first year of the war offer anything like the perfectly crafted words that the historiographer reports—in a style remarkably like Thucydides' own?

There is considerable irony here. Thucydides is one of the first historiographers to present his narrative as unequivocally factual, and to contrast his writing, as such, with what he saw as non-factual writing by prior historians. The term *historia* with which he would label his work, and what he calls its precision (the Greek word that he uses is *akribeia*) is offered in contrast to what he thinks of as *mythos*. This Greek word, from which our English word, "myth," is derived, had once referred to the kind of narrative that one finds, for example, in Hesiod's *Theogony*. That work, offering an account of the birth of the gods and of the world that they in turn shaped, must be—and this is what *mythos* meant in Hesiod's time (the 8th-7th century BCE)—a gods'-truth account. For Hesiod could only know how the gods were born if they themselves provided him with the information. He obviously wan't present at the event—and he cannot have made it up; the gods would surely punish such hubris.

By Thucydides' era, however, *mythos* was coming to refer to legend-bound, factually suspect accounts and *historia* to factual accounts. But what, then, of speeches or events that Thucydides didn't actually witness himself? Can he guarantee their facticity? And what, even, of the events we might suppose Thucydides actually witnessed—this or that battle, for example? Can we really believe that what he describes took place precisely as he describes it, as if he had been standing, god-like, above the fray, a witness in an objective manner to events on both sides of the battle lines? Could he have seen what was transpiring and what he then reports with such dispassionate calm, as he fought for his life in the heat of the moment? However competent his reconstruction of words and events afterwards, what he presents is historiography—interpretive writing about history, not history itself as some absolute. It is no surprise that classicists have been debating aspects of the war presented in that Thucydidean report for generations.

We can recognize the same sort of problem in more recent historical watersheds. Who was at the Battle of Hastings in 1066 and if so, in a position to know exactly what happened, to record the totality of circumstances surrounding the battle and its consequences? Who knows with absolute certainty, a mere four decades after the event, what exactly happened on that November afternoon in Dallas in 1963—and who exactly was responsible for the death of John F. Kennedy? There is a good deal of historiography about the subject, but no history, if by that term we mean a certainty about events and their causes and effects.[2]

History is a bit like revelation in religion in this regard. Religion is based on the belief that divinity reveals itself to and through certain individuals; through them we learn what it is that the Power that we believe created us—and therefore also believe has the power to destroy us—wishes us to think, say, do, be. But those to whom that information is revealed are soon gone and at the moment of their deaths their words become subject to our interpretation of them—even the issue of what words they spoke can be a matter of contending memory and interpretation.

If Ezra the Scribe redacted the Torah into the form in which we now have it only in 444 BCE; if the Torah became the central part of a canon of God's words to Jews, the Hebrew Bible, organized by Jewish leadership not until 140 CE; then neither Ezra the redactor nor the biblical canonizers six centuries after him were there when Moses came down from Sinai or Jeremiah spoke out in frustration before the gates of the Temple in Jerusalem. The decision as to which words would be included as divinely inspired—and which excluded—was made according to an interpretation that separated Judaism from, say, nascent Christianity, whose leadership asserted that words excluded by Judaism should be included. But the heart of those words, the Gospels, would be embraced along four parallel but not identical lines, written down (redacted) not until between 70 and 110 CE (in other words, several generations after the events they describe and the words they report); and the New Testament as a whole would move toward preliminary canonization until around 180 CE—its final, absolute canon not approved until the late fourth century.[3]

Moreover, writings regarded as divinely-inspired at that point by Christians but not by Jews, and today still regarded as revelationary by Catholics and Orthodox Christians, came to be thought of as non-Biblical by Protestant denominations in the sixteenth century. These books are called Apocrypha—the adjectival form of which, with a small "a" ("apocryphal") consequentially entered everyday English to refer to any story that some might believe but others recognize as historically false. Of course, long before then—by the seventh century—Islam had arrived on the scene and come to view all of these texts as having had a divinely revealed beginning, but as having become corrupt over time. For Muslims, the Qur'an is the final and only reliable revealed text—but its words were put into the form in which we have them a generation after the death of Muhammad, the prophet though whom they were revealed. The gap between certainty and relativity with respect to his words is filled by Hadith, a body of words spoken by or about Muhammad, as opposed to those spoken by God through Muhammad in the Qur'an.

It turns out, then, that history, religion and myth are much more interwoven with each other than our everyday use of these terms might suggest. Just as the Greeks began, at least by the fifth and fourth centuries BCE, to distinguish *historia* from *mythos*, so over the course of time, particularly as the polytheistic belief systems and their texts to which ancient peoples like the Greeks—and the Egyptians and Mesopotamians and Canaanites and Romans—adhered, came gradually to be supplanted by divergent forms of monotheism, devotees of the one form of belief began to refer to their own system as religion and to other systems as myth. Genesis is religion, a God's-Truth account of how the world came into being; Hesiod's Theogony is myth, a fanciful account of that process—as are the Mesopotamian Enuma Elish and the Mayan Popul Vuh as well as cosmogonic narratives found in the Eddas and the Rig Veda.

The narratives of the religion in which we believe are validated by us with the label "factual" or at least "allegorical," while the narratives of belief systems to which we don't adhere—which we thus term "mythology" or "superstition" or "cult"—are reduced by us to a lesser status by referring to those narratives as "mythological." The entire enterprise of wrestling with both divinity and the progressive development of humanity derives from what we believe as a starting point. And what we believe we call factual (history) or revealed (religion), although it is subject to a far greater process of interpretation than we may realize. For we have become accustomed to accepting as Truth the accounts we drank in with our mothers' milk and from our first teachers, before we reached an age when we might think and analyze.

The pages that follow may be seen ultimately to weave together aspects of history and religion which are both, in turn, interwoven with aspects of myth. The narrative follows a complex of instances, both geographically and chronologically diverse, that focus on a particular nexus of threads within the tapestry of religion, history and myth: the story of the Jews, mainly but not exclusively in relationship to Christianity. The particular thread within that nexus, woven through Western and Middle Eastern contexts, is that of legal—or what we might better call "quasi-legal"—proceedings. The phrase "Jewish Trials" offers a double definitional issue that crisscrosses the history/religion/myth matrix. Firstly, because the history of Judaism—its roots; its foundations—pre-dates the time when the words "Jew," "Jewish," and "Judaism" are in use in a manner that we would recognize. Secondly, because the history of legal consciousness and legal development predates the time when "legal trial" would be used in anything like our sense of that phrase. Thus from the outset we need clarification as we set out to interweave "Jewish" and "trials" into a coherent pattern.

Geographically, our focus moves from the Middle East to Western and Eastern Europe to America and back to the Middle East; from the Sinai Desert to Ancient Israel and Judah to the Diaspora to Modern Israel. Chronologically, we follow from Moses' day to the time of Jesus to the era of Torquemada to the time of Dreyfus to Eichmann's day to that of John Demjanjuk and Jonathan Pollard—which is our own time. Strictly speaking, the terminology centered around the term "Jewish" slips only gradually into place. For the issue shifts, from Israelite to Judaean law and justice in theory and action; from a Judaean (Jesus) tried by Pagan authorities—but more commonly and popularly pictured as a Christian tried, somehow, by Jews, or even as a Jew tried and executed by Jews—to the issue of Jews repeatedly accused of echoing or re-enacting that "Crime" (Blood Libel).

The narrative continues to the matter of Christians tried by Christians for "Judaizing"—but often mistakenly thought of in everyday thought as Jews tried by Christians (Inquisition)—to Jews tried in a world which had come to think of itself as secular (where one's religion would not therefore be a factor in determining one's fate, yet may well have been) for crimes of "treason" against the secular state (Dreyfus, Rosenberg). We follow to an account of a self-denying Christian (Eichmann) tried by a Jewish court for crimes against humanity and a practicing Christian denying that he is the one accused of such crimes (Demjanjuk) to a Jew found guilty of divulging the military secrets of his secular homeland to colleagues in his second, spiritual homeland (Pollard).

The word "trial" is used in a double sense. It refers to legal proceedings—the particular ones which are the focus points of the narrative. But it is also used, as becomes increasingly clear over the course of the discussion, in a broader sense, to refer to the Jewish condition in history. This is a story of the trials of the Jews as a minority of islands in diverse—primarily, in our narrative, Christian—seas, as those trials are observable from the varied angles of certain renowned legal and quasi-legal or imagined legal proceedings between antiquity and the present day.

Introduction:
What are "Jewish Trials"?

I. From Abraham the Hebrew to the Late Judaean Period

Let us begin by asking what is meant in these far-flung contexts by "Jewish"? Historically, Abraham in the Bible is referred to (by himself as well as by others) as a *Hebrew*—a term which Biblical scholars have recognized as socio-economic rather than ethnic—and so, too, his son Isaac and his grandson Jacob.[4] It is after Jacob's famous wrestling match (in Genesis 32) that he is called *Israel*—*Yisra-El*: "[one who] has wrestled/striven with God." And so his offspring are called Children of Israel. These enter Egypt, and it is their descendants, grouped into twelve tribes, also called Children of Israel, or simply *Israelites*, who are led forth from Egypt by Moses (ca 1400-1300 BCE). A tribal confederacy, variously led by Joshua and his successors, finally cemented together into a kingdom by Saul, David and Solomon in turn (ca 1050-925 BCE), splits up after Solomon's death.

The northern half of the kingdom, residence of ten of the twelve tribal groupings (a continued sense of tribal identity competing with the sense of national identity was one of the factors that enabled the united kingdom so easily to unravel) was now called "Israel", while the southern half was call "Judah" (after the dominant tribe resident in the south).[5] In 722-21 BCE, Israel (in other words, the northern kingdom) was overrun by Assyria; Samaria, its capital,

was sacked; its inhabitants were carried into exile. Due to a combination of circumstances, the ten northern tribes (aka the Israelites)
melted into the fabric of the Assyrian Empire. The circumstances are
easy to understand: on the one hand, already weakened attachment
to their faith—because of two centuries of hostile relations between
north and south and thus for northerners the relative inaccessibility
of Jerusalem and the Temple which Solomon had built back in the
10th century. On the other hand, the Assyrians put into play their
standard technique of breaking up the families and communities
of conquered peoples, in order to minimize the likelihood of revolt.
This break-up also eliminated the primary means of transmitting
a system of spiritual beliefs—the family and the community, with
their mothers and fathers and teachers—particularly when, in the
case of the Israelites, those beliefs stood out as different from those
of all the other peoples around. The ten northern tribes were never
heard of or from again as an identifiable ethnic or religious group.
They were lost to history and are thus referred to as the "Lost Ten
Tribes."[6]

It was only the southern realm, Judah, comprised of the large
tribe of Judah and the tiny tribe of Benjamin, which remained intact,
barely escaping the grasp of Assyria.[7] But Assyria itself succumbed
to the nascent power of Babylonia by 614-12. And Judah was in
its turn swallowed by the Babylonians, its capital at Jerusalem engulfed, its glorious Temple ravaged and the cream of its population
carried off into exile, in 586 BCE. From this time forth, the adherents
to the Covenant of Abraham and Moses with God, the bearers of the
historical tradition of the Davidic monarchy and the Israelite prophets, were called Judaeans.

But the Judaean community in Babylonia broke historical precedent: unlike the peoples around them who, in the face of defeat,
invariably abandoned their gods or synthesized them to those of
their conquerors, the Judaeans maintained their loyalty to the belief
system and sense of historical destiny of their ancestors. Thus, when
Babylon fell before the newly-honed might of Cyrus the Great of
Achaemenid Medo-Persia in 538, and the conqueror offered to the
Judaeans the opportunity to return to Jerusalem and rebuild their

Temple (constituting Judah as a subprovince[8] within his sprawling empire) a large number of them accepted the offer. By the year 515, the Temple had been rebuilt and the world possessed two major Judaean communities: one centered in Jerusalem, the other in Babylon. Two centuries later the Persian subprovince of Judah became a subprovince in the empire of the Macedonian Greek conqueror, Alexander the Great, after Alexander defeated the last Achaemenid Persian Shah, Dareius III, in key battles at Issus and Gaugemala.

At Alexander's death in 323 BCE, there was a generation-long scramble among his generals and colleagues and putative wives and progeny to assume power over all that Alexander's charisma had held together for a brief historical moment. By about 300 BCE the Empire had been carved into large chunks. For our purposes, the most important were that controlled from Alexander, Egypt, by the dynasty established by Alexander's friend and general, Ptolemy; and that which would come to be ruled from Antioch, Syria, by the dynasty established by another of Alexander's generals, Seleucis. Two mega-kingdoms, then, with Judah situated between them. At times, in the continual struggles between these two Hellenistic polities for dominance in the region, Judah was directly within the sphere of control of the Seleucids, at times within the ambit of the Ptolemies.[9]

In this polyglot, polyfaith world, the Judaean religious system was accepted as one among many. But what the Pagan faiths shared in common—a multiplicity of deities, addressable in different guises by different names, worshipped in sculpted and painted forms, visible and tangible—Judaeanism could not: it offered an uncompromisingly singular, invisible, intangible deity with its very Name ineffable in ordinary speech.[10] Among the Middle Eastern traditions absorbed by Alexander's successors, slowly asserting themselves with greater and greater emphasis, was that which included placing the ruler—initially, after earthly death, and later while still alive—among the divinities worshipped by their peoples. To this, too, Judaeanism could not, of course, adhere: to make a god of a man was anathema to Judaean religious doctrine.

So it was that by around the year 170 BCE, a problem arose:

Antiochus IV, ruler of the Seleucid domains who was regarded as a divinity in the eyes—or at least according to the lip service—of his pagan constituents, suggested that the Judaeans under his governance worship him. They were free to continue worship of their own God—but at least they should place his (Antiochus') image in their Temple, next to that of their God. It would have been inconceivable to Antiochus that they had no image of their God in their Temple: a god without a physical presence would be no god at all. Request in any case became demand; demand evolved into attempted imposition; attempted imposition engendered the response of insurrection. The struggle for complete religious autonomy, led by the (priestly) Hasmonean house of Mattathias and his sons, grew almost organically into a struggle for political independence. By the time of the death of Simon, last of the five "Maccabee" brothers, in 136 BCE, Judaea was, for all intents and purposes, an independent state.[11]

II. From the Hasmoneans to Herod to Rome; from Judaeans to Jews and Christians

By this time, the axis of Western and Middle Eastern political centrality—which, in the previous thousand years had shifted from Assyria to Babylonia to Persia to Macedonia and then broken into a handful of dominant locales from Ptolemaic Egypt and Seleucid Syria to the renascent Parthian (aka Arsacid) Persian power—had slipped further to the west: by the period focused, for us, around Simon Maccabee's death, Rome had swallowed Italy, razed North African Carthage (thereby engulfing the entire western Mediterranean), defeated Phillip V of Macedon at Corinth and encompassed Greece—and begun to reach hungrily eastward. The Seleucid Empire would succumb to Rome by about 65 BCE, and the last of the Ptolemies—Cleopatra VII—would ultimately yield both any remaining semblance of Egyptian autonomy and her life to Rome by 31 BCE.[12]

In the century or so between Simon's death and that of Cleopatra, Judaea would evolve from commonwealth to kingdom. The Hasmonean line would change from an elective to a hereditary leadership dynasty, would absorb the High Priesthood of the Temple into its control, spill blood within its house and within its kingdom in diverse struggles for personal and political power—until the last Hasmonean, the princess Mariamne, would be pulled by marriage into the blood-soaked arms of Herod. Herod's father, Antipater, a king of Idumaea (a people south of Judaea), was active in manipulating forces in the power struggles between the Hasmonean brothers Antigonus II and Hyrcanus II (ca 45 BCE).[13]

It would be left to Herod to covet the power, not behind the Hasmonean throne of Judaea, but of that throne itself. Friend of Julius Caesar, Marc Antony and Octavian-become-Augustus Caesar in turn, he would receive Roman political approval, and his own military and dynastic-murder skills (as opposed to dynastic-marriage skills, beyond Mariamne, second of his ten or more wives) would help earn him that throne by 37 BCE.[14] Initially, in order to legitimize himself in the eyes of the Judaeans he would force marriage on Mariamne. In order to seek the favor of those Judaean constituents who worshipped the God of Israel, he would glorify (not rebuild, as is often mistakenly assumed, but significantly refurbish) the Temple in Jerusalem and significantly expand the platform on which that structure stood: the Temple Mount. To appease the pagans under his rule (and Roman support for Herod had expanded the Judaea of his kingship beyond its earlier more modest bounds to encompass pagan populations), he would build temples and theatres at pagan centers such as the coastal town of Straton's Tower. This last he expanded, aggrandized with a magnificent harbor and renamed for his Roman patron: Caesarea.

In order to assure himself of a refuge from both Israelite-Judaean and pagan constituents, he would build up and beautify (it might as well be an attractive and comfortable refuge) a palace complex at Massada. In order to forestall the attempts on his life that he increasingly feared, he would gradually murder nearly every member of his immediate family—including Mariamne. Indeed, as Herod's paranoia increased, his taste and reputation for blood grew. The chaos that followed his long-hoped-for death in 4 BCE (apparently of a severe stomach ailment[15]) proved critical for Judaea's independence: there was no longer a personage on the Judaean throne respected by Rome. The result was the loss of what autonomy Judaea had possessed: she retained, in name, a degree of self-rule, but more and more that self-rule was undercut by the presence of the Roman governor—the proper term is "procurator"—to whom Judaean leaders ultimately answered, and who, in turn, answered to the Syrian governor, who answered to the Senate and Emperor in Rome.

Rome, the quintessential polytheistic culture, was inclined to be tolerant of the religion of Judaea. Indeed, when earlier Judea had still remained technically independent of her, Rome had accorded *religio licita* status to Judaeanism, under the sympathetic sponsorship of Pompey, Julius Caesar, Marc Antony and Octavian/Augustus in turn. Such status meant that the Judaean religion was accepted by the state; Judaean religious beliefs and customs and Judaean places of worship were not only respected, but protected if necessary throughout the growing Empire.[16] This became more significant with the passing of Herod and Judaean semi-independence: the entirety of Judaea and its capital in Jerusalem were under Roman protection. Even the annual contributions sent to the Temple in Jerusalem for its upkeep, by Judaeans living in Rome and elsewhere, were conveyed under the protection of the legions: to attempt to pilfer such sacred funds was punishable by death.[17] The antithesis of *religio licita* status was that of *superstitio*—at best an unrecognized, unrespected and unprotected belief system (a superstition, in our terms); at worst, a belief system regarded as sinister and politically subversive, illegal and with adherence to it punishable by death.

The legitimacy—the *legality*—of the Judaean *religion* in Roman eyes is an issue separate from that of Judaean *political* aspirations. Roman legions might protect the annual Temple contributions, but they also supported the ordinances and judgments set forth by the procurators. And if, as, for example, in the case of a certain individual named Pontius Pilate, the procurator was oppressive or cruel, Rome was experienced by the populace as an iron heel. Under Augustus, (i.e., until 14 CE), a procurator might well be possessed of a heavy hand, but he served for only three years, so an oppressed people would at least know that the suffering would be relatively short-term. Under Tiberius (14-37 CE) and his successors, however, since a procurator could serve for life (unless he was recalled for reasons of well-demonstrated malfeasance of one sort or another), should his inclinations be to squeeze a province, there would be little hope of relief for its inhabitants.

If one joins this reality to the larger one—that no matter how generous the particular procurator, the basic political fact of post-Herodian Judaea (after Herod himself had provided over thirty years of mercilessly oppressive rule) was subservience to Rome and her whims, a subservience in both spirit and practical matters that would lodge unhappily in many a Judaean heart—then one can well understand the slow but inexorable motion toward revolt. A rebellious movement that was not *religious* but *political*. A movement itself fragmented—not everybody would be desirous of upsetting the status quo, however uncomfortable in some respects: the consequences of upset might be worse. A movement that begins to swell during the Emperorship of Tiberius, with the change in the procuratorial system—historically coincident with the time of Jesus of Nazareth's life, preaching and death—and which a generation later would burst into a Judaean revolt against Rome, of four (almost five) years' duration, with a further three-year epilogue of siege and struggle at Massada.

The revolt against Rome broke out in Greater Judaea in 65-6 CE; Nero (54-68 CE) was Emperor by then, and Vespasian, his most capable general, was dispatched to quell it. A process that was expected to take a few weeks stretched into months and then years, as first the Galilee in the north and then Lesser Judaea proper in the south were painstakingly subdued.[18] By the time Jerusalem itself was under siege, Nero had been assassinated in Rome by his own bodyguards, and four different generals had vied for and succeeded each other on the Imperial throne in the course of less than a year (69 CE). The fourth, who would remain Emperor until his death from natural causes in 79 CE, was Vespasian; his son Titus undertook the siege of Jerusalem—while within the walls of the sacred city, factions of Judaeans fought among themselves for spiritual as much as political leadership.

It was with tremendous frustration that Titus' troops failed again and again to take the city. When it was finally overwhelmed, its contents were ravaged, its Temple Mount assaulted, the Holy Temple itself burned—in spite, his apologists would assert, of Titus' command to desist:[19] the intensity of frustration would seem to have smashed the cardinal Roman military rule, discipline. Three more years would be required for the Romans to squash the last hold-outs of revolt at Massada.

It is symptomatic of the dichotomy between the religious and political status of Judaea under Roman rule to which I have alluded above, that even during the siege of Jerusalem, annual contributions for the Temple's upkeep continued to be shepherded from Rome's ex-patriate Judaean community to Jerusalem. Judaeans living in various parts of the Roman-ruled world, as adherents to a belief system but uninterested in political independence, remained unmolested, to the best of our knowledge, both in Rome itself and elsewhere. Even the *fiscus judaicus* that emerged shortly after the quelling of the Judaean revolt, one can imagine, derived from Rome's political and economic logic, not its inclination toward religious or spiritual oppression: with no Temple, why would the Judaeans need to contribute to its upkeep? Why not turn that self-imposed tax unto a tax that would both benefit the Roman state and remind the Judaeans and others that rebellion against Roman authority is an impractical enterprise? Even the design of a coin with imagery that commemorates the Roman victory, offering a supine and bent-over female figure as an allegory of Judaea and an inscription, *"Judaea Capta"* —"Judaea captured/defeated" —reflects political, not religious concerns.

Indeed, when in the generation following the revolt, (two generations after the Crucifixion), Judaeanism's schism into spiritual factions—Christianity and Judaism—began to seek greater clarity with regard to what separated them from each other spiritually, it is instructive to recall that Judaism as a religion continued to be treated as a *religio licita* by the Romans, and would be for centuries, whereas early Christianity was regarded as a *superstitio*. This, as we shall later observe, is an important element in understanding the tension between early diasporic Judaism and early Christianity. The competition to establish themselves before the eyes of their Roman political masters as the legitimate heirs to the *religio licita* status of Israel-Judaea—as that status had been granted by Pompey and Caesar—would have ugly consequences for Jewish-Christian relations.

III. *Religio* Status and the Question of Who is a *"Yehoodi"*

The issue of *religio* status before Roman law brings us back to the center of our initial inquiry: what, for the purposes of "Jewish trials" is meant by the word "Jewish"? It also leads us to the other half of that inquiry: what is meant by the word "trials" in our context? In the first case, we have arrived from the terms "Hebrew" and "Israelite" to the term "Judaean." What follows is the pair of terms "Jew/ish" and "Christian." But the adjective "Jewish" and the noun "Jew" share with both the noun and the adjective "Judaean" the fact of being renderings of the Hebrew term *"yehoodi"* and its equivalents in Aramaic (*yehoodae*), Latin (*iudaeus*) and Greek (*ioudaios*)—which four languages are the primary ones operable in the Judaean ambit of the Roman Empire.[20]

"Judaism" and "Jewishness" as those terms are commonly thought of today, have no explicit connotation of political statehood—even the so-called "Jewish state" is called "Israel," not "Jewland" or some similar name, and its citizens are variously associated with the Jewish, Christian, Muslim and other faiths. Judaism has evolved as a religion—a *religio*—in the complex sense of a binding:[21] as a cultural heritage, a linguistic common ground, an almost ethno-familial identity, but above all, as a defined system of spiritual beliefs. Although there is a certain historical fluidity, yielding a series of definitions rather than a monlithic definition of those beliefs, they came to center on an agreed-upon canon of Biblical texts, commentaries, calendrical events and life cycle celebrations and rites of passage—all of which have parallels to but are different from what Christians and Christianity consider to be Biblical texts, commentaries, calendrical events and life cycle celebrations and rites of passage.

The adherents to the system defined as "Jewish" understand

their roots to dig into the Hebrew-Israelite-Judaean past and themselves therefore to be part of a continuum that carries from Abraham to Moses to Jeremiah to Ezra to Hillel the Elder to Rabbi Akiba. The early Christians believed the same of themselves, but saw their spiritual line as following from Abraham to Moses to Jeremiah to Ezra to *John the Baptist, Jesus of Nazareth and the Apostles*. Each group saw the other as having slipped off the main spiritual Hebrew-Israelite-Judaean road onto a path leading toward disaster.[22] To recapitulate: the remnant of the Israelite tribal confederation-become-kingdom, its Judaean leadership carried off into Babylonian exile,[23] clung to the idea of the land at the same time that it necessarily evolved modes of expressing its beliefs—its sense of involvement in the covenantal relationship between Israel and God—away from the land and the sacrificial center in Jerusalem.

They and their descendants called themselves Judaeans—derived both from a sense of association with the tribe of Judah and from an ongoing sense of attachment to the land it had inhabited: Judah (or as it would be called by the Hellenistic period, Judaea).[24] Consider, though: by the time of the Maccabees, adherents to the evolving faith of Abraham, Moses, David and the Israelite Prophets lived not only in Judaea; there were developed communities in Mesopotamia, Egypt, Syria, even in Greece and beyond, in Italian Rome. Neither Hebrew nor Greek, Latin or Aramaic offer what English provides: separate words to distinguish "Judaean" inhabitants of Judaea from what we might term "Jewish" inhabitants of, say, Egypt or Rome.

What makes the English distinction of terms confusing is that it misleads us to imagine that the features that we associate with Judaism to which I referred two paragraphs earlier are already in place in, say, 100 BCE, whereas they are not even fully in place by 100 CE! The non-English terms have the advantage of not misleading us: we realize, when we encounter *"yehoodi"* or *"ioudaios"* in a text from, say, 200 BCE, that we cannot be certain whether the reference is to someone dwelling in Judaea or someone who traces his ancestry to the tribe of Judah or someone in neither of these categories but who worships the God whose primary shrine is in Jerusalem.

Moreover, when Simon Maccabee's grandson, Alexander Jannaeus, conquered the Idumaea of Herod's grandfather shortly before the turn to the last pre-Christian century, he demanded that those he conquered choose between adherence to Judaean faith and death or exile. The Idumaeans chose conversion. Thus Herod, on his father's side, was a *yehoodi* in terms of his adherence (at least nominally) to the Judaean belief in One God, but was ethnically and nationally an Idumaean (and, for that matter, on his mother's side, he was a Nabataean). In other words, Herod was not, as is often mis-stated, half-Jewish; rather, he was simultaneously a *yehoodi*—but only spiritually and not ethnically—and an ethnically divided half-Idumaean/half-Nabataean.

It is ultimately the growing sense of *Judaism* as opposed to *Judaeanism* that would enable the former to survive and evolve apart from the state that the Romans in effect deprived of *political* freedom after Herod's death. This is why some Roman *yehoodeem* could continue quite logically to send contributions annually to the Temple, out of *religious* conviction, while exhibiting no interest in, or support for the struggle of other Judaean *yehoodeem* for *political* independence. It is this that enabled Judaism and Jews to continue long after Judaea the land, swallowed by the Roman Imperium, had become part of a politically independent dream past.

IV. "Jewish Trials"

In a strict sense, "Jewish" trials can only begin at a point after the destruction of the Temple (70 CE) and the final loss of active Judaean political ambitions (135 CE).[25] History refuses to yield to our desire for simplicity, however. Not only do we begin our narrative at a pre-"Jewish" point in time, but the title (to repeat) is intentionally ambiguous. It doesn't specify whether "Jewish" refers to the process, the judge, the judged, the accuser(s), the defendant(s). It doesn't distinguish between formal legal procedures and a more general sense of "trial": trying events, difficult experiences. But all of this ambiguity is not only intentional; it is necessary: as with most ideas that include the adjective "Jewish" as an attachment, changing the time and place often changes the import of the noun to which

"Jewish" is connected. The literature and art to which one might refer as "Jewish literature" or "Jewish art" do not fall into the same category when we ask "what is it" in fifth-century Palestine as opposed to thirteenth-century Poland as opposed to twentieth-century America.

Thus the ambiguity of the term "trials" is increased, both conceptually and practically, by its context in this discussion. The evidence for Jesus' "trial," for example, is both limited and not much focused on the *legal* procedure that we might hope for in speaking of "The Trial of Jesus." The "Trial of Jesus" is that of a *yehoodi*—a Judaean in the larger, Herodian sense (in the narrower, pre-Herodian sense he is in fact a Galilean, not a Judaean), who worshipped the God whose primary shrine is the Jerusalem Temple and who traces his genealogy back to the tribe of Judah—and the historical question centers around whether his accusers, interrogators, judges, defendants were Judaeans (and in *which* sense were they "Judaeans"?) or Romans. To what extent could the one group or the other have had the opportunity, both practically and conceptually, to have been connected to Jesus' earthly demise as that event is generally understood?

The discussion of events in Norwich, England, in 1144, never offers the semblance of a formal trial, either: rather, we encounter a multiplicity of claims, accusations, and questions which pertain to the inter-locked issues of sanctification and Blood-Libel. A community stands accused of enacting a ritual death for William—and the historical question centers on the relations between Christians and Jews in a medieval English context. The trial of Alfred Dreyfus is filled enough with formal legal proceedings and their record, but its legal details prove to be less significant, perhaps, than the historical iceberg of which it is only the proverbial tip. For Dreyfus' trial for treason takes place in a secular state in which the brotherhood of all Frenchmen had been proclaimed a century earlier—and yet the historical question focuses on the paradoxic surfacing of vehement anti-Jewish prejudices, both in bringing Dreyfus to trial in the first place and in the events that unfold beyond the series of legal and other trials that were part of that Affair.

The account of a series of historical events which constitutes this book is both the account of evolving legal sensibility within Judaism and within the worlds in which Judaism has wandered and often flourished, and the account of formal legal proceedings in the Jewish and non-Jewish realms. To accomplish these necessarily intertwined aims it is necessary to begin before the beginning of Judaism in the terms just defined. An understanding of the language basis for the concept "Jewish" introduces us to the complexity of that concept, but we cannot apprehend that complexity without turning to Judaean, Israelite and Hebrew history and religion. This will certainly be true for the specifics of "Jewish trials."

Thus from the bible and its Israelite sense of Law we turn to the Mishnaic (ca 400 BCE-200 CE) sensibility that carries from Judaean to early Jewish thinking about how law and justice co-exist—and how both concepts may and may not be formulated apart from direct Divine involvement and injunction. This discussion offers a backdrop for understanding the Trial of Jesus. That procedure offers the beginnings of a two-fold exploration: of the likely Judaean-Jewish role in the proceedings, based on our understanding of Judaean law; and of subsequent centuries of legal confrontations that result from traditional Christian historiographic assumptions both about that role and about the identity of Judaeans and Jews.

In moving through history, most of the course of this narrative finds Jews on the receiving end of some accusation. In more recent cases, such as that involving Julius and Ethel Rosenberg, the plot spreads out to encompass Jews in a variety of roles besides that of defendant, with what I will argue are distinct consequences—and the question becomes: why are there such consequences? Where the later Eichmann and Demjanjuk trials are concerned, the plot spreads still further: the accusers and the judges and juries are Jews, and yet in the courtroom of the world outside the courtroom it is as much the accusers as the accused who stand trial: can individuals like Eichmann or Demjanjuk be given a fair trial by a Jewish court? What is the just and fair punitive result of such a trial in such a court?

Ultimately, then, its seems that, regardless of the particular role(s) played by Jews in this case or that, in this legal or quasi-legal drama or that history proves to offer "the Jews on trial." In the end, as with any course of historical study, the point is to extract something from the past: a series of lessons that might guide our thinking toward the present and future. In the court of our own sense of history, we seek not absolution as much as explanation. To come full circle: a reconstruction of aspects of the past as present seeks to reinvoke the positive and excise the thoughts and actions that produced the negative, for the present and the future. We need to learn from it.

Chapter One:
From Biblical Law to Late Second Temple
Era Justice

I. *Religio* and *Lex*

One of the obvious changes over time with respect to the concept of "law" is the sense of what or who dictates it. When Hammurabi presents his famous law code to the Mesopotamian population that he governs, he offers all of its details inscribed on a stele surmounted by a powerful image. The image represents the king, as lawgiver, *receiving* a scroll—presumably containing the laws delineated below the image—from the sun god, Shamash, himself. In other words, the viewer of the stele is to understand that the laws derive from the realm of the gods, and that Hammurabi is a conduit through which those laws are transmitted to the people he governs, as opposed to understanding them to have been promulgated by Hammurabi himself, an exalted figure to be sure, but ultimately no more than a human being.

The same conditions apply to the Israelites as they are led through the wilderness by Moses and to the laws promulgated by him in the course of those forty years. Whether one associates Moses merely with the Ten Commandments that he is depicted in the Torah as bringing down from Mount Sinai or with the entirety of the 613 commandments that traditional Judaism counts up throughout the course of the Torah, the underlying principle of Moses' legislative efforts is that he is the conduit through which God Itself pours Its prescriptions for living a proper life. Moses is the mouthpiece—the Hebrew term for "mouthpiece" is *navi* and is eventually rendered in Greek as *prophetes* ("one who speaks before or on behalf of")— through which God speaks to the Israelites. As such, a contradiction of any of those laws would constitute an abrogation of God's will, not the will of Moses, and carry with it consequences for the individual appropriate to that abrogation. As a community tightly knit together by its embrace of a covenantal relationship with God articulated by those commandments, the entire house of Israel might be put at risk by the abrogation of God's will by an individual—or perhaps the specific tribe of which s/he is part.

One can see a jarring instance of how this works in a practical manner—how the contravention of Moses' leadership, which is ultimately an abrogation of God's will that Moses be the leader to whom the Israelites hearken, might result in a painful legal decision that derived directly from God and not from Moses. The text at the beginning of Numbers 16 introduces Korah, the son of Izhar, the son of Levi, who, together with Dathan and Abiram, the sons of Eliav and On, the son of Peleth, "took men; and they raised up before [literally: "in the face of"—i.e., "against"] Moses, with certain of the Children of Israel, two hundred and fifty men; they were princes of the congregation, the elect men of the assembly, men of renown; and they assembled themselves together against Moses and against Aaron, and said unto them: 'You take too much upon you, seeing all the congregation are holy, everyone of them, and the Lord is among them; wherefore then do you lift yourselves up above the assembly of the Lord?'" (Num 16:1-3)

The double context of this moment of rebellion is first, the conviction that, if the entire people Israel has been designated by earlier phraseology as a "nation of priests" intended by the Lord as a "light onto the nations" then there should be no hierarchy that places Moses and Aaron or anyone else at the top—they are all equally sacerdotal. Such a sentiment would particularly apply to Korah, who, as a grandson of Levi may be assumed to descend from the priestly tribe of the same name. The second contextual element that helps provoke the opposition is the no doubt growing frustration at this endless journey through the wilderness, bubbling up finally to and exploding over the surface of things, which at a basic human level causes Korah, Dathan and Abiram and their supporters to question the validity of Moses' get-them-nowhere leadership.

The response comes not from Moses himself, who merely suggests that "in the morning the Lord will show who are His, and who is holy, and will cause him to come near unto Him" (v 5), but from God Itself—in response to Moses' words, and in unequivocal terms. For indeed, the next day, "the Lord spoke unto Moses and unto Aaron, saying: 'Separate yourselves from among the congregation, that I may consume them in a moment.' And they fell upon their faces, and said: 'Oh God, the God of the spirits of all flesh, shall one man sin, and wilt Thou be wroth with all the congregation?'" (vv 20-22). Thus we see the destructive potential to the entire people through the actions of an individual. But God relents from the extremist intention of destroying all of the Israelites, either due to Moses' intercession, or, one might argue—having tested Moses' quality as a sacerdotal leader, who instead of saying "yeah, God, go get 'em all!" interceded to save those who might be innocent among the guilty—following what had been the more moderate Divine plan all along.[26]

Moses is instructed to call upon those who would follow his leadership to distance themselves from Korah and his associates, and "it came to pass, as he [Moses] made an end of speaking all these words, that the ground did cleave asunder that was under them [Korah and his followers]. And the earth opened her mouth, and swallowed them up, and their households, and all the men that appertained to Korah, and all their goods. So they, and all that appertained to them, went down alive into the pit; and the earth closed upon them, and they perished among the assembly... and fire came forth from the Lord, and devoured the two hundred and fifty men [who were Korah's supporters] who offered the incense [as an independent offering to God, as opposed to participating in the offering of Moses' words]." (vv 31-33)

There are several issues relevant to our discussion that need to be noted in this extraordinary passage. First, "all these words" that Moses had spoken began (v 28) with "hereby you shall know that the Lord has sent me to do all these works, and that I have not done them of mine own mind" — thus explicitly presenting the argument that God is the one who has "tried" Korah and the others, found them guilty and provided the means of punishing them. God is Judge, Jury and Executioner. Second, in order still further to underscore the unusual nature of this legalistic/judicial configuration, Moses' words continue (vv 29-30): "If these men die the common death of all men, and be visited after the visitation of all men, then the Lord has not sent me. But if the Lord make a new thing, and the ground open up her mouth, and swallow them up, with all that appertain unto them, and they go down into the pit, then you shall understand that these men have despised the Lord" — not "despised me, Moses" but "despised the Lord." So the punishment — the execution — that follows is not only divinely ordained but so out of the ordinary that it can only be perceived as divinely accomplished, and accomplished in response to Moses' request for back-up from God, thus demonstrating that Moses is the ultimate (and in the context of that time and place the only true) divinely-appointed *sacerdos* to whom God, as such, instantly hearkens.[27]

The context of this may be still more fully understood by jumping ahead toward the English language that has been providing our translated access to this text and the words "religion" and "law." More precisely, we turn to the Latin-language basis for these two words — that offers the identical basis for both. For the same "l-*V*-g" to which we have earlier referred (above, in fn #21) as the basis for "*religio*" is also the root of "*lex*" (a development from "leg-s", or more precisely, "l-*V*-g-s" wherein the "s" constitutes a suffix indicating the nominative singular case).[28] What the shared root helps clarify is the related role that *religio* and *lex*, as two *bindings*, play in a given society: the one binds a community together with regard to its God or gods, the other with regard to its human constituents. But in the world of the Babylonians of Hammurabi's time or the Israelites of Moses' time, the two concepts are essentially one and the same. If all laws are ultimately understood to come from God, then how we act vis-a-vis God in the offerings we bring or the divinely-decreed festivals that we celebrate are, on a practical level, no different from how we treat each other with respect to honoring parents, or not murdering each other, or offering truthful testimony whether in the gossip of the street or in the courtroom, or in not coveting each others' possessions.

It is no accident, then, that the text of the Ten Commandments offers prescriptions for both categories—that remembering the Sabbath Day and not committing murder are part of the same compendium—and that the far more extensive discussion of "do's" and "don't's" that carry throughout the Torah (613 of these, by traditional Jewish count) offers scores of injunctions that pertain to human-Divine relations and scores that pertain to human-human interaction. Nor should we be surprised that, in the post-Torah phase of Israelite history as we have that history presented in subsequent prophetic books, figures like Hosea and Jeremiah can speak in God's name of Divine agitation regarding how people treat each other even if and when they are bringing the proper offerings to the Temple of God and reciting the proper blessings when they do so.

The question that then emerges is: *when*, in Israelite history—or Israelite historiography, the Israelite sense of itself, of its history vis-a-vis God and vis-a-vis the world—do *religio* and *lex separate*? When do the prescriptions regarding human-human interaction come to be perceived as set forth by humans operating by means of their own brains, hearts, and consciences and not by means of God working directly through one or more of them?

Before answering that question we must note a further issue. The larger context of the Moses-Korah situation is a lengthy narrative which carries from Moses' descent from Mount Sinai with stones upon which Divinely-dictated laws are set forth (Exodus 20) to the statement in Numbers 15—just prior to the Korah rebellion—that includes the prescription: "As for the congregation, there shall be one statute both for you and for the stranger that sojourns with you, a statute forever throughout your generations; as you are so shall the stranger be before the Lord. One law and one ordinance shall be both for you and for the stranger that sojourns with you... both for he who is home-born among the children of Israel, and the stranger that sojourns among them; you shall have one law for him who does anything in error." (Num 15: 15-16, 29)[29]

We recognize in these passages a rather astounding concept, found nowhere else in the ancient world even a millennium after Moses and even, for example, in the vaunted democracy of Periclean Athens, ca 450-30 BCE. The concept is this: that *leges* set forth from God apply not only to the group that was present at Sinai, but to everyone who chooses or is forced to dwell among them and their descendants over the generations that follow. Such *leges*, in other words, do not discriminate in terms of ethnicity, nationality or gender. By contrast, in Pericles' Athens, (which is contemporary with Ezra and his redaction of the Torah), those fully enfranchised and thus fully protected by the *polis* laws were Athenian-born and free-born—and adult males—both of whose parents were free-born Athenians. Not only was the Athenian democracy a closed franchise, but it provided limited if any protection to those who fell outside this narrow category. Even a free-born Athenian male, should one of his parents have been a slave, lacked the full protection of the law, the more so a woman, child, or foreigner (even a *metoikos*: a foreigner whose family might have found work and lived in and around Athens for several generations).

The Israelite formulation marks a stunning departure from such a sensibility.[30] Even were we to assume that not a word of the Torah is historical—that it is all tendentiously historiographic or even mythological, that Ezra or others along the line made it up—the fact is that the society moving forward from the Israelite into the Judaean period, after the return from Babylonian exile and the rebuilding of the Temple, believed not only in the reality of the historical details that encompassed Abraham and Moses and Isaiah, but more importantly, in the reality of the Divine instruction set forth in the Torah and subsequent prophetic books. Thus, at the very least, the Judaean society taking shape in the last half-millennium BCE or so was shaped, in large part, by its conviction that—regardless of whether or not God was speaking to it through prophets in it own era—God Itself had laid down the injunctions that encompassed not only keeping the Sabbath and honoring one's parents and not committing murder or adultery, but respecting and protecting and embracing the stranger who dwells among you by the same laws that embrace the Israelite-Judaean.

Some of those laws expressed within the same Korah-centered narrative, were quite extreme. Thus in Numbers 15:32ff the community of Israel finds someone abrogating the Sabbath by gathering sticks on the Sabbath Day. "And the Lord said unto Moses: 'The man shall surely be put to death; all the congregation shall stone him with stones without the camp.' And all the congregation brought him without the camp and stoned him with stones and he died, as the Lord commanded Moses" (vv 35-36). The divine command works through Moses to the community that then acts as one in executing the one whose abrogation of God's commandment would have endangered the entire community—or perhaps *not* out of fear of such danger to them all but simply out of awe of God and the belief that one must do God's bidding without asking questions. Or without asking questions if one is not Abraham or Moses.

And *would* the community be endangered by one man's sin of disobedience to God's command? Apparently it is a given in a world where *religio* and *lex* are one and the same—because both derive from the divine force(s) that created and therefore can destroy us, that can help or harm, bless or curse us—that, in a community that defines itself as a community in terms of its covenant with that Force, for an individual to displease It by abrogating any of Its commandments will be disastrous for the entire community. Would not God have destroyed the entire community for the sin of Korah and his group of followers had not Moses interceded?

What if and when the world or our view of it has changed? What if and when, in the Judaean world, the mainstream leadership comes, in the time after Ezra, to believe that God no longer addresses them in such a direct manner. Should they respond to every individual's abrogation of the Sabbath in the way in which, as God once commanded through Moses, the congregation of Israel did in the wilderness when an anonymous individual abrogated the Sabbath by gathering sticks? Would it matter whether or not that individual in question was an Israelite? Not in the case of Numbers

15, apparently, when one law serves everyone dwelling among the Israelites, for better and for worse—but what about, say, the year 25 BCE in Judaea, with no prophets like Abraham or Moses or Jeremiah among the community, the High Priest in the Temple almost anyone appointed at his convenience by King Herod and increased complications of defining what it means to be a *yehoodi*? What if the abrogator were doing something else besides gathering sticks on the Sabbath: how would the congregation and its leadership even define what constitutes "abrogation of the Sabbath"?

Put otherwise: how is this issue to be adjudicated when and if the community, even the community of the Covenant, begins to see *religio* and *lex* as separate? How is it to be adjudicated when the conduits through which Divine prescriptions have been set out are no longer present; how do the descendants of those who lived when the prophets did engage the words revealed to the prophets? The answer is the answer that has been lurking in the background of this discussion all along: by *interpretation*. Once Moses is gone, his successors—assuming that all the words spoken by God through him have been precisely and accurately recorded, which in and of itself offers a challenge—may need to discuss and debate not only which words belong in the canon of Divine verbiage, but in many cases, what exactly those words mean. Not only God's words through Moses, but those spoken through all of the prophets and other figures who are believed to have been the recipients of Divine revelations of one sort or another.

II. From Apocrypha to Mishnah

If we re-examine the Judaean community between about 450 BCE and 100 CE with respect to this issue of parsing the line between revelation and interpretation—sibling to the line between history and mythology—we recall that its schismatic personality culminates in the separation into the communities we call "Jewish" and "Christian." And we recall that, among the issues that separate these progeny of the Israelite-Judaean parent is the question of what defines the point of transition from a period of Divine revelation and what follows that period. Thus Jews believe that the point falls

at or around the time of Ezra (ca 450 BCE) whereas Christians believe that the point falls well beyond what I am calling the "Judaean" period. Put otherwise: one group interprets the Torah, Prophets
and Sacred Writings to be the Bible in its entirety, all *written down*
before the time of Ezra, and the other believes that all of these works
are merely the prelude part of the Bible that culminates with a New
Testament of Gospels, Acts, Epistles and the Book of Revelation,
written down much later.

Someone standing outside both of these belief systems might
observe that they differ in their interpretation of what *constitutes*
revelation.[31] Indeed, there are other books that would eventually be
rejected by Protestant Christianity as non-canonical while embraced
by Catholics and Orthodox Christians as part of the canon. The one
group refers to these as "inter-testamental" (i.e., coming between
the Old and New Testaments) or as "deuterocanonical" (i.e., part of
a "second [part of the] canon"); the other labels them "apocryphal"
(literally: "hidden away," meaning that they *should* be hidden away
lest a believer mistake them for part of the canon and be spiritually
misled by them). Needless to say, this group of books, that includes
Maccabees I and II, Judith, Susanna and the Elders, The Wisdom of
Ben Sirach and others, is perceived by Judaism as Apocrypha, as well.
For our purposes, what is important to understand is that, if such
works were written, as they appear to have been, during the post-
Ezra Second Temple period then, divinely inspired or not, they may
offer some insight into general historical, spiritual—and even legalistic—developments during that era.

Thus a book like Susanna and the Elders—the more so if it is
not viewed as a divinely revealed text, as for Jews (and later, Protestants), it is not—offers a view of how a legalistic sensibility that
relies on human rather than Divine intervention is developing in the
Judaean world. Its narrative in a nutshell is this: that two Elders of
the community—judges, no less—conceive a passion for the pious
and beautiful Susannah and, when she refuses to satisfy their lust-
ful demands accuse her of adultery. They tell their lies to the community that—because the accusers are two venerable old men and
the accused is one young woman—believes them and condemns her

to death. But the young Daniel (presumably the same figure who would spend time in a lions' den in the Hebrew Biblical book named for him) intervenes and saves her life. While the Law of Moses had already insisted on a minimum of two witnesses to yield a guilty verdict in a capital case, Daniel examined the two "witnesses" (i.e., accusers) separately. As they contradicted each other, their perjury and her innocence were proved and Susannah was exonerated.

The book is conventionally dated to the last pre-Christian century, and offers this separate cross-examination as a simple—but at the time quite revolutionary—juridical principle. It also offers a slightly more subtle perspectival point: that justice is not necessarily conveyed by favoring the inherently stronger, and that "stronger" in the spiritual sense is not in any case related to age or gender. We may see this as a continuation of the principle articulated in Numbers 15. One might also wonder how, when the perjuring pair of elders is executed, for "they [the people] obeyed the Law of Moses and killed them" (v 62) they were executed. Were they stoned as happened to the abrogator of the Sabbath in Numbers 15: 36? If so, was the method the same as described in that verse from the Torah, or had the methodology of stoning evolved also?

Beyond the question of what books are believed—interpreted—to fall into or out of the canon, Jews and Christians differ with respect to how they interpret the texts that they both agree are revealed. In general terms, Christians might be supposed not to need to dig as deeply into the Torah, since it is only the prelude to the Gospels; Jews don't need to look at the Gospels at all, which are the primary focus of Christian interpretative attention, since they are not considered Biblical by Judaism. In more specific terms, each of the two groups might be expected to and does interpret the same passages differently—such as those prophetic passages which predict the arrival onto the stage of history of a future anointed figure (and the nature of that figure as "anointed") whom Christians see as encapsulated as Jesus of Nazareth and Jews see as encapsulated as nobody, to date.

This last issue—that of a divinely ordained anointed leader—is one, it behooves us to recall, that did not arise for the first time in the era and context of John the Baptist and Jesus of Nazareth. On the contrary, from at least the time of the return from Babylonian exile, in 538 BCE—and in some senses, one might suppose, from the time of the division of the kingdom of David and Solomon a few years after Solomon's death, around 925 BCE—the Israelite-Judaeans wondered and worried about the arrival onto the stage of their history of a descendant of David and Solomon to reunite the people and to redirect them toward a fuller, more righteous relationship with God.

That issue grew in insistence when, in the aftermath of the Hasmonaean success at regaining Judaean political independence, the renewed state found itself led by non-Davidic figures who were engaged in constant internal blood-letting; it expanded exponentially with the coming of Herod to the throne. Messiah-fever swept through late-Second-Temple Judaea, for surely the situation could not get worse than it was under Herod: this must be the proverbially darkest hour before the messianic dawn. Only it did get worse: after Herod's death the Roman heel descended strongly onto the Judaean political neck. Any number of individuals apparently asserted or had followers who asserted of them that they were descendants of David and Solomon (of the many wives and many offspring) ready to ascend the Judaean throne and to lead the people back to the sort of Golden Age that, from the retrospective distance of nearly a millennium, seemed to have defined the Davidic era.

Jesus was the last of these—and part of the question regarding him is that of what he himself actually asserted regarding his role in history, as opposed to what others would subsequently assert of him and his role. This is part of what would come to separate Judaism and Christianity and intersects the issue of his trial and death that we discuss below.

All of these issues also have both broad and particularized implications for the matter of *religio* and *lex*. Not only might we expect to find a difference of belief between these two groups regarding when the separation between these two concepts takes place. Even the question of how human fashioners of *leges* ought or ought not to be doing their work with a sense of what God prefers us to be as a community—how human *leges* might or might not effectively reflect the precepts and prescriptions of our *religio*—inevitably becomes an issue separating Judaism and Christianity from each other.

Thus: what does it mean to "murder"—as opposed to "kill" or "execute"—and what, therefore, does God mean by the Sixth Commandment? What are the means by which one might abrogate God's Fourth Commandment, to "remember the Sabbath day and keep It holy"? What might the commandment found three times in the Torah—the first time is in Exodus 23:19—not to "seethe a kid in its mother's milk" mean in practical terms, general cultural or specific gastronomic terms? With such questions in mind, the leadership of the Judaean community in the Late Second Temple period—paradoxically, away from the Temple itself, for its priesthood had in any case become increasingly farcical with respect to spiritual leadership—began to record orally an increasingly elaborate web of discussions of such matters. In the end these discussions would become part of the mainstream literary canon of post-Biblical Judaism, (whereas they would not become part of Christianity's different literary canon).

These interpretative debates not only focused on issues such as these just mentioned, but, starting, one might say, from the opposite conceptual end of legalistic thought, they sought to provide a means by which one might live one's life with a sense of God's abiding immanent presence. The first sort of thought, taking as its method to begin with a passage *from the Torah* (and *other canonical texts*), is called *midrash*. The second sort, beginning, instead, with a *practical problem*, and seeking to adjudicate the problem by interpretive *references* to the texts of the canon, was called *mishnah*.

The term *"midrash"* is built from the Hebrew root *"d-r-sh"* meaning "to dig" and midrashic literature is inherently interpretative: it seeks to dig beneath the surface of a sacred text for meanings that are not apparent on the surface. The primary body of midrash, the *Midrash Rabbah* ("Great *Midrash*"), focuses on the Torah and five works from the hagiographa that, for various reasons, were perceived as needful of discussion and commentary.[32] For example, the first discussion in the *Midrash Rabbah* centers on the opening words of the Torah: "In the beginning God created the heavens and the earth." The *midrash* addresses the question of which God created first, the heavens or the earth, and why—or whether both were created simultaneously.

The discussion segues from that question to others that are recognized as analogous, from elsewhere in the Torah, but which bring the issue closer and closer to practical, ground-level territory. Thus, do we honor Abraham more than Isaac and Isaac more than Jacob, Sarah more than Rebecca more than Rachel more than Leah? Do we honor father more than mother, given the order of the words of the commandment "honor thy father and thy mother"? In concluding (I have not given the various arguments, of course; I am jumping to the conclusion of the last question) that God would have us honor our fathers and our mothers equally, the *Midrash Rabbah* shows itself a worthy continuer of the equality principle set forth in Numbers 15 regarding laws and statutes. That principle is so different from the Greek worldview on such a matter: in the *Midrash Rabbah*, gender parity is emphatically articulated with regard to parental respect.

By contrast to midrashic literature, the mishnaic literature uses references to God's words to validate the view of the various rabbinic figures who debate within its pages but has as its starting point practical problems. How many times during the week is it incumbent upon a scholar to have sexual relations with his wife— as opposed to a carpenter or a brick-layer? When exactly does the day begin—so that we know when we will be maximally fulfilling the Divine commandment to recite the morning prayers? What are the optimal dimensions, configuration and details with respect to foliage used as roofing for a booth—a *sukkah*—such as the Torah prescribes as a week-long dwelling every fall season, in commemoration of the wandering of the Israelites in the wilderness during which time they dwelled in temporary booths? If two men are walking down the street and one sees a garment but the other picks it up, and the first says "it's mine; I saw it first!" whereas the second says "it's mine, I got to it first!"—how does one adjudicate the argument between them. And so on.

The term *"mishnah"* derives from the Hebrew root "sh-n-h," meaning "to turn," a reference to the idea of turning ideas over and over in order to arrive at an understanding of them and thus at a proper God-aware way of life. As with the *Midrash Rabah*, the *Mishnah* began as an oral tradition in the last few pre-Christian centuries and the first centuries CE. By the early third century, (the traditional date is 212 CE) Rabbi Judah the Prince organized the entire ocean of discussions and debates, commentaries and interpretations, into six over-riding "Orders," subdivided into 63 sub-set "tractates"—each collation based on a subject. By that time, too, a vast secondary group of commentaries—commentaries on and discussions of the *mishnah*—had been in the process of beginning to take shape. This secondary body of interpretive literature is called *gemara* (meaning "completion"). Eventually the two bodies of work, reflecting several centuries of discussions and debates—the first part focusing on an array of issues and the second on the commentary on issues—found their way under one written roof. Together, *mishnah* and *gemara* constitute the essential Talmud (which word means "learning").

Of course by that time, the Jewish community was already dispersed throughout the Middle Eastern and Mediterranean worlds, as it held its ground as a *religio* within the Roman realms in competition with its sibling rival, Christianity which, in the course of the third century, was suffering its most difficult historical period as a persecuted *superstitio*. The Jewish community of that era, however, had two primary centers of cultural, spiritual, and political activity. The smaller of the two was in and around Judaea—which, since the time of the Bar Kokhba revolt against the Romans of 132-5 had been known in the larger world as *Palestina*[33]—and the larger, by far, was (ironically enough, given earlier history) in and around Babylonia.[34] Each of these two communities produced its own *gemara* commentaries on the *mishnah*, so that one properly speaks of a Palestinian Talmud and a Babylonian Talmud. The first is much smaller than the second, both in the sense of not offering *gemaras* on all 63 *mishnah* tractates and in usually offering shorter ones, involving fewer commentators in its discussions.

III. Shaping the Sanhedrin and Tractate *Sanhedrin*

Among the most important talmudic tractates for the purposes of our discussion is the one called *Sanhedrin*. The term *"sanhedrin"* is an aramaicization of the Greek word, *"synhedrion,"* meaning (literally) "a seating with" — referring, in this case, to an entity that sits together to hear legal cases. For that term, in turn, is a rendering of the Hebrew phrase *"Bet Din,"* meaning "House of Judgment," which phrase refers to the institution that was evolving during these same post-Ezra centuries to adjudicate legal issues. As in much of what transpires in the Judaean world of increased *religio-lex* separation, there is a precedent from the Israelite tradition of the Torah for such an entity. In Exodus 18 Moses appoints others to assist him in adjudicating the issues that are brought before him by the people — following the suggestion of his father-in-law, Jethro, the former priest of Midian, who had embraced the God of Israel after witnessing the miracles affected by God through Moses.[35] "...The hard cases they brought to Moses, but every small matter they judged themselves." (v 26)

Thus one might say that not only is there a biblical basis for an entity that might be called a "House of Judgment" at a time when *religio* and *lex* are largely still joined, but a distinction between kinds of legal situations, some of which require God's intervention and some of which do not. If the formalized structure of the *Bet Din* comes into being more than a thousand years after the presumed time of Moses, by which time the Judaean community is no longer wandering as a tribal confederation through the wilderness, but is settled, if scattered through a defined national territory whose inhabitants are variously keepers of flocks, tillers of the soil and dwellers in towns and small cities, we might well wonder exactly how that formal judicial entity was configured by then. The source for that information would naturally be the tractate that describes the entity both in terms of its shape and in terms of its procedural functions — although further details may also be found in other tractates.[36]

Our information regarding exactly how, when and by whom the institution was operated in Judaean times is tricky — since Judaean-Jewish tradition ascribes the starting point to Moses, based on the just-mentioned passage in Numbers. Within the *Mishnah* itself, in the unique tractate known as the *Avot* ("Fathers"), the Torah—

which is the term used in Numbers 15:16 that is conventionally translated as "law" — is said to have been transmitted from Moses to Joshua to the Elders to the Prophets to the Men of the "Great Gathering" (*"Knesset Ha G'dolah"*), its contents summarized as a three-fold instruction: "to be deliberate in judgment (*"din"*), to raise up many pupils and to build a fence around the Torah." (chapter I:1). The first two questions that arise for us are: can we understand the "Great Gathering" to be the same as what elsewhere will be called the Sanhedrin—or is the first body something different from the second, and either way, what exactly were the issues encompassed within the purview of the latter?

When in any case does Judaean history arrive at the point referred to by the phrase "men of the Great Gathering"? We might interpret it to refer to those who led the community as early as the aftermath of Ezra's time or 150 years later. For the next line of *Avot* refers to "Simeon the Just [as one] among the survivors of the Great Gathering" and Simeon the Just might be the individual recorded as the High Priest in the Temple from 310/300 to 291/270—or he might be a second Simeon, grandson of the first, who was recorded as High Priest in 219-199. Josephus mentions both of these (in his *Antiquities of the Jews* [i.e., *Judaeans*] XII.2.5 and XII.4.10) but only to the first does he apply the epithet "the Just." So if we assume that the "Great Gathering" is a synonym for the "Great House of Judgment" and if we assume that the genealogy in *Avot* is correct and if we take Josephus to be correctly informed (for he is in any case not writing until the late first century CE); then the shaping of the entity would have begun a century and a half after the time of Ezra.

The text continues by referring to Antigonos of Socho "who received [the Torah] from Simeon the Just," and what follows is a succession of "pairs" — *"zuggot"* — Yossi ben Yoezer of Zeredah and Yossi ben Yohanan of Jerusalem first; followed by Yehoshua ben Perahiah and Nittai of Arbella; succeeded by Yehudah ben Tabbai and Simeon ben Shetah. If "Simeon the Just" is the older of the two Simeons, and if we take the genealogy at face value, then there is a long stretch between his time and that of Yossi ben Yoezer, who dies in 160, even with Antigonos of Socho sandwiched between them:

could there have been others not mentioned because they were not significant enough? The text ascribes sayings to each of the figures it mentioned; could there have been others who said nothing worth recording? Or should we assume that the Simeon referred to by the text is the younger Simeon, and not take Josephus to heart—in which case the shaping of the "Great Gathering" *cum* "Great House of judgment" began closer to 240 years after Ezra?

In any case, whereas all of the maxims ascribed to Simeon, Antigonos, Yossi and Yossi, and Yehoshua and Nittai pertain to general ethical conduct, those ascribed to Yehudah and Simeon ben Shetah might be called legal: "Yehudah ben Tabbai said: 'Do not make yourself as those who prepare judges...'. Simeon ben Shetah said: 'Examine thoroughly your witnesses...'" (vv 8,9). So could it be that the nature of the "Great Gathering" shifted over time and that its role as a "Great House of Judgment" was arrived at only later, during the Hasmonean period—around 100 BCE? The text continues with Shemaiah and Avtalion and thence to Hillel and Shammai. The latter were active during the second part of the reign of Herod and on into what we might approximate as the first decade of Jesus of Nazareth's life.

While the history and genealogy of creating the Sanhedrin is of interest to us, it is more important for us to understand three other issues that are part of this story. One is that elsewhere in the talmudic literature (*Megillat Hagigah* II.2) the *zuggot* are referred to as holding a pair of offices of *Nasi* ("President" or "prince") and *Av Bet Din* ("Father of the House of Judgment") respectively. These terms, together with a third term, *muflah* ("distinguished") are in use eventually with reference to the leadership of the Bet Din *HaGadol*—the Great Sanhedrin—which reinforces the notion that either this institution had a long Second Temple-era history, or in emerging relatively late in that era, grew out of an already-extant prior institution.

As for the functional meaning of these terms, it seems that the *Nasi* presided as the representative of the majority view on a given issue and the *Av Bet Din* represented the minority view—so that every issue that came under discussion (and we see this generally with the Talmud) was considered from at least two points of view. The *mufla* may have been a kind of expert adviser and in any case it is not clear how formal or informal any of these designations and their significances were. And there is no evidence that the high priest in the Temple held any of these roles inherently; his responsibilities in the Temple were distinct and separate from those of the *Bet Din HaGadol*.

The second issue is that, either from the time of the return from Babylon (ca 538 BCE) or the time of Ezra's redaction of the Torah (ca 444) or some time thereafter, the schismatic nature of the Judaean community was expressed by terms referring to contending bodies of leadership: Sadducee and Pharisee. Regardless of the origins of these terms[37] the Sadducees seemed to have tended toward narrower interpretations of the Torah, focusing on individual trees within the forest of divine dicta, whereas the Pharisees tended toward broader interpretations and focused on the larger spiritual forest landscape for those interpretations. More importantly, the two groups, although presumably originally associated with spiritual perspectives, became increasingly politicized, so that by the late second pre-Christian century they were in effect political parties. And in the course of the bloody progression of Hasmonean leadership between 104 and 63, the Sadducees as a group were completely wiped out. By the time we arrive at Shemaia and Avtalion and Hillel and Shammai, the term "Pharisee" would have become a synonym for the spiritual and legal leadership of the Judaean community.

That leadership (and this is the third issue) would have also been distinguished by that time from the religious leadership of the community with respect to formal *religio* at the highest level—the Temple and its program of sacrifices, supervised by the High Priest. If since the time of Simeon the Hasmonean (no relation to "Simeon the Just," of course) the High Priesthood had been arrogated to a ruling house that was not Tzadokite, which would have upset the religious purists, then by the time of Herod this situation had worsened from the perspective of even those who were not such purists: the High Priest was apparently appointed at his whim by the King and such a priest's fitness for representing the community to God would have been more than a little suspect. The

Pharisaic leadership of the Judaean *community*—which, to repeat, presumably but not certainly accounted for the *Bet Din HaGadol* to which we shall return in a moment—was also readily distinguishable from the leadership of the Judaean *state*. Herod's political authority must have butted up against the spiritual authority of the pharisaic leadership on more than one occasion.

All of which brings us back, then, to the unanswerable question of how to understand the historical relationship between what Tractate *Avot* refers to as the *Knesset HaG'dolah* and what is discussed in Tractate *Sanhedrin* as the *Bet Din HaGadol*—and the other *Batei Din*. At the very least we can say that, whereas in the first text it seems to have been the High Priest (Simeon the Just and his successors) in the Temple who was himself the head of the first institution, by the time we have arrived to the time of Herod and toward the time of Jesus—that is, to the time of the last two *zuggot* delineated in *Avot*—the institution that is described in *Sanhedrin* is not only not headed by the High Priest, it encompasses a realm of issues pertaining to the *religio*-based, *lex*-guided everyday lives of the Judaeans that was a complete antipode to the highly suspect *religio*-based activities theoretically carried out on behalf of the Judaeans by the High Priesthood.

And what does *Sanhedrin* say about the Sanhedrin? To begin with, it speaks of two of them—a Greater Sanhedrin of 71 and a Lesser Sanhedrin of 23—in addition to apparently more *ad hoc* adjudication boards comprised of only three judges. Thus monetary cases; cases of larceny and mayhem; claims for full or half damages, for example, may be tried by three judges (2a).[38] But concerning cases of rape, seduction and libel, whereas Rabbi Meir holds that they may all be tried by three judges, "the sages hold that a case of libel requires a court of twenty-three since it may involve a capital charge" (*ibid*). Conversely, "cases involving flogging, [may be tried] by three; in the name of Rabbi Ishmael [however] it is said, by twenty-three" (*ibid*). There are other issues for which the number of judges produces discussion or debate: "the intercalation of the month is effected by a court of three, and the intercalation of the year by three—so Rabbi Meir. But Rabbi Simeon ben Gamaliel says the matter is initiated by three, discussed by five and determined by five" (*ibid*).

There is no question concerning certain kinds of cases: "Capital cases are adjudicated by twenty-three..." and should someone be supposed to have been killed by a wild beast—thus constituting a murder whereby the beast is the murderer and therefore also subject to capital punishment!—even "the death sentence on the wolf or lion or the bear or the leopard or the hyena or the serpent is to be passed by twenty-three" (*ibid*). It must be admitted that in this last kind of case there is not a unanimous perspective: "Rabbi Eliezer says: whoever is first to kill them [such wild beasts, without trial] acquires merit; Rabbi Akiba, however, holds that their death is to be decided by twenty-three" (*ibid*). The ante is upped for certain issues. Thus "a tribe [that has become idol-worshipping], a false prophet and a High Priest can only be tried by a court of seventy-one. War of free choice can be waged only be the authority of a court of seventy-one.[39] No city can be declared condemned except by a court of seventy-one" (*ibid*).

In turn, the opening passage in the tractate speaks of various aspects of why each of the two kinds of Sanhedrins is formulated, not surprisingly, by way of reference to the Torah. Thus the Great Sanhedrin is composed of seventy-one members, since "it is said, [in Num. 11:16] 'Gather unto me seventy men'; with Moses at their head we have seventy-one" (*ibid*). And "How do we know that the Small Sanhedrin is of only twenty-three? [because] it is said 'and the *edah* shall judge... and the *edah* shall deliver.'[40] One *edah* [i.e., 10 adult male Judaeans] judges [i.e., condemns] and the other may deliver [i.e., acquits], hence we have twenty....and from where do we derive the additional three? By the implications of the text, 'thou shall not follow a majority for evil [i.e., for condemnation, Ex 23:2]' I infer that I may follow them for good [i.e., for acquittal]... [and] since for good [acquittal] a majority of one suffices, whereas for evil a majority of two is required, and as a court cannot consist of an even number, another one is added, making a total of twenty-three."

Within this Torah-laced discussion the underlying concern is how to effect justice. Thus the more significant the issues, the larger the number of judges prescribed by the *mishnah*. The idea expressed in all cases, however insignificant and however small the court adjudicating them, is that "a court may not consist of an even number [of judges]"—to avoid a decision of no-verdict due to the lack of a majority viewpoint (2b). The size of the court is in part determined by the size of the community it must serve. Thus, in order to qualify to have a small Sanhedrin (of 23, as opposed to an ad hoc group of 3) to adjudicate its issues, a town must be of at least a certain size: "one hundred and twenty. Rabbi Nehemiah says: two hundred and thirty, so that each member shall be a 'ruler' of [at least] ten"[41] (*ibid*).

The second chapter of the tractate covers diverse issues such as the rights and privileges of the High Priest and the King—the spiritual and political leaders of the state[42]—and various other subjects, including the matter of how Biblical commands may be reasoned into sense without simply relying on the idea that they are divinely revealed. One might well see in this part of the process of shifting away from assumptions or expectations of direct divine intervention in matters of law and justice, toward embracing full human responsibility for them.

As we enter the third chapter we return to the ins and outs of the court system, specifically the rights of parties to a suit to choose or reject judges and witnesses in the shaping of the arbitration process. Thus in indicating that "civil actions [are to be tried] by three," the text continues: "Each [litigant] chooses one, and the two jointly choose a third; so holds Rabbi Meir, but the Sages rule that the two judges [chosen by the two litigants] nominate the third" (23a). Furthermore: "each party may object to the judge chosen by the other, so holds Rabbi Meir, but the Sages say: 'when is this so? Only if the objector adduces proof that they are either kinsmen or [otherwise] ineligible...'" (*ibid*). We recognize the underlying issue in this discussion: that every effort be made to guarantee an objective, fair tribunal.

And the effort to assure a fair trial includes wide latitude with regard to accepting, rejecting and reversing one's viewpoint regarding prospective judges. Thus "if one [of the litigants] says to the other 'I accept my father or thy father as trustworthy [i.e., in spite of the normally inherently disqualifying status of fathers and other blood-relatives]' or 'I have confidence in three cowherds' [i.e., those at the bottom of the socio-economic and intellecutal ladder, and therefore assumed to be inherently unfit to serve as judges]' Rabbi Meir says he may [subsequently] retract, but the Sages rule that he cannot..." (24a).

Similarly, "each party may reject the witnesses produced by the other. So holds Rabbi Meir, but the sages say: 'When is this so? Only when proof is brought that they are either kinsmen or [otherwise] ineligible..." (23a). So the same principle operates for witnesses as for judges. And there shortly follows a statement as to what kinds of individuals would be not merely inherently inappropriate but outright ineligible to serve as either judges or witnesses. These include "a gambler with dice, a usurer, a pigeon-trainer, and traders [in the produce] of the sabbatical year... [and in the last case], Rabbi Judah said... that 'if they have no other occupation but this; but if they have other means of livelihood, they are eligible" (24b-25a).

We might note two things in this litany. The first is that what these variously-named professions share from the mishnaic perspective is an essential and inherent dishonesty. Userers are considered virtual robbers and thieves, and pigeon-trainers (for the purpose, presumably, of racing them), like gamblers, are presumed to be dishonest, since they are assumed to be willing to win at virtually any cost. The second is that the presentation of categories is connected back to the Torah. Thus the disqualification of gamblers, userers and pigeon-trainers is based on interpreting Exodus 23:1: "put not thy hand with the wicked to be an unrighteous witness" to refer to such categories of individuals as wicked. The traders in sabbatical-year produce are disqualified based on the dictum in Leviticus 25:6 that "the Sabbath of the land shall be for food to you"—interpreted to mean "for food and not for commerce." Thus a Sabbatical-year produce trader would be abrogating God's commandment.

The tractate goes on in chapter four to prescribe the methodology of the courts and then to distinguish different kinds of crimes and the different kinds of punishments that apply to each. It begins with the prescription that "both civil and capital cases demand inquiry and examination, as it is written: 'you shall have one manner of law'" (32a)—thus basing an interpretive turn to the notion of even-handedness (to refer to kinds of cases, rather than kinds of individuals) on Divine writ.[43] Yet key aspects of trial methodology distinguish civil from capital cases—the one involving a potential fine, the other a potential death. For the text continues by asking "what is the difference between civil and capital cases?" to which it responds, first of all, that "civil suits [are tried] by three; [whereas] capital cases by twenty-three" and then by asserting that "civil suits may be opened either for acquittal or condemnation; capital charges may be opened for acquittal, but not for condemnation" (*ibid*). Thus where a life hangs in the balance, the court is enjoined to place the first words it hears in the mouth of the defense.

Moreover, "civil suits may be decided by a majority of one, either for acquittal or condemnation; whereas capital charges are decided by a majority of one for acquittal, but [at least] two for condemnation" (*ibid*). So civil cases and capital case acquittals are both handled with a less decisive requirement for the outcome than a capital case condemnation, which requires a minimum of 13 for to 10 against—since if a 23-person court must decide by a majority of 2 then, as a practical arithmetic matter, it must decide by a minimum of 3. Further, "In monetary cases the decision may be reversed both for acquittal and for condemnation, while in capital charges the verdict may be reversed for acquittal only, but not for condemnation. In monetary cases all [meaning student judges][44] may argue for or against the defendant, while in capital charges, anyone may argue in his favor, but not against him. In civil suits, he who has argued for condemnation, may [i.e., should he reconsider and find his own arguments erroneous] then argue for acquittal, and vice versa; whereas in capital charges, one who has argued for condemnation may subsequently argue for acquittal, but not vice versa" (*ibid*).

There is more, with regard to what begins to emerge, point by point, as a sensibility that will bend itself considerably in order to assure that a life is not taken in error through less than a densely layered rigor of procedure.[45] Thus, whereas "civil suits are tried by day and decided by night, capital cases must be tried by day and concluded by day"—meaning that every moment of the discussion must be conducted in optimally open conditions—and whereas "civil suits can be concluded on the same day, whether for acquittal or condemnation, capital charges may be concluded on the same day with a favorable verdict, but only on the following day with an unfavorable verdict" (*ibid*). Thus on the one hand the judges have a night through which they may think and rethink the evidence, and on the other, new evidence might turn up in favor of the accused during the night. "Therefore trials are not held on the eve of a Sabbath of festival" (*ibid*)—lest, since the court adjourns for Sabbaths and festivals, protagonists before the court suffer the hardship of having to wait one or more days until their cases are concluded. The more so in a capital case that might lead to a guilty verdict: in that case the accused would be made to wait until his execution, since no executions may take place on a Sabbath or festival.

The text continues: "In civil suits and in cases of cleanness and uncleanness, we begin with [the opinion of] the most eminent [of the judges], whereas in capital charges we commence with [the opinion of] those on the side [benches]" (*ibid*). Thus the counterpoint to favoring acquittal in a capital case by making acquittal arguments the first that the judges hear is to save the argument offered by the most eminent of judges for last.

Chapter five goes into some detail with regard to rules for cross-examining witnesses, including issues such as potential retaliation against a witness and contradictions and discrepancies with regard to evidence. It also discusses procedures for voting on and promulgating a sentence, including the notion that the final argument in a capital case must be the argument for acquittal, so that both the first and the last words that the judges hear before they begin to deliberate are those seeking to exonerate the accused.

The sixth chapter then turns to a description of how a condemned man in a capital case is led to the place of execution and how a last opportunity is offered to him to offer an argument that will lead to his exoneration and the revocation of the sentence. Thus in a capital case, "when the trial is ended [and the accused found guilty], he is led forth to be stoned. The place of stoning was outside the court, even as it is written, 'bring forth him who has cursed.'[46] A man was stationed at the door of the court with the signaling cloth in his hand, and a horse-man was [also] stationed at a distance within sight of him [i.e., the signal man]; if one [presumably of the judges] says 'I have something[further] to say in his favor,' then he [the signaler] waves the cloth, and the horse-man runs and stops them [from carrying out the sentence until the new argument is examined]. And even if he [the accused] himself says: 'I have something to plead in my own favor,' then he is brought back [to the courtroom to consider the new argument], even four or five times—providing, however, that there is substance in his assertion" (42b). So, frivolous delays excepted, the procedure offers an enormous potential effort to save the condemned man from erroneous execution.

The exercise of this effort is further expressed in the next line (43a) where, in the case of a condemned man going forth to be executed, "a herald precedes him [crying out]: 'so and so, the son of so and so, is going forth to be stoned because he committed such and such an offence, and so and so are his witnesses. Whoever might know anything in his favor, let him come forth and state it.'" Thus virtually to the final moment before the execution the court will reconvene and consider new evidence that might save the life of the accused.

Two further issues might be noted for our purposes. The first is that stoning is used in chapter six merely as an example, because in chapters seven through ten four modes of execution are delineated, each connected to specific kinds of capital crimes. Thus, apart from stoning, burning, decapitation and strangulation are also prescribed and described, and the nature of the crimes requiring each form of execution explained. Thus, for example, burning is to be used in certain forms of incest, and decapitation for murderers. Hanging is also discussed in the later part of chapter six—but what is described is the momentary and posthumous exposure of the body of a criminal who has been already executed by stoning. This contrasts emphatically with the Roman mode of hanging—on a cross—of a still-living victim left to die slowly through all-day or longer exposure to the elements combined with hunger and thirst.

The second further issue is the precise nature of "stoning" that is laid out in the mishnaic context. An individual accused of a capital crime cannot be found guilty without a minimum of two witnesses convincingly attesting to his commission of the crime. If the accused is pronounced guilty he is placed in a pit and a large stone is rolled onto him, crushing him, and the two whose testimony led to the sentence are the ones who must push the stone onto him—as opposed to the biblical mode of stoning that, as we have seen above, involves an entire community in the act of casting stones at the victim, beating him to death from a distance, so to speak.

There is, incidentally, no record of a Sanhedrin actually ever sending anyone to be executed by *any* means throughout the course of its history. The entire discussion is hypothetical, as far as our historiography goes, to date. More importantly, this entire lengthy narrative in which I have engaged has implications for how we might understand the death of Jesus, as will become clear in the next chapter.

Chapter Two:
The Sanhedrin and the Trial and Death of Jesus of Nazareth

I have belabored three issues in the previous chapter—the complexities of the historical context that carries our narrative to the time of Jesus; the pains to which the *mishnah* goes to distinguish different kinds of crimes and different kinds of courts to address them; and the pains to which the *mishnah* goes to characterize different kinds of capital crimes and the varied modes of punishment associated with each—in order to begin to answer the following question: how might we understand the trial and execution of Jesus of Nazareth in Judaea around the year 30 CE, the period during which the *mishnah* was not only in formation but in which the still further and still more complicated discussions of the *gemara* were also beginning to take shape?

I. The Gospels and the Trial in Its Contexts

At first glance it would seem impossible that the Sanhedrin had anything whatsoever to do with Jesus' death. If he had been brought before a tribunal—be it of 23 or of 71 members—with a capital charge, then the procedures that could have led to a guilty charge would have had to be followed. Had he been found guilty, then one of the four means of execution described in detail by tractate *Sanhedrin* would have had to be followed—or more precisely, given specifics of his alleged crime, only one of the four methods could have been used.

So the question becomes: what was Jesus' supposed crime? And then, how was he tried and executed? Who tried and executed him? But underlying these questions is the more fundamental one: how do we know the answers? What are our available sources? The one source that would immediately spring to most people's minds, no doubt, is the text of the Gospels. In turning to this source the first issue which we might recall is that of the complicated and/or blurry lines between history and historiography, between history and mythology, between religion and mythology, between religious faith and historical fact. In remembering this issue, and in briefly examining the four Gospel texts that reside in the New Testament as we have it canonized between 180 and the end of the fourth century, we recognize of course that the four differ from each other with regard to the handling of details.

Thus the Gospel According to Mark is sixteen chapters long. The first fourteen verses of chapter 1 present John the Baptist in action; Jesus is introduced by reference to the temptations directed toward him for forty days in the wilderness. From verse 14 to the beginning of chapter 10, Jesus is depicted moving about in the Galilee. In the chapters that follow Jesus is seen preaching in Judaea, culminating with his Apocalyptic discourse in chapter 13. The Passion begins with the first verse of chapter 14 and the assertion that "the chief priests and scribes sought how they might take him by craft and put him to death." In verses 43 and 44, Judas and a multitude of followers "with swords and staves, from the chief priests and the scribes and the elders" arrive into the Garden of Gethsemane, "and he that betrayed him [i.e., Judas] had given them a token, saying, whomsoever I shall kiss, that same is he; take him and lead him away safely."

There is an inherent illogic to this moment in the narrative: why would it be necessary for Judas to point Jesus out this way, since presumably they all knew who he was (and in fact Jesus states in verse 49 that "I was daily with you in the Temple teaching and you took me not").[47] And why couldn't Judas just point Jesus out with the usual manual deictic gesture: pointing? In any case, the seizure is shown to take place in the darkest hour of the night, as they led Jesus "to the high priest, and with him were assembled all the chief priests and the elders and scribes" (14:53). We might ask whether these constituted the Sanhedrin and if not, why Jesus was not brought before that body. Nonetheless, the high priest is represented asking if Jesus is the Christ, and, in response to Jesus' affirmative response, tears his clothes and asks rhetorically: "what need have we of any further witnesses...and they all condemned him to be guilty of death" (14:63-64)—and (as chapter 15 opens), "straightway in the morning the chief priests held a consultation with the elders and scribes and the whole council [presumably this is the Sanhedrin], and bound Jesus, and carried him away and delivered him to Pontius Pilate [the Roman procurator]."

Pilate asks Jesus if he is the King of the Judaeans,[48] to which he responds "*You* [*scilicet*: not I] say it" (15:2). Pilate marvels that Jesus remains silent in the face of the "many things they witness against you" that we might suppose Pilate lists. There follows a strange passage, in which we are told that "at that feast [Passover] he [typically?] released unto them one prisoner, whomsoever they desired. And there was one named Barabbas, who lay bound with them who has made insurrection with him, who committed murder in the insurrection" (15:5-7). Pilate is represented as asking the people whom to release, and inspired by "the chief priests" they ask for Barabbas' release and, with regard to "the one whom you call King of the Judaeans, ...they cried out again, Crucify him!" (15:12-13).

What is strange about this last exchange is that there is absolutely no Roman record of such a custom under the procuratorship of Pontius Pilate or any other Roman procurator; and that the name, "Barabbas" means "Son of the Father" in Aramaic, suggesting that it is an artificial, made-up name, intended to mirror what and who Jesus is: Son of the Father. And to what "insurrection," and by whom, is the text referring, in which Barabbas killed someone? If from context we may take "with him" to mean "with Jesus" then does that mean that Barabbas and Jesus are being said to have participated in that insurrection for which this is the sole reference?

In any case the text continues that "Pilate, willing to content the people, released Barabbas unto them and delivered Jesus, when he had scourged him, to be crucified" (15:15)—this, only a few days after the people had been so enthusiastic about him that they were strewing palm branches in his path as he entered the city. The crowning with thorns follows, the bringing of him to Golgotha, with "one Simeon, a Cyrenian, who passed by, coming out of the country, the father of Alexander and Rufus, [compelled to] bear his cross" (15:20), and finally the Crucifixion itself, at "the third hour," with the "superscription of his accusation... 'The King of the Judaeans'" (15:25-26). There follow references to mockery of Jesus as he hangs there, and "when the sixth hour was come there was darkness over the whole land until the ninth hour, and at the ninth hour" he cried out and then finally died (15:33-37). Mark concludes with the arrival of the three Marys to the tomb, who find it empty, and the appearance of the resurrected Christ to Mary Magdalene, then to two others, then to the eleven remaining apostles (the missing twelfth is Judas), whom he sends forth to preach "everywhere, the Lord working with them and confirming the word with signs following" (16:20).

The Gospel According to Mark is by consensus the earliest to have been written down, in the early 70s—in other words, 35 or 40 years after the Crucifixion.[49] As such it may have been available as a model for the next two versions of the same narrative, according to Matthew and Luke, written down, in that order, in the mid-80s to early 90s. The version associated with St. Matthew is 28 chapters long, and begins with a genealogy of Christ that carries from the Israelite King David to "Joseph the husband of Mary, of whom was born Jesus, who is called Christ" (1:16). The miraculous Virgin Birth is recounted both in terms of its fulfillment of that "which was spoken of the Lord by the prophet" (1:22) and in terms of Joseph's acceptance of the miracle, and thus of Mary as his wife.

Chapter 2 begins with the birth of Jesus in Bethlehem, the arrival of wise men from the east looking for this newly born King of the Judaeans, and Herod's gathering of the "chief priests and scribes of the people" to inquire about this, culminating in his massacre of "all the children who were in Bethlehem and in the coasts thereof, from two years and under, according to the time which he had diligently inquired of the wise men" (2:16). The most obvious question that might occur to the reader is: which Herod?—if this is Herod the Great, builder of the Massada complex and refurbisher of the Temple, who died in 4 BCE, then when was Jesus actually born? Or could it have been one of his successors, such as Herod Antipas or Herod Archelaus?[50] A differently and equally interesting observation would be that, since Bethlehem is inland, then if the turn of phrase "and the coasts thereof" is to be taken straightforwardly, the swathe of Herod's slaughter of the children was a wide one indeed.

Matthew's second chapter continues with the observation that the Holy Family, having fled into Egypt to avoid Herod's sword, was able to return after the death of the king and thereafter dwelled in Nazareth. Chapter 3 describes the preaching of John the Baptist, the arrival of a now-adult Jesus to the Jordan where John was preaching and baptizing people, and the first twelve verses of chapter 4 describe Jesus' sojourn in the wilderness where he fasts for 40 days and nights and is tempted by the devil. From verse 13 through the beginning of chapter 19 we read of Jesus in the Galilee, and in the last nine chapters we follow him into Judaea, toward his Apocalyptic discourse, the description of the Passion and finally the narrative of the empty tomb and the resurrection.

There are many differences of detail in all of this between the two Gospels; generally speaking, Matthew is more extensive in describing events and in relaying the words of Jesus. The seizure in the Garden of Gethsemane is somewhat more detailed, and the name of the High Priest is specified as Caiaphas. More important is a number of aspects of the role of Judas in the narrative. He is shown repenting of his actions and approaching the chief priests and elders "saying, 'I have sinned in that I have betrayed innocent blood.' And they said, 'what is that to us?'" (27:4); after which he throws down onto the floor of the Temple the 30 pieces of silver that had been paid him to betray Jesus and goes off and hangs himself.

Two Marys, not three, are shown witnessing the empty sepulcher. Among the most important of Jesus' words is the statement near the very end of the book that "all power is given unto me in heaven and in earth. Go, therefore, and teach all nations, baptizing them in the name of the Father and of the Son and of the Holy Spirit, teaching them to observe all things whatsoever I have commanded you; and lo, I am with you always, even unto the end of the world" (24:18-20).

Luke—24 chapters long—parallels or shortly follows Matthew in time of composition and writing down, and begins, in chapter 1, with parallel descriptions of the annunciations to Zacharias and to Mary regarding the miraculous births of John and Jesus, respectively. Chapter 2 carries Joseph and the pregnant Mary from Nazareth to Bethlehem because as "one of the house and lineage of David" (2:4) Joseph needed to be in "the city of David, which is called Bethlehem," for the purposes of the Roman tax that had just been imposed by Augustus Caesar—as opposed to the change of venue having come about as a consequence of the massacre of the innocents and in the aftermath of the Flight in Egypt. The birth of Christ is accompanied by the Annunciation to the Shepherds, and the narrative of his childhood culminates with his engagement, at age 12, of the learned ones in the Temple, whom he amazes with his wisdom and understanding.[51]

Chapter 3 begins by picking up the thread of John the Baptist's story to the time when he is thrown into prison by Herod, and then picks up the story of Jesus at age 30, with the Holy Spirit descending upon him in the form of a dove; it culminates with a genealogy that carries from Joseph back through David all the way to Adam. Chapter 4 begins with Jesus' experience in the wilderness and the Temptation, and follows with his preaching in the Galilee; this continues through 9:50, after which he journeys to Jerusalem and then through Samaria (through 19:27) and arrives again into Jerusalem, where the Passion narrative begins with the Kiss of Judas at 22:47. In Luke 22:51 Jesus heals the ear of the high priest's servant that was cut off, as opposed to his statement to "put away the sword" that one reads in Matthew 26:52 or his rhetorical question in Mark 14:48, directed altogether away from that act toward his apprehenders: "Are you come out, as against a thief, with swords and with staves to take me?"—which question is repeated in Luke 22:52.

As in Matthew, Pilate is presented as finding Jesus innocent, and releasing Barabbas to the people, in chapter 23. There, some further specification is offered regarding the superscription—"This is the King of the Judaeans"—written over his head, to wit that it was written "in letters of Greek, and Latin, and Hebrew" (23:38). The last chapter begins with a reference to the empty tomb, only specifying by verse 10 that "It was Mary Magdalene, and Joanna, and Mary the mother of James, and other women who were with them, who told these things to the apostles." The book culminates with post-resurrection events that take place around Jerusalem—as opposed to their primary locus in the Galilee that one finds in Matthew.

These three gospel texts are referred to as the "Synoptic Gospels," since they offer a narrative with three very similar but not identical arrays of detail: "*ops*" in Greek means "eye" and "*syn-*", as we have seen in the previous chapter, means "with"; thus "seeing with" or "seeing together" is the connotation of the English-language adjective. If we revel in these texts as expressions of faith that address our faith, then we understand the differences of detail as reflections of the rich range of oral *midrash* on the life, times, circle and significance of Jesus of Nazareth that was passed down lovingly from follower to follower and group to group, ultimately taking definitive form in these narratives, imbued with and inspired by the Holy Spirit of God Itself. If, on the other hand, we are looking to these texts as factual, historical accounts of the events that encircle Jesus, his times and his followers, then we should be disturbed by the challenges that the differences of detail offer to our desire to know exactly what transpired.

The shape of the 21 chapters of the Gospel According to John, dated by New Testament scholars still later than Matthew and Luke—as late as the early second century—is formatted altogether differently form the three Synoptic Gospels. If, for our purposes, we jump to chapter 16, and the apprehending of Jesus in the Garden—referred to simply as a garden on the other side of the Cidron brook from Jerusalem—then we find the Pharisees mentioned, together with the chief priests, to seize him. Conversely, while Judas is with them, there is no kiss: they announce in response to Jesus' rhetorical question "whom do you seek?" (18:4) that they are seeking Jesus of Nazareth and he responds: "I am he" (18:5).[52] Here Peter is specified as the one who cuts off the right ear of the high priest's servant, who (the servant) is here named Malchus (18:10).

The essentials of what follows are similar to what we have noted in the three earlier Gospels: seizure in the pre-dawn darkness is followed by the bearing of Jesus to the high priest—but in this case "to Annas first, for he was the father-in-law of Caiaphas, who was the high priest in the same year" (19:13). Caiaphas is said to have given "counsel to the Judaeans that it was expedient that one man should die for the people" (18:14) although the text never specifies why such a sacrifice is necessary: from what do the people require salvation through the sacrifice of one individual?

The Judaean leaders lead Jesus to the House of Judgment— clearly the Roman court, since, as they wait in the early morning in the outer chamber, Pilate comes out to them to ask what the charge is. There follows an interesting exchange: Pilate tells them that they should judge him themselves, but they respond that it would be unlawful for them to put any man to death (18:31) so Pilate (in order, the text explains, to fulfill the prophecies concerning Jesus, that he should die) takes him into the judgment hall and asks, as in the other Gospel narratives, whether he is King of the Judaeans. To this question Jesus responds with a question: "Are you saying this yourself, or did others say this of me?" (18:34), to which Pilate answers that "your own nation and the chief priests have delivered you to me. What have you done?" (18:35).

We note that the response of the Judaean leadership that it is unlawful for them to put any man to death is ambiguous but in any case correct. The ambiguity is that, if this is indeed Friday morning, the Sanhedrin would be forbidden by its own laws from trying someone in a capital case—the more so if this is also the first day of Passover. But the turn of phrase might also refer to the shackling of the Sanhedrin by prevailing Roman law from acting on its own with regard to a capital case. In any event, the Judaean leadership cannot act, so Pilate has to choose whether or not to do so himself—which as procurator would be his legal right and responsibility, according to Roman law. He chooses to proceed, but the burden of the accusation is left on the shoulders of the Judaean leadership by the text.

Once again, the story of Barabbas and the custom of release follows; once again the leaders and people call upon Pilate to crucify him; once again Pilate himself is exculpated by the text, that presents him as saying to the people: "you take him and crucify him, for I find no fault in him" — to which the response from the Judaeans is: "we have a law, and by our law he ought to die, because he made himself the Son of God" (19:6-7). There follows a back and forth in which Pilate is represented as uncomfortable with the possibility of crucifying an innocent man, the Judaeans point out to him that Jesus' assertion that he is king is treasonous against Caesar, (and that therefore, obviously, he is not innocent). Pilate asks "'shall I crucify your king?' [and] the chief priests answered: 'We have no king but Caesar.' Then he delivered him therefore unto them to be crucified. And they took Jesus and led him away" (19:8-16). Thus not only does the responsibility for Jesus' death fall, in John's account, on Judaean shoulders, in that the Judaeans pushed Pilate to execute Jesus, but the Judaeans themselves, not Pilate or the Romans, are represented as actually crucifying him.

II. Historiographic Sources Outside the Gospels

There are at least four issues that this rapid review of key elements among the Gospel narratives presents to an astute reader, with regard to the death of Jesus and its consequences for subsequent history and religion. One is the fact of myriad contradictions among the four versions that, to repeat, should raise bright red historiographic flags with regard to that death and the events surrounding it, and how any or all of these narratives accord with or contradict what we might anticipate for a legal case such as that associated with Jesus, based on the text of tractate *Sanhedrin* and its mishnaic siblings. A second is the question of what other sources we might turn to for either corroboration or contradiction of the Gospels not only with regard to this detail or that, but to the overall picture of what transpired in Judaea around the Passover festival nearly two millennia ago. The third is the question of how and why, if there are important differences between the picture of events that the Gospels paint and other sources, those differences came into being. The fourth is what the consequences are, specifically for Christian-Jewish relations over the centuries that follow. For Christianity's embrace of these texts as God's word means that, in spite of whatever internal contradictions or contradictions of other external texts exist, they are to be embraced as *true* in the most fundamental sense of that word.

Thus we have seen that there are small discrepancies among the Gospel texts regarding the details of the seizure of Jesus in the Garden and his appearance before the High Priest in the Temple as well as his appearance before Pontius Pilate. More importantly, we find serious contradictions between what the Gospels offer and what we might expect based on *Sanhedrin*. The very manner in which Jesus is represented as appearing in the house of the High Priest in the first place, regardless of details, contradicts the role for a Judaean court: the Sanhedrin could not—and there is no evidence that it ever did—meet to exercise its jurisdiction in the house of the High Priest or anywhere else except within the court house established within the Temple precincts.[53] A night-time trial without any cross-examination by witnesses and a call for and carrying out of an immediate execution—by crucifixion, no less—directly abrogates what is laid out in *Sanhedrin*.[54]

Mark 15:42 asserts, moreover, that the day that dawned and brought about an immediate rush to execution was a Friday—the day before the Sabbath. That, too, would directly abrogate Judaean law. Not only must a full day elapse between condemnation and execution, but no capital trial can begin on a Friday, since the court does not meet on the Sabbath and therefore the procedure would have to pause, leaving the condemned and everyone else in an uncomfortable state of suspension until the trial and/or the consequences of its outcome, should that outcome be negative, could resume. So assuming that Jesus was apprehended just prior to dawn—at that dark hour without a specific name except, perhaps, in Spanish, in which it is called *la madrugada*—then the trial would have had to wait for Sunday morning, the proceedings concluded on Monday and the execution on Tuesday.

But there is a still further issue with the day of the trial: the

Gospel accounts all point to the seizure as happening during Passover. The Last Supper is represented as having been a Passover Seder, and, assuming therefore that that meal took place on Passover eve, the festival would have continued for a week thereafter—this was, we recall, one of the three major pilgrimage festivals on the Judaean calendar, and Jerusalem would have been so packed with Judaeans, Galileeans and others—so that the entire story of the seizure, trial and execution of Jesus would have taken place during the festival, in fact on the very first day of the festival. But no criminal proceedings were permitted on either the eve of a feast day or on the day itself.[55] Nor could a witness testify against himself which Jesus is depicted as doing, albeit in a somewhat roundabout manner—and a conviction, as we have noted, required the testimony of at least two reliable and independent witnesses, who had to attest both to having witnessed the offence in their presence and to their certainty that the offender committed the offence knowing that the act was a punishable crime.[56]

And what, again, is the capital crime of which Jesus is represented as being accused by the High Priest and/or others? Blasphemy. Fair enough—but what exactly constitutes "blasphemy" in the eyes of the Judaean court, according to Tractate *Sanhedrin* 7, 5? Blasphemy is only committed if those two truthful and independent witnesses testify that the accused has, in their presence, pronounced the Ineffable Name of God—which name might only be pronounced by the High Priest and by him only once a year, on the Day of Atonement, as he entered the innermost sanctuary—the Holy of Holies—of the Temple. This is not at all what is suggested in any of the Gospel texts.

Thus aside from internal differences of detail with respect to these and other issues, the Gospel texts clearly contradict the record in *Sanhedrin* and other mishnaic sources of what the appropriate procedures would be in a case like that of Jesus. Nonetheless, we could ascribe the internal issue of detail differences to variant recollections of those details and the varied times and perhaps even places of writing them down. We could ascribe the external issue of the relationship to *Sanhedrin* to the *sui generis* nature of Jesus himself and therefore of his alleged crime and therefore a willingness on the part of the Judean leadership and people to make a profound exception to the norms of Judaean law in his case—and his case alone. We might then be inclined to accept the Gospel account—which in general terms (regardless of internal contradictions of detail) ascribes responsibility for Jesus' death to the Judaean leadership and/or to the Judaean people, either directly (that they crucified him) or indirectly, (that the Judaean leaders and their followers both brought Jesus before Pilate, the Roman procurator and/or pressured him to crucify Jesus)—were there some corroborating testimony from available non-Gospel sources.

Put another way: if Jesus were, at the time of his life and death, such a central figure on the historical stage of Judaea in its position as a procuratorially-administered sub-province of the Roman Empire, we might expect to find sources outside the Gospels that offer some serious focus on his words and actions. In that case, we might be willing to embrace the notion that his case was so out of the ordinary that it caused the Sanhedrin to completely abandon its generations'-old, Torah-based procedures for dealing with individuals brought before it, from convening so late at night in the High Priest's house (at a time when the High Priest could hardly be more subject to being regarded as a mock-High Priest), following an unprecedented and never-again-tried juridical procedure and engaging in a completely uncharacteristic and illegal mode and manner of execution.

What are those other possible outside sources—that might or do make some mention of Jesus or individuals and events connected to him? The available ones to date[57] that speak of him in some way are works by the Roman writers Tacitus, Suetonius—both of them early-second-century historians—and Pliny, the late-first-century scientist; the early-mid-first century Judaean philosopher Philo of Alexandria; and the late-first-century Judaean-Jewish historian, Josephus. One might add to this array the so-called Dead Sea Scrolls, which are the only writings directly contemporary with the events described in the Gospels as far as physical manuscripts are concerned. But these last don't make any mention at all of Jesus, those around him, or any of the events summarized above, and their precise possible dating ranges from before to after the time of Jesus' life, encompassing it, one might say, as opposed to being clearly synchronous with it.

It is true that the so-called "Battle Scroll" speaks of a Good Teacher who will ultimately lead all the forces of Good against the forces of Evil led by the Wicked Priest, in an apocalyptic battle that will involve angelic hosts. But to construe the figure of the Good Teacher as Jesus, as one might, requires interpretation through faith—there is nothing wrong with that, as long as we remember that it is historiographic interpretation and not historical factuality—for nothing in the scroll makes such an equation explicit. And in any case, this is an apocalyptic text of the future, not a historical text of the present or past—and may have been written a generation or more before Jesus was born. So even if the Good Teacher were to be construed to be Jesus, the text is referring to what he will do, not to what he has already done.

What do the Roman and other Judaean sources offer us? Very different views of the story from that told by the Gospel texts—or the Acts of the Apostles, for that matter, about which more shortly. Thus where the Gospels represent the High Priest, Caiaphas, as believing in Jesus' guilt and bringing him to Pontius Pilate—virtually forcing him on the procurator, who is depicted as believing Jesus innocent—Josephus presents the High Priest as answerable to the procurator and notes that the latter has full power of appointment and dismissal, the implication of which is that the High Priest would not likely attempt to pressure or succeed in convincing the procurator to go against his own will, regardless of who the procurator and who the High Priest might be.[58]

But then again, Pilate is represented in the Gospels as a decent and fair ruler, who could be imagined easily enough to yield to the emotion-laden petition of the High Priest, the Judaean leaders and indeed the Judaean people, even if it went against his better judgment. But not only Josephus, but also Philo and Tacitus represent Pilate as a ruthless ruler who willingly and quickly consigned scores of Judaean victims to execution without trial. For example, in Book XVIII, Chapter III, Section 1 and 2 of his *Antiquities of the*

Judaeans, Josephus, writing around 93-95 CE, tells us how Pilate—who "removed the [Roman] army from Caesarea to Jerusalem... in order to abolish the Judaean laws," stirred up unrest among the Judaeans by pilfering sacred funds [contributed by Judaeans from around the empire and reserved for the upkeep of the Temple] in order to dig a channel with which to supply Jerusalem with water.

The resultant tumultuous protest led to the slaughter of a great number of Judaeans, unarmed in their crowded protest against the procurator, surrounded and attacked by Pilate's soldiers, who "laid upon them with much greater blows than Pilate had commanded them, and [who] equally punished those who were tumultuous, and those who were not; nor did they spare them in the least, and since the people were unarmed and were caught by men prepared for what they were about, there was a great number of them slain by this means, and others of them ran away wounded."

No source outside the Gospels, be it Josephus or anyone else, even hints at a Passover-period custom, under Pilate or any other procurator, of releasing a convicted criminal from prison selected by the people for release. What is more peculiar is the name of the individual whom, according to the Gospel text, the Judaeans chose to liberate: Barabbas. The name, to repeat, means "son of the father" in Aramaic. That is, of course, exactly who Jesus claims to be! Thus the son of the father was traded for the son of the father; one let free and the other executed by or under pressure from a howling crowd. This portion of all four Gospel texts smacks strongly of something made-up. Or perhaps there is merely confusion as to what was what and who was who, so that the story written down so long after events mistakenly divided Jesus the Son of God into two figures—which in any case, offers a mechanism for Pilate's exoneration. The question, to be addressed shortly, is: *why*?

Conversely, the image of the Judaean leadership—particularly the Pharisees—that is placed before the reader in the Gospels is of a group detested by the people (in contrast to the image of a Jesus loved by the people) and full of hypocrisy. Josephus not only presents the Pharisees as popular with the people, but their evolution over the last pre-Christian century is that of a "People's Party"—in contrast and opposition to the Sadducees, who were the party of the upper crust. All kinds of mishnaic interpretations of the Torah reflect Pharisaic concern for the common man.[59] If anyone would have been detested by those among the people who knew his falseness, it would have been the High Priest—but among those who would have best known and most despised him were the Pharisees.

What of Jesus himself, who in the Gospels is, of course, the center of events and widely known, and the dawning aftermath of whose trial attracts such an enormous crowd—and whose trial is as unique as he is? In the other sources he is barely mentioned—sometimes in a manner that suggests a complete misunderstanding of what and who he was or claimed to be. Josephus, in the passage in XVIII:III:3 that follows what was quoted just above, writes about how "there was about this time Jesus, a wise man, if it be lawful to call him a man, for he was a doer of wonderful works, a teacher of such men as receive truth with pleasure. He drew over to him both many of the Judaeans [in this context less a reference to nationality or ethnicity than to religion: i.e., believers in the God of Israel] and many of the Gentiles [i.e., pagans]. He was the Christ. And when Pilate, at the suggestion of the principal men among us, had condemned him to the cross, those who loved him at the first did not forsake him, for he appeared to them alive again at the third day, as the divine prophets had foretold these and ten thousand other wonderful things concerning him. And the tribe of the Christians, so named from him, are not extinct to this day."

Josephus is a Judaean insider, as it were, albeit very Romanized: one might suppose that his perspective and thus his awareness of Jesus and the issues surrounding him come from within the Judaean community—albeit not from within the nascent Christian branch of that community, since, regardless of the details he gives, he himself was apparently not drawn to become a follower, a member of the "race" or "tribe" of Christians. And his own sources for events that predated his birth (he was born in 37 CE) would have been like those of the Gospels: an expanding oral tradition that may, for him, have included the Synoptic Gospels themselves. He is the only source outside the Gospels that associate some of the leadership

of the community of which he was part with Jesus' demise, in suggesting that they helped push Pilate to condemn him—although he
gives no details by which one could judge Pilate's own mind in the
matter. And his reference to Christians as a "tribe" underscores the
lack of clarity with regard to classificatory terminology still in place
with reference to (what we would call) Christians and Jews at the
end of the first century.

What of the Romans themselves, whose procurator we could
easily enough imagine a little bit apprehensive as the population
within Jerusalem swelled to many times its normal size during the
Passover festival? This was, after all, not just any pilgrimage festival, but the one that was annually inspired by the celebration of the
successful "rebellion" against the Egyptians by the Moses-led Israelites, and the disastrous consequences for the Pharaoh in the swirling
waters of the Sea of Reeds. We might well imagine Pilate nervously
seizing someone who was led into the city as an anointed descendant
of King David and who, perhaps, regardless of that individual's own
peaceful, spiritual rhetoric might have been misperceived by those
drawn to him—or Pilate might have misperceived him as well as
misperceiving how Jesus' own followers perceived him—as a potential rabble-rouser, ready to inspire his followers to rebel against Roman power in emulation of their Israelite ancestors.

But what do the Romans themselves *say*? Nothing at the time
of the events in Judaea, and very little nearly a century later. Suetonius, a Roman, pagan outsider, writing around 120 CE, in his *On
the Lives of the Caesars* mentions Jesus and the Christians once each.
In section 25 of his "Life of Claudius" (Emperor between 41 and 54
CE), he discusses what was and was not permissible to foreigners,
then notes that because "the *iudaei* at Rome caused continuous disturbances at the instigation of Chrestus, he [i.e., Claudius] expelled
them from the city."

There are several different but related issues of confusion in
this passage. First, there had been *iudaei* in Rome since the early
Hasmonean period—ca 170-160 BCE—and that, combined with
the *religio licita* status of the Judaeans from a century later (ca 63
BCE) Judeans could not, per se, be expelled from Rome, particularly

not those who had long been resident there. So those expelled by
Claudius would have had to be recent arrivals. Second, given the
reference to "Chrestus"—a Latinized version of the Greek *"Chris-
tos"*—we must infer that those exiled at that time, ca 49 CE, were
Judaeans who were "followers of Chrestus," i.e., who believed in
Jesus as the *Mashiah/Christos.*

We might imagine that they had arrived in Rome preaching
their belief in Jesus as *Mashiah/Christos* and the concomitants of
that belief—perhaps one of their leaders was even invited to deliver a guest sermon in one of the synagogues in Trastevere, the area
across the Tiber from downtown Rome, where most *iudaei* lived—
and his sermon stirred things up to ultimately riotous proportions
between the two Judaean factions. From Suetonius' pagan Roman
perspective, even writing as late as 120, they are all *iudaei*; he cannot
distinguish "Jew" from "Christian." So it is most likely that proto-
Christians—or if one prefers, "Judaeans for Jesus"—were expelled.
Third, of course: Suetonius has no idea who Jesus of Nazareth is, to
whom some *iudaei* refer as the *Mashiah/Christos.* He imagines a mob
leader, in Rome in 49, stirring things up, who is named Chrestus,
and not an individual who has already been dead for more than a
decade and a half and was already remembered by his followers as
a soft-spoken spiritual leader.

In section 16 of his chapter on Nero (Claudius' successor as
Emperor, from 54 to 68), Suetonius makes reference not to Christ
but to Christians as "a kind of men given to a new, and criminal
superstitio, [who] were put to death with grievous torments." Thus
he evinces neither any sense of a connection between them and the
"rebel leader" to whom he had referred in his life of Claudius nor
any awareness of the continuity between those he labels *"Christiani"*
and the *Iudaei* of that slightly earlier, Claudian period. This, although
Nero's era was a time when nearly all of those who believed in Jesus
as the *Mashiah/Christos* would still have been *Iudaei*: religious history is only just beginning its turn to the process according to which
the "Judaeans for Jesus" have begun to reach out to the pagan population for converts.[60] Of course, by Suetonius' own time, Jews and
Christians themselves would have long arrived at incipient clarity

regarding their separation, in terms of beliefs, celebrations, and respective senses of sacred text.[61] The two terms would have been in increasingly frequent use, but it would take another decade or so for the distinction between the two groups to become apparent to pagan outsiders.

Tacitus actually writes his *Annales* a few years earlier than Suetonius writes his *Lives*—ca 115-117. In this work, essentially a history of Roman history from the beginning of the Empire to his own time, he arrives, in chapter XV, section 44, to the burning of Rome about ten years into the reign of Nero, and the issue of how Nero turned public suspicion away from himself. Thus in order to deflect that suspicion,

> Nero put in his own place as culprits, and punished with every refinement of cruelty, the persons whom the common people hated for their secret crimes. They called them "Christians." Christ, upon [whose name] the name was based, had been put to death in the reign of Tiberius by the procurator Pontius Pilate and the persistent *superstitio* was checked for a while.
>
> Afterwards it began afresh not only in Judaea wherethe mischief first arose, but also in Rome...
>
> In the first place some [of the Christians] were seized and made to confess; then, based on that information, a vast multitude were convicted, not so much of arson as of hatred of the human race.
>
> And they were not only put to death, but put to death with insults, in that they were dressed up in the skins of beasts to perish by the attacks of dogs or else put on crosses to be set on fire and, when daylight failed, to be burnt for use as lights at night.

So the first thing that we notice is the horrific consequences of Nero's false accusation for a group that, to repeat, at the time of Nero would still have been thought of as consisting of *iudaei*, but who were apparently already becoming recognized as *iudaei* who followed the ideology of Christ as articulated in the thirty years since his death by Peter, Paul and others—and whom Tacitus, by his era, correctly refers to as "Christian" (even if Suetonius does not). The second matter of note—which comes up first in Tacitus' text—is Tacitus' reference to Christianity as a *superstitio*, which term he uses to describe it as a pestilential political subversion. It is a subversion significant enough that he can construe the general pagan Roman populace as hating the Christians for their "secret crimes"—and by definition, anything Christians did, be it praying together or telling stories about Jesus together, would be construed as a "secret crime" since their faith was illegalized by its *superstitio* status.

Of course Christianity, as such, did not exist at the time of Tiberius and Pontius Pilate, as a *superstitio* or as a *religio licita*. The contemporary followers of Jesus, like Jesus himself, were simply *Iudaei/Yehoodeem* and their faith was centered on the God of Israel whose primary cult center was the Temple in Jerusalem. They, like he, saw his role as one of restoring a proper relationship between the *Iudaei* and God after centuries of erosion and schism. So Tacitus is retrofitting his limited understanding of Christianity not only onto Nero's era but onto Tiberius' era. This was appropriate to his own time-period to the extent that, in its emergent shape (as distinct from Judaism in *its* emergent shape), Christianity had come to be regarded as a *superstitio*.

Josephus, writing[62] in his *Antiquities of the Judaeans*, XVIII.v.2 [116-119], (to repeat: nearly a generation before either of these Roman historians—around 93-95 CE or so), speaks at several paragraphs' length about John the Baptist, observing that "some of the *Ioudaioi* thought that the destruction of Herod [i.e., Herod Antipas, one of the successors to Herod the Great]'s army was a divine judgment, a very just penalty for his murder of John the Baptist. For Herod killed him in spite of the fact that he was a good man, who taught the *Ioudaioi* to practice virtue, to show righteousness toward one another and piety toward God, and to form a community by means of baptism."

Later, in XX.ix.1 [200], he also mentions James [James the Greater, best-known as the patron saint of Spain, *Santiago el Mayor*] who—during the year 62, right after the procuratorship of Festus, who had died suddenly in office, and before the new procurator, Albinus, arrived—was apprehended by the bold and insolent high priest, Ananus. Ananus "convened a judicial session of the Sanhedrin and brought before it the brother of Jesus, the so-called *Christos*—James by name—and some others whom he charged with breaking the law and handed over to be stoned to death."

Up to that point in Josephus' text we might suppose that what happened to James in 62 had influenced the Gospel text with regard to its description of Jesus' seizure and death. James' fate so resembles, albeit in abbreviated form—and not insignficantly, with reference to a different mode of execution—the fate of Jesus as described in the Gospels. Or perhaps we might see Josephus as corroborating the Gospel account by offering the possibility of a second abrogation of the Sanhedrin's mode of operation. However, Josephus continues: "But as for those who seemed the most just among the citizens, and who were thus the most uncomfortable with this breach of [Judaean] law, they disliked what was being done [by Ananus]. So they sent [word] to the king [Agrippa II, one of the successors of Herod three generations after the latter's death[63]....], desiring him to send [word] to Ananus that he should act no more, for what he had already done could not be justified; nay, some of them went forth also to meet Albinus, as he was on the way [to Jerusalem] from Alexandria [to take up his post as procurator] and informed him that it was not lawful for Ananus to assemble a Sanhedrin without his [the procurator's] consent."

Thus one thing is clear: Ananus's attempt to subvert Judaean law in general and Judaean law specifically in its relation to Roman law ultimately failed. A second thing is unclear: whether Ananus' attempt failed before or after James was executed—and if James was executed, then by whom, exactly? And it remains unclear as to what relationship there might be between Josephus' account of James' fate and the Gospel accounts of Jesus' fate. What are Josephus' sources? If the subversion to which Josephus refers in the story of James actually mirrors what happened to Jesus, why wouldn't the writer have added something to that effect: "James, the brother of Jesus the so-called Christ, who suffered the same fate" or something of that sort? Which leads to a third issue that is *clear*: the scant mention of Jesus, only in passing, with reference to James, as the *so-called Christos*, sixty years after his death—and similarly, within Tacitus and Suetonius eighty years after his death—suggests that at the time of his life and death and in the century of its aftermath he was a minor figure on the stage of history as far as the general awareness of *who* he was and understanding of *what* he was were concerned.

This makes it far less likely that the Sanhedrin or the Judaean leadership or the Judaean people at large would have stepped so far outside their own legal system in order to assure Jesus' demise. Jesus' death by crucifixion would have made him one of hundreds or perhaps even thousands of individuals executed that way by the Romans, however, typically for political subversion. For that reason the cross took nearly half a millennium to emerge as a Christian visual symbol: until the faith prevailed, and until the memory of all those deaths could fade, one could hardly refer to Christ's uniqueness by an image that would merely evoke and connote the deaths of an endless array of individuals executed as political subversives by the Romans.

Thus, far from mocking him, the superscription referred to in the Gospels—"Jesus of Nazereth King of the Judaeans"—would, from the Roman point of view, have delineated his crime: that he was asserting himself as a king over a territory governed by a Roman procurator and, as such, that he was acting as a political subversive. This is, needless to say, a very different perspective from what one obtains within the Gospels, where he is emphatically nonpolitical, much less politically subversive in viewpoint: he enjoins his follows to "render onto God that which is God's and to Caesar that which is Caesar's" and warns Peter (or an unnamed follower) to "put away the sword...".

Indeed, broadly speaking, the Gospel accounts suggest a harmonious relationship between Rome and nascent Christianity—whereas all three Roman sources suggest the condition that would not change until Constantine's "Edict of Milan" in 313. That is, Suetonius, Tacitus and Pliny all represent Christianity as being at odds with pagan Roman authority. Later Christian hagiographers corroborate this: Rome persecuted Christians until the early fourth century. Of course, none of the Judaeans in the Gospels are *Christians*, just as none of them are Jews—yet. The distinction between the two groups as we would recognize them will not approach clarity until the end of the first century and the beginning of the second.

But by then Rome—even after the revolt that ended in the destruction of the Temple in 70 CE—had made a decision regarding how to treat adherents to the two sibling faiths. The Romans distinguished between *religio licita* and *superstitio*. The first phrase refers to a faith that is accepted by Roman authority as legitimate, that offers no threat to the state—that offers to its God or gods what is due It/them (prayers, offerings, celebrations, proper behavior) and to the Roman state and its leaders what is due them (blessings, taxes, celebrations, proper behavior). The second term refers to a faith that is not accepted by Roman authority because it is perceived to be dangerous to the state: we might translate *superstitio* as "subversion."

Now the Judaean religion had been granted *religio licita* status by the Roman authorities back in the time of Pompey the Great, around 63 BCE. In practical terms this meant not only that the Judaean religion was accepted and respected as such, but that Judaean sacred sites—most notably and obviously, the Temple in Jerusalem—were protected, that the half-shekel contribution sent annually by *Yehoodeem* from throughout the Roman world for the upkeep of the Temple were sacred funds to be protected by Roman officials, and that to attempt to pilfer them was punishable by death. That *religio* status for Judaea was continued by Pompey's successors in charge of Judaea, from Julius Caesar to Marc Antony to Augustus Caesar and his imperial successors—all the way to the time of Theodosius at the end of the fourth century.[64]

But the question would arise by the late first century: which child of the Judaean parent, Christianity or Judaism, should be the logical heir to the *religio* status of Judaeanism? The answer was made simple for the Romans by the linguistics of the situation and their own ignorance of the ins and outs of the inner ethno-religious politics of the Judaean world: in Latin, as in Greek, Hebrew and Aramaic, the word for Jewish, Jew, and Judaean are one and the same; the word for Judaism and Judaeanism are one and the same. Thus it would have seemed clear to the Romans that Jews were the logical heirs to the *religio* status of Judaea—of which Judaea was not deprived even after the revolt of 65-73! Roman authority continued to distinguish between the political nature of that revolt and the need and legitimacy of suppressing it; and the religion of the rebels as legitimate.

By contrast, the soon-to-be-called Christians, by virtue of being labeled with a different—a new and different—designation, were perceived to be a new group without a historical right to be considered *religio*. And, for whatever reasons, the Roman authorities saw the Christians as subversive, as a threat to the stability of the empire. Thus they labeled the new faith a *superstitio* and continued sporadically to persecute its adherents all the way through the time of Diocletian. It was only with Constantine's different perspective—that Christianity could be a glue to help him hold the empire together—that its status and its condition changed.[65]

This situation helps us understand the historiographic problems that the Gospels present. I reiterate: these are *not* problems if we look at those texts simply as centerpieces of faith, and internal differences are easily enough explained, also to repeat, by looking through the lens of faith. But the radical differences between the Gospels and the non-Gospel sources are understandable by means of the *religio/superstitio* issue and its concomitants. For from the last third of the first century until the second quarter of the fourth century, nascent and then developing Judaism and Christianity are locked in a double wrestling match with each other. They are not only increasingly at theological odds with each other; they are contending with each other for *religio* status under the Roman political authority to which they both answer.

Thus we might expect and find in the earliest Christian texts, the Gospels, and then the Acts and the Epistles and apocalyptic Revelation that fill out the New Testament, a depiction of the Romans as just, of the Roman procurator as just and completely guilt-free with regard to the demise of Jesus. Conversely, the Judaeans who did not come to recognize Jesus as the *Mashiah/Christos* can and do come to be thought of not as Judaeans like the proto-Christians and early Christians themselves, but simply as *Jews*. And the Jews are already being tarred as guilty for Jesus' demise just as the Romans are being exonerated by the time of Acts 3:14-15: "It was you who accused the Holy One, the Just One; you who demanded the reprieve of a murderer"—referring, presumably to the Barabbas story found within the Gospels.

Although Pontius Pilate would have had a motive for both fearing and destroying Jesus, and could also have destroyed him from within the bounds of Roman law; and the Judaean leadership could only destroy Jesus as described in the Gospels by stepping well beyond the bounds of Judaean law; the latter scenario would be more appealing to the Gospels since it is less anti-Roman and more anti-"Jewish."

The tendentious nature of the texts explains their narrative direction. And what of the consequences of this? As time went on, the doubly-founded rivalry between developing Judaism and Christianity would only intensify. In reading or hearing the Gospels in Greek or Latin, Christians of the second and third and fourth centuries—particularly as increasing numbers of them were non-Judaean pagans converted from among the far-flung peoples of the empire—would understand the term *"Ioudaios/Iudaeus"* to mean "Jew," not "Judaean." For as Christianity during these centuries became increasingly and aggressively proselytic, reaching out to the pagan populations of the empire—and eventually, with Theodosius, overwhelming the empire as its official religion—the tie to Judaean ethnicity would in any case be diluted further and further and ultimately disappear. To a Christian born in fourth-century Spain or Gaul, clearly the *Iudaei* referred to in the Gospels are the Jews.

And the firm placement of responsibility for Jesus' death on the shoulders of the Jews would have been essential both for political purposes vis-a-vis the Romans and for theological purposes vis-a-vis the Jews. They (the Jews) are those who have failed to see how the words of their own sacred texts are echoed and the promises of those texts fulfilled by the advent of Jesus onto the stage of history as portrayed in the Gospels.[66] And the ramifications of this—as the ancient world begins its shift toward the medieval world, as formerly pagan Rome is transformed into Christian Rome and the Roman Empire starts its shift toward becoming Europe—are profound.

A Christian world will, over time, forget that anyone other than Jesus (or perhaps Jesus and a pair of thieves to either side of him) suffered crucifixion—crucifixions will become The Crucifixion. The notion that the Jews crucified him, that they who refused to recognize him as the *Mashiah/Christos* (which, in English, will yield "Messiah/Christ") were responsible for his earthbound death will become almost as central to Christian thought as the notion that, as the *Mashiah/Christos*, Jesus was

God Itself become one of us, born miraculously by parthenogenesis. The hostility against the Jews as a consequence will reverberate down through the ages, and among the details of that consequence is a fascinating array of legalistic procedures—trials of various sorts—to which Jews will be subject in the Middle Ages, as we shall see beginning in the next chapter of this narrative.

But it should be noted that the implications will carry beyond the medieval period. Thus, not surprisingly, perhaps, Martin Luther, in his early sixteenth-century translation (into vernacular German) and commentary on The New Testament[67] responds to the passage in Matthew in which the exchange of Jesus for Barabbas is depicted, that "Matthew means to say that Pilate wanted to propose the most dreadful murderer so that the Jews could not ask for him. But they would sooner have pleaded for the Devil himself before they would have had the Son of God released. *Sic et hodie agitur et semper.* (Thus it happens also today and always.)" Thus the reformer did not reform the Christian conviction that the Jews were and remain nefarious opposers of Christ and his message.

More disturbing—because it comes so recently and in the aftermath, among other horrors, of the Holocaust that Luther's teaching regarding the Jews helped facilitate—is the comment made on March 21, 1985 in the official organ of the Passau, Germany Catholic diocese by F. Mussner: "The Jews are guilty of killing Jesus for without the Jews the trial against Jesus of Nazareth and without the trial the Passion of Jesus would not have taken place. Because of the trial of Jesus the Jewish perpetrators provoked punitive consequences for themselves, above all the destruction of the Temple and the Holy City of Jerusalem [in the year 70]. The punitive consequences for the killing of Jesus apply also to the "children" of the Jews, the enemies at the trial of Jesus, hence all Jews unless they make a profession of faith to Jesus. A 'collective guilt' weighs upon the Jews!... All Jews, unless they convert to Christ, are excluded from salvation... Every Jew has crucified Christ..."

Even the liberal and open-minded American theologian Harvey Cox, writing at virtually the same time (on Friday, April 5, 1985) in a *New York Times* Op Ed column about "The Trial of Jesus," while seeming to center that trial on Pontius Pilate, explaining how "he wanted more than anything else to avoid a bad report to the capital, where Sejanus, his patron, had lost influence,"[68] and observing that Pilate and the Sanhedrin "watched uneasily as thousands of unruly Jews streamed into Jerusalem for the Passover," misses the important linguistic, cultural and spiritual nuance that would distinguish "Jews" from "Judaeans," and takes the Barabbas story at face value: "One fervid ultra-nationalist, Barabbas, already was behind bars, but the festive crowd demanded that he be the prisoner traditionally amnestied on the holiday." And, while trying to "explain" it, nonetheless Cox also takes at face value the Gospel claim of a "traditional" Roman Passover release of a prisoner chosen by the people, and its ascription of responsibility to the Sanhedrin: "They moved quickly. Without the consent—possibly even the knowledge—of the rest of the Council, they seized Jesus at night, to avoid popular opposition, and interrogated, in clear defiance of established Jewish legal procedure...[but] when no witnesses could be found to make a blasphemy charge stick, his accusers decided to get Pilate to execute him for subversion."

So while acknowledging that what is reported in the Gospels contradicts what we otherwise know of the Sanhedrin, and asserting that the Gospel report, its internal contradictions properly pieced together, "completely discredits the stubborn myth that the Jews crucified Jesus for claiming that he was the Messiah," he apparently cannot help embracing the report. He imagines a portion of the Sanhedrin—presumably the unidentified "they" who "moved quickly"—acting first to apprehend Jesus out of fear that he was making such a ruckus that there would be bad consequences for the community, and then handing him over to Pilate when they suddenly decided to follow Sanhedrin procedures and found that those procedures would not yield the results that they needed in order to get Jesus out of the way. If such full-hearted misunderstanding comes from a Harvey Cox, what is to be expected of a less adept theologian or an everyday Christian or of a less open-minded Christian leader or follower?

Chapter Three:
Jewish Trials in the Christian Medieval World

I. Triumph and Trauma from Constantine to the Fall of Constantinople

Medieval Western history is in large part the story of the triumph of Christianity—but it is also the story of a varied array of traumas that, through the centuries, have nipped at the heels of that triumph. The Medieval Church, beleaguered by a range of issues is never, to begin with, the "seamless cloak" that Western historiography often alludes to in considering its condition prior to the Protestant Reformation of the sixteenth century—as if Luther and his successors were responsible for tearing it apart.

To begin, chronologically speaking, with the problem of heresy—misbelieving while calling and considering one's self a proper, believing member of the faith—was present within the Church, virtually from the beginning of its legalization under Constantine. Thus in the early fourth century Arius of Alexandria asserted that the Father and the Son could not be correctly construed as co-substantial,[69] since the one is eternal and unchanging and the other is depicted in the Gospels themselves as mutable, as being born, growing up and dying. This assertion produced a crisis, since the view taken by those led by Alexander and Athanasius of Alexandria was that not only the Father and the Son but also the Holy Spirit are co-substantial and share a uniquely tri-une condition of being. In brief, a council at Nicaea in 325 weighed the two perspectives and that of Alexander and Athanasius—perhaps, in part because of the support they received from Emperor Constantine himself—was decreed to be the correct Christian understanding of God.

Thereafter, however, although the non-triune view of Arius was in effect outlawed, it refused to disappear—somewhat as Christianity itself had refused to disappear during the centuries when the pagan Roman authorities viewed and treated it as a *superstitio*. As an internal *"superstitio,"*[70] Arianism was a heresy—to be distinguished not only from proper Christian belief, but from non-Christian, infidel[71] beliefs such as those that paganism continued to offer for many centuries and such as Islam would offer, barely beyond the time when ancient pagan infidel beliefs had disappeared. And heresy not only of the Arian sort, but of other sorts, would follow the Church—sometimes leading the Church—out into the worlds it sought to convert to its understanding of God.

It was primarily Arian Christians who ventured north to convert the "Barbarian" tribes in the third and fourth centuries, so that, beyond whatever hold Arianism retained in the Mediterranean basin, every wave of Germanic invaders—as the Western Roman Empire inexorably melted into a succession of aspects of emergent medieval Europe in the fifth through seventh centuries—brought new groups of adherents to the Arian viewpoint. The Arian heresy had its siblings and offspring: without getting side-tracked with details, the fact that 900 years later the Franciscan and even more so the Dominican order came into being to help the Church wrestle with heretical groups and individuals makes it clear enough that the problem had not been solved by that time.[72]

But other internal issues would come to challenge the issue of heresy as most problematic to the expanding Church as the centuries rolled forward. As the leader of the Church in Rome evolved beyond his position as Bishop of the Eternal City to that of Pope—Father of the entire Church, and heir as such to the position that tradition conferred upon St. Peter, as rock upon which Christ would build his new spiritual edifice[73]—the evolving hierarchy below him echoed the debased and then defunct Roman pagan senatorial bureaucracy as he echoed the erstwhile position of the Emperor. Eventually, though, the Papacy would find itself in periodic conflict with other would-be leaders of Christendom.

Thus there were secular figures who coveted that position directly or indirectly. From the facing down of the would-be sacker of Rome, the Lombard chieftain, Ariulf of Spoleto, by Pope Gregory I ("the Great") in 593; to the crowning of Charlemagne as Holy Roman Emperor by Pope Leo III on Christmas Day in the year 800; to the struggle for primacy between Pope Gregory VII and the young German Emperor, Henry IV, that culminated with a resolved confrontation at Canossa in 1077—a continuous series of issues confronted the papacy in its relationship with the secular leadership of Christendom, with varying results. Indeed the "exile" of the Papacy to Avignon in 1309-78 and the schism that placed one Pope in Rome and another in Avignon from the end of the "exile" until 1415 largely reflected ongoing political-secular struggles and manipulations toward hegemony.

Moreover, (and there is some irony in this), the very movement that had as its purpose to focus the pious most fully away from the material world of secular politics and economics—monasticism—became a source of crisis, in two ways. St. Benedict's rule, drawn up back in the late 520s, had introduced into the West a formal mode of withdrawing from the everyday world. But over the centuries, sons (and later, daughters) who chose—or whose families chose for them—a monastic life, but who found themselves unhappy in that vocation, introduced an increasing volume of worldliness into the world of the monastery and the convent. The first crisis was that monastic orders found themselves more than occasionally and increasingly corrupt— as a consequence of which, new sub-orders sprang up to restore proper spiritual conduct. One of these, the Cluniac order—and this became the second crisis—spread so far in the tenth and eleventh centuries that its Mother House was enormous and its Abbot powerful enough to challenge the Pope himself in ecclesiastical matters.

One sees this, for example, in the case of the second trial for heresy directed at Peter Abelard in the twelfth century, who was ultimately protected by Peter the Venerable at Cluny and was thus in effect beyond the reach even of Pope Innocent II. And here is the irony. Not only should the monastic tradition have offered among the strongest antidotes to heresy, but the creation of the Dominican and Franciscan orders in the 13th century was in part a function of the need for an instrument to assist in the *struggle* against heresy—and the Dominicans, as we have noted, emerged as the primary champion of the Papacy in counteracting heretics. But the Cluniac monastic order would be in a position to harbor the most important and notorious intellectual of his era who, thanks in part to the juridical assertions of another monastic—St. Bernard of Clairvaux—had been declared heretical by the Pope himself.[74]

There is yet more with respect to internal Church matters: the challenge that eventually emerged with respect to ecclesiastical, Christ-ordained leadership that came from the Eastern wing of the Church as that wing grew in step with the Eastern Roman—aka Byzantine—Empire. Thus the Orthodox patriarchs of Sees from Alexandria to Athens and from Jerusalem to Constantinople to Antioch arrived at a crisis in their relationship with the Bishop of Rome—the Pope—with regard to ultimate authority. The key issue that engendered the Great Schism of 1054 and separated Christendom into Western and Eastern Churches pertained to papal authority in ecclesiastical matters: the Eastern Bishops (otherwise referred to as Patriarchs) acknowledged the idea that the Pope, seated on the throne of St. Peter, is entitled to a greater measure of honor than other Bishops—but not to greater authority in the address of spiritual questions.

Thus the Eastern Church, that engendered progeny from Greece to Serbia to Muscovy and from Alexandria to Antioch to Nisibis, grew steadily apart from the Western Church after the middle of the eleventh century. In Constantinople, the continuing Eastern Roman empire offered a continuing sequence of Emperors who appointed the Patriarch in Constantinople even while continuing to jockey for power with this Western emperor or that and at times with that Pope or this. For the Papacy evolved, given all of these briefly-summarized issues, as political as well as spiritual—the Papal States became the polity of which the Pope was the secular as much as the spiritual leader, which did not preclude papal involvement in the internal affairs of other states—and was itself subject to varying decrees of outstanding leadership offering moments of grandeur and glory or periods of weakness and deep-seated corruption.

All these traumas within Christendom pulled at its otherwise triumphant expansion over Europe and the Mediterranean worlds; the multiple Reformations and secessions from Rome in the sixteenth century are thus the culmination and not the beginning of the tearing of its fabric. But meanwhile, from without, issues both spiritual and political also pulled. To the East the infidel faith of Zoroastrianism and its effective offspring, Mithraism, experienced resurgence and growth from the third through seventh centuries, although contact with it and threat from it was pretty much limited to the eastern flank of the faith. But poised to affect the center and west of Christendom at precisely the chronological point when Zoroastrianism and Mithraism were passing their zenith of success, the new infidel menace of Islam not only appeared on the scene, but spread its wings up out of the 'Arav and across the southern Mediterranean by the eighth and ninth centuries.

In the aftermath of the death of its founding prophet, Muhammad, in 632, Islam surged north out of the Arabian Peninsula. The dismantling of the largely Zoroastrian Sassanid Empire in Persia (Iran) by 651 was preceded by the conquest of the Holy Land and with it, the northeastern coasts of Africa. Spain fell to Muslim warriors who had swept gradually across the rest of North Africa in the two generations that followed, by 711-718—by which time Islam had spread to the east as far as India; Sicily and southern Italy became a center of Muslim power by the mid-ninth century. Christendom and the Dar al-Islam stood word to word and sword to sword at all the gated walls into Europe, from the Pyrenees to the Bosporus to the Caucasus Mountains.

While heresy and Church-State conflict gnawed from within and muscular Islamic expansion threatened from without, there remained a problem intermediate between these two—a group classifiable neither as infidel nor as heretic nor offering any sort of challenge to internal political or ecclesiastical Christian authority—which had its inception with the birth of Christianity itself, as we have seen: the Jews. The dispersed community of Christendom's sibling was to be found everywhere within the realm itself, yet always as an outsider group within: Judaism remained a far-flung archipelago within the expanding seas of Christianity. While the external threat is fairly clear-cut and addressable in fairly conventional military fashion—the *Reconquista* in Spain at the western-most edge of the European-Mediterranean world and the Crusades at the easternmost edge are the most consistent response to the perceived threat of Islam[75]—and while heresy, schism and Church-State conflicts fall within the spectrum of obvious Church jurisdiction, the anomalous problem of the Jews yields a complex of attempted solutions.

II. The Jews In-Between

To begin with, Medieval Christendom had to address the question of how to classify Jews in the Christian world because they were neither Christian heretics nor infidels the way pagans, Zoroastrians and Muslims were understood to be. We may recall the original conflict between emerging Judaism and Christianity at the end of the first and beginning of the second centuries with regard to their respective sibling claims to be the true carrier of the Israelite covenant and also the legitimate recipient of *religio licita* status under Roman pagan jurisdiction. A second revolt against Rome by Judaeans in 132-5 led by Bar Kokhba—this being the Aramaic epithet of Simon Ben Kotziba accorded him by Rabbi Akiva, meaning "son of a star" and reflecting the conviction that his would ultimately be a successful messianic uprising—produced a series of political martyrs. These martyrs who were executed (almost certainly by crucifixion)—in the course of the eventual Roman realization that the only way to terminate Judaean political/military unrest was to extirpate its religious roots—were also religious martyrs.

Christian religious martyrs scatter the second century, abound in the third and overflow into the first years of the fourth, as we have noted earlier. The sense of Christianity as a *superstitio*—as politically subversive—culminates with Diocletian, who saw the faith as tearing apart the empire that he was so desperate to hold together. The decree of his ultimate successor, Constantine, in 313 at Milan, recognizing Christianity as a *religio licita*, not only altered that understanding but changed the course of history. Speculation regarding the ratio of spiritual conviction to political astuteness in Constantine's decision is beyond what we need to consider here, but what is important for our purposes is how the Emperor's decree helps set the stage for Christian hegemony in what will one day be Europe. Add to this Constantine's role in the Council of Nicaea in the following decade and his place in Christian progress is unequivocal. Indeed, with the possible exception of Julian (whom Western Christian historiographers refer to as "the Apostate") in 360-63, every Roman emperor from the time of Constantine to the end of the Empire would be Christian.

How in such a context ought the Jews to be defined? They had rejected the notion that Jesus of Nazareth was the *Mashiah/Christos*, both in its original, simple connotation of "anointed one"—scion of the House of David and anticipated restorer of Israel's political fortunes—and its more complex, Pauline-evolved connotation of divinity: that Jesus of Nazareth, the *Mashiah/Christos*, was God Itself incarnate, made accessible to our understanding by means of the phrase, "Son of God." The term "*superstitio*" would be turned around and directed to Judaism. For to deny the divinity of Jesus and everything that goes along with that concept is to obstruct the shaping of a messianic kingdom on earth, and therefore to be politically as well as spiritually subversive—the two are sides of the same coin of posing a threat to the eternal souls of citizens of Christendom.

As a practical matter, Jews would become excluded from most of the workings of medieval Christian society. They would lose the right to own land, would obviously find no place in military or clerical service (the two most essential potential roles for sons of land-owning classes) and would be excluded from the evolving structure of crafts guilds. Since in order to join a guild—or more broadly, for even the simplest of agreements and every land transaction—one uttered some religious formula, usually swearing in the name of the Father, the Son and the Holy Spirit (*in nomine Patris et Filii et Spiritus*

Sancti) an oath that could hardly be uttered by a believing Jew; then Jews remained, by definition, economic and social aliens wherever they dwelled throughout Christendom.

Jews were limited to, and also able to benefit from, commercial and usurial enterprises. Their sense of being isolated islands in the vast Christian seas around them tended to induce a sense of fraternity which made their information and transaction of commercial ventures more readily successful. Their isolation *was* that of islands: connected, somehow, under the depths of those seas. Their primary legal text, the Talmud, specifically discourages usury,[76] but circumstances made such practice vis-a-vis *non*-Jews acceptable. At the same time, a virtual monopoly of money-lending was created by a paradox in church policy. For Luke 6:35 enjoins the faithful to "lend, hoping for nothing again"[77]—interpreted by the churchmen of the medieval period as forbidding the extraction of interest on a loan. Thus all forms of usury came to be theoretically forbidden to Christians, and avarice, as one of the seven Deadly Sins, is typically understood to encompass usury. This ban may have been evaded in small-scale matters, but not on the grand scale. How, for example, could a king tax his subjects, since that act could and generally was construed as part of avaricious usury?

But the king—or the nobleman of whatever substantial level— could tax the Jews who in turn would be granted the franchise of taxing the Christian populace. Thus the Jews would be guilty of acting in an avaricious, usurious manner and the king or lord would both protect them up to a point from the re-directed anger of the populace and punish them appropriately by taxing them and confiscating their goods periodically. This was most clearly the case in England from the twelfth century, but also elsewhere, such as Poland in the fourteenth century. The irony is that both the Christian interpretation of Luke and the rabbinic discussion in the Talmud ultimately point back to the same starting point, Leviticus 25:35-7: "When your brother-Israelite is reduced to poverty and cannot support himself in the community, you shall assist as you would an alien or a stranger, and he shall live with you. You shall not charge him interest on a loan... You shall fear your God..." But practical need could permit an abrogation of this sentiment outside "brother-Israelite" — i.e., fellow-Jewish or fellow-Christian — lines.

Ultimately, the socio-economic isolation of the Jews of Medieval Christian Europe was reinforced by the growing hostility engendered by the role of Jews as money-lenders shaped by this concatenation of circumstances. But that socio-economic alienation would be reinforced by further twists and turns in the popular theological perspective of the medieval Christian world. For at some point Christians began to ask themselves: if the Jews were rejecters of Christ (indeed, if they were actually responsible for his demise), whom must they by definition embrace, according to the internal logic of perceiving reality as comprised of spiritual blacks and whites and never grays?

Logic, in a medieval world dogmatically divided between forces of good and forces of evil, understood that the Satan was prominent as the adversary of God, and that his offspring was the Anti-Christ — the child of Satan and a Judaean harlot, as the Christ was the son of God and a Judaean virgin.[78] Logic would dictate that, as deniers of the Christhood of Jesus, the Jews must be embracers of the Anti-Christ, that the rejecters of the true God must be the servants of Satan.

They must, moreover, play a continuously sinister role in history as a kind of apocalyptic army bent on the destruction of Christendom. The extent of this feeling may be observed in the accusation that the Jews were aiding the Mongol invaders from the east, in the thirteenth century — an accusation actively lodged as far away as Germany.[79] The sentiment may be more fundamentally observed in the popular fiction that Jews have horns and tails — even cloven hooves — as if spiritual devil-traits might be observed in such physical characteristics, which fiction is reflected in art and literature perhaps as far back as the ninth century.[80] It may be observed in the double-edged idea of the Jews as doctor-sorcerers, whose medical and magical practices are intertwined and in turn interwoven with the strands of their allegiance to the dark powers of the Other: they can both heal and destroy.

Against this complex series of contexts, by what series of processes might Christendom shore up its rifts and defeat its variously configured enemies? The Muslim infidel might be fought without, by means of war and its concomitants—and the descriptions of the Crusaders' blood-lust are chilling—and as for the internal problems of heresy, schism and church-state conflict? Heretics and false-believers might be purged of their sinfulness by being burned. Schismatics might be fought like infidels are. Inquiries developed into the faith of those suspected of heresy or of state or church leaders who went astray from the proper course of faith: Hence, the Inquisition.

And what of the Jews? There are three legal (or quasi-legal) events or processes that shape the negative side of the Jewish experience within Christian Europe during the medieval period, at least one of which—the Inquisition, particularly as it developed in Spain—intersects the issue of heresy which should only indirectly have affected Jews, if at all. The other two are the disputation and the blood-libel/blood accusation. All three, one might argue, are based on two fundamental issues, even as they carry those two issues in such different manifestational directions: the continuous sense of the "otherness" of the Jew and the ongoing sense of threat from any "other" in a world offering complex modes of threat to human survival, both in the here and now and in the hereafter. Put another way, the demonization of the Jews and the sense of a Jewish conspiracy to impose evil on the world interweave. Each of the three "legal" processes addresses aspects of Christian belief and/or fear; each reflects different aspects of external Jewish-Christian relations and each has different ramifications for the internal development of Jewish religious legal thought.

III. The Blood Libel in and beyond Norwich

One might say that the blood libel is the "legal" proceeding that most directly connects the medieval Christian relationship to Jews and Judaism with the sense of the latter that grew out of the New Testament. That is, the notion that the "Jews" were responsible for the death of Jesus, which notion expands from the Synoptic Gospels to the Gospel of John to the Acts of the Apostles and various Epistles, lays direct conceptual groundwork for the blood libel—otherwise known as the blood accusation. There is a range of modes in which this fascinating notion manifests itself, but broadly speaking, it offers two aspects. The first part (strictly speaking, the "blood libel") is that a Christian child is mock-crucified by Jews; the second part (the "ritual accusation") is that they then use various internal body parts for this or that gastronomic purpose—the entrails, for example, for the *haroset* (sweet herbs) of the Passover meal—or to perform secret rituals.[81] The classic accusation is that the blood is drained from the victim and then used as a key ingredient for *matzah*, the unleavened bread that is the ultimate gastronomic aspect of and symbol within the Passover meal as well as of and within the entire Passover week.

There is both a certain logic and an irony to this. The logic is that Passover occurs in close proximity to Easter, the time of year when the Passion of Christ is being most intensely reviewed in the Christian community, with Passion Plays filling out Passion Week, culminating with the Gospel stories that represent the Jews as responsible for Christ's death. And if they crucified him once, wouldn't it make a certain perverse sense, in the ongoing folk-level theological battle between the sibling faiths, that they would symbolically repeat that act year by year, particularly since mocking Jesus as the messiah would represent a reversal of the messianic hope so rampant at Easter time? Wouldn't it make perverse sense that the Jews in their nefarious, betraying ugliness, would instill within the flat bread that they eat at Passover the very element that emerges from the wine and flat bread of the Eucharist? And on the other hand, wouldn't it make sense that, since it is a universal truth that both magical and medicinal rituals require absolutely pure components to be effective, they would take pure body parts from pure little Christian children to perform theirs?

The irony is that the blood libel reverses the significance of the eucharistic ceremony within Christianity, in which the wafer and wine are transubstantiated into the body and blood of Christ, consumed by his followers so as to merge his being with theirs in a literal way: so the Jews are accused by medieval Christians of doing what they, the Christians, do, albeit in an indirect, symbolic and negatively nuanced way! They consume food infused with the blood of an innocent, crucified in mockery of the ultimate Innocent—the pure Lamb of God. The second irony is that blood is the most basic element that must emphatically be removed from food in order for Jews to consider it edible, i.e., kosher—acceptable in God's eyes for human consumption.[82] In the Jewish tradition, meat is typically drained and drained, pounded and cooked until it is well enough done so that not even the suggestion of blood that might be visually conveyed by the red juices of rarer meat will be in evidence when it appears on the plate. How likely is it that Jews, who so carefully avoid blood or anything resembling blood in their food, would incorporate it within *matzah*—plain flat unleavened bread into which not even yeast has been added?

Yet the canard of the Blood Accusation has a long history in Europe, beginning as early as the eleventh century in Russia.[83] The first *detailed* account of a blood libel, however was in Norwich, East Anglia—in what is today called England—in 1144. In that year a little boy named William disappeared into the surrounding heath woods on March 21, the Tuesday before both Passover and Easter. The court system in place at that time included local jurisdiction for secret cases of killing (i.e., murder, as opposed to open cases of homicide) and therefore it was the responsibility of the local authorities to deal with the body of a victim where it was found, even if, say, the body were identified as that of so-and-so who was known to have been living in a different district. One might further note that it was not until the 1180s that the idea—found in the Book of Susanna and the Elders, as earlier noted—of interrogating independent, separate witnesses was introduced under Henry II, and even then the system was only sporadically utilized.

Jews, probably having arrived into what we now call England with William the Conqueror, in 1066, had been living in Norwich since at least 1086; reference is made in the Domesday Book to a certain "Isaac" among the Frenchmen (i.e., Normans) who arrived there around that time. By 1144 the small Jewish community lived in its own area of the town (although not forcibly confined to that area). In fact, the Jews were legally "owned" by the king, who afforded them

his protection while using them as middle men in his financial deal-
ings with the people. The down side of this relationship was that the
king could suddenly impose new burdens on them. Thus in 1159,
Henry II imposed on the Jews the burden of financing his expedition
against his rebellious subjects in Toulouse,[84] and one can in retrospect
see the increasing impoverishment of the community beginning from
that time. On the other hand they also seemed to have served in the
twelfth and thirteenth centuries as lenders of funds to the Christian
community—at exorbitant interest rates (but not unusual for that
era)—for major building projects, such as that of the Norwich cathedral. But while the debt and its interest might escalate, they might
never get paid back. There are several important instances in various
places of noblemen-debtors inciting massacres to encompass the Jews
to whom they owed spiraling amounts of money to avoid having to
pay borrowed funds back.

As elsewhere in Europe, ground-level resentment toward the
Jews derived probably not quite as much from religious sentiment
as from the economic role they played. To be sure, that hostility was
reinforced by the Church leadership, that—as a historical technicality, as it were—tended to emphasize the mocking of Christ's passion
aspect of the blood libel canard, rather than the aspect that fanta-
sized regarding the use to which the victim's blood or entrails might
be put. So, too, the Crusades helped reinforce hostility to the Jews,
as it also offered a means through which noblemen who had killed
Jews in order to avoid paying debts could avoid having to offer justice for their actions, instead devoting themselves to God by going
on a Crusade. The hostility toward Jews in England would culmi-
nate in the summary expulsion of them all in 1290.

But back in 1144 this long process was toward its beginnings.
William of Norwich (as he would later come to be known), son of
a relatively poor widow, was apprenticed in his village as an eight-
year-old to a skinner/tanner, a trade for which there was a good deal
of demand. The account by Thomas of Monmouth (about which,
more in a moment) tells us that William was "gifted with a teach-
able disposition and, bringing industry to bear upon it, in a short
time he far surpassed lads of his own age in the crafts aforesaid, and

he equaled some who had been his teachers."[85] Thus he moved on to the city of Norwich, where he lodged with a famous master and worked until he was twelve years old. The Jews of Norwich, good clients of the skinners/tanners, are said in Thomas' account to have preferred William to his colleagues.

Thomas goes on to refer to the assertion by a former Jew, who, after converting to Christianity came to be known as Theobold, perhaps at Norwich, that ancient Jewish writings claim that the Jews will never be free nor able to return to their homeland without the shedding of human blood, and that they must therefore offer an annual sacrifice of some Christian, in demonstrating their contempt for Christ and to avenge their sufferings on their Christian victim as a surrogate for Christ himself. Furthermore, according to this extraordinary narrative, the rabbinical and other leaders of the Jews meet in Narbonne each year to determine by the casting of lots where the human sacrifice of that year should take place: the first draw was to choose from among the countries inhabited by Jews and the second the location within that country. Norwich, Thomas quotes Theobold as asserting, was the location chosen for the year 1144.

One has to love the irony of Theobold's treachery. While self-hating former (or practicing) Jews are found in plenty of times and places in history, this particular mode of betrayal—concocting such an elaborate story regarding his former co-religionists, smack stunningly of what one might expect of an individual labeled by the denomination "Judas." And the consequences for the innocent victims of Theobold's assertion, whatever he gained by it either materially or spiritually, would be stunning. Interestingly, too, Theobold's story intersects—or, in retrospect, may be seen as a parent of—a different canard that will appear more distinctly several centuries later, the conspiracy story associated with the so-called *Protocols of the Elders of Zion*.[86]

In any case, Thomas goes on to claim that he learned from certain converted Jews that, at the beginning of Lent, the Jews of Norwich had determined upon William as their victim. The lad had begun to spend more time than the minimum necessary for business with the Jews—either because they were drawn by his charm and intelligence (and he either enjoyed their company or was too reticent to refuse their invitations to be more sociable) or because they were shaping their plans for him. Suddenly, for whatever reasons, William's uncle by marriage, Godwin Stuart, a priest, prohibited him "from going in and out among them any more." The Jews, perhaps concerned that this change reflected a change toward greater animosity in the general Christian mood toward them, sought to draw William once again among them—perhaps with the intention of finding out from someone young and guileless if something was amiss.

One might wonder why Godwin suddenly interceded between William and his lucrative contacts. It could certainly have been his concern not only or necessarily for William's physical safety, but for his spiritual well-being: in a world where the correct understanding of God and how God wants us to relate to Him is understood to affect the condition of both the individual and the community of which s/he is part, both while alive and, particularly from the Christian perspective, even more so in the world to come, then the possibility that an impressionable young boy, however clever, might be seduced into apostasy would have been an appalling thought for Godwin. Conversely, the sudden demurral of William with regard to being in their company, in a world where their situation was always tenuous and suspicions regarding them easily aroused—and in which stories of massacres of Jews in this place or that would have been familiar to them—could easily have led the Jews to seek William out more insistently, hoping that they could learn something from him regarding what, if anything, was afoot.

From this point, Thomas' account moves swiftly into the details of the alleged murder. The Jews are said to have sent a messenger to draw William in through deceit, "for he pretended that he was the cook of William, Archdeacon of Norwich, and that he wished to have him as a helper in the kitchen..." (Bk 1.4) He agreed to go with William back to his village to convince the latter's mother to allow the boy to go with him, and the following morning—so they apparently spent the night at William's mother's home, which either means that the unnamed deceiver was exceedingly clever in how he calmed her, or was no deceiver at all—"the traitor, the imitator in almost everything of the traitor Judas, returns to Norwich with the boy, and as he was passing by the house of the boy's aunt, he went in with him and said that the mother had entrusted the boy to himself, [again thereby leaving an ever-clearer trail] and then he went out again hastily. But the boy's aunt said quickly to her daughter, 'follow them at once and take care that you find out where that man is leading the boy.' ...she followed them...and at last saw them entering cautiously into the house of a certain Jew, and immediately she heard the door shut."

The narrative continues with the report that the Jews treated William kindly at first—one might wonder how Thomas knew this—keeping him in the house until the following day (which would be Wednesday). There is no statement of how William responded to this overnight detour on the way to the Archdeacon's kitchen, among the host of details of which Thomas asserts knowledge. The next day was the first day of Passover, when, "after singing the hymns appointed for the day in the synagogue, the leaders of the Jews assembled in the house of the aforementioned Jew suddenly seized the boy William as he was having his dinner and in no fear of treachery and ill-treated him in various horrible ways. For while some of them held him behind, others opened his mouth and introduced an instrument of torture which is called a teazle, and, fixing it by straps through both jaws to the back of his neck they fastened it with a knot as tightly as it could be drawn. After that, taking a short piece of rope about the thickness of one's little finger and tying three knots in it at certain distances marked out, they bound around the innocent head with it from the forehead to the back, forcing the middle knot into his forehead and the two others into his temples, the two ends of the rope being most tightly stretched at the back of his head and fastened in a very tight knot.

"The ends of the rope were then passed around his neck and carried around his throat under his chin, and there they finished off this dreadful engine of torture in a fifth knot... Having shaved his head, they stabbed it with countless thorn points, and made blood come horribly from the wounds they made... Some of them adjudged him to be fixed to a cross in mockery of the Lord's passion... and, having lifted him from the ground and fastened him upon the cross, they vied with one another in their efforts to make an end of him. And we, after inquiring in the matter very diligently, did both find the house, and discovered some most important marks in it of what was done there, instead of a cross, a post set up between two other posts and a beam stretch across the midmost post and attached to the other on either side. And as afterwards we discovered from the marks of the wounds and of the bands, the right hand and foot had been tightly bound and fastened with cords, but the left hand and foot were pierced with two nails... After all these many and great tortures they inflicted a frightful wound in his left side, reaching even to his inmost heart... and extinguished his mortal life."

Who provided Thomas with all of the details? A Christian servant girl, bringing the boiling water from the scullery, would claim to have seen the evidence of some of it—a boy tied to a post—through a crack in the door, with one eye, and later on found a boy's belt in the room, but even she did not witness all the details that appear in Thomas' narrative. In any case, this account is merely that of a blood libel—a mock crucifixion—and not one that includes a discussion of the subsequent use of blood or other elements of the victim for gastronomic or ritual purposes. For the next issue that Thomas of Monmouth takes up is the question the Jews had regarding the disposition of William's corpse. In the end, after exploring several options, they decide to take the body to someplace distant, so that, if it be found, "the Christians may think it a case of murder; and if the talk of murder becomes sounded abroad there is no doubt that the officers of the king's justice, eager for gain, will readily open their ears to the false rumor. Then, since the blame will be laid upon the Christians, we will be safe." So if the Jews could smuggle William's body to someplace where no Jews were living, by definition the murderer(s) would have to be located from among the local Christians of that place or, in the absence of sufficient evidence to produce a murderer, the local community would be required to pay a "murder" fine to William's family.

But it seems awfully strange that a murder planned according to anything resembling a prescribed program—even ignoring

Theobold's horrific assertions and the oddity that he himself was in
Cambridge and not Norwich at the time of the great annual event to
which he was allegedly privy—would not have included the fore-
thought of how and where to dispose of the body of the victim!
That issue would reduce the possibility that William died at Jewish
hands to a maximum of the death as an unforeseen accident, so that
even if one were to embrace that maximum, the religious significance of his demise for the Jews is reduced to nothing.

In any case, Thomas reports that the plan that emerged was
to wait until Good Friday, when most Christians would be making
the rounds of churches and there would be less chance of someone
noticing and wondering about the two Jews with the corpse-filled
sack that they would be carrying. But as they were entering Thorpe
Wood, they met Aelward Ded, one of Norwich's prominent Christian citizens, and his servant. Ded wondered why two Jews were
traveling "so far from home on a day when it was not the custom
of the Jews to leave their houses"—for the wood was on the opposite side of town from the Jewish section. Aelward also wondered at
the contents of the sack held across the saddle bow of one of them
and, touching it, realized that it contained a human body, but was so
focused on his goal of reaching St. Leonard's church that he didn't
follow up on the matter, even as the two Jews galloped rapidly into
the woods when "in their terror [they had nothing] to say" to his
inquiry.

The two Jews hung the body from a tree in a remote spot and
hurried home to relate the unhappy encounter to their colleagues.
They decided to seek the protection of John the Sheriff, to whom
they promised 100 horses if he would prevent Aelward Ded from
revealing what he had seen. This worked out all right. The Sheriff
was as good as his word in providing his protection, and Aelward
kept his lips sealed in spite of immediately subsequent events, until
five years later when, nearing death and having been admonished
by a vision of William—by then well-known throughout the area
and having achieved sainthood as a child martyr—Ded confessed
what he had seen to two priests whom he called to his deathbed.

That William was famous by then is a function of what Thomas understands to have been the hand of God already moving, barely after the boy's body been left hanging in the woods. For on Friday evening (Good Friday), "a fiery light suddenly flashed down from Heaven, which, extending in a long train as far as the place where the aforementioned body was, blazed in the eyes of many people who were in various places thereabouts" (Bk 1.9).

At dawn on Easter Saturday a group led by Lady Legarda went into the wood to the place where she thought she had seen the light and found the body of a boy lying in the thick bushes with his head shaved and his body punctured by many stab wounds. Two ravens kept alighting on the body and then withdrawing. Lady Legarda, convinced that the corpse must be that of someone extraordinary, drove off the ravens, went home in an ecstatic state—but did nothing further to follow up on her extraordinary discovery! Later on that morning the local forester, Henry de Sprowston, came upon the body, and noticing the wooden gag in its mouth and other signs of violence, immediately suspected that the murderers were Jews and that it had been the source of the previous evening's strange light. He, too, took no immediate action, other than to try to arrange for a burial site in the churchyard. But it was not until Easter Monday that Henry set out. Although he was intending to bury the body in the churchyard he somehow changed his mind and instead buried the body where it had been found—albeit with all due reverence, Thomas reports.

As word spread regarding the discovery—rather slowly, all things considered—so did the conviction that only Jews could have done such a thing, especially at such a time (i.e., Easter/Passover). Among those who heard the news was the priest Godwin Stuart, William's aunt's husband. On Tuesday he went into the wood with William's brother and his own son, Alexander, to dig up the corpse and see if it might not be William. Presumably the family was concerned about the boy's welfare: because he had supposedly last been seen entering a Jew's house? Because someone inquired at the Archdeacon's house and learned that William had never arrived there? Or that he had never been sent for in the first place? Thomas is silent on all of these important details that we might wish to have before us in some form or other. Although "so many days had passed since the time when they suspected he had been put to death, yet there was absolutely no bad smell perceptible emanating from the little corpse. But what seemed more deserving of their wonder was that—although there was never a flower nor any sweet-smelling herb growing in the area—yet there the perfume of spring flowers was wafted to the nostrils of all present" (Bk 1.13).

Godwin reburied his nephew's body, returned home and told his wife what had happened, who then recalled a dream she had had on the Saturday before Palm Sunday: she was standing in the Norwich market square when some Jews attacked her with a club, broke her right leg, tore it off and ran away with it. She now interpreted this to have been a warning that the Jews were about to take away one of her loved ones from her. She fainted at that point, and thereafter continued to lament the loss of her dear nephew and with that lament expressed the certainty that the Jews had been responsible for his death.

It is strange that no effort seems to have been made to find the individual who allegedly led William to the Jew's house where he was done in—this man who made a point of stopping with William in his mother's house and again in his aunt's house, yet whom nobody came forward to identify. The girl who had followed William and his "guide" to a specific Jew's house never came forward to point out that house when William's mother began crying out that the Jews had murdered him—nor did she point it out to William's mother. Indeed when she learned of her son's death, William's mother, according to Thomas, came directly to her sister in Norwich, but neither that sister nor her husband, the priest Godwin, could tell her anything other than that he had died strangely—whereafter she immediately seems to have leapt to the conclusion that the Jews had murdered him. The townspeople shortly took up her cry "with one voice that all the Jews ought to be utterly destroyed as constant enemies of the Christian name and the Christian religion" (Bk 1.15)— as opposed to directing themselves to the house where the murder was alleged to have taken place.

Thomas himself does not sound entirely convinced, observ-

ing how "with a woman's readiness of belief she [William's moth-
er] gave credence to these conjectures [that "it was not Christians
but Jews who had dared to the deed"]". But he (Thomas) does,
later on in his account, refer to the house where the murder took
place as belonging to a Jew named Eleazar—but by then Eleazar
himself had been murdered, and the Bishop of Norwich was attempting to protect Eleazar's Christian murderer, who was one of
the Bishop's knights, by using the death of William as a counter-
accusation: in other words, Eleazar's death would be construed
as a just punishment, an execution, as it were, rather than as a
murder.[87] Both the murder of Eleazar and the specific argument
associating Eleazar with William's demise took place in 1149, five
years after the latter's death. Nor does Thomas indicate when and
how this specific datum was discovered any more than he ever
explains how he was privy to such detailed information regarding how William was martyred (beyond the limited testimony of
the servant girl).

Indeed, Thomas' narrative gives us an accusatory story without whatever defense might have been articulated by the Jews. It
seems clear that William was murdered and it also seems true that
the Jews pretty quickly sought the protection of the Sheriff—which
means that, having heard of or knowing about the murder by whatever means, they knew that an accusation could be lodged against
them. If Thomas is both privy to and telling the truth about this
last detail, then they asked for the Sheriff's protection before it was
commonly known that a murder had been committed and before
William's mother set the town in a dither toward the Jews. They are
also alleged to have approached William's brother, Robert, who reported to Thomas that "he could have had ten marks from the Jews
if he had hushed up the charge concerning his brother's murder"
(Bk 2.10).

But all of these details must also be weighed within the various
limits of Thomas' account. To begin with, Thomas of Monmouth was
a monk in the cathedral priory of Norwich, who was asked by Bishop Turbe to draw up his account toward the end of the 1140s, several years after the event. By that time, several things had happened

that may have pushed both the Bishop's request and the viewpoint of Thomas' account. Whatever condemnation of the Jews—whatever trial by ordeal proposed by Godwin Stuart to the then Bishop Eborard—might have been sought by William's family and either part or all of the Christian community, failed to emerge, presumably because the Sheriff stuck to his word in protecting the Jews. This act seems one of unusual integrity for that time or perhaps any time, since the Sheriff apparently owed a good deal of money to some of them and could easily have had his debts erased by betraying them. (Perhaps they cancelled his debts in exchange for his protection). The case was supposed to be tried before the king himself at Norwich, but nothing came of that. Thomas asserts that the trial was postponed and then never materialized because the Jews had managed to bribe the king and his councilors.

Godwin Stuart managed to have William's body transferred from the wood to the monks' cemetery a month later (on April 25). By 1146, Eborard was succeeded by Turbe as Bishop. A few years later, in 1149, one of Turbe's mesne tenants (Sir Simon de Novers) murdered or arranged for the murder of the Jew Eleazar, and as the Jewish community demanded justice, the Bishop was prompted to recall William's murder, associate it directly with Eleazar, whose name only then enters Thomas' account. The Bishop's charge more generally stirred up the embers of the story —including, no doubt, the prompting of the deathbed recollections of Aelward Ded, and perhaps also prompting the Bishop to ask Thomas to take up the pen.

It is strange that Aelward Ded, who apparently kept his oath until he was on his death bed not to tell what he had seen, in confessing the recollection of that strange Good Friday morning, did not—or could not—identify the two Jews whom he encountered with a corpse in a sack. On the one hand, Thomas—but not using Ded as his authority—asserts that Eleazar was one of the two. But Eleazar was apparently the richest Jew in Norwich (Bk 2.13), so it is likely that Ded would have at least recognized him, if not both Jews. In retrospect, it is also somewhat odd that, having encountered two Jews out in the early morning heading into the woods with a corpse Ded would not have shared the story of that moment with others.

And of course his confession came under the weight of the intervening years and the accusation against the Jews, so the tale he told on his deathbed was based on the retrospecting of whatever happened that morning through the lens of the accusation—no doubt further encouraged by the priestly confessor whom he had called to his bedside, for reasons that I will soon review.

There are other interesting aspects of Thomas' report. He asserts that William de Hastings, former Dean of Norwich, (the same to whose kitchens William was told that he was heading at the outset of his fatal journey) heard two Jews engaged in a dispute and that one turned to him (i.e., to William de Hastings) and said, regarding the other, that he should not be "listened to by you who are a Christian, for he is the man who first laid hands upon your Christian William, whom you call a martyr, and killed him with his blood-stained hands" (Bk 22.12). An extraordinary but not impossible tale, particularly if the Jew who is quoted by Sir William were one of those who converted out of fear in order to gain amnesty for himself, and to further assure his own safety offered implicating testimony regarding others to Thomas. More phenomenal, perhaps, is the statement that Thomas makes that, confident that they would be well protected by the Sheriff, the Jews used to joke with the monks that "you should be very much obliged to us, for we have made a saint and a martyr for you!" (Bk 2.11). It is difficult to know whether Thomas himself recognized the unlikelihood of such a dramatic and dangerous interchange—or of many of the other holes in the stories that he relates.

Given the summary of events as I have thus far presented them, let us move in two directions. The first is to connect the events as Thomas of Momouth offers them to the point at which he becomes the scribe recording those events and also subsequent events. The second is to consider further the issues, problems and contradictions with Thomas' narrative as we have it for the history we are considering: of Jewish-Christian relations as those relations hinge on legal or quasi-legal events that carry us from the time of Jesus toward our own time. Thus to begin with, let us return to William's body, buried by Henry de Sprowston some time after he had seen it and after it had been earlier seen by Lady Legarda—who had been led to the spot by the fiery ladder-like light of the previous evening.

Lady Legarda, to repeat, was convinced that this boy was no ordinary child, due to the strange conduct of the ravens; and Henry de Sprowston immediately suspected that the Jews had murdered him. The story, of the light, the boy and the alleged murder at the hands of the Jews spread rapidly; townspeople began hurrying out to the woods to see the body. When William's uncle, the Priest Godwin, came out with diggers to identify the corpse because he thought that it might be William (nobody had yet identified the victim) the soil moved—perhaps from gases or the rigor mortis contractions of the body, or for any number of other reasons, but for Godwin this was extraordinary—and the area around smelled wonderfully of spring flowers, rather than of rotting flesh. At that time of year, in a wooded heath, one can be surrounded by acute and overwhelming earthy, vegetal and floral smells, but for Godwin, this also seemed extraordinary, at least as reported by Thomas.

All of these events marked the beginning not only of addressing the question of William's murder, but of elevating him to sainthood. In the matter of the murder, we have only the testimony gathered by Brother Thomas, who recorded the various assertions, claims and testimonies offered by the various individuals whom we have thus far encountered. We know little about him, except, to repeat, that he arrived in Norwich some time after the events he described, was there between 1146 and 1150 at the Cathedral priory—and, at the behest of the Bishop, wrote it all down, completing his record not until 1173, nearly twenty-five years after the event itself and its aftermath.[88] In other words, the testimony that he gathers and reports, since there appears to have been no prior written record, would have been offered by those still alive who recalled the events, with whatever reliability of memory, or lack thereof, reinforced by whatever convictions, intensified over twenty-five years and further reinforced by the sanctification of William that occurred in the interim, led them to tell Thomas what he wrote down.

The process that led to William's sanctification is connected to this but is also a separate matter. It is connected by deriving from testimony such as that which pertained to the murder, but it is separate since its basis is not alleged human action but an array of supernatural events. These begin with the story of the ladder of light and the sweet smell emanating from around the corpse and from the corpse itself and from there continue to the expanding accounts of miraculous acts of healing effected by the dead child, initially in the woods—where later, in 1168, Bishop Turbe built a chapel on the spot where St William's body had first been buried, which chapel became a local focus of pilgrimage.

But well before that construction effort, in Lent, 1150, Thomas of Monmouth himself asserted that he had three visions in which Herbert of Losinga (d. 1119), who had founded the Norwich Cathedral, appeared and ordered the translation of William's body from the monks' cemetery to the chapter house. Thus the body was actually transferred to the cathedral in July, 1151 and moved again to the apsidal chapel of the Holy Martyrs to the north of the High Altar (now known as Jesus Chapel) on April 5, 1154. The great enthusiasm of that final installation completed the initial phase of solidifying the cult of William as a saint, who was credited then and subsequently with many posthumous acts—visions and miraculous healings—worthy of sainthood.

In examining the murder through the lens of his sainthood, his death could be understood more emphatically than ever as martyrdom: William died as a martyr for the faith in which he became a saint. Two paths intersect: that of William as a Christian martyr saint and the role he would play as a martyred saint in the decades after his death; and that, not incidentally, of William's death as a necessary weapon in the fight by the Bishop of Norwich to protect his vassal, Simon of Novers, against prosecution for murdering the Jew, Eleazar of Norwich, to whom Simon had been indebted for a good deal of money. Put another way, then, the positive intersects the negative.

The twelfth century is heavily marked across Europe by the interest in and need for saints, for child saints, for martyrs and martyred saints. This interest and need were were quite strong in England of the twelfth and thirteenth centuries. William at the very least served that layered need, his innocence a symbol of the innocent lamb of God who was sacrificed on the Cross, his sacrifice an emulation of Christ's sacrifice in which all who, in an age of Christian hegemony, when the feasibility of emulating Christ through martyred self-sacrifice was not possible as it had been a millennium earlier, could participate. Vicarious participation would be effected by visiting the shrine of St William (and others like him), the reality of whose sainthood, attested to by the miracles with which the shrine was increasingly associated, could quite literally rub off on visitors.

Aside from the spiritual need that saints and miracles address, the renown of a saint with the power to effect cures would yield positive economic results to a town like Norwich: pilgrims coming to find help would spend money in the town while they waited for a chance to touch the shrine, or for the results of having touched it. Bishop Turbe and Richard de Ferraiis, who became prior in 1150, were not unaware of the pecuniary and not only the spiritual benefits of having a local saint interred in the cathedral. And it was not until the papacy of Alexander III (1159-81) that sanctification required papal confirmation—nor until the papacy of Urban VIII (1623-44) that papal confirmation was universally invoked within the Catholic world.

If fulfilling this need may be viewed as a positive underpinning for William's sanctification, the negative—the use to which his death was put to protect a feudal vassal of the Bishop—may be viewed as part of a larger negative: the fear and hatred of the Jews, for an interweave of spiritual, political and economic reasons. Which leads back to the question: what happened to William, and how did his death lead both to a Blood Libel against the Jews of Norwich and to his sanctification?

To be sure, he was murdered. He was apparently stabbed in the heart, in which case that wound would have killed him (and that wound is directed to the opposite side from that where Christ was wounded by the Roman centurion's spear point—which could be argued either to militate against William's death-wound as part of a mock-Crucifixion, or in favor of it, since the wrong side could imply mockery, depending upon one's interpretive predisposition one way or the other). He was apparently gagged and scalded, according to the testimony of those who saw the body some time after it was found in the woods. Apparently, his head had been shaved. Those who reported to Thomas asserted that there were wounds on the head suggesting a crown of thorns and evidence that the child had been tied up at the hands and feet, with a rope that had also gone around his neck.

But who murdered him and why? Let's suppose that it *could* have been "the Jews"—but *why* would they have murdered him, unless we assume that the assertion Theobold made had some truth to it? But there are too many holes (leaving aside intrinsic absurdity) to his tall tale. Or could they for some strange reason simply have been playing around with the idea of mock-Crucifixion, using William in a jocular if ridiculous (at least to our minds) manner and things got out of hand, so that he died, or had some sort of epileptic seizure and they thought he died and so they panicked? But there is absolutely no proof for such a notion except by cross-referencing this narrative with others of the same sort that early enough in history became embedded in the popular Christian imagination.[89] The cross-referencing becomes circular: we believe that the Jews did "x" somewhere at some time; therefore if "y" happens we assume that the Jews did "y" because we interpret "y" to be a form of "x". (We believe that somewhere sometime they mock crucified a Christian child—under whatever circumstances—therefore when a Christian child is found murdered, we assume that the Jews did it because we interpret the child's death to be the result of a mock Crucifixion.)

Could William's own family, as some have suggested, have attempted to gain spiritual "credit" for themselves and for him by causing him to undergo some form of symbolic Crucifixion on Good Friday, and when he had a fit or seizure, panicked and quickly buried him in Thorpe Wood—and then tried to blame the Jews? Was he wandering through those woods and ingested mushrooms or some other vegetation from which he had a poisonous reaction? In that case we would need to suppose that the story of all the wounds derived from the fact of the much later posthumous examination of the body, imposed on the telling in order to accord with the popular idea that the Jews might have, could have, and must have done him in. Could it have been a random murder, by a sadistic killer, Christian or Jewish, such as may be found in all times and places, who not only killed him but seems to have subjected him to torture along the way?

Regardless of the still-unknown and perhaps unknowable cause of William's death, we can make at least five observations regarding his demise and its aftermath. First, that his death subjected the Jewish community of Norwich and its vicinity to trying circumstances, which could have been still more trying had it not been for the fact that Sheriff John stood by them. Second, that there was no straightforward "Trial" in the legal or quasi-legal sense, of the Jewish community or particular members within it, due presumably to the Sheriff's protection and/or to the community's monetary "gift" to the king and/or his councilors. In part, there was no legal action because after a while things seem to have died down, and when they resumed their heat, it was when the focus fell on one of their leaders, Eleazar. But by then Eleazar himself had already been murdered, and the defense put up by the feudal protector of his murderer was that the latter was carrying out justice on behalf of William—five years after William's death—so that, perhaps content that vigilante justice had settled whatever score needed settling, the Christian community at large let the whole thing drop.

By then that community may be supposed to have started to become more focused on the positive side of having William as a saint within its own parish. But what of William's family: can they have been satisfied by the failure for a legal action if they were sincerely convinced of the Jews' guilt? Would Eleazar's death have sufficed for them? Interestingly, in the aftermath of William's sanctification, and apparently due to their relationship to the martyr, both his brother, Robert and his uncle Godwin were appointed officials in the monastery where William's body had lain for a time; and his mother was later buried in the monastery cemetery, apparently to the dismay of several of the monks resident there.

But the atmosphere of suspicion toward Jewish communities within England that spread thereafter—this is the third observation—led to a series of subsequent blood libels in the centuries that followed. In fact, whereas the story of William of Norwich offers as an accusation of the Jewish community that it mock-crucified William, it never offered the further assertion, that any of his internal body parts was used for this or that ritual or religious or magical purpose. Thomas' account—as opposed to the depiction of the mock-Crucifixion on the roodscreen in the Loddon Church, which shows one of the Jews catching the blood spilling from William's wounded side in a container, the implication of which could be that the captured blood would be saved and used for some purpose—never moves in that direction. Even the fact that William's death falls just before both Passover and Easter is never referenced other than as a chronological datum in Thomas' narrative: the accusers of the Jews neither associate the mock-Crucifixion with Easter, per se, nor do they take the next step to associate William's blood or any other body parts with Passover, gastronomically or in any way.

That sort of fuller-fledged accusation would evolve subsequently, with an increasing number of variations. Thus almost as popular as the Passover association with killing a Christian child was the association with the festival of Purim that typically precedes Passover by a month or so. I have already noted the earliest discussion of such an event (in fn #89)—reported for Imnestar, Syria in 415 by a fifth-century Christian historiographer, Sokrates. Ironically enough, medieval Purim celebrations lend themselves more naturally to association with excessive behavior than do medieval Passover celebrations. Purim is the one holiday on the calendar where Jews are not only enjoined to "let go" but where the culmination of the celebration focuses on the defeat of the enemy, Haman—who, intending to destroy the Judaeans strewn across the 127 provinces of the Persian empire as it is described in the Book of Esther, is instead himself destroyed and hanged from the very scaffolding that he had prepared for his enemy, Mordecai, the Judaean hero of the story. But while excessive zeal in "letting go" may well have been part of the celebration, including some degree of physical violence against the character chosen to play the role of Haman in the *Purimspiel* (Purim Play) it is inconceivable that that individual could have been a child or a Christian, much less a Christian child.

It may be somewhat more conceivable that there was some truth behind the charge rendered against the Jewish community of Manosque, in Provence, in 1306, that they had flogged one of their *own co-religionists* running unclothed through the streets, or of sponsoring the cross-dressing of another before he was flogged. Certainly dressing up has long been part of the Purim festival, and cross-dressing, together with other reversals of normal behavior are part of the reflection on the reversal of fortune that is the central theme of the Purim story. But in that case those volunteering to be "victimized"—which would only have come about if that individual were assuming the role of Haman—would be an adult, surely male, member of the community. One can imagine the jump in the Christian imagination from behavior strictly within the Jewish community to behavior spilling into the Christian community—but it is very difficult to conceive of a Jewish community being so foolish as to allow that spill-over from transpiring, given the relentlessly tenuous situation of Jewish communities within Christian Europe.

Differently, there is a strange account of how the Jews of Bray, France, in 1191 demanded justice from the Crown when one of his vassals killed a Jew. The story—difficult to believe unless one is predisposed either to general gullibility or to gullibility with regard to strange events pertaining to Jews and their relations with Christians—is that their own suzerain, the Countess of Champagne accorded them the right to execute the murderer, and since the events coincided with Purim, they placed *him* in the role of Haman. But they were said, further, to have crowned him with thorns (a detail having nothing to do with the Book of Esther and Haman's demise but plenty to do with the New Testament and the Christian sense of the Jewish responsibility for Christ's demise), and scourged him as he ran through the streets. Interestingly, the account doesn't indicate whether he was killed in the end—because that was obviously not its focus, but rather the emulation of Christ-torturing. The upshot, however, was that King Philip Augustus was so exercised over this blasphemous behavior allegedly permitted by the Countess that he marched into Champagne to subject it to his suzerainty—and burned more than 80 Jews at the stake.

The point is that such accounts interweave and overlap each other, tied together by the thread of the Christian conviction that the Jews both rejected and were responsible for the death of Christ, and that they are forever in league with dark anti-Christian forces; Christian animosity and its frequent violent expression against the Jews is transferred and translated into diversely articulated fables regarding hostile Jewish violence against Christians. Variations on a theme: in 1401 in Freiberg: the accusation took the form of an assertion that the Jews were using the dried blood that they obtained through the murder of a Christian child to spread it as a powder onto the fields of their Christian neighbors, so that the fields would not produce their crops. In 1476 in Baden a charge was lodged claiming that a pure Christian child's blood was being used to alleviate the wound of circumcision and for other medical purposes, such as easing labor pains. How appropriate that the most distinct physical mark that distinguishes Jewish from Christian males and thus the Old from the New Covenant should become the focus of suspicion!

There were, in fact—in backtracking to the century of William of Norwich—at least seven subsequent accusations of ritual murder of Christian children by Jews in the twelfth century: one more in England, two each in France and the German-speaking lands and one each in Poland and Bohemia. The number grows significantly in the thirteenth century, where at least 15 are recorded in German-speaking lands and 7 in England, and one each in France and Spain. In the fourteenth century the overall number drops to at least 16 across Europe, in the fifteenth century it rises again to at least 23, and continues to rise to at least 30 in the sixteenth century.[90] Most astonishingly, perhaps, is that, while the numbers appear to diminish in the seventeenth century, they begin to rise again in the eighteenth—and in the more secularistic nineteenth century the number explodes to at least 40.[91]

In England itself, the accompanying details of a blood libel might offer wonderfully perverse twistings and turnings. Thus Richard of Devizes implies that the martyrdom of a Christian boy in Winchester in 1192, whereby the boy might achieve sanctity, was accomplished by the Jews in order to *bring honor* to the city in which they had been so well treated, by gaining a martyred child saint for the city. Moreover, the boy's martyrdom "was shown by the indications of the deed, though by chance the deed itself was absent"—suggesting that the chronicler himself doubts whether or not the event ever took place. No doubt the most famous blood libel in England—more famous, even than that associated with William of Norwich—was that which focused on Hugh of Lincoln, who was murdered in 1255 and disemboweled posthumously. The Jew, Copin, in whose house the murder was alleged to have taken place was subject to torture, which, perhaps not surprisingly, in combination with promises that his life would be spared if he told his auditors what they wanted to hear, elicited a forced "confession" from him—in which he offered the kind of details that would already have been familiar to everyone from prior blood libels.

Hugh was renowned enough to find his way into Chaucer's 1400 *Canterbury Tales*. In "The Prioress' Tale," Chaucer offers a lengthy description of the murder by the Jews "in a great city in Asia" of a Christian child; the story is both based on that of Hugh of Lincoln and culminates with a direct reference to him, "also slain by cursed Jews, as everyone knows (for it was but a little while ago)." Of course the irony is that Chaucer (1343-1400) cannot have ever met a Jew or met anyone who had met a Jew in England. They had been expelled over a century before his "Prioress' Tale," in 1290, and that edict would not be revoked until the Cromwell era in the mid-seventeenth century.

That would help account for why there is a sudden drop to zero in the count of Blood Libels in England in the fourteenth century. In general the numbers are low in the fourteenth century—but then the horrific phenomenon of the Black Death in the middle of the century led to such wide-spread decimations, expulsions and destructions of Jewish communities accused of poisoning wells and the like that perhaps there was less energy for the specific complexities of blood accusations. In any case, the number drops to zero in the fifteenth and following centuries in France also—no doubt since the Jews were definitively expelled from French lands in 1394.[92]

The fourth observation, then, is that whereas the poisonous assertions of the Blood Libel spread eastward, like a slow-moving disease, first from England to France, and that the accusation perforce more or less ended by the time of the expulsions of Jews from those countries, the idea continued to grow and expand within Central and Eastern Europe, where the number of such accusations grew into the seventeenth and eighteenth centuries and even nineteenth centuries. As we shall subsequently see, Tsarist Russia would host an infamous Blood Libel Trial slightly before World War I.

A fifth and final observation offers inter-connected parts. The disease of this sort of animosity is very difficult to cure, particularly when it is urged on by local preachers and teachers. Many popes have directly or indirectly condemned the blood libel and none is ever known to have sanctioned it. In 1247, Innocent IV sent letters to Bishops in France and Germany asserting that "although the Holy Scripture gives the commandment 'Though shall not kill' and forbids the Jews from touching a dead body of any sort at the festival of Passover, there are people who falsely charge them with partaking in common at this festival of the heart of a child who they have killed. They believe that the law of the Jews enjoins this upon them, although precisely the contrary is the case; and if a dead body be found anywhere, the Jews are maliciously accused of having committed murder;" and Gregory X prohibited blood accusations in 1272. Yet on-the-ground Christian leaders in many times and places, whether for theological or political or economic reasons, did nothing to inhibit or prohibit such thoughts and their resultant words and actions from their flocks, in fact sometimes egging them on.

The unabated gut-level feeling regarding things that Jews can do, might do, or habitually do, may be found expressed in subtle ways in perhaps unexpected places. Thus one of the most effective and complete contemporary summaries of the story of William of Norwich, M.D. Anderson's *A Saint at Stake: The Strange Death of William of Norwich, 1144*, offers what is to my mind a rather remarkable series of comments in his chapter discussing "The Alternative

Verdicts" (to the verdict suggested by Thomas of Monmouth's narrative with its "testimony" by Theobold). Anderson seems to take it as a given that the Jews could have enticed William into their midst—in order to elicit information from him regarding some planned violence against the Jews, since William was being all of a sudden inhibited or prohibited from spending time among them—treated him nicely at first, became more insistent, and "once the child became frightened, and tried to escape, the Jews would have realized that to release him, and let him tell his tale of threatened, if not actual ill-usage, would have meant precipitating the attack they dreaded."[93]

Anderson goes on: "Since they could not draw back they might as well go on, and so they tied him to the posts of the house and re-sorted to torture." Why? What could possibly cause such behavior on their part—and if they had decided that they had no choice but to kill him, why would they need to torture him first? Why not just kill him—by strangulation or suffocation or some other bloodless method? Anderson continues: "Although Thomas does not tell us how he knew that a knotted rope was tightened round the child's head, it is quite possible that the marks left on the corpse by this common form of torture would have been recognizable. Unlike the pricking of his scalp with thorns, which followed it, this torture had no relation to the Passion of Christ and accords better with the theory of interrogation by the Jews than with that of blasphemous parody." Indeed!

Having observed that nobody examined the body in any manner approaching an autopsy for a month after its discovery, and that the initial discovery was accompanied by an automatic assumption by the discoverer that the Jews had murdered this child, regardless of markings on or not on the body, Anderson refers to these signs as if they are fact and then seeks to explain them—by exonerating the Jews from the specifics of ritual murder, while apparently not finding it at all difficult to believe that they did murder William.

Anderson discusses other details as if they are as factual as Thomas does—or does not—believe them to be, and arrives a few lines later to the statement that "if one assumes that the Jews carried out their attempts to force information from William to the point when he lost consciousness, or seemed to be in danger of dying in their house, the presence of the gag [which was never seen by anyone, but was part of the story as it was handed down to Thomas and is present in a second painting—on the roodscreen in Litcham] becomes quite logical. After such mishandling they would never have dared to release him in Norwich; their only chance of evading the consequences of their cruel acts was to smuggle him out of the city to some remote place in England, or on the Continent, whence trusted compatriots would ensure that he did not return."[94] So Anderson's "reconstruction" still offers as its central moment the murder of William by Jews, who were torturing him without intending to kill him but then had to kill him when they realized they could never let him go after they tortured him, and then had to get rid of the body, and planned a remote removal that was somewhat short-circuited: they only got the corpse as far as the nearby woods on the other side of town. If Anderson is an individual who is writing to debunk the blood libel as it applies to William, what might we expect of Christians with perspectives less charitably disposed toward the Jews?

The consequences of the William legend may indeed be felt less benignly and less subtly—well into the twentieth century. As we shall see in a subsequent chapter, a town in New York State came very close to becoming the site of a blood accusation in the late 1920s. And of course, in Europe, in that very decade, Adolf Hitler was penning his plan for resuscitating Germany from its post-World War I catastrophe by ridding itself of its Jews, a plan that would go into horrifying effect in the following decade. Is it mere coincidence that Hitler received such support for his plan from everyday Germans when the Blood Libel had reached such a stupendous peak in German-speaking lands in the thirteenth through sixteenth centuries—culminating with the time of Luther's vicious late-life remarks about the Jews, and the religious wars that followed—and the gut-level sentiments which (as we shall also see subsequently) show no evidence of having abated into the eighteenth and nineteenth centuries?

IV. The Disputation: Nahmanides in Barcelona and Others Elsewhere

What on the other hand, of the disputation as an instrument of legal or quasi-legal Christian-Jewish interaction? A disputation such as is depicted in the elaborate allegorical painting of that name by Raphael—*la Disputa*, one of the frescoes that the artist produced at the behest of Pope Julius II in the offices of the Vatican, in 1508-12—refers to a theological issue upon which all of the assembled figures ultimately agree. The issue in the case of Raphael's fresco is the miraculous transformation of the Host into the body of Christ during the ceremony of the Eucharist: transubstantiation. All of the individuals witnessing the display of the Host agree that the miracle takes place, the question is *how* it takes place, so that the word "disputation" really has the connotation of a *discussion*, a debate between or among co-believers regarding the details and inner workings of an issue regarding which none of them has any real doubts. The process is quite analogous to that in which the *tanna'im* and *amora'im* engaged, in the Jewish tradition, both its talmudic and its midrashic sides, debating and discussing the details of faith against a backdrop of faith that seems not to have wavered in the course of such discussions.

How very different the disputations that involved both Jews *and* Christians. In such cases the intention was for the one side to demonstrate the full legitimacy of its own spiritual perspective and the falseness of the perspective maintained by the other side. Except that neither the conditions promoting the discussion nor its conceivable outcome were balanced and even. Thus in the first place, it was the Christian majority and its leadership that demanded—as opposed to requested or suggested or invited—the disputation with leaders of the Jewish minority. The content might vary—Hebrew Bible ("Old Testament") versus New Testament; Talmudic interpretative literature versus Patristic and/or Scholastic interpretative literature—but the expected results and their consequences always led in one multi-valenced direction.

Thus it was a given from the Christian perspective that the priest arguing against the rabbi would be victorious. The expectation was that the Jewish community would embrace the defeat and turn to Christianity. But should the rabbinic arguments triumph against the most insistent of expectations, the usual consequence was a bubbling forth of frustration from the majority directed against the minority that expressed itself in massacres, expulsions and/or forced conversions/baptisms, particularly of children. Or put another way, the Jewish-Christian disputation was typically a no-win event for the Jewish community: win or lose the spiritual argument, it typically lost whatever degree of physical and emotional/mental comfort it might have possessed before the event.

In the twelfth-century England of William of Norwich we read in the contemporary historiography of William of Malmesbury how a disputation was held involving some Jewish leaders and some Bishops, before William Rufus, and of how the king joked that he would become a Jew if their leaders bested the Bishops in the discussion.[95] The Christians claimed victory but the Jews maintained that they had been bested not by argument but by force. It is more than likely that force played a role regardless of how successful the respective arguments actually were. Nonetheless, interestingly enough, there is a *number* of accounts of conversions to Judaism, including those of two Cistercian monks.

This sort of Jewish-Christian disputation seems to have been relatively and atypically benign. One might say that the "typical" Jewish-Christian disputation bore more of a resemblance to Christian trials for heresy than to Christian-Christian disputations. The unevenness of the playing field and the circumscription of the accused with regard to what he might say as opposed to what was being said about him—I am thinking, for example, of the two trials for heresy endured by Abelard, particularly the second one, at Sens, in 1141, in which his accusers[96] had actually not even read the writings that they were criticizing; or of the style evidenced in the late fifteenth-century heyday era of the Spanish Inquisition, as we shall shortly see—is a characteristic shared between heresy trials and Jewish-Christian disputations.

Yet no two were precisely alike. Three Jewish-Christian disputations have left behind detailed records: the Paris Disputation of

1240, the Barcelona Disputation of 1263 and the Tortosa Disputation of 1413-14. The first of these was limited both in that it focused only on allegedly anti-Christian passages in the Talmud; the last offered a broader debate regarding Jewish versus Christian ideas, texts and customs, but the Jewish participants were offered very little psychological space in which to maneuver, intimidated as they continuously were by their opponents. Of the three, the Barcelona Disputation is the most renowned, in large part because the Jewish spokesman was Nahmanides (Rabbi Moses ben Nahman), one of the outstanding Jewish minds of the medieval period, who himself also recorded the event for posterity in his own words. The Barcelona Disputation was also unusual in that the Jewish side was given more license than was usually the case to develop and present its arguments; the playing field was much closer to level—not entirely, by any means: Nahmanides was permitted to ask no questions of his opponent, only respond to questions, and anti-Jewish violence as an outcome always lurked in the background—than in other cases that are known.

We might note that both the Paris and Barcelona disputations took place during the momentous Christian thirteenth-century marked on the one hand by the development of Gothic art and architecture and thus a new departure point for the physical presence and power of churches and cathedrals; and by the towering intellectual edifices of St Thomas Aquinas' *Summa Theologica*, which sought to encompass the entirety of Christian thought within its pages; of Vincent de Beauvais' *Speculum Mundi*, which sought to encompass all of human thought in three or four areas of intellectual enterprise;[97] and of Jacobo da Voragine's *Legenda Aurea*, which offered the most comprehensive hagiography until the nineteenth century (and the first such work since Gregory the Great's work of that sort in the early seventh century). On the other hand it was marked not only by the entrance onto the stage of history of the Franciscan and Dominican Orders, but in the case of the latter in particular, the shaping of the Inquisition and its spread from Italy north into France, south into Sicily and ultimately west into Spain, largely in response to the spread of this heresy or that within the same era.

The same century was also marked by the sacking of Byzantine

Christian Constantinople by Western Christian warriors in 1203-4 as a culminating act of the fourth Crusade—that never reached the Muslims and the Holy Land, so preoccupied were its perpetrators with their Eastern brethren and the wealth of their capital. And from the Jewish perspective, the early part of the century was most obviously marked by the Lateran Council of 1215 in which it was determined that thereafter Jews would be required to wear a distinguishing mark on their clothing—be it a colored shape or a peculiar hat—to make certain that Christians would recognize them as resident aliens wherever they dwelled.

Nahmanides stands out as a late beacon within the growing night of the Jewish experience in Christian Europe of the next several centuries. In Spain in particular, the Jewish condition had been a relatively benign one for the previous five hundred years or so, and culturally and socio-economically the previous three had amounted to what has been referred to as a Golden Age. Of course, part of the reason for that was the counter-weight of the Muslim presence and power since 718—but after the Christian defeat of the Muslims at Las Navas de Tolosa in 1212, that weight had palpably shrunk.[98] Moreover, in the two centuries leading up to that battle, as the Christians kept chipping away at the Muslim holdings in Spain, the Jews were an important instrument for administering the newly conquered areas, as an educated middle class. But gradually the perception of the Jews as necessary in such a role diminished in the course of the thirteenth century.

The desire to cause the Jews to recognize the truth of Christianity, which desire one can recognize easily enough as present from the end of the first century CE forward, tended to bubble to the surface either at times of particular duress or ones when the Cross seemed to be succeeding in overwhelming the opposition. One might say that in Northeastern Spain and Southern France—from Catalonia to Provence—both of those conditions coincided in the mid-thirteenth century, between the crisis of the Cathar heresy on the one hand and the successes of the *reconquista* on the other. The bubbling to the surface was personified by Pablo Christiani, a former Jew who had embraced Christianity, become a Dominican friar and was eager to push his former co-religionists in the direction he had taken. Pablo was sent by his superior in the Dominican order, Raymundo de Penaforte, to request of King James I of Aragon that he command Nahmanides, as the chief rabbi of Catalonia, to appear on July 20-24 in Barcelona to debate with Pablo regarding three issues: whether the Messiah had yet appeared; whether the Messiah is to be considered human or divine according to the Israelite prophets; and whether the Jews or the Christians are in possession of the true faith.

The disputation was to take place at the palace of the King, in the presence of the monarch and his court as well as prominent ecclesiastics and knights. The fact that King James ("the Conqueror"), who in his successes in effecting parts of the *reconquista*, had many Jewish appointees in important administrative and other positions—and had up to this point all but ignored papal instructions to rid himself of them—agreed to the disputation is itself indicative of a subtle change of condition with regard to tolerating the Jewish presence and certainly Jewish prominence. It was a harbinger of further negative transformation. Nonetheless, Nahmanides was invited to the debate with all due courtesy—which distinguished this disputation from the harsh denunciatory event in Paris 23 years earlier—so it is only in retrospect that we can recognize that change. Indeed, Nahmanides was able to stipulate to the King that he be granted complete freedom of speech in his responses to Pablo's queries.

There is something else new at Barcelona, which is the goal of demonstrating the truth of Christianity by reference to Jewish writings themselves—hence the importance of a former Jew as the primary Christian disputant. Rather than merely the familiar passages from the Hebrew Bible, selections from the Talmud and *Midrash* would be adduced. Judaism would be attacked from within. The idea was that there would be material unpolluted by subsequent hostility to Christianity within the Talmudic literature (i.e., rabbinic discussions that carry through the fifth century) which, dug out carefully, would demonstrate why, from within their own post-biblical material, Jews should turn to Jesus. Christian scholars such as Christiani now was, or such as other Dominican students of the Talmud (as well as of classical Muslim literature) were, trained in the academies established by Raymundo de Penaforte, could pick and choose what passages they wished to adduce to prove their points—while refusing the same right to cherry pick to their Jewish counterparts. Moreover, the notion that the *Midrash Rabbah* often gives diverse and mutually contradictory interpretations of biblical passages and often views those passages as allegorical and not literal, seems to have been lost on Christian students and disputants—including Christiani, in spite of his Jewish background.

The fundamental differences between the Christian and Jewish views virtually guaranteed that the disputants would often talk at cross-purposes. For Christianity, the messiah has come in the person of Jesus who is God incarnate and the messianic arrival guarantees personal salvation for all who embrace him—who are otherwise damned eternally due to Adam's Original Sin of disobedience to God. The Christ's arrival into history also marks the beginning of shaping a perfect reality, however long it takes to complete the process. For Judaism, the messiah has not yet come and may never come—and certainly not necessarily in the form of any particular person who, if he is a person is in no way divine, but merely a descendant of the Davidic house.

The advent of a messianic individual or a non-person-based messianic era will result when we have all worked together to transform the world into a perfect reality. Since we don't inherit Adam's sin—although we share in the consequences as far as hard work and painful childbirthing are concerned—then Jews neither require nor worry about salvation in the hereafter. Indeed, there is no dogma regarding the configuration of the hereafter: no clearly described heaven, much less hell.

Moreover, whereas there is only one correct understanding of the messiah for Christianity—and that understanding is the centerpiece of Christianity—and to misunderstand or disbelieve is profoundly deleterious to the heretic or the infidel and dangerous to the community; for Judaism, the messianic idea is non-essential, and differing views of that idea are embraceable within the faith.

There have been a number of messianic pretenders through the centuries and even the most extreme efforts against some of them by Jewish leadership never encompassed violence.[99] Most of Jewish doctrine is open to discussion—that is what rabbinic literature is about—and it would be difficult to find a Jew who would be excluded from the medieval Jewish community based on his opinions or interpretations of the Torah and its commandments. In particular the aggadic material within the rabbinic literature is understood to be non-doctrinaire. (We will see in a later chapter how this can and will shift, in large part due to Christian influence, when we arrive into the era of Spinoza, in the seventeenth century).

We can see all this first exemplified at Barcelona. Nahmanides' opponent—who had never attained extended knowledge of rabbinic literature while being or after having ceased to be a Jew—in trying to argue in favor of the notion that the Messiah had already appeared by reference to aggadic literature failed to recognize how non-binding and varied the opinions expressed within its pages are for Jews. Christiani referred to the *aggadah* in *Midrash Ekhah Rabbah* 1:51 suggesting that the Messiah was born on the very day that the Temple was destroyed, to which Nahmanides replied first of all that the day of Jesus' birth was not that of the Temple's destruction. But he also observed that the birth of the Messiah is not the same as his advent: the Messiah, like Methusaleh, might live for nearly a thousand years—or more—before engaging in his messianic mission.

"Does [Christiani] mean to say that the sages of the Talmud believed in Jesus as the Messiah and believed that he is both human and divine, as held by the Christians? However, it is well known that the incident of Jesus took place during the period of the Second Temple. He was born and killed prior to the destruction of the Temple, while the sages of the Talmud, like Rabbi Akiva and his associates, followed this destruction. Those who compiled the Mishnah, Ravvi and Rabbi Nathan, lived many years after the destruction. All the more so Rabbi Ashi who compiles the Talmud, who lived four hundred years after the destruction. If these sages believed that Jesus was the messiah... then how did they remain in the Jewish faith and in their former practice? ... If these sages believed in Jesus and in his faith, how is it that they did not do as Friar Paul [i.e.' Pablo Christiani], who understands their teachings better than they themselves do?"

And more to the point, he added, in any case "I don't believe this *aggadah*"—underscoring the non-binding principle that Christiani missed. This, before continuing to point out that other aggadic passages in any case offer a different viewpoint, to wit, that the Messiah would be born near the time of the Redemption. Given both the norm within aggadic literature of posing different and often mutually contradictory viewpoints on any given subject, and the permissibility of individual judgment in the matter of accepting or rejecting the conclusions of *aggadot* in general, he, Nahmanides, accepted the *aggadah* with the pre-redemption viewpoint rather than that with the post-destruction viewpoint.

Nahmanides further argued that the horrific state of the world since the advent and triumph of Christianity is proof that the Messiah has not arrived, whereas his Christian adversary saw the messianic advent as the beginning of a lengthy process that has little to do with the world in which we reside as a species, since it ultimately focuses on the *individual*, not the *world* at large, in the *hereafter* and not in the *here and now*. Put another way, the argument from Christiani's side sees the Messiah as a figure bringing about salvation to the individual soul in the forever after of the world to come. The Jewish view articulated by Nahmanides is that salvation is *tikkun olam*—the mending of the world of the here and now, a bettering of humanity in the social, political, and economic senses, the accomplishment of which bettering will usher in the messianic era, with or without a particular individual as its harbinger, its agent or its culmination.

Of course, looking backwards instead of forwards, the urgency for the Messiah to be what he is for Christianity derives, in part, from the Christian understanding of the egregiousness of Adam's Original Sin: so profound that it reverberates through every human successor (except the Virgin Mary) and will lead to eternal damnation if not for the salvation effected by a divine Messiah. But for Judaism, as Nahmanides argued, Adam's sin was his own—we have inherited the twin curses of work and painful childbirth, but none of us is *marked*, per se, by his sin; none of us is doomed as a consequence of his action: there is nothing in Genesis that suggests Original Sin, eternal damnation and their concomitants to a Jewish reader.[100]

When Christiani argued in favor of the Messiah's divine nature by reference to an aggadic statement placing the Messiah at God's right hand, Nahmanides responded by asking: what of the placement in the same text of Abraham at God's left hand—is he, then, to be construed as divine?[101] Moreover, he referred to the worship of Jesus as an incarnation of God as idolatrous. "You, our lord king, are a Christian and the son of a Christian and you have listened all your life to priests who have filled your brain and the marrow of your bones with this doctrine, and it has settled into you because of that accustomed habit. But the doctrine in which you believe, and which is the foundation of your faith, cannot be accepted by reason, and nature affords no ground for it, nor have the prophets ever expressed it. [For it is strange to imagine that] the Creator of Heaven and Earth resorted to the womb of a certain Judaean woman, grew there for nine months and was born as an infant and afterwards grew up and was betrayed into the hands of his enemies who sentenced him to death and executed him, and that afterwards, as you say, he came to life and returned to his original place. The mind of a Jew, or any other person, simply cannot tolerate this..."

One of the questions that this last comment raises is whether Nahmanides actually uttered such bold words to his Christian audience. Since he wrote his own account of the Disputation, some have argued that he added to and embroidered upon his arguments when he wrote them down later. But given that he had elicited a promise from the king that he have full freedom to speak his mind, and that he is said to have uttered these words directly to the king, he may indeed have spoken thusly. He would go on—in the context of addressing the question of whether Jews or Christians possess the true faith—to ask rhetorically why, if he was the Messiah, Jesus had to hide from the Romans, and why it is that Rome declined after it embraced Christianity, and why currently Islam possesses the more powerful empire, not Christianity (a condition which, in retrospect, was in the process of becoming less true, especially in Spain, from this time)—and why Christianity has been responsible for more bloodshed than any other group in history?

Three days into the process, as it appeared that Nahmanides was getting the upper hand in the argument, the Jews of Barcelona begged him to desist, fearful as they were of the consequences of angering the Dominicans, but the king himself asked him to continue. And in the end the king rewarded Nahmanides with a prize of "300 dinars," declaring that he had never before heard "an unjust cause so nobly defended." While royal approbation suggested that Nahmanides had been victorious—moreover, James is said by Nahmanides to have visited the synagogue the following Sabbath, and respectfully preached the doctrine of Jesus as the Messiah while also permitting a response—the Dominicans declared victory. This is what impelled the Jewish scholar to publish the disputation with his remarks within it.

Royal support seems to have protected the community from violence against it or expulsion, but not Nahmanides himself, in the end—at least once he put his words into written form. Pablo Christiani selected certain passages from the Nahmanides publication, construed them as anti-Christian blasphemies, and denounced his disputational opponent to Raymundo de Penaforte. Presumably Raymundo did not require much encouragement to lodge a capital charge against the scholar and a formal complaint with the king. Distrusting the Dominican court of inquiry, James appointed a special commission and ordered the proceedings to be conducted in his presence. Nahmanides argued that he had not written down anything that he had not openly argued before the king, who had granted him freedom of speech during the disputation. Nonetheless, the compromise arrived at to satisfy the Dominicans was to banish Nahmanides for a two-year period and to burn all known copies of his pamphlet—and he was fined, although the fine was remitted as a favor to Nahmanides' brother, Benveniste de Porta.

Ultimately, though, the Dominicans were able to convince Pope Clement IV to extend Nahmanides' two-year exile into a permanent one. So he left Aragon, lived for a few years in Castile or

Southern France and in 1267 immigrated to Eretz Yisrael—where, in Jerusalem he established a synagogue that still stands.[102] He helped revive Jewish communal life in the city that had been disrupted by the Crusades and has remained unbroken since. Even well off and renowned and focused on the writing of his greatest work, a commentary on the Torah, he still felt the pangs of exile, who "left my family, forsook my house. There, with my sons and daughters, the sweet, dear children I brought up at my knees, I also left my soul."

V. The Evolution of the Inquisition

The court of inquiry that King James I of Aragon distrusted, in the hands of the same Dominicans whom the Jews of Barcelona so feared, is better known by the name "Inquisition." Such courts had only come into existence a few generations before the Barcelona disputation, not as a solution to the Jewish problem, but to deal with the problem of heresy. Part of the Inquisition's context was the problem of the Muslim infidel. If this last problem had as part of its "solution" the *reconquista* at the Western end of the Mediterranean, as we have observed, for which significant Christian progress carried from the mid-eleventh through early thirteenth centuries, it had, as another part, the Crusades at the Eastern end of the Mediterranean.

Beginning with the first Crusade declared by Pope Urban II in 1095, the stated goal of these efforts was to reclaim the Holy Land from the Muslims. That First Crusade may be said to have achieved success. But the second (1147-8), among whose most vocal supporters was St. Bernard of Clairvaux (the same who led the charge of heresy against Peter Abelard in 1141), was not. Part of the reason may have been that the German crusaders expended so much of their energy—and St. Bernard was distraught about this—attacking, massacring and expelling Jewish communities in the Rhineland. Two years after Salah-ad-Din (known to Europeans as Saladin) retook Jerusalem for the Muslims in 1187, a third Crusade was declared (1189-92) that involved, among others, the English king Richard I (the Lion Heart). It included some victorious battles against the Muslims, but ultimately failed. The Fourth Crusade, we recall, culminated with the sacking of Constantinople in 1204, and the establishment of a "Latin" (theoretically loyal to Rome and its Catholic papacy) Imperium in Byzantium for a century (after which the Greeks, i.e., Orthodox, re-asserted themselves).

This is the context in which Pope Innocent III (1198-1216) arrived at his papacy. In the very year when Constantinople was sacked and the Fourth Crusade came to an end, Innocent sent Diego de Acebes, Bishop of Osman, to preach in Southern France and Northern Spain, in the company of one Dominic of Calervega. The focus of their preaching was the growing problem of heretical beliefs, of which the most disturbing, widespread and best-organized was that known as the Cathar or Albigensian heresy. On the one hand, what is often referred to as the Albigensian Crusade was declared in 1209. Its purpose was ostensibly to eliminate the Cathars who had spread through much of Occitania—what is now known as southern France. The bloody struggle lasted for decades, and was as much or more about the politics of northern France and its desire to incorporate the south into its domains as it was about spiritual concerns, but in the end both the heretics and the independence of the south were exterminated. (See n 70 and n 72).

On the other hand, Diego and Dominic gradually gathered followers and so developed a mendicant order—a monastic order that moved, as preachers and beggars, from place to place, rather than establishing itself in a permanent monastic location, where it might become materially prosperous and, from the viewpoint of the Papacy, threatening—that was officially recognized by Innocent in 1215. This was the same year, as historical nicety would have it, when up in the England of King John, that monarch was being forced to agree to the terms of the Magna Carta drawn up by his rebellious knights at Runnymede. So, too, in that year, at the Fourth Lateran Council, as previously noted, a call went out for the first time demanding of Jews that they wear distinctive badges, yellow and otherwise, on the clothing, or horned hats, so that their neighbors would be able to recognize these adversaries of the faith, in league with the horned anti-Christ and his father, Satan.

At the same Lateran council of 1215, polemics against Islam led Pope Innocent to call for a Fifth Crusade to the Holy Land—an effort that was ultimately engaged in the year following Innocent's death, lasting form 1217 to 1221 and, while achieving initial successes, ending in the surrender of the Crusaders to Sultan al-Kamil of Egypt and the agreement to an eight-year truce. Meanwhile, the mendicant order of which Dominic of Calervega had quickly become the dominant leader continued to grow and spread until Dominic's death in 1221. At the same time, the mendicant order that had been established by St. Francis of Assisi in the early part of the century, that had begun seeking ordination from the Pope in 1209 and achieved it also by 1215, became an elite clerical force within the Church by the time of St. Francis' death in 1226.

The following year, Pope Innocent III's successor, Honorius III, died and was succeeded as Pope by Gregory IX who at the outset of his papacy pushed hard for a sixth Crusade—and excommunicated Emperor Frederick II for his failure to lead one in spite of his many promises to do so[103]—at the same time that he began to augment the struggle against heresy. In that augmentation the Pope initially called upon the Dominicans to be his primary instrument, who were joined by the Franciscans by the mid-1230s. These were the two orders which, as mendicant orders and perhaps because of the psychological disposition of their respective founders and their followers, were most loyal to the curia.

Obviously the issues with which they dealt and the procedures that they developed with which to deal with the issues had little or nothing, in theory, to do with Jews and Judaism. Heretics, misbelievers from within the faith, are not infidels, unbelievers from without. In fact, the most important Christian thinker of the thirteenth century—and arguably the most important Christian thinker of the entire medieval period—St. Thomas Aquinas, had argued strenuously against using force of any kind in trying to convince Jews of the wrong-headedness of their beliefs. "Belief is voluntary" he noted; to compel someone is to create a false believer. Only should Jews "hinder the faithful," must they be dealt with strongly.

So what, then, of Christians who, for one reason or another— perhaps as a consequence of this disputation or that—have *converted to Judaism*? By 1267, Pope Clement IV (the same Pope who extended

Nahmanides' two-year-long exile from Aragon into a permanent one) enjoined the Dominican and Franciscan orders to direct their efforts toward prosecuting former Christians who had apostasized and become Jewish. They were to be prosecuted as heretics—on the grounds that, once baptized, an individual is considered a Christian, so for a former Christian who practices as a Jew constitutes mis-Christian practice, or heresy. Moreover, Clement instructed his agents to punish any Jews believed to have *induced* such Christians into this form of heresy. ·

This redirection of the Inquisitional efforts of the two orders was repeated under the directing decrees of Popes Gregory X in 1274 and Nicholas IV in 1288 and again in 1290. We may recognize how all of these efforts—crusading against the Muslim infidel, inquiring into the faith of Christian heretics, and attacking rabbinic literature through disputations—were fundamentally linked. But beginning with Clement's decree of 1267 that linkage takes on a new, somewhat paradoxical twist: while the spiritual line between Christian and Jew is being drawn ever more emphatically (one cannot cross the line from the first to the second, period), the line of method regarding how to deal with heretics versus Jewish infidels is becoming more blurred.

The institution of the Inquisition, led by the Dominican order, having continued its growth, came to encompass all the Jews in southern France by 1297—meaning that any of them could be subject to its attention based on the assumption that any of them could be involved in drawing good Christians into heresy: the Judaizing heresy. With the same sort of concern in mind, the Christian authorities expelled all Jews from Apulia in southern Italy at around the same time.

Meanwhile, as for the Jewish community at large, we may recall that in the aftermath of the destruction of the Second Temple and the failed Bar Kokhba Revolt of 65 years later, the community of what the Romans were calling Palestine, (rather than Judaea), was beginning to shrink, both in size and importance. While there are Palestinian commentators on the *mishnah*, so that we speak of a Palestinian *gemara* and a Palestinian Talmud, by and the large the more significant—and certainly much more extensive—*gemara* and Talmud are referred to as Babylonian. For—ironically enough, given the Judaean history of the previous millennium—by the third century the greatest centers of Jewish life were in key cities of Mesopotamia, such as Sura and Pumbedita, that were developing what would shortly become the most important rabbinical academies in the Jewish world. The prominence of these academies continued through the end of the tenth century. By then the pendulum had begun to swing, geographically speaking, all the way west to Iberia.

Thus at just around the time when the great Muslim Ummayad Dynasty, with its capital in Cordova, was collapsing, and with that collapse, the *reconquista* was beginning to succeed after 300 years of relative stasis, the socio-cultural silver age of the Jews in Spain was beginning to turn golden. That golden age, as we have earlier noted, began the gradual process of tarnishing in the middle of the thirteenth century, culminating by the end of the fourteenth. For in 1391, on Ash Wednesday, prompted by the torrid sermonizing of a preacher named Vincent Ferrer, the Christian community of Sevilla effected a massacre on its Jewish community. The mood of violent anti-Jewish sentiment spread quickly through Christian Spain.

The unrest continued virtually unabated for a generation, until 1415, the result of which is that perhaps a third of Spain's Jewry— some historiographers have asserted that there were nearly a million Jews among Spain's 9 million inhabitants by that time, making it by far both the most Jewishly populous country in the world and also the one with the highest *percentage* of Jewish inhabitants—left Spain; another third are said to have embraced Christianity under the stress of the oppressive conditions that emerged for the first time in nearly eight centuries. Jewish law is ambiguous regarding how to view conversion from Judaism—a real enough issue from the fifth century forward. In general a distinction was made between a genuine conversion and one that was made under force and therefore might be viewed as fictitious rather than real. The very Hebrew word for "convert"—"*anoos*"—means "one who has been forced;" it is the same term used in contemporary Hebrew to refer to someone who has been raped.

The practical double question debated by the medieval Jewish authorities was how to adjudge a conversion real or fictional, and, in the case of the latter, whether to make it easier or more difficult for a convert to return to the fold of Judaism, should desire and circumstances permit. The Franco-German rabbis—the key figures among them being Rabbeinu Gershom (Gershonides) and Rashi—in focussing on this question, differed with regard to how extreme to construe the idea of forced/fictional: if one's life is at stake—but whether or not it *is* at stake may not always be clear. Gershom insisted that the convert be reminded of having converted out of the faith, emphasizing the inherent weakness and guilt in the act, as if to suggest that, at a fundamental level, death is to be preferred to apostasy. Rashi emphasized the meaning of the term *anoos*, thereby assuming that anyone seeking to return to the community had by definition been converted under duress and should therefore—provided his/her behavior was exemplary—be joyfully brought back in.

In Spain, the community tended to follow the lead of Maimonides' authority, who argued that Jews are enjoined "to live by the Torah and not to die by it," and yet he construed what it means to "die" by and for the Torah in extreme terms. A convert, particularly to Christianity, was viewed by him as having become an idolater, so that a returning former convert should be only very reluctantly accepted back into the community. Maimonides' further criticism was directed to the convert who did not immediately try to return to the fold when circumstances made such a return possible.

With the unexpected disaster of 1391 and its aftermath, and sometimes mass conversions, the question of how "real" or "fictional" the acts of apostasy were emerged with considerable vehemence. If not precisely my life, but my livelihood, say, were threatened—for as Christian Spain moved toward and through the fifteenth century, the role of openly professing Jews in the socio-economic and cultural infrastructure continued ever more swiftly in the downward spiral begun in the mid-thirteenth century—so that my ability and that of my family not to *live* but to live *well* was at risk, would my conversion to Christianity be construable as forced or willing? The community and its leaders wavered as to how to interpret such an issue in the face of such large numbers.

Meanwhile, the Christian community itself was not necessarily so happy with those numbers either, for at least two reasons. First of all, since many of those Jews who converted did do so for reasons more of livelihood than life, that meant in practical terms that the economic role that they played in late fourteenth-century through late fifteenth-century Spain was not diminished, to the chagrin of Christian neighbors who had hoped to profit by their demise. Second—and this must surely have sat in many Christian throats like a big bone—the conditions compelling such large numbers of conversions in Spain helped shape a phenomenon virtually unique in Jewish history (certainly unique on this scale and with this degree of obviousness): that of long-term fictional conversion.

This phenomenon had two aspects that defined it in Spain. One is that the fictional convert, while professing Christianity on the exterior—from having been baptized to going to church and celebrating Christian holidays—practiced Judaism on the interior: secretly praying on the Sabbath and on Jewish holidays, secretly baking and eating matzah during Passover and fasting during Yom Kippur. The second is that this complex double life might continue through several generations. The phenomenon was well enough known so that all *conversos*—all *Nuevos Christianos* (New Christians)—were at least theoretically suspected of being secret Jews: *crypto*-Jews. The frustration of "old Christian" neighbors who failed to reap the benefits they expected from the demise of their Jewish neighbors when that demise never set in, since those neighbors embraced Christianity, would have been exponentially greater if and when they suspected those neighbors of actually being crypto-Jews.[104]

Indeed, a specific term was directed toward *Nuevos Christianos*—or at least those suspected of being crypto-Jews: *marrano*. The word in the Castilian dialect of the time meant "swine," and it was applied both by Old Christians and also often by still-professing Jews whose non-converted status certainly doomed them to increasing poverty as the fifteenth century wore on. Of course, on the other hand, New Christians who were sincere in their profession of Christian faith—whether in the first generation or the second or third, as the strain of double-life marranism often led to gradual diminishment of or complete disconnection from spiritual or ritual connections to Judaism—might easily become more virulently anti-Jewish than their Old Christian neighbors, eager as they were to prove both to those neighbors and to themselves how fully Christian they truly were.[105]

The evolving Inquisitional process will intersect this morass along two parallel, but ultimately converging lines. First of all, if by the late thirteenth century, the Papal Curia and its Dominican instrument had already turned their concern with the problem of heresy toward the assertion that a Christian who becomes a Jew is a heretic, then what of a Jew who becomes a Christian but is accused of continuing Jewish religious practices? If once baptized, one is unequivocally and irrevocably a Christian, then obviously a baptized Jew has now become a Christian and any Jewish religious behavior—despised, perhaps, but tolerated in an openly professing Jew—is by definition heretical. And in Christian Spain, from 1391 onward, the number of individuals committing, or suspected of committing such a heresy—the Judaizing heresy—would have expanded enormously. So the urge to put the Inquisitional process in motion in Christian Spain would have been—and obviously was—irresistible.

Moreover, the ability of the Inquisition to have as a starting point an endless supply of informants willing to point fingers at such heretics was unprecedented, given the frustrating conditions outlined briefly in the previous few paragraphs. And given the hostility of genuine New Christians toward both false ones—crypto-Jewish marannos—and also to their former co-religionists, then a perfect set of conditions for a particularized reign of terror presented itself, particularly if and when some of those genuine New Christians achieved positions of prominence in Church and State.

Consider the following handful of events reflecting the growing ugliness with regard to the condition of *Nuevos Christianos* in the second half of the fifteenth century: in 1468, Henry (the Impotent) of Toledo—whose confessor preached emphatically against the *Nuevos Christianos*—decreed that no *converso* could any longer hold office within his domains. Five years later, in 1473, in Cordoba, the self-styled "Christian Brotherhood" claimed that, during the procession of the image of the Holy Virgin, dirty water was tossed onto the image from the window of a young *conversa* and riots broke out that spread elsewhere in south central Spain—the most intense riots since 1391.

The following year, King Ferdinand of Aragon and Queen Isabel of Castile, whose courtship and marriage five years earlier had been accomplished in large part—Ferdinand's wooing of Isabel was certainly financed—by key *converso* figures in the king's court, ascended together to the throne of a unified Aragon and Castile. As these were the two largest Christian states within the peninsula that had not experienced unity since the Roman period, Christian Spain was virtually unified for the first time in the history of the *reconquista*. Within three more years—by 1477—the Christian Spanish civil war was officially over and that unity was officially complete. Within two years, the *reconquista* would resume, having as its goal to divest the Muslims of their control of Granada and thus to bring the entire peninsula under one administrative roof.

But sandwiched between the official end of the Christian civil war and the resumption of the effort at *reconquista*, in 1478 an accusation was lodged in Seville that during the Passover Seder that coincided with Holy Week some Jews had blasphemed the Christian Religion. Evidence (there is no record as to *what* evidence) was brought before the state court, the result of which was that the king sent an ambassador to Rome asking the Pope to emit a bull establishing the Inquisitional authority in Spain. This was odd, in a sense, since, to repeat, the Inquisition dealt not with Jews but with heretical Christians—unless we assume that the "Jews" accused of blaspheming Christianity were actually *Nuevos Christianos*, labeled as or misunderstood to have been Jews, by authorities then or since.[106] Pope Sixtus IV hesitated, out of concern that the Institution could well fall outside his control given the realities of distance and actual power, but finally complied, so that by the late fall, on November 1, the Spanish sovereigns were instructed by way of a papal bull to appoint three bishops over the age of 40 to assume jurisdiction over the shaping of an Inquisitional Board.

In 1480 the first activities of that authority began in Seville and in February, 1481 the first *auto-da-Fe* was held: a public execution of unrepentant or confessed heretics who were burned at the stake (in order not to shed any blood, for the inquisitional policy called for death to be meted out "without effusion of blood"): six men and women were burned. All of them were *marannos*, accused of the heresy of Judaizing; the Inquisitional authority published a list of 37 signs by which such heresy might be recognized. The most obvious among these was evidence that an individual had celebrated the Jewish Sabbath by changing the bed sheets on Friday afternoon or not kindling a cooking fire on Saturday, or by reciting a Hebrew blessing over the wine or kindling candles on Friday evening and allowing them to burn out of their own accord; or by celebrating Passover by eating *matzah* or other foods associated with the Passover Seder; or by fasting and praying on the Day of Atonement.

By 1482, seven other Inquisitional centers had been established. The following year the entire system was unified under Tomas de Torquemada. Tomas was the personal confessor of Isabel—and had been since before she and Ferdinand were married. He was, moreover, the grandson of *conversos*, and therefore, perhaps, as fanatical an anti-*converso* individual as one could hope for, who now had the entire apparatus of the Inquisition in his hands with which to ferret out false *conversos*, the sort of crypto-Jewish *marannos* that gave his grand-parents and parents—and, should anyone know of his background, himself—a bad Christian name. His enthusiasm for his work naturally spread to the queen whom he confessed weekly. In turn that enthusiasm would have spread to the king, for two reasons. The first is that he, too, had *converso* blood flowing in his veins! His mother's mother was Paloma the Jewess, of Toledo (so that halakhically speaking, he would be considered a Jew by Jewish law)[107] and more to the immediate point, he would have felt it of profound importance that he demonstrate to his queen that his zeal to purify Christian Spain of heresy was as great as hers.

The second reason for Ferdinand's enthusiastic embrace of the

Inquisition was one of the key features of its methodology. One accused of heresy and arrested by the inquisitional authorities was immediately deprived of his home and all of his belongings, the value of which was divided among three principles: the Church, the State and the accuser. If the fact that the accuser remained anonymous is added to this matrix, then we understand why such a method encouraged a reign of finger-pointing terror. But we also understand how, spiritual issues aside, both Church and State would have been eager to arrest more rather than fewer of the middle- to upper-management kind of individuals whose confiscated property would help fill their respective coffers—and Ferdinand's were remarkably empty.

Which leads us to the issue of the methodology of the Inquisition and how to understand it in the context of the issue of "Jewish trials." Two aspects of this are relevant—the first having to do with "trials" and the second with "Jewish." Thus the individual arrested by the inquisitional authority was not being formally arrested by the state and there was no accusation lodged by the state. In fact, it was often the case that the accused was not presented with a single specific detail to account for the general accusation of heretical behavior—which of the officially published 37 acts-cum-signs-of-heresy had led to the arrest—any more than s/he was confronted with the witness of those signs and permitted to cross-examination that witness. The accused might in fact be placed in prison for anywhere up to a year before even being brought before the Inquisitional "court" to face the unspecified charges that had been leveled anonymously against him or her.

More precisely, the official process began with an "Edict of Grace" in which the accused was asked to come forward and confess, in exchange for a promise of merciful treatment; the "Term of Grace" allowed 30 days for this confession to come forth. This was accompanied and/or followed by an "Edict of Faith," in which the faithful were enjoined to come forth and denounce those guilty of heresy to the inquisitional authorities—and so the entire population was deputized, as it were, to be accomplices in rooting out heretics.

The tribunal itself was in theory objective and impartial;

charges were examined by a committee that pronounced them legitimate before an arrest was made. The trial was then not only conducted in secrecy, but any breaches in its secrecy were punished severely. The accused were segregated within dungeons—and bore whatever costs the process required. Since the trial process could take years—as many as 14 years in one case—these costs could obviously be considerable.

Meanwhile, of course, all of the property of the accused would have been confiscated and sequestered. One might suppose that the inclination to find him or her innocent would have been severely undermined by the idea that the court and its allies would lose that property, since if the prisoner were found guilty, all of his/her property went to the Holy Office—but apparently it was rare, even on the rare occasion when an individual was able to prove his or her innocence beyond the cynicism of the court, that his/her property would be returned anyway: it remained in the hands to which it had been remanded at the time of the arrest.

In any case, faced with a general but non-specific charge without the right to confront the accuser(s) or witness(es) and without witnesses for the defense being allowed (because such witnesses were assumed to be inherently untrustworthy) the accused—the victim—might go in one of two directions: to deny or to confess, with or without an explanation. In the latter case, the confession might comply with the charge or, more often, open up new avenues for the prosecution, since, say, the witness had asserted that the accused fasted on Yom Kippur and the accused, imagining that the charge was that she had changed the bed sheets on Friday afternoon, admitted to that (explaining, perhaps, that this was just the ordinary laundry day for her, having nothing to do with the advent of the Jewish Sabbath), to which the tribunal might then respond, "oh, so you were *also* committing *that* heretical act!"

The entire process was helped along by a range of physical tortures that the evolving inquisitional authority picked up along the way from the thirteenth to the fifteenth centuries, primarily in Sicily. The details of torture to elicit confessions I leave the reader to investigate through sources in the footnote concluding this sentence.[108] The point is that the entire procedure bore very little resemblance to what in most times and places would be considered a legitimate legal procedure or a fair trial. Moreover the results were almost invariably the same: if one confessed, one was punished; if one did not confess but the court was not convinced of one's innocence, one was punished. The only difference was whether one was unrepentant and thus burned alive at the stake or confessed and was therefore mercifully killed by being garroted first before being burned.[109] By November, 1481, 298 victims had already been burned and another 98 in prison awaited their audience before the tribunal.

Theatrical sermonizing typically accompanied the Autos-da-fe which, subsequently published, yield much of our information about this horrific period. The voraciousness of the Inquisition authorities under Torquemada and his successors is remarkable, from the eagerness with which victims were chosen without distinction of gender or age—from 10-year-olds to 97-year-old Anna Rodriguez, burned at the stake in Lisbon in 1682—to the tenacity of pursuit: a Portuguese family was burned in effigy in 1656, having managed to flee and change its name. But the Inquisition caught up with it in 1679 and was then able to subject its members in the flesh to what had only been accomplished in a surrogate manner 23 years earlier.

These last details lead once more to the question of who the victims were and how the Inquisitional trials might or might not be construed as "Jewish trials." The answer begins by turning back to the question of how to define who and what a Jew is. Strictly speaking, as we have already noted, the purpose of the Inquisition, from its inception in the thirteenth century, through its most horrific and extended development in Spain in the fifteenth century and beyond, had nothing to do with Jews, per se: it dealt with the problem of heresy, of misbelieving Christians, not of infidels, non-believers such as Jews or Muslims. But if late in the thirteenth century, as we have seen, its focus turned to former Christians who had become Jews, and because of the growing power of the Dominican inquisitional organization over the state, could encompass Jews who were accused of facilitating such conversion; how much more logical was it to turn, in Spain, to Jews who had become Christians—and from them to encompass

Jews who might be accused of encouraging backsliding into Judaizing heresy among their former co-religionists?

Interestingly, direct attacks on the still-professing Jews of Christian Spain seem not to have taken place all that often, if at all—although, to repeat, it is sometimes difficult to know who is a professing Jew and who a crypto-Jew in reading the record of that dark time and place, just as, conversely, for the *conversos* themselves, their self-definition as Jews or as Christians could represent a redefinition of both. That is: great-grandchildren of *conversos* might be fully believing and practicing Christians, but still be kindling a special set of candles on Friday evening without even realizing that the inherited "family" custom was the remnant of a distinctly Jewish process of welcoming the Sabbath; another great-grandchild of the same generation might fiercely still consider himself Jewish (albeit hidden) while not realizing that the pork he consumes especially on Saturday in order to celebrate the Sabbath is contrary to Jewish gastronomic legitimacy. The entire mood of antipathy to *Nuevos Christianos* was in part connected to the Spanish idea of purity of blood—*limpieza de sangre*—referred to a few pages back. That notion, in this context, suggested a blood-purity to Old Christians which, by definition, newer arrivals to the faith could not possess.

But where the authorities were concerned, inquiring into the proper faith of professing Jews was illogical and ultimately pointless. In the long run, rather, the recommended course emulated that of Apuleia of two centuries earlier: expulsion. In order to help assure an end of the Judaizing heresy, it would be wise, Tomas de Torquemada would have said to Ferdinand and Isabel, to remove heresy-influencing Jews from Spain. The concern for the consequences of allowing continued *converso*-Jewish interface was well expressed in the trumped up blood libel at Avila in the end of the 1480s which accused Jews and *conversos* jointly of complicity.

Of course until January, 1492, Jews and crypto-Jews alike could head south—and perhaps many of them did—to the relative safety of Muslim Spain: Granada. But the swelling coffers of Ferdinand, enlarged mainly through a decade of inquisitional activity, finally made it possible to mount the final assault on Granada at that time.

And with his victory, religious zeal must also have swelled. With the triumph over the Muslims Ferdinand and the Christians lost whatever incentive they may have had for conciliating the Jewish minority that had been useful for so long in both an administrative infrastructural and go-between capacity. So in spite of the promise the king had made prior to taking Granada—that a united Spain would be open to all faiths—he contrived an edict of expulsion by the end of March, published it in April and saw to it that it was carried out by the beginning of August, which late date was as much as the formerly powerful Abravanel family could extract from Ferdinand as a thanks for decades of service to the crown.

Interestingly enough, *conversos* were forbidden to emigrate. One might suppose that losing that population and the opportunities it offered for inquisitional confiscations of its material goods had something to do with that. For the Inquisition remained in place in Spain until the eighteenth century, was carried over into Portugal and into the New World by the colonial administrations of both Iberian countries, where it lasted an equally long if not longer time. Interestingly, any number of its victims who had been genuinely faithful Christians abandoned that faith and reverted to Judaism as a consequence of its procedures. Both openly professing Jews by being forced and *conversos* by stealth managed to leave in 1492 and in the years and decades to follow. Among the places to which many eventually went was Holland, which by the end of the sixteenth century had achieved its independence from Spain—with various consequences for our narrative, as we shall see in the chapter that follows.

Chapter Four:
Between Medieval and Modern Worlds

I. An Age of Exploration, Explosion and Intellectual Implosion

One might say that 1492 marks a multiple point of transition for our narrative. Christian Europe was in the process of undergoing significant developments along two parallel fronts. Between the time of Columbus' first journey and the completion of the journey of Ferdinand Magellan's crew in 1522, which circumnavigated the globe, the sense of the physical world exploded, and an increasingly aggressive age of European exploration of the planet began.[110] During the same time period Western Christendom was psychologically imploding through what evolved toward a series of challenges to the spiritual authority of the Papacy. What began with the issues raised by Martin Luther—in the 95 "Theses" that he tacked on to the door of a church in Wittenberg, Germany in 1517—expanded during the next twenty years or so into an extensive series of protests and demands for reforming the Church, led by individuals such John Calvin, Martin Bucer, Ulrich Zwingli (and in a very different, more personal and overtly *political* way, King Henry VIII of England), whose work as a compendium is commonly referred to as the Protestant Reformation.

The snowballing process of groups of Western Christians in different countries falling away from allegiance to the Church at Rome eventually provoked a Counter-Reformation. Among the most unfortunate consequences of the Reformation-Counter-Reformation processes was an endless series of religious wars that continued with relatively little respite until 1715. Nor was the interweave of war and both spiritual and political concerns limited to Protestant-Catholic struggles. On the one hand, the sacking of Constantinople several generations before Luther's day—in 1453—by Sultan Mehmet the Conqueror and the Ottoman Turks, who, as a group, had embraced Islam much earlier, opened the door to Christendom from Asia barely had the Crusades ended and only forty years before the *reconquista* finally removed Muslim political power from the Iberian peninsula. It was Mehmet's successor's successor, Beyazit, who eagerly welcomed Jewish refugees into his realms from Spain in 1492 and Portugal in 1496-7. In turn Beyazit's successor, Suleiman the Magnificent, carried Ottoman Turkish power—and the Muslim presence—into Europe, coming so far as Vienna, which he besieged but failed to conquer in 1529.

On the other hand, a series of no less than four wars defined the French-Spanish relationship in the mid-sixteenth century. Queen Isabel died in 1506 and was survived by Ferdinand by a decade. Their daughter, Juana, married a Hapsburg prince, Philip the Handsome, who died not too long after his arrival into Spain, but not before impregnating Juana (who was distraught enough after Philip's demise that she repaired to a convent for the rest of her life) with an heir. That heir, the grandson of Ferdinand and Isabel, became King Charles (Carlos) I of Spain, after his grandfather's death in 1516. Three years later he assumed the Hapsburg throne, as Emperor Charles (Karl) V. Between the two crowns his empire encompassed much of central Europe as well as the burgeoning array of Spanish colonies to the West, in the New World and to the East, in the south Pacific. Charles engaged in four wars with Francis I of France—each of them asserting himself to be the truer Catholic ruler, and therefore each expecting papal support for his cause. When in 1527 the Pope supported Francis, Charles' troops sacked Rome and the Vatican along the way to other battles.

In all of this, two issues of consequence for our narrative were beginning to play out. One was the expanding array of questions regarding religion and God: how could the true faith be such a constant source and center of slaughter (echoing, in implied terms, the explicit issue raised by Nahmanides in his Barcelona disputation in 1263)? How could God possibly be receptive to Christian prayer when it was offered in such brutal contexts? And if Christian theological certainty found itself with a new series of sources for doubt, then what exactly might that mean with regard to the fifteen-hundred-year-long nemesis of the Church, Judaism? The other was that, questions aside, in the array of wars and battles that peppered the sixteenth and seventeenth centuries, religion and politics interwove each other with sometimes significant on the ground results for the Jewish condition within Christendom.

Thus the struggle in the 1570s for independence from Spanish political control of the northern seven Netherlandish provinces—of which Holland was the largest, sometimes lending its name to the entire group—which resulted eventually in political independence, also separated those seven provinces from their southern lowland neighbors along religious lines. The Netherlands became Protestant—Dutch Reformed—while Belgium and Luxembourg remained Catholic. From a Jewish perspective this meant three things, potentially: that Jews whose families had been forced to leave Spain or Portugal at the end of the fifteenth century and had eventually made their way to the Netherlands—they were not forced out of later Spanish dominions in the decades following the 1492 expulsion from Spain proper and the 1496-7 expulsion from Portugal—could breathe slightly more easily now.

It meant that crypto-Jews whose families had managed to leave Spain or Portugal during the previous decades, but had had to remain wary of showing any Jewish affiliation in Spanish or Portuguese dominions where the Inquisition operated could now, as it were, come out of hiding and re-become openly practicing Jews, if they lived in places no longer under Spanish or Portuguese control in the New or the Old Worlds. And it meant that, in the decades that followed, crypto-Jews who managed to flee from Spain or Portugal could and did come particularly to Holland and re-open their Jewishly lived lives. For in entering the seventeenth century, we arrive at a period when Holland's material and colonial successes are chronologically coincidental with a policy of religious open-mindedness and tolerance unique and ahead of its time.

The northern Netherlandish provinces achieved extraordinary prominence in developing trading companies directed both toward the New World and toward Southeast Asia, in which enterprises they would eventually butt heads not only with the Spanish and the Portuguese but with the English; in establishing relations with the expansive Ottoman Empire—that, for example, afforded the Dutch a monopoly on the burgeoning tulip propagation and trade that originated in Turkey; and in particular in the visual arts of painting and engraving. For our purposes what is most important is that the evolving Dutch middle class, focused as it was on its material and cultural successes, was less inclined to worry about the particulars of an individual's spiritual direction if that individual were honest and energetic enough to be a contributing member of Dutch society.

Thus Holland in general and Amsterdam in particular became a distinctly multi-cultural, interfaith world in which Jews felt more comfortable than they had anywhere in Europe since, perhaps, Cordova back in the tenth century. Jews from Central and Eastern Europe migrated westward to Amsterdam—Jews whose general designation in terms of their liturgy, languages and customs is "Ashkenazi."[111] And Jews—or *conversos*/Crypto-Jews—from Spain and Portugal also found in Amsterdam a comfortable home. Such Jews would be called by the designation "Sephardi"—a term from the medieval Hebrew word for Spain (*Sepharad*)—and might come directly from the Iberian peninsula or from elsewhere to which they had migrated in leaving the peninsula, eventually to find in Amsterdam a new home. In 1657, Jews were formally recognized as citizens of the Dutch Republic.

Two unusual characteristics might be noted of the Spanish and Portuguese community in Amsterdam. One is that it seems never to have quite completely gotten over the fear that generations of Inquisitional experience had taught it. Since the Netherlands was either potentially or actually still in conflict with Spain or Portugal (or both) at times throughout the seventeenth century, and since there were in any case neighboring lowland countries (Belgium and Luxembourg) that had retained their Catholicism, if not their allegiance to the Spanish crown, there was always the danger that the new home of the Sephardim would lose its political and/or spiritual independence and/or open quality. Should that happen, former Crypto-Jews who had returned openly to their Judaism would be in danger of being dragged before the Inquisitional authorities which, it was assumed, would shift into place. This fear was reinforced by the fact that there were spies for the Inquisitional Authority who operated in the Spanish and Portuguese community of Amsterdam. So there was an underlying fear for the future that wove itself through the Dutch Sephardic communal tapestry of the seventeenth century.

The second feature of that community—more nuanced and ironic—is that it seems to have absorbed into itself certain features of the Inquisition-dominated world it had left behind. Thus the notions of heresy and excommunication enter into its vocabulary, as a direct borrowing from the Catholic world from which it fled. The specifics of this we may see if we explore the trial, for heresy, and the excommunication proceedings, directed toward Uriel Acosta[112] and Baruch Spinoza, that offer unhappy highlights for the community in that era.

II. The Trials of Uriel Acosta

Uriel Acosta was born ca 1585 to a *converso* family in Porto, Portugal. His family had originally converted in order to dodge the persecution of Jews but became devoutly Catholic—his father was a priest well-versed in Canon law. Uriel also held an ecclesiastical office—he became the treasurer in the Collegiate Church—having studied Canon law as a student. As a student he also began to study the Christian Bible and to have questions about contradictions that he saw in the Gospels. He began to study the Hebrew Bible as well, concluding that it is more logical than the New Testament. He was also struck by the fact that both Jews and Christians embrace the Hebrew Bible, whereas only Christians embrace the New Testament as Divine writ.

Fully aware of his family's Jewish past, he began to contemplate a return to the faith of his ancestors. With the death of his father, he began to discuss this idea with his family. In the end, in 1617 they all decided to return to Judaism; they fled to Amsterdam from Portugal.[113] But by then—or by the previous year, depending upon when exactly he had arrived—Acosta began rather quickly to recognize differences between modern Jewish life as he saw it being lived in Amsterdam and what his study of the Torah had led him to recognize as Mosaic law. There is an irony here: his expectations for Jewish life were based strictly on what he saw in the Torah, as often through history Christians have assumed that Judaism is strictly Torah-guided, without recognizing the centuries of rabbinic commentary and interpretation that have shaped Judaism as a dynamic, evolving organism across the centuries. So Acosta's view of proper Judaism is more Christian than Jewish, even after his conversion.[114]

Acosta in fact offered eleven theses—eleven *Propositions against Tradition*—that were published in Hamburg, Germany (another center of post-Reformation Sephardic life) in 1616. He argued (among other theses) that: 1, the use of phylacteries is not prescribed in the Torah; 2, circumcision as it is currently practiced corrupts the injunction commanding it in the Torah; 3, adding extra holy days while in exile (a second day to Rosh HaShanah, and an eighth day to both Sukkot and Passover, for example) is also contrary to the prescription in the Torah and therefore a sin; 6, the command to punish "an eye for and eye and a tooth for a tooth" should be taken literally and not yield to being replaced by monetary compensation from victimizer to victim; 7, oral teachings (i.e., the discussions in the rabbinic tradition) are fundamentally illegitimate, only written laws (i.e., what is in the Torah) are valid; 11, benedictions are illegitimate, since they do not derive directly from the Torah. If Acosta's "Mosaic" view may be seen as derived from the Christological mentality that he imported into his analysis of Judaism, the same might be said for the response to his publication.

In addition to publishing, he seems to have engaged in public disputes with the Sephardic rabbinic leaders—in which he referred to them as Pharisees, viewing them also from a New Testament, not rabbinic perspective. The consequence of this oppositional defiant behavior was that he was excommunicated in 1618.[115] More precisely put: the rabbinic leadership published a statement that extended from Venice to Hamburg banning him from the community and ordering the community to exclude him from intercourse with them. This form of forced separation is referred to as a *niddui* in Hebrew. It is a limited writ of excommunication, in both time and meaning: Acosta's exclusion was for a month and he was required to pay a fine to the community.

But a few years later, by 1623, he was publishing a new work, in which his view of the rabbinic authorities as Pharisees in the negative, New Testament sense, was amplified: the very title of the work was *An Examination of the Traditions of the Pharisees*. In this booklet he argued against the notion of reward and punishment beyond this world, contradicting the prevailing wisdom among the Sephardic rabbinate. The response of the leaders of that rabbinate, such as Rabbis Saul Levi Morteira and Manasseh ben Israel, was to accuse Acosta of denying God. Children were incited to hound him in the streets, yelling "heretic" and "apostate" at him. Needless to say, the import of both the *niddui* and this sort of harassment is a far cry from the torture and death meted out and eternal damnation promised by the Inquisitional and Papal authorities within the Church, but the influence of the Catholic methodologies on the Sephardic leadership is clear.

This second writ that banned Acosta from the community was formally delivered on May 15th. Its text included the injunction that "nobody, whoever it might be, is permitted to talk with him, neither man nor woman, neither relatives nor strangers, nobody may show him favor or otherwise be in contact with him, under penalty of becoming included within the same ban and being excluded from our congregational fellowship. And to his brother we grant a period of grace of eight days in which to complete his separation from him." The idea is one of complete, if temporary, isolation from the community.

There is more, however: the rabbinic leadership threatened Acosta with further action: that of bringing his case before the Christian (Dutch Reformed, essentially a branch of Calvinism) magistrate, as subverting the Christian church (for which the immortality of the soul and its suffering or salvation in the eternal afterlife are essential doctrines) and not only Judaism! They apparently did this, since there follows a record of Acosta having spent some 8-10 days in prison and paying a 300 florin penalty (he was released on May 31, 1624, so the entire process took over a year to complete). He was still affected by the *niddui* and ultimately fled Amsterdam and settled for a time in Hamburg, but found himself ostracized by the Sephardic community there as well. Eventually he felt that he had no choice but to return to Amsterdam, around 1631—he asserted that he would go back to being "an ape amongst the apes" (a less complimentary form of "doing in Rome as the Romans do," but seems to have found it difficult to do that. In any case his nephew accused him of abrogating the *kashrut* laws shortly thereafter, which seems to have led to a renewal of the *niddui* against him.

Moreover, he continued to speak out in ways found outrageous by the community of that time and place. Thus he openly questioned whether the laws of the Torah were truly divinely sanctioned or whether Moses simply composed them—and in the end concluded that all religion is humanly contrived, and overrun with empty ceremonies and rituals that are meaningless to God. For God resides in nature—which is peaceful and harmonious, whereas religion is stamped with blood, strife and incessant violence. Moreover, two would-be proselytes to Judaism came forth to accuse him of trying to dissuade them from their path. In response, the horrified rabbinate demanded of him that he read a statement of recantation that they drew up, and that he submit to a public whipping. His refusal led to a fuller and more definitive writ of excommunication by 1633: a *heirem*, which banned him from the community for seven years, dooming him to virtual isolation, shunned by his family and his loved ones, regardless of where he was living.

If even the *heirem* is far less extreme than a Catholic writ of excommunication, yet for Acosta it was psychologically and emotionally powerful enough that he eventually returned to Amsterdam—yet again—in 1640, desperate for reconciliation. He begged for mercy and reinstatement within the community. The conditions of that reinstatement were threefold: that he read a "confession" publicly; that he submit to a public flogging of 39 lashes (administered while the rabbinic leadership chanted Psalms of Praise to God!); that, as a consummate act of humbling himself, he lie across the threshold of the synagogue as every member of the congregation walked through the doorway, tramping on him as they passed through it.

He submitted to all of this and so was "welcomed" back into the community, but was so demoralized and depressed that he could not live with himself for much longer. He lived long enough to pen a brief autobiography, *Example of a Human Life* (which, interestingly, he wrote in Latin, not Portuguese, as if wanting to be sure that the scholarly community would have wide and immediate access to it). In this work he talked about his experience as a victim of intolerance and one last time addressed the matter of the Laws of Nature, which, he contended, contain the best of the laws found in Judaism, Christianity and Islam alike. He obtained a pair of pistols with which he apparently intended to shoot both his cousin and himself (it is not clear why his cousin was in his sights) but the gun aimed at his cousin misfired. He shot himself.

III. Baruch Spinoza and the Question of Heresy

That year, (1640), Baruch (Benedict) Spinoza was turning eight years old. His family had most directly derived from *conversos* in the town of Espino in Galicia (northwestern Spain, just north of Portugal) but may also have had Portuguese and even French branches to it—and *may* have included among its members Don Diego d'Espinoza, a Grand Inquisitor, which would simply add another thread of irony to the tapestry of this narrative. In any case, his father, Michael, a merchant of modest means, seems to have come in the 1620s from Galicia. Baruch was born on November 24, 1632 in the Jewish quarter of Amsterdam. Spinoza's mother, Hannah Deborah, Michael's second wife, died in 1638, when Baruch was only six years old. A few years later, in 1642, his father married a third time to Esther De Espinosa, whose family came from Lisbon, so even if

Baruch's bloodlines did not include a Portuguese branch, the step-side of his family certainly did.

As a young lad at the Talmud Torah—a school for Jewish boys, who were still taught separately from their Christian neighbors, in which he studied Hebrew and Aramaic by way of the Hebrew Bible and the rabbinic tradition (the tradition that Uriel Acosta had rejected summarily when he became a Jew)—he showed splendid promise. His most important teachers were none other than Rabbi Saul Levi Morteira and Manasseh ben Israel, who, as the key rabbinical figures in the Sephardic community of Amsterdam, had overseen the various excommunication processes involving Acosta. They shared the hope that Baruch would himself become a rabbi, and as he grew older he added to his repertoire a strong interest in the medieval Jewish rationalist philosophers, such as Maimonides, Gershonides and Chasdai Crescas and an interest in but apparent contempt for the mystical tradition of the kabbalists. Nonetheless, kabbalah and in particular the doctrine of the *sephirot* would have an influence on his thinking.

Manasseh ben Israel was the instructor who introduced Spinoza to Kabbalah. Manasseh was also the individual who, visiting England in the 1650s, convinced Oliver Cromwell to publish an edict in effect rescinding the 1290 expulsion of the Jews.[116] Morteira was a fanatical and conservative ecclesiastic. In retrospect, it was only a matter of time until conflict would erupt between these teachers and their pupil, brilliant and modest—but unafraid of expressing his rationalist viewpoint. It should be noted, too, that in 1648, when Spinoza was 16, several important events transpired within the broad European world of Christians and Jews. In that "messianic" year, two different individuals—David Reubeni, from central Europe, and Shabatai Tzvi of Ottoman Greece and Turkey—declared themselves to be the messiah, and stirred up, especially in Shabbatai's case, an enormous expectant reaction across the European Jewish world.

What helped facilitate the excitement was the Ukrainian war for independence against Poland led by Bogdan Chmielnitzki, beginning in 1648, that encompassed far-flung massacres of Jews along the way. (This was a precipitating factor in the migration of so many Ashkenazi Jews westward toward Holland). On the other hand, the Thirty-Years' War came to an end in that year, and in retrospect, one might chart the beginning of Oliver Cromwell's rise from the same year. So one might see a number of elements snowballing together to yield new directions for Spinoza's thinking into the 1650s.

By about 1651 the young Dutch Jew began to study the work of the French Catholic modernist philosopher Rene Descartes. Three years later, with the death of his father and no means—his family, his step-sister and her husband,[117] a zealous follower of Rabbi Morteira, all but cast him off at this point—he began to teach in the private humanistic school run by an ex-Jesuit and freethinker, Franz van den Enden, with whom he also studied Latin and through whom he came into contact with the thought of St Augustine, the medieval Scholastics, Christian Renaissance thinkers and modernists such as Thomas Hobbes, among others. Van den Enden himself would go to Paris later, in 1661, to further his own studies of Cartesian philosophy, where he became implicated in a plot to assassinate King Louis XIV.

Gradually most of Spinoza's friends were free-thinking Christians like Van den Enden. By 1656 he had been expelled from the Jewish community—but why? It seems that when his father died, in 1654, there was a struggle between him and his half-sister, Rebecca, over an inheritance, and in her deposition before the court she referred to him as a "renegade." More precisely, his brother-in-law denounced him as an apostate and a heretic to the rabbinical authorities. These were led by Rabbis Morteira and Mannaseh ben Israel, who were themselves presumably already disappointed that Spinoza had not followed the path that they had foreseen for him, and were acquainted with the intellectual vector along which he seemed to be traveling.

Spinoza in any case decided to fight for his inheritance— from all that can be determined, his motive was not the money itself, but rather the principle: that justice be done in the matter of his father's will.[118] But rather than acceding to a trial and judgment to be held before and through the rabbinic leaders—a Jewish

Bet Din (literally: "House of Judgment"),[119] he brought the case before the Dutch governmental (i.e., Christian) court. Such an act would have both insulted the sense of authority of the rabbis and also provoked their fear, since to have internal community strife aired to outsiders might lead, they thought, to a curtailing of Jewish rights within that outside world.

Within the *Bet Din* that was nonetheless convened at the insistence of Rebecca and her husband, Rabbi Morteira was in the uncomfortable position of confronting the pupil whose brilliance he knew so well and whose free-thinking had strayed to far from the path that he had expected and intended for him. Witnesses were called, since for someone to be found guilty of heretical thinking, there needed to be a minimum of two witnesses who could attest to it. In other words, the case was being treated as a capital crime, since removal from the community was viewed as tantamount to death. As in the case of Uriel Acosta, two erstwhile acquaintances of Spinoza came forth and confirmed the "fact" that he had uttered blasphemous ideas in their presence. Morteira interrogated Spinoza, requesting either denial or confirmation of the testimony offered by his two "friends."

Apparently disheartened by the betrayal by his two "friends," Spinoza apparently refused to respond, neither to confirm nor to deny. The result was a 30-day ban from visiting the synagogue and from receiving visits from fellow Jews—a *niddui*—together with a pleading, demanding, threatening request that he clean up his philosophical-spiritual act and renounce his heretical views. He remained silent in the face of the sermon delivered to him by the court. So having found his inheritance case twisted into a heresy case before the Bet Din, which case was lost by his refusal to comply with its demand that he speak up; and on the other hand having won the inheritance case before the Christian court and turned over the inheritance to his enemies, Spinoza began his life of increasing isolation from the Jewish community, and increasing interest in modernist thought.

That the writ of excommunication was no more than a short ban, a *niddui*, is evidenced by the fact that toward the end of the next year, on December 5, 1655, there is a record of Spinoza reading from the Torah in the synagogue. Around the same time, van den Enden tried to convince him to take on a more substantial teaching position at his school, but Spinoza refused. One might suppose from the grounds of his later refusal to accept a teaching position at the university that this was because he was wary of being beholden to any institution that might then expect him to think and teach in a particular manner—or perhaps he simply wanted to devote more time to his own thinking, and since he needed so little to live on, reasoned that a more substantial teaching job would get in the way.[120]

In any case, the hostility toward him and his views, and presumably his outspokenness about those views as he began more firmly to formulate them, led to the convening of another Bet Din. This one took place without his even agreeing to be present.[121] Yet a crowded congregation filled the synagogue lit by black candles, where on July 27, 1656 a fuller ban—a *heirem*—was pronounced against him. The text of the *heirem* gives us a sense of how far the Sephardic rabbinate in Amsterdam had come toward seeing itself as an instrument of God to which God in turn hearkened in a manner reminiscent of the Inquisitional authorities in place since the thirteenth century. Thus:

> The Senhores of the *Mahamad* [i.e., "governing council"] make it known that they have long since been cognizant of the wrong opinions and behavior of Baruch d'Espinoza, and tried various means and promises to dissuade him from his evil ways. But as they effected no improvement, obtaining on the contrary more information every day of the horrible heresies which he practiced and taught, and of the monstrous actions which he performed, and as they had many trustworthy witnesses who in the presence of the same Espinoza reported and testified against him and convicted him... they now excommunicate him with the following ban:
>> 'After the judgment of the Angels, and with that of the Saints, we excommunicate, expel, curse and damn Baruch d'Espinoza with the consent of God, Blessed be He, and with the consent of this Holy Congregation before the holy scrolls with the 613 precepts which are written therein, with the anathema with which Joshua banned Jericho, with the curse with which Elisha cursed the youths, and with all the curses which are written in the Torah. Cursed be he by day, and cursed be he by night; cursed be he when he lies down and cursed be he when he rises up; cursed

be he when he goes out and cursed be he when he comes in. The Lord will not pardon him; the anger and wrath of the Lord will rage against this man, and bring him all the curses which are written in the Book of the Torah, and the Lord will destroy his name from under the Heavens, and the Lord will separate him to his injury from all the tribes of Israel with all the curses of the firmament, which are written in the Book of the Torah. But you who cleave to the Lord your God are blessed.'

We order that nobody should communicate with him orally or in writing, or show him any favor, or stay with him under the same roof, or come within four ells of him,[122] or read anything composed or written by him.

So these rabbis clearly at least intended their constituents to imagine them to be operating with God's cooperation and approval. Their tone is quite Christological right from the start, with their invocation of angels and saints. On the other hand, we recognize their usage of a key passage from the Torah, (Deuteronomy 6:7), where the Israelites are enjoined to recite the words reminding them of God's oneness and loving relationship with them, "when you sit in your house and when you walk by the way, and when you lie down and when you rise up."

We also must recognize that in the procedures leading up to the articulation of the *heirem*, physical torture of the sort that was developed by the Inquisition was not part of the repertoire of the rabbinical authorities—even lashes, which were sometimes part of the procedure for returning to the fold, is miles away from that—and the *heirem*'s prevailing sensibility, even with the invocation of God's anger and non-forgiveness, was directed to this world and not the next. But this issue—of the similarities and differences between the Dominican Inquisitional operation and the Sephardic rabbinical operation of inquiry into faith leads to the question: what was it exactly about Spinoza's beliefs that so exercised everybody? We might assume that the content of his thought as it is found in his writings distressed members of the community or its rabbinic leaders. Certainly his short treatise on *God, Man and His Well-Being*, which discusses the issue of how we can have knowledge of God and thereby knowledge of truth might have contained ideas that were deemed heretical. But he wrote this treatise between 1656 and 1660, after his excommunication, so his views were in any case only available orally at the time of both trials, the first one when he remained silent before Rabbi Morteira's interrogation and the second one when he was not even present before the *Mahamad*.

That short treatise contains in seed form what would be the centerpiece of perhaps his greatest work, the *Ethics*, on which Spinoza spent the last fifteen years of his life—beginning his writing not before 1662, a good six years after the *heirem* was pronounced against him. In both the short and the long works God is associated with Nature. Put otherwise, Spinoza articulated a form of *panhenotheism*—a concept often confused with *pantheism*. Where the latter finds gods everywhere, the former finds the one (*heno*) God (*theos*) in all (*pan*) things. More specifically, Spinoza began to articulate the notion that God is Nature in the process of "naturing" (n*atura naturans*) and what the creation process yielded is nature "natured" (*natura naturata*): thus God is both separate from and yet identical with the universe.

While such an idea is not, in fact, so far from the Jewish and Christian notion that God breathes Itself into the first human, and as Adam and Eve's "progeny" we are "besouled" thereby[123]—we have a bit of God within us—Spinoza offers two problems for the conventionally-thinking Jew or Christian. One is that what I am calling "besoulment" encompasses more than merely humans, and by implication to ascribe souls to other than humans might be considered as heretical as, say, to argue that the earth moves around the sun rather than that the sun and all other heavenly entities revolve around the earth.[124]

The other problem for most of Spinoza's contemporaries could be that what he describes essentially eliminates the "personality" ascribed by Judaism and Christianity to God and with that elimination he eliminates the notion of a personal relationship between God and ourselves: *natura naturans* cannot be imagined to be "talking" to Moses and delivering to him commandments at Sinai, much less hearkening to our daily prayers. Spinoza observed that our embrace of the Bible and its teachings is based on belief, which should not be confused with reason; there is no rational proof of God as the deliverer of the Torah to Moses. He also argued that in our tight embrace of the God of Scripture—a God of laws and commandments—we have lost hold of the God of *Life* that he articulates as continuous *natura*, i.e., continuous in the barely discernible form of the nonetheless extant boundary between *naturans* and *naturata*.

The difficulty for us with all of this, however, is twofold. First, that new ideas and disagreements with ideas is a constant in Jewish intellectual history—the Talmud is built on diverse opinions expressing themselves without any authority threatening expulsion to someone whose views are considered extreme. So the very fact of the process against Spinoza (as against Acosta and others) offers a unique moment in Jewish history, in which this particular branch of Jewish leadership is so paranoid as well as methodologically influenced by the very institution that is the central source of its paranoia that it acts in an unprecedented manner.

The second difficulty is that Spinoza hadn't written any of his "heretical" thoughts down until well after the time of his excommunication, so it is difficult to know what those who accused him actually had before them as proof of his heretical thinking. They clearly observed an Inquisitional methodology of embracing assertions favoring the prosecution without worrying overly much about arguments for the defense. We might suppose that if, in the case of the first "trial," his sister and brother-in-law had money as a motive, in the case of subsequent "trials" it was the anger and frustration become righteous indignation of Rabbi Morteira and his colleagues that blinded them to the absurdity of the situation—aided and abetted by Spinoza's refusal either to return to the path that they envisioned for him, or even to rise to the bait of his pathetic accusers.

Equally intriguing is the issue raised by the fact that, when he did write down his thoughts, he used Latin. As the universal language of science and philosophy in his era, Latin would have made his thoughts accessible to intellectuals across religious and political lines. So one might suppose that in their concern that the non-Jewish majority would read Spinoza's writings and suppose from them that the Jewish minority was a group that not only denied the Christhood of Jesus but the Godhead in any form, the Sephardic leadership panicked and cast him out. But for fear related to the fact of his writing "publicly" in Latin to be the determining factor, he would already have had to write before the two trials leading to the *niddui* and *heirem* respectively had taken place. And there seems to be little likelihood that that had transpired.

So we are back to the more fundamental, word-of-mouth, gossip-based, jealousy-driven accusation and testimony; and a condemnation supported by the refusal to defend himself by a Socratic sort of character who was either humbly arrogant or intensely disillusioned, or both—the urge to condemn perhaps exacerbated by the fact that his judges were teachers disappointed and angry regarding where the brilliant young, potentially rabbinical Spinoza had gotten to. Where those rabbis were concerned, there may truly have been concern for the community's safety in general and in particular with regard to the possibility of reimposing the Inquisition upon it in the event of a Spanish or Portuguese victory. Casting out a Spinoza might be presumed to make the community less likely to attract the interest of the Inquisition in such an event.

They would have had at least one legitimate reason for that concern. The Dutch had been engaged for nine years in a war with the Portuguese for which the key prize was the city of Recife, on the coast of Brazil. In the very year of Spinoza's father's death and the inheritance struggle with his step-sister and her husband, 1654, the Portuguese took Recife. It was only the generous nature of the Portuguese captain that permitted a major catastrophe for the Jewish community to be transmuted into a more minor one. Many *conversos* had resumed their openly Jewish lives in the Dutch colony; they would now face the anger of the Inquisition with the assumption of Portuguese control. But the captain allowed the community many months to make arrangements to leave before the authorities moved in. So torture and death were commuted to expulsion. Among those leaving that summer were 23 Jews and/or former *conversos* who ended up not in Amsterdam but in New Amsterdam, marking the virtual beginning of the Jewish community in North America—about which, more anon.

But from the point of view of the Sephardic leadership in Amsterdam itself, the fate of the Jewish community of Recife served as an example of what could happen to their community should the conditions in the Christian majority shift. And anything that might rock the boat of the Jewish position within Christian Amsterdam, even while it remained staunchly Protestant, would have been unnerving and threatening. So Spinoza, one might say, had to be made an example.[125]

In spite of the totality of the *heirem* against him, Spinoza seems to have been largely unaffected by it (in this as in other ways he was different from Acosta) and content to live a pretty isolated life. He did respond to the charges by way of a theological essay, his *Apologia*, which the community was forbidden to read, of course. Many of his former Christian associates also began to avoid him, since the views he espoused—or was said to espouse—were as offensive to them as they were to Jews. Among those who did not abandon him was Franciscus van den Enden, in whose home Spinoza lived during the next few years (and with whose daughter, Clara Maria, Spinoza was in love, according to some sources.)

During this period Spinoza earned a comfortable and quiet living, to repeat, as a lens grinder. The community, when he passed through it, expressed open contempt for him and there was even an attempt on his life. His decision not to teach at a university—he had several offers to do so—was based both on his desire for absolute intellectual freedom (the universities were run by the monarchic state and he did not want to have to answer to the king for his views) and his concern that his ideas were not sufficiently formed at the time. But whatever threat he nonetheless represented to Rabbi Morteira—and it is not clear whether or not the other rabbis were involved in this, or felt as strongly as Spinoza's former teacher seems to have felt—Morteira appealed to leaders in the Dutch Reformed Church, who were able to influence the municipal court to ban Spinoza from the city of Amsterdam for a period of time.

He moved to Ouderkerk at first, just outside Amsterdam. By 1660 he had moved on to Rhynsburg, near Leiden. Installed in that location and subsequently in other locales he kept up correspondence with a close circle of friends and fellow scholars and wrote some of the most important treatises in philosophy and theology of the seventeenth century. He lived a very frugal life, having spurned his inheritance completely. He changed his first name from Baruch ("blessed") to its Latin equivalent, Benedict. His work continued to attract sufficient attention to be banned from publication as blasphemous by the ruler, William of Orange, in 1675. But he died peacefully, in his sleep,[126] on February 21, 1677 and was buried in the cemetery of the New Church in Amsterdam, although he never renounced his Judaism or became a Christian.

In one of his letters to Henry Oldenburg we get a brief summary of issues that are discussed in his Ethics, such as his comment regarding "God, whom I define as a Being consisting in infinite attributes, whereof each is infinite or supremely perfect, after its time. You must observe that by attribute I mean everything, which is conceived through itself and in itself, so that the conception of it does not involve the conception of anything else...by God we mean a Being supremely perfect and absolutely infinite."

We can hardly imagine someone with even a barely open mind reading this and finding it heretical with regard to standard Jewish or Christian (or Muslim) thought, so one might suppose that his further association of God with nature as I have briefly summarized that association was what would have angered his critics, as I have also observed above. But given that he had not yet written anything, I am reminded instead of how Peter Abelard was condemned at Sens in 1141 by a tribunal whose members, like Abelard's main accuser, St Bernard of Clairvaux, almost certainly had not read a word of what Abelard had written. So the miscarriage of justice is double: not only was Spinoza, like Abelard, misjudged (his beliefs are not heretical) but those who accused him were operating out of vicious and/or dishonest impulses masked as impulses intended to protect the community and offering the presumption of God's approval.

In the same letter to Oldenburg, Spinoza also goes on to respond to his colleague's inquiry regarding "errors that I detect in the Cartesian and Baconian philosophies." We are reminded by that aspect of his discussion that Spinoza is part of a larger upheaval with consequences for Western thought in general and our narrative in particular. The sixteenth century's explorations and Reformation-Counter-Reformation movements opened up new paths to questions regarding the world in which we live and the nature of Truth regarding the path to the God Who engendered the world. As the age of Religious Wars spilled from the sixteenth century into and across the seventeenth century, it carried those questions onto the territory engaged by Descartes in France and Spinoza in the Netherlands, as well as Francis Bacon in England and Gottfried Wilhelm Leibnitz in Germany. None of these thinkers disbelieved in an all-powerful, all-knowing, all-good and interested as well as interventionist God, but each added new nuances to the question of how to understand what God is, which nuances opened doors to others who might disbelieve. The consequences of the process of opening those doors for "Jewish trials" will be seen in the chapters that follow.

Chapter Five:
Moving Toward Modernity?

I. An Age of Revolutions

The seventeenth century is one of intense intellectual upheaval in Western Thought, as we have seen. A series of Jewish, Protestant and Catholic thinkers has unraveled a series of threads that could and did lead to an unraveling of theological certainty in the centuries that follow. Descartes is the beginning of this process. He raises the issue of doubting what we think we know about the world around us, ultimately reducing the matter of certainty to himself and the process in which he is engaged: "I am thinking, therefore I [must] exist" he concludes, since he could not be thinking if he did not exist.

From that starting point, voiced both in his *Discourse on the Method* (1637) and in his *Meditations* (1641), he reconstructs what it is about which one can be certain. Among the more important issues that he touches upon is that *outside* the world around us, but believed by us to have engendered both us and the world: God. If in the end he offers a confident and rational case for God's existence, yet the fact that he could doubt it in the first place might lead others to follow the path of his Cartesian doubt and not his rational argument to allay that doubt. Certainly, as we have seen, Spinoza nowhere suggests that he doubts God's existence, but he recasts "God" in a mode that moves against the everyday traditional terminology and thus the nuances of the beliefs of his contemporaries. Other contributions to this discussion are offered by individuals such as Bacon and Leibnitz.

Meanwhile, we might recall—the reminder will prove significant as we move forward—that the Jewish world is experiencing a new direction. This is aside from whatever one might suppose might have left its direct imprint on that world through Spinoza, the Jewish thinker cast out by his community. It is another branch of the Sephardic Jewish community that cast Spinoza out that is engaged in beginning to shape a new reality. For 23 members of that branch that had taken up residence in Recife, Brazil, found themselves in New Amsterdam, rather than Amsterdam in the late summer-early fall of 1654, as we have noted in the previous chapter.[127]

The colonial governor, Pieter Stuyvesant, was none too happy about their presence—but, in fairness, he was an equal opportunity bigot, not happy about the presence of anyone who was not part of the Dutch Reformed Church, such as Quakers, Catholics and even Lutherans. But as it turned out, he lacked the power to expel them of his own volition, since approval to do that was needed from the Board of Directors of the Dutch West Indian Company that was his employer—and as a practical matter, the 23 refugees apparently had no funds with which to buy passage out. In any case, given that no less than seven members of the Company Board were Jews—a practical symptom of the pluralistic reality of Amsterdam by the seventeenth century—it should be no surprise that Stuyvesant's request to deport the refugees was rejected by the Board. They remained and a Jewish community was in the process of being formed in what would one day be the United States of America.

Between the Pieter Stuyvesant/Baruch Spinoza era and that of American independence, several developments relevant to our narrative may be observed back in Europe and extending to America. The Age of Religious Wars that had yielded such slaughter across Europe along primarily Protestant-Catholic lines finally came to end, more or less with the death of Louis XIV in 1715. Industrial, technological and scientific revolutions were beginning to bubble from England toward the European mainland from about 1760 onward. The philosophical and theological revolutions that had, in retrospect, been percolating throughout the sixteenth and seventeenth centuries in the West continued to expand in the direction of the view held by some either that no particular understanding of God could be held as superior to any other, or that God is not to be understood as an all-powerful, all-knowing, all-good Being, interested and involved in human affairs, or that there simply is no God.[128] At its most extreme, this last, fully secularized view is expressed by someone like the French writer, Voltaire (1694-1778), who viewed anyone who stilled maintained a religious viewpoint as hopelessly anachronistic and intellectually primitive.

By the time of Voltaire's death, the 13 English colonies in North America—including territories like New Amsterdam that had been wrested by the English from the Dutch barely a decade after the arrival of the Jews from Recife—were on the verge of going to war to assert their desire for independence from the Mother Country. The American Revolution would in turn help inspire the French Revolution and in general one may add political revolutions to the litany of technological, industrial, scientific, philosophical and theological revolutions that define the Western and Central European landscape of the last third of the eighteenth century, spilling into the beginning of the nineteenth. In the context of all of this, what of the Jews? How might they and how were they affected by the myriad new paths of thinking about and being in the world?

In Western and Central Europe historiographers speak of Emancipation. By this we mean the following two propositions. One, that with the break-down of earlier certainties with regard to God and the human-Divine relationship—if we have arrived at a point of agreeing to disagree along Protestant-Catholic lines (and by implication, Catholic-Orthodox and Protestant-Orthodox lines) with regard to Truth in this matter; and if in some quarters we have even arrived at a point of doubting God's existence—then the notion that Jews must be kept outside the mainstream, disenfranchised and oppressed, for theological reasons, ceases to make sense. The more so, if we tout ourselves as entirely rational and thus enlightened in our approach to the world.

Two, as a consequence of this rationalist conclusion, bills specifically removing social, economic, cultural and eventually even political barriers to Jews were emitted in one country after another: thus, a "Jew Bill" was first proposed in England, in 1753—although it would be another generation or more until it would actually be put into play. A series of Emancipationist edicts were issued by the Hapsburg Emperor Joseph II across his territories in the 1780s. That series was echoed by a decree issued on September 28, 1791, in the aftermath of the French Revolution, that Jewish Frenchmen were indeed Frenchmen who happened to be Jewish and not Jews who happened to live in France, and were therefore entitled to the same measure of liberty, equality and fraternity to which all Frenchmen were entitled. The last of the major Western powers to accord Jews enfranchisement was Prussia, in 1812.

In theory, then, our narrative might be expected to come to an end here. The sort of "trials" that we have considered in the previous chapters of this text—all centered on the problematic Jewish-Christian relationship as that relationship is informed by the New Testament and subsequent teachings of the various Christian Churches, and in the case of Acosta and Spinoza by the manner in which Jews in one place and one period absorbed and applied issues that derived from that problematic—should fall off the pages of history as it moves forward. But history is rarely simple, and the case of "Jewish trials" well exemplifies that lack of simplicity.

Consider the following developments during the period we have reviewed thus far in the previous chapter and the beginning of this one. The formal designation of an area within a city to which Jews are confined not by choice, from which, often, they may not leave between sunset and sunrise; an area that is gated and walled—whether the confinement is construed as intended for their safety or not—is first arrived at in Venice, in 1516. That is, just a year before Luther posted his 95 theses onto the church door in Wittenberg, the Venetian authorities decided that all Jews within their city should dwell in a defined area near the former iron foundry. The word for "foundry" in the sixteenth-century Venetian dialect is *"gheta"*; in general Italian, it is *"gietto"* —yielding a term, "ghetto," still active in our vocabulary today.

For our purposes, one question we might ask is: when between 250 and 300 years later, Jews were formally permitted outside the ghetto in so many places in Western and Central Europe, would they be able to remove the ghetto from their minds? We have seen how the Sephardic rabbinic leadership in Amsterdam, free of the Inquisition could not free its mind of the Inquisition. To what extent would such a psychological complication apply in a broader context? Another question is whether the outside world would be as ready as it thought to accept and embrace Jews when in theory it emancipated them. How and where will it draw the line between "toleration" and "embrace/acceptance"?

Voltaire, for example, even as he saw himself as a champion of what he and others called the Enlightenment—a term referring to the rationalist perspective that he and those intellectually similar to him presented in opposition to what they regarded as the benighted mode of religiosity that had dominated Europe for millennia—maintained a strongly negative view of the Jews even without a theological basis, as a "greedy and selfish race." He contemptuously describes them swarming in dark and dirty ghettos without a hint of acknowledgment that the dark and dirty ghettos (and how dirty *are* they, however dark they might be?) to which they are confined are imposed and not chosen by them as places and conditions of residence. The German playwright, poet and philosophy, Goethe, another hero of the Enlightenment, referred to the Jews as an "inferior and degraded people"—this, too, without reference to their religion. Yet another German Enlightenment philosopher, Fichte, suggested that the practical solution to what he considered an unresolved "Jewish Problem" would be to send them back to Palestine and relieve Europe altogether of their presence.

Conversely, within Eastern Europe, which had come increasingly under the political domination of the Romanov Tsars of Russia, a new situation obtained in the matter of the Jews, by the late eighteenth century. The once far-flung kingdom of Poland was gradually carved up, from 1771 to the mid-1790s, in a series of three partitions in each of which pieces went to Prussia, Austro-Hungary and Russia. For Russia in particular, that meant a large influx of Jews—from the still-substantial remnant of the community in Poland that had flourished in the fourteenth through early seventeenth centuries. Thus the same Katherine the Great who corresponded with Voltaire and sought to bring the intellectual and cultural Enlightenment to Russia by means of establishing Western-style museums and academies within her domains, created the Pale of Jewish settlement in 1771. This region within western Russia defined the limits of where Jews could live and even travel, and within it, there were also limitations of both inhabitation and movement. So to the ghetto idea that was tied to a given city she added what was, in effect, an enlarged, trans-city ghetto.

These varied developments from West to East would have a range of effects on the narrative of Jewish life through the nineteenth century and into the early twentieth century as that narrative extends from Eastern to Western Europe and from Europe to America. There is one further sequence that carries through the eras of Reformation and Revolution of which we need to be aware before proceeding with that narrative and its specific "trials" repercussions. Thus we recall that during the Lutheran process of Western Christian reform, the reformer himself anticipated and expected that the Jews, who had resisted the embrace of Jesus as Christ for fourteen centuries, would come around by means of the new direction in which, by the 1530s, he was taking Christianity. But their refusal to embrace what he shaped, coupled perhaps with his advancing years and other mental and psychological factors beyond mere frustration, had led him to write what has been referred to by many—including the editor of the Nazi newspaper, der Stuermer—as the most viciously anti-Jewish pamphlet ever penned. The pamphlet in question is Luther's 65,000-word treatise, written in 1543, three years before his death, "On the Jews and their Lies."

One might suppose (as many have) that Luther's scathing comments affected the German Christian view of the Jews dwelling among them during the centuries that followed. Perhaps it is not accidental that Prussia, the dominant German-speaking Lutheran polity by the eighteenth and nineteenth centuries, was the last of the major powers to offer an edict of Emancipation.[129] Nor is it perhaps surprising that, between 1812 and 1870 the pendulum kept swinging back and forth between granting and rescinding various civil rights to Jews. One of the more famous written debates over the issue of whether the Jews have the right to expect civic equality with their secular Christian neighbors in a secular Christian state arrived in Prussia in the early 1840s. Bruno Bauer wrote against the legitimacy of that expectation—suggesting that, whereas a secular Christian could attend Church on Sunday and yet function independent of his Church-going the rest of the week, a Jew could not cease to be a Jew and therefore function independent of his synagogue-going on any day of the week. Karl Marx—whose father had in fact had him converted to Christianity at age six (in 1824) to help him dodge the prejudices still being meted out against Jews in spite of Emancipation, as he grew up—wrote against Bauer.

There are two interesting and relevant aspects of Marx's two essays "On the Jewish Question" that might be noted for our purposes. One is that he decries Bauer's unrelenting anti-Jewish view that in order for Jews to expect civil rights they must become secularized as Bauer has—but must first become Christian and *then* abandon Christianity for secularism. In other words, even in calling himself secular, Bauer retains his Christian perspective: that Christianity has superseded Judaism as the faith with a proper Covenantal relationship with God, and therefore, that the only proper path to an enlightened secular stance is through the Christianity that the secularist abandons. To come directly through Judaism will not suffice.

The second aspect is that, even in decrying Bauer's Christian prejudices and hypocrisies regarding Jews, Marx shows that in his own way, he has absorbed such prejudices on his own. He expresses them, albeit from an angle different from Bauer's. For in his second essay, Marx writes that the liberation of both Jews and Christians, whether religious or secular—the liberation of humanity at large—will come about with the liberation of them all from the obsession with money. And he equates that obsession with Judaism, asserting that the Jewish God is capital. So the condition forced upon medieval Jews, of fitting into the world by filling the niches of tax-farming and money-lending—even as that role was more than matched by the fourteenth and fifteenth centuries with the emergence of prominent Christian banking families in Germany and Italy such as the Fuggers, the Medici and the Monte dei Paschi di Siena—had been transmuted in Marx's mind as in the general Christian mind into an overall statement of Judaism as money-focused.[130]

The overarching issue that we observe in making our way through the ins and outs of this small sweep of history is that the precise definition of Judaism and Jews is finding itself less easily articulated in the Europe leading to and beyond Emancipation rather than being made easier. The gradual process of secularization may eventually and theoretically eliminate anti-Jewish prejudice that is theologically based. A religion-based conviction that the world is divided between the camps of God/Christ and Satan/Anti-Christ and that Christians are by definition in the first camp and Jews, by definition, are in the other may fade away as an unhappy memory. But anti-Jewish prejudice need not disappear, particularly if Jews and Judaism are re-defined: as race or ethnicity, as body of customs and traditions, as social and/or economic state of mind.

This sort of redefinition is what we see transpiring along various paths. None of these is more emphatic than that traveled by the secular Christian political pamphleteer, William Marr. In 1878-9, Mahr borrowed a coinage from the vocabulary of comparative philology—the term "semitic"—that had been in use by then for nearly a century as a term referring to a "family" of languages. Those languages, including (among others) Hebrew, Aramaic, Arabic, Ethiopic, Ugaritic and Akkadian, are understood to share certain traits in common, the way French, Italian, Spanish and Portuguese do, and also therefore assumed (at least by most students of Semitic philology) to derive from a common linguistic ancestor, just as these four "Romance" languages are understood to have derived from Latin. But the Semitic languages all originate and either died out or are still spoken in the Middle East, so Mahr translated that term into racial-ethnic use. He asserted that the Hebrew-using Jews are Semites—and, as such, native to the Middle East and strangers to Europe. They are not "one of us," and his strategy as a politician was to vow to push them out of the pure European Prussia which they were polluting with their blood lines.

Thus with Wilhelm Mahr the racialization of Jews is officially introduced to a wider public and the terms "antisemite" and "antisemitic"—and their rarer opposites, "philosemite" and "philosemitic"—are born.[131] Emancipation, justified along secularizing lines could find its antipode—Jewish rights could be rescinded or at least Jews could still be despised and anti-Jewish words and actions expressed—in a politically-based racial theory of Judaism. One of the important rabidly nationalist thinkers of late nineteenth-century Prussia, Heinrich Gotthard von Treitschke, asserted in a series of articles in the *Pruessische Jahrbook* (*Prussian Annual*) in the fall of 1879 that there was an increasingly powerful "Jewish solidarity" manifesting itself in Prussia—the emergence of a German-Jewish caste whose members were separate from other Germans. He warned his Christian countrymen that Prussia and its German-speaking satellites must be reshaped as a Lutheran *Kultur-staat* ("Cultural State"), that the state needed to be cleansed of non-nationalist, international—the precise word he used was "cosmopolitan"—influences. This last term was intended as a virtual synonym for "Jewish," for Treitschke further asserted that an international "network of Jews is using [political] liberalism to fasten a stranglehold on German life."

Nor was Prussia alone in the West in wrestling in increasingly ugly ways with an unanswered Jewish Question through the nineteenth century.[132] The country to which Prussia looked and to which, indeed, Bruno Bauer referred in his own essay as the most socio-religiously forward-looking of the major European powers, France, had its own interesting wrestling match. Thus in 1806—fifteen years after the Revolution had declared French Jews to be French, and far less than a decade after Napoleon came to power and transformed the former kingdom-become-republic into an empire—the French Emperor was strongly advised by one of his more anti-Jewish courtiers, Count Molé, that he need to inquire into the Frenchness (as opposed to the faith!) of his Jewish citizens.

So on July 29, 1806, Napoleon convened what he called The Great Sanhedrin—an assembly of French Jewish notables whom he charged with responding to a dozen questions that his court advisers laid before that assembly, the point and purpose of which was to determine whether the Jews in France saw themselves primarily and essentially as Jews or as Frenchmen. It was as if the Revolution and its own conclusions in 1791 had never happened, or perhaps as if the conclusions had been arrived at too precipitously, in the exhilarating aftermath of dismantling the monarchy, without looking into the issue in sufficient detail. To his credit, Napoleon's own motive seems to have been to resolve the issue of Jewish identity vis-à-vis French identity once and for all to the advantage, not the disadvantage, of the Jews.

The first three questions pertained to marriage (are both monogamy and polygamy permitted in Judaism?) and divorce (which takes precedence in granting one, the State or the rabbis?) and more broadly, to the Jews' attitude to their Christian neighbors: is intermarriage permitted or prohibited? The next three furthered the matter of attitude: do French Jews look upon non-Jewish Frenchmen as "brothers"? Do all French Jews consider it a sacred obligation to fight for France in the event of war? The next three asked about the process of naming rabbis—who names them?— and whether they are deemed to have policing power that would or could conflict with that of the government. Does their power as leaders within the community derive from Jewish law or custom? The last three questions continued along this last line but also took up the question of whether certain professions are prohibited to Jews and whether usury is forbidden, or whether it is treated differently when it pertains to Jews as opposed to Christians.

These questions were placed before the "Great Sanhedrin" by Napoleon and the assembly dissolved to be reconvened in February, 1807, when the 80 Jewish delegates returned with responses that were carefully crafted to underscore the community's sense of itself as emphatically French—many of whose members could trace their residence within France back to the Roman period. As such, they were affirming the idea that their Judaism was a function of religion alone, and not bloodline or any other allegiance. As Frenchmen who were Catholic went to church on Sunday, Frenchmen who were Jewish went to synagogue on Saturday.[133] As the one group celebrated Christmas and Easter, the other celebrated Hanukkah and Passover. The one group did not circumcise its male-children, the other did. But both shared an equal fervor for France as their patrimony. The upside of the Napoleonic inquiry was that Jews now felt definitively arrived as citizens of France and its ostensibly secular government.

And yet, as we have noted, the process of Enlightenment did not yield an unalloyed, problem-free positive consequence for the Jewish communities that it affected as far as their *own internal* questions of *self*-definition and place within the world were concerned. The insistent questions, discussions and re-shapings of Judaism from without merely offered an intensified prod to Jews to address their condition from within. How, as a practical matter, ought I, a French Jew, let's say, with a shop in Lyons, who have defined myself as a Jew exclusively by religion, to handle the following matter? My shop is not dissimilar from that of my Catholic neighbor across the street. His is open Monday through Saturday—by law, all shops must remained closed on Sunday, the Christian Sabbath, the Lord's Day, although the government proclaiming that law refers to itself as secular, not Christian. So my shop must remain closed on Sunday, as well. But what, then, of Saturday—*my* Sabbath? To keep my shop open is to abrogate that most fundamental of aspects of my Judaism as a religion. But to close it is to sacrifice one-sixth of my business, which, in a competitive world will surely in the long run force me out of business—especially if I add to the Saturdays the various Jewish holidays that may fall, year by year, on weekdays, when I should also therefore close my shop.

And what of the children whom I am now free to send to the schools that are attended by their little Catholic friends—rather than to the privately run Talmud Torahs of the sort that I (or my parents or theirs) was required to attend, since public schools were off-limits to Jews back then? Do I do send my children but keep them home on Saturdays? Ask them to go but not to write on Saturdays (since writing, in the interpretation of the Torah that the generations have bequeathed to me, is considered labor and that is forbidden by the Torah on the Sabbath)? Or that they only write on that day if there is an exam being administered? And what, indeed, when Yom Kippur is on a Tuesday or the first day of Passover on a Thursday?

One of the answers to these questions arrived at from within the German Jewish community was to reform itself and its concept of what Judaism entails. In Hamburg, in 1810-11 Reform Judaism was "officially" born, which looked at all of the layers of inter-pretation and discussion of the previous two thousand years of Judaean-Jewish history and saw many elements that fitted into the sort of category defined by Voltaire for religion in general: anach-ronistic and out-of-date. Thus the very notion that the Torah and the rest of the Hebrew Bible were Divinely-dictated was put into serious question; the notion that Jews are waiting for a messiah was rejected; the centuries of interpreting the Torah with regard to celebrating the Sabbath or with regard to what one might or might not eat were placed on a growing pile of literature regarded as interesting but without undue significance for how I should live my life as a Jew.

The response to such reforms was a revitalization of parts of the traditional Jewish community, that began to refer to itself as Orthodox—a Greek term meaning "correct (*orthe*) belief (*doxa*)"— even as the Reformers referred to the traditionalists by the same term, but sneeringly (because the Greek may also be translated as "*narrow* belief." An even more reformist version of Judaism shaped itself by the 1830s in Prussia. Calling itself "The Science of Judaism (*Die Wissenschaft des Judentums*)," the movement sought to eliminate all of the out-date religious/spiritual elements of Judaism but re-tain its cultural and ethical core. Of course, even the practitioners of reshaped, watered-down-relative-to-older-traditions version of Judaism would be found by Bruno Bauer undeserving of full civic rights in the Prussia of the early 1840s—and would be included by Wilhelm Marr together with still-traditional Jews in the "Semite" category that he hoped to remove from Prussia and ideally from Europe altogether by the end of the 1870s.

This rather complex amalgam of issues and developments—some of them, such as the convening of a Napoleonic "Sanhedrin," qualify as Jewish trials in their own right—together form the framework for a number of interesting legal procedures that carry us through the late nineteenth century and out into the twentieth.

II. Tiszaeszlar, Hungary: The Blood Libel of 1882-3

A century after Joseph II had gone to great lengths to articulate a detailed series of decrees of Emancipation for the diverse Jews scattered throughout the many provinces of his domains, a Christian child disappeared in the small town of Tiszaeszlar, in Northeastern Hungary in the early spring of 1882. Tiszaeszlar in the 1880s was a town of about 2700 souls, primarily Catholics and Calvinists—and about 25, fairly impoverished Jewish families. In the spring of 1882 the small community was looking for a new kosher slaughterer—a *shohet*—who could double as a cantor (*hazzan*) in the synagogue. A competition was held on April 1—three days before the advent of Passover—in which the competitors demonstrated their skills at both singing and slaying. On that same day, 14-year-old Eszter Solymosi disappeared while on an errand for her employer, Andras Hury, in whose home Eszter worked as a servant girl.

By the next day, her increasingly frantic mother was both looking everywhere and asking everyone. Among these was her neighbor, Jozsef Scharf, who is reported to have said, in an attempt to comfort her, "Don't worry, neighbor, your daughter will be found. She probably just wandered off somewhere. Something like this also happened once in Hajdunanas. There, too, a child got lost and the people began saying that it was the Jews who had gotten hold of her. But then the child found her way home. She'd fallen asleep among the tussocks." Of course Scharf's words of comfort yielded the opposite result, in a manner echoing all the way back to Norwich, England in 1144. Mrs. Solymosi embraced the notion unequivocally that the Jews had done her daughter in, without further thought.

Meanwhile, within another day the talk of Eszter's disappearance had spread among the townspeople to encompass the theory that the Jews had murdered Eszter in order to use her blood for the Passover holiday a day or two away. This, we must note, neither included the idea that they had mock-crucified her—so the spreading rumor lacked that specific and specifically religious aspect of the classic Blood Libel—nor did it speculate on the specific use to which the blood would be put (typically, as we have earlier discussed, to make *matzah*) so no gastronomic or ritual specifics filled out the slowly expanding hysteria within Tiszaeszlar's Christian majority.

The notion that the Jews might have had something to do with her daughter's disappearance, nurtured on its own internal illogic pushed Mrs. Solymosi to turn to the local authorities on April 3, although she merely asked for their help in searching for her daughter, at first, without mentioning her suspicions regarding the Jews. Later that same day she returned to them, brought up her suspicion and asked that the synagogue be searched. Gabor Farkas, the *biro*— the local administrator, somewhat between a mayor and a police chief in role and responsibility—for whatever reasons told her that he required a higher authority in order to undertake such a search, which was otherwise beyond his jurisdiction.

So the next day, Mrs. Solymosi traveled to the district seat, Vencsello, and went to see Jeno Jarmy, who as *foszolgabiro* (county administrator), told him of her suspicions and demanded that he authorize Farkas to undertake a search of the synagogue. Jarmy listened with disbelief and calmly but firmly impressed upon her the absurdity of such thoughts. He suggested that she ignore those who offered them, refused her demand but did send an official notice to Farkas to initiate a search for young Eszter.

In the following month, as no sign of her daughter appeared and rumors continued to swirl around her, Mrs. Solymosi's suspicions evolved into an obsession. Moreover, several other factors began to stir the pot further. On the one hand, locally, a few women came forth with assertions that fed Mrs. Solymosi's fire. Thus, for example, Mrs. Istvan Lengyel, whose house was right next to the synagogue claimed that on Saturday (April 2) she noticed that the

Jews began leaving the synagogue well after noon, whereas they usually finished their prayers by 11 AM. So, too, in the afternoon, she claimed to have heard three faint cries, in a child's voice—sounding as if they were coming from underground—coming from the direction of the synagogue.

On the other hand, the newspapers had begun to pick up the story. This enabled it to carry all the way to Budapest. There Geza Onody, Tiszaeszlar's representative to the Hungarian Parliament, and a leader of Hungarian nationalist agitators, together with Gyozo Istoczy (who later founded Hungary's anti-Semitic party)—who had earlier proposed in the House of Deputies the expulsion of the Jews from Hungary—began to stir up the public against the local Jews.[134] It was they who spread the specific rumor that the Jews had killed Eszter Solymosi in order to use her blood at Passover. All of the growing agitation and excitement, leading to violence against the small Jewish community of Tiszaeszlar culminated with Mrs. Solymosi's official accusation of the Jews for having murdered her daughter. She brought the charge to the local judge, demanding that he investigate.

On May 19, the county court of Nyiregyhaza sent the notary Jozsef Bary to act as the investigating magistrate and examining judge for the case that would be tried at Tiszaeszlar. A solid, confirmed anti-Semite, Bary was entranced by the Blood Accusation idea and decided to pursue it as the centerpiece of his investigation, which he followed through means more illegal than legal. Among the multitude of "witnesses" who were interrogated were members of Jozsef Scharf's family. The irony is double: first, because Scharf, Mrs. Solymosi's neighbor, was Jewish—in fact he was the synagogue sexton—and in alluding to a Blood Libel that dissipated quickly when the lost child turned up, back in Hajdunanas, Scharf had unwittingly planted the idea in his neighbor's mind that this is what had happened to her daughter; and second, because Scharf now became a focus of Bary's investigation into the possibility that Eszter's disappearance was the result of Jewish foul play.

Symptomatic of Bary's illegal and inappropriate mode of investigation was the initial focus of his inquiry: Scharf's five-year-old son,

Samuel. Apparently coddled by neighboring women and prodded with sweets the child was induced to assert to them that his father had called Eszter into their house where the new *shohet* cut off her head. To Bary he asserted that the *shohet* had, in the presence of Samuel's father and others, merely made an incision in the girl's neck, and that he and his brother Moric had caught the blood in a plate. Is it possible that none of these interrogators had ever listened to a five-year-old expound on events that never transpired, spinning marvelous fantasies, particularly if encouraged to do so by adults—no doubt asking very leading questions—who are bribing him or her with sweets? Or that the shift in the story—from chopping off the head to making an incision in the neck—is part of that process through which a five-year-old fails to distinguish fact from fiction? How could Bary possibly not order a careful search of Scharf's house, where surely blood stains would have remained as a result of such an event—after *either* version of that event recounted by little Samuel.

Both Jozsef and 13-year-old Moric—and all the others whom Samuel might have identified as present during the blood-letting, but none of whom was apparently aware of the stories that Samuel had concocted—strenuously denied any knowledge whatsoever of how Eszter could have disappeared, where she might have gotten to or what might have happened to her. Nonetheless, Bary had Scharf and his wife arrested, and Moric, who claimed that he had not even heard anything about Eszter's whereabouts from hearsay, was taken from them and put in the "protective custody" of one Recsky, Commisar of Safety. Recsky took the boy to his country house in Nagyfalu, where his "safety" was to be the specific job of the Court Clerk, Peczely—who had himself served 12 years in prison for murder.

It seems that the plan that Peczely and Recsky put into motion (either with or without Bary's knowledge), was to sufficiently terrify the boy—separated from his parents who had been arrested, as well as from his little brother, mostly or perhaps entirely unaware of what exactly was going on, away from home in a strange house out in the country—into a willingness to be the mouthpiece for the accusation which they would articulate. Thus the boy "confessed" that

after the Sabbath morning service of April 2 his father had called
Eszter into their house under the pretext of having her remove some
candlesticks (because, presumably, moving them would constitute
work forbidden to Jews on the Sabbath). Further, he asserted, a Jewish beggar named Abraham Wollner, who had been staying with
them, then led the girl to the synagogue and attacked her; that there
two *shohets*, Abraham Buxbaum and Leopold Braun, had undressed
her and held her down while a third, Salamon Schwarz cut into her
neck with a large knife and emptied the blood from that wound into
a pot.

Moric claimed to have witnessed this through the keyhole
of the synagogue door (recalling to our minds, perhaps, how the
Christian servant girl witnessed some of what happened to William
of Norwich, with one eye, through a crack in the door). Presumably
the three perpetrators were the three—or three of the—competitors
for the *shohet/hazzan* position who, having sung and slaughtered the
day before all stayed over through the Sabbath, with their knives
handy in the synagogue, and remained in the synagogue after the
morning service to accomplish this pre-Passover act (although nowhere in Moric's testimony does the fact that Passover would be
arriving on Monday come up). And presumably the story that five-
year-old Samuel had told, which set the action within his father's
house, was now being ignored.

Moric added that he remained outside the synagogue door, on
watch, and, while apparently spending much of that time watching
through the keyhole rather than watching for intruders, he also saw
them tie a rag around the neck of the girl and dress her again after
the blood-letting was finished (and she was presumably dead)—at
which time others were also present, to wit: Samuel Lustig, Abraham Braun, Lazar Weisstein and Adolf Juenger. Having coaxed and
coached this story from Moric, Recsky and Paczely sent for Bary, to
whom Moric repeated his account—adding the further detail that,
after the murderers had left the scene of the crime he (who had been
on watch and entrusted with the key) locked up the synagogue. Before doing so, he looked around and could find neither blood stains
nor corpse.

Bary pushed his investigation in the synagogue and into the homes of the various Jews who were named one way or the other—a dozen Jews were arrested now—and among the graves in the Jewish cemetery, but his investigative team also failed to find any trace of either blood or a body anywhere. And then a body was found: on June 18 the body identified by the district physician as that of a 14-year-old girl was drawn out of the Tisza River that flowed through Tiszaeszlar; the body was found downstream, near the village of Dada, and apparently it was sufficiently intact for many to assert immediately that it was the body of Eszter Solymosi. She had apparently either fallen in on that fateful April 1 or committed suicide (for reasons that nobody ever came forth to try to explain, including her mother). Given the likely familiarity with the river that flowed through the village in which she grew up for a 14-year-old girl who moved freely across that landscape from the time she could walk, suicide seems more likely than accident.

If she was murdered, it was not by any apparent physical violence except drowning. There was no marks on her neck that could come close to suggesting that anyone slit her throat. But the astounding thing—or perhaps not, given the point of anti-Jewish hysteria to which her mother had arrived, the constant prodding that she received to maintain that hysteria, by neighbors, by Bary and his associates, by the local Catholic priest, who would write an article in effect accusing the Jews of practicing ritual murder—is that Eszter's mother emphatically denied that this could be her daughter's corpse, although later on identified the clothes in which that corpse had been dressed as those of Eszter.[135] Thus what might have ended in a saner, less charged atmosphere, moved forward.

A committee of "experts" was organized—two physicians and one surgeon[136]—that declared the corpse to be that of a girl of 18 to 20 years, who had perished a mere 8 to 10 days earlier. Without anyone coming forth to assert that his or her daughter, sister, wife or mother had disappeared 8 or 10 days earlier, the authorities simply buried the body in the Catholic cemetery of Tiszaeszlar. The local Catholic priest and other agitators implied that the body had been smuggled in from elsewhere, dressed in Eszter Solymosi's garments (her body having been disposed of nobody could say where) in order to make it appear that this was Eszter's corpse and thereby conceal the ritual murder that they had committed. Later testimony by some of those who had discovered and drawn the body from the river indicated that threats and promises had induced them to renounce their original testimony regarding how they found the body and to change it to the claim that they had brought the body to the river after they had dressed it in the clothing provided them by an unknown Jewess (whom they unequivocally knew, however to be a Jewess!)

The result of this morass was that new arrests were made and formal charges finally brought against 15 people on July 29. The breakdown was this: Salamon Schwarz, Abraham Buxbaum, Leopold Braun and Hermann Wollner were accused of murder; Joszef Scharf (who first unwittingly planted the seed for all of this in Mrs. Solymosi's head!), Adolf Juenger, Abraham Braun, Samuel Lustig, Lazar Weinstein and Emanuel Taub were accused of complicity, of voluntary assistance in the murder; and Anselm Vogel, Jankel Smilovics, David Hersko, Martin Gross and Ignac Klein were accused of aiding and abetting the crime and smuggling the body away. No women were implicated — in spite of the revamped story by some of the discoverers of the body in the river that a woman had provided them with the clothes in which they garbed the corpse.

The unusually long time that elapsed between Bary's arrival on the scene in May and the formal preferring of charges may be ascribed to the examiner's mode of operation — interrogations without the presence of the state attorney, writing up of the record of those interrogations without witnesses (sometimes of the interrogation, sometimes of the recollection of the interrogation as it was shaped in his writing it up), to say nothing of the use of torture on both those accused and those suspected but not yet accused. During the whole time, Moric Scharf, who was, as it were, the star witness for the prosecution, was placed in the custody of the district bailiff, who in turn placed him in the custody of the warden, Henter. He was thus kept isolated and out of contact with any of the defendants, including of course his family, or with any of the Jews of Tiszaeszlar, as he was continually primed to present his testimony in court.

The lawyer imported from Budapest to represent the defendants was Karoly Eotvos, a non-Jewish journalist and member of the House of Deputies. He was supported by a team consisting of Benjamin Friedmann, Sandor Funtak, and Max Szekely of Budapest, and also Ignac Heumann of Nyiregyhaza, the county seat where the trial was held. The first issue taken up by Eotvos was the system of torture utilized by Bary, Recsky and Peczely to extract testimony; he appealed to the Minister of Justice, Pauler, that such testimony be categorically left out, but Pauler ignored the appeal—which seems not in the long run to have been lost on the tribunal, however, since it invalidated all of the false "evidence" that had been submitted through the efforts of Bary and his associates.

The process of the pre-trial investigation dragged on to the point that State Attorney Kozma came in from Budapest in September to help speed it up, and widespread coverage in the media stirred up agitation throughout the country. This is the point at which anti-Semitic pot-stirrers drew up and passed out a number of pamphlets in cities and towns across Hungary. It is also the point at which Lajos Kossuth, the renowned nationalist exiled by the Hapsburgs and living in Turin, Italy, spoke out loudly in castigation of the authorities who were permitting this travesty to continue and thus stirring up anti-Semitic sensibilities. He argued that the preoccupation with the idea of the ritual murder of a Christian child by Jews was a disgrace to Hungary, showing it to be mired in a medievalist mentality, and out-of-step with the modernity of which the nation was otherwise so much a part.[137] Kossuth's eloquent outcry was echoed by Erno Mezei, a member of parliament, in November, in an address directed to the Minister of Justice.

The address yielded results: the Attorney-General himself was dispatched to Nyiregyhaza, where he learned that, in spite of the assertion by the examining judge, those accused had themselves not yet had a single hearing. Some prisoners were released; in mid-November, Joszef Scharf's wife, who had not been one of the 15 individuals officially charged, but had remained in custody, was finally released. On December 7, at the request of Eotvos and his team the body found in the Tisza river was exhumed and re-examined by three professors of medicine brought in from the University of Budapest. These adjudged the conclusions of the first medical team woefully incompetent. While it was no longer possible to identify the body due to its state of decay, they asserted unequivocally that it was that of a younger girl—with no marks on her neck that would support any story of ritual murder involving throat cutting. Given that nobody had in all this time come forth to claim a missing loved one, they concluded that it must be that of Eszter Solymosi.

The denouement of the entire affair did not come until June 17, 1883, when a formal trial began, leading to discussions that lasted through thirty sessions of the court, although the only "serious" testimony that they had to evaluate was that of Moric Scharf, dominated by contradictions—including the question of what happened where and the absolute lack of physical evidence of wrong-doing in either the synagogue or any Jewish house—in spite of the careful coaching he had received. Over the next month, the tribunal examined witnesses whose memories of what did or did not, might or might not have happened fourteen and fifteen months earlier spoke more out of their stirred-up emotions than out of a sense that could in any way be labeled factual.

The procedure was very much the theatre entertainment of that summer for those who could make it. Special admissions fees were charged to those who wanted to sit in the courtroom. That audience numbered in the thousands, including as many as 2,000 Jews. Witnesses testified in various languages,[138] requiring the added complication of a small bevy of simultaneous translators. The court visited the alleged crime scene(s) on July 16 and on August 3 unanimously voted for acquittal. That is, the three judges concluded that the accused were not guilty—those accused of conspiracy were exonerated, since the judges argued that the theory of procuring a corpse had already been shown to be unproven in the pre-trial investigation—but those accused of murder, while found not guilty were not precisely pronounced innocent, either.[139]

For the wording of the verdict with regard to the four individuals actually accused of committing the murder (Schwarz, Buxbaum, Wollner, and Leopold Braun) was rather strange in its equivocal tone—as if the judges were reluctant to exonerate them. They stated that "the fact that the charge of murder against Salamon Schwarcz and his companions was not proved precludes the concealment of the act of murder." So the verdict of not guilty was more implied than declared. This decision to offer only the bare minimum of compliance with what the Hungarian criminal code calls for in the matter of acquitting a defendant of a charge in the absence of incriminating evidence—and in a case which everyone recognized had a much larger historical significance for Hungary and its place in the eyes of the world than an "ordinary" murder trial—is strange, to say the least.

Either the judges were simply not satisfied with the innocence of the defendants but could not find them guilty in the absence of any real evidence—or they could not embrace their innocence due to the nature of the charge and the religious identity of those charged. When the defense team went to thank the Chief Judge, Korniss for the "impartiality of the court and the verdict announced that saved the honor of Hungary's administration of justice," Korniss, according to Bary (who witnessed the moment), "responded icily, almost harshly." Bary himself would state that "the Jews, with the help of the government, prevent the exposure of the truth."

So the final chapter of this story is more about the explosion of anti-Semitic sentiment in a Hungary in which that sentiment had been brewing for a century or longer than about understanding how Eszter Solymosi died. Mrs Solymosi's attorney appealed the decision, knowing that the verdict was not likely to be overturned—the Supreme Court rejected the appeal the following year (May 10, 1884)—but by appealing it, he and the soon-to-be-formed anti-Semitic party that he would represent in the approaching parliamentary elections, would be able to keep alive the Blood Libel as an issue. They would be able to exploit it as a vital issue of national interest.

For the verdict of acquittal and the freeing of the prisoners, most of whom had been under lock and key for fifteen months or longer, were orchestrated by the anti-Semites into a series of violent outbreaks and attacks on Jews in Budapest, Pressburg and other cities throughout Hungary. The Tiszaeszlar case figured prominently in the politics of the newly formed anti Semitic party. Istoczy and his circle use the vicious language of the Blood Libel as a centerpiece of their anti-Jewish propaganda—a more useful instrument, drawing from old and familiar wells of fear, than the more sophisticated modernist political anti-Semitic rhetoric, in appealing to the masses.

They were successful in gaining 17 seats in the parliamentary elections of 1884. But the implications of this flourishing of anti-Semitism that the Tiszaeszlar Affair helped to facilitate would have implications felt into the next century, from the White Terror (1919-21) that followed World War I to the role of anti-Semitism in Hungary during World War II and the Holocaust.

III. Stepping Back Briefly: The Damascus Affair

The issue of a nineteenth-century event offering important implications for the position of the Jews in the world deep into the twentieth century is not limited, of course, to Central Europe, or even to Europe overall. While the Christian world is the logical nexus of this discussion—the problematic of "Jewish trials" finds its natural origin and development within Christendom, given the early "Christ-killer" idea—that problematic is not limited, particularly in the modern era, to the Christian sea with its far-flung Jewish archipelago. Indeed, before moving forward within Europe, I would be remiss in failing to make reference to the emergence of the Blood Libel in the Muslim world—albeit due, almost certainly, to the European Christian presence and influence there—by the nineteenth century. By that time, France, Britain, Prussia and to a lesser extent Austro-Hungary and Tsarist Russia were engaged in an aggressive imperialist policy of involvement in the Middle East, seeking political, religious and cultural footholds in areas where the Ottoman Turkish hold was weakening thanks to a succession of incompetent sultans.

In fact, the Porte had become sufficiently enfeebled that—to make a longer story relatively short—when the Albanian of Arab descent, Mehmet Ali, who had served the Sultan as an army officer at the time when Napoleon brought France into contact with the Middle East, became in effect the independent Pasha of Egypt by 1805, there was not much the Sultan could do. Eventually Mehmet Ali's power would extend up through Syro-Palestine and he was nearly in a position to depose the Sultan. Mehmet Ali's efforts and those of his son, Ibrahim Ali, were supported by the French; the British and the Austro-Hungarians preferred to help restore Ottoman Turkish power, out of a fear that French influence was extending too far.[140]

The Damascus Affair of 1840 brings these issues together. One might say that it exemplifies the meeting between West and East in the matter of Blood Libel-based prejudice. On February 5, a Franciscan Capuchin friar, Father Thomas da Camangiano, and his Greek servant, disappeared, never to be seen again. As a physician, Father Thomas was well known in the Muslim and Jewish communities of Damascus, and a few days earlier he was said to have had a dispute with a Turkish muleteer, who heard him blaspheme Muhammad, whereupon the Turk is said to have asserted that "that dog of a Christian will die by my hand." Nonetheless, when Thomas' disappearance was brought to the attention of the authorities, the French consul in Damascus, Ratti Menton—well-known as inimical to the Jews—began, after discussion with several Capuchins, investigating in the *Jewish* quarter.[141]

Not surprisingly, Menton found nothing there, but managed to turn the story in what he considered the appropriate direction when he managed to exact a "confession"—under torture—from a Jewish barber named Negrin. Negrin "named" a baker's dozen Jewish community leaders, who were arrested and also tortured— their skin burned, their teeth and beards pulled out—to induce a confession that Father Thomas and his servant had been murdered and their blood extracted for the purposes of Jewish ritual or to be used in the baking of *matzah* for the imminent Passover festival. The elderly Joseph Lanado and several other victims died from the ordeal; Moses Abulafia converted to Islam to escape it. Beyond some unclear ravings under the pains inflicted upon them, the remaining victims failed to offer Menton and the local Muslim ruler, Sharif Pasha, the sort of narrative that they were seeking.

Nonetheless, Sharif Pasha wrote to his overlord in Egypt, Mehmet Ali, asking for authorization to execute them all. Meanwhile, Menton was writing articles of the sort that anticipate the work of Edouard Drumont in the Dreyfus Affair more than fifty years later (see below, 174-75, 184-85) libeling the Jews. On the other hand, the Austrian Consul in Damascus, Merlatto, and the Austrian Consul-general in Alexandria, Eliahu Picotto, sought to defend the Jewish community from the accusation. They met with Ibrahim Ali Pasha, who ordered an investigation.

At the same time, the Damascus Jewish community appealed to its brethren in Europe and the United States. In what proved to be a groundbreaking act, 15,000 American Jews protested in six cities, and largely as a consequence, the United States Consul in Egypt lodged a protest in the name of President Martin Van Buren. More importantly for the fate of the accused, the lawyer Isaac Cremieux and the Orientalist Solomon Munk, both from France, and Sir Moses Montefiore, from England, were dispatched to meet with and plead with Ibrahim's father, Mehmet Ali. Arriving on August 4, they met several times with him, ultimately receiving from him the unconditional release and recognition of the innocence of the surviving nine Jewish leaders (out of thirteen who had been interrogated and tortured), on August 28.

This group followed their visits to Mehmet Ali with one to the Ottoman Sultan, Abdulmecid, who issued a *firman* (edict) declaring the Blood Accusation to be absurd, and asserting that, within the Ottoman domains, "we cannot permit the Jewish nation, whose innocence for the crime alleged against them is evident, to be worried and tormented as a consequence of accusations which have not the least foundation of truth."

One might observe two consequences of all of this activity. One is the organizing of the international Jewish community for the first time in its history, both as a general idea and with regard to the establishment of new organizations, such as the *Alliance Israelite Universelle* (in 1860). So, too, new organs of communication—a modern

Jewish press—such as *Les Archives Israelites de France* (which persisted from 1840 to 1935) in Paris and *The Jewish Chronicle* (founded in 1841) in London were born.

The second consequence is that, although the nine survivors were ultimately freed and the Jewish community officially exonerated, both in general of such an accusation and specifically with respect to the disappearance and presumed death of Father Thomas and his servant, yet riots broke out in Damascus at that time and the synagogue of Jobar (a Damascus suburb) was pillaged, its Torah scrolls destroyed. The funeral procession for Father Thomas (devoid of his body) through Damascus not only helped generate more emotion and hostility, but the inscription on his tombstone—in Arabic—still remains. It refers to his having been "assassinated by the Jews on February 5, 1840." And the spill-off in this direction was profound. Sporadic pogroms, with references back to Damascus, 1840, spread throughout the Middle East and North Africa through the end of the nineteenth century and into the twentieth.[142]

Nor does belief in that Libel end in the early—or late—twentieth century. Two articles by Mahmoud Al-Said Al-Kurdi appeared in the October, 20, 2000 and the March 25, 2001 issues of the Egyptian daily, *Al Akhbar* repeating the accusation made 160 years earlier. Syria's Minister of Defense, Mustafa Tlass, repeated the Libel as fact in his 2002 book, *The Matzah of Zion*. Moreover, as recently as January 20, 2007, the Lebanese poet Marwan Chamoun spoke in a television interview of the "...slaughter of the priest Tomaso de Camangiano... in 1840... in the presence of two rabbis in the heart of Damascus, in the home of a close friend of this priest, Daud al-Hariri, head of the Jewish community of Damascus. After he was slaughtered, his blood was collected, and the two rabbis took it away with them [to use it in the manufacture of *matzah*]."

If the blood libel cannot seem to die within the Christian West, how much the more so within the Christian and Muslim Middle East! Or rather, if in the West the terms of the Blood Libel, as we shall shortly see, may be recast in more socio-cultural, economic and political forms in the modern era, in the Middle East it seems that the older ethno-religious form still flourishes unalloyed. The implications of this extend into the question of the potential for peaceful relations within that region, specifically between Israel and her neighbors, where that question and those relations are tied to trust.

IV. The Dreyfus Affair and the—Incurable?—Disease of Anti-Semitism

The Western world of the late nineteenth century might have looked at the Tiszaeszlar affair, and seen it—as Kossuth knew it would—as symptomatic of the backward, medievalist mentality of a peasant-dominated Central European country, no matter how modernist its capital city, Budapest may have been. But certainly the same could not be said of France, the most Western, most socially modern of European states! France, which had moved from its September, 1791 declarations that encompassed the Jews as *citoyens* through the Napoleonic liberations that extended from France to the countries he conquered—and under whose regime the great convening of the Jewish "Sanhedrin" had, from the viewpoint of some, at least, put an exclamation point on the fact of Jewish inclusion within French society.

France, that had steered its way through the revolutions of 1830 and 1848 and, in the aftermath of the debacle against Prussia in 1870-71 moved unflinchingly toward a third shaping of itself as a republic. That France could never possibly follow the sort of course that led through Tiszaeszlar and Nyiregyhaza in the early 1880s (or anything resembling a re-directed course that led through Damascus in 1840)! This is why the trial of Alfred Dreyfus for treason, blown up into a cataclysmic *Affaire Dreyfus*, came as such a shock when it exploded in the 1890s.

Perhaps a closer look by the outside world at developments in France between the defeat at the hands of the Prussians and the 1890s might have made the *Affaire* less shocking to it. The country was divided between royalists and republicans, conservatives and liberals. The conservative, royalist side included, among others, the leadership of both the Catholic Church and the armed forces. The latter had been humiliated by the defeat by Prussia that opened the 1870s. Barely a decade after that debacle a major scandal sliced across those "party" lines, pertaining to the brilliant de Lesseps' plan to cut a canal across Panama and thereby connect the Atlantic and Pacific Oceans. The extraordinary undertaking ended up costing 22,000 French lives over the next several years, and remained unfinished—until the United States took it up in the early 1900s, completing the canal only by 1914.

But for France of the 1880s, the engineering trauma was accompanied by an equally politically debilitating corruption catastrophe: 104 members of the Chamber of Deputies were eventually implicated in a conspiracy to lie to the French public regarding the disastrous financial condition of the Panama Canal Company, which failure to disclose cost the government over a million Francs. Although many royalists were involved, the focus turned on two wealthy Jewish (and republican) families—in particular that of Baron Jacques de Reinach—who had supported the project and been part of the conspiracy; their involvement was treated by the royalists and their allies as symptomatic of prevailing Jewish financial corruption that was said to be undermining France.

So the same sort of anti-Jewish mood that emerged in the 1870s in Germany culminating in the will to be rid of them that was expressed in the racialization process articulated by Wilhelm Marr; the same mood that crystallized in Hungary in the 1880s, after the Tiszaeszlar Affair, with the shaping and success of an anti-Semitic political party by 1884—that same mood could also be seen in France in the 1880s. It was a mood most fervently articulated and promoted by Edouard Drumont. He was indeed the ringleader of those foisting the entire blame for the Canal disaster and its attendant corruption scandal on the Jews.

Drumont published a book in 1886 called *La France Juive*—Jewish France—in which he warned his Catholic compatriots of the threat to their country of the emancipated Jews among them. France, Drumont asserted, was being swallowed up by the corrupt, dishonest and dangerous Jews. He wrote it in a popular, accessible style, emphasizing how Jews could be easily identified by their hooked noses and unpleasant smell, and how the dangerous socio-political condition of liberalism was a function of their efforts. Drumont went so far as to suggestion that Protestants were actually half-Jews, lest his web of bigotry be construed as too narrowly spun.

Moreover, his assertions were not limited to a one-shot book; he was a journalist who published a *feuilleton* called *La Libre Parole* (*Free Speech*) in the 1890s, which he used as a constant platform from which to espouse his antagonistic view of Jews. The success that Drumont's book and his *feuilleton* experienced demonstrated to the anti-republican political forces how useful an instrument anti-Semitism could be for their cause. The royalist press, and not only Drumont's writings, pushed forward in the late 1880s with an increasingly vehement campaign of Jew-baiting. Yet because the government remained in republican hands, not well-disposed to support such a mood, the anti-Semitic campaign from the political right lost some traction by the early 1890s.

This is the matrix of issues that caught the French army Captain Alfred Dreyfus in their crossfire as the 1890s progressed, providing the royalists and their circle with perfect conditions for promoting their ideology. For in September, 1894, a French counterespionage agent claimed to have found a suspicious piece of paper in the wastepaper basket of the Prussian military attache, which he passed along to his superiors. The paper, later referred to as the *bordereau*,[143] apparently contained a promise, written in French, to deliver an important French artillery manual into Prussian hands. Its actual words were:

> Although I have no news that you wish to see me, I am sending you, sir, some interesting information:
> 1. A note on the hydraulic brake of the 120 mm. gun and the way in which this gun has performed;
> 2. A note on the covering troops (some modifications will be made under the new plan);
> 3. A note on the modification in artillery formations;
> 4. A note concerning Madagascar;
> 5. The projected Field Artillery Firing Manual (14 March 1894). This last item is extremely difficult to obtain and I only have it at my disposal for a very few days. The Ministry of War has sent out a fixed number to the various corps concerned, and the corps are responsible for them. Each office holding one must return it after maneuvers. If, therefore, you wish to take from it whatever

is of interest to you, and then keep the original for me, I will take
it back, unless you would prefer that I should have it copied *in
extenso* and send you the copy.
I am about to leave for maneuvers.

I say that the agent "claimed to have found" the *bordereau*, because the piece of paper, presumably intended for the attache, Lieutenant-Colonel Maximilian von Schwartzkoppen, (whose job it was
to gather information on French military matters), torn, unsigned,
undated, ended up in French hands without great clarity as to how
it got to them. The most commonly embraced version of this small
detail of history—or should I say, *historiography?*—is that a char-
woman working in the German Embassy, a Mme. Bastion, found
it in the wastebasket in von Schwartskoppen's office and it was she
who turned it over to the French agent who passed it on.[144]In any
case it ended up in the Statistical Section of the War Ministry offices
on the morning of September 27, where the first one to see it was
Major Hubert Henry, a career officer and one of five officers serving
in that office.

Henry showed it to his superiors. The handwriting of the *bordereau* was not recognizable either to the Chief of French Military
Intelligence, Colonel Sandherr, or to the handwriting experts he
consulted. But Colonel Pierre-Elie Fabre, Chief of the Fourth Bureau and his assistant, Lieutenant-Colonel d'Aboville concluded
that it had to have been written by a Probationer-Artillery Officer
on the General staff—"probationary" meaning that he would be
moving through a two-year program of serving for six months in
each of the four departments of the War Ministry, which multi-va-
lent knowledge seemed reflected in the note.[145] The small handful
of Probationer-Artillery Officers included Captain Alfred Dreyfus.
Eventually Major Henry seems to have persuaded Sandherr that the
most likely person to have written the note was Captain Dreyfus—
although there was little resemblance between Dreyfus' handwriting and that on the *bordereau*.

Colonel Fabre would later describe before the court-martial tribunal of 21 August 1899 (by then he had been promoted to the rank
of General) how "during the reading and discussion of the various
details we came to the conclusion that because of the mentioned

technical questions on artillery the document could only have come from an artillery officer who was at that time in the Fourth Bureau — that is, an office assigned to the General Staff. We attempted to re-member all the names of artillery officers assigned to the Bureau. The name Dreyfus was the only one we could think of *who had not made a good impression and who had received a bad report* [my italics]. That did not mean at all that we regarded him as a traitor. We were moved only by curiosity to compare his handwriting with that of the *bordereau*. I took out of my drawer a report of 1893 that he had filled out. We were struck by the fact that there was a similarity be-tween the word "artillery" in this report and in the *bordereau*. In both cases the "i" fell well below the other letters."[146] But any viewer with a modicum of handwriting analysis experience — not even ex-pertise — could and can still see how different Dreyfus' handwriting was from that of the *bordereau*.

As for Dreyfus' having not made "a good impression" and having "received a bad report," it is rather interesting to note the following biographical data on him. He entered the *Ecole Polytech-nique* in 1878, at not quite age 19, and two years late became a sub-lieutenant in the artillery. Reports on him as a lieutenant were consistently positive. He was labeled "intelligent" (1883), "consci-entious" (1884), "very energetic" (1885), "very courageous" (1886); was called "a good commander" (1887) and said to have an "ex-cellent memory" (1888) and to "command without blustering" (1889 — so much for the snobbery of which Fabre's description also accused him). The following year he was admitted to the *Ecole de Guerre* (War College), where he spent the following two years, con-tinued to receive good reports and was proclaimed "well qualified for staff duty." He graduated ninth in his class of eighty-one can-didates and was then admitted to the general staff.

During the following two years, 1893 and 1894, with one excep-tion, the reports at the end of each semester — and each one signed by a different commanding officer (three with the rank of colonel and the last with the rank of general) — were excellent ones. Thus Colonel Germiny refers to him as "a very intelligent officer [who] writes very well, already possesses extensive knowledge, can treat questions with originality" (first semester, 1893); Colonel de Dancy writes of him as "a very intelligent officer, quick to grasp affairs, works easily, perhaps a bit too sure of himself. Knows German very well"—an obviously useful sort of knowledge, but also one that could make him an object of suspicion if one were searching for one (first semester, 1894). General de Boisdeffre referred to him (second semester, 1894) as "a good officer. Alert mind, comprehends quickly, zealous, a worker who made *a favorable impression wherever he went* [my italics]. Only Colonel Fabre, in his report after the second semester, 1893, although he refers to Dreyfus as "very intelligent and highly gifted" states that he is an "officer of uneven ability...[and] a bit conceited, and from the point of view of character, conscientiousness and manner of work, does not fulfill the requirements for employment on the General Staff."

On the one hand, this last report is so diametrically opposed to the other three as well as to the reports on him while in the polytechnical school as to suggest that something other than Dreyfus' performance motivated Fabre. On the other hand, in recalling that it was in fact Fabre who later retrospectively reported why they had zeroed in on Dreyfus—by referring to bad impressions and bad reports, when it was only his own report that fit (and only partially) that description, over against the overwhelmingly positive array of reports otherwise—it is difficult not to imagine that Fabre didn't like Dreyfus for whatever reasons back when he wrote that report and therefore did not have to stretch very far to point the accusing finger at him later on. Why, though? In the absence of anything concrete, one might speculate, which is the basis of so much of historiography.

Dreyfus was Jewish, wealthy[147] and—at least in the opinion of Henry and his friends—snobby (hence, perhaps, the not making a "good impression" to which Fabre refers). Moreover, his family came from Alsace, part of the region on the French-Prussian border over which the war a generation earlier had been fought—and in which the French army had been so thoroughly defeated that it was still licking its wounds at the time the *bordereau* was discovered. This last aspect of who he was made him a suspect—someone who didn't know much about him might speculate that his sympathies fell onto the German and not the French side of that border. The first aspect, his Jewishness, however secularized, made him suspect almost by definition, because his very presence as a Jew was an irritant to the profound prejudices percolating within the Catholic, Jesuit-trained aristocracy that almost entirely accounted for the officers' corps of the French army—particularly in the Drumontesque atmosphere of that period to which I have already referred.

There is considerable irony in all of this. Why did the youngest son of a well-off Jewish family join the army in the first place? Part of the reason offered later by members of his family is that he was so struck by horror at the overrunning of Alsace by the Prussian army—he was eleven years old at the time—and the subsequent peace agreement signed in Frankfort that ceded Alsace to Prussia, that he made a pledge that when he grew up he would join the French army with the goal of avenging that defeat and reclaiming Alsace as French territory. And he kept that promise to himself; if the French army in general was still licking the wounds of that 1870-1 defeat, so was Dreyfus as an exemplary member of that army. Beyond that post-1871 frustration, his disciplined, loyal but shy nature may well have found in the military the sort of atmosphere in which his combination of psychological and emotional needs could be met.

As for his family itself, when Alsace was ceded to Prussia, all of that province's inhabitants were given a choice: leave, or take on German citizenship. The entire Dreyfus family left, with the exception of one uncle who needed to stay behind and manage the family factories—but he sent all of his children to France for their education, and also left as soon as it became feasible, requesting that his French citizenship be reinstated. So the notion that Dreyfus would have had some Germanophilic reason for betraying France could not be more preposterous. But in the context of an army for which the Franco-Prussian War humiliation felt as if it had occurred just yesterday, and not more than twenty years earlier, desperate for a scapegoat to explain the defeat and inherently hostile to Jews, Dreyfus was the perfect candidate.

On the evening of October 14, 1894, Dreyfus was at home with his family, and received a summons to appear at the office of the Chief of the General Staff the following morning—but the summons had a puzzling element in it. "The Divisional General, Chief of General Staff, will hold an examination of probationary officers during the evening of Monday, October 15. Captain Dreyfus... is asked to present himself on that date at nine o'clock in the morning at the office of the Chief of General Staff. Civilian dress." Dreyfus had to have been confused by the last two words: why *civilian* dress? Nonetheless, "on Monday morning I left my family [Dreyfus writes]. My son Pierre, who was then three and a half years old and was accustomed to accompany me to the door when I went out, came with me that morning, as usual... The morning was bright and cool... As I was a little ahead of time, I walked back and forth before the Ministry building for a few minutes, then went upstairs"—clearly not suspecting that anything was amiss. However, "...I was somewhat surprised at finding none of my comrades, as officers are always called in groups to the general inspection. After a few minutes of commonplace conversation Commandant Picquart conducted me to the private office of the Chief of General Staff. I was greatly amazed to find myself received, not by the Chief of General Staff, but by Commandant du Paty de Clam, who was in uniform.[148] Three persons in civilian dress, who were utterly unknown to me, were also there..."

> Commandant du Paty de Clam came directly toward me and said in a choking voice: 'The General is coming. While waiting, I have a letter to write, and as my finger is sore, will you write it for me?' Strange as the request was under the circumstances, I at once complied... After first requiring me to fill up an inspection form, he dictated to me a letter of which certain passages recalled the accusing letter that I knew afterward, and which was called the *bordereau*. In the course of his dictation the Commandant interrupted me sharply, saying 'You tremble!' (I was not trembling. At the court-martial of 1894, he explained his brusque interruption by saying that he had perceived that I was not trembling under the dictation; believing therefore that he was dealing with one who was dissimulating, he had tried in this way to shake my assurance). This vehement remark surprised me greatly, as did the hostile attitude of Commandant du Paty. But as all suspicion was far from my mind, I thought only that he was displeased at my writing it badly.

My fingers were cold, for the temperature outside was chilly, and I
had been in the warm room for a few minutes. So I answered, 'My
fingers are cold.'

So, unbeknownst to Dreyfus, he was being set up to produce
handwriting samples that, compared with that on the *bordereau*,
would point to him as its author. As du Paty kept trying to shake
Dreyfus up, but Dreyfus, confused as to what was going on but still
completely unsuspecting what was afoot, remained unperturbed,
du Paty decided that there was no point in continuing this part of
the game. Instead, as soon as the dictation was completed, he arose
from his chair, "placed his hand on my shoulder, cried out in a loud
voice: 'In the name of the law, I arrest you; you are accused of the
crime of high treason.' A thunderbolt falling at my feet would not
have produced in me a more violent emotion; I blurted out disconnected sentences, protesting against so infamous an accusation, to
which nothing in my life could have given rise."

At that point, M. Cochefert, head of the secret police, and his
secretary, seized and searched Dreyfus, who offered no resistance,
crying out, rather: "Take my keys, open everything in my house; I am
innocent!"—adding: "At least show me the proofs of the infamous
act you pretend I have committed!" To this they merely responded
that the evidence was overwhelming, but refused to state what it
was or precisely what the shape of the accusation was. We may recognize a familiar, Inquisitional methodology in the refusal to present the accused with the accusation, his accuser(s) or the evidence
of the accusation. Dreyfus was taken to the military prison on the
rue du Cherche-Midi by Commandant Henry—who had watched
the entire proceeding from behind a curtain, yet asked Dreyfus of
what he had been accused, as if he might thereby elicit something
from him that could be used against him—and one of the detectives.

Henry would subsequently write a report suggesting that he
had had a lengthy, incriminating conversation with Dreyfus on the
way to the prison—a clear fabrication, as so many subsequent aspects of this narrative would demonstrate. In any case, Dreyfus was
thrown into a cell where he was left by du Paty for three days virtually incommunicado, before he continued the victim's "interrogation." For seventeen days du Paty showed up—always late in the

evening, when he might expect his prisoner to be most fatigued, or asleep. He would cut up facsimile photographs of letters by Dreyfus and the *bordereau*, mix them together in his hat, and then order the prisoner to select some fragments for further interrogation—meanwhile steadfastly refusing to inform him of the actual charge, the precise reason for his arrest. Only two weeks after the arrest did du Paty show Dreyfus a photograph of the *bordereau* of which he was accused of being the author.

For the purposes of our discussion, there are three issues of consequence that proceed from this point: the court-martial and its aftermath; the attendant features that turned the case into "*l'affaire Dreyfus*" together with the consequence of those features for France and its Jewish population as it moved toward and into the twentieth century; and the eventual exoneration of the innocent man. Thus after some two weeks of incommunicado imprisonment with its nightly visit from du Paty, Dreyfus was brought before a military court-martial and formally accused of treason. Colonel Henry—who had first suggested Dreyfus as the culprit and fabricated the "confessional" discussion with Dreyfus, now informed the officers' panel that he had "other" information implicating Dreyfus, "of such secrecy" that it could not be revealed without jeopardizing France's military position. Given the psychological state of France's military since 1870-1, one can well imagine that such a statement would not have found many on the panel to oppose it as ridiculous (if this was a closed, military tribunal, why would it have been dangerous to confide to these officers what he, Henry, an officer in the same army, knew?)

Largely because of what was transpiring out in the streets and the media, beyond the courtroom and the nominal content of the issue it was debating—about which more below—the tribunal determined that it would be expedient to convict Dreyfus, in spite of the flimsiness of the evidence against him. On December 22, 1894, they found him guilty by unanimous vote. So Dreyfus was stripped of his position within the army and sentenced to life imprisonment in exile; he was transported in chains to a pestilent prison island—known as Devil's Island—off the coast of French Guyana in South America.

More fully: on Saturday, January 5, 1895, at 8:45 AM, an "execution procession" was organized in the main courtyard of the *Ecole Militaire* on Place Fontenoy, to which each regiment of the Paris garrison sent two units, one of soldiers in arms and the other of recruits. Diplomats, journalists and a few notables were invited to view the spectacle—the public jammed the streets and in some cases the roofs, outside the gates. General Paul Darras, waiting on horseback at the center of the space, drew his sword as Dreyfus was escorted toward him, and holding it high, proclaimed: "Alfred Dreyfus, you are no longer worthy of bearing arms. In the name of the people of France, we dishonor you!" Dreyfus responded by crying out: "Soldiers, an innocent man is being degraded; soldiers, an innocent man is being dishonored! Long live France! Long live the Army!"

Sergeant-Major Bouxin of the Republican Guard ripped the decorations from Dreyfus' cap and sleeves, the red stripes from his trousers, the epaulets from his shoulders. These badges of rank were tossed to the ground. His sword and sheath were confiscated and Bouxin broke the sword over his knee. Jacques St. Cere, Correspondent for the *New York Herald*, noted how again at this point Dreyfus cried out "Long Live France!" He was then required to march bareheaded before the troops and to make a tour of the entire military assembly in the courtyard. "When he arrived in front of the two hundred journalists and civil officials who were permitted to witness the ceremony, Dreyfus cried out: 'Tell the whole of France that I am an innocent man!' The way in which this cry was given, and the appearance of the prisoner, who held himself erect in his mutilated uniform, his red face, his bloodshot but dry eyes, produced a profound impression even on those who were the most thoroughly convinced of his guilt," continues St. Cere's account. But as far as most were concerned, the story was ended, awaiting only the epilogue of his transfer to Devil's Island.

But it turned out not to be ended, even after Dreyfus was remanded to Devil's Island. Sandherr retired as Chief of Intelligence the following year and was succeeded by Lieutenant Colonel Picquart. And in March, 1896, the same counter-espionage agent who had allegedly discovered the *bordereau* (or to whom it had been passed on by the cleaning woman at he German military attache's office) discovered—in the same office—a new piece of paper, a small special delivery letter the contents of which were a promise to deliver a new cache of French military secrets. The handwriting was identical to that on the *bordereau*. Given that Dreyfus was locked away on Devil's Island, and had been for over a year, that could only mean that someone other than he had been the author of the *bordereau*, was guilty of the treason of which he had been accused, and was still actively engaged in espionage activity.

Picquart managed to trace the handwriting to another officer, one Walsin Esterhazy, who had a reputation for being a profligate party-goer. Picquart discussed his findings with Henry (whom he had inherited as his assistant from Sandherr), and was shocked at Henry's response: how could the army admit that it had made an error? Such an admission would tarnish its honor! At this point the process leading to Dreyfus' exoneration can no longer be separated from the events that transformed the entire story into the *"l'Affaire Dreyfus."* For part of what had impelled the court-martial tribunal to conclude its business so quickly and find Dreyfus guilty without anything resembling substantial evidence to support that conclusion was the campaign being waged outside the doors of the courtroom. And that campaign's bombast continued to reverberate after the trial to the streets beyond the walls of the *Ecole Militaire* courtyard. It was a campaign to crucify the "Jewish traitor."

I have intentionally chosen the verb "crucify" in the last clause of the previous paragraph—albeit used metaphorically, of course—to underscore the vehemence that focused itself on Dreyfus *because* he was a Jew; because of centuries of teaching about and suspicion of all Jews as traitors in the image of Judas as betrayer of the crucified Christ; and because the various forms of obsession with an "international Jewish conspiracy" were reaching a new level and a new shape by the late nineteenth century—in France as elsewhere. More specifically, the furor outside the courtroom and the *Ecole Militaire* courtyard was led by Edouard Drumont by way of daily diatribes in *La Libre Parole*, and by other organs of the royalist, anti-republican press with which the army and the Catholic Church were in such strong sympathy. So Dreyfus was a magnet for diverse anti-Semitic groups and not only a scapegoat for the wounded army but a stand in for the republican cause that the royalists hoped to derail.

Seldom has such a far-flung, concerted and venomous campaign of word and image—caricature after caricature and cartoon after cartoon—been mounted against the Jews in the roughly two hundred-year history of *feuilleton*, newspaper and magazine journalism. What France spewed forth in the 1890s would have delighted the leaders of Nazi Germany in the 1930s. Images abounded, such as that of "The House of Dreyfus, Judas and Company, Selling Military Secrets to the Germans" or (on a cover of *Antijuif*—"*AntiJew*"—an image of the Grand Rabbi Zadoc-Klein, with a simian-looking secretary assisting him, standing before an enormous safe crowned by a golden calf together with Moses holding the Torah, who is shown distributing bags of money to Reinach and the liberal politician, Georges Clemenceau.

Drumont would editorialize in the weekly illustrated edition of *La Libre Parole* of November 3, 1894: "What a terrible lesson, this disgraceful treason of the Jew Dreyfus! A well-to-do man, the son-in-law of a wealthy merchant, officer in our Army, who holds one of the most sought-after posts, sells our mobilization plans and names of his comrades entrusted with foreign missions. Never have we had a similar outrage in our Fatherland. Concerning the Judas Dreyfus, for eight years I have been warning you each day!"

Nor was Drumont alone, of course, both within the royalist press and on the street. When in his humiliating, bareheaded walk around the *Ecole Militaire* courtyard Dreyfus arrived before the representatives of the press and cried out their obligation to inform "all of France that I am innocent," the response was "Silence, wretch! Coward! Traitor! Judas!" and "You know that you are not innocent! Long live France! Dirty Jew!" The crowd outside the gates yelled "Death to the Jew!" Leon Daudet, in writing about the procedure, described Dreyfus' face as "ashen, without relief, base, without appearance of remorse, *foreign, to be sure, debris of the ghetto*." [my italics]. Foreign? Whose family had been in Alsace for centuries? Debris of the ghetto? Whose family had lived in small towns in Alsace that had long been divested of ghettos? Daudet's anti-Jewish prejudices are simply imposed upon the face he describes.

So, too, Maurice Barres, who referred to Dreyfus' "foreign physiognomy." Barres would further ask rhetorically: "What do I have in common with Dreyfus. He is not of my race. He was not born to live in society... Be on your guard, patriots! When, then, will Frenchmen learn how to conquer France again?"[149] A century after the revolution and its assertions of liberty, fraternity, equality for all; a century after France declared itself a religion-blind, secular state; eighty-five years after the Napoleonic "Sanhedrin" had clarified the position of French Jews as Frenchmen—the animosity toward and suspicion of the Jew as an alien showed itself unabated when conditions allowed free rein to such feelings.

Jacques St Cere, in his previously-mentioned article for the *New York Herald*, asserted that "...here is some information that comes to me from a very good source. There is no doubt as to the prisoner's guilt. His arrest was decided on the unanimous vote of the eleven ministers, who at the time pledged themselves *not to reveal anything contained in the report demanding the prosecution of Dreyfus...*[my italics]. The secrets betrayed by Dreyfus are of such importance that the government will ask the chamber to pass a law providing for imprisonment... on an island of French Guiana... It is believed that Dreyfus was the center of the German espionage system in France..."

Why not reveal anything about it? Perhaps because the evidence was so spectacularly flimsy, and even the *bordereau* itself by itself so insignificant—it is what the *bordereau promised* that was potentially significant, but there was no evidence or even discussion as to whether the field artillery manual or any of the military information that was promised was ever *delivered*. When the young diplomat Maurice Paleologue expressed surprise at Dreyfus' calm restraint in the wintry courtyard of his humiliation to Colonel Sandherr, the latter observed that "it is clear that you do not know the Jews. The race has neither patriotism, nor honor, nor pride. For centuries, they have done nothing but betray."[150]

All of which puts Henry's response to Picquart into a context. The subtext of his concern for the Army's justice blunder included the concern for the royalist cause that would be damaged—and for himself who had, after all, virtually invented the story out of thin air of Dreyfus' guilt, with his reference to "secret" information, in order to feed that cause and to embarrass the Republic by investing the republicans with the taint of the "Jewish treason." The case had to be kept closed at all costs! More than that, when Henry realized the danger that Picquart's discoveries portended, he immediately did two things. He hurried to his office to forge new "evidence" against Dreyfus with paper, scissors and invisible ink (this became known later on); and he informed his superiors that Picquart was on the verge of opening an embarrassing inquiry into the original conviction. Picquart was suddenly transferred to North Africa.[151]

Fortunately for Dreyfus, history and justice, Picquart was able, just before his departure, to pass on the information that he had uncovered to his attorney, who passed it on to the liberal vice-president of the French Senate, Scheurer-Kestner. Confronted with what he recognized as an affront to justice and fair-play—equality for all before the law, as a principle undergirding the republican government, and understanding the obvious reason for the army's desire to keep the case buried and done with, Scheurer-Kestner initiated a campaign within the Senate itself for a re-trial. Mathieu Dreyfus, Alfred's brother, was able to procure a facsimile copy of the *bordereau*, which he submitted to a series of officials from the banks where the various artillery officers who might have been guilty of writing it did their banking—and Esterhazy's handwriting was as rapidly identified by them as it had been by Picquart.

From that point the *Affaire* entered the second phase of its development. The information regarding the relationship between Esterhazy's handwriting and the *bordereau* was released to the press—not all of which was conservative and royalist, of course—and the army had no choice but to bring Esterhazy before a court-martial. In his case, not only was the handwriting a clear match (whereas in Dreyfus' case the claim of a match was anything but clear, so that the weight of the charge rested on Henry's assertion of "secret" information) but, unlike Dreyfus, who was a quiet family man of some means (and therefore with no financially straitened motive for espionage on behalf of the Prussians), Esterhazy was both a playboy and a chronic gambler who was constantly short of funds. And his own diaries revealed his distaste for France, his *adopted* country (so who, then, is the "foreigner" — Dreyfus or Esterhazy?).

But the commitment to the idea of a "Jewish treason" and the unwillingness of the Catholic and conservative military tribunal either to acknowledge a miscarriage of justice on its part (for such an admission would have been an ironic and further humiliating horror to add to that of 1870-71 that had helped precipitate the miscarriage) or to convict a fellow Catholic military man—one of their own, whereas Dreyfus, in his Judaism, however secularized, was viewed as not one of their own—led to Esterhazy's acquittal.[152] But the scandal—as, step by step, it had already clearly become a scandal—refused to go away. By 1898 it was the most traumatic issue in French politics and society, from press diatribes to duels. On the royalist and anti-Semitic side the campaign was organized and led, as it was later revealed, by the staff of the Vatican Secretariat of State.

On the other side were Dreyfus' brother, Mathieu, who never stopped pushing to have Alfred brought back from Devil's Island for a re-trial; Bernard-Lazare, who was, outside the family, the victim's most insistent and consistent champion; politicians such as Clemenceau and Aristide Briand; and writers such as Anatole France, Charles Peguy and above all, Emile Zola. If earlier I have metaphorically referred to Dreyfus as a Christ figure—crucified for the sins of the French army that caused such spectacular failure in 1870-71 and of the French royalists and other conservatives whose world had been falling apart ever since—then Zola might be likened to Longinus, the Roman centurion who recognized in Jesus someone other than the political criminal which the Romans had accused him of being and for which they had executed him. The tradition of Longinus' utterance—*ecce homo*; "behold [this is] the man"—reverberates through history toward Zola's "*j'accuse*."

Zola wrote boldly: his most famous piece was presented as a long open letter to the president of the Republic on the front page of the January 13, 1898 issue of the publication, *l'Aurore*. The renowned novelist labeled the anti-Dreyfusard faction a conspiracy by the royalists to put the Army beyond the reach of civil procedures, and thereby bring down the Republic. He named names—accusing du Paty of deliberate malfeasance and Sandherr at least of incompetence, and Generals Mercier, de Boisdeffre and Gonse of having gotten "so caught up in this miscarriage that they would later feel compelled to impose it as a sacred truth that could not even be discussed"—in an eloquently libelous frontal assault that turned the flames of the *Affaire* into a conflagration. The generals who "at first... were merely careless and moronic... seem at worst to have given in to the prejudices and the religious fervor of their milieu. In the end, they allowed idiocy to prevail."

Zola's "letter" began with the title, *"J'accuse"* ("I accuse..."). It concluded with a rhetorical flourish, repeating those words eight times. Once they are followed by a summary description of du Paty as diabolical; a second time, followed by a summary reference to General Mercier as complicit; a third time, they are followed by a summary accusation of General Billot's deliberate withholding of the evidential proof of Dreyfus' innocence; a fourth by the names of Generals de Boisdeffre and Gonse as complicit; a fifth by the names of General de Pellieux and Major Ravary as villainous inquisitors; a sixth by the names of "the three handwriting experts, Messrs. Belhomme, Varinard and Couard, [whom he accused] of submitting reports that were deceitful and fraudulent;" a seventh, by the War Office in its use of the press "to conduct an abominable campaign to mislead the general public and cover up their own wrongdoing." And "[f]inally, I accuse the first court-martial of violating the law by convicting the accused on the basis of a document that was kept secret, and I accuse the second court-martial [Esterhazy's court-martial] of covering up this illegality... [and] knowingly acquitting a guilty man."[153]

By the summer, one of Esterhazy's relatives, apparently one of many whom he had swindled, asserted that the "secret" evidence against Dreyfus was fraudulent. The new army Chief of Staff, General Cavaignac—neither pro-Dreyfus nor by any means philosemitic, but honest—felt obliged to investigate. Henry was asked to produce the Dreyfus dossier and it took very little time to recognize the forged nature of all that Henry had produced. Henry was thrown into prison, where that very night he drank two bottles of rum and slit his own throat. His suicide was a further explosion within the French political-religious world. The royalists organized a "Henry Memorial Fund" to be used in the coming battle against the pro-Dreyfusards, the republican left, the Jews and their allies.

It took until June, 1899, however, for the 1894 verdict to be struck down and a re-trial ordered. Meanwhile Dreyfus had been rotting for five years in the island prison, completely unaware of the furor that had been billowing back in France over his case during that intervening half-decade. He was suddenly ordered to dress and board a ship for France, brought to Rennes, where he was told to prepare for a re-trial. A gaunt, bent, bald and very old man—all of 39 years old—entered the courtroom in Rennes, where the proceedings were mostly conducted in the public eye, rather than in secret as the first court-martial proceedings had been.

By then the Dreyfus dossier, which had been barely a dozen documents thick five years earlier, having been well-nourished in the intervening years, had fattened to a file of over 400 documents. But many of these were shown to the judges only *after* the courtroom proceedings had been concluded, as they began their close-door deliberations—in other words without permitting Dreyfus or his counsel to see them. Meanwhile the anti-Semitic outcries of five years earlier repeated themselves beyond the courtroom—including the warning that the Jews faced "mass extermination." The evidence of Dreyfus' innocence—from information regarding Esterhazy to evidence regarding Henry's forgeries—would have seemed irrefutable in an atmosphere of reason, objectivity and an interest in justice. But in a stunning verdict, the tribunal found him guilty by a vote of five to two of the crime of high treason for unspecified *"extenuating circumstances"* (my italics).

At this point the government itself intervened; headed by the liberal new President of the Republic, Emile Loubet, who offered Dreyfus a pardon. He accepted it on condition that he be free to prove his innocence. This took him seven further years to accomplish: only in July, 1906 did the Appeals Court annul the 1899 Rennes verdict and pronounce Dreyfus innocent. From a strictly legal stand-point this might be argued to have been "wrong" —only a military tribunal should have had the authority to overturn the results of a military court-martial. But from the point of view of justice—and given the unwillingness of the Army to change previous verdicts, as a point of "honor"—it was an appropriate outcome in every respect.

And it came in the wake of an explosive response from the liberal press to the re-trial of 1899 and a long campaign not only to support the verdict of Dreyfus' innocence but to more effectively silence the anti-Dreyfusard right and its clerical and royalist allies. A radical parliament was able, in the course of that time, to effect a permanent separation between Church and State. Dreyfus himself was honored, as if to cement his role in forcing the political show-down that brought the liberals to the fore, and to underscore the reality of France as a liberal philosemitic—or at least not anti-Semitic state—by being made a chevalier of the French Legion of Honor, on July 20. A week earlier he had been promoted to Major—and on the same day, July 12, Picquart, having been re-embraced by the army, was made a General.[154]

But the repercussions of the *Affaire Dreyfus* may be said to have echoed from the time of his first trial to our own time. Among those who covered the court-martial of 1894 and its surrounding events as a journalist was the Viennese Jew, Theodore Herzl. Having grown up in a comfortably assimilated family in a world in which Jews were significantly interwoven with the *fin-de-siecle* cultural and socio-economic Viennese world, Herzl had been shocked when the 1888 rally to mark the fifth anniversary of the death of the composer (and virulent anti-Semite), Richard Wagner, co-sponsored by the fencing fraternity of which he was a member, degenerated into a barrage of anti-Semitic vituperation in which several fellow-members of the fraternity were vocal. His sense of how insoluble a problem anti-Semitism is was galvanized.

The notion of anti-Semitism as a disease without a cure had first been articulated a decade earlier by the Eastern European Jewish physician and essayist, Judah Leib Pinsker. It was a notion for which Herzl had not had much sympathy as a child of an Emancipated Western Jewish community. If, like the Tiszaeszlar blood libel, the anti-Semitism of the Viennese could still, perhaps, be ascribed to a fundamental non-Western backwardness, surely such sentiments would not be found still lurking in the real West. So Herzl was one of the array of shocked foreign journalists who, sent to cover the Dreyfus trial in France—he was reporting for the Viennese *Neue Freie Presse*—instead found themselves shocked by the *Affaire* that dwarfed the judicial proceedings.

In short, one of the consequences of that shock was that, in the following year, Herzl sat down and in a white heat produced the pamphlet *Die Judenstaat (The Jewish State)* that analyzed why anti-Semitism would not and could not disappear as long as Jews were not the political masters of their own state, and why it could and would dissipate if they *were* able to accomplish that. The extended period of the *Affaire Dreyfus* runs on a parallel chronological track with the gestation period of the Zionist idea from Herzlean abstraction to the concretion not only of a series of international conferences but to the debate regarding what the intentions of that idea should be.

If Herzl's ambition as a political Zionist, worried about Jewish physical survival itself, was to create an independent Jewish polity—virtually anywhere—the goal of the spiritual Zionists was to create something with sufficient autonomy to be able to be genuinely Jewish. For that goal, only Eretz Yisrael would do as a location—which was under Ottoman Turkish control, so that meant negotiating for less than full political autonomy. Among the answers to the Zionist question—a kind of subset to the answer provided by spiritual Zionism—was the importance and self-conscious effort to create Jewish culture symbolized by the opening of the Bezalel arts school in Jerusalem in 1906—the year of Dreyfus' exoneration.[155]

V. The Blood Libel Still Lives: Romanov Russia and Mendel Beiliss

Meanwhile, the world east of the world from which Herzl had come, but to which he ultimately directed most of his energy and from which he hoped to gain the necessary numbers of participants in his Zionist idea to really countenance what he envisioned—that world to the east was moving toward its own crisis, in which Jews would be repeatedly caught in a cross-fire, at the same time that the world at large was moving toward the crisis of the Great War.

Tsarist Russia had, we recall, experienced a swelling of its Jewish population in large part due to the three partitions of Poland, in the late eighteenth century. In broad terms, the empire was experiencing significant changes in the course of the late nineteenth century. By 1861 Tsar Alexander II had issued an emancipation edict that undercut the centuries' long feudal system and enabled the serfs to move about in a way—as independent communal proprietors, not tied by law to the landlords—that had been impossible theretofore. Russia finally caught up, in this regard, to where most of Europe, and certainly the major powers, had arrived generations earlier. During the same period, the students at the St Petersburg Arts Academy rebelled and a movement to go out and find subjects across the countryside and among the people emerged—with a cognate goal of bringing art and culture to the people.

The shift in mood that these events bespoke, an attempt to emulate the shift in mood in the West that had been in process for a century, did not significantly affect the Jews, however, who remained largely still confined by the Pale of Settlement and its concomitant restrictions. The relatively liberal openness to which Russia became subject in the next two decades[156] would in fact boomerang, both against the Russian people as a whole and against the Jews, one might say. This came in the aftermath of the assassination of Alexander II in 1881 by a group whom some view as anarchists but others as revolutionaries dissatisfied with the slow, if steady, pace of liberalization to which Alexander II had acceded by that time. Where Russia in general was concerned, Alexander's son and successor, Alexander III, tore up his father's plans for a parliament—a *duma*—which would not come into being until 1905, under Nicholas II. Moreover, police brutality in the form of the *Okhrana* (Secret Police) and the suppression of civil liberties were restored at a fever pitch.

Where the Jews were concerned, a wave of pogroms swept

across much of Russia, in part in anger because one of those implicated in the assassination conspiracy, Gesya Gelfman, was "of
Jewish origin." While her role as a member of the revolutionary
group was exaggerated, it offered sufficient justification for blaming the assassination on "the Jews"—and thus for the pogroms that
followed. On the other hand, the government not only made little
effort to suppress the pogroms, but in fact, over the next 25 years
often orchestrated them at junctures when anti-government fervor
bubbled intensely toward the surface. Redirecting the animosity of
the Russian people—who had been nurtured for so long on anti-
Jewish ideology by both church and state—toward the Jews and
away from the repressive government became a survival tactic for
that government until it finally collapsed through a tight concatenation of events ugly enough to bring it to a fatal end in the Revolution
of 1917.

That concatenation of ugly events included the notorious
Kishinev pogroms of 1903 that were so stunningly orchestrated by
the government of Tsar Nicholas II—in the same year that the text of
The Protocols of the Elders of Zion was first published in St. Petersburg
in the Russian newspaper, *Znamya* ("Banner"). The *Protocols* claim
to be a secret Jewish plan for world domination, in which the Free-
masons will function as agents for the plan articulated by a cabal
of Jewish elders. The marvelously contrived text, purporting to reveal what in effect would be the minutes from a secret international
meeting of those elders—the twenty-four protocols are essentially
a series of instructions to a new member of the group regarding
the different areas that they will come to control and how—echo
in tone the sort of Jewish conspiracy assertions dating back to the
twelfth century and the canard regarding the annual use of Christian blood articulated in conjunction with the murder of William of
Norwich.[157] The surging popularity of the *Protocols* accelerated, particularly among the anti-liberal forces within the Empire, especially
after the second edition of 1905 that coincided with the disastrous
military encounter with Japan that year and also with the creation
of a constitution and a *Duma* (parliament).

The concatenation of anti-Jewish issues marking the late

decades of Tsarist history included the conviction by Nicholas II and the reactionary groups that supported his autocracy, that the revolution of 1905 that failed to overturn his throne was part of a Jewish plot. It included further violence the following year against Jewish populations, in the context of the disastrous war with Japan, for which the Jews were also understood to have been responsible, having presumably followed the prescriptions of the *Protocols*. The level of that violence dwarfed the violence in Kishinev of three years earlier. That same year (1906) was marked by the publication of an Imperial Edition of *The Protocols*, a copy of which Nicholas owned (his library contained a volume in the Imperial Edition) and must surely have read.[158]

But what we might call the high-water mark (which is to say, the nadir) of the anti-Jewish events so endemic to Romanov Russia under its last Tsars, the most stunning of the links in this ugly chain, and perhaps the most interesting of Blood Libels in European history—in that it was ultimately government-ordained and even -sponsored—was the case of Mendel Beiliss. In fact, one might argue that one of the differences between the Beiliss case and the Dreyfus Affair that had ended only a few years earlier, is that, for all of its inherent anti-Semitism, the French army cabal that framed, tried and condemned Dreyfus, in conducting the entire proceedings in private did not presumably intend to create an anti-Semitic furor across France—it was Drumont and his followers who shaped that furor. Whereas it was precisely the Russian government's goal to inflame the Russian people against the Jews in order once again to direct their anger and anxiety away from the government's failings (including that of the army, the disaster of which against Japan in 1904-5 is so very reminiscent of France's disaster vis-a-vis Prussia in 1870-71).

The most extraordinary aspect of the Beiliss case, that puts it into its own category, is its synthesis of the modernist anti-Semitic ideology of which Drumont was such an expositor and the medieval demonology of the Jews as cannibalistic in their anti-Christian activities—which particular demonological perspective had been abandoned in most of Europe by the twentieth century. And perhaps, what was new and therefore extraordinary was the success of Jews outside Russia in gaining support from the international non-Jewish community that turned what might have remained fairly local as an event into a shot heard around the world with effects on the (short-lived) future of the Tsarist regime and also on the configuration of anti-Semitism and philo-Semitism in the century to follow.

The Beiliss case played out from the Russian courtroom to the streets of Russia to the journalistic world stage between 1911 and 1913—ending on the eve of World War I and the eve of the final act in the pre-Revolution drama that would extirpate the Romanov dynasty. The case began with the disappearance of a 13-year-old boy, Andrei (Andryusha) Yushchinsky on March 11, 1911 from Slobodka, a suburb of the Ukrainian city of Kiev. He never arrived at school on that cold morning, apparently and uncharacteristically playing hooky to visit his friend, Zhenya Cheberyak. Andryusha's body was found out in the woods 8 days later—more precisely, in one of the Lukyanovka caves, about midway between Zhenya's home and the brickworks where the Jew Mendel Beiliss worked and lived with his family. The body was pocked with 47 stab wounds, the few clothes still on him were caked with blood, as were his school cap and jacket found nearby. In one of the jacket pockets was a rag—part of a pillowcase—also blood-stained and, subsequent analysis showed, with traces of semen on it. Andryusha's school notebooks (with his name written on them) identified him as the victim; his textbooks and other clothing were never found.

The body was removed to the morgue and was subject to two autopsies, one on March 22 and the second four days later (by which time the body had decayed considerably). Word spread of his murder, and by the time of the funeral on March 27, mimeographed pamphlets had been printed up and were being distributed by one Nikolai Pavlovich, a member of the Union of the Russian People and of the Double-Headed Eagle,[159] asserting that Andryusha had been killed by the Jews and his blood used for making Passover *matzah*: "The Yids have tortured Andryusha Yushchinsky to death! Every year, before their Passover, they torture to death several dozens of Christian children in order to get their blood to mix with their *matzahs*. They do this in commemoration of our savior, whom they tortured to death on the cross... Russians! If your children are dear to you, beat up the Yids!..."[160]

Since this sort of outcry was all too familiar from right-wing groups, the Jewish community did not panic, and, even given the gruesomeness of the crime and the fact that the accusation was further circulated in the anti-Semitic newspaper, *Russkoye Znamaye*, on April 17, no pogroms were forthcoming—the "pogrom policy" of the Tsarist administration seemed to have spent itself after 1906, the culminating year of the last and bloodiest phase of the policy, which disgusted not only the outside world but even many home-born anti-Semites—so that one might have imagined that the association of the murder with the Jews would pass. In fact, Nikolai Pavlovich was arrested for disorderly conduct, and the offices of the Double-Headed Eagle in Kiev were raided by the police.

The lack of pogrom activity in Kiev might be explained, in part, too, by the fact that the Tsar visited the city that year to dedicate a statue to his assassinated grandfather, Alexander II—and thus would-be pogromists wanted a calm ambience for the imperial visit. On the other hand, that there were no pogroms immediately *following* the visit is all the more extraordinary, given that the Prime Minister Pyotr Stolypin—who, as interior minister in the previous few years "devised one cruel anti-Jewish measure after another"[161]—was assassinated just a few feet from Nicholas by a Jewish anarchist named Dimitry Bogrov. But things were merely picking up pace. A 19-year-old student at Kiev University, Vladimir Golubev—a colleague of Pavlovich in both right-wing organizations mentioned above, and also a protege of the Duma deputy (i.e., member of parliament) Zamyslovsky, a notorious demagogue and anti-Semite—led a strong protest at the arrest of Pavlovich. Perhaps due to his national administrative connection through Zamyslovsky, Golubev was able to produce results: Pavlovich was released on April 15—but that, again, seemed to be the end of the Blood Libel part of the story, even with the demand by the *Russkoye Znamaye* on April 17, that the "Jewish ritual murderers of Yushchinsky" be found.

Meanwhile, the actual investigation into the murder was proceeding. Detective Mishchuk, head of the Kiev criminal secret police (as opposed to the *okhrana*, the *political* secret police) considered the apparently respectable parents of Andryusha and the far from respectable mother of Zhenya to be his prime suspects. The latter, Vera Cheberyak, had a very bad reputation; her apartment was said to be a den of thieves—and why would Andryusha have gone *there* on the only morning he had ever played hooky? Could his parents have sent him? Was it true that he had a trust fund that would revert to them in the event of his demise, as rumors suggested?

Mishchuk arrested not only Andryusha's parents, but a group of his relatives, and all of them—including Andryusha's five-months-pregnant mother—were subject to intense interrogation; none of them was even permitted to attend the funeral. But they all had legitimate alibis and the trust-fund story proved false. So Mishchuk prepared to move on, to arrest Vera Cheberyak, whose apartment, by coincidence—or not—had been raided two days before the murder. The police were looking for stolen goods, since there had been a spate of robberies in the previous month and she was known to operate as a fence. But—and this is where the straightforward investigation of the murder and the propagation of the Blood Libel begin to intersect—he was prevented from arresting her (the most he could do was bring her in briefly for questioning) by Nikolai Chaplinsky, the prosecutor of the Kiev Apellate Court, an upwardly mobile anti-Semite who saw a career opportunity in this case, were it to be spun in the right direction. Not that he was certain, yet, as to what that direction might be. Were the judicial and political powers that be in St Petersburg (the imperial capital) that had ordered Pavlovich's release ready to go all the way toward a charge of ritual murder in this case?

If so—and given, one might presume, Chaplinsky's awareness of how false such a charge would be—then, by a sort of investigator's paradox, it would be necessary to ascertain quickly who the true murderers were in order to be able to protect them from the law while a Blood Libel scapegoat was being found. That way, too, the true murderers would be in his hands, should St. Petersburg falter—and it was to be hoped that the new Minister of Justice Shcheglovitov would not falter.[162] But Mishchuk's stubborn straightforwardness stood in the way—although the interrogation of both Vera and Zhenya led nowhere at the outset of the questioning, except to a handful of what were later easily ascertained to have been lies they told regarding what they recalled from the morning of Andryusha's disappearance.[163]

Nonetheless, Mishchuk's report, which he refused not to publish, concluded that the murder had been committed by a criminal gang—in the Cheberyak apartment. He asserted that the motive for murdering the child in emulation of a ritual murder of the sort imagined in traditional Blood Libels, was to provoke a pogrom in order to take advantage of the looting opportunities that such an event would offer. It was never clear as to how Mishchuk arrived at his conclusions, beyond the reputation of Vera, and his association of the blood-clotted and semen-stained pillowcase in Andryusha's jacket pocket with her apartment, from which just such a pillowcase was missing, its embroidery pattern identical to three others in her living room.

At this point in the narrative, three elements shift into place, reminiscent of elements in the Dreyfus case that elevated it from a trial to *l'affaire*. One, that by mid- to late April, the right-wing press throughout the Russian Empire, and not only *Russkoye Znamaye*, began a vociferous campaign in favor of viewing the death of Andryusha as the result of a ritual murder committed by the Jews. "Our slobbering liberals seem not to understand what kind of species the Jews are with whom they are dealing... They are so dreadful because they are an exclusively criminal species..." asserted one editorial, in part.[164] Such sentiments were multiplied across a range of newspapers and *feuilletons*.

Two, that by the end of the month, right-wing members of the *Duma* began to engage the issue as well, asking rhetorically whether "the Minister of Justice and the Minister of the Interior [are] aware that there exists in Russia *a criminal sect of Jews* who use Christian blood in their religious ceremonies, and that members of the sect tortured to death the boy Andrei Yushchinsky in March, 1911?"[165] The italics in the last sentence are mine, to underscore the thin line between the "official" assertion referring to a *group* of Jews and the wide-spread, unofficial attitude that *all* Jews were involved in such activities.

The third issue that would complete the transformation of the legal case to a political affair was accomplished, so to speak, in several stages. First of all a Jewish perpetrator (or perpetrators) needed to be found upon whom to focus the Blood Libel spotlight, and thus to help further fan the anti-Semitic furor both within the Duma and on the streets. Otherwise, the liberal press and the liberal members of the Duma were bound to keep the situation under control until it finally died down.

And it should be noted that—unlike what emerged in France during the Dreyfus Affair—the sentiment on the street, in spite of the attempts at inflammation on the part of the right-wing press, was not nearly as hostile to Beiliss as one might suppose. And the Russian press was not by any means uniformly opposed to him— whereas nearly all the French media had viewed Dreyfus as guilty when he first came to trial and was convicted. Even confirmed anti-Semites found the Blood Accusation leveled at Beiliss difficult to be-lieve (no doubt even among the conspirators were those who, while willing to use the accusation for political purposes, found it difficult really to believe).

The movement on parallel tracks, Mishchuk's toward zeroing in on the murderers, and Golubev's growing agitation to promote a pogrom—his agitation joined by those in both the local Kiev and the national St. Petersburg administrations who were interested in promoting the Blood Libel—pushed toward the third element that was shaping this process into an affair with an international fo-cus and consequences. The two parallel tracks end up converging through the government's framing of Mishchuk as an incompetent and charging him with obstructing justice as well as with forging evidence. He was sentenced to prison for three months, but—anoth-er scandal within the larger scandal being shaped—the charges did not stick, when the one who framed Mishchuk confessed publicly that he had framed him. Nonetheless, Mishchuk, honestly driven to seek justice, however bumbling he may or may not have been, was now off the case.

This still left the double problem of finding the murderers[166] and keeping that information hushed up, while deciding upon whom, within the Jewish community, to foist the accusation of the crime. The first problem was solved by hiring ace detective Nikolai Krasovsky—popularly known as "the Sherlock Holmes of Russia." Unfortunately, the conspirators did not count on Krasovsky's integrity and professional pride. He was determined to solve the crime, but recognized the need to play along with Golubev and his allies in order not to be hampered—or to suffer Mishchuk's fate. To make a longer story shorter, as Krasovsky approached the truth—that three associates of Vera had, with her assistance, murdered Andryusha because they feared that he had informed or would inform on them for their criminal activities—he was suddenly transferred back to the rural post he had previously held; Chaplinsky pretended to ignore the evidence that had been placed before him. He now had the first part of what he needed—the real murderers—but had to figure out how to assure that the information remained privileged.

Then there was still the second problem: which Jew to accuse. That problem was apparently complicated by the fact—as evidenced in their testimony at the trial—that none of Andryusha's family members were willing to assume that his murderers were Jews, much less Jews engaged in a ritual murder. Andryusha had Jewish playmates and his grandmother didn't even object to that! The closest to anything that could be used in an incriminating direction toward the Jews was that a Jew by the name of Shneerson, who had served in the army, in the Far East, was alleged by some "witnesses" (not, however, by any of Andryusha's family members) to have promised to take him to see his real father.[167] And Shneerson apparently used to drop by at the home of Mendel Beiliss for meals from time to time.

Mendel Beiliss worked in the brickworks not far from the Cheberyak home, in the Lukyanovka neighborhood where Andryusha's family had also lived until about a year before his murder. The brickworks had been founded by a wealthy Kievan Jew named Jonah Zaitsev. He founded it so that half of its profits could be used to help support the hospital that he built for the poor in 1894, in honor of the accession to the throne of Nicholas II and his marriage to Alexandra of Hesse. In the brickyard was a clay mixer that was favored as a ride for the children in the neighborhood, from which they would be dutifully chased away by any adult on the premises if they were seen playing in or around it. This was said to have been the destination of Zhenya, Andryusha and some other kids on the morning of Andryusha's disappearance.

Beiliss himself was in his late thirties at the time, a former soldier and the father of five children. He was a dispatcher at the brickworks, where he had worked for 15 years. He was not a particularly pious Jew: he worked on the Sabbath and on all of the Jewish holidays except the New Year and the Day of Atonement. Nor was he particularly literate, Jewishly or otherwise. Yiddish was his native tongue, his Russian was poor, even after his stint in the army, and his Hebrew was pretty much limited to prayer book Hebrew. Prior to the death of Zaitsev in 1907, one of Beiliss' jobs was to oversee the two tons of *matzah*—made with wheat grown on Zaitsev's own estates—that the philanthropist distributed to family and friends just before Passover.

Beiliss was on good terms with his Christian neighbors, including the parish priest. He gained permission for the Christian funeral processions to cut through the brickyard as a shortcut to the cemetery—when the Christian brickmaker who was Zaitsev's local competitor refused to allow passage through his yard—and he had convinced the Zaitsevs to supply the bricks at less than cost when a (Christian) parochial school was being built, while the Christian brickmaker refused to budge on his price. Even during the 1905 pogroms, he and his family were untouched—they were protected as the local priest and the local leaders of the Union of Russian People themselves had assured him they would be.

Fixing on Mendel Beiliss as a fanatical ritual slayer of Christian children and user of their blood was a stretch, to say the least. Nonetheless, the lamplighter Kazimir Shakhovsky and his wife Yuliana between them provided enough of an opening in that direction for Golubev, Chaplinsky and the other conspirators. Kazimir mentioned that Beiliss and Vera Cheberyak were "very good friends," that Zhenya had told him that "a man with a black beard [Beiliss had a short black beard] had chased the [kids] away from the kiln at Zaitsev's" brickyard the Saturday before the murder, that "on the day of the murder the factory was empty and no workmen were there."

His wife added in her deposition that Kazimir "had told her that he had seen Beiliss carrying or dragging Andryusha away toward the kilns." None of this testimony—and more—could be made to stick. (For example, there was in fact loads of work going on at the brickworks on March 12, there were plenty of workers on the premises, and Beiliss had been busy overseeing the sending off of shipments—he had signed a good number of receipts for them on that day. Kazimir's habitual drunkenness and his Yulia's feeble-mindedness—and the fact that Kazimir hated Beiliss for catching him stealing wooden planks from the brick yard—would surely have undercut their testimony under reasonable conditions.[168] But the conditions, as we have been seeing, were far from reasonable.

Beiliss was arrested in the dead of night on July 22 by the local head of the *okhrana*, a Colonel Kuliabko, and fifteen gendarmes. The procedure was organized by Chaplinsky by invoking a legal article designed for a condition of martial law. The troops could find nothing incriminating in his modest home, but took him and his oldest son into custody. The latter was sent home two days later and Mendel was transferred to the city prison—where he sat for 26 months awaiting trial. Even at that, neither Beiliss nor any of his neighbors associated the arrest with the murder—they assumed, as the newspapers reported, that the arrest had to do with a residence issue.[169] Eleven days later, on August 3, he was charged, to his astonishment, with the murder of Andrei Yushchinsky—although no mention was made at that time of *ritual* murder.

By late September it began to become clear to certain Jewish leaders that there was a conspiracy afoot and a committee was formed to provide Beiliss with legal assistance and his family with support. The trial would not take place until 1913. Among the prosecution's star witnesses would be the lamplighter and his wife—the latter in particular offered highly incoherent and self-contradicting testimony, from which the only consistent detail was her recollection of having seen Andryusha and Zhenya playing together on the fateful and fatal morning. The battery of "witnesses" included Anna Zakharova, known popularly as Anna the Wolf-Woman, a slightly deranged, often inebriated homeless woman who slept out, during the summertime, in a place known as Wolf's Ravine (hence her nickname). Her inability to identify anyone to whom her attention was directed in the courtroom or to recall any names—including that of Andryusha, about whom all she recalled was that he was dead— was extraordinary, particularly given the deposition previously recorded by the magistrate which represented her as asserting details (such as having seen Beiliss dragging Andryusha away toward the kilns).

The prosecution's star witnesses also included a cellmate of Beiliss by the name of Kozachenko, who gained the confidence of Beiliss as someone sympathetic, who would help him as soon as he himself got out—which he did, shortly, since he had in any case been placed in that cell precisely for the purpose of gaining Beiliss' confidence, and for the consequent spin-offs of that confidence. He succeeded in his task, for Beiliss provided him with a letter of introduction to his (Beiliss') wife, suggesting how Kozachenko was to be trusted and given any assistance he required to help him help them, which made the story he then concocted regarding Beiliss' request to him that much more believable. According to his deposition, the request was to raise enough money from Beiliss' friends and associates "to pay me for poisoning two witnesses, a lamplighter, whose name he did not give me, and another one called 'Frog.' Beiliss said I could give them some vodka with strychnine..."[170]

If under the circumstances—of their supposed intimacy—the concoction might have made sense, the fact that the second supposed intended victim (the "Frog") was the very shoemaker, Nakonechny, who had stuck his neck out so boldly in Beiliss' defense meant either that Kozachenko was confused as to how properly to concoct his incriminating tale, or that the anti-Beiliss conspirators coaching him were. In any case, Kozachenko had disappeared by the time of the trial, so that he was not available for cross-examination the way others were.

If so much of the pre-trial testimony gathered by the conspirators to indict Beiliss as the murderer would prove absurd either on its own or in the context of the trial and its cross-examinations, what of the "evidence" that might support the assertion that the motive for the murder centered around the extraction of as much blood as possible for ritual and/or gastronomic use? There, too, the conspirators ran up against problems: neither of the two autopsies supported such a contention, since both referred to several different ways in which the murder was accomplished in a manner that minimized, rather than maximized the extraction of usable blood: many of the wounds were inflicted after Andryusha's death, blood accumulated in the organs that had been pierced (and was thus lost to his killers), and no instruments that might have drawn the blood out in an efficient manner had been used—hardly the evidence one would wish for if one were looking for proof that he had been murdered not only with ritual in mind, but by someone skilled in such an act, since his people had been committing that act annually for centuries.

The best the conspirators could do was to present a post-mortem analysis from the only forensic medical man willing to cooperate—the only one willing out of half a dozen they sought out. They found a Dr. Kosorotov, from St. Petersburg University, who was apparently willing to present findings either gained without ever seeing the body or long after it had deteriorated beyond anyone's ability to really understand what had happened to it in the sequence that would be required for a blood ritual.[171] Kosorotov asserted in his deposition that "the wounds were inflicted during the life of the victim...The body was left nearly bloodless... all [of which] makes one think that the wounds were inflicted with the purpose of obtaining the largest quantity of blood possible, perhaps for some special purpose."[172] The preparation of Passover *matzah*, perhaps?

The writers of the second autopsy report were pressured to

supplement it with suggestions that the wounds might have been inflicted to maximize the collection of blood. (The publication of their report was delayed for several weeks, presumably while this pressure was being applied). But the original conclusions of both autopsies, that contradicted this, could not be made to disappear. Nonetheless, while Mendel Beiliss was rotting in prison, by early 1912 the "medical" opinions collected by the administration conspirators, emphasizing the idea of ritual murder, were made public—and the Western press was becoming increasingly interested: the case was becoming an affair, a sequel to the Dreyfus story.

The conspirators also obtained a *psychological* analysis from an emeritus psychiatrist from the faculty of the University of Kiev, a renowned anti-Semite, I. A. Sikorsky. He spoke of "[t]he psychological basis of this type of murder... [as] 'the racial revenge and vendetta of the Sons of Jacob' directed against the persons of another race... [and] the fact of choosing young victims and also the letting out of their blood, according to Professor Sikorsky, [as the prosecution reported on his report] are the result of other considerations which perhaps have to the murderers the significance of a religious act."[173]

As the shaping of the case came to light, and then reached its final articulation during the trial, the international media and the responses of Western scientists was mockery—"Professor Sikorsky [reports] in a fashion which makes it difficult for one not to become satirical," commented one scientist—voices of protest and concern were also raised within Russia. Thus, for example, the Kharkov Medical Society passed a resolution stating that it is "shameful and degrading to the high standards of a physician to display racial and religious intolerance and to attempt to base the possibility of 'ritual murders' on pseudo-scientific arguments."[174] Even as early as December, 1911, nearly two years before the trial actually took place, a manifesto signed by 150 Russian notables, including 64 members of the *Duma*, railed against "[t]he false story of the use of Christian blood by Jews [that] has been broadcast once more among the people. This is a familiar device of ancient fanaticism..."

The case for the prosecution was so full of holes and absurdities that the trial in fact kept being delayed, which is why Beiliss was stuck in prison for over two years, awaiting his day—his six weeks, to be more precise, in the summer of 1913—in court. By that time, scores of intellectuals from Germany, England, the United States— even France, in its post-Dreyfus condition, yet allied with Russia and therefore concerned not to stir up trouble for her ally—were signatories to protests that there was even going to be a trial. And within Russia and even Kiev itself, collections were being taken up by working people to help Beiliss' family as well as to help cover his legal expenses—much of this from his neighbors, all of whom were non-Jews, who affectionately referred to "our Mendel" when queried about him.[175]

Even V.V. Shulgin, editor of a well-known conservative and an- ti-Semitic Kiev newspaper, *The Kievlyanin*, editorialized that the trial was a sham. He asserted that "one cannot help but feel ashamed for the Department of the Prosecution of the Kiev Court and for Rus- sian justice overall, which have dared to appear before the world with such paltry machinery."[176] Shulgin and other traditional anti- Semites expressed disgust both at the case and at the attempts to turn it into a motivator for pogroms, seeing the entire affair as a pathetic reflection on Mother Russia and its leadership. One of the Rightist leaders in the *Duma*, Purishkevich, asserted that "I cannot permit Russia to become another France through the Beiliss trial, that Russia share the fate of France during the Dreyfus period..."

No religious figure or Russian theologian of any note was willing to cooperate with the administration conspirators. But that didn't mean that someone not of note might not be willing to co- operate. Father Justin Pranaitis, who back in 1892 or 1893, when he lived in St Petersburg, had authored a pamphlet, *The Christians in the Jewish Talmud*, or, as it became better known in English, *The Tal- mud Unmasked: The Secrets of the Teachings of the Rabbis Concerning Christians*, in which he sought to prove that ritual murder is both practiced and advocated by Jewish leaders, was brought in from his home in Tashkent to testify as the administration's expert on the Jewish religion. He was regarded by his anti-Semitic supporters as an expert on both the Talmud and the Hebrew language.

The absurdity of this conviction became apparent when Pranaitis was cross-examined in the courtroom. A request for definitions of key talmudic terms elicited a consistent response: "I don't know." Thus terms such as *hullin*, ("ordinary produce" as opposed to "sanctified produce"); *eruvin*, (domains established by traditional Jewish communities within which items may be carried on the Sabbath without that act being construed as "work" and thus of abrogating the Sabbath); *yevamot* (childless widows as defined in the context of the discussion of Levirite marriages)—are all names of talmudic tractates of which, when queried, he clearly possessed absolutely no knowledge. My personal favorite was his "I don't know" response to the query, "when did *Baba Bathra* live and what was her activity?" The question plays on the Russian word, *"Baba,"* meaning "grandmother"—but in Aramaic it means "gate" and *"Baba Bathra"* is the name of a talmudic tractate of that name which means "the Final Gate." It is also one of the most basic tractates, one that that virtually every beginning student learns. So much for Pranaitis' talmudic "expertise."

Beiliss was defended by a team of five lawyers—one Jew and four non-Jews. He himself was hardly even mentioned until the 29th day of the 36-day long trial, so focused was the prosecution on the matter of proving that a ritual murder had been committed and by Jews. Whether or not it was Beiliss was ultimately, of course, irrelevant to them, although in the end a necessary element in their case if the case were to have any hope of success. Far more time was spent trying to exonerate Cheberyak and her three associates—who became popularly known as the *"troika"*—who were believed by everyone honestly connected to the case and interested in justice and not pogrom-incitement to have murdered Andryusha. What had also become clear for the unprejudiced and clear-headed was their motive for murder: in the heat of an argument at his friend Zhenya's house Andryusha had yelled that he would tell what he had seen transpiring in that household. From the legalistic standpoint, it is strange, to say the least: Beiliss is nominally on trial but the prosecution divides most of its time between trying to prove that a ritual murder took place and denying that the murder was committed by a group of individuals not on trial!

The summations began on October 23. The prosecution asserted that there were three possible answers to the question of who killed Andryusha: members of his family, Cheberyak and the troika or Beiliss. Since no suspicion rested any longer on the boy's family, that left the second and third possibilities. If Cheberyak could be proven innocent then that would leave Beiliss as guilty by default! It might be noted in passing that Cheberyak's children—Zhenya and his two little sisters—got deathly ill in the course of all the investigations and machinations, and that Zhenya and one of his sisters died. Shortly before his death, the defense reported, while his mother, the local priest and the investigating detective, Polishchuk, all hovered around him, he refused his mother's request to "tell them I had nothing to do with it." On the contrary, every time he seemed about to speak his mother leaned over and covered his mouth with a kiss—nonetheless he cried out at one point, "Don't scream, Andryusha! Don't scream!" The children were believed by most to have been poisoned, but whereas the anti-Semitic press wrote of the deaths as if the poisonings were somehow accomplished "by the Yids," the greater likelihood is that Cheberyak and/or her associates permanently closed the mouth of the little boy who seemed on the verge of offering damning testimony against them.

All of this perhaps helps to explain why the prosecution spent three times as much space discussing how "no serious evidence [was] found connecting [Chebaryak] to the crime" than they spent in trying to prove their conclusion, that it had to have been Beiliss who committed the murder. A good deal of space, however, was devoted to discussing the proofs for the existence of ritual murder as a Jewish practice. While the brief discussion of dissent—that no such practice exists—came from the two leading non-Jewish experts on Judaism, the star "scholar" offering an expert and much more extensively quoted opinion that the practice *does* exist, was Father Pranaitis. He was quoted as asserting that according to the Talmud, non-Jews are considered merely "animals in human form." Thus "...the Talmud allows and even commands the killing of non-Jews... The extermination of non-Jews is commanded as a religious act...[that] hastens the coming of the Messiah."[177] The uniqueness of

Pranaitis' testimony, one might say, was a perfect complement to the uniqueness of Kosorotov's medical testimony—purchased for 4000 rubles—which stood alone among the analyses offered by medical experts in interpreting the details of the autopsy to fulfill the conditions that could be construed as necessary for a ritual murder.

The prosecution's rambling document so affronted the sense of reason and justice of the president and secretary of the Board of Judges who needed to approve it before it could come before the court, that they resigned from the Board rather than sign the indictment when they were over-ruled by their colleagues. So the document came before the court, the witnesses came before the court, the testimony of which I have offered only a tip-of-the-iceberg summary came before the court, in all of its absurdity. The prosecution's team railed against the Jews in general as part of their incoherent but emotional accusation against Beiliss. The caricature of a trial was played out on the dual stage of the courtroom and the world press.

All along, in fact, as the farce built within the courtroom over a five-week period, the world press reacted for the most part by condemning what was an obvious conspiracy—from England's *Manchester Guardian* to Prussia's *Frankfurter Zeitung* to the *Neue Freie Presse* of Vienna (for which Theodore Herzl had been reporting on the Dreyfus Affair nearly two decades earlier) to the *New York Times*. But not the entire world press responded that way. Fascinatingly, all things considered, the loudest voices supporting the Blood Accusation came from France, out of the still-extant royalist and conservative press such as Drumont's *La Libre Parole*—still, one might suppose, searching for a Dreyfus who could be found genuinely guilty of treason against the human race. There were also publications, such as the *Yorkshire Post* that seemed neutral on what would have been a fabulous comic drama enacted in the courtroom, had it not been so nefarious and also so pathetic as a symbol of Tsarist Russia in the early twentieth century and the medievalist view of Jews still alive in so many corners of Europe.

In the courtroom the jury listened to the arguments and testimonies and cross-examinations with a particular sort of innocence. They had all been hand-picked by the Department of

Justice, whose leaders had sought the most uneducated peasants possible to serve, assuming that such jurors would be the most superstitious, most prejudiced and most easily intimated. It turned out that seven of the twelve were also members of the Union of the Russian People. Shcheglovitov also appointed in Judge Boldyrov someone who could be counted upon to tow the party line—and his charge to the jury was lengthy and unashamedly prejudicial. In fact, in spite of the spectacular absurdities that contoured the prosecution's case, the preliminary vote was 7 to 5 in favor of finding Beiliss guilty—and the final verdict regarding the nature of Andryusha's death, was that it had been accomplished in the "Jewish surgical hospital" adjoining the brick factory. But when the jury foreman went around for a final count regarding Beiliss' guilt, one pious peasant stood up and, crossing himself before the icon on the wall of the deliberation chamber, announced that "I don't want to have this sin weighing on my soul—he is not guilty." Others followed and Beiliss was acquitted.

The aftermath was largely one of jubilation across Russia, for Jews and non-Jews alike: "Strangers embraced on the streets with shining faces and streaming eyes; Jews and gentiles congratulated each other, proud of their country and its 'simple citizens,' gloating over the happy ending and the humiliation of the administration."[178] Astonishingly, the prosecution asserted that it had won a victory in claiming that it had proven in court that a ritual murder had taken place, even if Beiliss had not been the perpetrator. And of course, if by Beiliss' own count he received seven to eight thousand visitors daily over the weeks that followed his exoneration—and over 11,000 letters, 7,000 telegrams and 20,000 calling cards—on the other hand he also received messages from the Black Hundreds group[179] threatening death for him and his family. Enough of these led finally to his decision to emigrate—first to Palestine, in 1914, and then to the United States in 1922.

VI The Beiliss Affair's Ramifications into the Twentieth Century

The previous paragraph leads us in four observational directions.

The first is that the victory of liberal forces in Russia signified by the exoneration of Beiliss would not prove in the long run to be the dawning of a new, forward-looking era for the empire. Or rather, both where the Jews and the general population were concerned, there would be a revolution beginning in 1917 that would emphatically dismantle the Tsarist regime, and the father of that revolution, Vladimir Ilyich Lenin, seems to have envisioned a new reality in which social and economic classes, nationalities, ethnicities and religions would work side-by-side for the benefit and betterment of all. Yet in the long run this would not come to pass. Lenin would be dead by 1924 and Tsar Nicholas would appear a benign, fearless leader in comparison with Lenin's eventual successor, Joseph Stalin and the system of cold-blooded mass-murder that he put into place.

One of the most obvious events relevant to the rubric "Jewish trials" associated with the period of Stalin's rule would be the notorious "Doctors' Trials" effected by him in 1953. Minimally, as "Jewish trials" the Doctor's trials—that began shortly before Stalin's death and ended rather quickly after that sudden demise by a stroke, with not only the exoneration of all of those accused, but with an admission that the entire "plot" had been a fabrication by Stalin and his closest associates—were a function of Stalin's increasing paranoia about doctors and his desire to purge the Party leadership. Maximally, they were part of a larger, specifically anti-Semitic campaign that may be said to have begun back in 1948 shortly after the creation of the State of Israel and its pro-Western orientation as the Cold War was unfolding. This led to the elimination of the Jewish Anti-Fascist Committee and the launching of an anti-Semitic program against so-called "rootless cosmopolitans," which had as its final purpose the deportation of all two million Soviet Jews to Siberia.

The shifting from a general anti-Semitic tone to a more concerted program of persecution may be observed in Stalin's comments to the Politburo on December 1, 1952, in which he noted that "every Jewish nationalist is the agent of the American intelligence service... Among doctors there are many Jewish nationalists"[180]—thus articulating a relationship between treasonous thought and behavior, and both being Jewish and being a physician. The last in this trio of "crimes" was further specified three days later when Stalin brought up allegations that had been percolating inside his head for nearly a year, that a cabal of doctors had been decimating the ranks of Soviet leadership through false diagnoses and deliberately wrong drug prescriptions.

The official Communist Party newspaper, *Pravda*, printed an article on January 13, 1953, in which "the arrest of a group of saboteur-doctors" was reported. The article asserted that

> [t]his terrorist group uncovered some time ago by organs of state security, had as their goal shortening the lives of leaders of the Soviet Union by means of medical sabotage. Investigation established that participants in the terrorist group, exploiting their position as doctors and abusing the trust of their patients, deliberately and viciously undermined their patients' health by making incorrect diagnoses, and then killed them with bad and incorrect treatments...
>
> The majority of the participants of the terrorist group...were bought by American intelligence. They were recruited by a branch office of American intelligence—the international Jewish bourgeois-nationalist organization called "Joint."[181] The filthy face of this Zionist spy organization, covering up their vicious actions under the mask of charity, is now completely revealed...

A list of names—all but two of them Jews—was offered, including Stalin's personal physician, Miron Vovsi. Shortly thereafter 37 individuals were arrested, and subsequently several hundred were arrested. Scores of Jews were dismissed from their jobs and either transferred to the notorious Soviet Gulags or executed after swift, privately conducted trials.

Occasionally, a trial was held publicly in Moscow—a show trial—accompanied by anti-Semitic articles published in the state-run media. Jewish notables were tortured and thereby forced to offer statements of complicity in the "plot" so astutely uncovered by Comrade Stalin, or to join in the signing of a letter published in *Pravda* condemning its "perpetrators." Other, lower level "doctors' plots" began to be "uncovered" in February, in other places within the Soviet ambit, particularly after a February 9th explosion on the land of the Soviet Mission in Israel.[182] Meanwhile streams of telegrams flowed in condemning the absurd parade of show trials—reminiscent of the trial of Beiliss forty years earlier, and offering a "modern" version of the medieval Blood Libel of which the Beiliss case had been one of the last avatars—from notables around the world. But it was only after Stalin's death on March 5 that his successors admitted that he had invented the entire thing, and all the charges were officially dropped on March 31.

The consequence of the affair was an upsurge in Jewish emigration from the Soviet Union and a significant diminishment of support for the Leninist ideals still theoretically espoused by the USSR by Jews and others across the world: clearly the dream of the makers of the Russian Revolution had evolved into an unequivocal nightmare. The aftermath was a debate as to how purely the affair had been motivated by anti-Semitism—whether it was part of a larger plan, reminiscent of the various Tsarist plans from the time of Catherine the Great to that of Nicholas II, to solve the "Jewish problem" by relocation and expulsion projects, in this case by deporting all of the Jews to Siberia—or whether it had been motivated by growing Stalinist paranoia in general and/or specifically where doctors were concerned, many of whom, by coincidence, happened to be Jewish. But there is no reason not to suppose that both issues, anti-Semitism and other layers of Stalinist paranoia, met in the mind of the madman to create the debacle.

The second observational direction in assessing the consequences of the Beillis Trial, in considering it both as an event that bears comparison to the Dreyfus Affair and as a historical moment with broader implications for "Jewish trials" in the Europe of the twentieth century, is the following. Contrary to what one might suppose, the general tone across Russia, as we have seen—even among many who were known for their anti-Semitic sentiments—was both largely supportive of Beiliss from the time of his arrest to the time of his exoneration and downright jubilant in the aftermath of his acquittal. The prosecution conspirators had a very difficult time finding individuals who would testify in an incriminating way, whether under a personal or a professional aegis. By contrast, the mood in France had been much darker with regard to Dreyfus. Most of France both believed in his guilt—were eager, it seems, to believe in it—and connected his guilt and their anger over it to his Jewishness. Drumont and his followers had a much easier time ginning up anti-Semitic anti-Dreyfusardism on the streets of Paris than did the Russian right-wing press in trying to gin up anti-Semitic anti-Beilissism on the streets of Kiev and St. Petersburg, and Dreyfus' small team of supporters needed to fight a long, uphill battle to achieve even the succession of trials necessary to lead ultimately to his acquittal and exoneration.

One might say that a different stream of anti-Semitism flowed beneath the surface of Russia from that flowing beneath France, and subsequent twentieth-century events would not by any means demonstrate that the French form was or is more benign or less malignant than the Russian. By those subsequent "events"—and this is the third observational direction toward which one is pushed by the Beiliss Affair—I am referring to what began in the 1930s in Germany and Austria and spread with the Nazi-led armies across most of Europe. The Jews of these last two countries, so interwoven into the cultural, socio-economic and political tapestries that encompassed their Christian neighbors, felt comfortable in a way in which the Jews of Russia did not, in raising an outcry regarding what was happening to Beiliss. German and Austrian Jews and German and Austrian Jewish organizations were the most obvious sparks to the international conflagration of agitation on Beiliss' behalf that engulfed non-Jews and not merely Jews—which agitation helped stimulate the anti-anti-Beiliss sensibilities within Russia herself.

Interestingly, it has been argued that part of the motivation of German Jews was the opportunity that the Beiliss case offered to undercut the Franco-Russian alliance by discrediting Russia as a legitimate, modern European power.[183] This assertion underscores how emphatically *German* and *Austrian* Jews of those countries felt themselves to be—feelings that would have an overwhelmingly tragic consequence a generation later with the shaping of the Holocaust in those polities. By contrast with such communities, Jews in Russia and in particular the Jews of Kiev felt the need to be extremely careful in how and what they expressed; agitation of any sort, including that on behalf of Beiliss, had to be left to others. In recalling how the Pale still existed, how Kiev was mostly off-limits to Jews so that those dwelling in the city were there by special dispensation, we are reminded that Stolypin had managed to underline their marginality by forcing 1200 Jewish families out of the city in the spring of 1910 as part of his attempted crack-down on Jewish political dissidence. So the positive sentiments on Beiliss' behalf should not, to repeat, be mistaken for marking a comfortable condition for Russian Jews any more than it should be mistaken for marking the dawning of a new socio-political day for Russia.

Fourth—an observational issue raised by the fact that Beiliss relocated to the United States by 1922—is the issue of whether and how things might be expected to be different for Jews on the other side of the Atlantic. Our discussion to this point has swept geographically up out of the Middle East and into Europe and has carried chronologically out of antiquity and through the medieval period into modernity, where, to our dismay, we have found that anti-Jewish sentiments continue to abound, the terminology perhaps shifting, but the centuries' long fear, suspicion and animosity not apparently abated. But that, one might suppose, is a function of the inability of the Old World, like a leopard, to change its spots.

What of the New World? So many features of America in general and the United States in particular separate it and mark it as different from the worlds beyond the oceans that flank our continent. Might that difference be manifest in the matter of "Jewish trials" as well? No and yes, as we shall see in our next chapter, beginning with a Trial and a trial that were beginning as the Beiliss Trial and Affair were closing—with a much unhappier outcome than the Beiliss Affair yielded. For that matter, the Leo Frank Trial through which we shall turn to America had an unhappier ending than did any of the mid-nineteenth, late-nineteenth- and early twentieth-century cases in Central, Western and Eastern Europe and also the Middle East that we have been discussing in this chapter.

Chapter Six:
The Trials of a Brave New World

I. Jews in America

The first Jews are said to have arrived to what would one day become the United States in 1654, from Recife, Brazil. This group of 23 Jews was forced to leave Recife because, as we earlier observed, after a nine-year-long war between the Netherlands and Portugal in which the Portuguese were finally victorious, the Inquisition authority arrived into Recife in that year. These Jews were apparently former Crypto-Jews—Marannos—who, having left Portuguese territory, had been able to emerge from the closet of their Christianity as Jews once again. But now that the place of their residence was to fall under Portuguese control, they would be in danger of being tortured and executed as heretics, and so fled—back to Amsterdam, they thought (or at least that is the story in standard historiography), but found themselves dropped off, instead, by an unscrupulous French captain, in New Amsterdam. (See note #127.)

The Dutch colony of New Holland, with New Amsterdam as its capital—fated to become New York a few decades later, when it fell to the British—was governed by Pieter Stuyvesant as an agent for the Dutch West India Trading Company. Stuyvesant was not thrilled to have this group of penniless Jews dropped on his doorstep[184] and so wrote to the company Board of Directors asking permission to deport them. Unfortunately for Stuyvesant, that Board, formed in an Amsterdam that was well ahead of its time with regard to religious toleration, included seven Jews. He was commanded to extend them hospitality, and one of their leaders, Jacob Bar-Simson, together with a German Jew, Asser Levy, who arrived at around the same time, soon petitioned to be able to bear arms in defense of the colony—the petition met with success—which opened the door to citizenship rights. Before long the small Jewish community had acquired some land for a cemetery, and eventually it became substantial enough, as New Amsterdam increasingly became an immigrant destination, for a synagogue to rise within the expanding polity.

The—primarily Sephardic—Jewish community evolving in the New World peppered the eastern seaboard from Charlotte to Newport. By the time of the American Revolution perhaps as many as 7,000 Jews resided in what were in the process of becoming the thirteen American Colonies. Jews played a significant enough role in the War for Independence, both as soldiers and as supporters of Washington and his oft-beleaguered army. In the aftermath of independence and the putting into place of a brand-new government, Jewish communities, like others throughout the nascent republic, sent congratulatory messages to the new president, George Washington.

Just prior to the Revolution, arguably the most prominent Jewish community had been that of Newport, Rhode Island. Although like the city itself, the community had been devastated by the British during the War, its reputation as prominent and its place within the most pluralistic and religiously open-minded of the original colonies, were what perhaps led President Washington to visit the community and speak from the pulpit of its synagogue in 1790. Moses Seixas, sexton of the synagogue, had written the congratulatory note to the new president from which Washington quoted in his address to the congregation when he visited Newport, observing that ours is "a government which, happily, gives to bigotry no sanction; to persecution no assistance." That phrase was the first statement of such a principle enunciated by a leader of the new American government, for which mere toleration is presented as insufficient, "as if it were to be conferred by one class of people on another," as opposed to all being equal by law.[185]

Such a sensibility may be seen to mark a departure from the various European "emancipations" of the Jews taking place during the era of American independence. From England (tentatively) in 1753 to Prussia in 1812 those edicts implied the decision of various secularized Christian governments graciously to *allow* Jews a range of rights which approached but did not necessarily arrive at full citizenship rights. By contrast, Washington's statement made it clear that minorities, including Jews, were to be defined quite matter-of-factly as American citizens; they need only "demean themselves as good citizens, in giving it [the U.S. government] on all occasions their effectual support."

The declaration of such a principle could not have found a more appropriate venue for its articulation than in Newport, Rhode Island. Roger Williams, the colony's founder, had fled Puritan Massachusetts and its intolerance to those of other faiths. The laws that shaped Rhode Island were to be different, in recognizing that intolerance obstructed both civil peace and the search for truth. The colony's laws, already back in 1647, had pledged that in Rhode Island, "all men may walk as their consciences persuade them, everyone in the name of God."

The news of such open-mindedness, as it reverberated back toward Europe, encouraged Sephardic Jews to immigrate to Rhode Island. The first Jews seem to have settled there by 1658, only a few years after others had arrived to New Amsterdam. By the time of the American Revolution the bustling community, bolstered by the arrival of Ashkenazi Jews from Central and Eastern Europe, had dedicated a synagogue designed by the pre-eminent colonial architect, Peter Harrison, its dedication attended by Jewish and non-Jewish notables alike. The synagogue became a site for meetings of the General Assembly as well as sessions of the Court of Rhode Island during the early 1780s.

By the time of Washington's visit, the community of Newport was in decline, never really having recovered from damage it suffered during the Revolution, so his choice to visit the synagogue there reflected its past and symbolic role, rather than its current stature. Washington was a Deist, who believed that God's existence can be argued along purely rationalist lines—without recourse to some human authority or absolutist revelation mediated by various interpreters. Deism had become increasingly popular in the late 17th century and through the 18th century. As an adherent to this form of faith, Washington would have been drawn to the non-denominational notion suggested by Seixas' words, which the new president quoted in his letter to the congregation.

The small Jewish population grew and prospered as the American republic prospered and expanded—prosperity and expansion in part a result of the sweat of those not yet recognized as citizens, and therefore untouched by Washington's noble words: slaves imported from Africa; or through dispossessing others of the lands that they had inhabited for centuries, if not millennia, who were also not recognized as citizens: Native Americans. By the middle of the nineteenth century American Jewry had expanded to more than 50,000, demographically dominated by individuals who had emigrated from Central Europe—from places where the short-circuited Emancipation laws still imposed strong limits on what Jews could be and do. As active as Jews had been as participants during the American Revolution, they were involved—on both sides of the fence—in the war between the southern and northern states that had as part of its result the theoretical enfranchisement of African Americans as citizens.[186]

As with the general patterns of emigration from Europe to the United States, Jews who arrived most often as individuals, in the tens of thousands, from Central Europe in the mid-nineteenth century, were succeeded by the waves of those arriving from Eastern Europe, most often as families, by the hundreds of thousands and millions, in the last part of that century and the beginning of the next. In fact, the upsurge in Jewish immigration may be marked fairly specifically from the time of the pogroms in Tsarist Russia that followed the assassination of Alexander II in 1881.

In the sweep of Jewish immigration, from the "Sephardic period" of the mid-seventeenth to late eighteenth century through the "Central European Ashkenazi period" of the late eighteenth to late nineteenth century to the massive "Eastern European Ashkenazi period" of the late-nineteenth through early twentieth century, we may observe variations on an obvious theme. Nearly all of these groups were seeking what America seemed to offer: an opportunity to be an enfranchised citizen of the ever-expanding republic where they, like all of their neighbors, would be measured not by their religious affiliation but by their willingness to contribute socially, economically, culturally and politically.

The question was, as the waves of Eastern Europeans—and by no means Jews alone—flooded these shores, would America be able to live up to the promises that had first been articulated in documents like Roger Williams' Legal Code for Rhode Island, George Washington's letter to the Jewish community of Newport and the Declaration of American Independence, together with its sister document, the Constitution? Certainly in some key respects the promise seemed to be upheld, like the torch in Manhattan harbor, held aloft by the Statue of Liberty that dominated the harbor from the mid-1880s onward.

There have also been key times and places where the torch seemed to become darkened by mists of prejudice and bigotry. Where Jews in particular were concerned, voting as a measure of having arrived as a citizen with a voice in the workings of the government, while available at the federal level from the birth of the American Republic, was not available in every state for some time thereafter: The debate that began in 1818 lasted for eight years until Maryland's 1826 "Jew bill" rendered it possible for a non-Christian to run for political office there. In New Hampshire, a condition of political equality for Jews did not arrive until 1877.

It was only four years later that the enormous upsurge in immigration began. The volume of new arrivals from parts of Europe regarded as backwards within Europe itself coincided with the coming into their own of the central European Jews who had arrived a generation earlier. Thus on social, economic as well as cultural fronts the preserves of the Anglo-Saxon elites of previous generations were assaulted both from within America by Jews already here and from the outside by the sheer numbers of Jews arriving from the most benighted parts of the Old World. The growing resentment could be felt in exclusionary patterns in hotels, resorts and neighborhoods.[187]

The surge in immigration from the 1880s led many of those in the general population—who had forgotten how their own grandparents or great-grandparents had been immigrants, and often refugees, seeking opportunities and liberties not available in Europe (or simply in flight from persecution)—to seek ways in which to limit the numbers of new arrivals who had not been part of the earlier patterns of immigrant flow. The process of "scientifically" categorizing potential immigrants with regard to their viability as Americans, and developing "fair" quotas—based on a system of tying acceptance of would-be immigrants to the numbers of residents who had already arrived some decades before from a given place—reached a culmination point by 1921.

On May 19 of that year, the Emergency Quota Act—also known as the Johnson Quota Act—was passed by the U.S. Congress. The act limited the annual number of immigrants who could be admitted from any country to 3% of the number of persons from that country who, according to the U.S. Census figures of 1910, were living in the United States in that year. Given the overall population, this meant a total of 357,802 immigrants would be allowed in—just over half from Northern and Western Europe, and the remainder from Eastern and Southern Europe and elsewhere. In practical terms this meant a 75% reduction (over the previous year) in the number who could enter the United States as immigrants from Eastern and Southern Europe.[188]

While the Act, passed without record in the House of Representatives and by a vote of 78-1 in the Senate, was allegedly intended to be temporary, it turned out not to be. On the contrary: three years later, the 1924 Johnson-Reed Immigration Act reduced the quota from 3% to 2%—and based the percentage not on the 1910 census but on the 1890 census, thus further disadvantaging would-be immigrants from the "wrong" places.[189] As Representative Albert W. Johnson (from Washington state) whose name is attached to both Acts, expressed it: "...a nation great in all things, ... the United States is *our* land. If it was *not* the land of our *fathers*, at least it may be, and it should be, the land of our *children*. We intend to maintain it so. The day of unalloyed welcome to all people, the day of indiscriminate acceptance of all races, has definitely ended" (italics added).

This spectacular statement of hypocrisy and bigotry arrived at a time when the United States was midway between a sense of obligation to engage the world in a dominating manner and a desire to flee the world so fraught with centuries of ethnic, religious and national strife. It reflected that uniquely American brand of blindness to the realities of sociology, anthropology and history—even the sociology, anthropology and short history of the United States itself. The virtual slamming shut of the portal by which Lady Liberty awaits, her torch ever lit, would not only have obvious and horrific consequences within a decade of Johnson's statement—when so many were trapped in Hitler's inferno with no place to which to escape—but its effects are still felt to this day.

There is a double irony here. Where Jews were the object of prejudice in the early twentieth century, it was based less on traditional Old-World stereotypes than on the New-World stereotypes regarding all kinds of denizens of the Old World, be they Italian Catholic, Greek Orthodox, Polish Catholic, Russian Orthodox, or Russian or Ukrainian Jewish. Second, American Jews who had arrived in the previous wave of immigration were at this time initially as guilty of these prejudices, regarding their co-religionists, as other Americans were regarding all of those who came from Southern and Eastern European countries. The difference is that, having accepted the fact that millions of Eastern European Jews would be entering the country, the largely German and Austro-Hungarian Jews who were already well established in America soon launched an ambitious array of educational and cultural programs intended to Americanize the newcomers, rather than simply leaving them to find their own way.

We might recall our earlier discussion of the Sephardic rabbinate in Amsterdam and its handling of Uriel Acosta and, more famously, Baruch Spinoza (see above, 131-46). On the one hand, the Sephardic rabbis seem very clearly to have absorbed the mentality and even some (but by no means all!) of the methodology of the Inquisitional authorities operative in the countries from which they or their parents or grand-parents had fled. On the other, this imitation of the majority mentality that is also obvious in America 250 years after Spinoza derived, in part, from the fear that Spinoza-like thinking in the one case or that too many unwashed, backward immigrant Jews on the other, would upset the comfortable but potentially tenuous condition of the Jewish minority within the Christian majority.

Where the matter of race, rather than ethnicity, nationality or religion was concerned, the Civil War—fought largely to determine a more precise ratio of federal to state control over the lives of American citizens—offered as an important side-effect, the freeing of all those Africans still enslaved in the southern states. If on the one hand that did not guarantee a leveling of the white-black playing field of American citizenship rights, on the other, it did yield an enduring antagonism between north and south—particularly on the part of the south toward the north—that would have a presence and repercussions until the twenty-first century.

To the extent that a late nineteenth-century southern Populist leader like Tom Watson (about whom more below) might express hostility to an individual or group along religious lines, that hostility would be mainly toward Catholics. But northerners would be a profound source of southern regionalist hostility. Those northerners involved in successful industrial enterprises that were perceived to be stripping the rural south of its personality and, (as elsewhere), to be oppressing the workers (a particularly strong gripe given the sense that the workers were forced into the factories by the destruction of their rural world), would be an equally profound source of socio-economic anger. To the extent that a Jew might be either a northerner or an industrialist he might feel the verbal wrath of a Watson, but his Judaism, per se, was less than more likely to be the central object of that wrath.[190]

In fact, for Jews living in the south, of which, since the mid-nineteenth century there was a goodly number, the issue of their own attitude toward racial prejudice and persecution offered an obvious conundrum. The Jewish tradition for which the Passover celebration was an annual reminder militates strongly against legitimizing slavery, and the Jewish experience as an oppressed people for so many centuries would and should incline Jews to oppose the dehumanizing system of slavery that still persisted in the south up to the time of the Civil War and the still-prevalent demeaning attitude toward blacks that continued long after it. On the other hand, in order to be accepted as a southerner, one could hardly speak out against its cultural and societal norms, for which first slavery and then prejudice had evolved as a natural way of being-in-the-world.

Whereas the racial attitudes expressed by the Wilhelm Marrs and Edouard Drumonts of Europe grouped Jews with Africans and Asians as inferior non-Europeans, in the American South they were by and large accepted as Whites. Even the prejudices that might be expected to play out against them along religious grounds in a corner of the New World dominated by Bible-focused Christians were mediated by intra-Christian strife—in particular the hostility toward Catholics (and the fear of "papist" conspiracies to dominate the world) on the part of various Protestant denominations.[191] Thus a delicate calm persisted in Jewish-Christian relations across the South, a tranquility few Jews would wish to disturb.

The American equivalent of Marr and Drumont, Ignatius Donnelly (1831-1901), while he shared his European counterparts' hostility to the Jews, saw their nefariousness not as a consequence of race but of historical circumstance: having survived centuries of persecution, they have become "as merciless to the Christian as the Christian had been to them."[192] Nonetheless, regardless of his sense of the cause, Donnelly's negative stereotyping of Jews was spreading at a time when circumstances such as massive immigration made Christian Americans more inclined to embrace such images. Thus Jews as lecherous and unclean, and as lusting for Gentile women, were favorite themes of his. Such themes are echoed in the writings of others in the first decades of the new century. Thus the prominent sociologist, E.A. Ross would write in 1914 of "pleasure-loving Jewish businessmen [who] pursue Gentile girls."[193]

There is a certain irony to the fact that such an obsession is—albeit much later on, in the America of the 1960s and beyond—a focus of a number of well-known works of fiction by Jewish writers in America. Thus the *shikse* goddess appears a number of times in

Philip Roth's work (notably, *Portnoy's Complaint*, 1969) and later in *Joshua, Then and Now*, the 1980 novel by the Canadian, Mordecai Richler. During the same period the most infamous appearance of this construct in film, *The Heartbreak Kid* (1972, the screenplay by Neil Simon after a story by Bruce Jay Friedman, directed by Elaine May—all of them Jewish[194]) offers the idea. But all of these fictional cases, so much later than the events before us and their contexts, share the quality of being understandable as tongue-in-cheek responses to the stereotype that had so many earlier iterations in the Christian imagination.[195]

On the other hand, as in other historical situations (such as the case of Spinoza that we have discussed previously) Jews, like other human beings, were and are just as subject to taking on the very sentiments of those around them even if those sentiments create as negative a condition for Jews as they are emulations of positive social and cultural qualities. Thus there were certainly southern Jews who embraced the same prejudices toward Africans held by their Christian neighbors—and even a handful of Jews who owned slaves when that custom was still legal. As prominent a figure as Isaac Mayer Wise, who imported Reform Judaism to America in mid-century, and whose thoughts on most subjects were decidedly liberal, justified slavery as a protective measure for an inferior race.[196]

If northern Jews were decisively anti-slavery, southern Jews were largely either silent regarding or supportive of a system that had become endemic to the South two centuries earlier, and at the end of the century, racial prejudice and non-prejudice could both be found within the American Jewish community. The massive turn by American Jews toward progressive social thinking vis-a-vis Blacks and other oppressed minorities in the United States would emerge later, after World War I, when the United States itself was re-articulating its politically prominent position in the world; and after World War II, when the Jewish community was being transformed as a more suburban phenomenon than theretofore.

All of these issues, that encircle the question of the ability of the United States to step out of history in general and in particular where the history of Christian-Jewish relations are concerned, may be said to come to rest in the case—the accusation, trial, pardon and lynching—of Leo Frank.[197]

II The Leo Frank Affair

Leo Frank arrived from the north[198]—he had majored in Mechanical Engineering at Cornell University in upstate New York, from which he graduated in 1906—to Atlanta, Georgia, where, from August, 1908, he had worked as the manager of the National Pencil Company offices and factory, as he noted in a 1914 letter to a former college-mate, John Gould.[199] He had met, fallen in love with and married Lucille Selig, daughter of a well-off Atlanta Jewish family, in November, 1910, and for the next two and a half years led a life most noteworthy for its calm satisfactions.

Mary Phagan was a 13-year-old girl who had begun working at a young age in order to help support her widowed mother and five siblings. By 1913 she was working at the Pencil factory managed by Leo Frank, and the week before her death she had found her working hours reduced due to a shortage of supplies—she was thus making $1.20 a week. On Confederate Memorial Day— Saturday, April 26 of that year—she had come to the factory in order to collect her pay envelope from Frank (who, as an assimilated Jew, was habitually at work rather than in the synagogue on Saturdays) before going to see the Memorial Day parade; that was the last time anyone outside the factory saw her alive.

For at three o'clock in the morning of April 27 the factory's night watchman, a black man named Newt Lee, called the police to tell them that he had found the body of a dead white girl. The ill-trained officers—in a unit without the rudiments of crime-scene or analysis technology, not even a fingerprint lab—found what proved to be Mary Phagan's body in a dark and dirty basement littered with pencil shavings and coal dust. The girl's body was so covered with dirt that the officers at first thought that she was black; they had to pull down one of her stockings in order to verify her race.

She had been strangled with a seven-foot length of ¾ inch cord, of which there were plenty of pieces throughout the building.

It was still around her neck; blood apparently still flowed from her genital region when the body was discovered. She had a black eye, wounds on her scalp and below the knee; soot on her face and cinders in her eye—so much soot on the exposed parts of her face and body that, to repeat, her race was not immediately apparent to the police. In any case, the sloppiness of the officers who first arrived at the scene led to the loss of important evidence, including bloody fingerprints and a trail in the dirt that would probably have indicated from where the body had been dragged and dumped where Newt Lee found it. Nonetheless, elements such as the exit route of the murderer were readily ascertainable; whoever it was had pulled out an iron staple sealing shut a wooden sliding door at the rear of the basement and opening into an alley—the length of metal pipe used to forced it open was leaning against the basement wall.

The police initially investigated a number of potential suspects—Newt Lee and George Epps, a young friend of Mary Phagan, were both arrested, but were both soon released as, after some analysis, neither seemed likely as the murderer. A blood-soaked shirt was found in Lee's apartment, but the blood turned out to be on the inside; later on the prosecution claimed that the shirt was planted by Leo Frank to incriminate the night watchman. Strangely, Frank had, when he was first interviewed, asserted that Lee's time card had been punched, as it was supposed to be, every half hour, but later claimed to have forgotten that it was missing three time punches. It was in part the retrospect of that first interview with Frank that gradually drove the police toward suspecting him: having not answered the phone at 4 AM when they first called him he seemed (to their recollection) nervous when they arrived at this home before dawn and took him to the factory.

In fact—one recalls Dreyfus' initial "interview" after being called from his home to his superior's office—they claimed that he was trembling so strongly that he could not carry out simple physical tasks. Of course they had not informed him when they arrived at his house as to the reason for their pre-dawn call, so that—as he would later assert—the shock of being confronted with the murdered body of a young girl on the factory premises after having been rousted out of bed so early could easily have yielded such a strong physical reaction and account for his physical state.

In the next few days, Mary Phagan's murder became a *cause celebre*, dominated by an intense competition among the three main local newspapers, the *Atlanta Constitution* (which broke the story), the *Atlanta Journal* and the *Atlanta Georgian* (that had recently been purchased by the Hearst newspaper syndicate and turned from a low-key newspaper into an overt instrument of yellow journalism) to promote increasingly lurid accounts of what had transpired—including the publication of a doctored morgue photo in which the image of Mary's head was spliced onto the body of someone else in one of the more than three dozen "extra editions" that appeared that day. On the one hand, evidence disappeared, having been given to reporters by the police; on the other hand, newspaper offers of rewards for information leading to the apprehension of the murderer led instead to many false leads and wasting of the time of a police department already in over its head.

Among the pieces of evidence that the police had at their disposal was a neat, relatively fresh pile of human feces at the bottom of the elevator shaft, which however was squashed after the police used the elevator, generating a putrid stench throughout the basement. The relevance of this will be pointed out shortly. Of more obvious significance were two sheets of paper, found near the body, on which a pair of notes were either written, or intended to be perceived as written, by the victim as she lay dying—in fact, while she was in the midst of being raped. The first was written on an old National Pencil Factory order blank, with "Atlanta, Ga. 190_" imprinted across the top; the second was written on plain lined paper.

The first note accused a black man of her murder: "Mam that negro hire down here did this i went to make water and he push me doun that hole a long negro black that hoo it was long sleam tall negro...". So either a tall black man had murdered Mary Phagan or an altogether different kind of murderer had ginned up the note with its grammatical and spelling errors in order to point the police in such a direction. The second note asserted that "He (presumably the one raping and murdering Mary as she wrote) said he wood love me and land doun play *night witch* (my italics) did it but that long tall black negro did buy hisself."

Suspicion fell first (once Newt Lee—tall, slim and dark-complexioned as he was—and George Epps were let go) not on any black man, tall, slim or otherwise, but on Leo Frank, the Jewish Yankee plant manager who seemed so discomfited at the time he first viewed the victim's body. Frank was arrested on April 29. He was certainly in the factory on the day on which Mary was murdered, and had presumably handed her the money that she had earned, but which was nowhere in evidence around the body when the police got to the scene. George Epps, the 15-year-old newsboy first under brief suspicion together with Newt Lee, volunteered the information that Frank had flirted with and frightened Mary: "...She told me that he had often winked at her... He would look hard and straight at her, she said, and then would smile... She told me she wanted me to come down to the factory when she got off as I could escort her home and kinda protect her."

As suspicion began to devolve more seriously on Frank, the newspapers began to compete to spin appropriate tales, ranging from fictional descriptions of the salacious decor of the factory basement to what proved to be entirely fictional claims by a private detective of having seen Frank take a girl to an isolated wooded spot in the city. Stories expanded to fit the quickly arrived at conclusion, such as the tale from the madam of the local bordello asserting that Frank, a frequent customer, had called asking for a room in which to dump Mary's body. The madam, Nina Formby, soon fled to New York from which presumably safe distance she recanted, claiming that the police had gotten her inebriated and offered her cash to make such a statement.

Frank had alibis for the entire time during which the crime had presumably been committed—but any number of Frank's actions were interpreted toward his guilt, such as his hiring of Pinkerton detectives to seek out evidence that would confirm his innocence. The Pinkerton Agency was associated with violent oppression of workers by their industrialist masters, so Frank's use of them fueled whatever latent or blatant hostility toward him already existed that derived from the combination of his Jewishness, his Yankeeness or his identity as part of the industrial upper crust. But a contemporary witness noted that "it is ridiculous to protest that there has been prejudice against the Jew in the Frank case; the whole atmosphere of the case reeks of it," as events moved forward throughout the spring and summer. That Frank at the very least offered a more satisfying answer to the question of Mary's murder than a black man did, certainly for some Georgians, is surely and succinctly expressed by the pastor of the Baptist church that Mary Phagan had attended:

> My feelings, upon the arrest of the old negro watchman, were to the effect that this one old negro would be poor atonement for the life of this innocent girl. But when on the next day, the police arrested a Jew, and a Yankee Jew at that, all of the inborn prejudice against Jews rose up in a feeling of satisfaction, that here would be a victim worthy to pay for the crime.[200]

But Newt Lee turned out not to be the only black man who might have committed the act. Another possible candidate was Jim Conley, the 29-year-old factory janitor. In fact the day watchman, E.F. Holloway claimed that he had seen Conley scrubbing a shirt on May 1, trying to get a dark red substance out of the material. Conley at first tried to hide the shirt and then asserted that the stains that he was trying to wash out were rust stains. Although the police arrested him that day, they failed to have the shirt tested for blood (much less making any effort to determine whose blood).

Conley had a record of drinking and violence, he had served a sentence on a road gang, and when he was interrogated, he lied about an important aspect of his skills: that he had a grade-school education and could read and write, albeit slowly and poorly. For after repeatedly asserting his illiteracy for more than three weeks and through his first recorded statement, on May 24 he admitted that he *could* read and write—and that he had penned the murder notes.[201] He then went on to assert that Frank had called him into the office on Friday—the day *before* the murder—and had dictated the notes to him. (So either he was implying that the murder had been premeditated, or he got confused as to what happened on which day—or wanted his interrogators to believe that he was confused—or this is simply part of how his story shifted in accordance with his perception of what would serve his survival best.) This information was not transmitted to the Fulton County grand jury, however, which a few hours later indicted Frank for the murder of Mary Phagan. Frank was the only one of the more than a dozen individuals who had been arrested, including Conley, who was indicted.

Nonetheless, by May 28 common public opinion seem to have shifted in Conley's direction, who at that point suddenly offered a third narrative: that *on the day of* the murder a very agitated Frank had summoned him to his office to write the notes at around "four minutes to one o'clock," also repeating what he had said in his previous statements about having spent most of that morning visiting various saloons and drinking beer, wine and whiskey. He adds that Frank made him hide in a wardrobe to avoid his being seen by two women who stopped briefly in the office, and that after Frank dictated the note to him and plied him with cigarettes, he suggested that Conley leave the factory. Taking Frank's advice, he claimed, he left the factory, went out drinking some more and to a movie.

The following day, Conley gave a fourth version of events, for the first time asserting that Frank had led him to a dead girl on the second floor and admitted killing her, and claiming that he helped Frank carry the dead girl's body to the elevator and transport it to the basement. Thereafter they went back up to Frank's office—he by the elevator and Frank by the ladder to the first floor and then together by the elevator to the second floor—where the notes were written and where Frank gave him a cigarette package in which he later discovered $2.50 that he spent on liquor.

One of the obvious questions that this first mention of money raises is: what happened to Mary's $1.20 in pay? Might the murderer in fact have killed her for her money? If that had been the motive then Conley makes considerably more sense than Frank as the perpetrator. If the murderer was Conley, did he simply go out and expend Mary's money on drinking or on drinking and a movie? Given the scale of salaries for both the likes of Mary Phagan and Jim Conley, his subsequent assertion, in yet another version of his story, that Frank not only had asked for and received help in moving Mary's body from his office, but paid him $200, is astonishing.

Conley didn't have a penny on him when the police interrogated him; he casually claimed that Frank had taken the money back.

Conley made other rather odd allegations of what Frank said to him, either at his pre-trial interrogations and /or at the trial itself, such as that Frank had claimed that he "was not built like other men"—presumably referring to the fact that Frank was circumcised, but a comment it is difficult to imagine Frank making to the black janitor of his factory (or to anybody, for that matter). Conley also claimed that Frank had said to him—on Friday, the day before the murder took place, when, according to Conley's second statement, the notes had been dictated to him by Frank—that there was no reason why he (Frank) would hang, since "I have wealthy people in Brooklyn." In fact, Frank had no rich relatives in Brooklyn, only an invalid father, as he noted to the jury in his own four-hour-long statement.

There are at least two other "oddities" with regard to Conley's series of statements. He admitted to having defecated at the bottom of the elevator shaft on the day of the murder. But then those feces should have been squashed when the elevator was used to bring Mary's body downstairs, as they were the day the police were on the premises investigating. As for the infamous notes, it is at the least strange that the first was imprinted with an out-of-date superscription—"190_"—and not the more current "191_" that adorned the order blanks in Frank's office. The older, functionally useless forms were stored in the basement, where Conley admitted being (at least to defecate) on the day of Mary's murder.

And aside from the spelling, grammar and syntactic patterns of the notes—which accorded well with Conley's speech patterns but which would have required an imitative genius that Frank lacked for him to have dictated them—the reference to "night witch" is a reference to a folk-superstition common to specifically Black southern circles; it is a turn of phrase which Frank as a white Northerner who evinced no particular interest in Southern folklore is not likely to have known.[202] Yet with all these peculiarities and red herrings in Jim Conley's testimony, he was never indicted, serving instead (as we shall see) as the star witness for the prosecution.

Although Conley was provided with legal counsel by the *Atlanta Georgian*—William M. Smith specialized in representing black clients in which he had had considerable success—the beginning of the legal proceedings was a May 24 murder indictment returned against Frank by a grand jury that included four Jews, and that was unaware of Conley's confessions on that very day regarding the "murder notes." The panel's term expired in July, at which time there was a good deal of agitation among the new panel's members to indict Conley, but he never was, thanks in large part to the persuasive abilities of the prosecutor.

Formally, one might be reminded of the way in which the Beiliss case moved toward the courtroom: those who had been otherwise associated with the murder (and probably committed it) were never formally charged, but ended up in court as "witnesses" as Beiliss stood trial. Conley (who, as I will suggest below, almost certainly murdered Mary Phagan) would end up as a "witness" as Frank stood trial. The key differences, however, between the two cases were the Dreyfus-trial-like hostility to Frank that had built up by the time of his trial; the success of Prosecutor Hugh Dorsey at managing to arrange repeatedly for the police to find some reason for arresting one after another of the witnesses called up by, or who made statements for, Frank's defense so that they were either discredited or, under pressure, retracted their Frank-supportive statements;[203] and the inexplicable blunders committed by Frank's defense team before, during and after the trial, but most obviously in their cross-examination of Conley.

The trial of Leo Frank began on July 28, in conditions of sufficient heat that the courtroom windows were all left open, so that the growing audience outside had a fairly decent view of the proceedings—and conversely, its mood could also be emphatically felt within the courtroom. The consistent contrast between cheers for the Prosecutor's questions and jeers for that of the defense was part of an angry, electrified atmosphere.[204] Frank's defense team was led by Luther Rosser and Reuben Arnold. Prosecutor Dorsey argued the Conley's last affidavit statement offered the true story of events: that Frank had raped and murdered Mary—in the metal room where she typically worked, about 150 feet from Frank's office—and had dictated the murder notes in order to pin the crime on Newt Lee. The defense countered that Conley was the murderer, that the evidence offered against Frank was in many cases contradictory and that Frank's alibi—attested to by a large number of witnesses—was solid, leaving him no time to have committed the crime.

In the courtroom, Conley repeated the contents of his last pretrial statement, adding to it now that Frank was typically engaged on Saturdays in having sex with various women in his upstairs office while Conley kept watch—asserting that he had observed Frank performing oral sex on women to compensate for his not being "built like other men." The more Conley spoke, the more his story changed and doubled back to contradict itself and the more statements came out sounding like lies—but the more he elaborated on perverse sexual practices on Frank's part.

One of the women whom Conley had implicated was called forth and testified that she had never had sexual relations with Frank. Interestingly, where Conley's lies and self-contradictions seem not to have swayed the court to redirect its thinking, the fact that this woman was caught up in a lie with regard to an earlier run-in with the law (having nothing to do with Leo Frank) was felt to significantly weaken the value of her testimony on Frank's behalf—and surely the elaborations permitted by Frank's lawyers as they drew Conley out hoping and expecting (and ultimately failing) to trip him up pushed the jury into an increasingly anti-Frank frame of mind.

Other women from the factory testified to Frank's upright character. Two foreladies at the factory, Corinthia Hall and Emma Clark testified to having come to the building briefly, arriving at about 11:35 and departing at around 11:45—when Mary could not have arrived earlier than 12:11, given the streetcar schedule and the minimal time it would have taken her to get from the stop where she exited and the factory building.[205] Conley had stated that he had hidden in Frank's office after the murder, and after moving the body to the basement, when these two ladies were about to come into Frank's office. In that case the murder would have had to take place—in the Metal Room, 150 feet from Frank's office—and the removal of the body to the basement would have had to be accomplished, before 11:35, or more than forty-six minutes before Mary is said by one and all to have entered the building.

There was more that contradicted the timing of events as Conley presented it. Monteen Stover, a 14-year-old employee testified that she had gone to Frank's office to pick up her own wages and, arriving at 12:05, did not find him there, waited five minutes and left by 12:10. Regardless of where Frank might have been during those five minutes—and it seems that the prosecution put Stover forth in order to demonstrate that Frank was not in his office (and therefore busy murdering Mary Phagan) at that time—he could not have been with Mary Phagan, much less murdering her, since, as just noted, she cannot have arrived at the building earlier than 12:11. She obviously could not have been to Frank's office until a few minutes later than that, and if, after receiving her pay envelope she then proceeded to the Metal Room and he followed her there, (150 feet from his office), demanded sex and was refused, and then hit her, he would have had to have murdered her somewhere at most between 12:20 and 12:45.[206]

But Mrs. Arthur White, whose husband was doing some repair work on the fourth floor that day, asserted that she saw Frank in his office at 12:30 p.m. when she passed by his office on the way up to see her husband—and that, at 1 p.m. Frank had come upstairs to the fourth floor to say that he would need to lock up as he was going home for lunch and that, unless she left at that time she would need to remain in the building until 3 p.m., when he returned. So the possible window of murderous opportunity shrinks further: let us assume that Mary left Frank's office before Mrs. White passed by and headed for the Metal Room and Frank followed her there almost immediately after Mrs. White passed by: he would have had to accost and assault Mary between about 12:33 and 12:45.

The assertion that Frank declared that he was heading to lunch at around 1 p.m.—in other words, a mere four minutes after, according to Conley, Frank had called him to the office and he and Frank had been very busy together—dovetailed with the testimony of Minola McKnight, the maid of the Seligs (the in-laws of Leo Franks) regarding Frank's arrival home for lunch that day.

There are other timing issues. Conley claimed that, when he was sitting on a box under the stairs of the first floor of the building, watching as a few people came and went, he saw "Miss Mary Perkins, that's what I called her, this lady that is dead. I don't know her name... I heard the lady scream... and the next person I saw coming in there was Miss Monteen Stover... She stayed in there a pretty good while... I heard someone from the Metal department come running back their upstairs on their tiptoes, then I heard somebody tip-toeing back toward the metal department. After that I dozed and went to sleep.... Next thing I knew Mr. Frank was up over my head stamping and ... then I went up the steps..."

So Conley claimed that Monteen Stover arrived after Mary Phagan did, but according to Stover's testimony she would have arrived and left before Mary showed up—or at any rate, she (Stover) arrived at 12:05 or so and remained until 12:10 or so, which would once more mean that Mary would have to have arrived to the building some time before that, if Conley's version of the sequence of arrivals was to be believed. But according to her family, she was on the street-car that arrived at 12:07 at the stop near the Factory.

The defense also pointed out that the windows to Frank's office lacked curtains, and that there was in general constant activity in the factory on Saturdays, (certainly there seems to have been a good deal of activity on Saturday, April 26), both of which conditions made the new addition by Conley to his tale, of Frank's general Saturday sexual escapades, difficult to digest unless one were predisposed to do so.

Two witnesses came forward to implicate Conley, if only circumstantially. One was Will Green, a carnival worker, who said that he fled when, while he and Conley had been playing craps at the factory, Conley asserted his intention of robbing a girl who walked by. The second was William Mincey, an insurance salesman who said that he had met a rather inebriated Conley walking along the street, with whom he had a minor altercation during which Conley warned

Mincey off by asserting that "I have killed one today and do not wish to kill another."

So what *would* permit a southern white jury to embrace both the sequence of events and the nature of the events themselves as portrayed by Conley when other testimonies by various employees and other respectable citizens with no ax to grind one way or the other contradicted him, and when both his record and the assertions regarding things he did and said the day of Mary Phagan's murder all seem to point in the opposite direction? I would suggest that the reason was complexly simple: the notion that a Black man could come up with the story told by Conley, or that, coached by others, he could keep it in his head and more or less stick to it, even under cross-examination, was simply beyond what the majority of jurors would and could believe in that time and that place.[207] To tell the story that he told, with whatever the contradictions by himself or others, Conley would *have* to be telling the truth, or something close to the truth, because he simply wouldn't have the smarts to fabricate it.

That prejudice against the intelligence quotient of a black — particularly one who played into it by strongly playing down his education and his ability to read and write — overcame the prejudices that under other circumstances would have led a southern jury to regard the testimony of a Black man as inherently unreliable. Add to this the fact that the accused was both a Yankee and a Jew,[208] and a presumably rich one at that, and also recalling the viewpoint articulated by Mary Phagan's minister — and the reason for a predisposition to blindness to reason offers itself with some clarity. It might be noted that part of the failure of Frank's defense team was that they also underestimated the intelligence and cunning of Jim Conley as much as the jury presumably did and/or that the team did not think through carefully enough the problems in his story so as to point them out clearly to a jury as misguided as they.

The cross-examination indicated how selective Conley's memory was, but managed to allow him to continue to amplify his unconfirmed assertions regarding Frank's aberrational sexual behavior. And although among those whose testimony supported the Frank side of the case, Lemmie Quinn's statement that he unexpectedly came to the building at 12:20 and found Frank working alone at his desk—thus again contradicting Conley's assertion that at around that time Frank should either have been in the office with Mary or in the Metal Room with her—the fact that the defense waited more than two weeks into the trial to bring Quinn forward, apparently aroused some suspicion on the part of the jury. This was in spite of the fact that Quinn's place in the parade of witnesses for either side was not inherently strange, given the extended time frame of the entire proceeding.

Frank testified on his own behalf on the nineteenth day of the trial, although he never took the opportunity presumably offered him to confront Conley either within or outside the courtroom.[209] His speech lasted for nearly four hours, and in it he offered a painstakingly detailed account of his work on the day of Mary's murder, which showed how he could not possibly have had time to commit it. "...It must have been from 10 to 15 minutes after Miss Hall left my office, when this little girl, whom I afterward found to be Mary Phagan, entered my office and asked for her pay envelope... She continued on her way out and I heard the sound of her footsteps as she went away... She had left the plant hardly five minutes when Lemmie Quinn, the foreman of the plant, came in and told me..." This chronology accords pretty well both with the reports of Hall and Quinn and with the calculation by others as to when Mary would have been in Frank's office.

He noted that he had had no idea that Jim Conley was even in the factory on that fateful Saturday, and referred to Conley's allegations as "a monstrous lie..." He also explained his nervousness when the police brought him to the factory to see Mary's body, to which the prosecution had called attention. "I was nervous. I was completely unstrung. Imagine yourself called from sound slumber in the early hours of the morning...to see that little girl at the dawn of womanhood so cruelly murdered—it was a scene that would have melted stone."

The defense, in summing up, tried to play on the anti-black sentiments of the jury—but this may have backfired, for the reason I have suggested above: that that very sentiment militated against the jury's ability to see Jim Conley's testimony as false. And on the other hand, the prosecution suggested in its summary that Leo Frank was a Doctor Jekyll and Mister Hyde character who murdered Mary Phagan lest she reveal that she had been raped by him, which revelation would have resulted in a riot. It asked what motive Conley could have had for writing the notes and planting them by the body—which would impute too much cleverness to a black man, even one in desperate need of a means of dodging the accusation that he was the murderer. (But since Conley had never been indicted, he was not technically facing that accusation, and therefore his motive for writing the notes was severely undercut.) While Dorsey, in his three-day-long summary, did not play on Frank's identity as a Jew or a Yankee or a "rich industrialist," the crowds outside the courtroom apparently did so in a sufficiently vocal manner that Frank's lawyers asserted that the jury was being intimidated.

One might argue yes or no on this last assertion, but after the jury did find Frank guilty and Dorsey emerged from the courthouse, he was received as a conquering hero; "[t]he solicitor reached no farther than the sidewalk. While mounted men rode like Cossacks through the human swarm, three muscular men slung Mr. Dorsey on their shoulders and passed him over the heads of the crowd across the street" in triumph, as reported in the *Atlanta Constitution*. So at the very least it is obvious that the mob peering through the courthouse windows was thrilled with the verdict.[210] And it is noteworthy that Judge Leonard S. Roan arranged for Frank and his lawyers not to be present when the verdict was read, because he feared for their safety should the verdict be one of acquittal—and one must suppose that he considered it more than less likely that Frank would be acquitted based on his own assessment of the evidence, if he took such a precaution.

All of which leads us along a five-part path chronologically forward. Part one is the complex appeal process and its accompanying journalistic jousting. Immediately following Judge Roan's sentencing Leo Frank to death by hanging—fixing the execution date for October 12—the defense team began clamoring for a re-trial.

(Their first inexplicable error, incidentally, is not to have asked for a change of venue in the first place, given the atmosphere that, from beginning to end, seemed to make a fair trial impossible; they only complained about this issue after the trial and its verdict were done). The day of execution came and went as, torn between hope and hopelessness, Frank waited in his cell. On October 31, Judge Roan denied Frank's motion for a new trial, although oddly, he declared for the record that "I am not certain of this man's guilt. With all the thought I have put on this case, I am not thoroughly convinced that Frank is guilty or innocent"—yet he had condemned him to hang when, as Judge, he had several options regarding punishment in response to the jury's verdict. Was he himself influenced at that time by the clamor of the crowd?

Frank's lawyers filed an appeal to the Georgia Supreme Court in November, which failed; the court upheld both the conviction and the death sentence by 4-2, on February 17. While the dissenters noted that Conley's allegations regarding Frank's sexual habits were "calculated to prejudice the defendant in the minds of the jurors, and thereby deprive him of a fair trial," obviously the majority did not see it that way.[211] Once again a hearing was held on March 7 to fix a date for executing Frank; the date was fixed for April 17, Frank's 30th birthday. Three days after the hearing (on March 10) the *Atlanta Journal* published a heated editorial calling for a new trial:

> ...The *Journal* cares absolutely nothing for Frank, or for those who engaged in his defense or prosecution... [but] Leo Frank has not had a fair trial. He has not been fairly convicted and his death without a fair trial and legal conviction will amount to judicial murder... The very atmosphere of the courtroom was charged with an electric current of indignation which flashed and scintillated before the very eyes of the jury. The courtroom and streets were filled with an angry, determined crowd... The evidence on which he was convicted is not clear... In the name of Justice and in the name of the good people of the State of Georgia, who believe in fair play... let this man be fairly tried.[212]

As in the period following the murder and through the time of the trial itself, the various Georgia newspapers editorialized one way or the other, joined, now, by papers from different parts of the United States. Populist politician and journalist Tom Watson wrote his first *Jeffersonian* attack on Frank and his supporters on March 19, in response to the just-noted *Journal* editorial. In it he asked "does a Jew expect extraordinary favors and immunities because of his race?" To whatever extent it might be argued that Watson's general or specifically Frank-directed prejudices had not been focused on Judaism and the latter's Judaism theretofore, there is little question that from this point forward this issue is front and center in his thinking.

The day before he was to be executed, Frank filed a motion for a new trial and another to set aside the verdict. At a hearing on April 24, the defense introduced a new affidavit—from Jim Conley's girlfriend, Annie Maude Carter, who asserted that, when she had visited him in his cell, (during Christmas week, 1913, after Frank's trial and before Conley's trial), Conley had told her that he had murdered Mary Phagan, had written the two notes, and had taken the money he found in her purse. A series of salacious letters to Carter from Conley match both the hand-writing and, more importantly, the syntax of the Phagan "murder" notes. Nonetheless, Frank's motions were denied on May 6 and June 6, respectively.

In what seems a rather extraordinary turn, on October 2, William M. Smith, who had represented Conley from the outset, expressed his certainty that Frank was innocent, in an interview published in the *Atlanta Constitution*. He furthermore asserted his conviction that Conley's stories had been "a cunning fabrication" and that he, Conley, had been the murderer of Mary Phagan. At the end of November, Judge Roan—now dying of cancer in a Massachusetts hospital—recommended that Frank's sentence be commuted to life imprisonment, on the grounds of his uncertainty as to Frank's guilt, and his conviction that his accession to the verdict of the jury and the mood inside and outside the courtroom led him to call for an execution in the face of insufficient evidence of the defendant's guilt.

On December 7, The U.S. Supreme Court denied Frank's request for an appellate review of a decision on November 14 by the Georgia Supreme Court to uphold the motion not to set aside the guilty verdict. Twelve days later, both United States Supreme Court justices Joseph R. Lamar (a Georgian) and Oliver Wendell Holmes denied the writ of *habeas corpus* sought on December 17 at the federal level by Frank's legal team[213]—even though Holmes wrote an opinion in which he asserted his very serious doubt as to whether "the petitioner... has had due process of law... because of the trial taking place in the presence of a hostile demonstration and seemingly dangerous crowd, thought by the presiding Judge to be ready for violence unless a verdict of guilty was rendered." The question is *how*, in that case, Holmes at least, if not Lamar, could refuse to grant the writ? I find it difficult to answer this last question without recourse to assumptions regarding the Judges' prejudices.

Some time thereafter, (on December 28), though, Lamar did grant a writ of error, which would allow Frank to appeal his case before the full Supreme Court, and that appeal was heard in April, 1915. At that point, Tom Watson wrote in his *Jeffersonian* that "if Frank's rich connections keep on lying about this case, *something bad will happen.*" About this comment we might note that it furthers the issue of potential mob violence, reminds us of how times had changed in a generation with regard to prejudices, and certainly in Tom Watson's mind—but that no specific reference is made in *this* case to Frank's Jewishness by Watson, so the relationship between that aspect of Frank's identity (was it his religion or his socio-economic class?) and Watson's angry eagerness to preserve the certainty of Frank's guilt might remain a matter for speculation and debate, at least for some.

In any case, Frank's appeal was denied by a vote of 7-2 on April 19, with Justice Holmes and Justice Charles Evans dissenting. In writing the minority opinion, Holmes noted that "mob law does not become due process of law by securing the assent of a terrorized jury," suggesting that, at least as far as he, Judge Holmes, was concerned, justice had not been served in the Leo Frank trial, but that the very cry of injustice enunciated by Frank's lawyers had validity. Given the assertions by key figures in the process up to this moment—I am thinking in particular of William M. Smith and Judge Roan—that cry resonates loudly down the decades.[214]

This in turn leads to the second part of this post-verdict discussion. For Frank's legal team next sought a proposal for a commutation of his sentence from the three-person Georgia Prison Commission, on May 31, 1915.[215] A crowd of a thousand assembled in the Cobb County Courthouse in Marietta to protest any proposed commutation, and—whether under such pressure or out of conviction who can say?—the Commission voted 2-1 to advise against it. The decision would nonetheless be determined by the outgoing Governor of Georgia, John M. Slaton. In reviewing over ten thousand pages of documents, including further evidence that would incriminate Conley, including studies comparing Conley's speech pattern to the language of the "murder" notes, the Governor became convinced of Frank's innocence. Perhaps equally convinced that it would be at least pointless and at worst disastrous to the state to order a retrial, Slaton commuted Frank's sentence to life in prison on June 20, 1915. He acted, as he wrote, "assuming that Frank's innocence [will] be fully established and he [will] be set free" in the near future.

Slaton wrote further that "I can endure misconstruction, abuse and condemnation," (of which there was plenty, leading to a near-assault on the Governor's mansion, to disperse which assault the Georgia National Guard was called in), "but I cannot stand the constant companionship of an accusing conscience... I would rather be plowing in a field than to feel that I had that blood on my hands." He adds what for our discussion is an interesting, almost ironic point: "Two thousand years ago another Governor washed his hands of a case and turned a Jew over to a mob. For two thousand years that Governor's name has been accursed. If today another Jew were lying in his grave because I failed to do my duty I would all through life find his blood on my hands and would consider myself an assassin through cowardice."[216]

The commutation of Frank's sentence enraged the mob—the Governor's mansion was attacked on Slaton's last day in office; John Tucker Dorsey, chairman of the Georgia House of Representatives Penitentiary Committee called for his head;[217] Slaton was nearly assassinated after the inauguration ceremony of his successor. Tom Watson, who called for the lynching of both Frank and Slaton, wrote that "[o]ur grand old Empire State *has been raped!*" At this point, whatever distinction might possibly have remained for him previously between religion and socio-economics completely disappeared, as he further proclaimed that "Jew money has debased us, bought us, and sold us—and laughs at us."

Watson's words continued: "Hereafter, let no man reproach the South with "lynch law": let him remember the unendurable provocation; and let him say whether "lynch law" is not *better than no law at all!*" There is perhaps some irony in the fact that from both sides of the fence the law was felt to have failed to yield justice: Justice Holmes implying that Frank's trial had failed to be just and Governor Slaton asserting this unequivocally, and Tom Watson arguing that the Governor's commutation of Frank's death sentence, while legal, was an abrogation of justice.[218]

But the invocation of "lynch law" would play out in an ugly fashion—which leads us to the third post-verdict part of our narrative path. If lynching Governor Slaton could not be accomplished (although his political career had come to an unceremonious end the minute after he left the Governor's mansion) Leo Frank could be. A group calling itself the Knights of Mary Phagan began—openly—to shape a plan to kidnap Frank from the state prison farm and to lynch him in Marietta, right by Mary Phagan's grave. Led by a number of prominent citizens, including the former governor, Joseph Mackey Brown (who had all but called for the lynching at the time of the hearing that yielded Slaton's clemency decision) and John Tucker Dorsey and other leaders on the social and political scene, some 26 men set out for the prison farm late at night on August 16 with a caravan of seven cars. That morning Frank wrote to a friend that he was faring well, and was nearly recovered from his knife wounds of July 17.[219]

Well-armed, the group of men encountered little resistance from the prison guards and grabbed Frank, dragging him outside and forcing him into one of the automobiles. The kidnapping took all of ten minutes, so well-planned was it, (the kidnappers knew in advance exactly where they would find Frank). The caravan drove on back roads through the night; shortly before 6 AM on August 17 they arrived at Frey's Gin, about 2 miles east of Marietta. There—perhaps because they ran out of enough time to get to the site of Mary Phagan's grave—Frank was stood up on a table, a noose placed around his neck, the other end of the rope thrown over the branch of an oak tree (he was apparently allowed to write a short note to his wife, to go with the wedding ring that he asked be given to her—and at 7:05, the table was kicked out from beneath his feet. Frank died a slow death; the wound in his neck opened and blood slithered forth as he convulsed four feet above the ground.

The lynchers scattered quickly and almost as quickly word spread of the lynching. People swarmed the site from all directions; the *Atlanta Journal* reported that by 8 AM a thousand people had gathered and that the number soon swelled to 3,000—men, women and children. One man ran up to the swaying corpse and shouted: "Now we've got you! You won't murder any more little innocent girls!" The corpse was cut down at 10:17 and taken to the undertaker, where thousands of people surrounded the place demanding to be let in; some 15,000 viewed Leo Frank lying in the casket. They lingered in the streets, talking with excitement and sharing a sense of celebration, while vendors hawked photographs of Frank hanging from the oak tree.

In the aftermath of the lynching an "investigation" yielded no evidence as to who the perpetrators were.[220] Marietta Mayor E.P. Dobbs (in fact one of the lynchers) reports that "none of the officials had any intimation of such an undertaking until the body was found about two miles from the city this morning." On August 24, after a one-day-long hearing, the Cobb County coroner's inquest resulted in a simple verdict: that Frank had died "at the hands of unknown parties." The inquest was conducted by two of the lynchers, John Tucker Dorsey and Gordon Baxtor Ginn. On September 15, after two days of listening to "testimony" presented by prosecutor Eugene Herbert Clay (one of the lynchers) and his special assistant, John Tucker Dorsey, the Cobb County Grand Jury (which included seven of the lynchers) was "unable to connect anybody with the perpetration of the offense or to identify anyone who was connected with it... We... find it impossible to indict anyone."

All of this leads me to the fourth part of the post-verdict path through history. In the aftermath of the lynching there were newspaper headlines and editorials within and beyond Georgia most of which condemned the lynching. One of the few that did not was the *Marietta Journal and Courier*, which stated that "we regard the hanging of Leo M. Frank as an act of law-abiding citizens." Frank's widow, Lucille made her sole public statement on the front page of the *Augusta Chronicle* on October 1. She asserted:

> I am a Georgia girl, born and reared in this state, and educated in her schools. I am a Jewess; some will throw that in my face, I know, but I have no apologies to make for my religion. I am also a Georgian, and an American, and I do not apologize for that either...I only hope that those who destroyed Leo's life will realize the truth before they meet their God—they perhaps are not entirely to blame, fed as they were on lies unspeakable... Some of them, I am sure, did not realize the horror of their act. But those who inspired these men to this awful act, what of them?

However fearless Lucille's words may have been, fear of anti-Semitic repercussions motivated half of Georgia's 3,000 Jews to leave the state. Whatever one might try to assert regarding the objective reality of that fear, the close chronological proximity of these events to the conclusion of the Beiliss and Dreyfus Affairs—even as those Affairs had ultimately yielded a positive outcome for the Jews on trial—certainly helped American Jews to begin looking over their shoulders and wondering whether or not the United States would or could truly be different from what seemed to survive in Europe.

In any case, two organizations grew out of the Frank Affair. The B'nai B'rith organization founded its Anti-Defamation League in 1913, in part to assure that never again would a Jew unjustly accused of a capital crime be without appropriately organized resources for his defense—and in larger part to fight the bigotry, stereotyping and prejudice not only toward Jews but toward any number of minorities, particularly with the continuing upsurge of immigration, that inspire events such as the Leo Frank Affair. And on the other hand, the *Knights of Mary Phagan* became a take-off point for a reconstructed Ku Klux Klan by 1915—the earlier version having been effectively destroyed by the federal government during the Reconstruction period following the Civil War.

In the decades that followed the Frank Affair there was a handful of curious epilogues. Jim Conley was shot trying to break into an

Atlanta drug store on January 13, 1919. He recovered, was tried and convicted of burglary and sentenced to 20 years in prison. He was released in 1933, but was charged eight years later with gambling and public drunkenness (on October 20, 1941)—which is the last anyone hears of him. Monteen Stover was indicted on February 2, 1931, for luring men into a hotel room and then trying to blackmail them—further proof to some historians of the quality of the prosecution's witnesses at the time of the trial.

More extraordinary is the development of March 4, 1982. On that day, 83-year-old Alonzo Mann, who in 1913 had been employed as an office boy at the National Pencil Company building and had been in the building on the day of Mary Phagan's murder—he had testified briefly but without much consequence for the defense at the time of the trial—prepared a signed affidavit in which he swore that Jim Conley was the murderer.

> ...on the witness stand... I did not tell all that I knew. I was not asked questions about what I knew. I did not volunteer. If I had revealed all I knew it would have cleared Leo Frank and would have saved his life... Jim Conley... lied under oath. I know that... I am convinced that he, not Leo Frank, killed Mary Phagan. I know as a matter of certainty that Jim Conley—and he alone—disposed of her body.
>
> Jim Conley threatened to kill me if I told what I knew. I was young and frightened. I had no doubt Conley would have tried to kill me if I had told that I had seen him with Mary Phagan that day... [The lawyers] asked me practically nothing. I was nervous and afraid that day. There were crowds in the street who were angry and who were saying that Leo Frank should die. Some were yelling things like "Kill the Jew!"
>
> I came to work on that morning at about 8 o'clock... Although it was early in the morning, Conley had obviously already consumed considerable beer... He spoke to me. He asked me for a dime to buy beer... I told Jim Conley I didn't have a dime.
>
> ...I went upstairs to the second floor where my desk was located in the office of Leo Frank... I was supposed to meet my mother that day about noon and go to the Confederate Memorial Day parade. When I left the premises, just before noon, Mary Phagan had not come to the pencil factory...
>
> ...[I]t could not have been more than a half hour before I got back to the pencil factory... Inside the door, I walked toward the stairwell. I looked to my right and I was confronted by a scene I

will remember vividly until I die. Jim Conley was standing between the trapdoor that led to the basement and the elevator shaft... He had the body of Mary Phagan in his arms. I didn't know it was Mary Phagan. I only knew it was a girl. At that moment I couldn't tell if she was alive. She appeared to be unconscious, or perhaps dead. I saw no blood. He was holding her with both arms gripping her around the waist...

I believe for some reason Jim Conley turned around toward me. He either heard my footsteps coming or he sensed I was behind him. He wheeled on me and in a voice that was low but threatening and frightening to me said: 'If you ever mention this I'll kill you.'

...I am confident that I came in just seconds after Conley had taken the girl's money and grabbed her. I do not think sex was his motive. I believe it was money...

Leo Frank was convicted by lies heaped on lies. It wasn't just Conley who lied. Others said that Leo Frank had women in the office for immoral purposes and that he had liquor there... That was all false. Leo Frank was a good office manager. He was always proper with people who worked for him. There were witnesses who told lies and I remained silent.

Mann had nothing to gain by this confession nearly seven decades after the trial, except the expunging of his conscience. On the other hand, his confession supplies the last pieces of the puzzle—if any of it still seems a puzzle—where Jim Conley is concerned. For he was in the right place and the right time to have committed the murder, and was not only inherently "appropriate" as a candidate to have committed the crime—with a prior record of violence and drunkenness, and he had been drinking already that morning—but he had a clear motive: robbery.

Not only did he ask Mann for money that day. Leo Frank had much earlier noted that Conley could write, since Conley had specifically written him notes asking for money. So robbing a little girl who had just claimed her pay envelope was reasonable. And if he also sexually assaulted her, that would be consistent with his style as evidenced in his salacious letters to his girlfriend and her testimony about him. Conley was clever enough—and perhaps aware enough of the sorts of prejudices rampant in the specific world of the south in which he grew up and within its white male population in particular—to provide a story that would shift the blame from him to Leo Frank.

Case closed—but 69 years too late to save Leo Frank's life. One key witness failed to tell all he knew out of fear. The defense failed to push Alonzo Mann as they failed to push Jim Conley and others in their cross-examination, out of prejudice that didn't allow them to take Conley seriously enough as a wily liar and probably didn't allow them to take Alonzo Mann seriously, period. Nearly everyone else within and outside the courtroom was already predisposed to find Frank guilty and to act murderously on that predisposition out of complex prejudices and fears, regarding blacks and regarding northerners and regarding non-agrarian, industrial, white-collar labor—and regarding Jews.

Which leads us to the fifth and final part of the long post-verdict trail that reconfigures the Leo Frank *trial* as the Leo Frank *Affair*: the issue of anti-Semitism as a factor. In the aftermath of Alonzo Mann's confession, any number of newspapers throughout the south published articles asserting that Frank's innocence had finally been demonstrated unequivocally.[221] On January 9, 1983 three Jewish organizations filed an application with the Georgia Board of Pardons and Paroles requesting the grant of a full posthumous pardon that would exonerate Leo Frank.[222]

Astonishingly, on May 15, Randall Evans, a former judge on the Georgia Court of Appeals published a statement in the *Augusta Chronicle-Herald* asserting that the evidence of Frank's guilt "was overwhelming" and referring to Governor Slaton's commutation of Frank's death-sentence as "the rape of the judicial process"—echoes of Tom Watson's vitriol—and calling the application to request a posthumous pardon "completely ridiculous." Is such a commentary possible except by a spectacular *blindness* to justice and can such blindness have *other* than anti-Semitism at its heart? Or might it be due to some perverse sense that overturning a prior judgment would besmirch Georgian judicial honor—a psychology analogous to that evidenced in the concern of someone like Major Henry in the Dreyfus Affair that exoneration of the accused would besmirch French military honor?

Perhaps more astonishing still is the decision rendered on

December 22 by the Georgian Board of Pardons and Paroles to deny the application on the grounds that insufficient evidence had been supplied to prove Frank's unequivocal innocence. A year later Alonzo Mann himself wrote to the Board (on December 19, 1984) that "...Leo Frank... was innocent. He did not kill Mary Phagan... I hope and pray that I live to see the day the board clears his name... I know Mr. Frank should be cleared and God knows it too. I urge you to please grant him a pardon before I go to meet my God." Mann died three months later, on March 18, 1985, and it would be another year before the Board responded in the affirmative to a new application for Frank's posthumous pardon, on March 11, 1986.

But the Board's order states that the pardon is granted without "attempting to address the question of guilt or innocence; [it is granted] in recognition of the state's failure to protect the person of Leo M. Frank and thereby to preserve his opportunity for continued legal appeal of his conviction..." So Frank is placed posthumously in a position analogous to that of Dreyfus in the first phase of his rehabilitation, but, to date, has never had the chance to achieve the complete exoneration that Dreyfus eventually did. Perhaps predictably, the order of pardon was vociferously condemned by Tom Watson's great-grandson and also by Hugh Dorsey's son, Mary Phagan's great niece and a number of descendants of those who lynched Frank.

The unmediated conviction that Frank was the monster and murderer depicted by Hugh Dorsey with the able assistance of Jim Conley remains intact in many quarters and cannot be easily disconnected from the matter of anti-Semitism. Among the discussions of the Affair at the outset of the new millennium, among the more emphatic with regard to this issue is that offered in a June 13, 2000 article by law professor Jonathan Turley in the *Atlanta Constitution*, regarding the statue of Tom Watson that graces the Georgia state capitol building in Atlanta. Turney asserts that is should be removed, and replaced with that of someone like Martin Luther King, Jr.—for Watson "was a fervent anti-Semite who described Leo Frank as a 'satyr-faced New York Jew' and who asserted that Mary Phagan died '...defending her virtue against a rich, depraved Sodomite Jew,'" and thus Watson's image is inappropriate as a symbol of Georgia.

The accusation of anti-Semitism has also been leveled against the historian Albert S. Lindemann by Robert Wistrich, in Wistrich's February, 1998 article in *Commentary* magazine, "Blaming the Jews." Wistrich has a number of Lindemann's works in mind, but for our purposes the relevant book is his 1991 *The Jew Accused: Three Anti-Semitic Affairs (Dreyfus, Beilis, Frank), 1894-1915*. The work overall is an effective and interesting coverage offering inter-links among these three famous Jewish trials. In reading it (several years before coming across Wistrich's article), I was struck—particularly in the section on Frank—by a feeling that recalls what I have earlier expressed regarding M.D. Anderson's book on William of Norwich:[223] if this is an author who is sympathetic, what can one expect of those who are not?

I would not necessarily—at least not based on this one book—label Lindemann as Wistrich does. But I found it disturbing that he seems at pains to deny hardly any sort of anti-Semitism in the Frank Affair at all. Thus Tom Watson—where Watson's written statements make it clear that hostility to Jews had at least come to be interwoven with admitted other sources of antagonism by the time of and in the context of the Frank Affair—is spoken of in entirely other terms.[224] Similarly, Lindemann seems content with a narrative that arrives, in the end, at a pardon that does not embrace Frank's innocence, as if there had been no serious miscarriage of justice requiring redress. He (Lindemann) seems to ignore the evidence in hand, even before Alonzo Mann's 1982 confession, that seems to point so clearly both to Jim Conley's guilt and also to the *reasons* for the narrative that he contrived—as well as to the mood that pushed the jury and the populace at large toward its eager embrace. He simply does not want to see anti-Semitic and also, paradoxically, anti-Black, prejudice as a reality of that time and place and to acknowledge such sentiments as a factor in the shaping of the Frank Affair.

To point to factors other than anti-Semitism in the Frank Affair does not necessarily mean that anti-Semitism was not part of the matrix, but Lindemann seems eager to suggest that it was not. "Frank's Jewishness weighed *at least as much in his favor as against him*. Italians or Greeks enjoyed a distinctly less friendly press in

Atlanta and in the South generally... Certain negative stereotypes about Jews in late nineteenth-century America did come into play as the Frank case became an affair. *But they were not decisive*" [my italics].[225] Perhaps that would have been true had the trial taken place in the late nineteenth-century, but in general and certainly in the case of Tom Watson and his following, by 1913-15—given what was said in court by the prosecution and by Jim Conley, what was said and written by Watson and others in the context of Governor Slaton's commutation decision, and what was ultimately done to Leo Frank in the manner in which it was done—one can hardly see events as divorced from anti-Semitism, even if, by that time, anti-Semitism was socio-economically-based as much as religiously-based for individuals like Watson.

When Lindemann notes that "the detectives who came to suspect Frank had concrete reasons for doing so," what are those reasons, if not the enormous pressure to come up quickly with a murderer—wedded to prejudice and stereotype?[226] And what are the specifics of prejudice and stereotype at issue? While Lindemann legitimately refers to the accusations (that prove to be false) against Frank, he completely writes off his Jewishness as a factor in the willingness of those involved either to spread or to embrace those falsehoods. He asserts that, "if a different Jew had been in either Frank's or Dreyfus's position, a different course of events might have occurred," as if their trials were largely a function of how they looked and their personalities and, while asserting of Frank that he may or may not have looked "Jewish" but was certainly not "a more typical southern Jew," he considers it "not reasonable to maintain that blind prejudice, an anti-Semitism asserting that all Jews are the same, played a larger role than did the accident of personality."[227]

Blind prejudice does not always reduce so simply to the formula that all "X"es are the same! And while it is true that the anger after Frank's gubernatorial commutation was mainly directed toward Governor Slaton and Frank, rather than toward the Jews at large, if indeed half of them ended up fleeing the state, then they at least sensed something more dangerous than Lindemann does. I am not disagreeing with Lindemann's conclusion that a combination of factors wove a noose around Leo Frank's neck, but I am objecting to the ease with which he wants to dismiss nearly all evidence of anti-Semitism as one of those factors, as I am objecting to the conclusion that he presents which falls so short of exonerating Frank in favor of Conley as the murderer—and it seems to me that these two objections are linked together by the same near-sightedness on Lindemann's part, or perhaps "prejudice" would be a better word.

That near-sightedness, or prejudice, is either informed by or leads to his failure in an otherwise well-crafted book with a broad sweep, to mention important elements in Conley's testimony that all but prove his narrative(s) as false, or to present statements such as "that Conley had confessed the murder to his lawyer"[228] almost in passing, without acknowledging their potential weight, or passing lightly over information such as Hugh Dorsey's prosecution methods and suppressions of evidence that would have either compromised Conley or helped exonerate Frank, which information is well discussed in Dinnerstein's book written decades before Lindemann's as well as in Oney's book written a decade later.[229] And what can have prompted Lindemann to relegate Alonzo Mann's confession to a footnote far from the place where he draws his equivocating conclusions about who was and who was not guilty? If an academic who might be assumed by his readers to have some degree of scholarly objectivity is so near-sighted or prejudiced, what of others, then as well as now?

As in my comments on contemporary discussions of the Blood Libel and specifically of the murder of William of Norwich, it seems to me that the prejudices that led to many of the famous Jewish trials under discussion remain unresolved, sometimes even for those who offer discussions for the purpose of undercutting and resolving those prejudices. There is an obvious but odd thread that links Norwich—as well as Kiev—and Atlanta together: in all three cases, the impetus for the event is the murder of a Christian child, which murder unleashes a wellspring of anger and frustration in the populace at large and a sense of pressure upon the authorities to find and convict a murderer quickly.

But of course there is considerable divergence among these

three stories, not least of which is that the primary entity that acts on the anger and frustration and feeling of pressure is in the first case, arguably, the church, and in the second case, clearly the state, and in the third case, notoriously, the police department. Each entity had its own agenda and was able to reach in varying degrees into a centuries-deep well of distrust of Jews—whether for religious or socio-economic or other reasons becomes, in the end, irrelevant for our purposes—but the result of the effort is not, perhaps, what one might imagine: success in Norwich and Atlanta and failure in Kiev. Those varied results confound our assumptions with respect to changes in sentiments regarding Jews over time and to differences between those sentiments in this or that context in the Old World versus the New World. In this respect, William's Norwich and Mary Phagan's Atlanta (and her hometown, Marietta, near which the lynching took place) are tied closer together than either is to Andryusha's Kiev.

This is so in two ways. First, because the populace in both Norwich and Atlanta/Marietta were heavily in favor of finding the Jew under indictment guilty, based on whatever range of prejudices might be argued to define and/or differentiate those two communities an ocean and 770 years apart—whereas the populace in Kiev either from the outset or very shortly after the outset showed itself to be heavily in favor of seeing Mendel Beiliss exonerated, rejoicing in the streets when he was declared innocent in a manner turned 180 degrees from the rejoicing in the streets of Atlanta when Leo Frank was pronounced guilty.

Second, because, just as we have noted the need for saints in the medieval Christian world and the growing interest at the time of William of Norwich's death in child-saints in particular, and the manner in which William fit that bill in both spiritual and economic ways; so in the world that a populist like Tom Watson saw as slipping away, thanks to the influx of—northerners, industrialists, Jews, immigrants; take your pick—one might see in Mary Phagan a kind of child-saint. Her horrific death offered a rallying point to bring together the white, agrarian community with its increasingly politically and economically impotent male population, losing control over its women (who were passing out of its control into the control of the factories run by industrialists perceived to be all northern, Jewish or both) but also a rallying point for those women (who felt their traditional world being uncomfortably transformed). Mary became their martyred champion.

Mary's gravesite in Marietta became the goal of thousands of pilgrims, many of whom surely felt that "she died for us—but we have responded by destroying her destroyer." Conversely, Leo Frank offered a familiar sort of scapegoat in perhaps unfamiliar garb. His defeated corpse and the site of his hanging also became a focus of virtual pilgrimage for some time after his lynching. He became the demonic Other to the sainted, to-be-venerated Mary Phagan. As she expanded as a figure far too grand in conception to find its opposite in the person of some semi-literate Black rapist-murderer, Leo Frank presented a figure significant enough as an outsider who was yet tied in to the upper echelons of the community to fit the bill of martyr/saint-maker. He could be a modest Judas to her modest Jesus.

III. From South to North: Massena, New York, 1928

Parallels of this sort between events and their aftermath in the early twentieth-century United States and mid-twelfth-century England might be explained by some of the peculiarities of the American South. The unique fabric of southern society and the position within it of both Blacks and Jews, the particularities of its folk-lore—such as the tradition of night witches—might be assumed to offer an explanation for the ways in which the Leo Frank case could end up with as much or more in common with the William of Norwich case as that of Mendel Beiliss and even that of Alfred Dreyfus, with their various other parallels to the story of Leo Frank's destruction.

A question then arises: if significant parts of the Leo Frank story derive from unique features of the American south in the early twentieth century, could a similar sort of succession of events take place elsewhere in the United States or later in the twentieth century? Is the Frank Affair an aberration in this country's historical ethos with respect to the shaping of an Affair out of a legal or quasi-legal process involving a Jew? Further, how might things be expected to change in the years immediately following the Frank case with further developments in the position of the United States in the world? For in the aftermath of America's 1917 entry into World War I on the side of England and France, the war took a decisive turn in their favor, and in the aftermath of that war, the United States found itself a clearer, albeit for a time more self-isolating, world power than before.

One can certainly see how in the 1920s a new United States, bolder and brasher, was not only expanding its international muscles, but was also stretching those muscles internally.[230] Cities were burgeoning, skyscrapers were soaring, industry was growing, art and culture were beginning to find an increasingly distinctive American voice. Sentiment was, at least for a while, in favor of political self-isolation and a kind of distancing from the squabbles and issues that occupied Europe within itself and with respect to its imperial and colonial concerns in the Middle East. The British and the French were left largely on their own to divide up the remains of the Ottoman Empire in the decade after the Great War.

The other side of the isolationist coin was a distinct xenophobia. The fear of the "wrong kind" of immigrants, who might threaten the hegemony of "the old stock" of Americans (whose ancestors had themselves also been immigrants, of course), solidified. Moreover, the earlier mentioned Johnson-Reed Act of 1924 arrived in the midst of a decade of escapism—a twenties that roared less in celebration of the end of the Great War than in response to the horror of that war and what it meant for the human contention that, with our expanding scientific and technological powers we could perfect the world without Divine assistance. The Great War demonstrated that those powers could and without much pressure would be used as much for destructive purposes—on a scale unimaginable a mere generation earlier.

While the raucous sounds of paradoxically escapist/victory music and dance—this was the "Roaring Twenties"—dominated American, British and French cities, the cities of the defeated were dominated as much by frustration and anger at their defeat as they were by increasing poverty. Defeat and poverty alike could be and came to be tied together in the minds of the defeated Germans, for instance, first and foremost to "traitors" among them—such as Jews—and later to both unjust and overweening post-war reparations. Eventually both the victors and those who were defeated succumbed to a universal economic depression.

The consequences of the Johnson-Reed Act in the decade that followed its passage—which could not have been anticipated in 1924—would be profound, not only for the American people safe within the isolationist, xenophobic borders of the sea-to-shining-sea republic, but more so for those clamoring and unable to come within those borders when fascist regimes and their manipulations of frustration and anger toward focusing on "traitors" as scapegoats for defeat and poverty yielded ugly consequences that spread from Spain to Italy to Germany to Russia. Too many among such scapegoats would not be able to find refuge beneath the shining lamp of Lady Liberty.

Nor was all quiet on the American front. Well north of Leo Frank's Atlanta, Georgia, let us jump forward a decade and a half from the year of the Frank trial, to Massena, New York in 1928. This is the year when Al Smith, a Catholic running against Herbert Hoover for the presidency of the United States, had a good deal of difficulty— due to interference from the Klu Klux Klan that had experienced such a strong revival in the aftermath of the Frank Affair. And far from being limited to activity in the South, the Klan was active across the North, sponsoring an anti-Smith—i.e, anti-Catholic—rally in Massena in late autumn.

Massena was an ethnic mix, with a Protestant majority and a largely immigrant minority of French-Canadian Catholics whom many Protestants apparently feared as economic competitors— and a tiny community of 19 Jewish families. The first of these, Jesse Kauffman, had arrived in 1898 (in other words, in spite of his Germanic surname, he had arrived at the time of the great Eastern European Jewish migration toward America, rather than during the much more modest, mid-century period of immigration from Prussian and Austro-Hungarian Central Europe. A synagogue had been formed in 1919—right after the end of World War I—in the building that was formerly the First Congregational Church. The synagogue, named Adath Israel, housed an Orthodox congregation.

This was a Jewish community that by the 1920s perceived itself to be comfortably accepted by the larger community. Several of its key members—Kauffman, Friedman, Rosenbaum, Stone, Thulkin— were involved in retail stores; they were in the habit of granting credit to their customers in an age when cash transactions were the norm. It was a Jewish community whose members were either un- aware of, or chose to ignore, the quiet, behind-the-back anti-Semitic comments made occasionally by their non-Jewish neighbors—and not necessarily only those neighbors with some affiliation with the Klan and its activities.

But in Massena, with barely 8,500 village inhabitants and 12,000 altogether in the township, there were seven cross-burnings that year—by Klan members obviously active well beyond the am- bit of the south. And there in Massena, the weekend of September 22-23, 1928 led in a nearly fatal direction for the small Jewish com- munity. Those days fell toward the tail end of the Days of Awe—the ten-day period which, on the Jewish calendar, carries from the New Year (Rosh Hashanah) to the Day of Atonement (Yom Kippur). This is the most solemn period on the Jewish calendar, during which ten- day period Jews are expected to review their words and actions of the previous year and gear up for the 24-hour fast that, on the Day of Atonement, completes a spiritual cleansing process that will yield renewal in the year to come.

On that particular Saturday (September 22), Dave and Marion Griffiths were at their home half a block from the woods and fields known as the Nightingale Section of Massena. Their five-year-old son, Bobby was out playing in those woods, as he often did. As the day began its wane toward evening, their four-year-old daughter Barbara also headed into the woods to look for Bobby—also appar- ently not that unusual—but by evening had not returned. (In fact Bobby and his friends had exited at nearly the same spot where she entered, not long after Barbara headed into the woods). As the eve- ning moved toward nightfall, the Griffiths sought their little daughter in increasing desperation but failed to find her. The word of her disappearance began to spread back into the community.

That evening, on his way home from the store where he worked, Willie Shulkin stopped into the Crystal Palace ice cream parlor and cafe run by Albert Comnas, a relatively recent immigrant from Thessaloniki, Greece. Shulkin was returning from helping out in his father Jacob's store. Jake was highly respected throughout the community—as well as president of the synagogue—and Willie was a mildly retarded young man known by everyone in the community. Asked if he had heard about the disappearance of Barbara Griffiths or if he knew anything about it, Willie was apparently prompted by the questions to openly express his concern that it might be blamed on the Jews.

By then the place was already abuzz with discussion. Comnas—either with strong, accusatory conviction or perhaps with merely a passing casualness—observed how, in the old country there were constant rumors that Jews kidnapped Christian children and used their blood or their body parts for various rituals, especially those connected to important Jewish holidays. In fact, back in April of that same year, in Thessaloniki, the town from which he came, a Blood Libel had been leveled at the Jewish community. Comnas, who was well-known in Massena as hostile to the Jews, seems then to have speculated that this could explain Barbara's disappearance: perhaps the Jews of Massena had kidnapped her in order to murder her and to use her blood for rituals associated with Yom Kippur, which would begin on Sunday evening.

The zoning of Massena was such that the area in which Barbara Griffiths had disappeared fell under the jurisdiction not of the local six-man Police force but of the State Troopers stationed nearby. One of them was probably at Comnas' cafe when Willlie Shulkin showed up and began to respond to the questions, and brought him down to the police station for more formal questioning. State Trooper Mickey McCann was put in charge. By Sunday morning citizens were out in front of City Hall asking for action. The village mayor, W. Gilbert Hawes, began to put pressure on Trooper McCann to pursue the line of investigation that led to the

Jewish community. It should be noted that the issue was not mentioned in any of the sermons offered in Sunday morning church
services; the Christian leadership in Massena exhibited no interest
in pushing the narrative in an anti-Jewish direction, blood-libel-
related or otherwise.

But by the early afternoon, Barbara had still not been found, after an 18-hour search of the woods by scores of volunteers working
together with the State Police. At that point—just past noon, barely
five hours before Yom Kippur eve—the Lithuanian-born rabbi of
the small Orthodox congregation, Berel Brennglass, who doubled
as the community *shohet*,[231] was brought in by the New York State
Police for questioning and grilled for over an hour regarding Jewish practices with respect to human sacrifice and the use of blood in
food. He responded with indignance at the line of Trooper McCann's
questioning, and when he exited the police headquarters building,
eloquently shamed and scattered the crowd that had gathered there
eager, so to speak, for blood.

As it turned out, shortly after this interrogation was in process,
Barbara emerged from the woods and was found by two teen-aged
girls who had come in from the nearby town of Norfolk to help in
the search. It seems that she had gotten lost, taken refuge during the
night in some tall grass to keep herself warm and fallen asleep—so
soundly that she had not been awakened by the noise and lights of
the search parties. She had not seen any of the hundreds of people
who had been looking for her still searching the following morning
and had taken until the late afternoon to find her way out.

One might suppose that Barbara Griffiths' sound and safe re-
appearance would have brought the story to its close—certainly the
Jewish community considered her safe re-appearance shortly before
Yom Kippur eve a virtual miracle—but events proved and moved
otherwise. Many of the townspeople remained worked up. It seems
that, having gotten so exercised over the gruesome possibility that
had been laid before them, they could not so easily let go of what
had become a group psychology fantasy. Some suggested that the
Jews had indeed only released the little girl because their plot had
been discovered.

Rumors flew that they Jews got frightened after the Rabbi's interview at the Police Station, and so gave up their would-be victim.
"Scared you into returning the girl, didn't we?"[232] some said. Members of the Volunteer Fire Department who were affiliated with the
Ku Klux Klan called for running the Jews out of town.

That evening 100 "toughs" blocked the sidewalks near the
synagogue, forcing congregants to arrive by way of the streets or
an out-of the way route to services. Apparently, townspeople were
peering through the open synagogue windows during the services,
waiting for actions that would confirm their suspicions that untow-
ard things were going on inside. The manner in which some of the
older, more traditional Jews prayed, swaying, their *tallitot* (prayer
shawls) sometimes placed over their heads—and all, of course, in a
language (Hebrew) that was so obviously "foreign"—added an increased sense not only of oddness, but, in a xenophobic atmosphere,
of suspiciousness with regard to the Jewish congregation. Among
those who spearheaded this conviction toward the Jews was Mayor
Hawes himself. He organized a boycott of Massena's Jewish-owned
businesses.

The brief disappearance of a child who turns up unharmed—
a small, local event of the sort that can happen anywhere and any-
time—rapidly became an affair with national and perhaps international implications, and not only through the thoughts, words and
actions of the Christian community. On late Saturday afternoon,
as the mood darkened, the Massena Jewish community leaders—
in this case, specifically Shulkin, Kauffman and Stone—distressed
at the turn of events, recalled not only the Frank case but a riot
against Jews that had occurred in New York City on the eve of
Yom Kippur back in 1850 when the Irish inhabitants (including
the police) got it in their heads that a Christian streetwoman had
been murdered for the holiday and broke out in violence against
their Jewish neighbors. Unsure what to do, the Massena Jewish
leaders had called up Louis Marshall, head of the American Jewish
Committee. Marshall, who had taken on Henry Ford the previous
year—in a lawsuit for the libelous anti-Semitic words systematically appearing in the *Dearborn Independent*—had dispatched a

reporter, Boris Smolar, from the Jewish Telegraphic Agency, to assess the situation.

Meanwhile, as conditions remained tense on Sunday late afternoon, both before and even after Barbara Griffiths was found, the community leaders also called on Stephen Wise, chairman of the American Jewish Congress, to step in.[233] Wise called on his friend Al Smith, New York's governor—and running for President on the Democratic ticket, as noted above, in a heated atmosphere part of the heat of which derived from the fact that Smith was a Catholic— to speak out on behalf of Massena's Jewish community. The primary consequence of this decision, in the aftermath of having called on Marshall, was not only to bring a national Jewish (and non-Jewish) focus onto the events transpiring in Massena, but to turn the affair into a sparring platform between these two renowned Jewish American figures, vying for credit and the spotlight as efficacious national leaders.

Corporal McCann's superior, Lieutenant Edward Heim, had been dispatched to Massena Sunday evening and was one of those who in effect stood guard on the steps of the synagogue during the evening service. He also facilitated a meeting between Jewish community leaders and a now rather contrite Christian leadership, including Police Chief Floyd San Jule, Mayor Hawes and Town Supervisor Andrew Hanmer, on Tuesday—the day after Yom Kippur—in the synagogue. That initially cleared much of the air. But meanwhile the wire sent to Stephen Wise on Sunday, (after the call to Marshall on Saturday seemed to have elicited little concrete assistance), caused Louis Marshall to become more involved in the situation that very rapidly became a national *cause celebre*. Marshall wrote a long letter demanding an apology from Mayor Hawes in particular—the wording of which he would need to approve if it were to be accepted.

So the issue continued to expand, invoking and involving politics on several levels, from AJCongress versus AJCommittee, and Wise versus Marshall as effective national Jewish leaders, to Al Smith and his democratic campaign for President versus Hawes, a Republican, and his own impending re-election campaign. In fact,

Hawes had fairly quickly begun to feel pressure from within the national Republican Party not only to pull back but to apologize for having spearheaded the anti-Jewish campaign that he in effect initiated, even before Wise and Marshall became seriously involved. His public statement noted that "in light of the solemn protest of my Jewish neighbors, I feel I ought to express clearly and unequivocally... my sincere regret that by any act of commission or mission, I should have seemed to lend countenance... to what I should have known to be a cruel libel: imputing human sacrifice as a practice now or at any time in the history of the Jewish people."

It seems rather odd and interesting that Hawes' statement included the suggestion that his decision to recant an absurd accusation should have derived from "the solemn protest of my Jewish neighbors,"—as if without that protest he would not have recognized the absurdity of the accusation. In today's terms, Hawes might be said to have changed his stance in keeping with what he deemed politically correct, as opposed to what he deemed true and just. There is a general tone of questionable sincerity in Hawes' various statements, to Rabbi Wise and to the press, especially in comparison with that of Corporal McCann—who in effect became the fall guy, presented by those with more power or astuteness than he as the one who let things get out of hand—to Rabbi Brennglass.[234] Hawes was, in any case, elected to a sixth consecutive term as mayor.

On the other hand, the national publicity effected largely by the interest foisted upon the situation by the *New York Times*, continued to stew for several weeks. Louis Marshall in particular seems to have been reluctant to let the issue die an earlier, quieter death than it might have. Yet finally it did. And as Rabbi Brennglass reminded his congregation on the Yom Kippur evening after Barbara Griffiths had turned up safe and sound but the mood of the town had not yet quieted down: "...this happened in America, not Tsarist Russia, among people we have come to regard as our friends. We must show our neighbors that their hatred originates in fear, and that this fear has its roots in ignorance... We must show them that they have nothing to fear from us. We must tell the world this story so it will never happen again."[235]

IV. The Julius and Ethel Rosenberg Affair

The question is: *could* it happen again? And how might the story in Massena have ended differently, if Barbara Griffiths had not strolled out of the woods, safe and sound, but had suffered some mishap and been found dead or not been found at all? If the Blood Libel at Massena eventually faded, fifty years later there were still Christians in that town who apparently remained uncertain as to whether or not Jews do use Christian blood for some purpose or other.[236] And can suspicions continue regarding Jews, but with other, different directions from the specific direction of the Blood Libel in modern history—as most obviously in the Dreyfus Affair? Can such suspicions and their consequential charges against Jews repeat themselves not only in Europe or the Middle East but in the United States?

Did it happen again, but articulated in a less obvious manner than that of accusing the Jews of killing a Christian child and using his or her blood or body parts for one ritual or gastronomic purpose or another? Could it and did it happen on a more distinctly national scale than was offered by events in Atlanta or Massena—in the United States of America in the middle of the twentieth century? I believe that the answer to all of these interlocking questions is yes, and the articulation of the "yes" centers on the trial and execution of Julius and Ethel Rosenberg.

My intention here will be different from that in the discussions of Blood Libels and related accusations, affairs and events up to this point: I shall *not* argue *for or against the guilt or innocence* of the Rosenbergs or their associates. Others have done that, and I will summarize what seem to be the arguments to date in both directions. My point, though, is differently angled and differently intentioned. I would suggest that much of the process by which they were arrested, indicted, tried, found guilty and executed cut directly against the assertion that the American legal system inevitably leads to justice. More importantly for the larger narrative of which this story is part, I will claim that a significant factor in the failure of the government to operate according to just principles was that, not merely the Rosenbergs and their associates, but all of the principal individuals involved in their ordeal, were Jews.

Or put otherwise: the sort of assumptions, beliefs, fears and prejudices associated with centuries of blood libels that saw themselves transformed but not abandoned in the matter of Alfred Dreyfus and the Affair that bears his name is also evident in the Rosenberg Affair, half a century and an ocean away. In fact, the Rosenberg Affair offers some interesting parallels—in fundamental ways, antithetical parallels—to the Dreyfus Affair. The latter emerged nearly a generation after France had lost a war to the Germans, but at a time when the army was still licking its wounds and looking for a scapegoat in order to account for its defeat. It was also a time of political turmoil in France for other reasons, as we have seen, but which turmoil, coupled with newly-emergent theories of race and socioeconomic concerns—at a time when capitalist economics could be associated in particular with the Jews, even by a former Jew like Karl Marx—seemed to make it easy to point toward a Jew as that scapegoat and as a symbol of all that underlay the turmoil and the concerns.

By contrast, the Rosenberg Affair emerged less than a decade after a resounding victory by the Americans and their allies over the Germans and theirs. The most potent allies of the Germans, the Japanese, had been defeated ultimately by the new technology of the atomic bomb. But the ink of victory was barely dry and the fear of a new threat, from a new front—the Communist front, established, maintained and expanded by our erstwhile allies, the Russians— together with the fear that the Russian Communists might obtain that new technology, (the knowledge of which separated the United States from all other nations, allied or enemy), led to a psychological condition parallel to that in France sixty years earlier.

That fear has a somewhat paradoxic history. On the one hand Communism was simply present in the United States as one among several political viewpoints and alternatives within less than a decade of the Soviet Revolution of 1917. There was a candidate for the presidency from the Workers' Party—commonly understood to be the Communist Party—beginning in 1924. By 1936 a candidate—Earl R. Browder—ran openly as a Communist. But things began to change shortly thereafter. In 1944, the Communists were nowhere to be seen, although there was a Socialist Workers/Militant Workers Party that began running candidates in 1948. Thus the American concern regarding the USSR antedated World War II, particularly as Stalin increased his personal stranglehold on his country. That concern was necessarily pushed to the backstage of American foci as Hitler became a more substantial threat, but began to re-occupy center stage even before the war was over.

The psychological condition, paralleling that of France during the Dreyfus period, in retrospect, also reflected a broader xenophobic condition that we have earlier observed as arriving to a point of enshrinement in the Johnson-Reed Act of 1924—so solidly enshrined, in fact, that even when, as World War II was taking shape, shortly following *Kristallnacht*, a proposal for a bil that would permit 20,000 German (mostly Jewish) children under the age of 14 to enter the United States temporarily (above the German immigration quota) was submitted to Congress, that proposal was ultimately shot down by a coalition of paranoid, or perhaps merely hypocritical and self-obsessed, "patriotic" groups.[237] The Daughters of the American Revolution, for instance, voiced concern that the admission to our country of children from places where Socialist and Communist politics were at play could undermine our staunch opposition to such onerous political systems—thereby potentially depriving our own children of freedom.[238]

We must not forget that the 1930s began as an exceptionally difficult time for Americans as well as for others: the world-wide depression made it much easier for those with fascist impulses, regardless of the particulars of their political sensibilities, to find adherents eager to place the blame for their economic woes on someone else's shoulders. For a rising Austro-German politician like Adolf Hitler that someone could be labeled at first "Communist" and other terms referring to the political opposition to National Socialism, but soon thereafter, as "Jews." America also had its voices, none more rampant than that of Father Coughlin, the Detroit-area priest with a popular Sunday morning radio program in which he sermonized weekly against the Christ-killing, would-be-world-subduing Jews—who referred to *Kristallnacht* as a defense mechanism against the Jewish Communist conspiracy. No champion of anti-Semitism was more visible than Henry Ford, anti-Communist Capitalist *par excellence*, who provided copies of Hitler's *Mein Kampf* by the tens of thousands to his workers in America and his friends in Germany.

What Hitler, Coughlin and Ford had in common with most Americans was the fear that Communism, spawned by the Soviet Revolution two decades earlier but seeking to spread its tentacles across the planet, might accomplish its goals unless it met strenuous and concerted opposition. These three also shared in common a distaste for Jews—Hitler along Wilhelm Marr-inspired racial-ethnic grounds, Ford and Coughlin along religious-historical grounds—and a desire to gain the support of the German and American peoples respectively in a crusade to prevent the covert Jewish domination that they presented as the mirror of the overt Communist domination threatening good people everywhere. Why and how Hitler largely succeeded with the German people and Ford and Coughlin largely did not with the American people is a discussion beyond this one.

Conversely, it is also the case that many Americans—particularly American Jews—were initially sympathetic to Communism because of its socio-economic equity promises, even continuing to believe in it as an ideology after Stalin came to power. But most of these altered their view after the non-aggression pact signed in 1938 between Germany and the USSR. This virtual alliance seemed a betrayal by Stalin, given all that Hitler already openly espoused and was accomplishing, especially where Jews were concerned.

What is relevant for our narrative is the atmosphere of diverse upset, anger, frustration and paranoia in the United States of the 1930s that, among other things, underlay the formation of the House Un-American Activities Committee (HUAC) by the U.S. Congress, in May, 1938.[239] Texas Representative Martin Dies, Jr. was initially put in charge of the committee—designed to conduct public hearings intended to expose Communist and Fascist ties of individuals in public employment, education, labor unions and other fields with potential wide influence (such as, eventually, the Hollywood film industry). What was annually renewed as a temporary committee was converted to a standing committee in 1945, by which time its focus had completed its shift toward those with Communist, rather than Facist or Nazi sympathies.

The Committee had considerable subpoena power, and was thus able to compel suspected Communists to appear before it for interrogation about their own affiliations and activities and those of their friends and associates. Witnesses were inevitably confronted with difficult moral and/or legal choices in an Inquisitional atmosphere, where the Committee could lodge vague accusations, while witnesses received little or no opportunity to offer evidence on their own behalf or to cross-examine witnesses used against them. To admit membership in a Communist organization, even years before, (the more so, of course, at the time of inquiry), often led to "blacklisting"—the inability to be employed in a given profession. As such, careers and the lives built around them could be and were destroyed by the bushelful.

Of course, one could also refuse to testify, based on the Fifth Amendment—but this was assumed to be a tacit admission of guilt.[240] One could refuse to cooperate based on the First Amendment, but that could result in being criminally charged with Contempt of Congress.[241] On the other hand, one could exhibit remorse and prove one's rehabilitation by providing names of others—some have termed the decision to take this option "collaboration." The result was a chain-reaction of often unsubstantiated accusations which offered those accused not much with regard to saving themselves from disaster, except by engendering disasters for others—associates, colleagues, friends, even family members.

There was more. On June 28, 1940, the Smith Act was enacted by Congress. Its intention was to prosecute leaders of the Communist party in America for advocating the violent overthrow of the U.S. government. Put otherwise, Americans working for or advocating whatever a congressional committee regarded as radical solutions to the recession that had emerged in the previous two years could be investigated, fined and imprisoned as subversives.[242] Thus by the end of the war, two different governmental bodies were in full swing, with years of prior development, directing themselves at

Americans accused of involvement or believed to be involved with Communism. This direction of thinking had swiftly assumed the place occupied for a decade, in the minds of at least some Americans, by Nazism as the chief threat to freedom and the American way of life.

Nor, by the way, was the state of mind that completed a shift from focus on Nazism (back) to a focus on Communism limited to the United States. The British made a decision in 1948 to cease and desist from pursuing or prosecuting Nazi war criminals after August 31 of that year. The decision extended to all of the Commonwealth countries, including Canada, which in the previous year had been on the lookout for 154 suspected former Nazis. Commonwealth leaders were eager "to put World War II behind them in order to concentrate on the Cold War... [Further, a] confidential document dated August 13, 1948 cautioned that 'no public announcement' was to be made of this policy decision."[243]

The expansion of the Cold War on the heels of World War II re-enforced the sense of urgency to expose those individuals—huge numbers of them, in some politicians' estimates—who were working to overthrow the government. Fears deepened, as Stalin's post-World War II acquisitions within Europe led to the imposition of police states in Poland, Czechoslovakia and East Germany and support for Communist forces in the Greek Civil War; as by 1949 the Soviet Union showed its nuclear capacity, far earlier than had been predicted by U.S. Intelligence, exploding its first test bomb, fondly named "Joe 1"; as newly Communist mainland China intervened on the Northern side in the undeclared Korean War in 1950. All of this activity fueled the sense that an international Communist coalition was seeking to destroy democratic states and that there were spies within the heart of America willing not only to work for the overthrow of the government but willing and able to supply the Communists with U.S. nuclear secrets.

That sense was re-enforced by a number of cases—three in particular. Thus Elizabeth Bentley allegedly left the American Communist Party in 1944 and the following year went to the FBI with a list of 80 individuals who, she asserted, were part of an espionage ring on behalf of the Communists, 37 of them government employees. She testified before a federal grand jury convened in the spring of 1947 for the purpose of pursuing her claims, which after more than a year of deliberation was dissolved without a single indictment being handed down.[244] In part this was because most of those on the list quietly left the government before the indictment process could entangle them.

Bentley would also testify before the HUAC in July, 1948, and subsequently before Truman's EO 9835 Committee concerning loyalty and security investigations and other Senate and House committees, naming scores of people who she claimed had been Soviet spies while they were working for the American government. None of them was given the opportunity to face her or offer a cross-examination, and many lost their jobs as a consequence of her public accusations. The fact that very little of her testimony was verified—and that she was surviving economically by supplying her stories for pay to the *World Telegram*—did little to undermine the conviction of the HUAC or J. Edgar Hoover's FBI that the Communist threat was any less than they had initially supposed.

This HUAC testimony by Bentley is the second case that reinforced a widespread fear that Communist espionage was rampant within the country. The third case was that which, within 18 months of the Bentley testimony before the HUAC, culminated with the conviction of Alger Hiss in January, 1950. Moreover, one month later, the arrest and beginning confession of Soviet spy Klaus Fuchs, rang in the month of February in England.[245]

Fears and concerns pushed the HUAC and its sibling entities to new heights of influence as America moved into the 1950s, beginning with new legislation in the form of the McCarran Internal Security Act in 1950. The MIS required Communist organizations to register the names of their members and all financial contributors with the Subversive Activities Control Board. More notorious because of his gradual overstepping of all moral and legal bounds was Wisconsin Republican Senator Joseph McCarthy and his Permanent Subcommittee on Investigations—part of the Senate Committee on Governmental Operations. McCarthy leapt into national prominence when, in a speech to the Republican Women's Club of Wheeling, West Virginia on February 9, 1950—a month after Hiss's conviction—he held up a piece of paper claiming that on it "I have... a list of 205 names that were made known to the Secretary of State as members of the Communist Party and who are nonetheless still working and shaping policy in the State Department."[246]

In that very month—perhaps in part prompted by McCarthy's allegations—the Senate Foreign Relations Committee set up a subcommittee under the chairmanship of Democratic Senator Millard Tydings, to conduct a "full and complete study and investigation as to whether persons who are disloyal to the United States are, or have been, employed by the Department of State." In the end, the Tydings committee concluded that the individuals on McCarthy's list—he eventually came up with nine names, including several people who had never actually worked for the State Department—were neither Communists nor even Communist sympathizers. The Committee opined that the State Department had a very effective security program and Tydings summarized McCarthy's charges as "a fraud and a hoax."

Perhaps even more to the point, Tydings observed that the consequence of McCarthy's actions was "to confuse and divide the American people... to a degree far beyond the hopes of the Communists themselves." The Senate was itself divided along party lines as to whether or not to accept the report. (Three roll-call votes were necessary in order to do so). Against this chaotic backdrop, toward the beginning of his second term as a senator, in 1953, McCarthy was made chairman of the Senate Committee on Government Operations—an inherently banal committee appointment, (as opposed to the Internal Security Subcommittee), apparently designed to keep McCarthy from doing harm, as his methods became a matter of increasing concern for the Party leadership. But McCarthy merely transformed the CGO Committee's Permanent Subcommittee on Investigations into an instrument for furthering his search for Communists in the government.

This became the vehicle through which McCarthy pushed his accusations of Communist influence and involvement up into the Voice of America (administered at that time by the State Department's USIA)—against whose various employees not a single charge was substantiated—and the overseas library program of the USIA (the State Department succumbed and allowed McCarthy's thugs to remove all "materials by any controversial persons, Communists, fellow travelers, etc"—in some cases, burning the books. McCarthy went still further, using his committee in the fall of 1953 to attack the U.S. Army with stories of a dangerous spy ring among the corps of army researchers. He went as far as to butt heads with the executive branch of the government—as before with Democratic President Truman so now with Republican President Eisenhower.

A young lawyer by the name of Roy M. Cohn was taken on as legal council to the Committee—his job, in other words, to assure that nothing that the committee did would fall afoul of the American Constitution. But he evolved quickly—he was the primary individual who traveled around to U.S. embassies throughout Europe, stripping their libraries of "inappropriate" and "dangerous" books—into what Ed Kretzman, a policy advisor for the VOA, referred to as McCarthy's "chief hatchet man." Certainly McCarthy and Cohn offered, together, as dark a partnership as any in the political history of the twentieth-century United States.

The March 9, 1954 TV broadcast of journalist Edward R. Murrow's *See It Now*, which featured clips of McCarthy's rants, together with the televising of the McCarthy-Army hearings, created an anti-McCarthy backlash across much of America, and eventually, on June 11, Vermont Republican Senator Ralph E. Flanders introduced a resolution to have McCarthy removed as chair of his committees, and subsequently a resolution to have the Wisconsin Senator censured. On December 2, the Senate voted to condemn him by a vote of 67 to 22.[247]

But the end of Joseph McCarthy was not yet the end of the irrational fear (as opposed to rational concern, if I may make that distinction) regarding Communists within the America of the mid-1950s. It was not until June 17, 1957 (known by opponents as "Red Monday") that the Supreme Court, in a series of four decisions, sided with parties who had challenged governmental anti-Communist policies. Even then, the intervention by the Court was strongly enough criticized that it retreated and, as late as 1961 it upheld the prison sentence of a Smith Act Defendant. In fact it was not until 1962 that the Court began to make it clear that it would not tolerate prosecutions based on individuals' refusals to testify before legislative committees regarding Communist associations.

I have spent so much time in the discussion of the atmosphere leading up to, through and beyond the arrest, conviction and execution of Julius and Ethel Rosenberg because I believe that a significant element in all three of these aspects of their case may be traced to that atmosphere and the sort of activities that were permitted and even encouraged in the America of that era. In the mood that was building from 1938 to 1949—from the establishment of HUAC to the first Soviet nuclear test— with its desperation to find treasonous Americans, the emphasis, to repeat, reverted gradually but dramatically, from Nazism to Communism.[248]

One might see 1950 as a double turning-point. On the one hand, it was discovered in January—not long after the first Soviet nuclear tests—that Emil Julius Klaus Fuchs, a German refugee theoretical physicist at work for the British mission on the Manhattan Project, had been transmitting important documents pertinent to atomic research to the Soviets during and since the war.[249] Fuchs was arrested in England on February 2. On the other hand, on June 25, the Korean Conflict began, in which, over the following three years, thousands of Americans would die and in which the appearance of the Soviets on the other side of the conflict was perceived by some to have been made possible by their possession of atomic weaponry.[250]

If the unhappy progress of the Korean conflict could and would be used as an instrument with which to help further develop fear and with it hostile American public sentiment toward anyone believed to have been—or accused of having been—involved in transmitting information of any sort to the Soviets, the arrest of Fuchs offered a concrete beginning to a trail that would lead to the Rosenbergs by mid-summer.

Julius was born in 1918, toward the end of World War I. In

1936, at the age of 18 he became a leader in the Young Communist League in New York City. It may be difficult to recall—particularly given the Cold War that followed for so many decades thereafter—how attractive Communism appeared to many people, particularly young people, and perhaps to Jews in particular between the time well before the Soviet Revolution and the eve of World War II, when the nature of Stalin's iron-fisted regime had begun to reveal itself. (But there were those even then whose commitment to Communist principles was so profound that they never believed that the Soviet Union was really going in the direction in which, for others, it became clear that Stalin was leading). Communism argued that the key issue standing between the world as it is and a peaceful world of greater justice—and also one cured of the disease of anti-Semitism—is economic; that to redistribute wealth and with it, power, in a more equitable manner would be to cure the world of any number of its ills.

And of course, until the end of World War II, the Communist Soviet Union was not only our ally against the Nazis, but it had stood up to the Nazis alone for some time until we entered the fray on a new front. Thus Klaus Fuchs would later testify that after Nazi Germany invaded the Soviet Union in 1941 he began to transmit military secrets from the West to the Soviets, believing strongly that they had the right to know what the British (and subsequently, the United States) were working on. He asserted that he made his initial contact with the Soviets through a former friend in the German Communist Party. And, between the time Hitler invaded the Soviet Union in June, 1941, and the opening up of a new front by the allies, in France in June of 1944, the Soviets were largely alone in holding back Nazism—so idealists on both sides of the Atlantic were eager to help them.

For Jews drawn to Communism, it was not only a matter of social conscience and justice—the imperative to "fix the world" that is traced by many historians of Jewish thought back to the Israelite prophets—but that the movement's assertions included that of helping to rid the world of its anti-Semitism by repairing socio-economic inequities. The closing up of the great chasm between the few who possess so much and the many who possess so little (symbolized, in part, in Russia, by the theoretical elimination of the Tsarist regime and the redistribution of the wealth of the upper crust among the people),[251] together with the final and unequivocal elimination of religion as a false guide to living one's life, would lead to the elimination of Jew-hatred.

How could an idealist, particularly an idealistic Jew, not be drawn to that? In the first seven years after the Soviet Revolution, when Lenin was promoting a multi-cultural society that emphatically included Jews and was excoriating old-school anti-Semites—and for the decade following Lenin's death in 1924, before Stalin had solidified his power and began turning the USSR into an extended Gulag—Moscow appeared to offer as much of a hopeful humanist's glow as Washington, DC.

It was in the Young Communist League that Julius met Ethel, an aspiring actress and singer three years older than he, whom he married three years later. By then he had graduated from City College of New York with a degree in electrical engineering (in 1939); the following year he joined the Army Signal Corps, working on radar equipment. Julius and Ethel are said to have become full-fledged members of the American Communist Party—one of any number of socio-political parties outside the ambit of the primary Democratic/Republican dichotomy—in 1942.[252] This was the same year, according to his alleged former KGB handler, Alexander Feklisov, in which Julius, at age 24, was recruited, on Labor Day, by Soviet spymaster Semyon Semenov.[253]

Feklisov claims that the fact that both Semenov and Rosenberg were Jewish helped create a tighter connection between them.[254] Presumably the idealized view of Communism from a Jewish perspective would have been something they shared, while the concern regarding the potential spread of Nazism would also have been paramount to them both as Jews. The Rosenbergs are said to have dropped out of the party early the next year—allegedly so that Julius would be able to pursue his espionage activities without drawing the potential attention to himself that, as a member of the Party, he might have drawn.

On the other hand, Julius was fired from his job with the Signal Corps in 1945, when his prior membership in the Communist Party became known. If Feklisov's testimony is factual, then prior to his dismissal, Julius was able to provide good information to his bosses, including thousands of classified reports from Emerson Radio; he was also said to have recruited a number of individuals to serve the KGB, among them Morton Sobell. Feklisov also later asserted that Julius directed another of his recruits, William Perl, to supply their leaders with thousands of documents from the National Advisory Committee for aeronautics, including a set of design and production drawings for Lockheed's P-80 Shooting Star—and that through Julius, he (Feklisov) learned that Ethel's brother, Sergeant David Greenglass was working on the Manhattan Project at Los Alamos. And that he managed to recruit David to their service through Julius.

These would have been some of the key players on the team whose intention was to share atomic secrets with Stalin's Soviet Union in the aftermath of the end of World War II, the transformation of that aftermath into the Cold War and the first series of U.S.-Communist confrontations that evolved into the Korean Conflict by the early 1950s. In the aftermath of Fuchs' arrest in England, in February, 1950, and his subsequent interrogations and confessions, a series of individuals including members of this "team" were arrested that summer. Thus Fuchs' remarks offered sufficient weight against his "courier," Harry Gold, that Gold was arrested a few days after the FBI had interrogated Fuchs on May 20.

This was not because Fuchs referred specifically to Gold—in fact he did not recognize him in the still photo that the FBI showed him, (although he subsequently said that he *did* recognize him in film footage shown to him) and his description of his courier was considerably different from how Gold looked—but because the FBI concluded from Fuchs' identifying remarks about his courier that Gold must be the man. He was so-identified out of a list of 1200 chemists in the Philadelphia-New York area who might fit the bill that the agency compiled. Gold was arrested on May 23.

Gold would make his first court appearance not in the context of the Rosenberg trial, but as the star prosecution witness in what amounted to "the first actual trial of any of the nine Americans arrested during 1950 and linked with the Klaus Fuchs atom-spy ring," that opened on November 8, 1950. The defendants were Abraham Brothman—Harry Gold's former employer—and Brothman's business associate, Miriam Moskowitz. Brothman and Moskowitz were actually not accused of espionage, but of conspiring with Gold to impede a federal Grand Jury investigation back in 1947, and that Brothman had induced Gold to lie about their association, at that time and subsequently.

There are at least three aspects of that earlier trial that would have implications for the Rosenberg-Sobell trial of 1951. The first is the nature of Gold's testimony and his own comments about himself as a fabulist. His story kept changing, and with each iteration, Brothman and Moskowitz appeared in a darker and darker light and he (Gold) appeared to have spent more and more uncompensated time heroically if misguidedly assisting their espionage efforts. This allegedly culminated in a series of blueprints that his Soviet handlers returned to him, finding them incomplete, and the gathering of material over a period of a year and a half that was never even handed over, because the processes that the material "revealed" were already known to the Soviets and the information was therefore useless to them.

Meanwhile Gold had spun tales about his personal life when he first met Brothman—that he was married with children (he was a bachelor)—allegedly at the behest of his Soviet handler, Sam. He admitted to having continued to spin tales after he was no longer working with Sam. These were elaborate, not simple fantasies. His wife was named (Sarah O'Ken) and he had met her while courting another girl with one blue eye and one brown eye, they lived in a small apartment with their two twin children—and so on, typically basing his stories in part on aspects of the lives of real people whom he knew. He had a marvelous ability to keep all the fabricated details, however complicated, straight, and proudly exclaimed, regarding his fabulist skills, that "[i]t is a wonder steam didn't come out of my ears at times."[255] Nor were his weavings limited to reports on his personal life; he simply seems to have made up "facts" regarding his associations, his motivations and role within the American Communist world and his modus operandi as a spy.

The case against Brothman and Moskowitz relied primarily on the testimony of Gold and that of Elizabeth Bentley, the by-then widely known ex-Communist "spy queen" who had testified frequently in the previous several years before this Congressional committee and that Federal Grand Jury, as we have earlier noted. True to form, Bentley had little to offer that one could consider seriously legitimate. She had no idea—"not the least idea"—about *anything* regarding the blueprints in question, yet managed to have the strong "impression" that they had been stolen. She had had them copied, but could not remember where. She could remember nothing about what she had asserted two years earlier in her testimony before the HUAC. It seems astounding—and this is the second aspect of this trial that would have implications for the Rosenberg-Sobell trial—that anyone with a rational bone in his or her body would do other than arrive at the conclusion that, like Harry Gold, Elizabeth Bentley spun virtually whatever came into her head and would help prolong her moment in the sunlight of notoriety.

The second issue of particular interest is that the prosecutor was U.S. Attorney Irving H. Saypol, who would subsequently play the same role in the Rosenberg trial, and that among his three assistants was Roy M. Cohn—the same Roy M. Cohn who would play such a prominent role not only in the Rosenberg trial but also as legal counsel to Joseph McCarthy's Sub-Committee a few years later. What makes this particular issue interesting is that it might cause one to wonder as to how and why certain individuals choose to become "specialists" at prosecuting or assisting the prosecution of a particular sort of crime, such as that of being accused of being a Communist spy. If Gold and Bentley became professional ex-Communists and experts on Communist espionage, Saypol and Cohn became professional courtroom takers-down of alleged Communist conspirators.

Similarly—the third issue of interest—the trial judge was Irving R. Kaufman, who would not only preside over the Rosenberg trial, but gave every evidence of being prejudiced in advance in *both* trials in favor of the prosecution, thus facilitating Sapol's and Cohn's success: one might call it a team effort. That is: Kaufman was fully supportive of the notion that the country, its freedom and its democratic system were under profound assault and that it would be more dangerous to allow anyone accused of association with the assaulters to go free in error than to convict such a person in error. When in the Brothman-Moskowitz trial defense attorney William Kleinman asked the Judge for permission to examine Elizabeth Bentley's pre-trial statements regarding Brothman for inconsistencies vis-a-vis her in-court testimony, Kaufman refused, asserting that Kleinman's cross-examination of her had failed to reveal inconsistencies—as well it probably could not have helped failing to do, since her testimony was so entirely vague. But given her importance to the case, this is an extraordinary refusal, reflecting a strong anti-defense bias.

In the face of testimony of two individuals—one of whom admitted that he made things up, often along elaborate lines, and the second of whom had testified on two prior occasions against scores of individuals about whom no evidence could be found that they were guilty of that of which she accused them—the jury deliberated for three and a half hours and then found both individuals guilty. Astonishingly, Judge Kaufman turned to the prosecution team to congratulate it for the U.S. Attorney's "ingenuity in searching the statute books and finding the obstruction of justice statute, because there was a serious question about the statute of limitations having run on the matter of espionage itself."[256] In other words, Kaufman was thrilled to find *some* way of finding Brothman and Moskowitz guilty of *something*. For the original assumption that had led to their being hauled into court—their association with Klaus Fuchs—had been completely abandoned for lack of anything resembling legitimate testimony.

Judge Kaufman went on to speak of his distress at the limits of the punishment that he was permitted to impose upon them, "for I consider their offense in this case to be of such gross magnitude. I have no sympathy or mercy for these defendants in my heart, none whatsoever."[257] What might one suppose of the mindset of such an individual when offered the opportunity to preside over the Rosenberg-Sobell trial some time thereafter—with the same two star witnesses as the lead-off batters in the prosecution line-up? Thus the nature of the charge against Brothman and Moskowitz as it was articulated before the court, the kind of evidence deemed admissible and/or reliable, the jury's decision within the atmospheric conditions of its operaton, and Judge Kaufman's words in handing down the sentence—all of these elements reflect forward on the trial, verdict and punishment of Julius and Ethel Rosenberg and Morton Sobell.

If the significance of Judge Kaufman's words for our narrative is that they suggest a frame of mind that would impinge upon the Rosenberg affair—both making it difficult for them to receive a fair and just hearing and leading to what might be considered an excessive penalty—then the significance of the nature of the testimony of both Gold and Bentley is that they, with their courtroom track records, would be two of the key links in the chain that would permit the Rosenbergs and Morton Sobell to be found guilty of the charges leveled against them by the prosecution.

Harry Gold would testify damningly against the Rosenbergs, although the details of his testimony, as in the previous two trials in which he had been involved, kept changing.[258] It doesn't seem as if his notorious tale-spinning diminished—including his invention of imaginary recruits as spies about whom he provided imaginary reports. (There are names he named of individuals who simply did not to exist.) It is impossible to know whether his FBI interrogators had an influence—or how *much* influence they may have had—on the way he shaped the words that he ultimately offered in court, or how much of his testimony reflected his own delusions, or how much of it might have been true (for, as with his fabrications regarding his personal life, some of it might have had a basis of one sort or another in fact). Astonishingly, the Rosenberg lawyer, Emanuel Bloch, would fail to cross-examine him—and one wonders why.[259]

Gold asserted that he had been a link between Fuchs and Rosenberg and between Rosenberg and David Greenglass, initially making contact with Greenglass not far from Los Alamos in Albuquerque by way of the words "I came from Julius." He claimed that he matched part of a jello box that had been cut in half along a curving angle, the second half of which was in Greenglass' possession—the simple but clever ruse was like fitting together the two halves of the Passover *afikomen matzah*.[260] Having established each other's legitimacy within the espionage circle by matching box parts, he then became the transmitter of information between Los Alamos and New York. Oddly, however, Gold, with his memory of all the details of stories he made up about himself, had no initial recollection of having met Greenglass in New Mexico until the FBI interrogators provided him with a short list of possible names and Greenglass's was at the top.

He had neither mentioned nor written about his mission to Albuquerque prior to the time when David Greenglass signed his initial statement to the FBI in the early hours of June 16. This was ten days after Gold's lawyers conducted their first lengthy interview with him in Holmseburg County Prison and three weeks and 102 hours since his first conversation with the FBI. Even more astonishing—given the importance of this transaction for the prosecution's case, as the "necessary link in the chain that points indisputably to the guilt of the Rosenbergs"—is the fact that, whereas Gold referred, on the witness stand, to the phrase "I come from Julius" and to the jello-box recognition procedure between Greenglass and him, there was absolutely no mention of the procedure in his recorded pretrial interviews or written statements.

In fact, when his lawyer, Hamilton, asked him during their pre-trial conversations whether there had been any means for him to identify his contact in Albuquerque, (because Gold had not even volunteered that there was any recognition procedure until prompted), Harry responded that there was, "and while this is not the exact recognition sign I believe that it involved the name of a man and was something on the order of Bob sent me or Benny sent me or John sent me or something like that."[261] During the trial, Gold mentioned various encounters with the Greenglasses and others in which the name "Julius" was essential—six times he mentioned "Julius," to be precise—but in all of the extended pretrial testimony that he wrote or was recorded, he never mentioned the name at all.

Before he sat on the witness stand, he had forgotten trips to the Greenglass apartment in Albuquerque, forgotten the password "I come from Julius," forgotten about the jello box—nor did he recall having had a vital meeting in New York with Anatoli Yakovlev prior to going to Albuquerque, which is when, according to his courtroom testimony, Yakovlev supplied him with his instructions and his half of the jello box side.[262] He also had forgotten to turn over Greenglass's data to Yakovlev, according to his pre-trial testimony. Everything in that pretrial testimony points to his never having met the Greenglasses before their arrests. All of his revived recollections that served to corroborate statements by Greenglass seem to have emerged from his memory *after assistance* from the FBI interrogators and after the arrest of the Greenglasses.

There is indeed an amazing array of details that are entirely missing from the hours of pre-trial discussion and testimony to which the Rosenberg and Sobell defense attorneys did not have access that, as Gold sat on the witness stand, helped corroborate aspects of David Greenglass' story damning Julius Rosenberg.[263] Nearly all of those details lacked actual physical evidence—perhaps the mockup of the jello box is the exception to this—but were entirely dependent on the coincidence of the Gold and Greenglass testimony for validation. And whereas the jello box could easily enough have been created *post facto*, once the story had been shaped, there seems to be no record of all of the trips to and from New Mexico claimed by Gold—neither train ticket stubs nor employment records showing absences—that would concretize in a more objective way his claims of meetings with Greenglass in Albuquerque.[264]

Elizabeth Bentley would also testify—although in no courtroom other than that of Judge Irving Kaufman had anyone found a whit of her testimony truthful previously, even when backed up by months of FBI investigations pursued specifically in order to find corroboration or at least some support for her claims. In her testimony she asserted that, in her Communist days, she had gone under a variety of aliases—Helen, Joan, Mary—and that she had transmitted messages from "Julius" to her superior and lover, Jacob Golos. Judge Kaufman noted to the jury that they might infer that

"Julius" meant Julius Rosenberg—who was apparently unique, in that in spite of his importance to the Soviet espionage enterprise, he used no aliases while everyone else around him did. That "Julius" who initiated five or six telephone conversations conducted back in 1942 and 1943 with Ms. Bentley, always very late at night, by identifying himself: "[t]his is Julius."

Perhaps most important among the prosecution's star witnesses was the next of the alleged principals within the Klaus Fuchs spy ring to have been arrested—on June 16—David Greenglass. Greenglass had been a machinist at Los Alamos—a simple mechanic with little if any scientific training, who, it was claimed by the prosecution, had been recruited to select, assimilate and memorize secrets of decisive importance to the Atomic Bomb project. Greenglass confessed to having passed such secret information on to the Soviet Union through Gold and implicated his sister and brother-in-law. He asserted that he had handed over atomic bomb data to Julius; he went on further to describe a Rosenberg spy ring that had gathered information on a series of other projects—a space platform and an atomic airplane—and to claim that Julius had told him that he had stolen a proximity fuse from Emerson radio.

David asserted that Julius always knew things—such as the fact that David would be working on an atomic bomb project in Los Alamos well before David left New York for the Southwest—from "the boys." Thus, for example, he "told me he had gotten information about the sky platform from one of the boys, as he put it... He said that it [the so-called sky platform] was some large vessel which would be suspended at a point of no gravity between the moon and the earth and as a satellite if would spin around the earth."[265] "The boys" were never named, although according to David, Julius was absolutely swashbuckling in the information he shared. Julius' steady stream of boasting certainly contravened standard operating espionage procedures.[266]

He initially denied that his sister, Ethel had been involved at all, but that Julius had convinced her to recruit David on a visit to New Mexico in 1944—and that Julius had also passed secrets to the Soviets through Gold. By the time he was testifying in the courtroom,

Greenglass asserted that Ethel had typed notes containing nuclear secrets, (although the notes she was alleged to have typed up proved to contain little of relevance to the atomic bomb project), that she did this in the Rosenberg's apartment in September, 1945—and that he had himself made a sketch of a cross-section of the implosion-type atom bomb (the sort that was dropped on Nagasaki, as opposed to the sort that was dropped on Hiroshima) which he had turned over to Julius at that meeting.

Perhaps even more so than Gold and Bentley, Greenglass seemed either not to be able to distinguish fact from fiction or was susceptible, under pressure, to creating facts out of fiction. His own wife, Ruth spoke of his "tendency to hysteria" and of how, in all the years she had known him—since he was ten years old—"he would say things were so even if they were not."[267] Where he elaborated a long story of how Julius had pushed him to leave the country after the arrest of Harry Gold, Julius asserted on the witness stand that David had come to him in a very agitated manner and asked for money and information regarding what kind of injections were required if one were to go to Mexico. David asserted that he and Ruth and their kids had passport photos taken in order to follow the plan that Julius laid out for them, but the photographs produced in evidence (as exhibit #9) are not passport photos, but ordinary family photos—and two of the sets are dated more than seven months *after* David's arrest—and husband and wife contradicted each other with regard to how many groups of photos were taken.

Not a word offered by David Greenglass could be proven or disproven—it was simply his word against Julius' word—except for his story of the stolen proximity fuse. That "fact" was amenable to some sort of objective verification, but the records at Emerson Radio indicated that no such object had ever been stolen, or misplaced, or gone temporarily missing. Later—after Julius and Ethel had been convicted and executed in large part due to David Greenglass' testimony—while David was serving his own brief term in Lewisburg Penitentiary[268]—he was interviewed for a Senate Subcommittee hearing, once before the Subcommittee, (in 1956), once in prison (in 1957). Each time he further elaborated on his brother-in-law's alleged crimes, expanding well beyond what he had "remembered" at the time of the trial, including moneys that Julius was expecting from his well-paid spy associate who was working on the Aswan Dam project, in 1948. Except that there was no such project at that time.

Interestingly, Greenglass was not able to distinguish between more and less improved types of explosion molds on which he was supposed to have been working at Los Alamos that were alleged to be of decisive importance to the project. He was also said by Feklisov never to have supplied any information of value, since he "had only a rudimentary grasp of the work on the bomb." That assertion by the Soviet agent, while it may do little to change the view of Julius Rosenberg and David Greenglass as both involved in espionage for the USSR, raises that other perennial question: what was the value of the information transmitted from Los Alamos; was it as significant as the prosecution and trial judge made it out to be—and did it justify a death sentence for both Julius and his wife?

Julius was arrested on July 17 and Ethel on August 11. Suffice it to say that they defended themselves in court on the witness stand against the accusations made by David and Ruth Greenglass. Indeed, the narrative that they offered was not only different from that offered by David, but it suggests that David was in increasing trouble—whether espionage-related or otherwise they could not determine—and came to them for help. Put another way, Julius' version of events, if it is to be believed, suggests that David, in his desperation and his proclivity for expansive fantasy, not only transformed his role into that of a major supplier of atomic bomb information to the Soviets, through Julius, but transferred the role he had attempted to play to Julius' shoulders, once things began to catch up with him. For the jury then and for us now it becomes a matter, largely, of whom we find more credible, Julius (and Ethel) or David (and Ruth).

Another key alleged conspirator, Morton Sobell, the only other "conspirator" to stand trial with the Rosenbergs, was arrested a week after Ethel was, on August 18. The accusation against him was to have *agreed to supply* (as opposed to having *supplied*) national defense information to the Soviet Union. Sobell was on vacation with his wife and two children in Mexico City when the Rosenbergs were arrested. The prosecution would claim that he had fled precipitously to Mexico, (with the implied intention of continuing on, presumably to Russia) which precipitousness would point to his guilt as a spy.

But he had gone through the formal process of requesting a leave of absence from his employer, went through all the usual procedures for a family trip out of the country—visas, plane reservations and the like—and packed up and left in an orderly manner. He made sure that his camera equipment was checked out by the customs agents in Texas before crossing the border, so that he would not have to pay duty on it when he came back into the country, and rented an apartment in Mexico City where he and his family resided (openly, under their own names) for more than a month.[269]

It is true that he later asserted that he was trying to figure out if he could get to Europe without a passport, in a panic after hearing that Julius and Ethel Rosenberg had been arrested and that everyone and anyone who had been close to them was under suspicion. He went to two different port towns in Mexico, used aliases, thought about whether flight was feasible or even necessary and, ultimately abandoning the idea as crazy, remained in Mexico—until he was kidnapped from his Mexico City hotel and brought to the U.S. border, where he was arrested. The U.S. government claimed at that time that he was deported by the Mexican Secret Police, not kidnapped, but the Mexicans disavowed that claim in 1956—and in any case, he was in American hands by late summer, whatever the specifics of how it came about, and would ultimately stand trial with the Rosenbergs.

It is difficult, perhaps nearly impossible, for Americans who did not live though that time period to grasp the scale of paranoia and repression that held the country in its grip during a terrifying era. With increasing power and vehemence, a range of governmental agencies, from the FBI to the congressional committees in place since 1938—culminating with those associated with Joseph McCarthy's activities—were not merely engaged in dismantling entities involved in Communist support or sympathy, but in disemboweling careers and destroying lives of thousands of everyday Americans. An atmosphere of terror prevailed in which most people were afraid to speak their minds or express their beliefs. This was an era unique in American history, its only precedent the geographically circumscribed time of witch hunting in part of New England a century before the American Colonies asserted themselves against the mother country.

Studies of people under the pressure of intense fear for their safety show that individuals will tell the boldest and baldest of lies if they feel it is necessary in order to save themselves. It is also a truism of witch-hunting conditions that they offer opportunities to individuals who have grudges, to settle them, since the atmosphere makes it relatively easy to lodge charges against someone without the same degree of need to substantiate them as would be the case under "ordinary" circumstances and conversely it can often be difficult if not impossible to defend one's self against them. This is evident throughout history—from the Spanish Inquisition to the Salem, Massachusetts Witch Trials to the Stalin and Hitler eras in Soviet Russia and Germany, to name a few obvious examples in relatively recent history.

To what extent this double verity operated as the trial of the Rosenbergs and Sobell began on March 6, 1951 is of course an ongoing matter of debate. David Greenglass, for example, who gave direct testimony related to the crime of conspiracy to transmit information, about whom his own wife Ruth said that he "would say things were so even if they were not"—would he more emphatically say things even if they were not so, if he felt that his life or the well-being of his family (wife and two children) were under threat? What was his relationship with his older sister and her husband—there is no evidence that it was particularly close, but could he have found in this process the first opportunity in his life to step out from under their shadow or to even some old score (and could he possibly have known, given the leniency and limits of his own experience, what their fate would be, based in part on his testimony)? It is impossible to know for certain.

It might be noted that Greenglass was spared execution in

exchange for his testimony—he was sentenced to 15 years in jail, of which he served a mere 5 years—and his wife, Ruth (who according to conventional interpretation of the VENONA transcripts even possessed a code-name, where, oddly, given the presumed guilt of the one and innocence of the other, Ethel Rosenberg did not) was never even indicted.[270] But Greenglass in fact recanted in 1996, asserting that he had committed perjury when he testified regarding the typing activity of his sister. He claimed to have lied in order to lessen his own jail sentence and to protect his wife and children. But then, were there other details that he offered—and if so, which ones—that were false?

In fact when one reviews not only his testimony but subsequent information he supplied from prison, several years after the Rosenberg executions, one is hard put not to see him as a hapless fantasist, desperate in the first place to protect himself and his family, and willing to continue to elaborate further, over the years—based initially on suggestions and encouragements from the FBI interrogators, who easily recognized a scared dupe—one far more comfortable with science fiction than with the science he was supposed to have overheard, absorbed, integrated, interpreted, remembered and transmitted—when they saw one.[271] But we will most likely never know for sure.

What of the apparently most damning testimony from among the 23 witnesses brought before the jury by the government, that of Max Elitcher? Elitcher was a close friend of Morton Sobell—they became friends while attending Stuyvesant High School and City College together. They remained close friends thereafter, both moving to Washington, DC where they both got jobs as engineers in the Navy Bureau of Ordnance, even sharing an apartment together. Elitcher had in fact left the government in 1948 to take a job at Reeves Instruments; he and his wife moved into a house in Queens, where his backyard neighbors were the Sobells.[272]

Both Sobell and Elitcher had met Julius Rosenberg at City College, and Elitcher asserted that Julius had attempted to recruit him as an agent during the period 1944-48. While he claimed to have been sympathetic to the political beliefs espoused by both Julius and Morton, he denied having ever passed any secret information to either of them, although he subsequently claimed to have been present when Sobell passed what he took to be a roll of film to Julius, at Catherine Slip in New York. Elitcher had lied on his loyalty oath, regarding having been a college-age member of the Communist Party—because he feared the consequences of admitting ever having had Communist sympathies or connections.

One can imagine his terror that this lie had come back to potentially bury him when the FBI came knocking at his door three years later and, in the course of interrogating him, noted that they were aware of his past membership in the Party. He claimed that Sobell discussed espionage on several occasions, and that he had once seen Sobell visit Julius Rosenberg. But there is no corroboration for any of this—could he have lied about any of it, in fear for himself and his own family?—nor is it clear that the discussion of espionage would have had any connection to performing acts of espionage.

Julius and Ethel apparently did little to play to the sympathies of the jury. They both pleaded the Fifth Amendment when asked about either their involvement in the Communist Party or with others who were involved in it. Since at the very least the Prosecutors made a fairly convincing argument for that involvement, the refusal to acknowledge it led to a general sense for the jurors that the Rosenbergs were lying across the board regarding what they had or had not done and how they had or had not been involved in espionage—or at least "conspiracy to commit espionage"—on behalf of the Soviet Union. The fact that, in any case, that "conspiracy" had occurred years earlier, when, during wartime, the Soviets were our *allies*, would not have mattered to them any more than it apparently did to the prosecutors or the trial judge.

Morton Sobell was condemned by Judge Kaufman to the maximum sentence—30 years—in Alcatraz. Given the lack of any criminal record and the paucity of evidence against Sobell—Elitcher's testimony of the delivery of a small can that looked like a 35mm film can and therefore might be supposed to have had film in it, to Julius; and the assumption regarding the family trip to Mexico that it was a flight from justice, none of which led toward the sort of accusation being leveled at the Rosenbergs—the only explanation for the sentence can be Judge Kaufman's predisposition to believe Sobell guilty of conspiracy, of *intent*, to engage in a crime that he (Kaufman) considered heinous, since there was no proof that he had engaged in any crime.

In fact, in pronouncing his sentence, Kaufman observed that "I do not for a moment doubt that you were engaged in espionage activities; however, the evidence in the case did not point to any activity on your part in connection with the atom bomb project." *What* activity did it point to, then, that warranted 30 years in Alcatraz? None that someone who refused to hear Sobell's account of the Mexico trip, and who ignored all the factors that might have led to Elitcher lying in his testimony, would be able to find, without a more than *reasonable doubt*.

The Rosenbergs were convicted on March 29, 1951 and on April 5 were sentenced to death by Judge Kaufman, under Section 2 of the 1917 Espionage Act, which prohibits transmitting or attempting to transmit to a foreign government any information "relating to the national defense." Doubts as to the legitimacy of their conviction and more so, of the decision to execute them began to mount in August, 1951 with a series of articles by William A. Reuben, in the *National Guardian*. There followed the formation of a defense committee and a series of pleas for clemency, from within the United States and even more so, internationally, including one from Pope Pius XII directly to President Eisenhower—but this last one, was refused, on February 11, 1953, like those that preceded and followed it.

The Rosenbergs were to be executed on June 18, 1953, but a stay of execution was granted by Supreme Court Associate Justice William O. Douglas after an appeal by Fyke Farmer, a Tennessee lawyer whose previous suggestions and offers of advice and assistance had been met with rejection by Emanuel Bloch, the Rosenberg attorney. Interestingly, rather than allow the execution to be delayed for the usual months it would have taken while the appeal worked its way through the lower courts, the seven-member Supreme Court rushed into special session that same day, rejected the appeal and vacated Douglas' stay on June 19.[273] The execution was rescheduled for that night, but Bloch filed a complaint noting that the timing offended the Jewish heritage of the Rosenbergs, since the Sabbath would have begun by then. He obviously hoped to buy another twenty-four hours of delay while perhaps some further appeal or at least discussion might intervene, but the court simply moved the time of execution forward.

The Rosenbergs were thus executed in the electric chair, just before sundown on June 19, 1953, at Sing Sing Correctional Facility in Ossining, New York. Their espionage conviction helped fuel the fire building in the Senate, being fanned by Joseph McCarthy, with regard to the investigations into anti-American activities by U.S. citizens. Both their conviction and their execution had resulted in massive protests within and even more so, beyond the borders of the United States, and for the next forty years, discussions and debates, articles and books, symposia and conferences wrestled with the question of their guilt and if so, of its precise nature, and if that were clear, the validity of the punishment meted out to them.

In the mid-1990s, in the aftermath of the collapse of the Soviet Union and the end of the Cold War, information began to emerge from classified government files and archives that has affected the view of many as to how to answer this triple question. Nikita Khrushchev's memoirs, published posthumously in 1990, praise the Rosenbergs for their "very significant help in accelerating the production of our atomic bomb." On the one hand it is difficult to know what exactly Khrushchev knew, since he was not the man in power at the time of the alleged espionage. On the other hand, Alexander Feklisov, the former KGB officer, as we have previously seen, while corroborating the role of the Rosenbergs in providing various kinds of information to the Soviets, asserted unequivocally, in 1997, that the information that they provided was "meaningless" as far as furthering the atomic bomb project was concerned.

The most potentially damning documentation—not in terms of *what* was transmitted, but in terms of the fundamental question of their involvement in espionage, of information *having been* transmitted—is that contained in the VENONA project that was released to the public by the National Security Agency in 1995. VENONA was the code-name for the effort—jointly by the United States and the United Kingdom—to decrypt intercepted communications between known or suspected Soviet agents and the NKVD/KGB, mostly during World War II. The project was so secret that not even Presidents Franklin D. Roosevelt or Harry Truman knew about it, and it would provide a good deal of information as to who was doing what as the war moved toward its end and the Cold War began.[274]

The VENONA transcripts suggest a wide network of espionage on the part of the Soviet Union within not only the U.S. but other countries—American, Canadian, Australian and British spies were identified—as early as 1942. In the United States, spies were alleged at places that included Los Alamos National Laboratories, the State Department, the Office of Strategic Services (OSS) and even the White House. Among those identified is one referred to in a 1944 memo from New York City to Moscow by the code name ANTENNA, and subsequently referred to as LIBERAL, whom the FBI later inferred was Julius Rosenberg. "LIBERAL's wife" is also referred to—and identified by her first name, Ethel, but the only reference to her asserts that "she does not work," (i.e., is not engaged in espionage).

The preponderance of opinion is that "ANTENNA/LIBERAL" is Julius—but not universal opinion, since never does an actual name, Julius or otherwise, appear. But if that view is correct, then the transcripts would corroborate at least the fact that Julius was engaged in some sort of espionage on behalf of the USSR, while they were our ally against the Nazis during World War II. But in that case, they similarly corroborate Ethel's innocence—which was further corroborated by Feklisov, although he opined that Ethel knew what Julius was engaged in. Did she in fact type up information for him, as David Greenglass claimed? For that we have only Greenglass's word.[275] VENONA also demonstrates that, however extensive his espionage activities were, Julius never transmitted vital atomic information. Others, codenamed "QUANTUM" and "PERS" apparently facilitated the transfer of atomic and nuclear weapons technology information from within the Manhattan Project to the Soviets.

In general, the VENONA material is, to repeat, the most decisive—assuming, as not everyone does, that it is authentic (as opposed to having been forged by the NSA to discredit the Communist Party of the United States and its membership) and assuming that the inferred names identified by the decrypting process are correct—not only with regard to the Rosenbergs and their associates, but with respect to the larger question that remains unanswered to this day, one might say, regarding how virulent the threat of Communism was to this country and its allies in the 1940s and 1950s and since, and therefore how legitimate the sort of anti-Communist activity in which individuals like Joseph McCarthy were engaged.[276]

For our purposes, let us review what, in the end, are the questions and issues to which we have arrived. Were the Rosenbergs active Communists? There are relatively few who would doubt that—and except for those who are hypocritical regarding the importance of democracy and freedom, there are few who should *object* to that: Communism was and is one among any number of sociopolitical perspectives and/or political parties with which members of a free democracy might choose to be affiliated. Were either or both of them and Morton Sobell actively engaged in espionage on behalf of the Soviet Union as a symptom of their commitment to the furthering of Communism and its ideals? There is less consensus on this second question, although most likely many more students of the Affair today would be inclined to answer in the affirmative than would have been the case half a century or even twenty years ago, due to the opening of certain files—most obviously, the VENONA transcripts—and revelations offered by certain individuals, most obviously, Feklisov.[277]

But even this cannot be determined absolutely: the same questions that one might have regarding testimony in 1951 from the likes of Elizabeth Bentley or Max Elitcher, and certainly the likes of Harry Gold and David Greenglass, might be raised of Alexander Feklisov—especially when we recall that he was in the throes of writing a book on the subject, that he obviously hoped would sell, around the same time that he was making his claims—even if one might assume that, at the point in his life when he spoke out he would have had no motive other than bringing out the truth.[278] The more one reads about these individuals, their lives, and about the pressure under which the FBI and others placed them, the more one wonders whether they were spinning a constantly evolving web of fantasy.

But is Feklisov a different matter, commenting post-Cold War, to reporters in Brooklyn? It is impossible to know. Let us assume, for the sake of argument, that Feklisov and others who placed Julius at the center of an espionage ring are correct—and let us assume whatever degree of complicity on the part of Ethel we wish—we might wonder whether his motive was treason or idealism, particularly at the time he (they) was (were) alleged to have been engaged in that activity, (*during* World War II, when the Soviet Union and United States were *allies against* the Nazis). We might even wonder whether we can separate those two inclinations.

Further, we might view such actions, in the context of "Jewish trials," as symptomatic of one way in which Jews in the twentieth-century West have translated and enacted their Judaism: neither in ritual nor in formal, traditional God-focused terms, but in terms of fixing the world: secular, political *tikkun olam*. This would by no means justify espionage, but might explain involvement in that activity especially during the Nazi period, through most of which it seemed clear that no nation, including the United States, was overly concerned about saving Jews.

That last double question, of treason versus idealism, is one for which we do or don't possess the luxury of even asking it, depending upon the answer to the one that follows: if Julius was spying, what exactly did he ultimately transmit to the Soviets? That question, too, will not easily be answered with any certainty. Most of the testimony that offers some weight in favor of Julius' role as a spy would suggest that he might have engaged in industrial espionage, as opposed to having had access to and transmitted highly valuable and classified information with military implications, obtainable only from a unique place such as the Atomic Laboratory in Los

Alamos, New Mexico. Yet it is the latter most particularly which was the focus of the prosecution and certainly of the judge in his trial.

But let us assume that, with David Greenglass—who failed 8 out of 8 (yes, all eight) of the engineering courses that he took as a brief student at Brooklyn Polytechnic Institute, who in the courtroom couldn't identify which type of "high explosive lens molds" constructed in his shop at Los Alamos was an improvement over any other types; who didn't know the kind, quality, or combination of high explosives from which the lenses were made; whose description of the atomic bomb before the court was sketchy at best; who in fact testified that, before going to Los Alamos he received a description of an atom bomb from Julius, so that he would know what to look for there—as his mole and Harry Gold as a courier, Julius was actually transmitting information from Los Alamos: what was the level and weight of significance of that information for the arms race that was in the midst of its start-up phase at the time not of transmission but several years thereafter? Scientist after scientist in a position to judge has offered the assessment that the information as it was represented by the prosecution was inconsequential.[279] So of what crime, exactly, did Roy Cohn, Assistant D.A., possess "immutable evidence" that the Rosenbergs were guilty, "as confirmed by a long series of circumstantial and independent corroboration"—assuming that the evidence in his possession was indeed "immutable"?

This leads, then, to the obvious next question: was the prosecution correct and did it demonstrate beyond a reasonable doubt that the Rosenbergs were ultimately able "to steal through David Greenglass this one weapon, that might hold the key to the survival of this nation and means the peace of the world, the atomic bomb." The answer seems a much more unequivocal "no" than the answers to the previous questions. Among many other subsequent statements, that of James Beckerly, Director of the Atomic Energy Commission Classification Office—made on March 17, 1954, less than 9 months after the Rosenbergs were executed—stands out. He observed that it was time to stop "kidding" ourselves about atomic "secrets," that "the atom bomb and hydrogen bomb were not stolen from us by spies... atom bombs and hydrogen bombs are not matters that can be stolen and transmitted in the form of information"—certainly of the sort allegedly transmitted to the Soviets by the Rosenbergs.

A month later, the director of the atomic bomb project, General Leslie R. Groves further noted that "I think that the data that went out in the Rosenberg case was of minor value. I would never say that publicly." In which case, Judge Kaufman's summary statement, that "I believe your conduct in putting into the hands of the Russians the A-bomb...has already caused in my opinion the Communist aggression in Korea, with the resultant casualties exceeding 50,000, and who knows but that millions more of innocent people may pay the price of your treason" is off the mark on several grounds.

For how can he assert what it is that led to "the Communist aggression" or anything else regarding the Korean Conflict with such clearly minimal knowledge of that conflict and how it was shaped and by whom? And even supposing he were correct in connecting the disaster of the Korean War to the fact that the United States was not alone in possessing such weaponry, if it seems so clear that whatever the Rosenbergs and Sobell and their associates provided to the Soviets was not, per se, the wherewithal to manufacture an atomic bomb—the wherewithal did not require the work of the Rosenbergs and what the Rosenbergs provided was, at its most "generous" of negligible value for such a project—then how could a rational judge of history and their role in it make such an emphatic pronouncement?

In fact, if one reviews who shaped the conclusion that the "Rosenberg ring" had transmitted such critically dangerous information about atom bomb technology to the Soviets, one realizes something odd. The determiners were the FBI, the Justice Department, the prosecution team—and Judge Kaufman. One might add to that list, the Press, to which information and opinion were being carefully fed by the Justice Department and the prosecution team. Nobody among that series of groups had a scintilla of expertise in the matter, and nobody with scientific expertise, from the AEC, for example, or any other scientific agency or laboratory, was called upon to render an opinion.

Many might now argue that previously classified or otherwise inaccessible information such as that provided by the VENONA intercepts, made available to the public in 1995, or assertions made in 1997 by Alexander Feklisov, that he was Julius' Soviet "handler" and that the two met at least 50 times between 1943 and 1946 for the purposes of espionage—most specifically regarding industrial information and information dealing with military electronics—proves Julius' culpability as a spy. Yet Feklisov himself, while asserting Julius' extensive participation in industrial espionage, has argued, in his same 1997 remarks, that Julius played only a peripheral role in Soviet atomic espionage (and the VENONA intercepts corroborate this perspective)—which was the espionage for which he was charged and executed at Judge Kaufman's command. Feklisov is another key participant in the espionage circle who has observed that Judge Kaufman's contention that the Rosenbergs "altered the course of human history" and that their actions "caused in my opinion the Communist aggression in Korea" cannot be seen as anything less than entirely unjustified.

This in turn leads to the next pair of questions: why could General Groves not speak out publicly on such a matter? And cognate with that question: did the Rosenbergs receive a fair trial—which question is also cognate with yet another: if justice were to be served, should they have been given the death sentence? Was the sentence carried out with or without sufficient recourse to appeal? The answer to the first is that, in reviewing both the atmosphere of the trial and its aftermath and the atmosphere in the country in general in the time leading up to and away from the trial and executions, it is clear how even—perhaps especially—someone as well-positioned to have an opinion and to offer an opinion as General Groves, whose view would carry some weight, was afraid, or simply refused, to speak up. Either because the winds of McCarthyism as they had blown toward the Rosenbergs were so strong that Grove was fearful of being swept off his own feet by them if he spoke up; or he felt that the Communist threat was so powerful that to sacrifice two everyday American citizens to the gods of battle against Communism, in order to turn the tide in that battle, was necessary or even desirable.[280]

The answer to the second question and its further cognate—were they justly tried and should they have been given the death sentence (and should the various petitions for retrial, reconsideration of the verdict based on new evidence, or clemency, have been so quickly and unequivocally turned down)—seems fairly simple: no, not according to the dictates of the American legal system and certainly according to the dictates of justice. What are those dictates? To begin with, the guilt of an accused individual needs to be established beyond a reasonable doubt—and in a capital case, aside from the even more pressing importance of supplying that proof, it needs to be clear that the crime is one worthy of the death penalty. Given the doubts in the minds, for example, of three U.S. Supreme Court justices regarding the guilt of the Rosenbergs—as charged, as asserted by the prosecution and subsequently by the trial judge—the rush to execute them after the defense petitioned the Court would seem to contradict the American legal system as it in theory should operate in such a case.[281]

Given the quality of information for the transmission of which Julius might have been responsible, the quality of which, it seems, those decreeing death had to have known—or should have made it their business to know—in comparison, say, with the far more valuable information transmitted by Klaus Fuchs (who, in Britain, received a jail sentence of 14 years as his punishment), something other than rational justice must have been operating to yield such an unrelenting sentence, with its accompanying verbal justification by the sentencer.[282]

In fact, we might further ask: whose job was it to be the sentencer: legally speaking, who should have determined that they receive the death sentence or some other sentence, assuming that they were guilty? Judge Kaufman decreed the death sentence, not the jury. Some have pointed out that the Rosenbergs' deaths were "a gross miscarriage of justice" because, with the complicity of virtually the entire American legal system, they were tried, convicted and executed under the wrong statute.[283] The law that was used by the government was the Espionage Act of 1917, which gave the trial judge the sole discretion to impose the death sentence once the jury had found the Rosenbergs guilty—which discretion he exercised in no uncertain terms. The refusal of the courts, including the U.S. Supreme Court, to acknowledge convincing evidence that the law that the government should have used was the Atomic Energy Act of 1946, which would have limited the trial judge's power—Kaufman would not have been permitted to impose a death sentence unless the jury so-recommended—offers what seems an extraordinary failure of justice to prevail.[284]

Methodologically speaking, were the Rosenbergs given a fair trial? The Assistant District Attorney, prosecutor Roy Cohn, later stated in his autobiography that he had influenced the selection of the judge—something theoretically not feasible in an American court—and Judge Irving Kaufman (as we have seen, in part) was not only a veteran of this sort of case, but arrived into the courtroom with clearly documented prejudices and preconceptions on the "Communist" issue, and was predisposed against the defendants.[285] One can see this repeatedly in his rulings between prosecution and defense throughout the trial, but nowhere more obviously than in his statement the day following his imposition of the death sentence on Julius and Ethel.

For he noted then that David Greenglass had "testified to the vital character of the information which he gave to Julius Rosenberg" and that characterization, Kaufman asserted, had been affirmed by Walter Koski and John A. Derry, who "attested to the tremendous importance of this information." But Greenglass never testified regarding the vital character of his transmissions, nor could he have, given the incredibly limited knowledge and understanding that he consistently demonstrated, even of the materials upon which he was directly working, much less the larger atomic picture. Nor did either Koski or Derry make any reference whatsoever to the "tremendous importance" of the information.[286]

To make such a statement, the judge would have to be profoundly prejudiced in how he heard testimony. Kaufman's prejudices remain crystal clear when one further notes the following. The Atomic Energy Commission, after reviewing Greenglass' sketch and testimony, had no objection to allowing them to be made public, since the information that they presented was so inconsequential, hardly requiring that it remain classified as sensitive. Yet when in researching their book the Schneirs requested that Judge Kaufman lift his impounding order—in 1962, eleven years after the trial—he refused. Without citing any evidence (in fact all evidence would suggest that, in an open and free democracy, where no dire consequences could obtain from the release of such information, it should be available for study), he declared that he still adhered to the view that it was "in the best interests of the country that the order stand."[287]

Other aspects of how the trial was conducted are troubling. Crucial information was withheld from the Rosenberg defense attorney—it was even apparently withheld from President Eisenhower—to which the Prosecution and the Judge were privy. At the last moment, Prosecutor Irving Saypol brought in Ben Schneider, who ran a photo shop not far from the courtroom, as a witness. His testimony was considered crucial, but raises rather serious questions from two angles. For from among the scores of photo shops across New York City the FBI managed to find the one—and the day before the trial, right near the courthouse—to which the Rosenbergs were alleged to have gone for passport photos (thereby implying that they were planning an immanent flight from the United States).

Moreover, although he could produce no documentary proof (no negatives, no billing receipts, nothing), Ben Schneider was able to identify Julius Rosenberg in the courtroom, without prompting, as the one among his many customers who had come in with his wife and two boys to have those photographs taken months before. Nobody realized until later that Schneider had been brought into the courtroom by detectives the day before he testified, while Julius was on the witness stand. So his ability to identify Julius "unprompted" and without question, after the passage of so much time and in spite of the volume of Schneider's clientele—and the methodology of the prosecution—are somewhat suspect.

There is more that makes one wonder about the methodology of the courtroom as just. William Perl—another former college classmate of both Julius Rosenberg and Morton Sobell—was arrested. The arrest was for perjury, but as it was expressed to and by the

Press, Perl had been a Communist agent, whose testimony would immanently be used to validate elements in David Greenglass' testimony, thereby providing further "evidence" of a conspiracy outside the courtroom at the precise moment when Ruth Greenglass was on the witness stand within the courtroom.[288] Coming right in the middle of the trial, the timing of the arrest, as Sobell's Defense Attorney, Howard Meyer, would insist, was intended to further prejudice the jury. While Prosecutor Saypol asserted that "the indictment was returned in the regular course of criminal practice," and Judge Kaufman backed him up ("You have the word of the United States Attorney"), this hardly seems true, given both the statements to the press by him at the time regarding how Perl's testimony would be used and the fact that it required another 21 months until Perl was himself tried, in spite of his repeated demands to have his day in court.

In a city crawling with Jews fitting a socio-economic profile similar to that of the Rosenbergs and Morton Sobell, not a single Jew was placed on the jury: could this be considered the "jury of their peers" by which every American citizen has the right to be judged? What was Judge Kaufman's involvement in the jury selection, given the federal nature of the case, and how were his prejudices against the defendants a factor in the jury configuration?

There are other questions that one might pose, but the answers may simply reflect mistakes in strategy reminiscent of those made by Leo Frank's legal team. Why did Emanuel Bloch commit such key blunders, such as not cross-examining a character like Harry Gold, whose story within the court shifted so dramatically from testimony he had given to the FBI before—was that information withheld from Bloch or did he not think to examine it? Why did he move to impound exhibit #8—the Greenglass sketch purporting to show a cross-section of the implosion-type atom bomb, thereby acquiescing, in effect, to the prosecution's charge that the sketch was "the secret of the atom bomb" when it was far from that? How could an unschooled jury, being pushed not only by the prosecution but by the trial judge to think in such terms, not assume that the sketch was of cataclysmic significance and thus arrive at an unequivocal conclusion that the Rosenbergs were guilty of a profoundly serious crime if that information was hidden from view as if it were too sensitive to be seen?[289]

Cognate with the question of what exactly the crime of the Rosenbergs—if any—was, and the appropriateness of the punishment meted out to the Rosenbergs for it, Roy Cohn also asserted in his autobiography that he had successfully pushed Kaufman to impose the death penalty on both Julius and Ethel Rosenberg, and if that is so, the endgame of Kaufman's court procedures seems to have been seriously corrupted. The issue of that endgame returns us to the ultimate question—that of whether or not the Rosenbergs should have been executed, as opposed to imprisoned, even if we assume that nothing about the Affair was tainted by injustice or error. With respect to this issue, even Ronald Radosh, who as co-author of the 1983 book, *The Rosenberg File: A Search for the Truth*, maintained that the Rosenbergs were guilty of espionage,[290] has asserted that it is clear that the Rosenbergs did not give the Soviets the 'secret' of the bomb, and they should not have been executed."[291]

So, then, why *were* the Rosenbergs executed? Why were *both* of them and *nobody* else executed? If Morton Sobell and Max Elitcher, David and Ruth Greenglass and Harry Gold were part of the cabal, why were their respective positions treated so differently? In Sobell's case, the charge was differently shaped, but he received the maximum sentence and was incarcerated in the most uncomfortable of prisons—both of which aspects of his sentence might also raise eyebrows. The other four plea-bargained by means of acknowledging their guilt and then testifying against the Rosenbergs, and received sentences that ranged from light to none. Why, most obviously, did Klaus Fuchs receive such a relatively lighter sentence, particularly when the nature of what he was sharing with the Soviets was so much more serious? Since English law and American law are virtually identical in these matters, what might we assume about English versus American mores—or Jewish versus non-Jewish objects of the Anglo-American judicial system?

One can only speculate. Was it merely a matter of the Rosenbergs' unwillingness to admit their guilt and then to assist the authorities to tie up more threads in the government's conspiracy theory? Since whatever evidence was claimed against Julius was lacking with regard to Ethel, then some have supposed that the idea of tying her into a situation that would lead to her execution was intended to force Julius to admit the guilt that he denied to his death—in order to save her. But if that was a strategy, it failed; both Rosenbergs went to their deaths insisting on their innocence, and leaving two small boys behind to be raised by others. Why were they executed and not condemned to life sentences in Sing Sing penitentiary? Alive, they could have continued to be the subject and object of doubt and the legal system—the justice system—might have continued to examine their case. One cannot help but think back to the Dreyfus case: had he been executed instead of imprisoned, at the very least his eventual exoneration would have been functionally irrelevant to *him*—and at most he might never have been exonerated, since, once dead he may have not stirred the consciences of those who were so mindful of the ugliness of his place of incarceration and worked so hard to save him.

Dead, the guilt or innocence of the Rosenbergs became irrelevant in a certain sense. For the government the case and the Affair that revealed to the entire world a fear-based merciless inflexibility of which the United States can surely not be proud—defensive and arrogant, but not genuinely proud—could be considered definitively closed with the deaths of Ethel and Julius Rosenberg. So were the executions in the face of so much doubt by so many with regard to their guilt intended to close the uncomfortable case? If so, *that* effort failed; it has remained open for more than half a century.

Nor does the case and its implications show signs of being closed any time soon. Beyond the question of Rosenberg *guilt*, there is the issue of the *weight and significance* of their actions if guilty, which issue encompasses the problem of interpreting the significance of any sort of information—particularly atomic information.[292] And that issue is also interwoven with the question of *legal malfeasance* in the discussion of the *demise* of the Rosenbergs. This array of complications may be seen even as, in looking beyond the actual matter of the Rosenbergs' trial and execution, we arrive at discussions, and discussions of discussions that would be amusing were it not for the fact that they are connected to the deaths of two people. For example, two reviewers of Joseph H. Sharlitt's 1989 *Fatal Error* (to which I refer in n 227) offer absolutely opposed analyses of a key aspect of the book's assertion. Linda Greenhouse's August 6, 1989 review in the *New York Times Book Review* notes that Sharlitt's

> focus on the Supreme Court is a distortion because he fails to account for the many "fatal errors" that left the Rosenbergs seeking the Court's mercy at the last moment.
>
> To cite just one example, his treatment of the Rosenberg's lawyer, Emanuel Bloch, is puzzling. Bloch failed to raise the statutory issue on his own, and his effort to prevent the outside legal team of Fyke Farmer and Daniel Marshall from presenting it left those would-be helpers on very shaky procedural ground. While describing Bloch as "fair and decent" and "honest and candid," Mr. Sharlitt makes little effort to explain the "mystery" of the lawyer's strategy.

Thus Sharlitt is implicitly criticized for not effectively discussing what she understands to have been Bloch's miscues that set the stage for the Supreme Court debacle. But Bernice Green, in her March 30, 1990 review of the same book in the *Cleveland Jewish News*, writes—regarding the failure to note that the Rosenberg case should have been brought to trial under the 1946 and not the 1917 law—that

> Sharlitt faults Emanuel Bloch, the Rosenbergs' attorney, for not noticing this crucial difference [regarding jury-sentencing as opposed to judge-sentencing that distinguished the two laws]. Although he was a "decent human being," Bloch was beyond his depth in this case, Sharlitt notes again and again. Bloch made a number of tactical errors during the trial itself and, afterwards, he did not furnish fresh evidence which might have mitigated the sentence.

Thus Sharlitt is credited with fully recognizing Bloch's culpability. A reader of the first review will come away with a greatly different perspective on the book from a reader of the second. How much more profound the range of interpretive possibilities for understanding absolutes in the Affair itself!

What do all these questions have to do with a narrative that has "Jewish trials" as its focus? The answer to that question is contained in further questions and observations. The first observation is the reminder to a reader who was not alive at that time: the condition of fear under which the country operated—fear of annihilation should the Soviets in particular and the Communists in general get the upper atomic-nuclear hand; fear that traitors among us might effect their acquiring the upper hand; fear of being suspected of being such a traitor and having one's livelihood and/or one's life destroyed as a consequence—was inestimable.

The second is that there were key figures in the government—such as Attorney General Brownell—who virtually equated Communism with Judaism, or, put less extremely, perceived a vast number of Jews to be interested in or very much involved in Communism. Such Jews could be assumed and in effect were assumed to be potential or actual spies for the Communists. Brownell repeated in several memos that it was essential both that Julius and Ethel Rosenberg be found guilty and that they be executed, in order "to convince other Jews to leave the Communist party." The same sentiment was expressed in an alleged CIA plan to use the couple—hold their lives hostage, as it were—to convince Jews to get out of the Communist movement in exchange for their freedom.[293]

On the one hand, as previously noted, Communism as an idea would have been attractive to Jews in the 1920s and early 1930s. On the other, the rise of Stalin, his pact with Hitler and ultimately the developing Doctors Plot (see above, 212-13) had soured most Jews on the idea by the early 1950s. Moreover, there were also non-Jews who appreciated the positive ideas contained in Communism—and most Jews and non-Jews who were Communist sympathizers did not become spies, because they were loyal Americans first, regardless of the particuars of their political viewpoint (and initially, as we have noted, Communism was one among several acceptable and openly espoused political viewpoints).

Like Brownell, the assistant District Attorney Kilsheimer was eager to hurry up and be done with the case, out of concern for the "propaganda bath [that we are enduring] here and abroad" that the case was affording. Put in other words: it was more important to him that it be over and done with than that more time be spent that might alter the conclusion he was pushing, even if there were reasonable doubts as to the Rosenbergs' general and specific culpability, which doubts should have figured significantly in the decision as to their guilt and the appropriateness of their punishment.

Moreover, Brownell, in order to yield the results to which his preconceptions or prejudices hoped the court would arrive, maneuvered illegally behind the scenes—as did Chief Justice Vinson of the United States Supreme Court. How else can one explain the desperate rush to convene a special session of that Court in the face of the stay of execution allowed by Justice Douglas, rather than waiting the few weeks until the Court would have naturally re-convened—which would also have afforded more time to the justices to examine both the case and their souls? What was the nature of the pressure that yielded such a travesty?

One thinks back to the response by Henry to Picquart's realization that Dreyfus had almost surely been framed, when memos clearly intended for the Prussians appeared written in the same handwriting as that on the *bordereau* while Dreyfus was imprisoned on Devil's Island: Henry was horrified that the re-opening of the case would besmirch the honor of the French Army that had found Dreyfus guilty. The honor of the French army was more important to Henry than the life or well-being of one individual or than the truth. Those in the American government who refused to reconsider, in the face of so many not-clearly answered questions—at least the absoluteness of the punishment if not the very verdict of the Rosenberg trial—placed their sense of America's honor above truth and the lives of two individuals. Certainly this is the only reasonable way I at least can account for Judge Kaufman's refusal to dis-impound the sketch and testimony of David Greenglass even after the AEC determined that there was nothing sensitive about the information such material offered, without any explanation other than that it would not be "in the best interests of the country" to do so.[294]

The concern extended all the way to the top that the government's case must prevail—in the face of whatever questions and protests from around the world were sounded between the time of Judge Kaufman's choice of the death sentence for the Rosenbergs and their execution two years later. Determined to use the case as a banner against the perceived Communist threat to freedom and democracy, our political leadership, ironically enough, instead offered a strong statement to the world and to thoughtful Americans of the functional failure of those two ideas in a terrified America. In a desperate attempt to suggest otherwise, President Eisenhower was forced—I am giving him the benefit of the doubt, that he was misinformed, rather than that he chose to do this—to lie to the Pope and to other world leaders about the irrefutability of the charge against the Rosenbergs and the justification for their deaths, claiming falsely that all the courts had affirmed the fairness and appropriateness of the death sentences. If one compares Eisenhower's handling of this case with the handling of the Frank case by Georgia Governor Slaton, the president's heroic integrity—whether as a student of the case or as one who tows the party line; we cannot know which— does not shine.

How comfortable were *Jews* in the aftermath of the Holocaust in asserting themselves against implications by their government that too many of them were sympathetic to or involved with Communism, particularly as the Cold War (to repeat) rendered the "Communist threat" so overwhelming as an issue that Nazism was virtually forgotten, dozens of its facilitators embraced due to their presumed potential value in the fight against Communism?[295] When the National Committee to Secure Justice in the Rosenberg Case began to reach a wider public by late 1952, and the Committee put out a "Fact Sheet" that included a charge that religious and not only political bigotry helped lead to the conviction of the Rosenbergs, leading Jewish organizations denied that this had been the case—out of conviction or fear?

Authors Radosh and Milton[296] certainly argue strongly in their book that fear—of an explosion of new anti-Semitism—pushed Jewish leaders to go out of their way to argue against the clemency campaign as it was building. Earlier, shortly after the arrests of the Rosenbergs in 1950, the American Jewish Committee, for example— the very agency that had been so vocal a generation earlier in the Massena context—prepared a long memorandum, entitled "Public

Relations Effects of Jewish Atomic Spies," that voiced concern regarding the potentially dangerous situation for Jews engendered by the appearance of so many Jewish names among those accused of Communist sympathies and/or spying. But Jews also desisted out of conviction, for some contended that the Communist party was indeed trying to use American Jews "as it had long used Blacks as part of its war on America," and voiced their cognizance of Soviet anti-Semitism.

It is interesting that so many key players on both sides of the drama, but most importantly, the Judge and the most emphatic member of the prosecutorial team, Roy Cohn—at least so his autobiography and other roles in other cases and places during that era would suggest his emphatic role—were Jewish. Did that affect their approach to the matter at hand? Given the association being made in the highest political circles between Jews and Communists, would they have felt pressure to bend over backwards to be as harsh as possible with the Rosenbergs—and with Sobell—lest they be accused of the very sort of protective favoritism toward fellow Jews about which, in the Leo Frank Affair, Tom Watson had written regarding Jews and their expectations in general?[297]

Could *that* sort of concern have continued to press on Judge Kaufman even more than a decade later in his refusal to open the Greenglass file to public scrutiny? Was Emannuel Bloch hampered by the fact that he was Jewish? Did his concern about the Jewish/Communist equation affect his thinking and limit it, allowing a number of key blunders in his clients' defense? Would a non-Jewish defense attorney for the Rosenbergs have felt freer and done better? Mendel Beiliss' defense team consisted of one Jew and four non-Jews, we may recall. In short, would the Rosenbergs' fate have been what it was had they not been Jewish and/or had the Judge and prosecutor and/or their own attorney not been Jews—or conversely, had some members of the jury *been* Jewish? Or would the latter, had they been Jewish, have also felt obliged to bend over backwards to offer a condemnatory view of the defendants to their fellow jurors in order not to be accused of favoring a pair of co-religionists?

These are all questions for which it is impossible to arrive at definitive answers, and without the evidence of Brownell's memo, perhaps it would not even be worth asking them. But the mood suggested by that memo makes it difficult to avoid speculating—particularly when one juxtaposes the fate of the Rosenbergs with that of so many others whose efforts were far more deleterious to the United States who did not suffer that fate: the Rosenbergs remain, to date, the only individuals executed for espionage in U.S. history. When John Walker Lindh—a nice California Catholic boy who, having embraced Islam, joined the Taliban and began to work actively as a terrorist against American citizens—was arrested and tried there was no question of executing him, although his treason against the United States was clearer by far than that of the Rosenbergs.

In fairness, was that because it happened at a different time and within a slightly less panicked atmosphere than had been the case during the Rosenberg era—or because of what he came from, ethnically, racially, religiously? Would one call the post-September 11 atmosphere less panic-stricken than that of the early 1950s? Certainly the Bush administration used fear of terrorists as a consistent weapon to drown out opposition to its policies, including the alleged torture of numerous inmates at various U.S.-military-run facilities. But would anyone in the Bush administration have dreamed of drawing conclusions relating to the matter of John Lindh regarding Catholics and Islamic extremism the way Eisenhower's Attorney General so automatically made the equation between Judaism and Communism as that equation related to the matter of the Rosenbergs and Morton Sobel?

This can probably never be a matter of more than speculation. Like so much of history—and religion—we cannot be definitive, but we should not therefore not feel free to ruminate about it. There is an interesting little historical irony that might strike one, by the way, if one thinks back toward the beginnings of this narrative, and the context of the trial and execution of Jesus of Nazareth. An important element in that context was the contrast offered by Roman law between *religio licita* and *superstitio,* whereby the second of these categories applied to belief systems deemed politically subversive. Thus Christianity was regarded as politically subversive, as we recall, until 313 CE; and after ca 380 CE, when Christianity became the only form of faith accepted and embraced by the *Imperium* as *religio*, all others, including Judaism, were reduced to *superstitio* status.

The fear of Jews and Judaism that dominated the Christian medieval world, as we have seen, stemmed from a conviction that, as a *superstitio*, Jews and Judaism are actively engaged in a widespread subversive conspiracy to destroy the Christian European world that seeks to bring about a kingdom of God-led heaven-on-earth. That fear gives evidence, as we push into the modern secular age, of not dying an easy death—of even spreading not only into secular, "post-Christian" Christendom, but beyond Christendom—as we have also seen, moving by way of Wilhem Marr and others to Syria and Hungary, France and Georgia and Massena, New York.

At the very least, the equation made consciously between Judaism and Communism by individuals like Attorney General Brownell suggests that in the ongoing transformation of the particulars of that fear, anti-Jewish fear was still alive in a distinct if different iteration in the America of the post-World War II, Cold War era. For some, the communist *superstitio* could be understood as synonymous with what had once been officially referred to as the Jewish *superstitio*.[298] At the most, the equation could help account for the manner in which Julius and Ethel Rosenberg and Morton Sobell were tried and punished—as a sacrifice on the altar of a fear that looks to God with a cynical hope to save us from ourselves.

There is, of course, something amazing about the timing of this. If I am right—and it is not I alone who assert this, but there are also those who would disagree strongly with the assertion—that the Judaism/Communism equation, and the fact that so many of the principal *personae* were Jews, affected the conduct and outcome of the Rosenberg-Sobell trial; then given the fact that the ashes of 6 million Jews had barely cooled by the time of the trial should give one pause. Whatever sympathy for Jews might have arisen after and because of the Holocaust, and whatever effect that sympathy might or might not have had on other events, such as the confirmation of Israel's statehood, it was, like the horrors of Nazism, quickly forgotten, as we have earlier noted, with the rise of the Cold War and the emergent sense of Communism as the new existential threat to American democracy and freedom.

By that logic, the shortness and selectivity of human memory might be said to have combined with the Will to Fear (not to be confused with the Will to Freedom or any other kind of Will discussed by nineteenth and twentieth century Western philosophers) and with age-old, atavistic prejudices, to doom Julius and Ethel Rosenberg to death and Morton Sobell to a lifetime in Alcatraz.[299]

Epilogue: Since the time of my completing the original manuscript for this book, an interesting article, directly relevant to the discussion of the Rosenberg case, emerged in the media. Thus a front-page article on the Friday, September 12, 2008 edition of *The New York Times*—"57 Years Later, Figure in Rosenberg Case Says He Spied for Soviets"—presents 91-year-old Morton Sobell, who served, in the end, more than 18 years in Alcatraz and other federal prisons, and throughout those years and in the nearly forty years since, maintained his innocence, as

> dramatically revers[ing] himself, shedding new light on a case that still fans smoldering political passions. In an interview, he admitted for the first time that he had been a Soviet spy. And he implicated his fellow defendant Julius Rosenberg, in a conspiracy that delivered to the Soviets classified information and what the American government described as the secret of the atomic bomb.[300]

If one were to read no further into the article, at least the view of the Rosenbergs' and Sobell's guilt would be confirmed—although when at the end of the following paragraph the journalist asks Sobell whether he "was, in fact, a spy," Sobell's response is less than emphatic or clear: "'Yeah, yeah, yeah, call it that,' he replied. 'I never thought of it as that in those terms.'" At the very least the assertion of the article's first three paragraphs sounds less certain, although the notion of long-maintained and absolute innocence also seems to have lost defendibility. In any case, the entire discussion in the article would not definitively undermine the present discussion, but would certainly suggest a rereading of at least some of the questions raised in that discussion.

My interest, to repeat, is not to argue the Rosenbergs' and Sobell's guilt or innocence, but to argue that due process was compromised in myriad aspects of their case, and that the size of their crime was enormously exaggerated so that the possibility, say, of clemency—rejected by President Eisenhower on the eve of the Rosenbergs' execution—was eliminated. And my further suggestion is that the fact that both the Rosenbergs and Sobell and so many of the other prinicipals involved in the case were Jews was a factor—among other factors, the primary one being a hysterical fear of Communism and/or of being thought a Communist—in the failure of due process and the concomitants of that failure.

The astonishing thing is that if one reads the Sobell *New York Times* article through to the end, the black-white simplicity of its headline and first few paragraphs dissipate back into the grays that have accompanied the issue all along. Sobell goes on to assert that the materials that they handed over to the Soviets—during the war, when they were our allies and were bearing the brunt of the Nazi military onslaught—were defensive in nature; that the materials gleaned by David Greenglass from Los Alamos and what Julius gave to the Soviets "was junk."

Judge Kaufman's assertions regarding the earth-shattering nature of that information are confirmed as having been either naïve or mendacious, out of fear or ignorance, but certainly out of preconceived prejudices. And in any case, as we may recall, "the charge was conspiracy,... which meant that the government had to prove only that the Rosenbergs were intent on delivering military secrets to a foreign power. 'His [Julius'] intentions might have been to be a spy,' Sobell added."[301]

Moreover, the innocence of Ethel Rosenberg in all but her *possible* knowledge of her husband's activities; the outright lies told about her by her brother, David Greenglass—most damning, the assertion that she had typed his notes about the bomb; the notion that the testimony offered by Ruth Greenglass before the grand jury directly contradicted the charges that sent Ethel to the electric chair; the spectacularly unreliable nature of Harry Gold's testimony; and the various ways in which the judge, prosecution and FBI colluded to pressure such lies out of key witnesses, in order to *find* Ethel guilty — all of this sounds tragically confirmed. So by the end of the article, one feels that Julius and Morton Sobell were *guilty* of passing on what would prove to be relatively insignificant military information to the Soviets while we were allied with them, before the end of World War II and the beginning of the Cold War, and that their entire circle was deluded with respect to the promises of Soviet-style Communism toward shaping a better world — ie, toward some sort of *tikkun olam* in which they, as Jews, however secular, felt the need to be involved — but that the major villains in the story remain those who worked so hard to do them in.

One still ends up at the same place, with the sense that the darkest and not the brightest side of American democracy showed up in the Rosenberg affair, that they were sacrificed — or at least Ethel was — to our own system's delusions regarding how to protect freedom by subverting it. As the Rosenbergs' son, Robert Meeropol observes at the end of the article, in accepting Sobell's new revelations: "It's not the end of what happened to my mother and it's not the end of understanding what happened to due process." And my speculation with regard to the Jewish issue remains intact.

Chapter Seven:
The Return to the Promised Land

I. The Holocaust, Jews and Israel

Much has been written regarding the relationship between the Holocaust and the coming into existence of the State of Israel.[302] The discussions have ranged from the political and practical—did the State come into being because of the Holocaust; would it never have come into being without the Holocaust?—to the religious and spiritual: if the Holocaust is the darkest hour in Jewish (and perhaps human) history, and the darkest hour precedes the dawn, then is the founding of the state of Israel shortly after the Holocaust symbolic of the dawning of a new, glorious era, a messianic era, for Jews and for the world?

For the purposes of our discussion, these questions may be left to others, as we focus our attention in a slightly different direction. The relationship between the Holocaust and the coming into being of an independent State of Israel offers two related legalistic issues that impinge on our narrative. The first is that, for the first time since the generation before Jesus of Nazareth stood before his Roman judges, there is an independent Jewish—Jewish, in fact, and not Judaean[303]—polity that might hold legal proceedings. Should someone accused of having murdered Jews during the Holocaust find his or her way as a defendant into an Israeli court of law, then arguably for the first time in history, Jews would be engaged with that presumably Christian, or secular, or secular Christian, defendant—as prosecutors, defense attorneys, jury and judge.

Of course, this need not necessarily be absolutely assumed. While it is true that the majority of Israeli citizens are Jews, there is a substantial minority of Israelis who are Christians of any number of denominations, as well as Muslims, Baha'is[304] and members of any number of other faiths. And from the outset, the State has wrestled with its dual identity as a Jewish state—and what that phrase means, in general and in specific legal contexts, such as weddings and divorces and laws governing what may or may not be done on the Sabbath—and as a secular democracy that is governed by a constitution reflecting biblical, rabbinic, Ottoman, British and post-British-mandate Israeli sensibilities.

In that democracy, Christians and Muslims serve, for example, in the legislature—the Israeli *Knesset* (Parliament)—in a manner analogous to that which finds Jews serving in the British Parliament or the United States Congress. Thus the "Jewishness" of the "Jewish State" is only somewhat more obvious and definitive than is the Christianity of the United States, although the latter has throughout its history championed the theory that the American commonwealth consistently separates church from state.[305] So it would certainly be possible, if not overly likely in pure demographic terms, that a Nazi war criminal brought to Israel would find him/herself in a courtroom where any number of the key participants would be non-Jews.

The second, related issue is potentially raised by the first. One might ask the question of how objective the trial judges were capable of being at Nuremberg, when an array of mostly unrepentant Nazi leaders were brought before the tribunal to be tried for their crimes—their gratuitous destruction of human life well beyond the bounds of such destruction as it might be expected to happen as the "collateral damage" of war (to use a phrase coined half a century later).[306] The same question could be asked, many decades beyond Nuremberg—but with somewhat less conviction, since the passage of time might be supposed to have somewhat undercut the raw emotion that might otherwise hamper the smooth revolution of the wheels of justice—with the occasional trial in some other place of an alleged Nazi war criminal from some other place, such as Klaus Barbie, (whose identity nobody questions), who was brought to trial in France in 1987; or John Demjanjuk, brought to trial in the United States in 1983 (whose defense was that he was altogether being misidentified as "Ivan the Terrible.")[307]

If one then applies the question to Israel and Nazi war criminals tried there, the question might be more intensely focused, since Jews were so particularly and systematically the focus of the Nazi destructive impulse. Could an Israeli court, particularly if one assumes that most or all of the principals participating in it *would* be Jewish, provide a fair trial? The question might be asked the more so if one were to assume that there would be a good chance that any number of the individuals involved in such a trial might have lost personal family members to Nazi murderousness. In pure historical terms, such a trial would have no precedents: never before had a Jewish court with a Jewish prosecutor stood face-to-face with an oppressor of Jews and the opportunity to judge his acts and determine whether they were worthy of punishment and if so what sort of punishment.

The matter is complicated, theoretically, by the terms in which the issue of guilt or innocence first became couched at Nuremberg. The Nazis on trial were judged not for their crimes against Jews or any other particular group but, in recognizing the far range of their destructive accomplishment, for crimes against humanity. Would a trial in Israel of a Nazi war criminal be couched in the same terms? How would the formulation affect the trial? How would the world, watching the proceedings, refer to and respond to it: would the primary question remain "did so-and-so commit the crimes of which s/he is accused" or might the media and their audience turn their focus more sharply toward the question "can so-and-so receive a fair trial *in Israel*"? One might ask further: should such an individual be found guilty of his or her crimes, what *would* be the most appropriate punishment?

Given the questions left unanswered by the Rosenberg Affair, there is some irony to this last query, regarding the possibility or impossibility of fairness and regarding the nature of an appropriate punishment for someone found guilty of a particular crime. And as history and circumstance would have it, a case would emerge within Israel within a decade of the Rosenberg trial, while the discussion was still very heated regarding both the innocence or guilt of Julius and Ethel and the appropriateness of electrocution as punishment for their alleged crime. I am referring to the trial of Adolf Eichmann, the man often called the "Author of the 'Final Solution'" to rid the world of Jews unequivocally and once and for all.

II. The Capture and Trial of Adolf Eichmann

I have deliberately included the word "capture" in the title of this section to underscore the first legal and practical issue regarding Eichmann. There had been any number of alleged sightings of him in the fifteen years since the end of the war, primarily in Argentina, whither scores of Germans and Austrians had fled who were either Nazi sympathizers and/or had concerns regarding what their fate would be after the war due to those sympathies. Eichmann was ultimately and definitively identified in Buenos Aires by an odd— some might say accidental, others might say fate-decreed and still others God-directed—event.

His older son was dating a Jewish girl, and the relationship had become serious enough that the two children were eager for their fathers to meet. The girl's father was blind—having lost his sight during the Holocaust. But as often happens, the loss of one sense sharpens the senstivity of others, and when introduced to his daughter's boyfriend's father, this survivor recognized with an unequivocal nasal specificity the aftershave exuded from his opposite parental counterpart: he had never forgotten the particular aftershave odor of Adolf Eichmann.

Identified then, living under an assumed name—Ricardo Klement—working in a fairly non-descript job and living with his family in a fairly non-descript neighborhood, Eichmann was theoretically immune from the only entity that might try to bring him to trial for his role in the Holocaust, the Israeli government. Argentina had not yet established dipomatic relations with Israel; there was no extradition treaty of any sort under which the Israeli government could request that he be handed over to them—so his retrieval and transfer for trial would itself constitute an illegal act were the Israeli government to be involved in it in any offical manner.

As it turns out, the organization of Israelis involved in seeking out Nazi war criminals and bringing them to justice operated outside any such official circle (although, as in the television series and movie, *Mission Impossible*, with the imprimatur of a few key figures in the government). It was a finely-tuned organization, much of its training and guidance provided by Peter Z. Malkin, many of the members of whose family had been killed during the Holocaust, including his older sister and her son who had been his favorite childhood playmate—who was himself trained not only in various martial arts and in explosives but in make-up and disguises.[308]

In brief: a lengthy period of surveillance made it clear that Eichmann's quiet, systematic, bureaucratic sensibilities—so useful, among other things, for the maintenance of a virtually infallible train time-table necessary, during the war, for his Final Solution—had not changed since the war. The precision of his personal schedule made it relatively simple to spirit him away one evening, as he walked, after work, from the bus stop to his home. He was then kept in one "safe" house after another, until a clear plan of how to extract him from the country could be finalized. Simply summarized: he was drugged, disguised by Malkin to appear to be a very different-looking man, dressed in an El Al flight attendant's uniform and moved past the Argentine customs authorities and to the waiting plane—El Al, Israel's nascent national airline, had only recently opened up a route between Buenos Aires and Tel Aviv's Lod Airport—as if he were slightly drunk and not quite capable of moving under his own force.

If the first part of the story of the Eichmann trial, in terms both of drama and of law, was that of capturing him and bringing him before a court of law—one could in fact argue that his removal from Argentina was illegal, certainly according to Argentinian law; but then the question becomes whether his case required a larger, more international scope than was offered by Argentina—the second part was that of determining how to shape the indictment against him. And by whom and how should that indictment be formulated? How might one most legitimately articulate the crime for which he was to be charged—who probably himself never personally pulled a trigger or wielded a truncheon? After Prime Minister David Ben-Gurion announced to the stunned Israeli *Knesset* on May 23, 1960 that Eichmann had been found and brought to Israel to be tried, both legal and political questions blossomed within and beyond Israel.

Given the fact that the figure in question was not some low-level Nazi lackey but one of the individuals just half a notch below Hitler himself in the Nazi hierarchy, and the one credited with the most direct and substantial role in formulating the process of the Final Solution, the question of how his trial might serve as a symbol clearly presented itself to the prosecution as well as to the Israeli political leadership. Put otherwise: for various reasons, the Holocaust had been a subject *non grata* for the most part in the fifteen years between its end and the capture of Eichmann. Not only within the United States, as we have already noted, but in Israel itself the subject was hardly discussed. Survivors were not eager to discuss it for the painful memories it evoked; the Zionist leadership wasn't overly interested in discussing it, for as often as not they viewed the Holocaust as the culminating symbol of Jewish weakness and *self-victimization*, qualities from which they wished to distance themselves and the state.

If Israel were to offer, by contrast, the vision of a new kind of Jew, who furrowed his fields and not his brows, then reminders and discussions of a generation that "went like sheep to the slaughter" had not been a desideratum during the previous decade and a half.[309] And in any case, with the Zionist leadership, the younger generation had been entirely preoccupied with building and protecting the nascent state from the circle of would-be destroyers who surrounded it. On the other hand, the consequence of all this was that the younger generation had a serious hole in its knowledge of Jewish history. It had little sense of the world from which its parents had come and the kind of struggle many of them had endured in order to survive, and perhaps it possesed less of a sense of the desperate necessity for the continued existence of the state. And meanwhile, a dozen years into its independent existence, Israel still found plenty of opposition to or at least non-acknowledgment of the legitimacy of its existence in the world at large.[310]

The trial of Eichmann could offer the opportunity to place the Holocaust in the forefront of human consciousness by way of the far-flung web of television communication. As such, it could remind the world of what Jews had suffered while so many others either actively participated in pain-inducement or sat idly by, and remind the world and not just young Israelis of why the existence of the State was so important. A trial that offered a just and objective, even-keeled hearing both to the charges against Eichmann and to his defense would, moreover, underscore the extent to which Israel was a modern, justice-driven state, worthy of admiration and support.

So the framing of the charge for the purposes of a trial might be seen in the end to have had a number of motivating aspects. One might see this as the other side of the coin of the Rosenberg-Sobell conviction and punishment—and for that matter, of the Frank, Beiliss and Dreyfus trials. The nature of what eventually transpired within the courtroom was profoundly affected by larger issues outside the courtroom. Thus the charge of "crimes against humanity" connected the trial to those at Nuremberg and reminded the world of the breadth and depth of the events with which Eichmann was associated, while at the same time the Jewish context—against whom, after all, he had master-minded a systematic "final solution"—was underscored.

The norm in the Israeli legal system is to place the investigation of a crime in the hands of the police—by contrast, war crimes had been handled by lawyers and historians, even at their incipient stages in prior cases in other places—and Israel did just that. A special unit was set up by the police—Bureau 06—under Commander Abraham Selinger. He and his associates all spoke German, so that they were all able to communicate with the prisoner—and establish that he was in fact ready and willing to tell his own story of his involvement in the activities of the Third Reich. The investigation that followed occupied eight months and included endless taping and transcribing—on 3,564 type-written pages—Eichmann's extended statement of his life and the career leading to and encompassing the activities for which he would be charged when the trial finally began on April 11, 1961.

One of the observations offered in his memoir of the trial and events surrounding it by Gideon Hausner, leader of the prosecution team, is that Eichmann's testimony regarding most of his life revealed a prodigious memory for minute details. The only area where his memory seemed consistently to fail him was where the issue of the Jews and his role in effecting the demise of so many of them were concerned. His skill and pride in remembering so much else led those listening to or reading his signed statements to find such memory lapses difficult to accept as real.[311] In fact, Police Captain Avner W. Less, Eichmann's primary pre-trial interrogator, in his introduction to the English-language edition of the transcripts of Eichmann's testimony, noted specifically that "as time went on, I noticed that each time Eichmann said 'Never! Never! Never, *Herr Hauptmann* [Mr. Captain]' or 'At no time! At no time!' he was lying. That was always a cue for me to ask my colleagues to search for additional material with which to probe the sensitive spot."[312]

Nor would Eichmann end up ever provoking whatever sympathy he might have found by evincing some sense of regret or sorrow. This extended from the time of his capture to the time of his execution. On the one hand, Peter Malkin, in his account of the capture is astonished at the banal, bureaucratic personality of his prisoner, and tries to grasp what the face of evil might look like[313]—how is it that the destroyer of so many hundreds of thousands of people is such a grey, nondescript individual? Malkin broke protocol by engaging in brief conversations with Eichmann, trying to dig, but with little satisfactory result. When Malkin noted that his favorite playmate, his older sister's son, had been around the age of Eichmann's younger son (with whom Eichmann could be seen playing by Malkin in the evenings before his capture) when that playmate had been murdered by Eichmann's machine, Eichmann's reply was simply "but he was Jewish, wasn't he?" — as if his Judaism made the logic of his death obvious, requiring no emotion, no further explanation, certainly no apology.[314]

On the other hand, when confronted in prison by the Reverend William Hull with the suggestion that he confess his moral error in writing, his response was that "I did nothing wrong," and moreover, in taking refuge in the legal questions raised by his trial, observed calmly that his brother, a lawyer in Linz "wrote me that on the evidence submitted there was only one verdict possible, and that I should be set free. Any other judgment would be illegal.... [but] if I say now that I am sorry, they [the prosecutors] will pounce on that and say: 'Where there is sorrow there is guilt.'" Eichmann's Will to Survive would attach itself to whatever legalities might serve that end. Besides, as he stated to Hausner while being cross-examined in court: "...regrets do not help nor do they change matters. They cannot bring the dead to life. Repentance is a matter for small children."[315]

Indeed, "[i]t soon became clear enough how Eichmann wanted to portray his particular function in the Final Solution machinery. He was a mere pipe or conduit through which orders and instructions were relayed, he said; whatever he received from above he passed on to those below. He was not answerable for the orders of his superiors, over whom he had no control, nor for the execution of these orders lower down, which was the responsibility of other people. 'I never took part in deportations, not a single time.'"[316] And thus his guilt should be viewed as minimal — he was a mere transmitter, a bridge between orders given by others and actions committed by others.

While Captain Less was interrogating Eichmann, the Special Police Unit was busy collecting, sorting, organizing and preparing the mountains of documents that would offer evidence of Eichmann's culpable activities, and which also provided Less with the basis for much of his direction in questioning the prisoner. Bureau 06 found useful material by sifting through the thousands of documents contained in the prosecution and defense briefs from the postwar trials. Commander Selinger made the circuit of documentation centers in the Netherlands, France, England and the United States, seeking information and assistance from archivists and historians.

Important biographical data on Eichmann was available in Tuvia Friedmann's Documentation Center in Haifa, and a wide range of data was found in the archives of Yad Vashem, in Jerusalem, where mimeographed copies of material from the German Foreign Office dealing with Jewish Affairs, (and going back to 1870), captured intact in various hideouts by the U.S. Army, were piled high: some 485 tons of paper were available for sifting through. This included the Final Solution dossier, and together with it Yad Vashem had obtained copies of the personal dossiers of the SS Head Office from the Berlin Dcomuent Center Archives. Interestingly, from a legal point of view, while all of this material would serve a historian well enough—there was nothing to suggest that its authenticity might be suspect—in order for it to serve as incontrovertible evidence in the courtroom, it was deemed essential to obtain affidavits from the individuals in Jerusalem, Britain and the United States who could validate these as undoctored copies of the originals that had been returned to Germany.[317]

This last issue is tied to the larger one that I raised several paragraphs back: that in trying Eichmann, *Israel was on trial* in the court of world opinion. Although any number of countries had promulgated laws to encompass the trying of Nazi war criminals, the "legality" of Israel's laws to do the same was questioned by some.[318] Others, (to repeat), questioned the feasibility of a fair and objective proceeding by Jews. Others asserted that Eichmann was a small cog in the Nazi machinery, whose role was being artificially inflated in order to create what would be a fundamentally illegitimate show trial.[319] Argentina came before the United Nations Security Council and asserted that bringing Eichmann to trial in Israel constituted a threat to world peace. That issue continued to be discussed in the media and through Gallup polls, long after the UN had pushed it aside.

Thus the prosecution first of all faced the task of addressing the inherent problematic of a mistrial before anyone reached the courtroom since the endless public discussion could be said to have effectively made an impartial trial impossible. The case that they would have to make would need to be so factually solid—regarding not a particular criminal act but regarding the culmination of a criminal career with an entire nation-state as its context—that the fairness of the verdict could not be perceived to have derived from other than an immaculately impartial judiciary, in spite of all of the issues that would cloud that conviction among both neutral and sceptical observers.

And the clock was ticking at too great a speed for comfort; the citizens of the State of Israel were on pins and needles waiting for the court procedure to begin and be done. For the endless discussions and debates within and outside the state generated enormous tensions. And the conclusion of the trial of Adolf Eichmann would encompass conclusions drawn across the world regarding the State of Israel—the Jewish State—and its citizens.

Where the review of documents was concerned, a fairly straightforward, unemotionally presented parade of evidence was easily enough possible, offered by a professional prosecution team led by Gideon Hausner. But it would be more difficult to place before the court an array of witnesses who had suffered, in this way or that, at the hands of Eichmann or the machine that he created, without emotions taking over. But conversely, it would be the spilling over of human emotions that would capture the imagination of humans across the world—in a manner not evident, but also not as necessary, in the Nuremberg trials where documents dominated and witnesses played a minimal role in the proceedings—and contribute to the educative purposes of this unprecedentedly difficult exercise within the context of "Jewish trials." Thus,

> [i]n order merely to secure a conviction, it was obviously enough to let the archives speak; a fraction of them would have sufficed to get Eichmann sentenced ten times over. But I knew we needed more than a conviction; we needed a living record of a gigantic human and national disaster, though it could never be more than a feeble echo of the real events.[320]

The audience to which Hausner understood the trial to play—and it is clear that Prime Minster Ben-Gurion, among others, perceived things similarly—was, (to repeat), both that of the world and as importantly, that of the younger generation within Israel, which

knew so little about the Holocaust as a consequence of the long silence on that subject that had characterized most public and private
discourse since 1945.

Nearly all the witnesses were Jews—except two. One of these
was an evangelical Christian pastor from East Berlin, Probst Heinrich Karl Grueber, who had not only hidden Jews during the war
and organized an underground movement to smuggle them out,
while so many of his colleagues acceded to the prescriptions of Hitler's regime, but actually went and faced Eichmann himself in order
to plead on behalf of some of them. He was eventually jailed by
Eichmann and sent to a concentration camp where his teeth were
knocked out and he developed heart disease, but at age 70 he was in
the courtroom facing Eichmann once again—and offering testimony to the power of faith and courage in the horrific world of which
Eichmann had been one of the creators.[321]

The second non-Jewish witness was Michael Angelo Muman-
no, an American Catholic, a judge in the State Supreme Court of
Pennsylvania, and one of the American judges at Nuremberg. Prior
to that, just before the war ended, he was engaged in trying to find
out whether Hitler was dead and if not, to capture him, and in the
course of doing so, became aware of the mass-extermination of Jews
in which the regime had been engaged—and in nearly every interrogation or conversation of note, with individuals who ranged from
Goering to Hitler's barber, the name of Eichmann kept surfacing in
conjunction with the responses to his persistent question to them
all: how could such a massive act of murder have transpired? Who
organized it?

The question of how to balance documents and witnesses
was counterposed by that of whether to frame the charges in a
more limited fashion—specific deportations, for example—or to
push for a more all-encompassing charge reflecting all of Eichmann's activities.

> After a great deal of thought, I decided that we would draft a
> comprehensive indictment, charging Eichmann with guilt for the
> Final Solution in all the occupied territories, including the Polish
> and Soviet areas. There were two reasons for my decision: First, he
> was the head of the Jewish Department of the RSHA and Heydrich's

departmental chief charged with carrying out the Final Solution, "irrespective of geographical boundaries." So by the very nature of his position he was directly linked with what was done anywhere for the attainment of that object. This, coupled with the documentary evidence we possessed, would provide the factual proof of our allegations.

Moreover, his central position also carried a legal consequence, owning to the well-known principle of complicity in crime. Every man who counsels, aids or procures a criminal is guilty along with the actual perpetrator... Every member of an armed gang is in law as guilty of murder as the man who actually pulls the trigger that kills the cashier...[322]

Thus Eichmann, as "the central staff officer of the center's headquarters," was criminally answerable for all the millions of acts committed in pursuance of the criminal undertaking, even if he were to claim that some acts had 'bypassed' him.[323]

Eichmann was charged "'together with others' with the various crimes enumerated in our law of 1950 for the punishment of the Nazis and their collaborators."[324] It was a fifteen-part indictment. The first dealt with the murder of millions of Jews; the second with first placing them in conditions intended to destroy them; the third with causing them great physical and mental harm; the fourth with devising sterilization procedures and preventing childbirth among them; the fifth with causing their enslavement, starvation and deportation; the sixth with their general persecution on racial, religious and political grounds; the seventh with the spoliation of Jewish property as an addendum to the enactment of inhuman measures; the eighth summarizing the previous seven as punishable war crimes. The next four charges in the indictment broadened it to encompass the extermination of non-Jews: point nine dealt with the deporation of half a million Poles, the tenth with the deportation of 14,000 Slovenes, the eleventh with the incarceration in concentration camps of tens of thousands of Romany (Gypsies), and the twelfth with the deportation and murder of aproximately 100 children from the village of Lidice in Czechoslovakia.

The last three counts of the charge dealt with Eichmann's membership in three organizations declared to be criminal by the International Military Tribunal at Nuremberg: the SD, the Gestapo and the SS. These last three were the only ones not carrying the capital penalty as the maximum punishment. And interestingly, the indictment was drawn up in the longer style to which a German court is accustomed—and to which a German defense lawyer would be more accumstomed—rather than the shorter formulation that is the norm in Israeli courts. This was done to help facilitate the efforts of Dr Robert Servatius, the lawyer from Cologne, Germany whom Eichmann had appointed to represent him.

It should be obvious from much of the foregoing discussion that appointing an Israeli as defense counsel would have been extremely problematic—from the matter of client-lawyer confidence, to that of the potential conflicting pressures that an Israeli lawyer would no doubt feel, to that of assuring that the world would view the conduct of the trial as accomplished with judicial fairness and impartiality. A number of offers came from abroad from law firms and individuals interested in taking Eichmann's case, but he chose Dr. Servatius—who had considerable experience defending war criminals before various courts—since his (Eichmann's) half-brother, the aforementioned lawyer in Linz, Austria, had recommended him. He could adduce proof of never having been a member of the Nazi party—he had served as an officer in the German army from 1935 to the end of the war—and so provided no complication on that front.

Servatius called in Dieter Wechtenbruch, a sharp young attorney from Munich, to be his assistant defense counsel. It seems not only that a cordial relationship was established between prosecution and defense but that the former bent over backwards to make certain that the defense attorneys were familiar and comfortable with the particulars of the Israeli court system (essentially based on the Anglo-American court system) and that they received full cooperation in defending their client. Any information they required was made available as was full access to the library of the Law Faculty at the Hebrew University in Jerusalem. The conduct of the two sides and the judges leading up to and during the trial contrasts rather starkly with the manner in which the Rosenberg-Sobell pre-trial and trial were conducted.

There remained two further complications. The Israeli *Knesset* agreed to pass a special law waiving the normal requirements of jurisdiction: that only a lawyer who is a citizen of Israel can appear in an Israeli court. Then it turned out that the Eichmann (Klement) family apparently had no funds to pay for lawyer's fees. For various reaons, this seemed less than likely (for one thing an article had appeared shortly before in *Life* magazine for which it is likely that the family was very well compensated; for another it seems strange that someone as careful and well-placed within the Nazi hierarchy had failed to secret funds to provide for himself and his family as the Reich was collapsing, as so many Nazis did), so that Israeli public opinion was not overly sympathetic to providing state funds with taxpayers' money to cover his legal expenses.

Nonetheless, in the end the Israeli government agreed to pay the $30,000 fees requested by Dr. Servatius—who promised to return it if he succeeded in his suit to the German government that they be held legally responsible for covering the defense costs. He never succeeded in that suit, however. The trial finally began on April 11. Aside from other extensive security precautions, Eichmann was placed in a booth open in the direction of the judges, who could thus observe him without any obstruction, and formed of bullet-proof glass on the other three sides. The chief concern was that some member of Nazi or neo-Nazi circles—the first out of concern for the information he possessed regarding other Nazis still in hiding, the other out of anger that he seemed to be collaborating with the Israelis—might try to assassinate him during the proceedings.

Overruling the objections of the defense counsel, the court agreed to allow the trial to be filmed for television purposes, provided the filming did not interfere with the functioning of the court in any way. Thus one company was permitted to videotape and then to distribute the tapes to others. The consequence was that the progress of the trial was witnessed in considerable detail around the world. Throughout the several months that followed, broadcast companies in the United States, Britain and West Germany provided weekly one-hour summaries; in some cases—such as New York—there were half-hour summaries five nights a week. Over five hundred journalists and well-known writers and historians arrived from around the world to report on the trial.[325]

In at least two obvious respects, the judicial structure of the case resembled that of non-capital cases tried by the Sanhedrin in Judea two millennia ago more than, say, the judicial structure in the American courtrooms where Leo Frank and the Rosenbergs were tried. Thus the case was tried not before a jury but before three judges, as described in Tractate *Sanhedrin*.[326] And the defense was permitted to make the opening statement. As a potentially capital case, the proceedings, in conformance with Israeli law, had to be presided over by a Supreme Court judge. Justice Moshe Landau—at 47 years old the youngest member of Israel's Supreme Court, born in Danzig and educated in London, with twenty years of judicial training and serious scholarship behind him—presided. He was assisted by Dr. Benjamin Halevy, President of the Jerusalem District Court (and subsequently elevated to the Supreme Court) and Dr. Yizhak Raveh, of the Tel Aviv District Court. Both Halevy and Raveh were graduates of the University of Berlin.

There were some unusual procedural elements to the trial. Obviously the case had to be conducted minimally in two languages, German and Hebrew, and in fact simultaneuous translation (with whatever flaws are inherent in that process) was available to both participants and viewers into English and French, as well.[327] Contrary to the usual custom in an Israeli court (but not in Germany) Dr. Servatius offered only a brief oral argument (either because this is the customary procedure in Germany or because he felt more comfortable doing so since he would not be arguing in Hebrew) and then submitted to the court the extensive written plea of which it was the summary. Gideon Hausner, the lead prosecuting attorney, had received a copy of the document that morning and chose to follow the Israeli custom by responding to it orally—a process that took four court sessions to complete.

Hausner notes in his book that he was encouraged by a friend in the government to limit the time of his response, both so that he would not inadvertantly accord more weight to the defense objections than they deserved and so that the media would not lose interest before the proceedings moved from preliminaries to the the substance of the trial itself. It was, he admits, a reasonable pair of concerns, "but this was a trial, not a show; it could not be helped."[328] For Servatius' initial summary did not address issues of the case's substance or even how Eichmann would plead, but the legality of procedural matters. Not surprisingly he noted that the judges, as Jews, given the issues before them, could not be objective (and recommended that the venue be shifted to Germany); and that the overweening presence of politics and the press prior to the arrival of the case in the courtroom—wherein the accused had already been condemned without a hearing (he argued)—would have further influenced the judges.

He argued, moreover, that the 1950 law under which the prosecution would be lodging its charges was contrary to international law both in making someone like Eichmann liable for acts committed outside Israel and in making him accountable for deeds committed at a time when they were "legal" in the time and place when and where they were committed. He asserted, moreover, that the 1950 law offered little that was different from simple revenge; that it would hold an individual responsible for injuries committed by his state, and that only the state could make amends for such injuries— which, he contended, the Federal Republic of Germany had been doing by paying reparations to the State of Israel. He concluded by objecting that the abduction of Eichmann from Argentina deprived the court of jurisdiction.

The prosecution responded that no judge could ever be expected to be impartial toward a given crime, but that nonetheless all judges were expected to deliver justice—and certainly one would be hard put to argue that in Germany the judges would be any more or less impartial than those in Israel. They argued further that, with regard to the matter of the 1950 Israeli law in its relationship to acts committed beyond Israel's borders, aside from the obvious, under the circumstances—that with the dissolution of the Nuremberg and Tokyo tribunals after the post-war trials that they conducted, no international court to address criminal complaints *exists* (for the International Justice at The Hague has no such jurisdiction)—there are dozens of precedents (which he reviewed for the court) to show that territorial limitations on jurisdiction are not an accepted principle of international law. The prosecution showed that countries as varied as Austria, Brazil, Denmark, Finland, Germany, Holland, Italy, the Soviet Union, Switzerland and Turkey have adopted legislation and/or acted according to the principle that would permit them to try and even punish foreigners for deeds committed beyond their borders that affect citizens of, or more broadly, have consequences within, the legislating country. And Israel would surely qualify as the country most powerfully affected by the disappearance of European Jewry.

There was one more twist to this argument that Hausner added, which in retrospect set a precedent still being followed nearly half a century later. And that is that there are crimes which have always been "considered to strike at the welfare of humanity at large, for they are not limited to specific geographic units. Piracy is an example" of this. And it has always "been the law that a pirate can be tried by a country into whose hands he falls, for he is 'an enemy of mankind at large.' The perpetrator of a crime against humanity is considered to be on a similar level."[329] Thus Eichmann, as one standing accused of crimes against humanity at large, could legitimately be tried anywhere, and certainly in at least 18 different states directly affected by his deeds, but none of these had done so; all had recognized Israel's prior claim—none had requested Eichmann's extradition.[330]

Similarly, with regard to the matter of guilt for crimes committed in a time and place when and where they were not considered crimes, and of making the individual responsible for crimes committed by the state, Chief Prosecutor Hausner observed that this was precisely the sort of argument used by the defense in post-war trials such as that at Nuremberg. There and at other post-war tribunals, the precedent was set of diverging from a formalistic legal viewpoint and as a consequence such a plea was rejected. For, "the fact that Hitler had created a pirate state and called crime by the name of virtue could not render his followers immune from personal responsiblity. Otherwise we would arrive at the absurd result that a ruler merely has to be ruthless enough to abolish all moral prohibitions and create a legal vacuum to enable his followers to commit the most heinous crimes with absolute impunity."[331]

Hausner further argued that the reparations being paid by the German state were intended to help resettle displaced survivors in Israel, but were not viewed by either side as expiation or atonement for crimes that could not be forgiven through any number of payments. Finally, he brought before the court examples drawn from more than a century of precedents of English and American legal decisions that make it clear that the court does not concern itself with how someone accused of a criminal act ended up before it, but with the question of the act itself. Thus the attempt to delegitimize the case against Eichmann through the argument that he was illegally displaced from Argentina to be brought before the court in Israel was a false objection.[332] The discussion and counter-discussion proceeded for some time, but in the end the court overruled these preliminary objections. The same might be said of the court of world opinion, for, as one observer commented: "How could this [the notion that the Jewish court not be capable of impartial justice] be when every word, every gesture in court is being scrutinized by 500 trained and suspicious men, while the whole attention of the world is focused upon it as through a burning glass? Indeed, far from being unfair, it is already evident that the Israeli Attorney General is leaning backwards in his determination to ensure that scrupulous justice is observed and the defense given every conceivable latitude."[333]

All of which then leads to the actual trial: the framing of the charge under historically unprecedented circumstances, and all that followed in and beyond the courtroom. Hausner's most profound question—historical and conceptual, almost theological, rather than legal—was how to focus a charge that was being proffered, in effect, on behalf of an entire people, one third of whom were the putative victims of the accused. This was not a case where there was a single victim, such as William of Norwich or Andryusha Yushchinsky or Mary Phagan, with the question before the court as to which individual was responsbile for the demise of that victim; nor was it a case where there was no actual, concrete victim beyond what the judge or jury imagined as the consequence of the accused's actions, as in the Dreyfus or Rosenberg-Sobell trials. This was a case with an astronomical number of victims—six million or more of them[334]—with the question before the court as to *how* culpable (as opposed to *whether* culpable) the accused was for facilitating that mass murder.

And the question within the question was: what could possibly effectively avenge the deaths of those victims? Hausner noted that the answer proved in a sense simple: see to it that the man in the dock, among those chiefly responsible for the torture and murder of so many innocents, receives a scrupulously just trial. The colossal injustice of the system that he authored would be counter-balanced, with a full sense of historical irony, by its absolute opposite.

Hausner's opening words reflected his sense of the uniqueness of the moment: "As I stand before you, Judges of Israel, to lead the prosecution of Adolf Eichmann, I do not stand alone. With me, in this place and at this hour, stand six million accusers. But they cannot rise to their feet and point an accusing finger toward the man who sits in the glass dock and cry: 'I accuse.' For their ashes were piled up in the hills of Auschwitz and in the fields of Treblinka... Their blood cries out, but their voices are not heard..."[335] Aside from the powerfully emotive quality of his words overall, one cannot ignore the stunning juxtaposition of one phrase ("their blood cries out") that echoes the book of *Genesis*, and God's words to Cain after he has denied culpability in the death of his brother, Abel;[336] and a second that echoes Emile Zola's words ("I accuse!") with regard to the miscarriage of justice in the Dreyfus case.

Hausner's opening statement went on to observe how different the cold and calculated slaughter of masses of people shaped by murderers sitting calmly behind a desk with paper and pencil in hand—how different this mode of murder, arrived at in the twentieth century is from the kind of moment of passion leading to a singular act such as is expressed in the story of Cain and Abel. He offered a short, sweeping history that carried from anti-Semitism and racism to the Final Solution, with particulars of Eichmann's career interwoven with that history—and culminating with the recitation of a lullaby composed in the Vilna (Vilnius, Lithuania) ghetto. If one can imagine the silence in the courtroom that followed, one cannot imagine another courtroom or another kind of case in which such a combination and juxtaposition of elements would shape the opening statement of the prosecution.

The next day that opening statement was continued with a further depiction of the history of the Jews within Europe, particularly in the previous few centuries and with specific focus on the evolution of German Jewish involvement in their nation—from cultural output to military service in World War I. Reviewing the fifteen-count charge, Hausner concluded: "Adolf Eichmann will enjoy a privilege that he did not accord to even a single one of his victims. He will be able to defend himself before the court. His fate will be decided according to the law and the evidence, with *the burden of proof resting upon the prosecution.*"[337] I have added the italics both to underscore the determination of the Israeli court that such norms—going all the way back to tractate *Sanhedrin* in the Judaean period—be followed in this abnormal affair, and perhaps to suggest to the reader a comparison (yet again) with the Rosenberg-Sobell trial, in which such norms seem to me to have been abrogated.

Eichmann's voluminous statement was introduced into evidence, in which, among other things, he referred to himself as "only a minor transport officer" and later offered to hang himself in public "as a greater act of expiation...[and] as a deterrent example for anti-Semites of all the countries on earth." Oral testimony was heard, both from scholars such the historian Salo Baron, who fleshed out the picture of what had been and was no more with regard to Jewish Europe; and from eyewitnesses to the persecutions begun in Germany in 1933 and to the subsequent expulsions. The third of this group, Moritz Fleischmann, was the last survivor among the Viennese Jewish community leadership during the Nazi era. He was the first witness who specifically referred to Eichmann as the individual who had called the meeting with that Jewish leadership in which he announced to them that he would finally clear the whole of Austria of Jews—and identified the man in the glass booth as one and the same Adolf Eichmann, "though he was younger then and wore no spectacles."

Witness after witness, story after story, detail after gruesome detail, moving with the Nazis across Europe, from country to country, from ghetto to ghetto and camp to camp, marched through the testimony of the weeks that followed. Among the most important of the witnesses was Dean Grueber, whose testimony made it clear that Eichmann had been a powerful functionary who made independent decisions on actions of far-reaching consequence for his victims. This view was corroborated by Musmanno, who testified that at Nuremberg he had heard nearly everyone, including Goering, refer to Eichmann as one of the few who could be labelled responsible for what had happened to the Jews. Goering, in fact, "made it clear that Eichmann was all-powerful on the question of the extermination of the Jews. He went into that at great length: that Eichmann had practically unlimited power to declare who was to be killed."

The prosecution kept supplementing oral testimony with document after document, signed by or referring to Eichmann—or in one particular case the lack of a document. For in both his pre-trial and court testimony, Eichmann claimed that he asked to be transferred from his onerous assignment and that he was refused. But a good deal of documentary evidence showed that one could indeed be transferred, usually to the battle front, if one were not eager to follow the exterminationist program of the SS, yet there was not a single document to show that Eichmann had made such a request.

The defense chose rarely to cross-examine the witnesses. In its attempts to draw Grueber and Musmanno off their statements, it merely offered a greater opportunity for both of them to supplement their original testimony, and further cement their presented views of Eichmann's guilt. Eichmann apparently evinced no sign of being affected by any of this. He took notes, in an array of colored pencils, occasionally asking that a note be passed on to his attorney, watching the witnesses and sometimes the judges but almost never peering toward the courtroom at large. The court, in its passion to accord the defendant justice as absolute as humanly possible, was strict as to what it would and would not accept as admissable evidence from the prosecution, and in its insistence on absolute decorum within the gallery.[338]

Yet even the judges apparently could not completely hold back the water in their eyes as the prosecution showed an hour of documentary film—some shot surreptitiously, some by intention by the Nazis, some shot during the liberation by the allies. This was imagery of the kind that has since become somewhat familiar, at least to those versed in the subject of the Holocaust—of the pits, the mass shootings, the trains, the camps, the piles of emaciated bodies—but in 1961, it was new to most people's eyes. If this material was a novum, so was the culminating section of the Prosecution's presentation, which briefly but strongly reviewed the efforts—the successes—of Jews who were given the opportunity to fight against the Nazis both in the various armies of the allies and outside such formal frameworks. Not directly relevant, one might argue, to the case, but Hausner recognized that "[t]he trial was recording history, and it would be unpardonable if the superb military effort of the free Jews went unnoticed."[339]

After ten weeks of testimony, the prosecution rested its case—on June 19, 1961—and the defense was given a week to prepare before taking over. Its goal was to show that Eichmann's involvment "in the persecution of the Jews was a necessity and a result of the political leadership of the state"—thus offering a variation on one of the themes offered both by the defense at the Nuremberg trials and as part of the preliminary objections offered at the outset of this trial. Servatius would argue that the various Ministries of the German state "issued the instructions, directions, orders and directives. This was the legal basis and preliminary condition for those persecutions. Without them the accused could not have taken even one step, and *he did not take one step without them*."[340] The italics that I have added are intended to underscore the continuum of Servatius' double-pronged intention: to suggest that Eichmann's deeds were legal when he committed them and that he only committed them in *compliance* with and under *pressure* to comply with the legal directives of the state.

The Defense would further assert that Eichmann had sought to "stop the persecutions and bring the exterminations to an end by offering, through the usual channels, to enable one milllion Jews to leave the country."[341] These arguments would be presented through the testimony of Eichmann himself, who took the stand in his defense and asserted consistently that many of the procedures with which the prosecution and others associated him were a coincidence or accident of the office over which he presided, but with which he himself had no direct connection. Thus since the records of Jewish affairs were kept in his offices, everything having to do with the Jews was archived accordingly for filing purposes, but not necessarily with his knowledge or connection to such matters; his deputy, Rolf Guenther, received "special assignments" directly from the Gestapo Chief (Heinrich Mueller) that then implicated his office—such as the supply of poison gas to the camps or of skeletons to Strasbourg, or the massacre of the children of Lidice. So, too, he was required to be present at the sterilization conferences in order to take and distribute minutes, but he had no part in the conversations at those conferences.

He continued to use a technique that he had developed during his pre-trial interrogations: admitting to some far less egregious crime—or some part of some less egregious crime—in order to be able to assert his truthfulness, and then under that blanket, in an almost wounded manner, to appeal to the inherent credibility of his denial of the more serious crime of which he was being accused. He asserted how, in the wake of his reading of Zionist literature he had set up institutions which reflected his desire to promote emigration of Jews from Austria to Palestine. "*Kristallnacht* shattered all this," he asserted—an event with which he had no connection; the reason for the reporting to him on the progress of burning synagogues at 2:20 AM was that "I kept all sorts of files and archives in the outbuildings of the synagogues, and had to rescue the correspondence, which was absolutely necessary for further emigration work."[342]

His responses to questions or to the documents from which his lawyer read, presumably to elicit some comments as he sat on the witness stand, often became long and convoluted lectures, in a German so tortured, with sentences so long, that several times Servatius had to try to curb him, since the judges and even the simultaneous translators were findng him very difficult to follow. If in the old days Eichmann had been well known in Nazi circles for his capacity to lie convincingly, the range of his prevarications and the convoluted distances his narratives would travel to shift blame away from himself—from his statement that "the Wetzel letter on poison gas was forged," to his assertion that all the witnesses deposed at Nuremberg who referred to him were lying, to his claim that everything except for the train time tables that pertained to the successful removal of half a million Jews from Hungary to Poland in July and August, 1944 "was done by my superiors... The Hungarian gendarmery did not need German advisers"—rang hollow and unconvincing in the courtroom.[343]

The culmination of all this was the submission of twenty different charts of the various offices and authorities of the Reich that dealt with Jewish affairs in Germany and the occupied countries of Europe. Marked with heavy arrrows and lines, suggesting marvelously complicated channels of command, none of which seemed to pass through Eichmann's department, they suggested that just about everyone of any authority in the regime except Eichmann had a direct hand in the extermination of Jews.

The prosecution's cross-examination managed effectively to poke holes in his assertions, and to "remind" him of damning statements that he had suddenly "forgotten"—such as one that he made to his men shortly before the collapse of the Reich that he would jump joyously into his grave, knowing that he had taken 5 million Jews with him, to which he had referred in a signed document in the police interrogation. Sometimes it would require as much as a half hour to tease out an answer that would confirm a fact that placed some responsibility on his shoulders, such as that he was indeed the only head of the department of Jewish Affairs in the RHSA, or that his department was centrally responsible for preparing and drafting the Madagascar plan.[344] Surely the most damning means of breaking down Eichmann's account of his role would have been to play the tapes of the Sassen talks, in which "he could hardly have been able to deny his own voice," but those in whose hands the tapes resided were only willing to sell a copy of them—for $20,000—on condition that they *not* be made public in any way until *after* the trial, so that effort failed.[345]

Some of the moments of interchange between Eichmann and Hausner are remarkable for the interweave of elements they reveal. Thus on the one hand Eichmann admitted to practicing deception on all sides—which would reinforce the possibility that he was lying, now, in the courtroom, particularly since he included among those admissions lying to the Reich authorities around and above him. But on the other hand he asserted that the cause for most of his lies was because "it was so ordered" (by which comment he intended to refuse responsibility). "Didn't you assure the Slovak authorities that all the stories about the awful fate of the Jews were just horror tales?" "Yes, there was an order for that." "And when the Red Cross wanted to inspect a camp you showed them Theresienstadt?"[346] "Yes." "And you were telling the Jews that no harm would befall them. In Hungary you promised them they would not be deported if they cooperated." "Yes, I was so ordered."

Gradually, in the course of two weeks of cross-examination, his calm demeanor was breached a number of times by a hint of rage and anger: "under the livid and hollow mask, under the habitual prudence and pretence, there now appeared the true Eichmann."[347]

So, too, there was a number of features of the trial that reflected its unprecedented nature. When the cross-exmaination was completed, the three judges also took some time to ask Eichmann questions, in order to clarify certain issues. After Judge Raveh finished, Judge Halevy took over and, presumably to assure that his communication with the defendant was absolutely pellucid, departed from convention and interrogated him in German (it was Halevy's questioning that helped clarify that chief among Eichmann's concerns was leaving a record that would not make it overly difficult for his family to deal with—quite in line, as it turns out, with the pattern of focus and concern among the Nuremberg defendants). Judge Landau also spoke to Eichmann in German, translating himself into Hebrew. It was Landau's questions that elicited the remarkable assertion that one did not have to be an anti-Semite to be an "orthodox National Socialist" or to be particularly tough to run the

Gestapo—and that Eichmann had not thought that the Nuremberg Laws would be fully implemented.[348]

Even more unusual than the bi-lingual post-cross-examination interrogation by the judges was the manner in which the defense was permitted to bring forth its own witnesses. Since any number of them might be former high-ranking Nazis who would not be willing to travel to Israel—or who might well find themselves before the very tribunal trying Adolf Eichmann—an arrangement was organized according to which they would testify in a courtroom wherever they lived, with depositions taken in the presence of a local judge and representatives of both the prosecution and the defense counsels, which depositions would then be sent to the court in Jerusalem.

This would, of course, deprive the court of seeing the faces, expressions, and body language of the witnesses as well as of hearing testimony offered in a courtroom packed with the public and the press—and leave more potential doors open for doubt, which typically plays (or should) to the advantage of the one accused.[349] As it turned out, none of the defense's offered testimonies accorded sufficiently with Eichmann's to incline the judges toward his innocence. In their eagerness to whitewash their own respective positions and cases, these witnesses left him largely swaying in his own breeze. Nobody was willing to take a chance on his behalf—even those who had already been tried, sentenced and imprisoned and could presumably have done so without much risk. It turns out that his arrogance and rough treatment of his associates disinclined any of them from a wish to assist him. In the end he was no better off and possibly worse off than he had been before all of these testimonies had been offered.[350]

Ths summing up by the prosecution began by emphasizing both the unimaginable horrors of the Nazi regime of which Eichmann had been an integral part and his remarkably consistent lack of any apparent regret—consistent with his role as a Nazi, for "[i]t is horrifying to realize that whoever set his foot on this path no longer has a path back to human values... If there is sorrow, it is because the means that were chosen were not effective enough to complete [their destructive] task... This was no mass hypnosis in which men were gripped without the possibility of liberation. It was an act of the will, deliberate and conscious." To whatever extent Eichmann may have tried to present himself as the victim of a machine in which he was a helpless cog, was contradicted by the Sassen text, recorded 12 years after the war, when there was no fear of orders and punishments. For the only regret he expressed to Sassen was his profound regret that Jewry had somehow survived, despite all his efforts.[351]

This observation served as a segue into a detailed discussion of Eichmann's career as an enthusiastic Nazi leader, and one whose interest in the Jews was consistently destructive and not related to their welfare. Both the testimony of witnesses—even those brought forth in his defense—and the documents laid before the court indicated his fervent carrying out of, indeed his masterminding of, the plan summarily articulated at the Wannsee conference, every element of which shows the evidence of his involvement, his complicity in the devastating crime committed against the Jews of Europe. Eichmann's overarching authority in the organization of the concentration camps and the means of supplying them with Jews—to which even Rudolph Hoess attested—and his culminating activity in Hungary, in which he exceeded the scope of his orders, against the will of the Hungarians and even the directive issued by Hitler, was carefully reviewed.[352]

The defense took up its case after a weekend recess—the last word, therefore, going to the defense, particularly in capital cases, as prescribed by Israeli law and consistent with the prescriptions set forth in Tractate *Sanhedrin* two millennia ago. Its argument centered largely on the question of scope: could and should Eichmann be held singularly responsible for the acts that constituted the Holocaust when those acts were a consequence of an enormous machine in which he was only a—reluctant—element. Indeed Servatius argued toward the outset that Eichmann's membership in the SS, SD and Gestapo could not make him guilty for their acts—guilt, he maintained, is an issue pertaining to individuals, not to groups— and that they could in any case not be labeled per se as criminal organizations. With no lack of irony he observed that to suggest otherwise was to do what Hitler did: make every Jew guilty for being part of Judaism, which he (Hitler) regarded as a "criminal organization."

He contended (as he had in the preliminaries, before the trial began) that Israel was functioning outside its legal jurisdiction with regard to charges dealing with Poles, Slovenes, Gypsies and the Lidice children; that the deportations were mere population exchanges for which Eichmann's responsiblity in any case was only to affect smooth transport, not to propose or organize the idea; that the plunder of Jewish property was merely an *exchange*—of property for emigration visas—in which he was not in any case a central figure. However, "[t]hanks to the endeavors of the accused it was possible for two-thirds of the Jews of Austria to emigrate at that time, and they were in a position to leave the country. True, their condition, previously, was desperate, but this was not the fault of the accused. The same applies to the accused's activities in Germany, as well as in Bohemia and Moravia."[353]

So what the prosecution had presented as a negative— the transfer of masses of Jews to concentration and extermination camps—was presented virtually as a salvational act, on the grounds that Eichmann was merely moving them out of harm's way; he had no association with the locations and conditions to which they were being removed. Further, he noted that "[p]eople earmarked for deportation were not singled out by the accused; this was determined in accordance with Chapter 5 of the German citizenship law, and the accused had no influence whatsoever on this particular law."[354] This reference to the Nuremberg Laws is instructive in an obvious way: part of the methodology of the Nazi system was simply to *change* the laws in accordance with their needs, thereby in the technical sense—the very sense argued by Servatius on behalf of Eichmann—one could argue that no law had *ever* been broken by them. It could be said that Eichmann did not create any of those laws, he merely obeyed them with fervent enthusiasm until the last possible moment.

Servatius repeated both what he had argued from the beginning and what had been argued repeatedly by those in the dock at Nuremberg, that it was the politicians who were ultimately reponsible for shaping what became the Holocaust; that Hitler's will was unopposable; that Germans and Austrians such as Eichmann were as much his victims as those like the Jews were. Repeatedly the defense argued that Eichmann had no responsibility for this or for that, and went on to comment that those who testified gave testimony that was either mistaken, unverifiable or deliberately false. Thus Rudolph Hoess, for example, made charges—"that the accused passed on to him the order for extermination in the summer of 1941"—that cannot be proven, since there is no corroborative evidence. Similarly other charges made by others, including those called by the defense as witnesses: every damning assertion was waved aside as deriving from this motive or that; all assertions shared the lack of an interest in the truth as a motive.[355]

By contrast, he noted how cooperative Eichmann had been and how willing to confess to any number of charges leveled against him, thus demonstrating his integrity, his willingness to aid the legal process and his interest in arriving at a true account of events and how they took shape. He shrugged aside the Sassen material as false, overembellished, its details driven by alcohol-induced exaggeration, having sensation rather than factuality as its purpose. Ultimately he turned to the legal principle, enshrined in Israeli law, of "a guilty mind." Thus a criminal has to have known and willingly performed the criminal act of which s/he is charged in order to be found guilty. But Eichmann, Servatius asserted, knew neither the beginning nor the end of the process of which he was a mere, small part, and "it is very difficult to extract one part of the act from the causal train of events; the act of an individual is directed to the whole in which he takes part"—thus his actions do not add up to a criminal offense; he was "only a link in the chain."[356]

He offered the familiar argument that Eichmann's obedience derived from his sense of honor, having taken an oath of loyalty to the regime—and that, had he disobeyed, regardless of what it would have cost him to do so, others would have done what he refused to do, so his failure to obey would have been pointless. But disobedience was psychologically impossible in any case—and to the presiding judge's query as to whether there had been internal rebellion against the orders he followed, Servatius speculated that Eichmann had always opposed the unhappy orders which he nonetheless felt obliged to follow. (We have seen how what scant evidence exists points in the opposite direction—including during the time period between his capture and execution.)

The defense offered a last pair of arguments. The first was that Israel was not the appropriate legal venue for the proceedings—Argentina was, from which venue Eichmann had been abducted. Since in Argentina the statute of time limitations had already passed for such a trial, Israel should altogether suspend the proceedings. The second was to call for reconciliation, for allowing the time that had already passed since the Holocaust to be part of a longer sweep of time in which wounds might be healed. There was again an irony in the nature of this last appeal, couched as it was in terms of the Jews having "formulated the idea of 'a holy year' which brought peace and the abandonment of claims. He appealed to the court to render 'a Solomonic verdict that will astound the world with the wisdom of the Jewish people.'"[357]

There is a marvelously hollow ring to this last appeal to the conciliatory side of the heirs of the victims and surviving victims of Nazi atrocities, a cynical twist to the entirety of Jewish-Christian history, and not only to the denouement of that history in the Nazi period, given the profound lack of regret that seemed to emanate from Eichmann for the crimes with which he was associated (whether he was fully responsible, or partially responsible, or even, hypothetically, not responsible at all for them). The more so, given the trial testimony that had suggested that Eichmann himself (regardless of how large a role he was argued to have had) was completely immune to mercy, to allowing a single one of his victims to escape the deathtrap as far as his part (however large or small that part) of that trap was concerned.

The court adjourned for four months to await the decision of the judges. Their task had been a difficult one throughout the proceedings: to remain impartial and nonpartisan—with enormous pressure upon them not to conduct the proceedings in a manner that could even hint at the kind of prejudices that seemed in particular to have marked the Rosenberg-Sobell trial so deeply. Now, on December 11, 1961, eight months to the day since those proceedings had opened, they returned their verdict, which was to find Eichmann "guilty of crimes against the Jewish people, of crimes against humanity, of war crimes and of membership in criminal associations."

The judges complimented the counsel teams on both sides for their efforts, before turning to the issues. They began with the matter of scope—that the crimes under question are considered crimes within the legal thinking of all civilized nations, including Germany, and so the argument that the temporary abandonment of that legal sensibility by Nazi Germany could not free criminals of that era from responsibility for knowing that they were in fact commiting crimes; and that the nature and international quality of the crimes by definition transcend particularized national borders or time frames. Therefore, Israel in 1961 was as appropriate a place as any in which to carry out these proceedings—particularly given the acknowledged link between the coming into existence of the State of Israel and the extermination of six million Jews. The trial could legitimately be held in any number of countries, but none had come forth requesting that Israel cede the role of venue to it.

In a similar manner, the judges reviewed the sorts of objections that the defense had offered to finding Eichmann guilty as charged, from his relationship with the Jewish community in Austria as he represented it (as opposed to how others did), to the various programs of deportation in which he had been involved in a key manner, to the "increased energy, initiative and daring, and stubborn determination to complete the work in spite of all the difficulties in his way" that characterized his role in the destruction of the Hungarian Jewish community toward the end of the war. They reviewed the questions regarding his importance in the shaping and liquidation of ghettos, the facilitation of packed transports to the death camps, the eventual implementation of gas as a more efficient instrument of destruction than other means in those camps.

They noted the evidence of his willingness and ability to act with independence, initiative and responsibility—neither in blindly following those few above him in the Nazi hierarchy nor by any means being blind to the actions of his subordinates—in "all the acts perpetrated during the implementation of the Final Solution of the Jewish problem." Those acts "are to be regarded as one single whole, and the accused's criminal responsibility is to be decided upon accordingly;" that reponsibility is reflected in the fact that "the accused was privy to the extermination secret plan as of June, 1941. As of August, 1941, he began to be active in the furtherance of the extermination campaign, occupying a central place in it..."[358]

In short, the judges unanimously considered that all fifteen charges had been proven beyond a reasonable doubt—even to the matter of Eichmann's inner attitude that, had it been at all disturbed by the acts in which he was so intimate a part, might have led him to seek re-assignment or at least to have utilized his position in a less overwhelmingly negative way. But he evinced no evidence of having wished to work otherwise or elsewhere within the Nazi bureaucracy, and was merciless in all his deeds, "energetic, full of initiative and active to the extreme in his efforts to carry out the Final Solution."[359]

The question now became what would be the appropiate punishment to propose—which was the echo of the question regarding how to frame the charges against Eichmann, with which the prosecution's problematic had begun. Hausner and his associates weighed carefully as to whether the maximum penalty was obligatory and concluded that, even if it were not, the death penalty was appropriate—given that, were it hypothetically possible to execute Eichmann thousands of times, his multiple deaths could not match the deaths that he had made possible. So it was not a matter of balancing an account, as much as completing a powerful historical and moral lesson that had begun on the first day of his trial. Dr. Servatius argued—still—that Eichmann had been subject to "political hypnosis," but that he had changed, and that he would serve as a more effective educational instrument were he to live out the duration of his life in prison, writing the memoirs that would warn youth to beware of the kind of course he had taken.

Eichmann himself was offered the last word, in which he

expressed disappointment in his hopes for justice, asserting still that "the witnesses have been most untruthful" and that "legally, I am innocent." He continued: "Today of my own free will I would ask the Jewish people for pardon and would confess that I am bowed down with shame at the thought of the iniquities commited against the Jews and the injustices done to them, but in the light of the grounds given in the judgment this would, in all probability, be construed as hypocrisy. I am not the monster I am made out to be. I am the victim of a misconception."

The following day—December 15, 1961, the court reconvened. The judges announced that, while there was substance to the argument that the death sentence be pronounced as mandatory, they preferred, in the presence of some doubt, to treat it as discretionary. Nonetheless, based on their conclusions regarding Eichmann's culpability for the crimes articulated in the indictment, they sentenced him "to death for the crimes against the Jewish people, the crimes against humanity and the war crimes of which he has been found guilty."

An appeal to the Israeli Supreme Court followed and an Appellate Tribunal[360] was convened on March 22, 1962 to hear the appeal which began with the assertion that the mass of publicity had made it impossible for the court to remain objective, and ended with the interesting turn to the Rousseauian observation that there is no culprit who cannot be saved from sin. Thus Eichmann, his attorney claimed, was no longer a danger to anyone—and if spared might in fact serve as an instrument for the "obviation of dangers."

The prosecution's response noted that, given the conversation with Stassen of not that long before—and the regret that Eichmann expressed therein that he had not completed his "task" of destroying the Jews—it was by no means clear that the accused no longer represented a danger to the Jews or to the world at large. The arguments brought forth by the defense had all been brought forth before and been shown lacking, concluded the prosecution. And the notion that sparing him would serve any purpose with regard to other would-be criminal acts was deemed unlikely at best. These were the conclusions to which the Supreme Court justices arrived, as well. It took them three and a half hours to deliver their judgment, which affirmed both the lower court's verdict and its decision regarding punishment—exactly two years after the legal process had begun.

Dr. Servatius left Israel the following day, repeating his assessment of both the original trial and the appeal, to wit, that the proceedings were fair and justly accomplished. This left Eichmann with one last chance: to appeal to the President of Israel, Yitzhak Ben-Tzvi—to whom he wrote "I abhor the atrocities committed on the Jews as the greatest crime, and consider it just that the people responsible should be brought to justice now and in the future. But a line should be drawn between leaders and tools like myself." While the President sequestered himself with the written materials most relevant to his decision, the world outside his doors, both within and outside Israel, offered its commentaries.

Most of the media argued in favor of execution, while there were those who feared that his death would be interpreted as exonerating the German nation of the crimes that had been reviewed before the eyes of the world during the previous months. Others feared that Eichmann's death would offer a false finality to a narrative that humans deem finalized at our peril. In the end, and after many hours of deliberation, President Ben-Tzvi decided not to accede to Eichmann's application for clemency. The prisoner was informed of that decision at about 8 PM on May 31, 1962. Asking for a bottle of wine, Eichmann spent the last few hours of his life writing letters to his family and receiving the Reverend and Mrs. Hull—who reported that he neither evinced regret nor an interest in reconciliation with religion. He was hanged at midnight and his body cremated; his ashes were carried by police boat beyond the three-mile limit and tossed overboard into the Mediterranean Sea.

III. From Eichmann Forward?

Among the obvious significances of the Eichmann trial is what it offered, for better and for worse, for the first time in Jewish history: a Jewish court within a Jewish state meting out justice—and to a non-Jew whose crimes were most specifically directed at Jews—rather than that process being dependant on an entirely non-Jewish (be it

Christian, Muslim, Hindu or whatever version of secular one might choose) framework. Thus the trial of Adolf Eichmann, as it played out from beginning to end, was, perhaps more than any other of the trials upon which we have focussed, centered more distinctly on issues of history than of law—even as its self-conscious shaping was so emphatically punctilious regarding the law and justice. Put in more specific terms, Gideon Hausner observes that "important also was the realization that the only reason it was possible to hold the trial at all was that there was now a Jewish state on the map."[361] It is indeed difficult to imagine that, had Israel not existed, Eichmann would have been captured and brought to trial in the first place: who would have done it? Surely in the pregnant atmosphere of the Cold War in which, in so many ways, most had chosen to forget about the Nazis and the Nazi period, the major players on the world scene would not have been interested in opening such a can of worms.

Perhaps Eichmann would have been found and assassinated, but what would that have accomplished beyond revenge? The submission of Eichmann to the judicial process, as we have already noted, offered an important and extended pedagogic moment for much of the world. Moreover, somewhat more subtly nuanced is the futher observation offered by Hausner, that "fifteen years earlier Dr. Chaim Weitzmann had pleaded with the American Counsel at Nuremberg, Robert Jackson, to be allowed to appear as a Jewish witness to unfold the great tragedy at the trial of the war criminals.[362] Jackson politely refused... 'I am convinced,' he wrote Dr, Weitzmann, 'that for the future position of the Jews in Europe, it has been better to prove our case in this manner [i.e., by way of documentary evidence] than to have it proved by testimony.' Now it was the Jews themselves who could decide what was best for their position."[363]

Hausner's point is not to argue one way or the other with Jackson's assertion, it seems to me—as to whether the Jews would be better served by having others than they speak on their behalf, or by having documents with their cold, rational language placed before the court rather than the eye-witness testimonies with the intense emotions that they would inevitably bring to the surface—but that it would be desirable for Jews to make that decision themselves, especially in the context of addressing the destruction of so many Jews at the putative hands of those being tried in the courtroom. With the existence of Israel and its legal system—to say nothing of its organization, formally or not, of bodies positioned to locate and capture the various Eichmanns living with false identities in different parts of the world—that desideratum was in place as it was not at the time of the Nuremberg trials.

The other side of this *novum*, to repeat, is that Israel as a Jewish state with a Jewish court was as much on trial before the court of world opinion as Eichmann was on trial before the Israeli court—or more so. This was particularly evident at the outset, when a number of media—notably, American media—attacked the proceedings as inherently wrong. Thus the May 27, 1960 *Washington Post's* editors wrote that "anything connected to the indictment of Eichmann is tainted with lawlessness," and that the "State of Israel is doing a disservice to Jews of other nationalities." If the first part of this assertion smacks of cynical irony, and of the fear that the trial would be a sham, the second part suggests an embrace of the centuries-long notion that the only way for Jews to survive is by keeping a low profile, by rocking no boats and stirring up no tempests (to shamelessly pile on metaphor after metaphor).

Taking a somewhat different critical tack, the June 18, 1960 *New York Times* asserted that "no immoral act justifies another; the rule of law must protect the most depraved criminals" —referring to the illegality of Eichmann's abduction. To my hypothetical question of four paragraphs above, the *Times'* comment apparently provides an answer. For apparently a mass murderer, by this reckoning, should simply be left alone if he has taken refuge in a country where the justice system has no interest in pursuing him. The abduction of a mass-murderer is more disturbing than the murders—at least if those murders are of a particular racial or religious or ethnic or national group.

Such voices were in the minority, as others—with the not-surprising exception of Nazis, neo-Nazis and Nazi sympathizers—recognized the complicated necessity of balancing between the actual needs of justice and the theoretical dictates of law. This was expressed in so many words by the *Journal-American* in its editorial of June 2, 1960 and by the *Herald Tribune* in its June 11, 1960 editorial. And among the eighteen states that had been occupied by the Nazis who might therefore have laid claim to the right to try Eichmann, not one—including both Western and Eastern Germany—asserted the right or desire to try him; all were content to see the process proceed in Israel. Moreover, as the trial wore on, the conviction that Eichmann was being given every conceivable courtesy of law and justice could hardly be denied. So that the verdict within the world at large was even more strongly affirmative that the Israeli court had acquitted itself admirably and justly in the process than that the Israelis were correct in trying Eichmann in the first place.

On the other hand a major consequence of the trial, as evidenced in letters to the prosecution and to various news outlets during and after the procedure, was that it opened tens of thousands of eyes that had been closed theretofore to that black hole within history known as the Holocaust. It was not only those from various parts of the world who expressed dismay and astonishment both at what the Nazis had perpetrated and at the fact that they had known nothing about it theretofore. But Israeli youth, having grown up after events about which they had been taught little or nothing, with at best a sense of contempt for their parents' generation for having been led to the slaughter, were shocked to hear all that they heard in radio transmission after radio transmission and one newspaper report or summary after another.[364]

The broader Jewish response to the Eichmann trial and execution is itself worthy of a brief discussion, both in general terms, and in particular as it pertains to the writing of Hannah Arendt. There was at the outset the same range of concerns within the world Jewish community as within the world non-Jewish community: should some sort of international tribunal be convened or should Eichmann be tried in Germany—or in Argentina—rather than in Israel? By and large the view among Jews was that Israel was indeed the most appropriate venue for the trial—and the conviction in its aftermath was that he had received the sort of trial that could only positively impinge upon international Jewish life, due to the forthright manner in which it had been conducted. There was, as we have seen, dissent regarding what

Eichmann's punishment should be, based on varied interpretations of how this moment should serve history and human conscience, but no dissent regarding the propriety of punishment. Those seeking clemency for him included the Central Conference of American Rabbis and a group of Hebrew University professors who were led by the esteemed philosopher of religion, Martin Buber.

Among the most compelling arguments for staying the executioner's hand—but this argument appeared afterwards, in a brief article in the July-August, 1962 issue of the Israeli periodical *Ammot*— was that offered by the renowned Hebrew University professor of Jewish mysticism, Gershom Scholem. He argued that an execution would offer to the world a sense of finality, and offer it the excuse to return to businesss as usual, rather than doing what life-long incarceration (Professor Norman Bentwich, in England, had suggested that Eichmann be deported to Germany for that purpose) would do: keep the issue alive as an ongoing reminder of what had happened and a warning of what can happen when religious, ethnic, racial and other kinds of animosity are given free rein.

Scholem made a distinction between the legal/moral aspect of the situation—which asserted that "he deserved to die a thousand deaths each day," even as "[t]he laws of human society are [ultimately] at a loss as to adequate punishment for Eichmann's crimes... [for t]here can be no possible proportion between this crime and its punishment"—and its larger public, moral/historical aspects. In this latter realm, to execute Eichmann

> falsified the historical significance of the trial by creating the illusion that it is possible to conclude something of this affair by the hanging of one human or inhuman creature. Such an illusion is most dangerous because it may engender the feeling that something has been done to atone for the unatonable...
>
> One fears that instead of opening up a reckoning and leaving it open for the next generation, we have foreclosed it... If we wanted to prove that justice is being done and that a great historical reckoning is being effected, then a living Eichmann—whether imprisoned by us or put into the hands of the Germans (who had good reasons for not wanting him)—was not likely to stand in the way of such a reckoning.
>
> But it is to be feared that an Eichmann who has been hanged will indeed stand in the way—very much in the way."[365]

One wonders only why this eloquent argument was offered by Scholem *after* the fact, although he may well have offered this argument privately and/or orally before the execution took place — and he *was* among those professors at the Hebrew University who signed the letter to President Ben-Tzvi pleading for a commutation of the sentence.

Scholem's discussion is, in any case, presented from the perspective of a committed Jew, steeped in Jewish history and philosophy, who is concerned in a constructive manner with the implications of the Eichmann trial and execution for the Jews and for the world. Hannah Arendt seemed to come from a very different realm of thinking in her unique and disturbing exception to the positive conclusions that by and large emerged within the Jewish community (and, for that matter, the world community) during the trial and after it. For she was unrelenting in her negative view of the proceedings, from beginning to end. Where others who had begun with a negative viewpoint changed their perspective as the proceedings moved forward, she remained antagonistic to the feasibility of a serious and dignified legal process taking place in Israel for a prisoner such as Adolf Eichmann. "By the end of the trial, indeed, it was clear that Eichmann was a far stronger and more malign character than many of us had supposed. Miss Arendt, however, could not abandon her theory about his banality because it was essential for her main theme," wrote Richard Crossman in a strongly negative article reviewing her book.[366]

Arendt was initially writing in a five-part series of articles for *The New Yorker* magazine that subsequently became the basis for her book.[367] In it she argued that Eichmann was not only a grey bureaucrat, a banal exemplum of evil, but of an everyday evil of which anyone is capable — as opposed to seeing him as someone who carried evil to an unprecedented level. Thus she seemed to see little substantive difference between the role he played in the catastrophe and the conditions that informed that role and the role played by, among others, Jewish leaders "drafted" by the Nazis to do some of the work of organizing, keeping the calm within and selecting deportees from their communities. She displayed remarkably little sympathy either for the weight felt by the court in wrestling with the issues presented by the trial—for the necessary balance between the demands of law and justice in the narrowest sense and history in the broader sense—or for the victims who came forward as witnesses.

The notion of the widespread banality of evil as she considers it and her lack of sympathy for the victims is particularly well expressed—and, given both what the trial and so many subsequent studies and discussions of the Holocaust have brought out, rather diabolical—in her choice of focus on "the weird fact that in the death camps it was usually the inmates and the victims who had actually wielded 'the fatal instrument with [their] hands'." By this emphasis she presumably means both to ignore the Nazi organization and running of the gas chambers (for example) and to express sympathy for Eichmann's presentation of himself as innocent of hardly any direct deeds of death-dealing—who himself perhaps never wielded the fatal instrument in his hands, unless we understand that the pen in his hand was a powerful and fatal instrument.

Conversely, she asserted that the Israeli court—and Jews in general—"[n]ever arrived at a clear understanding of the actual horror of Auschwitz, which is of a different nature from all the atrocities of the past, because it appeared to prosecution and judges alike as not much more than the most horrible pogrom in Jewish history."[368] Thus—remarkably—Arendt interpreted the historical framework presented by Hausner to the court as if it offered the totality of his arguments, and ignored the myriad times and ways in the course of ten weeks of initial and subsequent assertions in which he discussed the Holocaust and Eichmann's role in it as unprecedented. She asserted that all of the participants in the trial failed to recognize that the gas chambers (as she asserts) are both politically and legally "crimes" (she places that word in quotation marks, and one wonders why) "different not only in degree of seriousness but in essence" from prior murderous anti-Jewish acts in history.

Nonetheless, there is something odd in the manner in which she insists early on that the case "was built on what the Jews had suffered, and not what Eichmann had done"[369] that suggests she missed much of the opening objections lodged by Dr. Servatius and both the responses to those objections and the whole point that Gideon Hausner felt needed making—Eichmann's clear and unique (and not banal) guilt for his crimes—throughout the trial. Her "report" on the whole was delivered with a glib and constantly tongue-in-cheek style that made light of the very weight that the affair carried for Israel, Jewry and the world.

One wonders how Arendt—a brilliant intellectual, a Jewish refugee from Nazi Germany who remade her intellectual life in the United States—arrived at her supremely unsympathetic viewpoint. The most obvious answer was provided by an article in the April 1963 issue of *The Jewish Spectator*, which suggested that "[i]n fairness to herself, she should disqualify herself from writing on Jewish themes to which she brings the *pathology* and confusion of the Jew who does not *want* to be a Jew and suffers because 'the others will not let him forget that he is a Jew.'"

One might add a number of comments to this summary statement. The first is that such a psychoanalysis of Arendt as suffering from *selbsthasse* (self-hate)—a condition to which any number of Jews and members of other minority communities have been subject over history—could in fact be traced not only to the high level of assimilation of the German Jewish community of which she was part, but also specifically to the Nazi condition which forced her out of the rarified academic world of which she had been part in Germany, that turned her into a refugee, and, however honored in her new home, that left her angry (as many refugees can be, no matter how uncomfortable the old and comfortable the new home might be) at having had to shift from an old to a new home, language, culture, frame of reference. The interesting thing is that such anger was directed not at the perpetrators who created the circumstances of her discomfort but at the victims—the group of which she was herself an ineluctable part—whose political powerlessness made it possible for it to be victimized by the perpetrators.

Moreover, as has emerged in more recent biographical discussions of Hannah Arendt, the blind spot which she evolved over time regarding Jews and Nazis was nurtured earlier on by her personal life: as a graduate student she was—and seems never to have ceased being—in love with her professor, Martin Heidegger, the brilliant German existentialist philosopher who also turns out to have been a Nazi. So if her "report" seems to offer more of a negative view of those shaping the trial and more of a positive perspective on the man in the glass booth, perhaps the reasons are not so obscure.

Arendt's critique of the Eichmann proceedings provoked a slew of responses.[370] Among these the most definitive was the extensive, point-by-point discussion/rebuttal offered by Jacob Robinson, in his 1965 book, *And the Crooked Shall Be Made Straight.*[371] More accessible simply in its brevity is one of the first responses to her, an open letter dated June 23, 1963 and printed in the January 1964 issue of *Encounter,* from an old friend and fellow scholar, also formerly from Germany—the same Gershom Scholem who had written the previous year on the impropriety of having hanged Eichmann.

Scholem takes on the unsympathetic perspective of Arendt's work by noting that "[a]t each decisive juncture...your book speaks only of the weakness of the Jewish stance in the world"—lending some credence to my suggestion that her viewpoint is derived, in part, from her anger at that weakness of the victim, the more so because she was one of them. It is also notable that in so doing she ignored what Hausner was at pains to point out—even at the cost of veering somewhat from what was most directly germane to the case before him—i.e., the manner in which, given the chance, Jews did acquit themselves as warriors against the Nazi regime.

Scholem is most critical of the tone of her writing, the flippancy (his word) in which he finds "little trace" of *Avahat Yisrael*: "Love of the Jewish people." He notes her choice of the term *"Fuehrer"* to refer to Leo Baeck. It is, he asserts, an attempt, in appropriating a Nazi term and applying it to a Jewish leader, to imply some sort of parallel between Baeck's role as a Jewish leader in the Terezin concentration camp and the role of Nazi leaders like Hitler and Eichmann in shaping the world of such camps, an implication that works "to the benefit of those Germans in condemning whom your book rises to greater eloquence than in mourning the fate of your own people."[372]

So, too, in the extended attention offered by Arendt to the issue of the *Judenraete*—Jews put in charge of their communities by the Nazis, to whom often fell, among other responsibilities, that of selecting who would be deported and who not, at a given time — Scholem finds Arendt's intention to wash over all such individuals equally ("some among them were swine, others were saints") and all of them in a manner making them essentially equal to Eichmann (i.e., part of the widespread banality of evil) more than overly simplistic and ill-informed — "for I do not know whether they were right or wrong. Nor do I presume to judge. I was not there." Scholem acknowledges the truth of the assertions that such Nazi machinations help "to blur the distinction between torturer and victim" but criticizes how that blurring becomes for Arendt a reason to be less sympathetic to the victims and less critical of the torturers.

In the end, Hannah Arendt restates the judgment meted out to Eichmann in her own terms rather than reporting on that of the Judges, in arguing that the prosecution did not succeed in proving what it set out to prove. In her own conclusion she refers to Eichmann as a "convert to Zionism" — but, as Scholem observes, her "description of Eichmann as a 'convert to Zionism' could only come from somebody who had a profound dislike of everything to do with Zionism. These passages in your book... amount to a mockery of Zionism." There is ample evidence elsewhere that Scholem was at least correct here — that Arendt was not at all sympathetic to the Zionist idea.

If there were many who took Arendt to task for her analysis,[373] on the other hand there were those few who were extremely sympathetic to her book and took critics like Scholem to task. Thus Dagme Barnouw — a professor of German at Brown University, which fact might, for some, raise questions as to her own perspective on the larger issues of which this discussion is part — wrote famously in a 1983 article[374] that Arendt's "description of Dr. Leo Baeck, former Chief Rabbi of Berlin, as someone who was 'in the eyes of both Jews and Gentiles the "Jewish *Fuehrer*",' was not due primarily to an appaling lack of sensitivity but rather resulted from her desire to help her readers understand certain issues... In contradistinction to Scholem, however, unprejudiced readers of Arendt's report may very well be able to understand Arendt's motivations in using the term *Fuehrer*, namely to establish a certain perspective on the victims who had *allowed themselves to be led so totally.*"[375]

To *help* her readers, or to prejudice her readers toward her own viewpoint? Understand *what* issues? Barnouw not only obviously agrees with what she reports as Arendt's conclusion—that (in Barnouw's words) "the crime against humanity committed on the body of the Jewish people does not, in her view, have the dignity of tragedy" but that "there are criminals and there are victims, and it is in the nature of this particular crime that the distinction between criminal and victim is not always clear." She writes Scholem off as a critic of such conclusions, who "simply rejects this insight with the comment: 'What perversity!'."[376]

Even were one to give Arendt the benefit of the doubt for her viewpoint—on the grounds that at the time of the Eichmann trial and its aftermath, the time of her writing, so little had yet really been written, said, or apparently thought about the Holocaust—certainly that benefit cannot be offered to Ms. Barnouw. She is writing at a time by which so much ink has flowed under the bridge on the subject of the Holocaust, that to speak simply (to use her term) of "victims who had allowed themselves to be led so totally," or of the Holocaust of over a million Jewish children as lacking "the dignity of tragedy," or of the blurred distinction between perpetrator and victim as other than perverse, is itself perverse. Such a sympathetic read of Arendt, as Barnouw articulates her sympathy, can derive only from a profound lack of compassion, a profound ignorance of the history of the Holocaust, or a strong will to feel moral sympathy with the Nazis at the expense of their Jewish victims.[377]

There is a particular appropriateness to the fact that the denouement of the unfinished discussion of the Eichmann trial is a series of discussions of Hannah Arendt's discussion of evil as it pertains to Eichmann and the trial that judged him. For one of the prevailing obsessions of Peter Z. Malkin, the man who captured Eichmann, as he and his colleagues held their prisoner in capitivity, awaiting the opportunity to smuggle him out of Argentina, was indeed the very grey, bureaucratic banality of his appearance. Malkin could, as he said, understand evil as visually expressed in the fire of Hitler's visage as he ranted from the speaker's platform time and again, but Eichmann's face offered no hints of how evil—profound evil—might or ought to look. He found himself not only asking Eichmann questions (as I have noted above, 322-323) but simply staring at him trying to find the visual evidence for what resided within.

If our discussion of the trial of Adolf Eichmann may be said to have traversed the periphery of a particular circle, pertaining to the question of evil—in leading from Malkin to concluding with Arendt—the discussion that shapes that circle also leads us in two obvious further directions. One is the matter of subsequent captures and trials—in Israel or elsewhere—of Nazi war criminals. The other is the larger matter of law and justice as it has been in the process of playing out in the State of Israel for the past half century, particularly given the unusual conditions under which Israel has existed during all that time and the decade or more before that time, essentially surrounded by those whose avowed goal has been the destruction of the State.

In the very year in which Dagme Barnouw's article defending Hannah Arendt's discussion of the Eichmann trial appeared, the extradition of John Demjanjuk, an auto worker from outside Cleveland, Ohio, was being sought by the State of Israel so that he might stand trial for his wartime role—as the Treblinka Concentration Camp guard known as "Ivan the Terrible"—in the Nazi anihilation of Jews. But Demjanjuk would end up experiencing a very different fate from that of Eichmann, as we shall discuss in the opening pages of the chapter that follows.

Indeed, to begin with, Demjanjuk's case was different from that of Eichmann in a fundamental way. For while the trial of Eichmann centered on the question of how to assess the defendant's role and guilt in the mass-murder of millions of Jews—and the capacity of Israel as the "Jewish State" to engage in that assessment—the trial of Demjanjuk centered on the question of whether the defendant had been correctly identified after so many years as the perpetrator of crimes that nobody doubted were commited by "Ivan the Terrible." It is in fact to a *series* of trials of John Demjanjuk that we must turn first in the next chapter of this narrative.

Chapter Eight:
Old and New Circumstances,
From Demjanjuk to the Next Millennium

The case of John Demjanjuk, with its starting point and penultimate point of discussion in the United States, is the most famous of the trials of suspected Nazis in this country that began to emerge in the late 1970s and 1980s.[378] Among the others, perhaps the best known are those of Andrija Artukovic, Frank Walus, Viorel Trifa and Otto von Bolschwing. All of the cases involving these individuals— and others—have in common with each other two related features. In each instance the individual was eventually believed to arrived as an immigrant to the United States under false pretenses—either as a refugee or simply as an aspiring American with an innocent past whose past turned out to have been far from innocent. And that lack of innocence was, in each case, associated with concerted efforts of one sort or another on behalf of the Nazis.

Each of them arrived into the United States at a time when Americans were obsessed with the danger of Communist infiltration and the threat to our freedoms of that infiltration, and entirely forgetful of the oh-so-recent Nazi past. The same atmosphere that was so deleterious to—among many others, but to none so egregiously—Julius and Ethel Rosenberg offered an ironic twist with regard to forgotten Nazis. "One [American] Legion member had a proposal to [look around for members of the 'secret battalions' of 75,000 'trained Communists' all over the United States]: 'a system whereby in each block in the city and in each neighborhood in the country someone can be made responsible' for exposing the Communists on his block.

"The irony is inescapable: in such a vigilante network, who would be better suited to stand watch than the displaced persons, the refugees from Communism, those whose homelands [such as Ukraine] had been 'incorporated' by the Soviets?"[379] Thus it was that between the end of World War II and the 1970s, while the Immigration and Naturalization Service (INS) joined with other agencies such as the FBI to remove *thousands* of "internal security" suspects, the Service "filed no more than ten cases against persons suspected of Nazi collaboration or of persecuting the innocent."[380]

Moreover, the INS was so poorly organized with regard to this issue, its handling so lackadasical, that "among the first cases brought by INS against Nazi collaborators, the defendants were not Nazis at all. They were three Polish Jews, Heinrich Friedmann, Jakob Tencer, and Jonas Lewey."[381] Of the nine deportation cases filed against alleged Nazi collaborators prior to 1973, three were lost at trial—the government did not appeal any of them—and six resulted in deportation orders, generally on grounds of having lied on their immigration applications, rather than for any other reason. Of these, three were reversed by the Board of Immigration Appeals.[382] A key issue that emerged in these cases was whether the act of having lied on one's immigration application due to fear of the consequences in the country from which the refugee came—fear of telling the truth, of not being viewed as a refugee, and therefore being denied a visa into the United States, and having to stay in, or being sent back to, the country in question—merited forfeiture of American citizenship and/or deportation.

Another issue was that the INS was essentially without a policy regarding (former) Nazis. And so the Demjanjuk case not only represented a watershed in the way in which it offered a new direction for the INS toward a policy but it also found—as so many other aspects of dealing with the Holocaust had begun to, in the America of the late 1970s—a cadre of concerned individuals who would both shape and push that newly directed policy.

John Demjanjuk—born Ivan Demjanjuk in Ukraine, at that time part of the USSR, in 1920—was a retired autoworker who immigrated to the United States in 1951, settling in Seven Hills, a western suburb of Cleveland, Ohio, becoming a citizen seven years later, changing his first name to "John"[383] and living a quiet life with his wife and three children, while working for the Ford motor company, for the next few decades. In 1976 he was unexpectedly identified by survivors of the Treblinka death camp as a brutal operator of the camp's gas chambers to whom they referred as *"Ivan Grozny"*: "Ivan the Terrible."

Treblinka was a hell on earth in Poland—about 50 miles east of Warsaw—that operated between July, 1942 and the fall of 1943, in which perhaps as few as 850,000 or many as 1.2 million people were systematically gassed and their bodies burned by the Nazis. The work force at Treblinka consisted of German SS officers—no more than 20 of them at any given time—and about 80 Ukrainians selected by the Nazi overlords from among the myriads of prisoners captured in the sweep of the *Wehrmacht* across the East, and chosen, apparently, "for their brawn, their viciousness, their willingness to exchange the hard life of a POW for three meals a day in a death factory."[384]

Below these on the camp hierarchy were work-Jews, several hundred on a given day, pulled at random from the arriving transports to do the ugliest and most undesirable work—sorting clothing, fountain pens, eyeglasses, tools, valuables, money—and dragging bodies out of the gas chambers and into the burning pits. These work-Jews could survive for days or weeks—rarely, if ever, longer—until they were placed in the gas chambers and a new group was selected from the latest arrivals to replace them as work-Jews. A group of these, astonishingly, managed an uprising against their oppressors in August, 1943. With crude weapons they surprised and overwhelmed the Ukrainians and SS and made for the woods around the camp—perhaps fifty of them were not mowed down by machine gun fire, making it into the forest to relative safety.

Treblinka was shut down shortly thereafter—its work of annihilation done, anyway, and all of its material aspects bulldozed into oblivion. But with the eventual liquefaction of so many only partially burned remains, the earth began to shift some time thereafter, and the gases released by putrefaction blew the topsoil off the pits: Treblinka revealed itself to the world. Of those few who had survived, intense memories followed them through the decades. Of all of the cruel figures associated with the horror that they remembered, one above all stood out, the man who operated the gas chamber and favored wielding a six-foot pipe like a club, shattering the skulls of those who displeased him in any way. They knew only his first name, Ivan, but gave him their own sobriquet, *Ivan Grozny*.[385]

The identification of Demjanjuk as *Ivan Grozny* came about almost by accident. The first moment in that identification process came in autumn, 1975, in an article in a Ukrainian-language, rather pro-Soviet, weekly published in New York City by an American Communist of Ukrainian descent, Michael Hanusiak. He referenced a report that he claimed to have located in a Soviet archive in Kiev. The report recounted a 1950s war crimes trial, in which Ignat Danylchenko, a former guard at the Nazi labor camp, Sobibor, referred to one Ivan Demjanjuk as having been a fellow camp guard. That article, and a list of more than 70 suspected Nazi collaborators of Ukrainian descent living in the United States, were passed on to the INS by Hanusiak.

Hanusiak specifically placed Demjanjuk as a trainee at Trawniki—where the Nazis prepared primarily Ukrainians to be guards, gas chamber operators and to perform similar services at death camps, particularly Treblinka—and thereafter as a guard at Sobibor (from March to October, 1943) and subsequently at the Flossenberg, Germany concentration camp until early 1944. He had no further information that would corroborate the allegations, nor did he know of any witnesses in the United States who might be able to do so. Soviet archives remained inaccessible to outsiders at that time, so U.S investigators were not in a position to verify Danylchenko's allegations.[386]

An important breakthrough in the process of pursuing such individuals came in 1980 in the wake of a visit to the Soviet Union by Allan A. Ryan, Jr. and Walter Rockler, of the INS, to request Soviet assistance in the prosecution of potential deportation cases involving alleged former Nazis that were taking shape at that time. In a period when the two countries remained Cold War adversaries, the memory of having been allies against a common foe 35 years earlier was sufficient for the Soviets to agree to have witnesses deposed, or even, were they healthy enough and willing to do so, flown to the United States to testify in court—not only to testify for the prosecution, but for the defense, should the defense so request. They agreed to supply original documents and not just photocopies.[387]

The list passed along by Hanusiak, of both names and specific allegations with regard to those names, did not include Treblinka among the sites associated with Demjanjuk. It mentioned Sobibor, 100 miles south of Treblinka—like Treblinka, a death camp operated by a small SS force and Ukrainian guards trained at Trawniki, but *not* Treblinka. So INS, in opening its case agaisnt Demjanjuk, referred to him as a former guard at Sobibor. In 1977 he was identified as—or accused of—having lied on his immigration application back in 1951, specifically regarding his role in the Nazi death camps.

Demjanjuk had also been unexpectedly identified—this was the second moment in the arrival at the indictment against him—by a number of Holocaust survivors in Israel, by way of a photo spread sent by INS to the Israeli police, during the investigation of Treblinka Concentration Camp Guard, Feodor Federenko.[388] Thus Eliyahu Rosenberg, one of the survivors/escapees of the Treblinka uprising, was asked—according to the custom of presenting the photospread in a "non-suggestive manner"—whether he recognized anyone. After a slow pass over the images, he identified Federenko, stating that he did not know his name—but then pointed to the photo of Demjanjuk and asserted that this was Ivan, who was also, he said, at Treblinka. The investigating officer insisted that this second man had not been at Treblinka, but Rosenberg was insistent that he was, although, he said, the image seemed to offer a "more mature" version of the face than the one he recalled from Treblinka.

The same procedure followed with Pinchas Epstein—who also identified Demjanjuk as Ivan, and, unsolicited (and obviously having no way of knowing the date of the photograph) observed that the face seemed a bit older than what he remembered of Ivan. Chaim Rajgrodski, a third Treblinka survivor, was brought in to examine the photo spread toward identifying Federenko but also, unsolicited, identified Demjanjuk as *Ivan Grozny*.

The information sent back to Washington was that Federenko had been positively identified, but that so had a second individual who had been at Treblinka, named Ivan. At the time the INS was too busy with Federenko to worry about this second suspect, but two years later, when the new Office of Special Investigations (OSI) took over this aspect of INS work, the Demjanjuk case re-surfaced from the files. And in late summer, 1979, the OSI sent a cable to the American Embassy in Moscow, asking for assistance in ascertaining whether or not the Soviets had records pertaining to Trawniki, where Ukrainian POWs were trained as guards in the death camps—and if so, if there was mention of an Ivan Demjanjuk among those records.

The result was twofold: one was that, in January, 1980 an envelope arrived at OSI from the embassy with a photocopy of an identification card issued by the SS authorities at Trawniki, culled from the Soviet Archives. "It bore a clear photograph of a serious young man with close-cropped hair... The man in the photo was born on April 3, 1920 in 'Duboimachariwzi' in the Ukraine. 'Face: oval; hair: dark blond; eyes: gray. Scars: on his back.' His father's name was Nikolai. And the name on the card was Ivan Demjanjuk."[389] The other result was the visit to Moscow by Ryan and his associates to which I referred above, toward the end of that month, which forged the cooperation agreement that would be so important to both the Demjanjuk and other cases.

Where Demjanjuk is concerned, it should be noted that the point and purpose of the legal exercise in the United States was merely to prove that he had lied on his immigration application regarding who he had been and what he had done, and, simply put, whether or not he had therefore been eligible for DP refugee status at the time of his immigration proceedings—and if not, to reverse that decision of nearly three decades earlier. It was not to try him for any of the crimes of which he might now stand accused. He could be deported—and the question that might arise was: to where?—

but not imprisoned, much less executed for those crimes, however egregious they might be and however clear his guilt might be.

The starting point of the prosecution's case was twofold: to gather enough expertise that the Trawniki ID card was authentic—and not fabricated by the Soviets as part of a conspiracy to get at "traitors" who were taken prisoner by the Germans, rather than commiting suicide, and more importantly, left for the capitalist West as the Cold War was beginning to unfold—and to gather witnesses who could attest to the actions of Ivan *Grozny* as well as to identify Demjanjuk as Ivan, from a new photospread. Its goal was to demonstrate incontrovertibly—without a scintilla of reasonable doubt—that Demjanjuk had lied during the immigration process regarding who he had been and what he had done: for to strip someone of American citizenship was a major legal issue.[390]

Demjanjuk's trial began on February 10, 1981 in a Cleveland courtroom presided over by Northern Ohio U.S. District Court Chief Justice Frank Battisti. The prosecution[391] began with witnesses—the first, Otto Horn, was a retired German nurse who had been assigned to Treblinka—the only one of 12 associated with Treblinka tried in Duesseldorff in 1964 to have been acquitted of participating in crimes against humanity. At the behest of the prosecuting attorney, Horn described the horrors of Treblinka and the presence of Ivan as the Ukrainian who assisted the two key SS officers in operating the gas chamber. Confronted with a photospread and without prompting, he was asked if anyone among those depicted could possibly be Ivan. He studied the photographs and then pointed to the image of John Demjanjuk from his 1951 visa to America. He then also pointed to a second image—that of the "serious-looking young man" from the Trawniki ID card.

The next witness, Chiel Rajchman, had written a memoir of his experience in Treblinka while hiding in a Warsaw ghetto bunker in 1944. He, too, was asked about and described what had transpired at Treblinka, culminating with a reference to the two Ukrainians who ran the gas chambers. "The biggest devil, who engraved himself in my memory, about whom I wrote 30 years ago, was called Ivan. His assistant was called Nikolai."[392] He described the apparent joy with which Ivan beat inmates with a lead pipe, usually just before they were gassed. Presented with a handful of photographs, he identified the 1951 Demjanjuk visa photo as that of Ivan.

The cross-examination of Rajchman by the defense attorney, John Martin, backfired: he asked about the process by which Rajchman had identified the same man a year earlier, hoping to be able to argue that American officials had pushed the witness suggestively toward that photograph—but Rajchman responded that he had had no idea what or whom the case concerned when he had made the identification. Moreover, when Martin showed another spread, with the 1942 Trawniki photograph, about which a year earlier Rajchman had not felt certain, (Martin was hoping thereby to inject some doubt into the proceedings), this time Rajchman pointed to it quickly and certainly, and asserted that this, too, was indeed Ivan. Whatever doubt had lingered in Rajchman's mind a year earlier had dissipated completely.

The third witness, Eliyahu Rosenberg had, we recall, identified Demjanjuk unexpectedly in the Federenko photospread he had been shown in Israel. He told his Treblinka story, culminating with reference to Ivan and Nikolai and to some of the specific cruelty of Ivan. And again, confronted with the two photo spreads, he asserted that the 1942 and 1951 Demjanjuk images both depicted Ivan. The fourth witness to make the photo spread connection between Ivan *Grozny* and John Demjanjuk was Sonia Lewkowicz. The fifth was Pinchas Epstein, who, like Rosenberg, had unexpectedly identified Demjanjuk in Israel while examining the Federenko photo spread. He offered more testimony regarding Ivan's activities—"Ivan split one skull after another. Every blow of his arm with an iron pipe split the person's head..."[393]—and, as he had done several months earlier in Israel, and as did the other four witnesses, he picked out the same two photos of John Demjanjuk as two images of Ivan.

Even with such compelling testimony from the witnesses and the failure of defense cross-examinations to do other than strengthen it, the case could have collapsed for lack of sufficient certainty, had the defense argument been sufficiently compelling that the Trawniki identity card was a forgery—that the Soviets had in fact released only a photocopy because they did not wish to subject the original to scientific analysis. Several requests from the OSI to the Soviets to borrow the original had, in spite of the successful January, 1980 Moscow meeting, yielded no response.

But halfway through the trial the Soviet embassy called the OSI offices to inform them that the original Trawniki identity card had been flown in from Moscow. The trial recessed so that both prosecution and defense could travel to Washington to examine the card in the company of their own experts. The ink, paper, signatures and photogaph were all tested by each side — without the participation or even the presence of the Soviets.[394] And then the card was flown to Cleveland when the trial resumed so that Judge Battisti could see it with his own eyes and hold it in his own hand.

The role of Treblinka in the annihilation of European Jewry, the role of Ivan *Grozny* in the functioning of Treblinka's torture and annihilation machinery and the identification of John Demjanjuk as Ivan having been accomplished to the satisfaction of the prosecution, they moved on to face the legal question of the appropriateness of revoking Demjanjuk's U.S. citizenship. In brief, the testimony of those who had served with the International Refugee Organization or the Displaced Persons Commission or the other branches of the government dealing with refugees and immigration, was clear: that nobody who had served on the staff of Treblinka or any other death camp would or could have been eligible for a DP visa to come to the United States. And so the prosecution rested on February 25, 1981.

The defense centered on John Demjanjuk himself, who took the stand to tell his version of his story. The critical issues upon which he needed to comment were regarding his whereabouts in general during the period leading up to and during the war — and in particular during the period from summer 1942 to early fall, 1943, when Treblinka had been in full operation as a death camp — and regarding the truths or lies that he told in gaining a DP visa to America and why, if he lied, he did so.

With regard to the last issue, he asserted both to Martin and, in cross-examination, to Prosecutor Horrigan, that he had been afraid that he would be executed by the Soviets if he were forcibly repatriated to the Soviet Union, "because I had been a soldier of the Red Army and there was a regulation that if you were going to be taken prisoner of war, you had to shoot yourself, and I hadn't done so."[395] He specified that the period of his fear was 1945-47—but the visa had been granted in 1951, by which time that fear-provoking condition presumably had eased.

Moreover, whereas on his application for that visa he had indicated that "from 1934 to 1943 you were [a farmer] in Sobibor, Poland" and that "from 1943 to 1944 you were in Pilau, Danzig," he now admitted that neither of these acounts of his whereabouts had been true, although he had signed the application under a written oath.[396] If he had lied under oath out of fear of the consequences of telling the truth at that time, why would one not suppose that he might be lying now out of fear of the consequences of telling the truth?

Demjanjuk's fall-back assertion—once he admitted that his original declaration to the immigration authorities had been false—was that he had been moved about from one POW camp to another during the central period under examination, whereas the prosecution believed that he had been captured in the Crimea in May, 1942 and sent to POW camps in Rovno and then Chelm, before being recruited by the Nazis at Chelm in the summer of 1942 to be trained as a camp guard at Trawniki, whereafter he was sent on to serve at Treblinka.

After a period of questioning that produced evasive and unclear responses, Prosecutor Horrigan returned to specific dates; Demjanjuk testified that he had been a prisoner at Chelm until October, 1944. He also turned to the Trawniki identity card; Demjanjuk conceded that the photo *could* be a photo of him. Importantly, Demjanjuk, under earlier questioning from his lawyer, had asserted that he had blue eyes—which might undercut both witness assertions (that Ivan's eyes were gray) and the card's description of Ivan Demjanjuk as having *gray* eyes. But in his visa application, Demjanjuk had himself written that his eyes were gray.[397] So, too, Demjanjuk possesses a scar on his back and his father was named Nikolai—details that are delineated on the Trawniki card, and the birth date on the card is the same as that which Demjanjk claimed for himself.

The following day, the prosecution produced as an expert

witness one Professor Ziemke, considered to be one of the ultimate authorities on the movement of the Russian front during the war. He asserted, rather simply, that Demjanjuk could not have been a POW in Chelm until October, 1944 because the Russian army had advanced far enough westward that by January, 1944 at the latest, the camp had been abandoned by the Germans. There remained nothing for the defense to assert—except, perhaps, that the Trawniki card was a fake, but Martin did not make that assertion, presumably convinced by his own experts that it was genuine. The trial was over.

In June, 1981, Justice Battisti handed down his 44-page exposition of the facts of the case and the law that applied, and his verdict. In sum, he concluded that, after "[t]horough cross-examination of each witness failed to depreciate in any way the certainty of the identifications," the "court must conclude that defendant was present at Treblinka in 1942-1943."[398] He asserted that Demjanjuk had been ineligible for a visa under the Displaced Persons Act and that his citizenship had therefore been illegally procured—and so, judging in favor of the U.S government, he declared Demjanjuk's American citizenship formally revoked.

The astonishing thing, perhaps, is that the conclusion of that legal process of 1981 proved to be merely the beginning of a longer legal process that continues to this day, as I write these words. Demjanjuk did not go to jail while awaiting deportation; a year later the appeals court upheld Judge Battisti's decision. Soon thereafter the U.S. Supreme Court turned down the request by his attorneys for a review. The question of whether and whither he would be deported was obviated when the State of Israel then put in a request to have Demjanjuk extradited to Jerusalem to stand trial for charges similar to those argued against Eichmann two decades earlier.

That request leads our own narrative back to one of the important issues with which this segment of our discussion began: the Jewish issue within the Demjanjuk and similar trials. It should be noted, first of all, that at the time of the first days of testimony in the Cleveland trial, there were two pickets who marched back and forth outside the courthouse. The first identified himself as the Imperial Wizard of the Ohio branch of the

Ku Klux Klan.[399] The Imperial Wizard carried an American flag and a sign that said "Jews killed Christ." He noted to reporters having worked "next to John Demjanjuk for twelve years at the the Ford plant" and that "[h]e's a kindhearted person and well-liked at the plant."[400] The irony—of wrapping the American flag, rather literally, around his venomous view of Jews—is palpable. His presence also underscores the larger, outside the courtroom implications for the Demjanjuk case as part of "Jewish trials."

The second marcher, from Toronto, further confirmed those implications. He carried signs noting that "Communism is Jewish" and that "[t]here were no gas chambers."[401] He thus combined a viewpoint that, as we have noted in discussing the Rosenberg-Sobell trial, was expressed for decades in the highest echelons of the American government, with an ideology of Holocaust denial that would achieve prominence in the years and decades that followed the Demjanjuk trial—and continues to find support in some corners of America and elsewhere, from Britain to Iran, to this day.[402]

The second "Jewish" issue pertains to the bringing of Demjanjuk to Israel and the question of how the legal process would operate there: an Eichmann redux, as it were—except, to repeat, that in this case the assertion by Demjanjuk's attorneys would focus on the question of his identity as Ivan *Grozny*, not on the question of what Ivan did or how such crimes should be addressed. The attorneys were new ones to Demjanjuk's case, for in the aftermath of the trial in Cleveland, and facing extradition to Israel, he and his family felt it essential that he begin anew with regard to legal representation as he continued to fight the deportation verdict. In 1983, Mark O'Connor of Buffalo was taken on as the primary defense attorney, as the deportation proceedings were still being fought.[403]

That is precisely when—in November, 1983, in the midst of those deportation proceedings—the Israelis asked to extradite Demjanjuk. And here it should be noted that by no means all Israelis were in favor of requesting extradition. "Quite the contrary. The Israelis resented the notion that they should, in effect, become the dust bin again and sweep up all of the world's debris, and have to put them on trial in Israel... The crimes were committed in Poland,

Germany and France; that's where the trials should be," asserted one commentator.[404] Similarly, an editorial in *The Jerusalem Post* noted that "Truth to tell, there can be little satisfaction for Israelis in the coming trial here of Ivan Demjanjuk." So, "what then is the point of the coming trial? The point, very simply, is that Israel had no other choice."[405] That reality reflects the condition of the Demjanjuk case as a "Jewish trial."

In any event, back in the United States, the deportation process continued until May, 1984, at which time Demjanjuk was finally and definitively ordered out of the United States. He refused to be deported—but in any case, in April, 1985, Judge Battisti ruled that he should be extradited to Israel. At that point Demjanjulk was sent to a federal prison in Springfield, Missouri as O'Connor tried some last-minute appeals, which failed. The defendant was finally flown to Israel at the end of February, 1986.

He was accompanied on the flight by U.S. marshalls, whose responsibilities included recording whatever the prisoner said, since it could be of potential use in any future legal proceedings. The transcript of his casual, in-passing remarks during the flight—in the context of what the marshalls referred to as his assuming a rather odd smile—includes a statement that he had in fact committed the crimes of which he had been and would again be accused, but those transcripts remained classified for years afterwards and have, to date, played no role in subsequent proceedings.[406]

The Israeli request for extradition having ultimately been honored by the United States government—which, to repeat, simplified the matter of *whither* Demjanjuk might be deported—O'Connor eventually hired the Israeli lawyer, Yoram Sheftel, to assist in addressing the Israeli legal system on behalf of his client. And the State of Israel ultimately prepared a 26-page indictment of Demjanjuk for "crimes against the Jewish people, crimes against humanity, war crimes and crimes against persecuted minorities." The trial would not begin until the beginning of October, 1986; Demjanjuk waited in an Israeli prison—the same Ayalon prison in which Eichmann had been held—for about six months until proceedings began. The prosecution by then had accumulated testimonies in their indictment from 53 witnesses from five countries—eight of them survivors of Treblinka—as well as from a former member of the SS who claimed to have served with Demjanjuk in the camp.

O'Connor would assert that his client was/is a victim of mistaken identity; that 40-year-old survivor memories were faulty evidence of Demjanjuk's identity as Ivan and the guilt that comes with that identity—precisely the kind of claim that had failed in the court over which Justice Battisti presided in Cleveland. O'Connor's additional twist to that claim, however, was that the real Ivan the Terrible had perished in the camp uprising that took place in summer, 1943. The trial process in Israel will be familiar to the reader from the Eichmann case—three judges, no jury—and it should be noted that O'Connor, interviewed the day before the trial began, asserted his confidence that his client would receive a fair hearing: "If there is anywhere Demjanjuk will get a fair trial, it's in the land of Zion."[407]

Justice Minister Avraham Sharir expressed his own certainty that the identity issue would be resolved through the trial process, and his hope that that process would (in an echo of sentiments expressed by key Israeli leaders a generation earlier, at the time of the Eichmann trial) help "to remind ourselves of what happens to people without roots, a homeland, an army and institutions to protect it. We have to remind the young generation that they have to guard and protect the state."[408] Others in the political worlds of both Israel and the United States—from Milton A. Wolf, who had served both as President of the Jewish Community Federation of Cleveland and as American Ambassador to Austria; to Patrick Buchanan, at that time an advisor to President Reagan—offered their comments on their confidence in the Israeli judicial process.

Buchanan remained convinced of Demjanjuk's innocence, and proceeded to write about it, asserting his convictions in a January, 4, 1987 op ed article in the Cleveland *Plain Dealer*. He mistakenly claims there that the original of the Trawniki I.D. card was only now going to be seen, in Israel, (it had been extensively seen and studied during the Cleveland trial, as we have noted),[409] and also asserts that Demjanjuk's name was not to be found on the Trawniki camp roster or on the transfer list to Treblinka—although he offers no source for that information. Buchanan's article sought to debunk the legitimacy of key witnesses—claiming, for instance, that Eliyahu Rosenberg had given a sworn statement back in 1947 to the effect that Ivan the Terrible had been beaten to death during the 1943 Treblinka uprising.[410] Several of the key witnesses are referred to by Buchanan as a kind of cabal that travels from trial to trial, offering testimony that, he implies, has been honed by their experience in many courtrooms, rather than by clear and honest memories of events that took place four decades earlier.

Buchanan provides his own explanation for what truth actually lies beneath the Demjanjuk affair: that the figure is, in effect fictional; "a composite of Ivan, the gas chamber operator mentioned by Wiernik,[411] the 'enormous brute,' the 'sadistic giant,' of Jean-Francois Cohen-Steiner's *Treblinka* (1966), the huge mesomorph that Polish villagers remember—a monster of a man who wenched and drank in their village near Treblinka, and who either died in the August uprising or perished in the Balkans with other Nazi survivors of the death camp" and "...a German, a Nazi, a middle-aged veteran of Hitler's 'euthanasia' program, a man Alexander Donat describes as a 'hot-tempered, brutal individual...' seen 'running through the camps brandishing his whip and his gun...' [whose] name was Christian Wirth, but [who] was known to inmates by a nickname—'Christian the Terrible.' Wirth was killed by partisans near Trieste on May 26, 1944."[412]

Clearly there is a strong divergence of opinion on the matter of John Demjanjuk's identity and its relationship to the historical figure—or quasi-historical figure—"Ivan the Terrible," but at least where Buchanan's opinion is concerned it is odd that he publicized it six years after the Cleveland trial in which Ryan and his staff were involved, and only after the trial had been repeated, as it were, in Jerusalem, and not before. As the indictment in Israel developed, however, further details emerged beyond what had been discussed in Cleveland five years earlier.

Thus Demjanjuk asserted that he was transferred from Chelm to Graz, Austria—sometime in 1944—where he served in a unit of the Ukrainian National Army organized by the Nazis to fight the

Russians. Having lived through the famines and purges of the Stalinist thirties and early forties, it was not necessarily that unusual, particularly for non-Russians, to view Stalin as a bigger villain than Hitler, (at least at first)—to even see the Germans as liberators—and therefore to switch allegiance if the opportunity presented itself. Demjanjuk claimed that in Graz he received the tattoo under his upper left arm that identified his blood group, shortly after which he was again transferred, to Heuberg, Austria, where he guarded a captured Russian general from November, 1944 to May, 1945.

The Israeli indictment, on the other hand, asserts that Demjanjuk was transferred, sometime before July, 1942, from Rovno to the Trawniki, Poland, training camp, where he received a blood group tattoo and swore an oath of allegiance to the SS. It asserts that he arrived at Treblinka no later than October, 1942, where he remained until at least September, 1943. Although the original allegations leading to the trial in 1981 had put Demjanjuk at Sobibor, not at Treblinka, subsequent identifications by witnesses from Treblinka placed him there, so that, in the citizenship revocation trial it was not necessary to pursue the matter of Sobibor. But Israeli prosecutors felt it important to pursue this matter as offering a key documentary piece of evidence of who John Demjanjuk is, and their indictment placed him in Sobibor for a short period of time in late March, 1943, presumably leaving Treblinka briefly and then returning there from Sobibor—a meandering picture not inconsistent with the Nazi tendency to move its Trawniki-graduate personnel about.

The matter of lying on his visa and citizenship applications remained, obviously, part of the heart of the contention: Demjanjuk continued to claim (as he had in his Cleveland trial) that he had lied because he feared being returned by force to Ukraine. The Israelis (like the OSI lawyers) asserted that he lied in order to hide his role in Hitler's Final Solution program. After months of delays in framing the precise details of the indictment, the prosecution and defense were deemed ready and the trial formally began on October 1, 1986. Even at that point there was an appeal—from Demjanjuk's lawyer, Mark O'Connor—that Demjanjuk's detention be terminated on the grounds that the Israelis did not have enough material to determine that John Demjanjuk and Ivan *Grozny* are one and the same, but the Israeli court turned down that appeal.

The prosecution was ordered to turn over all of its evidence to the defense by October 31, but O'Connor claimed that he had not seen all of the documents—but with a sudden alacrity the court announced that the trial would begin on November 26. On that day, Demjanjuk waived the right to hear the indictment read in court, asserting that he is not Ivan the Terrible. O'Connor then asked that his client's plea be postponed, since he had not had time to review the evidence, but one of the three presiding judges, Dov Levin, denied that appeal, stating that Demjanjuk's statement would already be taken as a plea of innocence—and the court adjourned until January 19.

But as of December, O'Connor still lacked an Israeli lawyer to assist him, so on December 29 the court granted him a 30-day extension, postponing the opening of the trial until February 16. It was in visiting his client in Ayalon prison that O'Connor met the Israeli lawyer, Yoram Sheftel, who agreed to be his co-counsel—on "condition that the defense does not deny or downplay the severity of Ivan the Terrible's deeds."[413] Clearly conditions had changed since—and perhaps due to—the Eichmann trial, with respect to the comfort/discomfort level for Israel, of having an Israeli serve as a key part of the defense team in a major Nazi war-crimes case (although O'Connor would remain, at least initially, the lead counsel for the defense team).

As the trial date approached, prosecution and defense offered preludes to aspects of the struggle that would take place in the courtroom. The prosecution intended to call eight witnesses who had identified Demjanjuk from photo spreads—including four whose testimonies would be read in court because they had died by the time the Israeli trial was gearing up—and it would produce the original Trawniki I.D card; the defense expected to offer "solid evidence to refute the Trawniki card's authenticity, but so far [as of eight days before the trial] it has not been able to locate witnesses who can place Demjanjuk where he claims to have been during the war."[414]

At least two of those who might have served as witnesses for Demjanjuk's claim were apparently reluctant to come forth because of fear of exposing their own false war-time claims when gaining entry into the United States. So, too, O'Connor claimed at the time that the Polish government would not permit him to interview three potential witnesses from a little town near Treblinka—he did not say why—two of whom claim to remember Ivan as a carousing visitor to their village who had bushy hair and was at least a decade older than Demjanjuk would have been in 1943. This assertion by O'Connor must be the source of Patrick Buchanan's inspired "reconstruction" of a composite, somewhat mythical Ivan *Grozny*.

In fact two Poles, Eugenia Samuel and Jozef Wujek, who were presumably the individuals to whom O'Connor referred, had been granted visas to testify in the United States as the deportation proceedings continued into 1984, but those visas had then been revoked, apparently without explanation—at least according to O'Connor. In any case, their testimonies were still offered in written form, and were accepted by the judge, Adolph Angellili, in that last American appeal proceeding—but the deportation order against Demjanjuk was nonetheless upheld. So it is not clear whether or how their testimony would be able to help Demjanjuk in Jerusalem.

As the trial date in Israel approached, it is interesting that *The Jerusalem Post* reported that while no one wants to see war criminals go free, some Israelis are concerned about the unpredictable effects the trial may have on their society and on the country's national image. Some also fear that it will diminish the historical impact of Adolf Eichmann's trial. Eichmann represented the Final Solution's evil plan, of which Demjanjuk, even if guilty, is 'a mere devil's apprentice,' the *Post*'s editorial stated." Thus two new wrinkles enter into our own discussion with regard to "Jewish trials."

One is the concern for how this sort of trial—a trial for Nazi war crimes; for crimes against the Jews as a people and against humanity—will psychologically effect both the Jews and humanity in general. The other is the self-consciousness of Israel as a Jewish state with regard to the effect on humanity in its *attitude toward* Jews. A long history of hostility interwoven with ambivalence—a starting point of which, as we have seen toward the outset of this narrative, is an array of suppositions pertaining to the trial and death of Jesus on the part of a substantial portion of humanity—had certainly left its legacy not only on Christian sentiments toward Jews but on Jewish sentiments and concerns regarding Christians and others.

Such concerns notwithstanding, the sense of historical and public-interest consciousness was paramount enough for the court to reserve the 400-seat "small hall" in Jerusalem's enormous *Binyanei ha'Ooma* ("people's buildings") auditorium, which at the outset of the trial overflowed with viewers. The trial dragged on, punctuated by a series of document examiners brought in from various parts of the world. For the main argument that the defense would adduce before the court in Jerusalem—which the defense had not made an effort to claim in the Cleveland deportation trial in 1981— was that the Trawniki identification card was a fraudulent concoction of the Soviets.

And thus each side sought expert witnesses to back up its position. The prosecution, aside from its assertion that the I.D. card is legitimate, and aside from its contention that John Demjanjuk fit all the expected criteria of those selected by the SS to be trained at Trawniki and sent to a camp like Treblinka as a guard,[415] also sought to demonstrate that the witnesses who had identified Demjanjuk as Ivan had spent enough time in Ivan's presence and witnessed enough of his actions to correctly identify him and recall those actions thirty or forty years after they were committed by him.

Specifically, the defense would assert that while Demjanjuk concedes (as he did in Cleveland) that the photograph on the card might "possibly" be a photograph of him, nobody can prove definitively that it is. In a deposition taken in Germany, former Trawniki administrator Rudolph Reiss had testified in 1984 that he had never seen a document like the Trawniki card—but the year before the Jerusalem trial stated that "all POWs who came to Trawniki had photographs taken for the purposes of issuing an ID card," and that the photographs had a small white strip with a number matching the number on the card, which is exactly as the Demjanjuk image appears.[416]

Demjanjuk's defense claims that he was never at Trawniki and never wore a uniform such as is depicted on the ID card photograph. The prosecution would note that camp recruits were shown wearing the same uniform in photographs taken when Heinrich Himmler visited Trawniki as is worn by the defendant in the photograph on the Trawniki card. The defense noted that Demjanjuk is two inches taller than is indicated on the card. The prosecution noted that such mistakes were commonplace: why would a forger produce that error when so much other personal information was correct?[417]

The defense further would claim that their documents experts noted two apparent staple holes in the photograph that could indicate that the photo had been attached to some other document, from which a forger could have removed it to place it on this card. But Reiss, who had primarily testified for the defense, nonetheless asserted that there were so many new recruits to Trawniki that officials often stapled their photos to their ID cards until there was time to glue them on.

Document experts verified the signatures of Trawniki Commandant Karl Streibel and quartermaster Ernst Teufel. But defense expert documents examiner Edna Robertson asserted that the ink on the official seal of the card "luminesces" — that is, it shows different levels of light, indicating the use of different inks — a possible sign of forgery. The prosecution responded by showing — in the courtroom — that the ink of any number of undisputed documents, including Demjanjuk's 1947 driver's license, also luminesces.[418] The prosecution forensic experts noted that the materials used to create the card date back to the proper time period; the defense asserted that blank forms and ink could have been found at the Trawniki site and used to forge it.

But the prosecution observed that it is ridiculous to suppose that such forms would have borne the signatures — not stamps, but actual signatures — of Streibel and Teufel. To which comment the defense suggested that the signatures could have been forged. To which the prosecution responded by asking how it is that their signatures were forged so well that experts could not detect the forgery — while Demjanjuk's, which he would not accept unequivocally as his, was done so poorly? Why would a KGB agent, who presumably is aware of the geographical designations of the areas under his/her jurisdiction, make errors such as misspelling the name of Demjanjuk's birthplace and placing it in the wrong district in Ukraine? Surely it is much more reasonable to suppose that such errors would have been made by Germans in a hurry to complete the registration process that included so many individuals from places with names not so familiar to the Germans.

There is even a change on the card: a numeral "1" is crossed out and replaced by a numeral "2" next to the words "undershirts" and "underpants"—a change that the defense saw as suspicious. The prosecution brought out documents showing that initially it was deemed sufficient to issue one set of undergarments to recruits, before that viewpoint was changed and two sets were issued. The culminating statements by the prosecution were that the card had already been pronounced indisputably authentic seven years earlier at Demjanjuk's denaturalization trial in Cleveland and so the new assertion that it is a KGB forgery in any case would carry no legal weight; that three experts refused to testify for the defense since they did not regard the card as forged and did not wish to compromise their integrity; and that those experts who did testify all testified outside their fields of primary expertise.

The "expert" brought forth by the defense after Robertson— Anita Pritchard, a "graph-analyst" (meaning that, by looking at someone's face, she could ascertain certain personality traits) working on her doctorate at the University of Columbia Pacific—proved even less useful to Demjanjuk's claim. Brought forward to assess whether the Trawniki photo could be that of John Demjanjuk, she was queried as to her familiarity with anthropology, morphology, anthropomorphy, physiognomy, neurology, optics—all relevant fields to her alleged area of expertise—and consistently responded that she did not know those fields.

The proceedings continued for a year. More "experts" were brought forth by the defense, every single one of whom was shown to offer arguments that ranged from the absurd to the ridiculous. The prosecution did not sum up until early February, 1988. In addition to the matter of the card's authenticity and the validity of survivor memories—and their ability to translate those memories not necessarily to the individual in the courtroom with them, but to the one depicted in photospreads—the key prosecuting attorney, Michael Shaked pointed out that the photospread procedures went beyond the norm to assure that they would be beyond reproach. Instead of the usual eight images, sometimes seventeen or as many as thirty were shown to witnesses. A claim that the defense had lodged, mid-trial, that Ivan *Grozny* was actually Alfred Bielitz, and not John Demjanjuk, was refuted on the grounds that Bielitz was German and Ivan was Ukrainian.

Three additional points of significance were offered. The first was that when the Israeli police had interrogated Demjanjuk regarding some towns and villages in the area of Treblinka—the exchange had occurred on April 4, 1986—the defendant had exclaimed, "You're pushing me toward Treblinka," suggesting that he knew that area well and thus that he had spent a reasonable amount of time there. For the interrogators had never mentioned Treblinka in asking about those other locations. The second was that the fact that Sobibor and not Treblinka is mentioned on the Trawniki card, which reflected the fact—proof of this was brought forward in court—that there were personnel exchanges between the two camps. The discussion and records of this were often accomplished by telephone and without bureaucratic smoothness and order, as opposed to offering a source of doubt as to Demjanjuk's whereabouts.

Third, with regard to Demjanjuk's claims regarding his whereabouts, prosecutor Blattman asked how it was possible—regarding his memory lapse pertaining to his alleged stay at Chelm—that "Demjanjuk remembers in impressive detail the intricacies of Rovno, where he spent only two weeks, yet about Chelm, where he claims to have spent about a year and a half, he remembers nothing, including the name of the camp?"[419]

Virtually as the prosecution was resting its case, the Demjanjuks were in the process of firing chief counsel Mark O'Connor, leaving the end game of the defense in the hands of Sheftel and O'Connor's co-counsel, John Gill; these two were shortly joined by a Canadian former prosecutor, Paul Chumak. That change did not improve the quality of Demjanjuk's defense team, it would seem. Non-experts were brought forth as experts, and still referred to as such in the defense's summation, even after having been seriously debunked by the prosecution. The defendant was poorly enough prepared that he could hardly give convincing answers to his own attorneys, much less to the cross-examining prosecution.

But there was at least one point that, at first glance, seemed particularly significant. In cross-examining survivor witness Rosenberg—who had identified John Demjanjuk as Ivan *Grozny* in both photospreads and the courtroom—Chumak returned to Rosenberg's 1947 written statement that Ivan had been killed during the Treblinka uprising.

> "You wrote this and is it correct?" Chumak asked. "What I said there I didn't see. I heard," Rosenberg said... 'That's right. I wrote it—but I didn't see it." Rosenberg explained that he was too busy escaping to see those other things. "Escape. That was my purpose, The bullets were shrieking all around us... I wanted to believe and I did believe. It was a symbol for us, it was a wish come true. It was a success...I wanted to believe, to believe that this creature... Unfortunately, to my great sorrow, he managed to survive."
>
> Proof that he didn't see it himself, Rosenberg said, was that his 1945 account of Ivan's death was different from his 1947 one; and still different from that he had heard from survivor Chaim Steir. But he'd never corrected any of them, he said, because until 1976, he believed that Ivan was dead. But there he was. Now, sitting across from him, alive![420]

The defense's summation asserted that there were flaws in the prosecution's "three streams of evidence—the survivors, the card, their historians."[421] Sheftel asserted that the photo line-ups were based on identification procedures and not on recognition. He noted contradictions among the survivor witnesses, particularly with regard to whether or not Ivan had been killed in the uprising. He claimed that the witnesses were biased and had "obviously" colluded.

Sheftel claimed that the Trawniki card had been well argued to be a forgery and that the prosecution's experts were insufficiently expert, and that the prosecution historians were less expert than those of the defense. Among the more interesting twists to these two parts of the discussion was that both the very imperfections that were evaluated by Shaked as proof against the Trawniki card being a forgery, had been argued by the defense to be symptoms of a forgery that was so perfect that it could not be detected!

The defense ultimately argued that there were in fact at least three Ivans: the Ivan of Treblinka, the Ivan of Sobibor and the Tranwiki card and Ivan Demjanjuk. Sheftel posited the theory that "the original KGB conspiracy was to accuse Demjanjuk of having served at Sobibor via the card, and then return him to the Soviet Union. That plan had derailed when the survivors, due to the suggestive photospread, accused Demjanjuk of being Ivan of Treblinka."[422] But the court asked Sheftel whether only the survivors who identified Demjanjuk in the photo spread were biased, or those who did not, as well? And whose photo was on the Trawniki card, if it was not Demjanjuk's? And whom, then were the suvivors identifiying when they identified the photo from the card as Ivan? Someone else altogether?

While Sheftel didn't respond to these questions, Chumak did, in a sense: he noted "that Demjanjuk had no identifiable morphological features—he was arguing, in effect, that all Ukrainians look alike."[423] Chumak went on to speak of the motivations of the KGB, with regard to its wish to promote hostility between Ukrainians and Jews as the two groups most inimical to the USSR. He went on to suggest that "this trial has all the earmarks of the Dreyfus trial"— which equation, with all of the weight that the Dreyfus trial offers for a Jewish court, of which weight Chumak was clearly unaware,[424] raised a few hackles on the judges' necks.

But Chumak, while he sought to apologize to the extent of declaring that "at stake is not only the name and quality of Israeli justice," continued the following day by asserting that, were Demjanjuk to be acquitted in Jerusalem, were "the three Israeli judges [to] have the courage to say not guilty, Israeli law [would] stand as a beacon."[425] As such, he underscored what he took, without a scintilla of irony, to be a larger historical place for this trial, equal in significance to that of Dreyfus. What he failed to recognize is the actual basis for the equation he was making, between a Jew famously on trial for crimes he did not commit against the French people; and Jews on trial with regard to their ability to confront enormous crimes against both humanity in general and the Jewish people in particular and to judge whether the accused committed those crimes.

Chumak concluded his remarks by asserting that the prosecution had had an unfair advantage that amounted to an unfair prosecution. Shaked rose to respond to this serious accusation by noting how offensive it was that such an assertion should be made virtually at the end of the trial, and that "your two colleagues, who have been with the trial much longer, cannot look us in the eye and make such a claim. They know better." Chumak refused to withdraw the comment, causing the prosecution to review all of the ways in which it had gone out of its way and beyond where it needed to, in order to assure that Demjanjuk had a good defense.

The trial ended on February 18, 1988. In mid-March, Sheftel called for an "extraordinary session of the court" to consider new evidence: 12 reports of interviews with Treblinka survivors from Camp One, and the 1979 deposition of Danylchenko.[426] Judge Levin decided to reopen the summation by both sides. In reviewing the new material, Shaked noted that all of the prosecution witnesses had seen Ivan *Grozny* day in and day out for some period of time, but that none of the 12 "new" witnesses, all from the lower camp, had seen him for long—some for as little as a few hours. Sheftel argued that the testimony of these 12 was significant, and in refering to "Ivan" in various capacities, from watchtower guard to truck driver to ranking officer, demonstrated the fallacy of survivor identification—that by his count there were at least six "Ivan"s at Treblinka.

The Danylchenko statement specifically referred to the guard Ivan Demjanjuk with a detailed physical description and reference to his having been trained at Trawniki; and to his pushing and hitting Jews with his rifle butt (which was not uncommon) but stated that he had not personally seen him shoot anyone. He claimed to have served with Ivan at Sobibor from his own arrival there in March, 1943 until spring, 1944, and that, together with other guards, they were sent in autumn, 1944, to accompany 200 political prisoners from a camp in Flossenberg to one near Regensburg, where they guarded prisoners until spring, 1945. As the allies were approaching, they were all evacuated to Nuremberg, but Danylchenko said that he escaped along the way while Demjanjuk continued to guard the prisoners and that thereafter he had no idea of Demjanjuk's fate.

Danylchenko had picked out images of Demjanjuk in several photo spreads laid out at the time in the Soviet Procurator's office—his 1941 Red Army photo, the Trawniki card photo, and his 1951 visa photo. If Danylchenko's account was accurate, then Demjanjuk would not have been in Treblinka at the time when the prosecution claimed he was. Shaked noted, however, that there were historical problems with this account. Most obviously, Sobibor was dismantled in Novmber, 1943, but Danylchenko claimed that he had served there until spring, 1944. Sheftel responded that all the defense needed to do was cast doubt on the prosecution's association of John Demjanjuk with Ivan *Grozny*, and that the Danylchenko account accomplished that purpose.

One of the judges, Dahlia Dorner, suggested that Ivan could have gone to Sobibor after the gassings began to slow at Treblinka, in January, 1943—but then how would he have been at Treblinka until it was dismantled—a few months after the summer, 1943 uprising? Shaked suggested that, since the Trawniki card places Demjanjuk at Sobibor after March 27, by which time he was already an experienced guard and trusted enough by the SS that he was given leaves from the camp, that he must have gained that experience at Treblinka.

The evidence submitted showed that guards—especially those with a skill such as Demjanjuk possessed, as a driver—were shifted back and forth among various camps all the time, so that he could easily have moved between Treblinka and Sobibor, could easily have spent a good deal of time with Danylchenko in several places, such as Flossberg, could have been remembered at Treblinka as late as the revolt and yet remembered at Sobibor (indeed, misremembered to have been there four or five months beyond the time of its dismantling).

On April 18, 1988 the court—in an extensive and carefully wrought verdict, 440 pages long in Hebrew and 768 in English translation—found Demjanjuk guilty as charged. The judges asserted that there were no grounds for believing that Ivan had been killed in the

Treblinka uprising and that Demjanjuk's alibi failed to instill even a scintilla of doubt that he was not Ivan. He could not at first remember the name of Chelm, where he claimed to have spent 18 months, could not describe the camp in any of its parts nor remember or describe anyone who had been there with him. The other aspects of his alibi were similarly flawed, including the time of his acquiring skill and experience as a driver.

The court stated its conviction that the Trawniki card is authentic; its errors—most fundamentally, that it does not list Treblinka as the place of Ivan's posting—reinforce its authenticity, since a forgery would surely not have contained such errors. The judges found the testimony of the survivor witnesses and others who had identified Demjanjuk from the photo spreads completely convincing—they noted in particular Epstein's identification of Demjanjuk/Ivan's walk. And the likelihood of two Ivans who looked so similar that Danylchenko was identifying one while the suvivors and Otto Horn were identifying another—all by essentially the same characteristics—is impossibly slim.

"The Ivans are one and the same: Demjanjuk who operated at Sobibor from late March 1943 and Ivan *Grozny* who operated in Treblinka during the second half of 1942 and early 1943, the Ivan identified by Danylchenko and the Ivan identified by the other identification witnesses are one and the same."[427] Rather interestingly, given the larger scope of this discussion, is that Judge Levin, as he read the decision and arrived at a statement of how different a world Treblinka provided, referred to *Deuteronomy* 28.[428] One might say that we have come full circle, back to the Torah as a starting point both for our discussion and for Jewish legal and moral thinking.

Thus—to summarize—the essence of the basis for the court's conclusion was the identification of Demjanuk in the various photo spreads by ten Holocaust survivors and one German SS officer, the Trawniki ID card, and the lack of a convincing alibi posed by the defense. A week after the proceedings, on April 25, in the reconvened court, the prosecution called for the death penalty. The defense refused to counter-propose a mitigation, since to do so would be to admit guilt and the defendant admitted none. Demjanjuk himself offered a closing statement reasserting his innocence of the horrible crimes which he acknowledged had been committed in the Nazi camps against the Jewish people—but not by him.

Three hours later the court reconvened and Judge Tal read the decision, reiterating that "in our verdict we established unequivocally and without the shadow of a doubt that the person before us, the accused, is Ivan the Terrible of Treblinka." In alluding back to the Eichmann trial and the inadequacy of any punishment, truly, to balance the crimes committed by the architect of the Final Solution, Judge Tal noted that "true, the accused is not Eichmann... However, he served as a henchman, who with his very own hands killed tens of thousands, humiliated, degraded, victimized and brutalized persecuted innocent human beings zealously. It is for this reason that we sentence him for the aforementioned crimes, to the punishment of death by hanging, as stipulated."[429]

From a purely legal viewpoint, in a compelling article appearing later that year in *The American Lawyer*, Susan Adams discussed the incompetence of the Demjanjuk defense team and raised the question of whether a better job by them would have yielded the exoneration of their client, or at least raised sufficient doubt that he could or would not have been found guilty and condemned to die.[430] In weighing between the legal and larger-than-legal implications of the range of events that we have considered in these pages, it is appropriate to review some of the key elements in Adams' narrative.

She begins by noting how remarkably unqualified Mark O'Connor was for the task that he took on—which he took on surely knowing that it could put him on the map—and how, for example, he took co-Counsel John Gill's dabbling in document examination to be a professional expertise that it was not. The two had worked together previously, on the Frank Walus case, and "[t]heir pleadings were riddled with weak arguments, mistakes in grammar and spelling, and incomprehensible sentences"[431]—and Walus had been adjudged guilty and lost his citizenship in his 1978 Chicago denaturalization trial.[432] In Demjanjuk's case, the fact that the Trawniki card never mentions Treblinka was never brought up in the Cleveland proceedings, (as we have seen): O'Connor stuck simply to the Soviet conspiracy/

forgery defense—and, as in the Walus case, riddled his arguments with grammatical and spelling errors and specious assertions.

When Demjanjuk was extradited to Israel, he was without legal representation for two months, which was the extraordinary amount of time it took O'Connor to follow his client. It then took O'Connor four months to hire Yoram Sheftel—barely a month before the trial in Jerusalem was due to begin. Once the trial began, and after an emotional sweep of witnesses, O'Connor chose to cross-examine them with questions that the judges themelves often found rambling and convoluted, and which sometimes seemed to contribute to the prosecution's case. For example, it was on cross-examination that Epstein, a key witness, in response to one of O'Connor's queries, "told the court how, when he watched news coverage of Demjanjuk's arrival at Ben-Gurion Airport, he had recognized the defendant's stride. 'I recognized him among other things by his walk... just as in Treblinka.'"[433]

Meanwhile, O'Connor and Sheftel were becoming increasingly disenamored of and argumentative with each other. Their conflicts ranged from procedures (in which O'Connor would have had little idea of what is and is not permissible in an Israeli court, which was part of the reason for engaging Sheftel in the first place) to issues like translations of witness testimony (although O'Connor knows none of the languages in use in the courtroom besides English) to the fact that O'Connor had apparently prepared no defense witnesses by the time the court adjourned in April for Passover.

It seems that O'Connor got increasingly desperate as the case slipped further from his control and his competence, so that he became both more focused on convincing the family that he should stay on as Demjanuk's lead counsel than on preparing the case—and threatened the family that without him, Demjanjuk would die. But by June, Sheftel and Gill both agreed that they could not go forward if O'Connor remained on the case, and managed to convince the Demjanjuk family that it would be disastrous for their husband/father to keep O'Connor on. But the latter refused to accept the letter dismissing him, so that the entire proceeding paused so that the court could judge whether or not Demjanjuk understood what he was doing in dismissing O'Connor. In the first of two hearings, Demjanjuk was indecisive and confused—not surprisingly, all things considered—but in the second hearing stuck with the dismissal decision.

O'Connor's departure now led to a frantic search for a replacement: finally Paul Chumak, a Canadian of Ukrainian descent was selected—and the proceedings continued, but with barely time for Chumak to be brought fully up to speed. And as it turned out, O'Connor had never prepared Demjanjuk to testify, who, as in Cleveland, would be the primary witness for the defense. Significantly, he could remember intricate details about his youth, but little about the war years, and in particular very little about Chelm, the camp in which he claimed to have been a prisoner when Ivan the Terrible was active at Treblinka. Indeed, prosecutor Blattman asked him why he had failed to remember the name of the Chelm POW camp no less than three times during his 1978 testimony to United States immigration officials.

After Demjanjuk, the first of the defense "experts" was put on the stand—Edna Robertson—whom, it turns out, Gill had met through one of the document examination societies to which he belongs, but who had very limited expertise—who spoke, we recall, of the luminescence of the seal, and also of stains on the card that indicated that it was forged. The judges rejected her testimony as not credible. The next "expert witness," Anita Pritchard, who claimed expertise as both a psychologist and document examiner, collapsed under cross-examination (regarding Demjanjuk's facial structure and what was supposed to be its mismatch with the face on the Trawniki ID card) and on the second day of her testimony took back everything that she had said on the previous day.

As we have seen, and as Adams points out, one after the other of the defense witnesses failed either to offer a credible validation of Demjanjuk's testimony or a cogent argument for the invalidity of the Trawniki ID card. In the end the defense asserted, on this last issue, that the KGB forgers were so experienced and skilled at their work that the flaws in the card before the court could not be detected—which, of course, contradicted entirely their year-long (or, one might say, going back to Cleveland, years-long) assertion that flaws in the card proved that it *was* a forgery!

After pronouncing a death sentence on the defendant, the three-judge panel advised the defense that it had 45 days to file an appeal. By then, Gill had withdrawn from the case, leaving Sheftel essentially to write up the appeal on his own—the salient new points in which were that the judges were biased and that slanted media coverage created "a lynch atmosphere." Given the sweep of our overall narrative, and considering in particular some of the key trials we have reviewed in the century leading up to the trial of John Demjanjuk, specifically with regard to the matter of the atmosphere in and outside the courtroom—from Dreyfus to Frank to Rosenberg—Sheftel's accusation should have an ironic (there's that word again!) ring for us.

The question becomes, however: is the accusation by Sheftel an act of histrionic grasping at straws or does it have any merit? It is in part to consider this question that I have spent as much time as I have in reviewing the problems and issues within the defense counsel team raised by Adams, in the aftermath of noting concerns within the Israeli press and population prior to bringing Demjanjuk to Israel to be tried. As in the Eichmann case, it would seem that the Israelis bent over backward to accommodate the defense, but that the defense counsel was, from beginning to end, incapable of mounting a sustained argument. To repeat: not the kind of argument made by Eichmann's defense regarding the nature of his actions, but in this case regarding whether the accused was actually the individual who had committed the acts the significance of which nobody denied.

There was a final aspect to the ironies embedded within this matter: Judge Levin, the lead judge of the three trying the case, at one point, as the defense was making its summation, asked Demjanjuk if perhaps he wished to *change* his alibi, to acknowledge that the Trawniki card was real. Because since the card made no mention of Treblinka, then a different, perhaps *stronger* argument could have been made that he had never served at Treblinka. Even the allegation that he served, instead, at Sobibor as a guard, and that he committed crimes against Jews and against humanity there, could have let him off, since from a legal (as opposed to moral or historical) viewpoint, if the charge was tied—as it had clearly become—specifically to Treblinka by way of the Ivan *Grozny* story, then Demjanjuk, had he been at Sobibor and not at Treblinka, could not be Ivan, which was (and is) where and how the matter ultimately centered and continues to be centered.

But the defense chose not to go that route.[434] In December, 1988, Sheftel, Chumak and a new Israeli co-counsel, retired Judge Dov Eitan—who after 17 years on the bench had, since 1983 worked as a criminal defense lawyer—appealed Demjanjuk's case before a new panel of five judges from the Israeli Supreme Court. While that appeal was still being framed the family was busy back in Cleveland, working with a solo practitioner, David Eisler, to sue the U.S. Attorney's office, the commissioner of the INS, the director of the OSI, and the Attorney General in Cleveland federal district court with fraud, in pursuing the original case against Demjanjuk. They alleged that these entities had concealed evidence relating to the facts of the case and to the credibility of the survivor witnesses. The complaint was not well put together and went nowhere. But the point is that the Demjanjuk trials (note the plural) story bifurcates at this point, moving forward more or less simultaenously in Israel and the United States—before, as we shall see, the paths reconverge and the story moves toward its inconclusive conclusion in America.

The appeal was scheduled for December 5, but the week before that date, defense lawyer Eitan died mysteriously. On November 29, an hour after making an appointment to meet his wife at 11 AM that morning to buy a new suit, he apparently jumped out of the 15th-story hotel window three blocks from his Jerusalem office, where he had been working on the case.[435] Moreover, an enraged 70-year-old attendant to Eitan's funeral on December 1 hurled hydrochloric acid at Sheftel, crying out that Eitan's death "is because of you!"[436] Sheftel was rushed to the hospital but fortunately the damage to his face was minimal. Nonetheless, the damage to his left cornea required two operations to repair—thus, the appeal was delayed a year to give Sheftel time to recover, and then another year's delay for him to study new material received from the Demjamnjuk defense FOIA suit and other sources.

For, most intriguingly, a new piece of evidence had surfaced the day before Eitan's suicide. It was a letter written in March, 1978, by Franz Suchomel, a former SS Sergeant at Treblinka.[437] In it he twice refers to "Ivan" and "Nikolai"—once as working in Trieste, in a concentration camp for Jews, the *Riseria* ("rice factory") at San Sabba; and once, noting that "[b]efore the end of the war, the gas chamber-fillers from Treblinka, Ivan and Nikolai, were probably shot—though it has been said that they slipped over into the partisans, which I don't believe."[438]

If this report is accurate (and presumably refers to the very Ivan, Ivan the Terrible, who has been coupled with Nikolai at Treblinka in various accounts), then it undercuts an important piece of evidence presented in the last days of the trial, after the defense had argued that the Americans had concealed information in the Demjanjuk deportation trial. The evidence is that Danylchenko, questioned by the Soviets in 1979, asserted that Demjanjuk had been in Sobibor for six months in 1943, and that, with the end of *Aktion Reinhard*, and after extermination camps such as that at Treblinka were dismantled, Ivan and he were among those who were sent to serve in concentration camps in southern Germany until the end of the war.[439] But Suchomel's claim is that Ivan was in Trieste at that point.

Sheftel asserted that he had seen the Suchomel letter, presented to the defense by the prosecution, together with a packet that included other information, and that within the packet were also two statements by Italian survivor witnesses who had identified Demjanjuk *qua* Ivan by means of the same photo spreads that had been shown to the Treblinka survivors. So, too, Ivan's boss at the Treblinka gas chamber, SS Sergeant Gustav Munzberger, interrogated back in the 1960s, had referred to the transfer of a group that included Ivan "from Treblinka to Trieste in September, 1943." The question is why, on the one hand, the prosecution apparently seemed rather eager not to have Trieste, by way of the Suchomel letter, enter into the conversation regarding the scope of Ivan's whereabouts; and why the defense—which was, according to Sheftel, discussing it at great length the night before Eitan's death—chose not to bring the letter into evidence.

More to the point, with the Suchomel assertion before the defense, the opportunity would seem to have improved to have Demjanjuk change his plea; in effect, to admit to having been a guard at Sobibor, but not at Treblinka. This would have reinforced his claim not to be Ivan *Grozny*, even if it would have confirmed the fact that he lied on his immigration papers—for *whatever* reasons. Meanwhile, instead, the prosecution could legitimately propose that John Demjanjuk, as Ivan, had been at both Treblinka and Sobibor, and it was a matter of faulty memory of specific details that accounted for the apparent suggestion that he had been in both places simultaneously, in the first place according to the survivors and in the second according to Danylchenko.

In fact, a close comparison of the Suchomel letter's assertion and the Danylchenko assertion and the assertions of survivors still leaves the following: that Danylchenko and the Trawniki card both place Demjanjuk at Sobibor after March, 1943, and the crimes of which he was found guilty were said to have taken place at Treblinka between September, 1942 and February, 1943. Where he was subsequently—in Trieste or somewhere else—does not undercut the notion of his having been at Treblinka as the gas-chamber operator during that six-month period. And when historian Gitta Sereny, who uncovered the Suchomel letter, traveled to the Soviet Union to learn more about Danylchneko, she found no evidence that contradicted survivor testimony or that provided Demjanjuk with the necessary alibi for the time period of Ivan's activities at Treblinka.[440]

Demjanjuk's appeal before the Israeli Supreme Court finally began on May 14, 1990—more than two years after the death penalty had been pronounced by the Jerusalem district court. A five-court panel heard arguments for over seven weeks—the longest appeal in Israel's then-42-year-long history. Sheftel began by arguing that the lower court had used a press-clipping service to monitor coverage of the trial for violations of the *sub iudice* law (the treatment of a case under consideration)—which, he argued, was itself a violation of the law. The response to this accusation was that the District Court judges, far from being influenced by the media were trying to protect the integrity of the case by maintaining a rein on media contact by the principals engaged in the case.

Of course, as with so many of the cases that we have discussed, in the Demjanjuk case the media played a large role in mediating between the legal matters handled within the court and the historical and political issues being addressed by the wide world beyond the courtroom. And indeed, in the two years leading up to the appeal, the media was very active in raising issues—most often, questions and doubts regarding Demjanjuk's culpability. This was how the Suchomel letter surfaced, with whatever questions its existence might be said to pose for the case.

So, too, the American television program "60 Minutes" interviewed a Polish witness, Mrs. Maria Dudek, who claimed that she knew intimately an Ivan—Ivan Marczenko—from the Treblinka death camp, whom she called "Ivan the Terrible." It is not clear how or why Dudek was suddenly uncovered as a witness for the discussion. But Demjanjuk's son-in-law, Ed Nishnic, who had by then become the primary spokesperson for the family, argued while the Israeli Supreme Court was still in session that Marczenko was Ivan *Grozny*. This idea was based first of all on two 1955 affidavits of a former Treblinka guard, Piotr Dmitrenko, that were admitted into evidence during the appeal process. Dmitrenko, who died in 1985, claimed that he had been assigned to Treblinka together with a brutal rapist known as Ivan Marczenko, whose physical features ("very tall, dark or black hair, dark complexion") did not match those of John Demjanjuk at all.[441] It was based, second of all, on the Dudek testimony.

A week before the appeal hearing began, the justices accepted testimony from Kazimierz Dudek, who claimed that his wife—the same Maria Dudek interviewed on "60 Minutes"—had slept with the so-called Ivan *Grozny* during the war years in order to get money to survive. Ivan had frequented the liquor store owned by Dudek that was located in Wolga Okralnik, a village near Treblinka. Dudek *also* claimed, as his wife did, that Ivan's family name was Marczenko. Nishnic stated to the media that he had visited Maria Dudek in Poland soon after her TV appearance in February, and asserted that she described Ivan as "tall, much taller than me, and I'm 6-foot-2. Mr. Demjanjuk is maybe 6 feet tall, 6-1 at most."[442]

There are further interesting twists to this aspect of the story. Maria had earlier been afraid to testify before the Polish authorities at the time when her husband did. His 1986 affidavit was followed by an identification of Ivan by way of a photo spread of eight different Treblinka camp guards. The photo to which he pointed as Ivan Marszenko—as Ivan *Grozny*—was none other than the Trawniki ID card photo of John Demjanjuk.

The next twist to the question then becomes: is it a mere coincidence, and if so, what sort of coincidence, that Demjanjuk's mother's maiden name was Marczenko, by which name he may well—as, for example, at Treblinka or in moving about outside Treblinka—have sometimes gone? The prosecution would argue that Demjanjuk may have taken on his mother's maiden name to protect himself by concealing his real identity. But Nishnic would observe that Marczenko is a common Ukrainian name. A few months later, a claim was made that the marriage certificate of John Demjanjuk's parents had been uncovered, and that his mother's maiden name was not Marczenko at all.

The marriage certificate states that her name was Tabachuk. But Demjanjuk had himself written "Marchenko" as her maiden name on his immigration forms. [443] He would assert in the midst of the early 1990s discussions that he had simply forgotten her maiden name and, embarrassed to admit such a memory lapse, had randomly chosen another. But to prosecutors, this seemed too much of a coincidence— especially when linked to all the other "coincidental" memory/forgetting aspects of Demjanjuk's varied alibi testimonies.

By mid-1992, the U.S. federal appeals court—in the sixth U.S. Circuit Court of Appeals in Cincinnati—was beginning to review the question of whether or not Demjamjuk should have been extradited to Israel in the first place, based on the new evidence that caused some to begin to question the previous certainty that Demjanjuk was Ivan. Defense counsel Sheftel, arguing now before the Israeli Supreme Court, insisted that the American Justice Department's OSI knew of the Marczenko testimony and chose to ignore it—

while Israeli prosecutors were still arguing that this changed nothing, since "Demjanjuk used the name Marchenko as an alias."[445] As it turned out, the Israeli prosecution had not been informed of the Marczenko papers at the time of Demjanjuk's trial in Jerusalem, which had been filed away by the OSI as inconsequential.

There were yet further media discussion and speculation, based on these developments potentially affecting the appeal. By July, 1993, Michele Lesie, writing in the Cleveland *Plain Dealer*, could conclude that there were two Ivans, with similar facial features, and that "what is now known about Marczenko, whose KGB file was also made available recently by former Soviet authorities, does not by itself prove Demjanjuk never served at Treblinka. It merely clears away the chaff by separating the two 'Ivans,' one of whom ran Treblinka's gas chambers until they were razed in the fall of 1943, then accompanied the camp's German officers to Italy to work at the death factory in Trieste."[445]

And the other? Offered the chance to change his alibi by reference to the Trawniki card's placement of him at Sobibor, Demjanjuk preferred to stick with his prisoner-of-war alibi, although to date no forensic evidence had (or has) pointed to the card as a forgery, and although there were so many holes in his alibi. As of the time of Lesie's 1993 article, she speculated that sufficent doubt as to Demjanjuk's alleged role at Treblinka had been cast for him to win his appeal; that the court would not likely start from scratch and try Demjanjuk for other, Sobibor-related or Flossenberg-related or Trieste-related crimes; that his by-then seven years in Ayalon prison would have fulfilled the maximum sentence for "membership in an enemy organization"; that even Israel's "Nazi law" sets a maximum penalty of 10 years for someone who was "instrumental in delivering up a persecuted person to an enemy administration"—which could certainly be the manner in which Demjanjuk's actions as described by Danylchenko could be construed.[446]

At that juncture the question would still be: where can he go? The Ukrainian ambassador to Israel had offered him citizenship shortly before this, but apparently Demjanjuk turned that down. The U.S. Justice Department said that it would oppose his return to the United States as a citizen. Four days after the Lesie article appeared—on July 29, 1993—the Israeli Supreme Court in fact *did* overturn the lower court's conviction, based on reasonable doubt that John Demjanjuk was the notorious gas chamber operator known as Ivan the Terrible, in a 405-page ruling. At the same time the court also ruled that "there was compelling evidence that Demjanjuk had served as an SS guard at the Sobibor death camp and at the Flossenberg and Regensburg concentration camps,"[447] as well as at Treblinka—but not as "Ivan the Terrible."

At that point, as the court sanctioned a two-week delay in Demjanjuk's deportation from Israel—during which Holocaust survivors and their supporters (including groups outside of Israel, such as the Simon Wiesenthal Center in Los Angeles) could and did prepare arguments to be heard before an expanded judicial bench as to whether the now-former defendant should be tried for war crimes other than those for which he had just been acquitted. The Israeli state Attorney, Yoseph Harish, had originally recommended against a new trial when the petition was first put forth after the Supreme Court appeal verdict had been heard, arguing that it would not be in the best interests of the state, and that a conviction would be uncertain.

The 15-day ruling by Chief Justice Shamgar was lauded by the Wiesenthal Center's dean, Rabbi Marvin Hier, who noted that "we have to remember that the Demjanjuk defense team was granted many such delays during the trial, and it is only fair to give the same opportunity to the Holocaust survivors."[448] At the same time, an editorial in at least one American Jewish publication excoriated Israeli media coverage as offering a kind of "Holocaust denial mentality" in its tendency to argue against retrying Demjanjuk for his deeds at Sobibor, Flossberg and Regensberg.[449] Aside from the larger picture of Israel as a Jewish state in the eyes of the world, this last turn in the twists of the Demjanjuk affair suggests the reality of how the various world Jewish communities—particularly the two most significant ones, that in Israel and that in the United States—were coming by the last fifteen years of the twentieth century to diverge from each other on any number of issues.

Meanwhile American survivors and their supporters were organizing a campaign directed toward President Clinton and Attorney General Janet Reno to prevent Demjanjuk's return to the United States, but a three-judge panel of the sixth U.S. Circuit Court of Appeals ruled on August 3 that the government could not bar Demjanjuk's re-entrance into the country—which decision was then appealed by the U.S. Justice Department. The Sixth Circuit Court of Appeals ruled that Demjanjuk must be brought back on the grounds that he was needed for a proper review of the case against him with new counsel; because his life was said (ironically enough, all things considered) to be in danger in Israel (where the question of whether or not to retry him had not yet been answered); and because otherwise he would be "stateless and homeless."

The matter of Demjanjuk's return to the United States was somewhat incidentally complicated by the fact that the French announced that they would not permit him to pass through French territory; at that time, most American planes coming from Israel stopped in Paris. But in the end the Israeli court opted not to retry him, noting that a further trial would violate the legal principle of double jeopardy, and he was released and allowed to return to the United States.[450] The Sixth Circuit Court of Appeals had meanwhile ruled that he was a victim of prosecutorial misconduct, asserting that federal prosecutors had deliberately withheld evidence that would have aided his case—although not that they deliberately tried to frame him—and the original deportation verdict of so many years earlier was overturned.[451]

But in that decision, Justice Thomas Wiseman noted that "Mr. Demjanjuk's alibi was so incredible as to legitimately raise the suspicions of his prosecutors that he lied about everything." The Sixth Circuit Court ordered Demjanjuk temporarily readmitted to the country, but "temporarily" became, effectively, permanently. On February 20, 1998, Federal District Court Judge Paul Martia ruled that Demjanjuk's citizenship could be restored.

By the turn toward the new millenium, however, the Demjanjuk affair was still by no means over. On May 20, 1999, the Justice Department filed a new civil complaint against him. No mention was made in the new complaint of his earlier-alleged role at Treblinka. Instead it argued that Demjanjuk had served as a guard at Sobibor and Majdanek in Poland and Flossenberg in Germany, and that he had been a member of an SS-directed unit that participated in the capture of nearly 2 million Polish Jews, which action led to their destruction. He was put on trial in 2001 and in February, 2002, Judge Matia ruled that Demjanjuk had not produced any credible evidence of his whereabouts during the war and that the Justice Department had in fact proven its case against him.

Thus on May 1, 2004, a three-judge panel of the Sixth U.S Circuit Court of Appeals ruled that he could again be stripped of his U.S. citizenship since the Justice Department had offered "clear, unequivocal, and convincing evidence" that he had served in Nazi death camps and therefore had both lied on his immigration and citizenship applications and been ineligible for citizenship as a refugee. Demjanjuk appealed that decision, without success, and on December 28, 2005 an immigration judge ordered him deported to Ukraine. The chief immigration judge, Michael Creppy, ruled that the defense had provided no evidence that Demjanjuk would be mistreated if deported to Ukraine, particularly given the political reconfiguration of that state in the aftermath of the break-up of the former USSR in the early 1990s.

The deportation order was upheld by the Board of Immigration Appeals a year later, on December 26, 2006, arguing that "the respondent's arguments regarding the likelihood of torture are speculative and not based on evidence in record."[452] That ruling was appealed, but on January 30, 2008, that decision was upheld; or rather, the Court of Appeals for the Sixth Circuit denied Demjanjuk's request for review. By the time these words are read, there will almost certainly be one or more further developments.[453]

Meanwhile, at the time when most of this was being written, John Demjanjuk remained in the United States, in his home and in his community—most of whom believed him innocent and a victim of varied forms of Soviet and American persecution. If, as seemed likely at the time, (early 2009), no other country was willing to accept him—the Ukrainian offer of 15 years earlier was not likely to be renewed, nor was it likely to be accepted—then he would remain in America, although as a stateless alien he would lose all Social Security benefits that he accumulated as a working American citizen.[454] The larger questions—of his guilt or innocence and of whether or not justice was done—remained unanswered, and must always remain unanswered. Only he really knows, and either one believes his protestation of innocence (and disbelieves the claim by U.S. marshalls on his flight to Israel that he had offhandedly "confessed") or one does not.

Given the likelihood that Demjanjuk participated in some way, shape or form in the working out of the "Final Solution"—regardless of whether he was or was not Ivan *Grozny*—this unresolved outcome may, perhaps, be appropriate: since there is no real way in which one can define a punishment appropriate to such participation, then perhaps the most appropriate ending is no ending. Some will see him as having escaped punishment; others will see him as having suffered unfairly through all of the years in and out of prison and in and out of the courtroom. If nobody is truly satisfied, then maybe that's how it should be. Gershom Scholem's lament regarding the Eichmann execution—that it offered the illusion that the book of Holocaust atrocities could be and was somehow closed—does not apply to the Demjanjuk case. The book is still open, thirty years after its cover was first cracked—and after his last trial, in Germany, the court's findings, and his eventual death shortly thereafter.

To end this chapter where it began: Demjanjuk's case is the best-known of the small but steady accumulation of cases in which quiet American citizens in various communities have suddenly found themselves accused of having lied on their immigration and/or citizenship applications regarding a serious Nazi past. These cases can obviously end in one of three ways: the defendant is found guilty—of having lied on the application forms, as opposed to having committed the specific crimes of which s/he might or might not be accused—or the defendant is found not guilty; or, as in Demjanjuk's case, the case continues forward without resolution (even its final "resolution" in a court in Germany, given the subsequent appeal that was interrupted by Demjanjuk's death in a nursing home at age 91 doesn't fully resolve it for most of those on both sides of his guilt/ innocence fence).[455]

Allan Ryan lists forty cases that had been filed by July, 1984 in the appendix to his *Quiet Neighbors*, but others have developed since. Occasionally it seems that the will to prosecute and deport can lead and has led to errors. Thus, for example, Frank Walus was a factory worker living on the southwest side of Chicago, who had come as an immigrant from Poland to America in 1959. The INS caught up with him in 1977. This was four years after an argument in which he evicted a boarder named Michael Alper, who then alleged to a Chicago Jewish agency that Walus had, several months before evicting him, bragged about having been a Nazi in the Polish cities of Kielce and Czestochowa.

The INS was by then feeling appropriate pressure—finally—to deal with the issue of former Nazis living in America. By the time the U.S Attorney filed suit in federal court on January 26, 1977, Walus had been "identified" by several Israeli survivors of the two Polish cities, but by way of a grainy enlargement of his 1959 visa photo, and with the name having been suggested beforehand, and no comparison images. He was identified as a former Gestapo officer—but it apparently did not occur to the investigators that a Pole could not be a Gestapo officer; this was a profession reserved for members of the master race.

In brief, in the Walus story everything points to his having been exactly what he had claimed when he applied to come to America as an immigrant: a Polish forced laborer on a number of German farms through the war years, hundreds of miles from the cities in question. But his trial was presided over by Judge Julius Hoffmann (best known for his role in the trial of the "Chicago 7" in the late 1960s), and handled by the judge as if Walus' guilt were a foregone conclusion, and resulted in a verdict in May 1978 whereby the defendant was stripped of his American citizenship.

Walus' legal counsel appealed—and still more evidence in his favor arrived shortly after the verdict—but Hoffmann refused to order a new trial. Nonetheless, the court of appeals both sharply criticized Hoffman's handling of the case and called for a retrial. Meanwhile, the OSI was coming into existence at around that time, and took the case on as a top priority—recognizing that it would need stronger evidence than that presented in the first Walus trial, if the conviction were to stick. "The case took nearly nine months to complete, but when it was over the answer [completely the opposite of what we anticipated] was clear... There was no trace of Walus in any records, here or in Poland, dealing with Nazi activities in that country."[456] Ryan called the U.S. attorney in Chicago, Tom Sullivan, and shared the OSI's findings, and both agreed that the case should in fact not even be retried, but withdrawn.

The consequence of this early—for the OSI—case was a series of lessons regarding methods of gathering testimony and evidence (particularly with regard to photo-spreads: it bears repeating that those in which Demjanjuk was identified included images of a range of individuals, images of him from different sources at different periods, and that his name was never mentioned to witnesses before or while they were examining the spread) and regarding the matter of how solid the evidence against a suspect must be, so that the guilty be convicted and the innocent protected.

One could argue that the case of Andrija Artukovic was the opposite of that of Frank Walus. He was convincingly suspected of having been actively engaged during the war as the number two man in the Croat-controlled government of Yugoslavia, and, as such, having organized a series of concentration camps in which somewhere between 200,000 and 830,00 persons—Jews, Serbs and Roma—perished "through exposure, starvation, bullets, and blunt instruments."[457] Artukovic managed to flee from Zagreb to Austria in 1945, where British authorities found him and interrogated him but released him after a month; he went to Switzerland after a year, adopting the alias, Alois Anich, and thence to Ireland in 1947, finally requesting and receiving a tourist visa as Alois Anich—the visa was valid for 90 days—to come to the United States the following year.

In the America of the late 1940s and early 1950s, as we have earlier noted—and quite different from what had evolved by the 1970s and the era of Frank Walus—the emerging Cold War and growing fear of Communism was coming to dwarf all other "persecution policy" issues, and certainly dwarfed the interest in worrying about former Nazis. Moreover, someone with enough smarts could take advantage of the American legal system, once he had gotten into the country, to pretty much avoid ever having to leave it. Artukovic's brother had left Croatia back in the thirties and become well established on the coast of California, where Andrija arrived with his expanding family (his third child was born in Ireland) in mid-summer, 1948, and where he was immediately employed as a bookkeeper in the family contracting business.

On September 15, 1948, a few weeks before his tourist visa expired, Artukovic applied for an extension, which was granted *pro forma* until February 3, 1949. He applied in January 1949 for another extension, revealing for the first time that his real name was Andrija Artukovic. But the name would have meant nothing to the clerks who routinely approved the second extension. When the April 17, 1949 expiration date of that extension arrived, Artukovic simply did nothing, instead applying to became a permanent resident based on the Displaced Persons Act—but the cut-off date for that appeal had been April 1, 1948, three months before Artukovic had first arrived into the country.

The long and the short of the events that followed is that, when through his brother's powerful friends, the Justice Department took up Artukovic's case, and passed it on to INS for a routine investigation, his past came to light. (Irony once more rears its head!) But the case against him, who "as Minister of the Interior... gave orders for the arrest and complete extermination of Serbs and Jews in the independent state of Croatia and ordered the establishment of concentration camps where masses of Jews and Serbs of Croatia were deported, kept under the most inhuman conditions, ill-treated and eventually exterminated,"[458] never really took full shape.

The INS sent its report to the congressional liaison at the Justice Department on February 6, 1950—directly to the number two man at Justice, Deputy Attorney General Peyton Ford. But remarkably, the government did nothing to pursue the case. "For over a year the government's paralysis continued. No one said anything;

no one did anything."⁴⁵⁹ Meanwhile the state of Yugoslavia—Tito's Yugoslavia, independent of the Soviet Union but nonetheless a Communist state—had gotten wind of Artukovic's presence in sunny California and requested extradition so that he could be tried for war crimes.

To summarize briefly: the deportation hearings and extradition hearings interwove each other. One arm of the United States government, with a good deal of solid information regarding who Artukovic was, waffled and waited on the deportation issue to see what the other arm was doing regarding the extradition request. Peyton Ford's assistant went so far as to write that "unless it can be established that he was responsible for the deaths of any *Americans*, I think that deportation should be to some non-Communist country which will give him asylum. In fact, if his only crime was against Communists, I think *he should be given asylum in the U.S.* (my italics)."⁴⁶⁰ Clearly in 1951 anti-Communism more than trumped anti-Nazism, and an atmosphere prevailed in which even the murder of tens or hundreds of thousands of people was regarded not only as inconsequential, should they prove to have been Communists, but a mass-murderer who was now at risk from Communists was worthy of American asylum unless non-Communist Americans were among those he had murdered!

Artukovic and his legal team were very clever at playing on these prejudices and fears while also playing up the good, quiet inhabitant of California that he had become and the family—by then further expanded—that he was raising in America. This certainly helped the American assessors of his situation to do virtually the opposite of what Judge Hoffmann had done in the case of Frank Walus. Artukovic was viewed as inherently worthy of clemency even before the evidence was heard by a judge: for he was pre-viewed as "a prominent and influential cabinet minister who had sworn eternal opposition to the ruthless Communists and had done everything in his power to oppose them"⁴⁶¹—not the ally of the Nazis who had murdered so many Jews, Serbs and Roma.

In the interview in which deportation was being considered, Artukovic spectacularly recast his role during the war, which the

INS representative, in possession of dozens of documents demonstrating otherwise, said virtually nothing to refute. Nonetheless, the hearing officer surprisingly ordered him deported in his judgment of June 27, 1952. This did not mean that he would have to return to Yugoslavia, merely that he would have to leave the United States— sooner than later. Meanwhile the extradition case was gearing up between Yugoslavia and Artukovic. Judge Peirson Hall determined that the only viable basis for extradition, a 1901 treaty between the United States and Serbia, did not apply, regardless of what the American government, using that treaty as a reference point to approve the extradition request, believed.[462]

Then again, in April 1953, the Board of Immigration Appeals reaffirmed the order of deportation, declaring itself unconvinced that Artukovic had been a public servant in a freedom-loving democratic state. This "was, really, a courageous opinion... [The year] 1953, very near the apogee of McCarthyism, was by no means the best year for a panel of Washington bureacrats to order deportation of a man for imprisoning and executing Communists... But the Board had no power to enforce its own decision."[463]

And the INS and Justice Department decided not to enforce the deportation order until the extradition case—which, after Judge Hall's verdict, was being appealed by the Yugoslav government— was finally decided. The process moved slowly forward: on February 19, 1954 the U.S. Court of Appeals overturned Hall's decision invalidating the 1901 treaty with the Kingdom of Serbia. But Hall came onto the scene in favor of Artukovic yet again, as the latter appeared once more in his courtroom. He concluded that the crimes ascribed to Artukovic by the Yugoslav government were "political" in nature and therefore not covered by the extradition treaty. So the extradition hearing itself still failed to take place.

At that point, the INS stepped back into the picture, deciding to repeat unequivocally its decree to deport—but oddly enough noting to Artukovic that if he did not depart on his own he would be directly deported to Yugoslavia. "Oddly," that is, since deportation orders typically do not need to specify the country to which deportation will follow (as opposed, of course, to extradition) and it would have been more logical for Artukovic to be deported to Ireland, since that was the country from which he directly came to the United States. The consequence of the new and geopolitically specific order was that it provided the defendant with an obvious out: he could claim that deportation *to Yugoslavia* amounted to a death sentence.

And in the procedures that followed, as the final disposition of Artukovic's case was to be determined—time had moved forward toward 1956—he not surprisingly touted the greatness of the America in which he had found a haven for so long, and underscored the threat of international Communism in which struggle he himself had been an important soldier. Such words found ready ears in the California in which he was living and where his deportation case was again being adjudicated. Meanwhile—as the deportation issue was still before the court, arriving at a verdict of "decision to be rendered as soon as it is practicable"—the Yugoslavs were still seeking the still-unresolved (and in any case unenforced) extradition.

By late 1958 an actual hearing with regard to extradition finally took shape—seven years after the Yugoslavs had first filed their request. The case would be heard by Commissioner (Judge) Theodore Hoecke. Oddly, the INS—nearly two decades before the OSI would come into existence, and in other words, ill-equipped methodologically and otherwise to deal with such a case—did not call a single witness, simply offering a substantial pile of affidavits. The defense responded with a parade of live witnesses, Croatian sympathizers from the United States and Argentina—all of whom insisted that Artukovic had essentially been a powerless figure sandwiched between his boss, the Chief-of-State, Ante Pavelic, and his subordinate, "Dido" Kvaternik.

Artukovic's defense counsel wisely chose not to have their client testify and therefore be subject to cross-examination. So nobody except those sympathetic to him actually addressed Artukovic's activities in person. Not surprisingly, the verdict of January 15, 1959 by Commissioner Hoecke was that there was no evidence that Artukovic had committed murder, and that there were no grounds for extraditing him to Yugoslavia. Hoecke had viewed the affidavits against the defendant as too insubstantial—and had on the other hand ignored the fact that the eight defense witnesses were all Croats, six of whom had held positions in the same government in which Artukovic served, and at least six of whom were rabid nationalists and bitter foes of Tito's government.

So after eight years, Artukovic was not extradited, and the mood offered by that decision was carried into the latest—last—deportation hearing, where the defendant argued eloquently that he would be killed were he to be deported to Yugoslavia. He argued in a closed room where only he, his lawyer and the judge sat—with nobody, not even an INS officer, to challenge his words. In the end, after years of legal wrangling—during nearly all of which he remained comfortably ensconced in his California home, surrounded by family and friends, a church-going anti-Communist—Artukovic was permitted simply to remain in America, even as the illegality of his status[464] was recognized by the court.

Among the entities that responded to this baleful conclusion was the president of the Association of Yugoslav Jews in the United States, who observed that the "position taken by the Department of Justice in handling this case caused great surprise among the members of our community." He noted the unhappy comparison between genuine refugees who had and were still being nonetheless deported and Artukovic, who had lied about being a refugee and was allowed to remain, how those in particular "who came from the Jasenovac concentration camp, which had been established through Mister Artukovic's decree and where they had been subject to most inhuman treatment... simply cannot understand the protection accorded to a man who is responsible for the killing of many thousands of innocent victims, while refugees from communist oppression still have to languish in [DP] camps...for years and years without any possibility of coming to this blessed country."[465]

The key issue in this last case, in comparison with the Frank Walus case, is its timing, both—to repeat—in the sense of what was transpiring in the United States in the 1950s with regard to Communism and with regard to the not-yet formed OSI branch of government subsequently created to deal with former Nazis two decades later. From the perspective of our discussion it is the first issue that is of particular interest, particularly when we juxtapose a case such as that of Artukovic with what was happening on the other coast of the continent during the era when his case was developing, to the Rosenbergs and others.

With respect to the second issue—the eventual formation of the OSI—it should be noted that the INS made two half-hearted attempts to deport Artukovic, (but not to Yugoslavia), in late 1959: to Ireland and Switzerland. But neither country would take him. The INS continued to pretend that it was "working" on the case well into the 1960s. But after the creation of the OSI a renewed and truly energized effort was begun with the reinstatement of a deportation order for him in 1981—which was reversed by the U.S. Court of Appeals for the Ninth Circuit in 1982—and then a motion filed by OSI to reopen proceedings in early 1984. The aftermath of this last effort was that Artukovic was finally deported to Yugoslavia, where he was tried and in 1986 sentenced to be executed. But a year later the Yugoslav authorities determined that he was too ill to be executed— he exhibited an advanced state of Alzheimers disease—and he died in a prison hospital in Zagreb in 1988, of natural causes.

And so on. To repeat: there are many more cases that have surfaced since the end of the 1970s. Among the obvious features that these cases tend to have in common—falsifying one's position and role during World War II in applying either for immigration and/or citizenship status to the United States and then living a quiet, unassuming, often extremely neighborly life somewhere in our vast republic—two linked meta-features stand out. The first is the willingness and ability to take advantage of the almost uniquely American capacity for moving swiftly from past to future, so that the will to leave World War II and the Holocaust behind in dealing with new issues—particularly the very effective new issue of Communism as a threat—created an atmosphere in which subverting one's Nazi or Nazi-related past was relatively easy, especially between about 1945 and 1960; and maintaining the fictions that such subversion necessitated was also relatively simple.[466]

After all, in so many parts of the United States, communities are both mixed and filled with individuals and families who have newly arrived from somewhere else—we are not only a nation of immigrants, but surely the most internally mobile polity in the world—and as a culture, in most times and places Americans tend to be willing to accept new neighbors, if they are nice, quiet neighbors, without asking too many questions about them.

The second meta-feature is that the American legal system typically assisted such individuals, once their stories had begun to unravel, to enjoy years or even decades of freedom before arriving at the actual moment of deportation. This is both because the legal system simply moves so slowly, and also because that system is by-and-large at pains to protect the rights of the individual and to err in favor of not executing or deporting someone who is guilty of the crime that merits such punishments, rather than mistakenly condemning someone who is actually innocent—as it should be, and as Tractate *Sanhedrin* no doubt would be, confronted with such legal situations.

There is, perhaps, some irony to the fact that this last feature, which helped keep someone like John Demjanjuk safe and warm in his Seven Hills home for so many decades, (aside from his time in the Ayalon prison)—even if he was technically a stateless person throughout that time—was not operative in the case of Julius and Ethel Rosenberg. They, who were accused of being Communist spies, were summarily executed in the face of various layers of doubts; he, whose supporters claimed that the case against him was a Communist plot, was well protected from exile and possible death due to thin slivers of doubt.[467]

Chapter Nine:
Epilogues: Jews on Trial

There are two directions in which one might carry an epilogue of the unresolved and unfinished Demjanjuk case in a narrative that can have no end. One is to consider some of the legal events that have repercussions for our overall discussion in the past forty years or so—the last third of the twentieth century and the beginning of the twenty-first. The other is to re-affirm my argument throughout, as we review the historical sweep of the discussion, that the Jew seems to be almost inevitably on trial regardless of the particular role he or she plays in the courtroom. This, I would assert, is because the courtroom that involves Jews *qua* Jews is inevitably larger than a given courthouse building, but encompasses streets that open beyond the courthouse walls and windows onto roads that extend across the planet and across the history through which Jews have been dispersed.

In the time between the Eichmann case and the beginning of the Demjanjuk case, and in the decades since, aside from the prosecution in the United States and Europe of a handful of Nazi war criminals, like Conrad Schellong[468], Klaus Barbie[469] and Karl Linnas[470], there have been other legal proceedings that continue to unravel specific threads of earlier history. Thus, for example, in the Soviet Union that put itself on the map with regard specifically to "Jewish" trials by way of Stalin and the so-called "Doctors' Plot,"[471] the ice of all kinds of anti-freedom strictures moved through phases of thaw and freeze between Stalin's death in 1953 and the collapse of the Soviet Union in 1991.

Embedded in the middle of that four-decades-long process of back and forth on various fronts, and sandwiched between the time of the 1967 Six-Day War in the Middle East and the fuller development of the "Free Soviet Jews!" movement of the late 1970s, among the more significant legal proceedings was that recalled by Hillel Butman in his book, *From Leningrad to Jerusalem*. That extended memoir recalls a period that began with a meeting of six friends in a park outside Leningrad in November, 1966 to create a Zionist group, culminated four years later with a series of legal trials, and achieved a denouement with the release—and "expulsion" to Israel—of those incarcerated at various times in the decade that followed.

The small group that had been formed in 1966 expanded over the next few years and its members, in some cases, came and went. They engaged in activities which might be considered standard for Jewish groups eager to raise Jewish consciousness among Soviet Jews and, at least, desperate to live their lives and express themselves as Jews while having no desire to leave the Soviet Union—or, at most, desperate for a freer life than that available in the Soviet Union of Leonid Brezhnev. They acquired, copied and distributed Jewish (by definition, "subversive"—*samizdat*) poetic and prose literature,[472] and they managed to teach themselves a fair amount of Hebrew and Jewish history. This particular group dreamed not merely of living as Jews or of leaving the USSR, but specifically of making *aliyah*, of immigrating to Israel.[473]

But a core within the group went still further in their thinking and their actions: they shaped a plan, which they called "Operation Wedding," to hijack a Soviet plane on May 2, 1970, fly to Sweden, and hold a press conference there that would draw international attention to the condition of thousands of Jews desirous of emigrating and undertaking *aliyah*. As, having shaped their plan, some of the group began to be enmeshed in doubt, they agreed to go so far as to delay the plan while seeking advice from individuals in Israel with whom they made contact—who advised them against it.[474]

Both the plan and the advice proved moot for some of its formulators. In the early morning of June 15, KGB agents at the Smolny Airport just outside what was then called Leningrad arrested a small group of Jews about to board a plane headed for Sortavala, near the Finnish border. The group—of both men and women—had in fact intended to carry out the sort of hijacking originally outlined as "Operation Wedding," which had been abandoned by its first formulators, Hillel Butman among them, in response to the advice from Israel. The "Smolny" group had proceeded with a different version of the original plan even as the original formulators had not only abandoned it, but had no idea that some of their erstwhile colleagues were proceeding with a version of it. Later that day, KGB agents arrested other Zionist Jews, including Butman, even if they had not been part of the hijacking scheme.

Butman's memoir recounts his participation in the Zionist group that he first helped form in 1966; in the creation of the "Operation Wedding" plan, his abandonment of it and his arrest nonetheless at the hands of the KGB; and his trial and prison time that followed. For, as he points out in his introduction, "[t]he KGB used the attempted hijacking as a pretext to smash Zionist groups throughout the Soviet Union. In addition to those arrested at the airport, about two dozen others were arrested and tried for anti-Soviet agitation and propaganda; some were charged with treason."[475] While apparently the KGB had become aware of the intended June 15 hijacking as much as two months before, they preferred not to do anything to prevent it from going forward; "evidently, the [KGB] plan had been finalized to use "Operation Wedding" as an excuse for a pogrom against *aliyah* activists, and to prevent the escape of potential victims."[476]

Butman describes his ignorance, at the time of his arrest, of what had transpired at Smolny Airport that same day or of most of what had led up to the almost-events. He writes of his brief preliminary interrogation and his refusal to speak to his captors—as much earlier, he and his colleagues had agreed to remain silent should they end up arrested. He understood at that point, on the other hand, that if there were no proof of whatever accusation against him had been shaped, "[i]n three days, the sanction of the investigations department would end. If there was no proof, he would have to release me."[477] So however totalitarian the regime, there were laws in place that offered some limited theoretical hope of protecting even someone such as he.

Of course, for Butman, part of the initial question was: "with what am I being charged?" since on the one hand the Operation had long been cancelled but on the other hand he *was* still guilty of the subversion of studying Hebrew and reading books—such as Howard Fast's *My Glorious Brothers* (a dramatic novelized retelling of the Hanukkah story and the revolt against the Seleucids led by the five "Maccabee" brothers in 168-5 BCE), which he was reading at the time of his arrest. A day into his incarceration he was told that he was being accused of masterminding the failed hijack attempt at Smolny Airport on June 15. He signed a statement at that point, in which he declared that "I know nothing about the attempt... And I know nothing about the participants. I refuse to answer any questions as a sign of protest against my illegal arrest and demand my immediate release."[478]

The next question for Butman was how and who had included his name among those associated with the Smolny plan about which he genuinely *did* know nothng. "Well... sooner or later it would get straightened out. The days of Stalin were over."[479] Perhaps, but that did not prevent Butman from being reclassified by the end of the third day of his initial incarceration—and the daily day-long interrogations for which he consistently refused to answer questions—as a defendant, rather than as a suspect.

Thus his incarceration continued, as did the daily interrogations. After a time he was convinced that it made more sense—both because it seemed that, from the interrogator's comments, others were talking, and because it seemed better for those about whom he cared who were still on the outside—to talk, at least up to a point. "There is a time to be silent and a time to speak. [But o]nce I started to speak, I realized the importance of not renouncing our ideals. It was up to us to turn the investigation and trial into a continuation of our struggle against forced assimilation and for free emigration."[480]

The interrogators orchestrated a range of inducements to talking, from direct suggestions that so-and-so had already confessed such-and-such (and there is thus no reason to continue to withhold such information) to casual, "mistakenly overheard" references to some datum that the prisoner would infer had been garnered from someone else's statement. Butman writes of the "aiming the cannon" strategy: referring to a piece of information that only the prisoner and one other individual know, in order to imply that that other individual has revealed it—so why continue to hide the information?—except that it turns out that the KGB has garnered that tidbit otherwise, from eavesdropping or wild guess, and not from the other individual. Such information was not admissible in a Soviet courtroom unless corroborated by the official testimony of one of the defendants—who may have been tricked into offering just such a corroboration. Butman found himself on the wrong end of a number of "cannon fire" questions.

While the goal may be different, I am not certain that the method is so different from what goes on behind the scenes in pre-courtroom American interrogations. It certainly resembles aspects of what we know to have transpired in the Rosenberg-Sobell case—with, in fact, a goal that was the mirror image of the Soviet goal in Butman's case: to prove that the defendant was engaged in nefarious activity that was both treasonous and potentially deadly threatening to the State.

It was, indeed, some time before Butman was informed as to exactly how his actions were being viewed, and thus how he would be charged—not, as it turned out, as part of the group that would be tried for the attempted airplane hijacking, but rather as a member of the illegal Zionist/Jewish Committee of which he had been an original organizer. From his point of view the significance of this, above all, was that his crime would almost certainly not be deemed a capital crime, whereas that of the hijackers could lead to a death sentence.

Thus officially designated as a defendant with regard to the crime of participation in a Zionist organization, he understood that his role had become not one of disputing or withholding facts, but of reshaping the *interpretation* of those facts: "it was important to stress that we were struggling for free emigration, to which we were entitled under the United Nations Declaration of Human Rights... I felt that the Soviet government was on the threshold of making important political decisions—decisions that could be influenced by our responses to questions during the interrogations... The goal of "Operation Wedding" had not yet been achieved, but it had not been abandoned by like-minded people who were demanding, *Let my people go*."[481]

This, of course, is where he and his co-defendants are subtly separable from the Rosenbergs and their colleagues. Butman denied none of the Zionist/Jewish activities of which he was accused. But he argued that they were not anti-Soviet as much as pro-Jewish—to the extent, even, that they might be called pro-Israel, he argued that they were still not anti-Soviet, and reminded his accusers that the Soviet Union had been among the first states to recognize the legitimacy of Israel as a state. By contrast, the Rosenbergs denied many of the key actions of which they were accused; had they engaged in those actions to the extent that the prosecution asserted, then the secondary, also arguable issue was how dangerous to the state, how anti-American, the actions were. One might say that Butman is distinguished from the Rosenbergs in a manner analogous to how Demjanjuk was distinguished from Eichmann: in Eichmann's case it was a matter of how the actions of the accused were to be judged, in Demjanjuk's a question of whether he had in fact committed the actions of which he stood accused.

The Smolny Airport trial took place beginning on December 15, 1970. Butman writes of the trial as theater—the first of a series of show trials over the next several years, echoing those of the Stalin period—a theater of the absurd in which all of the actors were carefully cast in their roles. The prosecutor, Leningrad District Attorney Solovyev "was already senile... [b]ut he had a trusty helper who never forgot anything—Inessa Katukova. The presiding judge, Ermakov, was a qualified executioner... The theme of the production was to be 'Destroy the gang. Destroy cursed Zionists, those who were responsible for harming Mother Russia...'"[482] Aside from the

chief prosecutor there was a pair of people's prosecutors to represent the Soviet people as the offended victim of the defendants' offensive aggression.

The defendants asserted that they were not anti-Soviet but
merely wished to leave for Israel, and, since they were not free to
do so legally as in other countries they would have been, that they
had sought desperate means to get out. But they "had not wanted to steal a plane. What would they have needed a plane for? If
the group had flown to Stockholm, then the Swedes, as is accepted
and proper would have returned the plane to the Soviet Union."[483]
Their intention, therefore, had been merely to borrow the plane. The
court responded that they had indeed wished to steal, "on a large
scale"—and that, under the criminal code of the Soviet State, the
proper punishment for such as crime is execution by shooting.

Butman was called upon as a witness, who merely testified regarding his own understanding of what he had originally planned,
since he could not say what the Smolny plan had become: to wit,
that his intention had been to get to Stockholm and hold a press conference in which he would cry out to the world that Soviet Jews desirous of emigrating and going to Israel were being prevented from
so doing by their government. The defendants were sentenced on
December 24: the prescribed punishments ranged from capital punishment with confiscation of property to four years of gulag imprisonment "without confiscation of property in the absence of such."

Meanwhile, his own trial had been scheduled for December
23—the day before the "Smolny" sentencing—but ended up delayed for several weeks. He refused to take on a defense lawyer, but
the state insisted that every Soviet citizen must be provided with legal defense and supplied him with one, "a pleasant Jew, tired, with
a slight tremor. He had never defended a political prisoner, but the
rules of the game were clear to him.... We agreed that he would defend me as he saw fit, as long as he did not defame what was dear
to me... Not once did he slander or revile either Zionism or Israel.
Instead, he limited himself to a declaration that he could not share
the political views of his defendant."[484]

We surely must recognize in this identity configuration of

personages and issues a mirror of the Eichmann and Demjanjuk trials in Jerusalem. In Eichmann's case, we recall the concern—felt by the Israelis and emphatically expressed by the world media—as to whether Israel could provide him with an effective defense lawyer, so the court reached outside Israel and provided and paid for a German defense lawyer, Dr. Servatius. In Demjanjuk's case, the American lawyer, O'Connor, began as the head of a defense team that included an Israeli lawyer, Yoram Sheftel, whose primary initial purpose was to make sure that the American team did not get tangled up in Israeli legal threads. In both cases, the defense counsels evinced no discomfort at assailing the Israeli court and the very shaping of the prosecution's case when they felt it appropriate or advantageous to do so.

We might presume that the Soviet government deliberately selected a Jewish lawyer for Butman in a manner superficially analogous to the appointment of a German lawyer for Eichmann—although we cannot be certain, and Butman does not assert this—who on the one hand was loyal to his client as far as possible, but on the other hand understood where the line of his defense needed to be drawn as far as his own survival was concerned and the political conditions under which the trial was taking place. It is inconceivable that Butman's lawyer would frame things to the Soviet court in an aggressive manner similar to that of Servatius and certainly O'Connor to the Israeli court.

In any case, while the bills of indictment were still being prepared, Butman and his lawyer were given access to all of the material that had been gathered through the interrogations of the previous months—forty-two thick volumes of it—and thereby learned, for the first time, something of what had happened at Smolny Airport on June 15 and of the hundreds of individuals who were subsequently interrogated or discussed in the interrogations.[485]

Meanwhile, interesting developments outside the courtroom were in process. The day after the sentencing of the airport group, a telegram of protest sent by 18 Muscovites was sent to Nikolai Podgorny, president of the USSR; subsequently "waves of protest and solidarity for the defendants in the two trials rolled into the Kremlin from all sides,"[486] somewhat reminiscent of those waves that washed over the proceedings six decades earlier during the Beiliss trial—and inconceivable not quite two decades earlier during the Stalin era and the "Doctors' Plot" trials. Those waves, nonetheless, were smaller than those that rolled in toward the White House and Supreme Court of the United States in the aftermath of the Rosenberg verdicts—but more effective, as it turned out.

The protests built. Jews from Riga and Kiev and Moscow wrote, and also representatives of the Russian human rights movements—non-Jews, who asserted that "[e]veryone who wishes to leave should be permitted to emigrate..." [and that] "[c]apital punishment and intimidation do not testify to the strength of the state." It is noteworthy that all of this initial activity came from within the Soviet Union—it was the Soviet Zionists and their supporters who recognized this as an opportunity to put pressure on the Soviet leadership, not the Israelis or the West. Among the individuals who wrote was the renowned physicist, Andrei Sakharov, one of the fathers of the non-Jewish political dissident movement. [487]

Meanwhile, as might perhaps be expected in a country with state-controlled media eager to crush both Jewish and Zionist sensibilities, the Soviet press as it covered events, before, during and after the first trial, referred to the would-be highjackers as "Zionist murderers" who, heavily armed with guns, knives, axes, brass knuckles, ropes and gags, had in mind to murder Soviet pilots—with getting to Israel as a decidedly secondary goal—although in fact both the plan hatched by Butman and his colleagues and that planned for Smolny Airport were as blood-free as one could imagine. Both hijacking teams opted to carry no lethal weapons at all, only implements that would intimidate the crew, in the end.[488]

Eventually, the West and the Israelis caught on to what was transpiring, and the need for action from without and not only from within the USSR. The Israeli *Knesset* (Parliament) met in special session and even the representative of the Communist party within Israel's multi-party system (that *includes* a Communist party) spoke out in condemnation of the Soviet government's actions. Significantly, a group of Basque terrorists on trial at around the same time in Spain, had also been sentenced to death, and world opinion was aroused to support a mitigation of their sentence.[489]

The two groups of death-sentence verdicts, in Leningrad and Burgos, were linked by the media. From the perspective of Brezhnev and Podgorny, being thereby connected to Franco—their mortal enemy—by an increasingly hostile world community was ironic and uncomfortable, and the thought of having a range of trade and industrial opportunities with the West scutted was recognized as potentially disastrous. On December 31, they decided to alter the verdict of the Smolny group, whose members were summoned to the office of the director of the prison where they were all being held and told to sign appeals.[490] The two condemned to die had their sentences commuted to 15 years of imprisonment, and all of the other sentences were variously reduced.[491]

Among the repercussions of what, in retrospect, would be a sea change in the political climate of the Soviet Union with regard to various forms of "political subversion" was a shift in the putative fate of the second group of Zionists, including Butman, who had been scheduled to go on trial on December 23. They were told that one of the lawyers had not had time to read the case, so it was postponed, first of all, until January 6. At that point, one of the defendants, Lev Yagman, was said to be ailing and the trial, the others were told, would be postponed until he was healthy. He did not recover from his chest cold until May.

In the interim, the 42 volumes of material were sent to Moscow for scrupulous review. "The authorities had decided that they wanted us, at our trial, to look like straying lambs who had been deceived by Zionism and saved by Soviet justice. Then our sentences could be lighter than those of the airplane group. This scenario required that all of us 'deeply acknowledge our errors and sincerely repent.' So in Moscow they examined the [pre-trial] testimony that each of us had given,"[492] although this changed perspective would only be known by Butman and his isolated, imprisoned associates, afterwards.

That *something* had changed must have seemed evident by the fact that the authorities permitted Butman's wife, Eva, to bring him a copy of Shapiro's *Hebrew-Russian Dictionary*, as he was spending much of his time between December and May studying Hebrew and English (and mathematics). That dictionary "accompanied me through all the islands of the Gulag Archipelago... After long years together, we parted one beautiful day shortly before I left the Archipelago. It is a *zek* (prisoner) custom to leave such books in the zone because it is very difficult to receive them behind the barbed wire. My dictionary became the friend of Natan Sharansky, who still had a long and tortuous road between the Gulag and Jerusalem."[493]

The day of the trial, May 11, 1971, arrived, and Butman and eight of his colleagues were brought to court—several others were tried shortly thereafter in Kishinev, in Moldavia, rather than in Leningrad. Unlike the airplane-group trial, which had been conducted behind closed doors, with a carefully selected group as its audience, this procedure, to the surprise of Butman, was conducted as an open trial. Thus press and the outside world in general had access to it. This did not mean that most of the audience was not, as in the closed trials, hired to respond as the government preferred—as representatives of "the people," who could "seethe with indignation" on cue. And many key members of the defendants' families, such as Butman's only sister, were not actually permitted within the courtroom itself.

Judge Nina Isakova presided. "She knew that all of the attorneys, Jews and non-Jews alike, would perform their roles as expected. Looking into the hall, Judge Isakova saw the relatives of the defendants. They wouldn't applaud, she knew, but they wouldn't start a rebellion, either. Each one of them had a job. Each had children. The habits ingrained in them in Stalin's day had not faded."[494] And again one thinks in comparative terms of other trials, such as those of Beiliss, the Rosenbergs, Eichmann and Demjanjuk. Was the fact, as earlier noted, of Jewish lawyers, part of the carefully orchestrated theater event which had as one of its goals to suggest the fairness of the proceedings—specifically, the lack of any anti-Semitism to them?

How comfortable or intimidated were such Jewish lawyers—and how more or less comfortable, intimated, sympathetic or unsympathetic than their non-Jewish colleagues? Were they genuine believers in the absolute righteousness of the Soviet State, and not at all convinced of the anti-Semitic aspects to which people like Butman sought to call everyone's attention, or were they simply acting as safely—for themselves and their families—as they thought possible, by participating in these proceedings exactly as they were told?

Interestingly, the courtroom seems, in Butman's description (and the descriptions by others of similar Soviet courtrooms of that period) more potentially dangerous for lawyers of whatever faith who were too energetic in defending their clients than had been the case for the Beiliss trial in the waning days of the Romanov era sixty years earlier. On the other hand, I am not convinced that the particular pressure felt by the Jewish lawyers in Leningrad was as different as one might wish to suppose from the pressures felt by Jewish lawyers and other key Jewish figures in the Rosenberg trial in New York City in the 1950s. Whatever particular pressures would have been felt in Jerusalem, for the judges and prosecuting attorneys, in both the Eichmann and Demjanjuk cases, by contrast, would seem to derive from the position of Israel, as the *Jewish* state, within the world—but that position and the nature of that pressure changed in the two decades between the first and the second of these two cases.

As the trial of Butman and his eight colleagues proceeded, the secretary of the court, Logvinova, who had already been known for her lack of principles back at the Law institute where Butman had studied, repeatedly recorded statements with regard not for precision of content or correctness of nuance but with focus on promoting the political position of the state. Thus for instance she would record "confessed his guilt" when a defendant's comments offered nothing of the sort.

The indictment read out to the court at the outset—from creating "in Leningrad, an underground anti-Soviet Zionist organization," beginning in November, 1966; to engaging in activities "to propagandize Zionist ideology, slander the international and national policy of the Soviet regime and incite feelings for emigration among people of Jewish nationality and so encourage them to emigrate to Israel"[495]—would be precisely echoed by the sentence at the end of the trial, as if "the sentence [had been] predetermined. Even a plagiarist will at least bother to change the order of words he is stealing. Can it be simply that the judges are lazy?"[496]

One of the features of the trial as "open" was that the defendants were permitted statements—lengthy ones, if they so desired. Butman pleaded guilty to having concealed some stolen machine parts in order to build a printing/copy-machine (in order to print and distribute *samizdat* literature), but not guilty to treason or anti-Soviet propaganda and agitation. As a lawyer, he was aware of some of the ins and outs, the important distinctions, between this and that article within the Soviet criminal code. Thus for having been an organizer of "Operation Wedding"—even though the Operation had been abandoned and never carried out and he was thereby able quite clearly to plead innocent to the range of charges that were connected to the carrying out of the Operation—he hoped "that punishment would come from within the framework of Article 70 of the Criminal Code... for anti-Soviet propaganda and agitation. For this, the maximum punishment would be seven years of imprisonment."[497]

Even this, he recognized, from the strictly legal point of view, would be inappropriate, "just as it was for the other defendants.... [T]he independence of the state was not damaged, nor was its territorial inviolability or its military power"[498] by their meetings, their teachings, even their hijack plan (had it been carried out). Such threats to the Soviet state were necessary, according to its legal code, for someone to be found guilty in the way that the court would find the defendants guilty and punish them. Indeed, in what turned out to be a six-hour—albeit unplanned—speech, Butman placed an emphasis on the anti-Semitism still rampant in the Soviet Union as the prime mover behind all of the actions of which he stood accused, leaving open the question as to whether anti-Semitism remained part of state policy or was merely a function of individuals within and outside the government who remained tainted by that disease.

Each of the nine defendants addressed the charges in his own way, and each asserted his innocence. Two of them had joined the Zionist Committee a mere 39 days before their arrest, and thereby had had little to do with the activities that were the basis for the charges against them, although neither of those two, Lev Yagman and Lassal Kaminsky, referred to that fact to help prejudice the case in their favor. None of the defendants exhibited the "sincere confession" and "heartfelt repentance" that the State hoped for as an excuse to lighten their sentences in the face of both internal Soviet and worldwide outrage.

Witnesses were called, ranging from those who, in a generic manner, could attest to the objectionable character of this or that defendant, to one who could not identify a defendant (Butman) whom she was *supposed* to identify as having committed some objectionable act—for which failure to compromise her integrity, the witness "probably paid a high price."[499] At least one witness changed his pre-trial testimony before the court, regarding anti-Soviet sentiments that he at first alleged that he had heard from Butman and others—a permissible but dangerous action. Witnesses who, in the course of their testimony, referred to "former Soviet citizens" thereby let the defendants know—for everything in the world of the Soviet Union and in the subworld of engaging the Soviet Union required coded words and actions—that those individuals had managed to leave, to go on *aliyah*: that the Zionist movement's goal was already in the act of being fulfilled.

The existence of the movement and its activities, as defendants and their lawyers made clear with references to both the particulars of their activities and the details of Soviet law, offered no violation of any Soviet legal code. Nonetheless, and in spite of the five-day charade of statements by defendants and testimony by witnesses—that implied a genuine legal proceeding—the State Prosecutor Inessa Katukova read out her demands for punishment. Five days later—on May 20, 1971, the judge pronounced both the verdict—guilty, of a sliding scale of charges—and the sentences precisely as requested by the prosecution: prison terms varying from ten years to one year. The pre-selected audience applauded on cue.

A month later Butman and several of his fellow convicts were flown south to Kishinev to serve as witnesses in the third of this group of trials, under similar conditions and with similar results for the defendants. Thereafter he began his journey through the Gulag (labor camp) Archipelago and the occasional prison cell. He was moved from one location to the next—dozens of camps and prisons, in fact—over the following nine years. For reasons unknown, his sentence ended up reduced by one year. Like the others, after serving his sentence, he was allowed to leave the USSR and arrived, with four of his colleagues, to Ben Gurion Airport on April 29, 1979. Of the group of which he had been a central figure, some others had arrived earlier and some arrived somewhat later.

He was met at the airport by the then-Prime Minister of the State of Israel, Menachem Begin; as well as by his (Butman's) wife, Eva and his two daughters—one, Lilya, four years old when he had last seen her, was now 13; the other, now five-and-a half years old, had been born in Israel. His wife had been permitted *aliyah* some time after her second and last annual conjugal visit with Hillel, in 1973. This second daughter is named Geulah, which means "redemption" in Hebrew.

Butman writes: "[t]he fact that I am a Jew determined my life as a Soviet citizen—from my experiences of personal and institutional anti-Semitism to the years I spent as a prisoner in the gulag." [500] This does not, of course, mean that *only* Jews were sent to the gulags—one needs merely to think of Nobel laureate Alexander Solzhenitsyn to understand that. It *does* mean that Butman, and others like him, were sent to the gulags *because* they were Jews who chose in one way or another to assert their Judaism in an environment that, in its fear of Judaism, recalls the Roman era with which this book's narrative began.

In Rome, we recall, a legal distinction was made between *religio* and *superstitio*, whereby the second of these two terms referred to a belief system that was regarded as politically subversive—as a threat to the well-being of the state. Whereas for two centuries or so, nascent Christianity was treated as a *superstitio*, by the end of the fourth century that unhappy baton was passed to Judaism, with consequences that are still being felt more than sixteen centuries later—including, but not limited to the specific events in the Soviet Union of the 1970s and the general atmosphere there at least until the 1990s. To enact one's Judaism as Butman and his associates did was to be part of a *superstitio*.

The series of farsical trials that brought Butman and others to prison terms proved to be the beginning of a succession of legal events through which the USSR sought to eliminate dissent, particularly of the Jewish and/or Zionist sort. Individuals of all walks of life were the focus of these trials, which, to put it simply, and in the same terms as those offered by Butman in his memoir, were a direct result of the Judaism of the defendants—specifically, of their will to enact their Judaism in general and in particular in seeking *aliyah*, as Zionists.

Among the most famous of those who eventually succeeded in making *aliyah* was the dissident who became the recipient of Butman's precious Shapiro's *Hebrew-Russian Dictionary*, who in a small prison on the outskirts of the town of Christopol had been in the cell next to Butman: chess prodigy and computer scientist Anatoly (subsequently, in Israel: Natan) Sharansky. Sharansky had been originally denied an exit visa to Israel in 1973—on grounds of "national security"—and subsequently served as an English-language interpreter for Andrei Sakharov, also becoming an increasingly outspoken human rights activist.[501] He was sentenced to 13 years of prison in 1977—two years before Butman was released—and five years later, in Christopol prison once more after a "tour" of several different prisons and labor camps, he undertook a hunger strike to protest the confiscation of his mail and the refusal of the authorities to allow visits by his family.

Ultimately, the international furor that by that time was becoming more and more pronounced led to the Soviet decision to rid the state of Sharansky by exchanging him—across the Glienicke Bridge separating East and West Berlin—for a pair of Soviet spies, Karl and Hannah Koecher, in 1986. As a Prisoner of Conscience—for so the Jewish/Zionist political subversives in the Soviet Union had come to be called by the end of the seventies—Sharansky had been particularly noted for his impish wit and the combination of sarcastic retort and scrupulous reference to facts as weapons of annoyance to the Soviet authorities. His humor in particular, he later noted, helped him to survive his years of incarceration.

Sharansky is unusual among the array of Prisoner of Conscience luminaries and unknown figures alike because of the course of his life after his exodus form the USSR. He was awarded a U.S. Congressional Gold Medal in 1986 and twenty years later the U.S. Presidential Medal of Freedom. Meanwhile, he rather rapidly became involved in Israeli politics. By 1996 he was in the government as Minister of Industry and Trade—a post he held until 1999, when he became Interior Minister. He resigned from that post in July 2000, and the following year became Minister of Housing and Construction and then rose to the position of Deputy Prime Minister. Sharansky was made Minister without Portfolio in March 2003, under Ariel Sharon, with particular responsibilities for Jerusalem, social and diaspora affairs, but resigned from the cabinet in April-May 2005 to protest the plans (which were subsequently fulfilled) to remove Israeli settlements from the Gaza strip.

Nonetheless, he was re-elected to the *Knesset* as a member of the Likud Party in March 2006—but announced that he planned to retire from politics in October of the same year and left the *Knesset* that November. Since June 2007, he has been president of Bet HaTfutsot, the Diaspora Museum outside Tel Aviv.

Sharansky's 2005 resignation from the *Knesset* over the issue of withdrawing from Gaza points us in another direction with respect to the rubric "Jewish Trials." While we have taken note of the issue of Israel and the matter of its ability, as a Jewish state, to handle the cases of Adolf Eichmann and John Demjanjuk, in the decades between those two historic junctures and our own an altogether different legal and moral web has wound itself around our rubric by virtue of the circumstances of Israel as a "Jewish" state surrounded by states that have been hostile to its very existence throughout most of its history, and the evolving direction of the manifestations of that hostility.

In general historical terms the Sharansky stance on the Palestinians raises the issue of how those who were previously oppressed view those who are currently oppressed. Are Jewish Israelis like Sharansky—and Sharansky in particular—less sympathetic than they *should* be, given their own experience, to Palestinian

aspirations? Or is the view he articulates simply and fully legitimate: that the Palestinians cannot accede to the independent status
they seek unless and until they abandon groups like Hamas whose
avowed goals are inherently destructive of Israel, and abandon the
anti-Semitism and not merely anti-Zionism that is endemic in their
society?[502] Are Sharansky's Zionistic views and his humanistic,
freedom-loving views compatible or inherently at odds with each
other?[503]

In more specifically legalistic terms, the condition of the Palestinians within Israeli-governed territory has raised repeated issues
on the same two fronts that we have seen as twisted in a constant interweave in at least the last century encompassed by this narrative:
the front within the courtroom and the one, outside the courtroom,
of media-shaped and politics-driven world opinion. Thus every legal issue within the State of Israel that has involved Jewish-Arab
or Israeli-Palestinian relations faces the double question of whether
it is being adjudicated in a just and objective manner in the Israeli
court system, and of whether the court of world opinion is judging
the conduct of that court system in a just and objective manner, or
using a standard of judgment with regard to Israel that is different
from the standard applied elsewhere and otherwise.

One sees this in a range of legal "events," from the trial of this
or that individual—usually Palestinian Arab Muslim or Christian
and occasionally Israeli Jewish[504]—accused of terrorist activity, to
the matter of Israeli housing construction in this or that area outside
the pre-1967 borders of Israel, to the construction of a security fence
gerrymandering through the territory within and beyond those borders to protect Jews within them and Jewish settlements that have,
since 1967, been developed beyond them.[505]

One sees it in the struggle within the Israeli government in the
early 1980s to reject or embrace a judicial inquiry into the putative
role of Israeli soldiers in the massacres by Lebanese Christian soldiers of Muslims in the Shatila and Sabra refugee camps—and then
in the conduct of the judicial inquiry itself. It has been noted that
one key political scientist commented that "world opinion had little
to do with [the decision to enact the investigation.] 'We investigated

the massacres for ourselves.' [The political scientist] pointed out that Jews have not only a religious tradition but a political one as well. 'Our tradition assumes that people have a right to know and to be heard.'"[506]

One sees it in an article such as that by Greg Myre that appeared in 2003 in *The New York Times*, reporting on the trial in Israel of Palestinian leader Marwan Barghouti, the West Bank head of Yasir Arafat's Fatah movement, who was "charged with orchestrating 26 killings in the current violence between Israel and the Palestinians."[507] The article notes that "[t]his case is the centerpiece of an Israeli effort to show it can counter violence and still run an open legal system that meets internationally accepted standards... Israel has previously handled such cases in military courts... where the rules are somewhat more favorable to the prosecution."

Within Israel itself, there was considerable criticism from human rights activists that the military tribunals operating in Gaza (at that time) and the West Bank were not observing "international legal norms."[508] The Israeli Supreme Court had outlawed torture in 1999 (although critics asserted that it was still taking place) but upheld detention without trial and the legitimacy of demolishing the houses of terrorists' families "while setting criteria to limit the practices... 'We have recognized the power of the state to protect its security and the security of its citizens on the one hand,' Aharon Barak, [Israel's] chief justice... wrote... 'On the other hand, we have emphasized that the rights of every individual must be preserved.'"[509]

There are obvious comparisons to be made—and Myre's article alludes to them, but does not discuss them (much more information for comparison has only come to light in the past few years, well after he wrote his article)—with the treatment of defendants accused either of terrorist activity or of preparing terrorist activity in or against the United States since the time of the September 11, 2001 attacks. Clearly the American justice system has either not drawn lines where the Israeli justice system has—has not even appeared to struggle with the issue, or at least has not asserted its authority over the Executive branch of the U.S. government and over the

American military—with respect to issues ranging from imprisonment without legal representation to incarceration without trial to
the extensive use of torture.

Indeed, as Myre notes, "[o]ne of the most unusual aspects of Israeli law is the rapid access that petitioners, including Palestinians,
can gain to Israel's highest court... One evening [during the fierce
fighting in April 2002 in and around the Jenin refugee camp], Palestinians in the West Bank, working with Israeli lawyers, petitioned
the court to halt the army's use of attack helicopters in the refugee
camp. The next day, after hearing the army's case, the court upheld
the use of helicopters." The point, of course, is that it was not a giv-
en that the court would uphold the army's point of view, and that
it stood ready to hear both sides of the argument without lengthy
delays, in the midst of the battle, before offering its viewpoint—regardless of what some might think of the court's decision.[510]

Raji Sourani, then-director of the Gaza-based Palestinian Center for Human Rights, who "has been battling the Israeli legal system for more than a quarter century..., despite his many frustrations
with the Israeli courts, remains 'constantly amazed by the high
standards of the legal system.'" Perhaps the most salient point is
the last one made in Myre's article, by an unnamed Israeli military
officer and student of the issue of balancing the needs of a just legal
system with those of protecting the population from terrorism: "the
problem is prevention, not punishment. How do you stop a suicide
bomber before he reaches Tel Aviv? International law is silent on
this"—but, I would argue, international legal and political commentators are very willing to weigh in as judges of the Israeli system
from the convenient safety of courtrooms, classrooms, homes and
shops thousands of miles away and not threatened on a daily basis
by suicide bomber-terrorism.

Most recently the Israeli courts have been in a continual condition of wrestling with the legality of the "security fence," or its particular parts in particular places—and having to weigh strict legality
against larger issues of morality that derive from the problem of security.[511] It is not by any means clear that most of the world community recognizes that wrestling match—including many Americans

and American media, who think nothing of the well-patrolled fence constructed to prevent Mexicans from entering the United States in search of employment but condemn the fence designed to prevent would-be suicide bombers from entering Israel in search of victims.

Is this simply how things happen to be, or is it related to the fact that Israel is regarded as "the Jewish state"? If it is the latter, then why does the Jewishness of Israel as a state affect the tenor of world opinion? Does the moral sensibility that too often judges Jews one way and others another way not begin with the misunderstood narrative of Jesus' demise?[512] Does it not proceed through centuries of the "Teaching of Contempt" which, even in the aftermath of substantial break-throughs in breaking down such teachings, have yet to take hold along a wide enough swath of primarily the Christian (and Muslim) world?[513]

One might turn the legal screw one further turn with regard to both Israel and the United States and thus the "Jewish trials" question, by reference to Jonathan Pollard—an American Jew arrested in November, 1985 and subsequently convicted for passing American military secrets to the State of Israel.[514] There are, in the context of our discussion, three issues in particular that the Pollard case raises for us. The first, of course, is: of what exactly was Pollard guilty (as opposed to *found* guilty)? The answer to that simple question, as so often in such matters, may not be so simply answered in the absolute sense. Nobody disagrees that Pollard, a six-year-long U.S. Naval Intelligence researcher and analyst, passed classified military defense information on to Israel. The question that I would like to address is both why he did this—in the double sense of what he would gain and what the Israelis would gain by this transfer—and what damage his actions did to the United States, in terms of security or in terms of image in the world or in any other terms.

Specifically, the materials apparently passed on to the Israelis pertained to the development of Syrian and Iraqi chemical, biological and nuclear weapon build-ups, as well as the missile development and deployment programs of these two states. It might be noted that the United States and Israel—staunch allies—had a full exchange-of-information agreement in place at that time;[515] that the United States could be understood to have been in contravention of that agreement by withholding the sort of information that Pollard passed on to the Israelis—U.S. Naval Intelligence was selectively deciding when to ignore and when to adhere to the agreement.

It turns out that not too many years after this Saddam Hussein used gas and other chemical and biological weaponry in his suppression of the Kurds; that, shortly thereafter, the United States attacked Iraq, at which time, as the Israelis stood militarily aside, a number of scuds were fired from Iraq into Israel, for which the Israeli response was for its inhabitants to take refuge in "safe" rooms, using gas masks that had been distributed earlier on, in large part arguably due to the information received from Pollard[516]—although there is little likelihood that Pollard could have anticipated any of this when he was passing along his information to the Israelis, so it would not be fair to exonerate him because of a fortuitous by-product of his actions.

In a letter from Pollard to a rabbi who had written to him and asked him why he had committed the espionage for which he had been imprisoned—the letter was written about a year before Saddam marched into Kuwait—the prisoner wrote, in part:

> In retrospect, rabbi, I know that there may have been other ways in which I could have exposed [Secretary of Defense Caspar] Weinberger's treachery. At the time, though, I was so scared of what might happen if the embargoed intelligence did not reach Israel that I threw caution to the wind. But tell me, Rabbi, what would you have done in my situation? Go to the press and run the risk of having sensitive information inadvertently leaked?... Convince yourself that the security of 4 million hard-pressed Jews was worth less than your loyalty to a man pledged to destroy them? The decision I made may have been illegal, but I honestly thought that I was doing something morally right.... So what was I supposed to do? Let Israel fend for itself?... [W]hat would be the difference between what they did and a decision on my part to have kept silent about the Iraqi gas threat to Israel?[517]... Was I really expected to let history repeat itself without doing anything to protect our people from this calamity?... Granted, I broke the law. But, to tell the truth, I'd rather be rotting in prison than sitting *Shiva* [sitting in mourning] for the hundreds of thousands of Israelis who could have died because of my cowardice.[518]

If we take Pollard's words at face value—then at least two issues emerge from his words. The first pertains to his conviction that
the American government—specifically its Defense Secretary—was
in the process of betraying Israel, and that the consequences could
be dire for millions of Jews living there. Given what had happened
18 years earlier on the eve of the Six-Day War and what would happen, scud-wise, a few years after Pollard's capture and trial—and
given Weinberger's larger role in all of this (see below)—Pollard's
convictions, even if misguided, may not be as over the top as some
might assert.

The second issue pertains to his consciousness not only of an
obligation to help fellow Jews, but to the fact that that consciousness is in large part informed by his sense of history: specifically the
history of forty years earlier, when the United States, even as it was
fighting World War II against Germany and the Axis powers, was
little concerned about saving Jews from the fires of the Holocaust—
at which time most American Jews dutifully toed the simple patriotic line of supporting the war effort and did not wish to seem to be
undermining it by pushing for a more aggressive struggle against
the perpetrators of the Holocaust.[519]

The question is whether one *can* take his words at face value.
One might argue that one should, since he was writing privately,
not publicly, toward no apparent purpose than to answer the question, as opposed to writing in order to gain freedom or some other
tangible end. But on the other hand, it is not psychologically uncommon for someone to justify his illegal or immoral actions retroac-
tively, even in private. Primo Levi eloquent addresses this in his last
work, with regard to those who committed ugly acts during the Holocaust and, surviving the experience (perhaps as a consequence of
those acts) develop a narrative of events that reverses their position
from scoundrel to hero—which they themselves end up believing,
more and more firmly with each telling.[520]

Thus Pollard was guilty of passing on classified information
to the Israelis, apparently for fear that, based on the information to
which he was privy, Israel's survival was at risk unless they were
made aware of the facts that he was passing along to them—or

because he had an 007 complex (Ronald Olive's turn of phrase) and a massive ego and was looking for an opportunity, any opportunity, to spy, which opportunity Israel eventually provided (also Olive's assertion). It is not absolutely clear that he was paid for the information, or if so, how much he was paid. The Justice Department would assert that their investigators uncovered evidence that, over the 18 months of his espionage activities he was paid a total of more than $45,000, although little concrete proof of this assertion has found its way into the light of day.[521] U.S officials at the time of Pollard's trial also are reported to have claimed that the documents passed on to the Israelis pertained mainly to the military capabilities of Egypt and Jordan, not the biological, chemical and other warfare capabilities of Syria and Iraq.

So our information on what Pollard was paid, if anything—and even the precise nature of what information he passed along—is not definitive, in part for reasons relevant to the second issue of interest for our narrative: how, once he was apprehended, was he handled and by whom in the legal proceedings—including the pretrial investigation which we have repeatedly seen as important to the conduct of a trial itself?[522] This is the issue wherein facts become even more murky. A day after Pollard's arrest his wife, Anne, was also arrested and charged with being an accessory after the fact to her husband's possession of classified national defense documents. In early 1986 a plea bargain arrangement was proposed by the Department of Justice, to which the Pollards agreed: if he would plead guilty to the charges against him, they promised that he would not receive a life sentence.

His agreement was also motivated by the fact that Anne was being held in prison without access to the medications she required for a serious intestinal disease—she had already lost 50 pounds during three months of incarceration—and the government made it clear that they would not help her out if he did not plead guilty. This sort of prosecutorial tactic is not particularly unusual, of course.

They both pleaded guilty—he to having passed classified information to an ally; she to being an accessory. The grand jury spent several months reviewing the information on the case and, significantly, never brought any charges against Pollard for having harmed the United States, its people or its security; he was never accused of or indicted for treason. He cooperated fully with the authorities in their inquiry and, specifically, its damage assessment.

Part of the reason for the non-definitive nature of the available information regarding Pollard's actions and their consequences as well as that regarding his rewards is that the government asked that Jonathan and Anne not have an open trial, but rather a hearing *in camera* (in secret; literally "in chamber")—promising once again that things would go easier for the pair if they were cooperative.[523] So they agreed to the arrangement—which arrangements is not all that unusual in this sort of case, in order to avoid further damage by making the proceedings public—trusting in the just nature of the American government.

Among the documents from that hearing that are still not available to public scrutiny was a 46-page classified memorandum to the judge from Secretary of Defense Weinberger—the contents of which were apparently not shown to Pollard's attorneys. Then again, there are those who assert that both he and his attorneys saw the memorandum, but not the four-page supplement—handwritten and delivered to the judge one hour before sentencing was scheduled on March 4, 1987—that Weinberger added to it.[524] That memorandum, or perhaps, more specifically, the hand-written supplement, is in any case supposed to have demanded the severest punishment possible "commensurate with the enduring quality of treason"—although Pollard was never (to repeat) accused or convicted of treason.[525]

It seems that Weinberger was particularly wroth with Pollard because his actions upset the image that the Defense Secretary wished to convey within the Middle East, that American policy was even-handed, and that "Israel should not be too strong in relation to her Arab neighbors." At the time, the Israeli government publicly denied that Pollard had spied for them and there remain questions to this day regarding the official versus unofficial position of the Israeli recipients of the information that he provided. Where one report suggests, to repeat, that he provided information regarding Syria and Iraq, and another that the information primarily focused on Egypt and Jordan, yet another suggests that the information covered the entire region, from Morocco to Pakistan, and one Israeli source allegedly reported to *Time* magazine that he "was selling the Israelis everything he could get his hands on. The range was unbelievable—from U.S. Navy cipher keys to breakdowns of the Saudi air force."[526]

Others asserted that he was trying to sell the information to which he had access not only to Israel, but to four other countries besides Israel, including Pakistan. Overall, to read the mainstream media coverage of the case is to gain a fairly dark view of his intentions and actions.[527] The general media, in fact, seemed, at the time, quite eager to follow a lead that would have placed Pollard—in a manner reminiscent of the Rosenberg affair, in its way—at the center of a much larger conspiracy. The Prosecuting Attorney, Joseph DiGenova subsequently noted the pressure that he was under to find evidence of an extensive Israeli spy network in the United States, but all of the polygraph tests and other aspects of the inquiry to which Pollard was subjected instead yielded proof—assuming in any case that such tests are reliable—that no such network exists.

Nonetheless, the same *Time* magazine article that quotes the anonymous Israeli source regarding the nature and direction of the information that Pollard was transmitting also noted that the Justice Department's account of his activities "strongly suggests the existence of a broader operation." Such innuendo without substantiation would reach hundreds of thousands, if not millions of American eyes and minds in short order. Clearly there were those in and beyond the Reagan administration for whom, for whatever reasons, the darker the sense of the extended context of Pollard's activities, the better.[528] On the other hand, it should be noted—and this is very relevant to our overall narrative—that the darkness of the Pollard Affair seemed (and seems) in the long run to have cast only a minimal shadow on the general view by non-Jewish America either of their Jewish fellow-Americans, or on the shape of American-Israeli relations.

Weinberger's memorandum is widely cited as a major reason why the sentencing judge, Aubrey Robinson, ultimately condemned Pollard to life in prison without parole—in what appears to be a direct contradiction of the attitude and promises of the Department of Justice all along. Interestingly, no fine was imposed on him. Pollard was immediately transferred to a prison hospital in Springfield, MO, where he was incarcerated in a ward for the criminally insane.[529]

Congressman Lee Hamilton was able finally to effect Pollard's removal from that ward—ten and a half months later—and he was subsequently confined to a sealed room for the six months that followed. Among other noteworthy data in this narrative is the letter written to Hamilton by the Director of the Bureau of Prisons, Michael Quinlan, stating that Pollard required no treatment as a patient that would justify his placement in the criminally insane ward, much less a sealed room—and that Pollard was the single prisoner in the United States being treated in such an inappropriate manner. Following his half-year in the room, he was once again transferred—to the U.S. Penitentiary in Marion, Illinois, the most severe, highest security prison in the United States at that time. After a lockdown in 1983, there were claims that the prison violated International Human Rights standards.

Pollard was kept in a basement room in solitary confinement at the Marion Penitentiary for 23 hours a day (he was permitted an hour per day of exercise in an adjoining room), where the temperature often reached 107 degrees in the summertime. In the midst of that period—on September 10, 1991—his case was appealed before the Appellate court in Washington, DC. Pollard's lead attorney at that time, Theodore Olson argued that he should be permitted to change his plea to "not guilty," since the government had reneged on its plea-bargain agreement with him: rather than treating him leniently in exchange for his full cooperation, it had pushed to ensure that he "would never again see the light of day." Indeed, rather than commending him for his cooperation, U.S. attorneys had denigrated the value of his help—although admitting that they gained information from him and from his wife that they were then able to turn against them.

Olson argued that the use of the word "treason" by Weinberger in his memo was designed to exacerbate Pollard's position in the eyes of the District Court, which tactic he labeled as "an outrageous abuse of power." The Appellate Court agreed with this and other Olson assertions—but returned its verdict on March 21 with a vote of 2-1 against permitting Pollard to retract his guilty plea so that his case could be reconsidered. Interestingly, those who voted against him were Ruth Bader Ginsberg and Lawrence Silberman—both Jewish—and the dissenting vote was cast by Steven Williams, who is not Jewish. One might speculate that their respective ethno-religious identities affected their views of the case, but that would be no more than speculation, perhaps worth considering given the larger context of this narrative, but leading to no definitive conclusion.

The two majority judges asserted that his case had merit but offered their negative ruling based on two technicalities: that they did not wish to offer an opinion on the validity of the life sentence that Judge Robinson had decreed for Pollard, and that the case should have been brought before the Appellate Court earlier. While it is certainly not unusual for one judge to refrain from commenting on the decision of a second judge, it strikes me as odd that such professional courtesy—and a technicality—would prevail in a case involving the entire life of an individual, particularly when the shifting of a case from a lower court to an upper court is designed to promote that sort of review. Judge Williams' dissenting opinion recalls that expressed regarding the Rosenberg proceedings by U.S. Supreme Court Justice William O. Douglass, that a fundamental miscarriage of justice had occurred (or that the possibility of a miscarriage, in their case, at least merited a delay in the process of sending them to death).

In Pollard's case, the Supreme Court refused to hear an appeal when it convened next in October, 1992. He remained in the Marion Penitentiary in the basement solitary confinement chamber for seven years. He was then transferred to the Butner Federal Correctional Facility in North Carolina, where he continues to serve his life sentence. Aside from the more than occasional agitation on his behalf on the part of the committee organized to push for a commutation of his life sentence—based on the conviction that the crime does not justify the harshness of the punishment, and that the government reneged on its agreement with him when he agreed to cooperate—there have been periodic attempts to extract Executive Clemency from Presidents Clinton, Bush (*fils*) and, more recently, Obama, that have all come up against strong opposition from the Defense Department, CIA and ultimately the majority of all three presidents' advisers, and thus failed.

This fact and the series of data regarding Pollard's prison experience leads directly to the third issue of particular interest where this book and its foci are concerned, which is how both the deed and its punitive consequences compare with other, analogous deeds and punitive consequences in the history of the United States, especially in the late twentieth and early twenty-first centuries. One might begin with Caspar Weinberger himself, who contrary to the clear mandate of the Reagan government for which he was serving as Secretary of Defense, participated in the process of transferring United States TOW antitank missiles and other armaments to Iran during the notorious Iran-Contra Affair—and as the disclosure of that affair grew, was ultimately forced to resign his post on November 23, 1987. Weinberger was indicted following his resignation by Independent Counsel Lawrence E. Walsh—but he received a presidential pardon from outgoing President George H.W. Bush on December 24, 1992.[530] Not exactly the mirror of Pollard's fate.

The Iran-Contra Affair, one may recall, blew up in the Reagan administration's face in 1986. It revolved, in a nutshell, around more than merely the illegal sales of arms to the Iranians—using Israel as a go-between—at a time when the President and Congress had asserted that the U.S. could and would have no relations with Iran. The affair remains covered in secrecy, and administration officials destroyed huge volumes of documents and/or withheld them from investigators at the time the scandal came to light. But a sufficient sense of its weight may be readily assessed even from the limited information that is available. When the arms sales were revealed, President Reagan appeared on national television (on November 6, 1986) to deny that they had occurred; a week later he re-appeared in the media asserting that the sales had occurred but not as part of a hostage-exchange plan; three months later, on March 4, 1987, he addressed the nation to take full responsibility for "what began as a strategic opening to Iran [that] deteriorated, in its implementation, into trading arms for hostages."

The hostages in question were seven Americans who were part of a larger group of 30 Westerners taken captive in Lebanon by Iran-backed Hizb'allah in 1983. The arms shipments were varied and extensive, and took place in 8 stages between August 20, 1984 and October 28, 1986. But even in admitting to the alleged strategy of arms for hostages—which, incidentally, failed in any case; only one American hostage was actually released during that period— Reagan was either lying or had been lied to by his own staff. For the real purpose for selling arms to Iran as it was engaged in a lengthy war with Iraq was to provide funds to the anti-Sandinista rebels— the Contras—in Nicaragua. Both the sale of arms and the funding of the Contras not only circumvented and contradicted administration policy, but went specifically against the congressional legislation known as the Boland Amendment, so its perpetrators were breaking several laws at once.[531]

One might argue that—given the layers of complication pertaining to the relationship of Iran to both Israel and the United States and between the United States and Nicaragua—the Iran-Contra Affair had a far more nefarious series of ramifications for the United States' position in the world and for Americans both within and outside the country than whatever it is that Jonathan Pollard did.[532] One might also disagree with that assessment. But in any case, none of the Iran-Contra Affair's principal movers and shakers was punished in any way resembling the punishment meted out to Pollard for his actions.

Weinberger, to repeat, received a presidential pardon, (an executive act that, requested several times for Pollard from various directions, has to date not come close to happening, through a succession of administrations—for precisely what reasons we cannot know without the revelation of more information than we currently possess). The Affair's primary architect, Oliver North, who lied before Congress and later admitted to having done so, asserting that he regarded the Contras as "freedom fighters" and therefore that whatever he could do to assist them was morally even if not legally justified—and who earlier had been involved in the importing of drugs into the United States (marijuana and cocaine) from South and Central America to help fund the Contras—*was* brought to trial in the wake of the Affair.

His verdict of guilty yielded a three-year suspended sentence, a $150,000 fine and 1,200 hours of community service—all of which elements of his sentencing were then subsequently vacated in 1990, with the help of the ACLU, on a technicality. North would go on to write best-selling books regarding his experiences and earn large sums of money as a lecturer—and run, albeit without winning, for the U.S. Senate from the State of Virginia in the mid-1990s.

There are other cases, more precisely comparable to that of Jonathan Pollard, because they involve spying and the transmission of information, that bear noting. Thus John Walker, to whom I earlier referred in the context of distinguishing espionage from treason,[533] was the center of a spy ring the principal other members of which were his son, Michael, his brother, Arthur, and his former student, colleague, and friend, Jerry Alfred Whitworth. They were all present or former Navy men arrested in May, 1985 and accused of having supplied military secrets to the Soviet Union—for more than seventeen years. The case was referred to by then-Admiral Elmo Zumwalt, Jr., former Chief of Naval Operations, as "a breach of security as serious as any I can recall."

John was arrested some months after his estranged wife, Barbara, had pointed the FBI in his direction.[534] FBI agents followed him and listened in on his conversations for several weeks, nabbing him on May 18, after he made a drop in rural Maryland. The drop included some 129 documents that had been supplied by his son, Michael—who was arrested shortly thereafter while working as an operations clerk on board the U.S. aircraft carrier *Nimitz*, which at the time was off the coast of Haifa, Israel. At that time, he seems to have become the primary supplier of most of the information that his father transmitted to the Soviets.

Earlier, John had served on two nuclear-missile-carrying submarines from 1962 to 1967, after which he was posted to Norfolk, Virginia, where he was privy to communications codes for the entire U.S. Atlantic submarine fleet and quite able to procure the information himself. Soon after retiring from the Navy he recruited his son as well as his brother, Arthur, who was still in the Navy, in order to be able to continue his work. Arthur was arrested in Virginia Beach at around the same time that Michael was being arrested on the *Nimitz*.

Over the years John Walker and his associates were paid somewhere between several hundred thousand and several million dollars for the information that they supplied—through the heart of the Cold War—to the Soviets. His former wife, Barbara, was not prosecuted in exchange for her help, although she had allegedly known about John's activities—and may have occasionally helped him out—for some fifteen years before she finally went to the FBI in November 1984. Her decision to turn her former husband in was apparently in large part because of his consistent failure to pay alimony while living in a luxurious lifestyle that (as she well knew) was derived from the proceeds of his spy-work. By then John had not only recruited his son as well as his brother. He had also tried to recruit his daughter, Laura, also a communications expert—but in the Army, not the Navy—earlier, as far back as 1979. She refused, indeed helping to implicate her father with her mother's encouragement.

The key other figure in this group, Jerry Whitworth—arrested in California shortly after the Walker arrests were made—had served as communications watch officer aboard the nuclear-powered aircraft carrier *Enterprise* and had been in charge of communications security at the Alameda, California Naval Air Station. He had also served, twice, in a top-secret location in the Indian Ocean, giving him an intimate knowledge of U.S Naval movements and capabilities throughout the Pacific and Indian Ocean expanses. Like Walker, he had worked as a cryptographer on ships engaged in spotting Soviet subs. The two first met at the Navy Communications School in San Diego in the early 1970s and became fast friends. By

1975 Whitworth was answering to Walker as his spymaster boss—and, ironically enough for him, had written to Walker not too long before the arrests that he was unhappy and ready to quit dealing in government secrets.

The upshot of the somewhat longer than one year of legal procceedings, which included a plea bargain from John Walker in which he agreed to give testimony against Whitworth in exchange for a lesser sentence for his son—is that Whitworth was sentenced to 365 years of prison—eligible for parole in 2046, after 60 years; John Walker was sentenced to a life term, eligible for parole in ten years; his brother Arthur was sentenced to three life terms, but also eligible for parole in ten years; and Michael was sentenced to 25 years, but was eligble for parole in 8 years and four months. The greater severity of Whitworth's sentence was based on the allegation that he was "the principal agent of collection" for the secrets relayed to the KGB.[535] Michael's lighter sentence was based on the plea bargain of his father, his cooperation after his arrest, and the assertion that his work had been less damaging to the country than that of the others—although when he was arrested, he had 15 further pounds of documents hidden around his bunk awaiting transmission, which gives some sense of the enormous volume of information that he was engaged in transmitting.

To this day it is not fully clear precisely what and exactly how much material was passed to the Soviets, beyond what was picked up at the time of the arrests, although at the time Secretary of Defense Weinberger noted that the Navy sustained "very serious losses that went on over a long period of time." It was a matter, over seventeen years, of thousands and thousands of documents—of over 200,000 encrypted messages—and the Pentagon subsequently spent close to a billion dollars to replace code machines and to make other alterations in military hardware as a consequence of the secrets disclosed to the Soviets by Walker's spy ring.

John and Arthur Walker (and Jerry Whitworth) all remain in prison to this day; they have not received the parole to which the Walkers already, in theory, have been eligible. At least in John's case, perhaps this is related to the fact that he has not evinced any regret for his actions—his best childhood friend described him as "intrinsically evil"—exulting, rather, it would seem, in the infamy he gained, and asserting that, in any case, the Cold War was "all a game... How much damage did John Walker do? None. Absolutely none. The Russians never invaded." He at one point asserted that the data that he initially sold to the Soviets was already compromised by the U.S.S. *Pueblo* incident (in which a Navy communications surveillance ship was captured by North Korea and its crew held for nearly a year).[536]

Yet a 2001 study at the U.S. Army Command and General Staff College—based on information from Soviet archives and other sources—suggests that the Pueblo incident may have happened because the Soviets were eager to study equipment described in Walker-supplied documents. Various intelligence experts have argued that the information supplied by him was sufficient to "alter significantly the balance of power between Russia and the United States." In Moscow, Walker was celebrated by KGB officer Vitaly Yurchenko as "the greatest case in KGB history. We deciphered millions of your messages. If there had been a war, we would have won it." Similarly, Walker's KGB supervisor referred to him as the "most important" spy ever recruited by the Soviets, who gave "us the equivalent of a seat inside your Pentagon where we could read your most vital secrets."

The losses by all estimates yielded the USSR enormous military advantages at a time when the United States and the Soviet Union were in what amounted to a constant state of nuclear facedown. Most disheartening, the motive for the treason committed by Whitworth and the Walkers was purely material: the money they earned for their efforts yielded the possibility of a fast-lane life style that was otherwise beyond their reach. Perhaps the exception to this is Michael, who asserted that he did it both "for money and to please my father."

But the point is, they were not motivated by any ideological thought such as defined the presumed espionage efforts of the Rosenbergs and those of Jonathan Pollard—and were engaged with an enemy, not with a former or current ally as was the situation with these two cases. I earlier noted that Walker's sentence, so much more lenient than that handed down to the Rosenbergs and even to Morton Sobell, (who was sent directly to Alcatraz for 30 years but became eligible for parole only after 18 years), might perhaps be understandable as a function of coming at a different time in history, and perhaps under different conditions. (Was the fear of the USSR greater during the Rosenberg era than during the Walker era? Would that difference have affected the perception of how deleterious the Rosenbergs' actions were, as opposed to those by the Walker ring?) But one cannot offer that justification in comparing his fate to that of Jonathan Pollard. How did Pollard's actions and punishment compare to those of the Walkers?

Moreover, Michael Walker was paroled, after serving 15 years of his 25-year sentence, in 2000. Pollard was imprisoned at virtually the same time as Michael was—under more egregious conditions of incarceration—and continues to serve his life sentence. Whereas Michael was part of a 17-year-long espionage effort that transmitted uncountable piles of information to an enemy, Pollard had transmitted a limited volume of material to an ally which information, according to a 1983 agreement with that ally, should arguably have been transmitted to it in the first place—although if Ronald Olive's book is accurate, the volume of material was more extensive than I am supposing.

Where Michael's efforts had serious ramifications for the security of the United States—and cost the American taxpayer a billion dollars to repair—Pollard's efforts had no ramifications for American security (at least as far as we know). Where Michael committed treason for money (and to please his father), Pollard committed an act that was not labeled as treason by those prosecuting him, for an ideology that only diverged from American ideology to the extent that the latter apparently functioned dishonestly with regard to an ally.

In the internet reprinting of the Associated Press article of February 17, 2000 reporting on Michael Walker's release from prison—obviously without prompting from the words I am writing—the commentator identified as "Justice4JP" observes, in his/her blog entitled "What's Wrong with this Picture?" that, among other things, "there is not a shred of evidence of any damage done by Pollard to US national security... The damage done by Walker, however, was vast, observably blatant and supported by an abundance of evidence."

More to the point, "Justice4JP" notes that "in the Walker case the Government honored the plea agreement it made with John Walker and did not oppose Michael's early release.[537] In the Pollard case, the Government violated the plea agreement it signed and continues to oppose Pollard's release from prison at any time. CIA [then-]Chief George Tenet and his agency had not said a word to protest the early release of Walker, in spite of the enormity of the crime he committed, and the vastness of the damage done. Congress as well has had no comment about Walker's early release. This is not the case with Pollard. Every time it looks like Pollard might go free—after serving just as long as Walker—there is a huge outcry by these Government agencies..."[538]

The blog has the tone of Zola's "*J'accuse*" of more than a century ago in the France of the Dreyfus affair—and saves me the trouble of having to articulate the question that "Justice4JP" raises for the reader of this narrative. While it is true that an anonymous blogger can ask questions and raise issues without identifying his/her sources, the comments, statements and questions have not been contradicted by any sources currently available to us—including Ron Olive's book. Thus one might legitimately ask: is there a "Jewish" connection between the obsession (and it certainly seems to be an obsession) with keeping Pollard so impenetrably behind bars and the insistence that the Rosenbergs be executed without awaiting further discussion of the nature of how they were tried? Is there a parallel between the limited willingness at the time of their impending deaths to discuss their crime and its consequences for the United States further—at a time, in their case, that was marked by anti-Communist hysteria—and the unwillingness for government representatives to discuss Pollard leniency possibilities?

Do the two legal cases reach deep into the secular (or not so secular) Christian souls of those government notables who maintain that obsession and maintained that insistence; also affecting the Jewish souls of those Jewish notables involved in both cases—which might be traceable all the way back to the Gospel of John and its indictment (at least in the post-Hebrew, post-Greek, post-Aramaic, post-Latin translation) of the "Jews"?

Would such a statement be either too extreme—stepping out onto a psychoanalytical limb with regard to those government notables, or unfair in terms of the larger picture of recent American espionage history?[539] Were American Jews and U.S.-Israeli relations, in the end, largely unaffected by the Pollard case? Would that negate this hypothesis? Just as the Walker case was surfacing, another espionage case was ending, that of former Northrup engineer Thomas Cavanagh. Cavanagh was sentenced on May 23, 1985 to life in prison for attempting to sell "stealth" aircraft technology to FBI agents posing as Soviet embassy officials, in order to make himself rich. It's not clear when and if he can be up for parole.[540] And it is also true that in the wake of the Walker-Whitworth affair—and the aftermath of 38 American espionage charges and 21 convictions between 1975 and the apprehension of the Walkers in June, 1985—the Senate brought to a culmination a decision to clamp down on spies more vigorously. The proposed bill would have mandated execution or life imprisonment without parole for anyone convicted of espionage on behalf of a Communist country.

But that has certainly not happened. On the contrary, even someone such as John Walker Lindh, a Maryland-born, California-raised former Roman Catholic who converted to Islam and eventually became a soldier for the Taliban with which, among other anti-American terrorist activities, the events of September 11, 2001 are associated—and who was charged with conspiring to kill Americans and support terrorists (but pleaded guilty to lesser offenses, such as carrying weapons against U.S. forces)—is only serving a twenty-year sentence.[541] And in early 2007 his father and lawyer asked President Bush to commute his term, arguing in large part that the sentence is unfair in comparison to that meted out to Australian David Hicks by his government, for the same crimes. Hicks was asked to serve less than a year in prison for aiding terrorism. The President did not comply with the Lindh defense team request.

Yet another and very interesting case with "parallels" to that of Pollard—more relevant to the matter of parole than to the specifics of guilt—came to my attention between the writing of this manuscript, including the previous paragraph, and the present time, as I review it for publication. A front-page *New York Times* article from Friday, January 20, 2009[542] notes that convicted and jailed CIA Mole, Harold Nicholson (whose original case I have not discussed),[543] who, since 1997 "has been locked in a federal prison in Oregon, the highest-ranking officer of the Central Intelligence Agency ever convicted of espionage," has been accused of continuing to "sell more secrets to the Russians over the past three years," by working through his 24-year-old son, Nathan, "using jailhouse visits, coded letters and clandestine overseas meetings" to do so.

The elder Nicholson apparently began training his son in spycraft from his jail cell in 2006 and provided him with the necessary contacts to meet with Russian handlers in Mexico, Peru and Cyprus. The elder Nicholson—who had received some $300,000 for his efforts by the time of his arrest—was given a 23-year sentence in federal prison. He asked to be imprisoned near his three children, who were sent at that time to live in Eugene, Oregon with their grandparents. So he was placed in a medium-security facility in Sheridan, Oregon. It's not clear, particularly based on this new turn of events, how his sentence might be affected, or what the legal consequences for his son will be. But it does seem odd that Pollard's incarceration remains so airtight parole-wise when Nicholson's, for a more egregious act of spying in all respects, has been so filled with air holes; when the one exhibits recognition of having committed a crime, and, if not remorse then acknowledgment of having committed a crime, even if it was due to the conviction that the cause he had served was that of millions of lives as opposed to his own profit-margin; and the other has schemed to continue his treasonous activity for no other end than his family's profit-margin.

Unless, of course, my assumptions regarding Pollard in this

last regard are wrong. They are based on information, including the above-quoted letter to his rabbi, which was available through 2006. In fairness to this discussion, along comes the already-mentioned book that year, *Capturing Jonathan Pollard*, written by Ronald Olive, a retired Naval Investigative Service counter-espionage officer, who was intimately involved in the investigation that brought Pollard to court and prison.[544] Olive asserts in his preface that the volume of what Pollard transmitted—over a million pages of classified material, according to Olive's estimation—dwarfs any previous or subsequent American spy effort, and that "what the public doesn't realize is that Pollard was a master of deceit and manipulation who repeatedly beat the system. Nor does the public realize the extent of the damage he inflicted."[545] He goes on to claim, in the words of a 2009 interview with *The Investigator*, that Pollard "still clings to a delusion that he was merely assisting an ally who had the right to U.S. defense secrets. He uses this rationalization to mask a sociopathic mind and 007 complex..."[546]

All of this may be true. Very few individuals would be in a position to make these judgments—in large part because, as Olive readily reminds us, the case was tried in secret—or technically, never went to trial—and so much of the information surrounding it remains classified as of this writing. This, of course, is also the problem with Olive's book as well as the interview. His goal "in the following pages is to set the record straight,"[547] and he asserts both his desire to be objective and the lack of animosity he feels for Pollard, who, as he puts it, "lost his way because of a misguided notion that it was okay to sell his nation's secrets."[548] But if so much remains classified, in spite of the list of sources he uses, how is he able to arrive at a definitive conclusion, and how, given the classified nature of so much of the story, can he give us an unequivocally "objective" analysis—particularly given that he was so subjectively involved in the case?

Should the fact that the government gave him the green light to publish his book, as he also points out in his preface, make the reader more or less confident that he has published the objective truth, as opposed, say, to a version of the truth that, his assertions notwithstanding, will further demonize Pollard and undermine his efforts to gain parole? I don't know, but I confess that his emphasis on Pollard's "exercise [of] his 007 complex and fuel[ing of] his mammoth ego"[549] feels less than calm, cool and objective.

I also confess to feeling some discomfort at all the psychological and other details about Pollard's growing up that, as with all of the information provided by Olive, is unfootnoted. Anyone can say anything about anyone if that person is not in a position to defend himself. We might recall how the Spanish Inquisition operated, or the French military tribunal in the Dreyfus trial—and particularly the manner in which Henry operated, among other ways, in reporting Dreyfus' "confession" to him. Every word of Olive's text might be true, but I'd be happier knowing what his sources for such omniscience regarding his subject are. [550]

This should not be construed as a plea on my part for Pollard—either for his innocence or for embracing the circumstances in which he spied—but to underscore my lack of certainty regarding Olive's objectivity. I must add another source of discomfort at the startling image Olive chose to use in closing his tenth chapter: "For the incredible volume and quality of intelligence Pollard was feeding them [the Israelis], the money he received amounted to nothing more than thirty pieces of silver."[551] It is a nifty image, but, given the context—Pollard the Jew accused of betraying the United States on behalf of the Jewish state—and particularly given the starting point of this narrative, it is hard for me to turn away from the image of 30 pieces of silver as the price for betrayal without certain doubts as to the purity of Olive's intentions, even, to repeat, as he specifically articulates them back in his preface as not to "demonize Israel and its intelligence agents"[552] nor with a grudge against Pollard, but simply to fire a warning shot over the bow of the American intelligence community for its laxness. If I were to uncritically embrace the entirety of the content of Olive's book, I would still be disturbed at his choice of a nuance that seems to me resonates with particular themes that have haunted Christian-Jewish relations for nearly two millennia.

And the question remains: is the story of Jonathan Pollard the account of a "Jewish trial" in the sense that he was handled differently from how he might have been had he not been Jewish—and had the State of Israel, albeit a staunch American ally, not been "The Jewish State"? One cannot answer this question with any absolute conviction, but it would be as unreasonable to simply brush it aside as it might be to embrace it unquestioningly as valid. Interestingly, Pollard's rabbi, Avi Weiss, in an article that appeared in *Viewpoint* magazine all the way back in spring, 1993[553] likens Pollard's incarceration to that of Natan Sharansky in the former Soviet Union. He acknowledges the illegality of Pollard's action, but observes that he "is serving well beyond the time served by others who have committed comparable offenses, [and] remains incarcerated because of improprieties, prejudice, downright anti-Israelism and elements of anti-Semitism that still exist in the U.S. Departments of Defense and Justice," so that now he has become, as Sharansky was, a political prisoner—a "Prisoner of Zion."

We can agree and also surely disagree with this sort of formulation: it certainly seems specious to compare Sharansky's struggle against the Soviet state, the context of which offers fairly clear anti-Semitic implications, with Pollard's struggle for a shortened sentence from a state with a considerably more benign track record regarding Jews—and Israel—even taking into account individuals like Herbert Brownell who have darkened that picture somewhat from time to time.

One might certainly write off Weiss as too subjective. I would, particularly in the light of even a part of Ronald Olive's book. But others have also made the same sort of comparison. And those calling for Pollard's release by the time of that speech and article included 570 rabbis representing the spectrum of the American Jewish community who were all signatories to an open letter in *The New York Times* to Former President Bush (the elder) expressing similar thoughts—albeit in a less strident manner—and an *amici* list of 160 prominent Jewish and non-Jewish organizations in the United States, Europe and Israel. So, for what it is worth, Weiss is not alone in his viewpoint. Conversely, earlier, soon after the Pollard affair—and the concurrent Iran-Contra affair—hit the media, Israeli academic and former Director General of Israel's Foreign Minstry Shlomo Avineri, in commenting on the distancing from Pollard that he perceived on the part of much of the American Jewish community, offered the sort of self-reflective Jewish "*J'accuse*" that has been discussed in the context of the Rosenberg affair.[554]

Avineri referred, in a *Jerusalem Post* commentary, to "a degree of nervousness, insecurity and even cringing on the part of the American Jewish community... You would expect that in a free and open society no guilt by association should be presumed, that nobody except Pollard himself should be held responsible for his deeds. Instead, we see some senior American Jewish leaders falling over each other in condemning Pollard and distancing themselves—and the Jewish community—from him."

Avineri continues: "Why must American Jews as Jews feel the need to distance themselves from Pollard?... I do not know Colonel North's religious affiliation—but have any of his co-religionists distanced themselves from him? And did any WASP have to distance himself from Alger Hiss's perjury and presumed spying for the Soviet Union?"[555] The same rhetorical sort of question might be raised of the co-religionists of the Walkers and the Lindhs, might it not? And thus the question is: why and whence that "nervousness, insecurity and even cringing," if Avineri was correct in his claim of perceiving it? I am not sure that Avineri is correct: it would seem that the opposite is at least partially true—that many more Jewish American leaders—I earlier mentioned B'nai B'rith's Seymour Reich (above, n 539)—took up and continue to take up Pollard's case. [556]

Or to turn the question back in the other direction: did Pollard and did the Rosenbergs receive unique treatment at the hands of American justice, and if so, why? Is the answer to be found in a story that wends its way through Massena, NY to Atlanta, Georgia and thence to St. Petersburg and Paris and Tiszaeszlar and from there to Barcelona and Norwich and all the way back to the Jerusalem of nearly two millennia ago—a story that still has not come to an end?

One cannot but wonder and perhaps one may find a disheartening kind of validation of such an unhappy viewpoint in reports,

such as that in the February 23, 1990 *Cleveland Jewish News* that Canadian anti-abortionists, at that time, were shaping a new form of
blood libel—asserting that specifically Jewish physicians were plot-
ting to kill Christian babies through abortions.[557] Or in the publication by a church in Tuscany, Italy, in 1989 of a book promoting the
blood libel.[558] Or in an Op Ed piece in *The New York Times* of Friday,
April, 1985, by Harvey Cox, one of the most important of American
Secular Christian theologians—a renowned Harvard professor. In
his pre-Easter article, intended to undercut centuries of Christian
hostility toward Jews that have a natural bubbling up point at that
season, he carries us full circle back to where this book's primary
narrative began: the trial and death of Jesus. (I briefly commented
on it above, at the end of Chapter Two.)[559]

Cox's reconstruction of events, based on "piecing together the
sometimes contradictory evidence of the Gospels with more recent
knowledge about Roman-occupied Palestine still leaves questions
unanswered, but it completely discredits the stubborn myth that
the Jews crucified Jesus for claiming that he was the Messiah. What
emerges is a story of intrigue, power-mongering and buck-passing
that might have happened anywhere and still goes on today." Fine.
But as Cox's brief narrative moves forward to "Pilate and the Sanhedrin watch[ing] uneasily as thousands of unruly Jews streamed into
Jerusalem for Passover, [and] one fervid ultra-nationalist, Barabbas,
[was] already behind bars, but the festive crowd demanded that
he be the prisoner traditionally amnestied on the holiday" we hear
echoes of historically questionable assumptions regarding events
that have echoed down the centuries unchanged.[560]

Barabbas is referred to as if his existence is an incontrovertible fact. The "traditional amnesty" is referred to as if it is an incontrovertible fact. To what festive crowd does Cox refer? By obvious
implication, the Jews—not, by the way, the Judaeans. And what do
they do? We shall see. Cox continues: "to make matters worse, a
young rabbi from the north who had won support from the poorest,
most unstable elements by announcing the dawning of the kingdom of God was among the pilgrims. There could be problems."
Moreover, [Jesus—that young rabbi] "arrived riding an ass while

his followers hailed him as 'Son of David'—a title with clear monarchical overtones."

So what did they—"some of the most jittery members of the Sanhedrin"—do, lest the disturbances being engendered by Jesus rile the Romans up?

> They moved quickly. Without the consent—possibly even the knowledge—of the rest of the Council, they had Jesus seized at night, to avoid popular opposition, and interrogated, in clear defiance of established Jewish legal procedure.... [and] when no witnesses could be found to make a blasphemy charge stick, his accusers decided to get Pilate to execute him for subversion.[561] Aroused from his bed, Pilate at first refused to condemn Jesus... [H]e adroitly tried to palm the case off on [Herod, but] in the end he would not take Jesus off Pilate's hands.
>
> Exasperated, Pilate told Jesus' accusers he could find no cause for capital punishment, and suggested that he be flogged and released. Here the trial might have ended, but Jesus' antagonists, now joined by a crowd recruited from Temple merchants and employees who had reason to oppose Jesus, told Pilate: This man claims he is a king. We have no king but Caesar. If you let this man go, you are no friend of Caesar's. Free Barabbas... Pilate complied. The life of one more Jew seemed a small price to pay for a little stability.

So only some members of the Sanhedrin acted illegally, even if it is acknowledged that they abrogated Judaean law. And then—still, the same canard is repeated, for the umpteenth time in nineteen centuries—the Jewish rabble demanded what Pilate reluctantly agreed to give to them: the blood of Jesus. And the Romans still come off as pretty innocent in the affair.

In short, Cox's narrative has returned us full circle to the beginning of this history and the problematic both of the account of what happened to Jesus and the consequences for subsequent history and in particular the history of Christian-Jewish relations as they have been affected by Christian beliefs regarding that account. And as much as he may conclude that "[Jesus'] death tells us nothing in particular about Jews or Romans," it takes very little subtlety to see that that is not correct. The villains in the tale remain the Jews; the narrative repeats the centuries-long exoneration of the Romans and guilt sentence on the Jews for Jesus' death. This is clear even if the narrative acknowledges Jesus as a Jew, and explains that his crucifixion was a function of the charge of political subversion against Rome—rather than his having been stoned by the Judaeans or Jews as a blasphemer against the Judaean God. Cox's version—to repeat my comment at the end of Chapter Two—tastes of very old wine in a recycled goblet.

If Cox is writing as a philo-semite, as an educated and scholarly student of religion and religious history, and serves up this goblet as a peace-offering—at the very season of Passover and Easter—what may we expect of those less benignly inclined and/or less scholarly than he? To paraphrase Jesus' words quoted in Luke 23:31, as he was led to Calvary: if these things are written when the wood is green, what will be written when it is dry? And what then, of the perspective that has been voiced regarding Pollard—and the Rosenbergs? Can we conclude that their treatment was different because they—and in the Rosenbergs' case, so many of the principals involved in the proceedings—were Jewish and the powers that be were Christian? That they were, indeed, less theologically astute, less historiographically reflective and less benignly inclined than the likes of Harvey Cox? What of the notion that Israel was on trial in Jerusalem as much as or more than Eichmann and Demjanjuk—and remains on trial every time a legal issue involving Israel or Israelis and Palestine or Palestinians comes into the media-and-world-opinion courtroom?

There are—by way of pushing this conclusion—two further twists that connect the larger question of Israeli-American relations and "Jews on trial" to the Pollard issue. They are separate— one more media-related, the other government-related. While these should not be confused, they may be seen as connected by the general discussion of Jews on trial. One is the periodic but ongoing media coverage of theories of a network of spies for Israel that began with the revelation of a Defense Department security office memo warning of Israeli spying, which revelation drew the ire of the Anti-Defamation League of B'nai B'rith.[562] The Defense Department memo accused the Israeli government of trying to steal U.S. military and intelligence secrets by using its "strong ethnic ties" to the U.S. in order to recruit spies—although the warning was withdrawn after senior officials determined that the memo had improperly singled out Jewish "ethnicity" as a specific counter-intelligence concern.

But that's the point: it doesn't take much to understand the meaning of "strong ethnic ties"—Jewish Americans—or to wonder whether such a group was being singled out, even if the singling out process was subsequently officially discontinued. Similarly, we may recall, in the Rosenberg affair, Jewish Americans were singled out—at that time by a State Department memo suggesting that they were particularly to be associated with the Communist threat. On any number of more general occasions, American Jews have found themselves suspected of dual loyalties, or of preferring loyalty to Israel over that to the United States in a manner almost no other ethnic or religious group has found itself accused of in American history (witness the non-prejudicial attitude toward German Americans before and during World War II).[563]

The second twist, a rather ironic one, is that, in the wake of the secret conviction of an Israeli army major for espionage for the United States, it was revealed—in 1993, a decade after the Reagan administration had vigorously denied it—that the United States had been in fact using that spy, Yosef Amit, in Israel's officer corps in the early 1980s. Indeed, then-Defense Secretary Caspar Weinberger had publicly chastised Senator Dave Durenberger (R-Minnesota) in 1987—in the midst of the Pollard affair—for having suggested that the American government had "changed the rules of the game" by spying on Israel. Durenberger, shortly after stepping down as chairman of the Senate Select Committee on Intelligence, had referred at a fund-raising event in Palm Beach, Florida, to the fact that former CIA director William J. Casey had used an Israeli military spy after Israel's invasion of Lebanon in 1982.

Durenberger's comments in fact emerged in the context of the Pollard prosecution—and one cannot help (or at least I cannot help) wondering whether the attempts to expand the perceived scope of Pollard's actions and also to see them as the center of a larger phenomenon of spying on behalf of Israel were not a smoke screen to draw any potential interest away from the activities of our own government vis-à-vis one of our closest allies. It is of note that immediately after Pollard's arrest and four months before Amit's arrest, then-Prime Minister Yitzhak Rabin noted that Israel had quietly—to avoid embarrassing their ally—expelled five Americans caught spying back in the 1970s and early 1980s. It is also of note that Amit was sentenced to 12 years in prison—obviously considerably less than the sentence meted out to Pollard. Indeed, the revelations of 1993 spurred forces working on Pollard's behalf to suggest that both he and Amit be released as a mutual goodwill gesture by the two allied nations, but that plan went nowhere.[564]

Pollard remains behind bars, with no likelihood, as of this writing, that his situation will change, although his sentencing guidelines should in theory cause his release by the year 2015.[565] Eichmann is long dead and so is John Demjanjuk, at 91 years of age—still, however, in limbo with respect to whether or not he was Ivan the Terrible. Leo Frank was exonerated, but never officially, for a crime he did not commit. The Inquisition no longer exists in Spain or elsewhere, but the sort of fear that informed the Sephardi community leadership of Amsterdam in its actions against Spinoza may not have gone away; it may instead have simply been transformed—perhaps occasionally making itself felt even in, of all places, the United States of America. The roodscreen and its narrative are there in Norwich for any visitor to study and inquire about; blood libels continue to resurface from time to time here and there across the planet, as we move deeper into the twenty-first century.[566] The texts of the Gospels, with whatever internal contradictions, are nonetheless God's incontrovertible word for hundreds of millions of inhabitants of this planet, very few of whom worry about those contradictions, or about the problem of reading God's word in translation, whether it applies to or refers to "Jews" rather than "Judaeans" or to anyone or anything else.

My narrative is intended as an exploration of an important aspect of history, not as an act of finger-pointing in any direction—none of us is so innocent as to begin throwing stones, to paraphrase Jesus. And there is any number of cases and historical moments that I have not discussed that could have further expanded the details of this narrative, although not its essential conclusions. For it strikes me as arguable that, in the courtroom of history—or, rather, the courtroom of historiography, with its ever-changing, never-changing interpretations of history—the Jew is nearly always on trial, whether occupying the role of defendant, prosecutor, jury or judge. If I am correct, then if the courtroom of history is to become more just, we must begin by recognizing that peculiar and disturbing truth. That is one way of becoming part of the process of repairing the world. Learning from history, we may perhaps multiply its triumphs rather than simply repeat its mistakes.

Bibliography

Acosta, Uriel, *A Specimen of Human Life*. New York: Bergman Publishers, 1967.

Adams, Susan, "Ivan the Terrible's Terrible Defense," *The American Lawyer*, October, 1988, 148-157.

Albert, Phyllis Cohen, *The Modernization of French Jewry: Consistory and Community in the Nineteenth Century*. Hanover, NH: Brandeis University Press, 1977.

Anderson, M.D., *A Saint at Stake: William of Norwich*. London: Faber, 1964.

Arendt, Hannah, *Eichmann in Jerusalem: A Report on the Banality of Evil*. New York: The Viking Press, 1963.

—, ed. Ron H. Feldman, *The Jew as Pariah: Jewish Identity and Politics in the Modern Age*. New York: New York: Grove Press, 1978.

Ashtor, Eliahu, *The Jews of Muslim Spain*. Philadelphia: Jewish Publication Society, 1979.

Babylonian Talmud, (Rabbi Isidore Epstein, transl. & ed. Bi-lingual Edition, 30 Volumes). Brooklyn, NY: Soncino Press, 1991. Especially Tractate *Sanhedrin*.

Baeck, Leo, *Judaism and Christianity* (transl. by Walter Kaufmann). Cleveland and New York: Meridien Books, 1961.

Baer, Yitzhak, *The Jews of Christian Spain*. Philadelphia: Jewish Publication Society, 1961.

Barnouw, Dagme, "The Secularity of Evil: Hannah Arendt and the Eichmann Controversy," in *Modern Judaism*, Vol 13, No. 1 (February, 1983), 75-94.

Baron, Salo W., *The Russian Jews Under the Tsars and Soviets*. New York: Macmillan Press, 1964.

—, *Steeled by Adversity* (Jeanette Meisel Baron, ed.). Philadelphia: Jewish Publication Society, 1991.

Barres, Maurice, *Scènes et doctrines du nationalisme*. Paris: Felix Guven, 1902.

Berkovits, Eliezer, *Faith After the Holocaust*. New York: Ktav Publishing House, 1973.

Bernstein, Herman, *The History of a Lie: The Truth about "The Protocols of the Wise*

Men of Zion." Chicago: University of Illinois; Project Gutenberg, 2006 (reprint of original 1921 publication).

Blum, Howard, *I Pledge Allegiance: The True Story of the Walkers: an American Spy Family.* New York: Simon & Schuster, 1987.

Brandon, S.G.F., *The Trial of Jesus of Nazareth.* New York: Dorset Press, 1968.

Bredin, Jean-Denis, *The Affair: The Case of Alfred Dreyfus.* New York: George Braziller, Inc., 1986.

Butman, Hillel, *From Leningrad to Jerusalem: The Gulag Way. Hijacking Plot and Trial.* Berkeley, CA: Benmir Books, 1990.

Chazan, Robert, *Barcelona and Beyond: The Disputation of 1263 and its Aftermath.* Berkeley: University of California Press, 1992.

—, *Daggers of Faith: Thirteenth-Century Christian Missionizing and Jewish Response.* Berkeley: University of California Press, 1989.

Cherkashin, Victor. *Spy Handler.* New York: Basic Books, 2005.

Cohen, Jeremy, *The Friars and the Jews. The Evolution of Medieval Anti-Judaism.* Ithaca, NY: Cornell University Press, 1983.

—, *Living Letters of the Law: Ideas of the Jew in Medieval Christianity.* Berkeley: University of California Press, 1999.

Cohen-Steiner, Jean-Francois, *Treblinka.* New York: Simon and Schuster, 1967.

Cohn, Haim H., "Reflections on the Trial and Death of Jesus," *Israel Law Review,* Vol II, no. 3.

Cook, Fred, *The Nightmare Decade: The Life and Times of Senator Joseph McCarthy.* New York: Random House, 1971.

Coulter, Ann, *Treason: Liberal Treachery from the Cold War to the War on Terrorism.* New York: Crown Forum Books, 2003.

Crossan, John Dominic, *Jesus: A Revolutionary Biography.* San Francisco: Harper SanFrancisco, 1994.

—, *The Historical Jesus: The Life of a Mediterranean Jewish Peasant.* San Francisco: HarperSanFrancisco, 1991.

—, *Who Killed Jesus?* San Francisco: HarperSanFrancisco, 1996.

Deutsch, Akiva W., *The Eichmann Trial in the Eyes of Israeli Youngsters.* Ramat Gan, Israel: Bar-Ilan University Press, 1974.

Dinnerstein, Leonard, *The Leo Frank Case.* Athens, GA: University of Georgia Press, 2008 (reprint of original 1997 study).

Dubnow, Simon, *History of the Jews in Russia and Poland* (Three Volumes). Philadelphia: Jewish Publication Society of America, 1916.

Fackenheim, Emil L., *God's Presence in History: Jewish Affirmations and Philosophical Reflections.* Northvale, NJ: Jason Aronson Inc., 1997.

Feklisov, Aleksandr and Sergei Kostin, *The Man Behind the Rosenbergs.* Enigma Books, 2001.

Fischer, Lynn F., ed., Security Awareness Division, Education Programs Department, *Security Awareness in the1980s: Feature Articles from Security Awareness Bulletin, 1981-89.* Richmond, VA: Department of Defense Security Institute, 1990.

Fleischner, Eva, Ed., *Auschwitz: Beginning of a New Era? Reflections on the Holocaust*. New York: Ktav Publishing House and The Cathedral Church of St. John the Divine, 1974.

Florence, Ronald. *Blood Libel: the Damascus Affair of 1840*. Madison: Wisconsin University Press, 2004.

Frankel, Jonathan, *The Damascus Affair: "Ritual Murder," Politics, and the Jews in 1840*. Cambridge & New York: Cambridge University Press, 1997.

Friedman, Saul S., *The Incident at Massena: Anti-Semitic Hysteria in a Typical American Town*. New York: Stein and Day, Publishers, 1978.

Fricke, Weddig, *The Court-Martial of Jesus: A Christian Defends the Jews Against the Charge of Deicide*. New York: Grove Weidenfeld, 1990.

Gerber, Jane S., *The Jews of Spain: A History of the Sephardic Experience*. New York: The Fre Press, 1992.

Golden, Harry, *A Little Girl is Dead*. Cleveland, OH: World Books, 1965.

Goldstein, Rebecca Newberger, Betraying Spinoza: The Renegade Jew Who Gave Us Modernity. New York: Schocken Nextbook, 2006

Goulden, Joseph C., *The Best Years*. New York: Atheneum, 1976.

Greenberg, Louis, *The Jews in Russia: The Struggle for Emancipation*. New York: Schocken Books, 1976 (paperback re-edition edited by Mark Wischnitzer).

Handler, Andrew, *Blood Libel at Tiszaeszlar*. New York: Columbia University Press, 1980.

Hausner, Gideon, *Justice in Jerusalem*. New York: Schocken Books, 1968.

Herman, Arthur, *Joseph McCarthy: Re-examining the Life and Legacy of America's Most Hated Senator*. New York: Free Press, 2000.

Hertzberg, Arthur, *The Jews in America*. New York: Columbia University Press, 1997.

Hertzberg, Steven, *Strangers Within the Gate City: The Jews of Atlanta, 1845-1915*. Philadelphia: Jewish Publication Society, 1978.

Hilberg, Raoul, *Destruction of the European Jews*. New York: Viking Press, 1981.

Holloway, David, *Stalin and the Bomb: The Soviet Union and Atomic Energy, 1939-1956*. New Haven: Yale University Press. 1994.

Hsia, R. Po-Chia, *Trent 1475: Stories of a Ritual Murder Trial*. New Haven: Yale University Press, 1992.

Hunter, Robert W., *Spy Hunter: Inside the FBI Investigation of the Walker Family Case*. Annapolis: Naval Institute Press, 1999.

Josephus, Flavius, *Antiquities of the Jews* (Louis H. Feldman, transl.). Cambridge, MA: Harvard Universuty (Loeb Classical Library), 1965.

Kamen, Henry, *Inquisition and Society in Spain in the Sixteenth and Seventeenth Centuries*. London: Weidenfeld and Nicholson, 1985.

Kayser, Rudolf, *Spinoza: Portrait of a Spiritual Hero*. New York: The Philosophical Library, 1946.

Klausner, Joseph, *Jesus of Nazareth. His Life, Times, and Teaching*. Boston: Beacon Press, 1925.

Kluger, Richard, *Members of the Tribe* (novelized account of the Leo Frank Case). Garden City, NY: Doubleday & Co., 1977.

Kneece, Jack, *Family Treason: The Walker Spy Case*. New York: Paperjacks, 1988.

Kostyrchenko, Gregorii, *Gosudarstvennii Antsemizm v'SSSR* [State Anti-Semitism in the USSR]. Moscow, 2005.

Levi, Primo, *The Drowned and the Saved*. New York: Summit Books, 1989.

Levin, Dan, *Spinoza: The Young Thinker who Destroyed*. New York: Weybright & Talley, 1970

Lindemann, Albert S., *The Jew Accused: Thee Anti-Semitic Affairs (Dreyfus, Beilis, Frank)*, 1894-1915. Cambridge: Cambridge University Press, 1991.

Lukacs, John, *Budapest 1900: Portrait of a City and Its Culture*. New York: Grove Weidenfeld, 1988.

Luther, Martin, *Die gantze Heilige Schrifft* (Der komplette Originaltext von 1545 in modernem Schriftbild. Hrsg. von Hans Volz unter Mitarbeit von Heinz Blanke; Textredaktion Friedrich Kur). Munich: Rogner & Bernhard, 1972 (New Edition: Ed. Lempertz, Bonn 2004).

Maccoby, Hyam, editor and translator, *Judaism on Trial: Jewish-Christian Disputations in the Middle Ages*. East Brunswick, NJ: Associated University Presses, Inc., 1982.

—, *Judas Iscariot and the Myth of Jewish Evil*. New York: The Free Press, 1992.

Malamud, Bernard, *The Fixer* (novelized account of the Beiliss Case). New York: Macmillan & Co, 2004 (reprint of original 1966 novel).

Malkin, Peter Z. & Harry Stein, *Eichmann in My Hands*. New York: Grand Central Publishing, 1990.

Marrus, Michael R., *The Politics of Assimilation: A Study of the French Jewish Community at the Time of the Dreyfus Affair*. Oxford: Oxford University Press, 1971.

Markle, Gerald E., *Meditations of a Holocaust Traveler*. (Albany: State of University Press, 1995), chapter two: "Banality."

Meeropol, Robert and Michael Meeropol, *We Are Your Sons: The Legacy of Ethel and Julius Rosenberg*. Chicago: University of Illinois Press, 1986.

—, *An Execution in the Family*. New York: St. Martin's Press, 2003.

Melinkoff, Ruth, *The Horned Moses in Medieval Thought and Imagination*. Berkeley and Los Angeles: University of California Press, 1970.

Mendelsohn, Samuel, *The Criminal Jurisprudence of the Jews*. New York: Sepher-Hermon Press, 1991.

Morgan, Ted, *An Uncertain Hour: The French, the Germans, the Jews, the Klaus Barbie Trial and the City of Lyon, 1940-1945*. New York: Arbor House/William Morrow, 1989.

Morse, Arthur D., *While Six Million Died: A Chronicle of American Apathy*. New York: Ace Publishing Corporation, 1967.

Morse, George P., *America Twice Betrayed: Reversing 50 Years of Government Security Failure*. Silver Spring, MD: Bartleby Press, 1995.

Netanyahu, Benzion, *The Marranos of Spain, from the Late 14th to the Early 16th Century*. New York: American Academy for Jewish Research, 1966).

—, *The Origins of the Inquisition in Fifteenth Century Spain*. New York: New York Review of Books, 2001.

Nizer, Louis, *The Implosion Conspiracy*. New York: Doubleday & Co., 1973.

Olender, Maurice, *The Languages of Paradise: Race, Religion, and Philology in the Nineteenth Century*. Cambridge, MA: Harvard University Press, 1992.

Olive, Ronald J., *Capturing Jonathan Pollard: How One of the Most Notorious Spies in American History was Brought to Justice*, Annapolis, MD: Naval Insititute Press, 2006.

Oney, Steve, *And the Dead Shall Rise: The Murder of Mary Phagan and the Lynching of Leo Frank*. New York: Random House, 2003.

Paleologue, Maurice, *An Intimate Journal of the Dreyfus Case*. New York: Criterion Books, 1957.

Peukert, Will-Erich, Peukert, "Ritualmord," in *Handwörterbuch des deutschen Aberglaubens*. Berlin: Walter de Gruyter, 1931, vol. 7, cols. 727–739.

Radosh, Ronald and Joyce Milton, *The Rosenberg File: A Search for the Truth*. New York: Henry Holt, 1983.

Renan, Ernst, *The Life of Jesus*. New York: Carleton Presss, 1864.

Roberts, Sam, *The Brother: The Untold Story of the Rosenberg Case*. New York: Random House, 2001.

Robinson, Jacob, *And the Crooked Shall Be Made Straight: The Jewish Catastrophe and Hannah Arendt's Narrative*. New York: The Macmillan Co., 1965.

Roth, Cecil, *A History of the Marranos*. New York: Harper Torchbooks, 1966 (reprint of the 1932 Jewish Publication Society of America edition).

Rubenstein, Richard L., *After Auschwitz: History, Theology and Contemporary Judaism*. Baltimore: The Johns Hopkins University Press, 1992, (Second Edition).

Ryan, Allan A., Jr., *Quiet Neighbors: Prosecuting Nazi War Criminals in America*. New York: Harcourt Brace Jovanovich, Publishers, 1984.

Samuel, Maurice, *Blood Accusation: The Strange History of the Beiliss Case*. Philadelphia: The Jewish Publication Society, 1966.

Schappes, Morris U., ed., "Leo Frank's Letter from Prison, 1914," in *Jewish Currents*, Vol. 37, No. 2 (404; February, 1983), 9-12.

Scholem, Gershom, *On Jews and Judaism in Crisis*. New York: Schocken Press, 1976.

Schneir, Walter and Miriam Schneir, *Invitation to an Inquest: Reopening the Rosenberg 'Atom Spy' Case*. Baltimore: Penguin Books, 1973.

Schwarzfuchs, Simon, *Napoleon, the Jews and the Sanhedrin*. London: Routledge & Kegan Paul, 1979.

Sharansky, Natan, *Fear No Evil: The Classic Memoir of one Man's Triumph over a Police State*. New York: PublicAffairs, 1998.

Sharlitt, Joseph H., *Fatal Error: The Miscarriage of Justice that Sealed the Rosenbergs' Fate*. New York: Scribner Publishers, 1989.

Snyder, Louis Leo, *The Dreyfus Case. A Documentary History*. New Brunswick, NJ: Rutgers University Press, 1973.

Sobell, Morton, *On Doing Time*. San Francisco: Golden Gate Naational Park Association, 2001.

Soltes, Ori Z., "Columbus, Catholics, Marranos and Jews: Who Was Who and What Was What?" in *Lexington Theological Quarterly*, Vol 28, No 3, Fall, 1993, 177-201.

—, *Untangling the Web: An Everyperson's Guide to Why the Middle East is a Mess and Always Was.*. Columbia, MD: Bartleby Press, 2009.

Speiser, E.A., *Oriental and Biblical Studies* (Collected writings of E.A. Speiser), edited by J.J. Finkelstein and Moshe Greenberg. Philadelphia: University of Pennsylvania Press, 1967.

Strack, Hermann L. *The Jew and Human Sacrifice. [Human Blood and Jewish Ritual]. A Historical and Sociological Inquiry*. London: Cope and Fenwick, 1909 (translated from German).

Strickland, Debra Higgs, *Saracens, Demons and Jews: Making Monsters in Medieval Art*. Princeton, NJ: Princeton University Press, 2003 (especially chapter 3).

Suetonius, *The Lives of the Caesars* (John C. Rolfe, transl.). Cambridge, MA: Harvard University (Loeb Classical Library), 1965.

Tacitus, Cornelius, *The Annals: The Reigns of Tiberius, Claudius and Nero*. J.C. Yardley, transl. Oxford: Oxford University Press, 2008.

Tager, Alexander B., *The Decay of Czarism: the Beiliss Trial*, Philadelphia, 1935.

Teicholz, Tom, *The Trial of Ivan the Terrible: State of Israel vs. John Demjanjuk*. New York: St. Martin's Press, 1990.

Thomas of Monmouth, *The Life and Miracles of St. William of Norwich* (A. Jessopp & M.R. James, eds.). Cambridge: Cambridge University Press, 1896.

Thucydides, *The Peloponesian War* (transl by Rex Warner). Harmondsworth, Middlesex, England: Penguin Books, 1954.

Trachtenberg, Joshua, *The Devil and the Jews*. Philadelphia: Jewish Publication Society, 1984 (reprint of original 1944 edition).

Von Long, Jochen, ed., *Eichmann Interrogated: Transcripts from the Archives of the Israeli Police*. New York: Vintage Books, 1984.

Ward, Rev. Caleb Theophilus, *Gospel Development: A Study of the Origin and Growth of the Four Gospels by Mutual Comparison*, (Brooklyn: Synoptic Publishing Co., 1907)

Wexley, John, *The Judgment of Julius and Ethel Rosenberg*. New York: Ballantine Books, 1977.

Wiernik, Yankel, *A Year in Treblinka*. New York: General Jewish Workers' Union of Poland, 1945.

Wilson, Nelly, *Bernard-Lazare*. Cambridge: Cambridge University Press, 1978.

Zeitlin, Solomon, *The Rise and Fall of the Judaean State*. (Three Volumes). Philadelphia: Jewish Publication Society, 1967.

Endnotes

Preface

1. See Thucydides, *The Peloponnesian Wars*, Book I:20-22.

2. The literature on the Kennedy assassination—and the careful analysis of who was responsible for the president's death—is by now legion. Many books and many scholars have questioned the factuality of the lengthy *Warren Commission Report* which is the U.S. government's official analysis of the tragedy.

3. There seems to have been an agreed-upon canon by all those calling themselves Christians by about 180 (perhaps a decade or two earlier) but was only formally approved by the Synod of Hippo (in North Africa; this is the town of which St. Augustine eventually became Bishop) between 393 and 397.

Introduction

4. The root, *'-v-r*, means to pass (from place to place); the biblical patriarchs and their families were itinerants: the first purchase of land is not made until the time of Sarah's death, as described in Genesis 23, when Abraham negotiates with Ephron the Hittite to purchase the cave of Machpelah as a burial site for Sarah, and is induced to purchase the entire field on which the cave is located. There have been any number of scholars in the past few centuries who have questioned the very existence of Abraham and these other figures. For our purposes that issue is irrelevant. For a traditionalist timeframe context, assuming that they were historical personages, Abraham, Isaac and Jacob—and their wives, Sarah, Rebecca, Rachel and Leah—would have lived ca 2000-1750 BCE.

5. There are certain problems with the simplicity of this formulation given how one might read the geographic disposition of the tribes in Joshua 12, but again this is beyond the scope of this book's interest. What is important is the evolving terminology that carries us from "Hebrew" to "Israelite" to "Judaean"—to "Jew/Jewish" and "Christian"—and what those terms imply ethnically, religiously or otherwise.

6. This, by the way, is a perfect example of the often problematic coalescence/confusion of history, myth, and religious tradition. If we analyze the allotments of land made by Joshua (in Joshua 13-19) to the various Israelite tribes, it seems that three were in the south and therefore nine, not ten should have disappeared and three, not two survived the Assyrian period. But tradition has settled on ten and two—the two, interestingly enough, of course, being the tribes from which kings Saul and David derived.

466 • Jews on Trial

7. Jerusalem survived a long siege, it seems, but the second largest city in the south (after Jerusalem), Lachish, was destroyed, its walls and gates pierced by Assyrian battering rams and catapults and its inhabitants carried into exile.

8. Judah became a subset of the province—"satrapy" (derived from "khsha-thra") is the transliterated Persian word—of Abar Nahara.

9. "Hellenistic" means "Greek-like" and is the term used to refer to the world after Alexander, in which so many features of Greek culture spread from Libya to India and evolved in various ways.

10. The various pagan faiths could intertwine their strands into a singular if varied tapestry without great difficulty: the Greek Zeus and the Egyptian Amon Ra—the latter already a combined form of two once-separate Egyptian deities—could (and did) become Zeus Amon Ra, worshipped in Macedonian Egypt in a single shrine, for instance. Judaeanism could not hyphenate in this manner.

11. The term "Hasmonean" refers to the family as priestly, albeit not part of the High Priestly line of Aaron-Tzadok. The term "Maccabee" was merely a nickname—meaning something like "hammer" or "hammer head"—presumably a nickname applied to Judah, perhaps due to a notable physical trait, such as a very short, bullish neck, that tradition eventually associated with his entire clan. (See Solomon Zeitlin, *The Rise and Fall of the Judaean State*, Vol 1, 96). "Judah" would be a more "correct" English "translation" of the Hebrew Yehoodah, but by the Hellenistic—which is to say, Greek-culture-dominated—era, and its cultural coninituation into the Roman period, it seems more appropriate to use the Greco-Roman version of the same name, "Judaea."

12. Cleopatra had maintained that autonomy by sheer personality—which had held Julius Caesar and Marc Antony in thrall, in turn, but in the end availed her not at all against Octavian-soon-to-be-Augustus Caesar.

13. I am following the convention of offering Greek names through Latin-based transliterations. Strictly speaking, the names would be *Antigonos* and *Hyrkanos*.

14. Regardless of whatever earlier doubts had been rampant regarding the Hasmoneans—who had arrogated to themselves both kingship and High Priesthood when they were descended neither from the House of David nor from the family of the High Priest in Solomon's original Temple—by the time of Herod they were by and large regarded as the most legitimate Judaean leaders around, certainly far more so than Herod who was not a Judaean at all, ethnically speaking. This is a more complex story than we have space for here; suffice it to say that the schismatic condition of the Judaean community was continuing to worsen on all levels—spiritual, political, social and economic—as the community leadership shifted from Hasmonean to Herodian. See Zeitlin, especially Vols I and II.

15. Zeitlin refers to it as stomach cancer; others have suggested kidney disease complicated by Fournier's Gangrene. Josephus merely refers to the excruciating pain as "Herod's Evil." (See *Antiquities of the Judaeans*, 17.6.5).

16. Rome technically considered itself still to be a Republic. Even Augustus Caesar, after he had ceased to be called Octavian and had certainly completed the destruction of the Republic in substance if not in form continued to refer to the state that he led as a Republic. The more so, then, a generation or two early, when the Roman generals Pompey and Julius Caesar were swashbuckling east and west across the Euro-Mediterranean world.

17. There were even Judaean troops in the Roman army whose gastronomic needs and Sabbath were both respected and accommodated. See Zeitlin, Vol. II, 316.

18. We recall that the Judaean state originally governed by the Hasmoneans

grew by conquest through the century of their rule and grew still further under Herod, so that the term "Judaea" really may be said to have two meanings by the time of Herod. The double meaning would still be in play subsequently, by the time of Jesus and even still later, by the time of the revolt: Lesser Judea around Jerusalem and the "Greater Judaea" that included Samaria and the Galillee to the north, parts of Nabataea and Idumaea to the south, and areas across the Jordan River as well.

19. Josephus, in Bk V, ix, 1-3 of his *Judaean Wars*, asserts that Titus backed off on his siege activity for a while, to give the inhabitants of Jerusalem the opportunity to think things over and surrender without experiencing wholesale destruction of their city. Josephus claims that he himself was designated by Titus to be the one to try reasoning with his compatriots to give in and receive Titus' clemency. He further claims (in Book VI, ch VI, sect 2)—by way of a long speech that he records, made to the Judaeans by Titus after he had taken the city—that the conqueror offered the Jerusalemites clemency even at that point, but they refused. Only after that did the Romans respond by setting fire to the city. As for the Temple itself, Titus is represented as having had no intention of destroying it: in Bk VI, vi, 5-6 a soldier is said to have tossed a firebrand into it through a window, without intsrutcions to do so; and Ttius is said to have come running from his quarters yelling instructions to quench the fire—but nobody heard him in all the chaos that ensued. Over the centuries Josephus was lightly regarded as a historian, viewed by many as a traitor, who went over to the Romans and then presented them in an overly generous light. But in the last several generations he has come to be regarded much more seriously and his historiography is seen as offering a good deal of truth to it. How exactly we might understand the detruction of the Temple should at least be up for discussion.

20. There were, of course, many other languages extent across the empire, and the *yehoodeem* (plural of *yehoodi*) on its easternmost front would have been using Persian as a language among others, but in and around Judaea, it is these four that are primarily relevant to our discussion. But Persian in any case shares with these four the non-distinction that English offers between "Jew/ish" and "Judaean."

21. In the broad sense, "*religio*" is based on the Latin root "l-V-g", meaning "bind" and *binds us back* ("*re-*" means "back" or "again") to the god(s) that we believe made us. The Romans subsequently appropriated the term for the narrower, more politicized usage to which I have referred above.

22. Put otherwise, the two forms of faith—as I shall later repeat—are siblings from a common parent, each viewing itself as the legitimate child and the other as the bastard child.

23. Note that it seems to have been only those of use or threat to the Babylonians who were actually exiled; the lower classes, as so often in war and conquest, remained where they were—perhaps some of them going with Jeremiah temporarily down to Egypt, from which they trickled back as the dust of destruction settled.

24. The Hebrew term is in any case, "*Yehoodah*" but whereas one tends simply to transliterate that term as "Judah" when referring to the pre-Hellenistic-Roman era, it is conventional to use the Greco-Roman rendering "Judaea" in referring to the region after about 300 BCE.

25. The last concerted political effort to re-establish Jewish political control in Judaea until the twentieth century was the Bar Kokhba revolt of 132-35 CE. But that's another story for another day.

Chapter One

26. The brief Divine-Moses interchange recalls the more extensive one in

Genesis 18:23-33 between God and Abraham, regarding the forthcoming destruction of Sodom and Gomorrah, and with it the question: can it possibly be the case that Abraham offers moral instruction to God, or is it not more likely that God is testing Abraham's "righteousness quotient"—which proves to be extremely high: instead of simply cheering God's destructive intention on, Abraham expresses eloquent and bold concern for the innocent who might be embedded within the communities guilty of many crimes, not least the treatment of Lot and his family (described in Genesis 19).

27. A *sacerdos* is a being—priest, prophet, pharaoh, hero, pope, emperor—who serves as an intermediary between his/her constituents and (the) God(s). The Latin term *sacer*, ancestor of the English word "sacred," refers not only to the realm of divinity, but of death, dreams, night, wilderness—the unknown and perhaps unknowable in all of its aspects and manifestations.

28. In the various other cases, both singular and plural, other suffixes are added to the same base, thus leg-is (genitive singular), leg-i (dative singular), leg-em (accusative singular), leg-e (ablative singular), leg-es (nominative plural), etc... The fact that the "s" and "g" in the nominative case end up combining as one letter, "x" is another linguistic story beyond the scope of this discussion.

29. "Law and ordinance" translates the Hebrew "*Torah ooMishpat,*" thus using the term that will come to refer to the entirety of the Pentateuch—and eventually will also be used to refer to the entirety of the Hebrew Bible or even the entirety of the rabbinic tradition of which that text is the centerpiece—to refer to a justice-bound legal system that does not distinguish native from foreigner, citizen from non-citizen.

30. And the formulation is repeated a number of times, including shortly before the pre-Korah narrative, in Num 8:14.

31. Thus who exactly decided when which books would be accepted into either canon? And are the individuals who made that decision to be construed by their constituents as divinely inspired or merely smart or scholarly? How do we construe the shift in part of Christian thought in the sixteenth century that eliminated certain books from the canon for Protestants which books are retained as canonical by Catholics and Orthodox Christians? We believe what we believe and the proof of the correctness of our beliefs is simply that we believe as we believe.

32. The five "scrolls" as they are called, are Lamentations, Ruth, Ecclesiastes, Esther and Song of Songs.

33. The Romans hoped to undercut Jewish nationalist ambitions by depriving Judaism of a territorial focus with an obvious, familiar name. They adapted and Latinized the name of the area today known as Gaza, but then still known as Philistia, since it was the area associated with the Philistines, (going back over a millennium to the time of the Israelite kings Saul and David), and applied it to the entire area of greater Judaea. They also briefly proscribed the Jewish religion, astutely recognizing a relationship between Jewish religious beliefs and Jewish nationalism. But that proscription lasted only three years; after the death of the Emperor Hadrian in 138, his successor Antoninus Pius restored Judaism's *religio* status.

34. Judaeans and Jews continued to call the area by that name since the first Exile, even as it underwent any number of political name-changes. Today it is Iraq.

35. We are thereby reminded, by the way, that even during the Israelite period one could be a spiritual member of the House of Israel without being an ethnic member of the House of Israel. The term "Israelite" therefore admits of a distinct ambiguity; how much the more so the term "*yehoodi*" which we have discussed in the introduction.

36. Thus tractate *Makkot*, for example, also offers a good deal of information on criminal law, and tractate *Baba Metzia* also offers information regarding who is fit to serve as a judge or witness in a court of law.

37. This issue falls outside this discussion. But for what I regard as the most convincing analysis, see Zeitlin, Vol I, section 3, part 2 and section 4, part 5; and Vol III, section 3, part 1.

38. The Talmudic tractates are typically paginated 1a, 1b, 2a, 2b, etc., so any such number-letter combinations I use in my narrative are page references.

39. This refers to any wars in which the people might engage for whatever reason that fall outside what they take to be their divinely-ordained responsibility to conquer Canaan and the so-called "seven nations" dwelling in Canaan.

40. The word *edah* is used in Num 35:24 to refer to a congregation of Israelites, for which the minimum is ten men, thus the *mishnah* is taking *edah* to mean "ten." One to judge and one to deliver would equal twenty.

41. The *Mishnah* is using as its model Exodus 18:25, in which Moses' selection of judges to assist him breaks down into "rulers of thousands, rulers of hundreds, rulers of fifties and rulers of tens." So ten is recognized in *Sanhedrin* as the minimum constituency to be able to speak as a communal leader as opposed to speaking merely for one's self.

42. Clearly the beginning point of the *mishnah* of Tractate *Sanhedrin*—and thus we might suppose of the institution itself—dates from within the Hasmonaean time frame; and refrains from commenting on the legitimacy or illegitimacy of either the High Priest or the monarch, as Davidic or not and as Tzadokite or not. It concerns itself with these offices as if the incumbents are legitimate.

43. The specific reference to treating monetary and capital cases in a methodologically equal way is Leviticus 24:22—"You shall have one manner of law, as well for the stranger, as for one of your own country; for I am the Lord your God"—which is also echoed, as we have seen, in Numbers 15:15-16, 29; and the notion of examining witnesses takes as its specific starting point Deuteronomy 13:15: "Then you shall inquire and make search."

44. The term "judges" that we have been using refers in practical terms to the group (of 3 or 23 or 71) who serve as judges, jury and in effect as lawyers for the two litigants: a charge will be brought against someone by someone else, the accused will defend himself, but the task of cross-examining the accuser, defendant and whatever witnesses there are will also fall to these same judges, who will then finally argue with each other toward the outcome on which they ultimately vote. If there are not 23 fully qualified judges available at the time of a given trial, some of their pupils—students of the law, meaning of the Torah and its exposition and of the thus-far extant legalistic discussions—may sit in to fill vacancies. They are invited to give opinions for acquittal but not for condemnation in a capital case. As to who is "qualified", the end of 32a in chapter four notes that "all [who are properly trained in the study of the Torah and related literatures] are eligible to try civil suits, but... in capital charges, only priests, Levites and laymen with whom priests can enter into a marriage relationship [i.e., Israelites of pure descent]. Such individuals are presumed to have a closer relationship to God and therefore a clearer sense of justice than the rest of us. So there is, as it turns out, an element of old-fashioned ethnoreligious sensibility in play here.

45. This principle is based, according to the later interpretation of the 12th-century scholar, Rashi, on the mishnaic interpretation of Numbers 35:25: "The congregation shall deliver the slayer out of the hand of the revenger by blood...,"

to mean that all effort should be exerted by the court to effect deliverance, i.e., acquittal.

46. The quote is from Lev 24:14, and the phrase "bring forth" is interpreted to prescribe an action to take place outside the court.

Chapter Two

47. For the purposes of this discussion we are not even considering the bold and important thesis put forth by Haym Macoby that the Judas figure is in effect as fictional as that of Barabbas. Is it the case that the coincidental linguistic association between the name "Judas" and the word "Judaism" and its cognates led to a conceptual association of the one with the other—he, the ultimate betrayer, is the conceptual parent and symbol of practitioners of Judaism, who are the ultimate betrayers of the communities around them in the midst of which they dwell through the centuries—or was the conceptual association retrofitted linguistically: did the Gospel narrative impose the name "Judas" on the betrayer in order to suggest and emphasize an ugly association between the Jews and Judas (who is, by the way, almost always represented in visual depictions as looking different from the other Apostles and stereotypically "Semitic")? See Hyam Maccoby, *Judas Iscariot and the Myth of Jewish Evil*.

48. This phrase is typically rendered—misrendered—"King of the Jews." Recalling our discussion above in Chapter One, the term that most accurately accounts for what both Pilate and Jesus have in mind as a point of reference is "Judaean."

49. While many books have discussed this issue in the last century, a nice concise discussion will be found in Caleb Ward's *Gospel Development: A Study of the Origin and Growth of the Four Gospels by Mutual Comparison*, 192-224 and 284-305.

50. After Herod the Great's death, his kingdom was divided by the Romans. Herod Archelaus became ruler of (Lesser) Judaea, Samaria, and Edom (Idumea); Herod Antipas became ruler of Galilee and Perea; and Herod Philip became ruler of territories east of the Jordan. Herod Antipas is in any case associated with both the beheading of John the Baptist and the Crucifixion of Jesus.

51. The Latin for "learned" is "*doctus*," hence the usual term used in English translations to refer to these gentlemen is "doctors." However I find the term misleading for most English readers, so I have preferred to refer to them as "learned ones."

52. It should also be noted that neither does John—or Mark—offer an account of Judas' death. On the other hand, where both Luke and Matthew suggest grief and repentance to be his end with his throwing the money onto the Temple floor and hanging himself, the Acts of the Apostles presents him bursting asunder in a field that he purchased with his 30 pieces of silver: unrepentant, he perishes through an act of God.

53. This is discussed both later in tractate *Sanhedrin* (86b) and also in *Mishnah Middot* 5,4.

54. As we have seen above, and as discussed in *Sanhedrin* 32a.

55. This we also find indicated in *Sanhedrin* 32a.

56. These important details come from two additional mishnaic sources: the non-permissibility to testify against one's self from *Tosefta Shavuot* 3, 8 and the discussion of witnesses from *Tosefta Sanhedrin* 11.1.

57. By the phrase "to date" I mean to suggest that one never knows what might suddenly be turned up by some archaeologist's spade in that part of the world. Had I been writing these words in, say, 1907 instead of 2007, the world would still be 40 years away from anybody knowing of the existence of the Dead Sea Scrolls.

58. On the other hand, why or how would Jesus—not a Roman citizen, since at that point in time, Judaeans and Galileans were not Roman citizens—have been brought before Pontius Pilate at all, since according to Roman law at that time, trials by Roman magistrates were reserved for Roman citizens?

59. For example: the decision to celebrate the bringing of the first fruits of early spring as an offering to the Temple. The Sadducees argued that the festival should be on the first day of *Shvat*, (ca February), the Pharisees that it should be not until the fifteenth, thus making it more likely that even a poor man with only a small plot of land would have found something growing on it by then that he could bring to the Temple, thereby participating in this important communal event. It was the Pharisaic interpretation that won out.

60. This is, of course, mainly thanks to the conversion of Saul of Tarsus as a believer in the late 40s or early 50s, who not only took on a new name—Paul—but succeeded in overcoming the objections by earlier leaders, notably Peter and James, to the notion of outreach. Whereas they believed that the *mashiah/christos* had come for *iudaei* alone, Paul preached the more universal message that would ultimately become Christianity's signature.

61. Keep in mind, by the way, that ethnicity would not offer a viable distinction: non-Judaeans not only converted to Christianity but also converted to Judaism and, until the late fourth century, Jews were nearly as aggressive as Christians in seeking converts. So there could be Judaean Jews and Judaean Christians and non-Judaean Jews and non-Judaean Christians.

62. A reminder that, whereas the Dead Sea Scrolls are written in Hebrew, and Tacitus and Suetonius wrote their relevant works in Latin, Josephus wrote in Greek. The Gospels, written as far as we know, in Greek, would be translated by Jerome into Latin, centuries later—and many scholars believe that the Greek texts are translations of Aramaic originals. So even the question of what languages are our primary instruments for unraveling all of this is not simply answered.

63. Agrippa II was the son of Agrippa I (who is the Herod referenced in the New Testament's Acts of the Apostles) who was one of Herod the Great's grandsons.

64. And we can therefore understand the context of Josephus' account of how, at the time of Pilate's pilfering of those funds, even for a building project that would benefit Jerusalem, the Judaeans would have risen up—for Pilate would have been abrogating the Roman law he was supposed to uphold, as well as undermining a generations'-old Judaean custom.

65. The exception to this comparative condition for Christianity and Judaism proves the rule: in the aftermath of the Bar Kokhba Revolt of 132-135, Judaism was declared a *superstitio*—it was illegal for Jews to study the Torah, celebrate the Sabbath or even visit Jerusalem—by the Emperor Hadrian. He correctly perceived a by-then intimate relationship between Jewish religious and nationalist beliefs, and figured that if he suppressed the one he could eliminate the second. But upon Hadrian's death in 138, his successor, Antoninus Pius rescinded the Hadrianic decree and Judaism resumed its *religio* status. All too often the condition for Jews of the last three years of Hadrian's reign are retrofitted onto the condition at the time of the first revolt of 65-73, mistakenly transforming a struggle for political independence into one against religious oppression.

66. For our purposes, details are not necessary for what I mention only in passing: that in recent decades other texts have emerged from obscurity that offer still other apparent "alternatives" to the narratives of events contained within the four Gospels, such as the "Gospel According to Thomas." What the putative legitimacy of

such texts reminds us is that the very question of what texts constitute God's Truth-bearing canonical words is a matter of interpretation within the nascent Abrahamic faiths: the process of deciding (and who decides?) what stays in and what is rejected precedes the process of interpreting and understanding what is found within (and who interprets and canonizes our understanding?).

67. The "definitive edition," first published in 1545-46 and fairly recently in a 1982 edition (Stuttgart: Deutsche Bibelgesellschaft), 61.

68. Sejanus was the horrific creature who ran Rome for nearly a decade on Tiberius' behalf (ca 26-36 CE) while the Emperor, for reasons beyond this discussion, spent his time cavorting and besotting himself on the island of Capri near Naples.

Chapter Three

69. Made of the same substance—which is how we typically translate the Greek term *"ousia,"* which means "isness." Arius thus asserted that they are not, therefore of the same pure, immutable "isness."

70. Heresy also constitutes a kind of *superstitio*. It offers a threat to the survival of the Empire, once the Empire has defined itself as adhering to a specific form of faith that focuses on a single God and therefore understands that there is a single correct *path* to that God. To follow a different path is to risk the disfavor of God and therefore to be subversive. What appears spiritual has political implications, or rather, the line between the spiritual and the political is rather blurry—for ultimately, not only the survival of the Empire in the here and now but of its constituents in the hereafter is perceived to be at stake.

71. From the Latin word, *fidelis*, meaning "faith" or "faithful." The "in-" prefix negativizes, thus *"infidelis"* means "non-faith(ful)" or "faith-less."

72. Perhaps the second-most notorious consequence of this struggle (the most notorious, in Spain, we shall arrive at shortly) was that which pitted the Dominicans against the Cathar heretics. Also known as the Albigensians, perhaps because their primary locus was Albi, in the south of France, the Cathars—the word probably comes from Greek, *katharos*, meaning "pure"—asserted that many of the sacramental acts central to Christian life were antithetical to the purpose intended by sacraments: to connect us more effectively to God. They are antithetical because they involve physical, material substance that is by definition not God-connected but Satan-connected—dross intended to pull us *away* from God. Thus Baptism, which uses the material substance water, can hardly be imagined to purify us spiritually; and the process of the Eucharist, which uses bread and wine, can hardly be imagined to connect us to Christ—to give two obvious and popular examples. But to eliminate such sacraments would be to undercut the importance of the Church and its priesthood. The Dominican order was empowered by Pope Innocent III to engage in an intense effort that centered between the years 1209 and 1229, to extirpate the Cathars. Whole towns and large groups of men, women and children were burned throughout Languedoc as the more nefarious processes of what would come to be called the Inquisition began to take shape—officially established at the culmination of this period, in 1229. In 1244, after the siege of the Moisegur fortress, some 200 Cathar prefects were burned at the foot of the castle; the last known Cathar to experience that fate was Guilaume Belibaste, burned in 1321.

73. This puns on Peter's name—*"Petrus"*, which means "rock" in Latin—and emerges as part of the post-biblical tradition in which Christ is building a new edifice, as opposed to the Gospel depiction of him as repairing the old edifice of the Hebrew-Israelite-Judaean tradition.

74. The fact that the denunciation of Abelard was misguided and incorrect and that St. Bernard was, in this instance at least, being a narrow-minded fanatic, is irrelevant for the purposes of this discussion.

75. I am oversimplifying at that. The first, called for by Pope Urban II in 1095 had as its ostensive purpose to regain full control of Christian holy sites to which pilgrims were beginning to make their way in increasing numbers; and was called for by the Pope with reference to the burning of the Church of the Holy Sepulcher—back in 1009, when the Muslim leader in Jerusalem was acknowledged by most Muslims to be mad; and whose successor promptly funded the rebuilding of the church, so that the turn to the remembered destruction as an inspiration for the crusade was rather extraordinary. But given the Great Schism of 1054, the crisis that culminated at Canossa in 1077 and the new heights of power attained by the Cluniac order by the 1080s, one cannot avoid the hypothesis that the papal declaration had more to do with internal Christian issues—and focusing away from them—than with Muslim governance of Jerusalem and its environs.

76. A usurer, for example, is not considered fit to serve as a witness in a judicial proceeding, in Tractate *Sanhedrin* III, 25a; and Tractate *Baba Mezia* devotes most of chapter V to a discussion of different types of actions and transactions that may be considered as tantamount to usury and are therefore forbidden.

77. This translates Jerome's Latin vulgate's *mutum date, nihill inde sperantes*; the Septuagint Greek has it:"...expecting nothing back (*meden apelpizontes*)."

78. We might note two interesting issues here. One, that the only overt appearance the Satan makes in the Hebrew Bible—where he is referred to as "the Satan," which Hebrew term means "questioner" or "adversary"—is at the outset of the book of Job, in which his challenge to God sets up the extended text of Job's faith. Two, that the idea of good and evil, symbolized by light and darkness, locked in an eternal struggle, is at the heart of the Zoroastrian faith where the two are referred to in Persian as Ahura Mazda and Ahriman. It is conceivable that a sense of black-white duality was brought back from Perso-Babylonia by Judaeans returning form the exile, some of whose descendants were the founders of the "Dead Sea Scroll" sect—one of whose texts, the Battle Text to which I have earlier referred, presents just such an absolutist, apocalyptic struggle. If, as many scholars believe, the years when John the Baptist and Jesus are not accounted for by the Gospels were years when one or both resided with that sect, then that would help account for the further transmission of such an ideology into early Christianity.

79. Though there is no evidence of any historic truth to this allegation, it is interesting to recall that, on the other hand, when the Arabo-Muslims successfully overran Spain, back in 711-18, the Jews may very well have assisted the invaders. But that should not be a surprise, since, after centuries of comfortable Jewish-pagan and Jewish-Christian co-existence, conditions had undergone a strong change between 589 and 616, (for reasons that fall outside this discussion), after which Jews spent the following century under considerably oppressed and circumscribed conditions. So the arrival of the Muslims would have been perceived by them as a decided improvement (and by and large it was, for the next four centuries, at least).

80. See Ruth Melinkoff, *The Horned Moses in Medieval Thought and Imagination* (especially 76-93); Debra Higgs Stricklan, *Saracens, Demons and Jews*, ch 3; and Joshua Trachtenberg, *The Devil and the Jews*. One might note that the early image in the West of Christ, particularly as the Good shepherd, evolves from the image of figures such as Apollo and Orpheus, pagan youth-gods of reason, while images of the goat-horned Jews, and that of Jews turned backwards astride goats may come,

as the image of the horned-Satan and his demons may come, from imagery associate with Pan and his satyrs, pagan field and wood paragons of unreason.

81. Connected to the notion of the Jews as in league with dark forces, and with the idea that, after all, black magic is tied to white religion—the most obvious linguistic reminder of this sensibility is the derivation of the magical phrase "hocus pocus" from the phrase that offers the culminating eucharistic moment in the mass: *hoc corpus est* ("this is the body [of Christ]")—there evolved a conviction that the Jews require Christian blood for their rituals and magical activities. Thus not only for preparing *matzah*, but in this place or that, for anointing rabbis, for circumcision, for curing eye ailments, preventing epileptic seizures, removing body odors, stopping menstrual bleeding, stopping bleeding from wounds, as well as to ward off the evil eye in general, and thus to fabricate amulets and love potions, as well as to anoint the bodies of the dead. See Peukert, *"Ritualmord,"* HWDA, vol. 7, col. 734.

82. *Kashrut* as it evolves ranges with regard to the gastronomically impermissible from foods that are inherently off-limits, as stipulated in the Torah, such as pig meat or shellfish, or animals that don't have cloven hooves or chew their cud up and down instead of side to side; to animals that are not slaughtered according to a prescribed method; to meat that has not been prepared properly; to the mixing of certain foods, most notably milk and meat or even milk and meat products (no cheeseburgers!).

83. In the context of the 1096 Polovtzian raid on Kiev, the monk Eustratus was said (in a later, thirteenth-century account) to have been sold to the Jews, who crucified him four years later in celebration of the Passover.

84. Which is located in the south of what is today France. So we are incidentally reminded that the geo-political configurations and concepts of England and France that we possess today were by no means in place at that time.

85. Thomas of Monmouth, *The Life and Miracles of St. William of Norwich,* (1173), Book I.3.

86. See below, Chapter V, v.

87. In twelfth-century England, just as the political side of the feudal ledger was socio-economically shaped as a hierarchy, whereby the king had his knights who answered to him, and they in turn had theirs who answered to them and these in turn had theirs who answered to them; the religious side yielded an Archbishop with his Bishops and the Bishops in turn not only had priests who answered to them spiritually, but knights who answered to them politically. Abbots, should the abbey complexes that they controlled be significant enough, could also play a Bishop-like or even Archbishop-like role. The feudal system of homage could offer a complex formula of loyalties, but the basic issue is that the lesser knights were sworn to serve their lords in battle and/or under other specified circumstances and the upper knights were sworn in turn to protect those and the interests of those below them.

88. There is also a depiction of the martyrdom of William on the roodscreen of the Loddon church (near Norwich). For our purposes the significance of the image is that it furthers our understanding of how strong an impact the alleged martyrdom of William had on the Christian community in the area of Norwich. There are details on the image that contradict details offered in Thomas of Monmouth's discussion and vice versa, but that is less important for our purposes.

89. I am referring to allegations that Christian children died by accident, through excessive zeal, during the Purim celebration: A fifth-century Church historian, Sokrates, wrote that in Imnestar, Syria, in 415, the Jews, overly inebriated during the Purim holiday "...began deriding Christians and even Christ himself and

...took a Christian child and bound him to a cross and hung him up...in a short space they lost control of themselves and so ill-treated the child that they killed him." It is hard to imagine a Jewish community within the by-then Christian Roman world so foolhardy, no matter how drunk, as to deride the Christian community—that one can hardly imagine not immediately turning on the Jews—much less stringing up a Christian child with nobody intervening. Incidentally, the Jews are enjoined to be sufficiently drunk on Purim so as not to be able to distinguish the phrases "blessed is Mordecai" (the hero) and "cursed is Haman" (the villain)—but the two phrases in the numerology of Hebrew are identical, so in fact the injunction is not to be that drunk at all. But one can well imagine Sokrates assuming that the Jews became altogether alcoholically undone on that festival. His tale, confirmed by no source but his own narrative, seems simply to be part of the growing array of canards regarding Jews that lead to and from the Blood Libel and in turn have as their starting point the New Testament depiction of the "Jews" as villains vis-a-vis Christ, multiplied by the theological and political atmosphere of the next several centuries with its wretched effect on Jewish-Christian relations.

90. Certainly one of the most notorious of the Blood libels of the fifteenth century—and the one about which we possess the largest body of information—was that in Trent, Italy, in 1475, where the dead body of a two-year-old boy named Simon was found in the cellar of a Jewish home on Easter Sunday. The ensuing arrest of nearly two dozen Jews, the charge that the child had been murdered in order to use his blood for Passover *matzah*, the extensive use of torture in order to extract "confessions," the association made between the child's death and a larger, worldwide Jewish conspiracy to accomplish such dastardly deeds, the equivocating role of Pope Sixtus IV (who was at that time engaged in overseeing the decoration of the Chapel that bears his name (the Sistine Chapel), and the transformation of Simon into a saint—are all drawn from the vocabulary begun at Norwich and carried forth through the world over the ensuing centuries.

91. I keep using the phrase "at least" because different sources suggest different numbers. The classic article on the subject by the folklorist, Will-Erich Peuckert, "*Ritualmord*," in HWDA, makes use only of secondary sources and does not dig into archival records, and follows the numbers only as far as the sixteenth century, for example. But one can certainly get a sense of a spreading disease-like phenomenon.

92. Not to be confused with the earlier expulsion of 1182. Philip Augustus, coming to the throne at age 15, and needing to fill his empty coffers, imprisoned all the Jews within his direct domains in 1180, freeing them only after a heavy ransom, and then canceling all Christian loans to them in 1181, instead directing those debtors to pay 20% to him. The expulsion of 1182 was alleged—in two separate accounts of it—to have derived from his conviction either that Jews kill a Christian at Easter time (see the monk Rigord's 1186 *Gesta Philippi Augusti*) and/or that they eat Christians. It is not clear whether the expulsion extended to the baronial lands not directly controlled by the king. It is also not clear whether or not he believed the versions of the blood libel that he supposedly referenced in his edict of exile. He allowed the Jews to return in 1198, regulating the banking, lending and taxing business to which they were limited so as to provide a substantial income for the throne. Even the definitive 1394 French expulsion must be understood by us as limited by the geo-political realities of that era. Thus it would not have included the areas around Avignon which were under papal jurisdiction and in which the Jews found themselves under papal protection.

93. M.D. Anderson, *A Saint at Stake: The Strange Death of William of Norwich, 1144*, 103.

94. 103-4

95. William of Malmesbury was born in Wiltshire of an Anglo-Saxon mother and a Norman father in ca 1080/95 and lived until 1143. Most of his adult life was spent in the Malmesbury monastery, where he wrote what is considered one of the best-written histories of England (*Deeds of the English Kings*, 1120; revised in 1127) and also a superb *Deeds of the English Bishops* (1125). The anecdote regarding the disputation is found in the latter work.

96. Primarily St. Bernard of Clairvaux who, interestingly, given the discussion in the previous paragraph, was one of the main forces behind the growth of the Cistercian order.

97. Vincent's work is divided into four areas—nature, doctrine, history and human salvation—but many scholars have argued that the fourth area was added subsequently and is not part of Vincent's original work.

98. One could certainly argue that Muslim power had in fact been in gradual wane since the eleventh century, with the collapse of the Umayyad Dynasty by 1031 and the capture of a number of key cities by the Christians, most notably Toledo in 1085. But the Battle of Las Navas de Tolosa of 1212 marked a more distinct and substantial turning point.

99. Medieval Jewish thinkers debated in a friendly manner recalling Christian-Christian disputations as to whether the messianic idea should be considered essential or not for Jews. Maimonides included it in his list of essential elements within Jewish thought, whereas both Joseph Albo and Judah Crescas did not. But for any and all of them, other issues, such as the reality of the Exodus from Egypt and the shaping and articulation of the Covenant, were regarded as far more essential.

100. Ironically enough, there is a statement in the Talmudic tractate *Avodah Zarah* 22b that comes close to the Christian doctrine of Original Sin, to wit that Eve had sexual relations with the serpent, and thus *zohama*—translated either as "impurity" or as "lasciviousness"—was injected into humankind, but Pablo Christiani missed it. Nicholas Donin brought it up at the Paris Disputation—but it is certainly not as profound as the notion of Original Sin, and is in any case an *aggadah* and therefore by no means a Jewish doctrine, per se, but rather a story offered by one among many rabbinic figures.

101. In the interests of space, I am somewhat oversimplifying the discussion that grew out of Christiani's reference to Psalm 110:1, where "The Lord said to my lord: sit at my right hand," and who and what the "lord" referred to might be.

102. It was damaged by the Jordanians in and after the 1948 Arab-Israeli war, to the degree that only the shell remained, but was restored by the Israelis after the 1967 Arab-Israeli war.

103. Nonetheless, Frederick finally undertook the Sixth Crusade the following year (1228) and, ironically enough, managed through diplomacy rather than warfare to gain concessions from his Muslim counterpart who handed over Jerusalem, Bethlehem and Nazareth to Christian control for a ten-year period.

104. What I mean by this statement of Christian expectation is that formerly Jewish *Nuevos Christianos* in the fifteenth century were disproportionately prominent in the law, as middle-level administrators of all sorts, in the army, the university structure, among the literati, even within the hierarchy of the Church. So Old Christians could or would have been irritated by the fact that all of the positions that the former Jews (aka New Christians) held, but would have lost had they not

converted, which positions would in that case have gone to Old Christians, did not go to them—especially if they suspected that some or all of their New Christian neighbors were falsely professing their Christianity.

105. As a practical matter, it is difficult for the historian looking back at this period (1391-1492) to identify exactly who is who, religiously speaking, in Spain: Aside from Old Christians and Muslims (still mostly inhabiting an independent state in Granada) are three categories that cannot easily be distinguished from each other: New Christians who are genuinely Christian, New Christians who are actually crypto-Jews and may be referred to either as Christians or Jews depending on circumstances—thus, say, the Abravanel family, due to its importance in the court of King Fernando of Aragon, while nominally Christian, probably, was known by everyone including the king to actually be Jewish, and thus was referred to as Jewish—and openly professing Jews. See the concise discussion in Ori Z. Soltes, "Columbus, Catholics, Marranos and Jews: Who Was Who and What Was What?" in *Lexington Theological Quarterly*, Vol 28, No 3, Fall, 1993, 177-201.

106. One might recognize a parallel between this "who is *actually* a *Jew*?" issue here in fifteenth-century Spain and the "who is a *Yehoodi*?" issue discussed (above, n 9-11, 20, and 22), for ancient Rome.

107. According to the Jewish legal understanding, an individual's Jewishness is carried through his mother. To the extent that this is understood in purely bloodline terms—in a literal sense, as the blood of the mother courses through the fetus and is carried by it out into the world beyond the womb—such an individual does not cease to be a Jew through the mere act of religious conversion. Given the notorious obsession with the idea of blood line—purity of blood (in Spanish: *limpieza de sangre*)—in Spanish culture, Ferdinand's condition is fraught with irony (as is Tomas de Torquemada's).

108. Two very accessible soures are chapters IV-VI of Cecil Roth's *A History of the Marranos*. For a detailed discussion of the *Marranos* in general, see both Roth and also Benzion Netanyahu's *The Marranos of Spain*. Also see his *The Origins of the Inquisition in Fifteenth Century Spain*. A more recent general discussion of the Sephardic Jews within and beyond Spain will be found in Jane S. Gerber's *The Jews of Spain*; regarding the Inquisition and its effect on Spanish life see Henry Kamen's *Inquisition and Society in Spain in the Sixteenth and Seventeenth Centuries*.

109. The theoretical justification for preferring burning over other means of execution was that no blood would be spilled.

Chapter Four

110. Magellan himself died in the Battle of Mactan, in the Philippines, in April, 1521; only 18 members of the original crew of 270 made it all the way back to Spain.

111. "Ashkenazi" is a word originally referring to Jews from the Rhineland area. Thus one of their most obvious defining characteristics is their middle-high German language—augmented by elements of Hebrew, Aramaic and a smattering of Romance language elements—known as Yiddish (meaning "Jewish"). Such Jews carried that language east (where it developed in its own, non-German direction) when, in the era of the crusades they were expelled from the Rhineland in the twelfth through fourteenth centuries. Many headed toward the growing Kingdom of Poland. By the fourteenth century, the Jagolowian king Kazimir I was in fact opening wide the door to his kingdom to Jewish immigration for reasons that fall beyond this discussion. But by the seventeenth century—also for reasons that fall

outside our discussion—conditions for Jews in Poland (particularly in its western-most area, known as Ukraine) had taken a distinct downward turn, and Holland presented itself as a safe haven to Jewish refugees from the East.

112. He is also known as Uriel da Costa and as Gabriel Acosta and also Gabriel da Costa.

113. There are some chronological details in this that are not clear. It seems that Uriel himself converted earlier, in secret—meaning that he would have had himself circumcised—when he was 27 or 28 years old, around 1612-13. That would have been extremely difficult to accomplish in Portugal, so if this is true, then he either went to Amsterdam well ahead of his family, or they all went much earlier than 1617—in which case, did they all convert earlier, as he did, or not until 1617, although they may have been in Amsterdam well before that year? For our purposes, these details and their accompanying questions are not crucial.

114. Or one might say that his view is more kara'ite than rabbinite; the Kara'ites are Jews who reject the rabbinic layers of Judaism completely, and seek to live their lives according to what they understand to be the precepts of the Torah and the rest of the Hebrew Bible. Their story falls outside the range of this one, but for information on them, see Yaron, et al, *An Introduction to Karaite Judaism* and Leon Nemoy, *Karaite Anthology*.

115. If he arrived into Amsterdam in 1617, then it took Acosta all of a year to run seriously afoul of the Jewish leadership there!

116. He was able to accomplish this by focusing on Cromwell's messianic hopes and ambitions. Cromwell had been supported in his rise to power by a group that called itself "Fifth Monarchy Men." This group believed that the Cromwellian "monarchy" would be the fifth and last in a series of world monarchies extending from that of the Babylonians to that of the Persians to that of the Greeks to that of the Romans; The fifth monarchy was to be the final one, yielding ultimately to the return of the messiah. But since a prerequisite condition of the messianic return was believed to be the "ingathering of the exiles"—the dispersed Jews—into the Promised Land, and since England was now to be regarded as the real Promised Land, (this is a subset of the Christian supercessionist idea), then rescinding that writ of exile in order to ingather all the Jews (back) into England was an essential part of the messianic vision that Cromwell shared with these followers.

117. Michael's third wife pre-deceased him as did Baruch's full sister, Miriam. There may also have been a half-brother, Gabriel, who was still alive at this point, but if so, he was sufficiently disengaged from the others that he doesn't figure into the narrative that follows at all.

118. This sense of Spinoza's thinking may be inferred from the fact that, when he won his case, he then turned around and handed over virtually all that he had won to his step-sister and her husband. He took only a bed and a blanket, and departed his father's house where he had been dwelling up until that time.

119. Such a *Bet Din* is modeled, at least hypothetically, on the *Bet Din* structure discussed in Tractate *Sanhedrin* that we have discussed above in Chapter Two.

120. He made his modest living as a grinder of lenses, a still rather new profession. The great Catholic "heretic" Galileo Galilei, we may recall, was engaging the Roman Inquisitorial courts earlier in the century, and part of what led to his strained relationship with the Church authorities was his improvement of lens magnification strength, his use of that improvement for "stargazing," and what he concluded regarding the physical relationship between the sun and the earth as a consequence of that activity.

121. Nor was Manasseh Ben Israel present, since he had left for England the previous year to meet with Cromwell and would not return to the Netherlands until 1657.

122. An ell is a somewhat indeterminate length, once used mainly by tailors; it is typically the distance between the shoulder/armpit and the wrist, but ranges from 27 inches (a Flemish ell) to 45 inches (an English ell).

123. In Latin terms we can see this easily enough, since one of the Latin terms for "soul" is *anima*—Adam and we are *animated* with God's *breath* (*anima*)— which is St Jerome's rendering of the Hebrew *n'shama* (meaning both "breath" and "soul") in the Vulgate translation of Genesis.

124. This is, of course, the sin of the Copernican "heresy" that earlier got Galileo in trouble with the Church.

125. Nor was he the only one. The year that followed the *heirem* against Spinoza included a proceeding against Dr. Daniel de Prado, "having been accused before the Senhores of the *Mahamad* of reverting to his evil and false beliefs against our Sacred Torah and of having corrupted through those beliefs young students..." Once again the precise nature of de Prado's beliefs is not stated in the writ of excommunication, but the point is that the process of removing someone from the community perceived to be spiritually subversive—unimaginable through most of Jewish history and across most of Jewish geography, even within the neighboring Ashkenazi Jewish community of Amsterdam—is very much part of life of the Sephardic community of Amsterdam for several generations.

126. He apparently died of a lung ailment, perhaps tuberculosis or silicosis— if the latter, it was most likely brought on (or at least exacerbated) by the constant ingestion of fine glass dust through his work as a lens-grinder.

Chapter Five

127. The reasons are not historically certain, but historiographically speaking, the prevailing understanding is that the French sea captain who took their money and agreed to transport them to Amsterdam, deceived them and instead dumped them in New Amsterdam and that was that. Fair enough to suppose that they were dumped, but I find it difficult to imagine that, arriving at the relatively new colonial town of New Amsterdam, the 23 refugees could have been deceived, believing themselves to be in the major city of Amsterdam, even sight unseen. So either they knew where they were going and believed that it would be a good place in which to get a new start, or they were forced off the ship at New Amsterdam against their will.

128. Seen from another angle: the traditional Abrahamic religious viewpoint is *teleological*: to wit, that God not only created us, but did so for a purpose—the Greek word for "purpose" is *telos*—and in a sense, a large part of our purpose is to figure out what that purpose *is*. By the late eighteenth century a counter-view was being offered by some: that either through "God" or simply through chance, the world began its progress and simply keeps going and going like a well-wound up watch or machine—which viewpoint is, accordingly, termed *mechanistic*.

129. The Austrian center of the Hapsburg domains was the other dominant German-speaking polity, of course, but it remained primarily Catholic.

130. It should be noted that Marx must have been as confused about himself as he seems to have been about Judaism. Converted at age 6 and growing up in the secular Christian atmosphere of Berlin, he was nonetheless spending summers with his Orthodox rabbinical grandparents, out in the country. Is it any wonder that the

first issue he addressed as a post-PhD academic was "the Jewish Question"—or that he both defended Jewish rights and misunderstood Jewish history as it relates to economics?

131. I use the phrase "introduced to a wider public" because the concept of racializing the Jews—and also declaring them inferior—was already in play along an interesting series of interwoven religious, linguistic and political lines. See, for example, the fascinating and disturbing book by Maurice Olender: *The Languages of Paradise: Race, Religion, and Philology in the Nineteenth Century.*

132. I am merely offering the tip of the iceberg in mentioning Bauer, Marr and Treitschke. There were plenty of others who contributed to this discussion between the time of Voltaire and that of Marr—and since that time there have been many more.

133. There were virtually no French Protestants, in effect, since the Huguenots had been expelled in the early eighteenth century by Louis XIV.

134. As so often in the modern era, nationalists view the Jews as not being part of their nation. In the case of Hungary, it is fairly certain that the Jews arrived into the territory that became Hungary side-by-side with the Hungarians—properly known as Magyars—themselves, in the eleventh century, around the time of the collapse of the Khazar Empire north of the Black Sea. As such, the Jews per se would be as Hungarian as Catholic and certainly Calvinist Hungarians, and also got along perfectly well with their Christian compatriots at least until the seventeenth century. But the influx of "foreign" Jews—from Vienna whence they were expelled by the Hapsburg Emperor, Leopold I, in 1661; from Bohemia and Moravia (more or less the Czech and Slovak lands) through edicts of the Hapsburg Emperor Charles III, in 1760; from Galicia (more or less southwest Poland), after the first partition of Poland in 1771-2; and again from that region due, more simply, to unrest, in the period 1840-80—changed all of that, and also led the nationalists to view all Jews as "foreigners." There emerged champions of the Jews as an integral part of Hungary, such as the renowned patriot Lajos Kossuth; and "Defenders of Hungary" who saw Jews as an unmitigated problem that could only be solved by expulsion.

135. Perhaps the face and body were sufficiently decomposed that the hysterical mother—also perhaps in still-hopeful denial that her daughter was dead—could not recognize her.

136. We are speaking of a time and place in which there is still a distinction between surgeons, who wield knives, and physicians, who wield medicines.

137. In fact, in approaching the twentieth century, Budapest was in advance of cities like Vienna, Paris and London as a contributor to modernism in a range of technological and cultural ways. See John Lukacs' wonderful *Budapest 1900.* Budapest also, incidentally, had a Jewish population of over 200,000 toward the end of the nineteenth century (nearly 30,000 more than resided in Vienna)—about 23% of its overall population.

138. Minimally, German, Hungarian (Magyar) and Yiddish were used.

139. What of Moric Scharf? He was returned to the bosom of his family, although not surprisingly, experienced a spiritual and psychological crisis. The family moved to Budapest and he with them, but he eventually left Hungary altogether, settling in Amsterdam, where he married and raised a family along traditional Orthodox Jewish lines.

140. For more information about this situation and its implications for the next two centuries of the history of the Middle Eastern conflict, see Ori Z. Soltes, *Untangling the Web: A Thinking Person's Guide to Why the Middle East is a Mess and Always Has Been.*

141. There are perhaps two issues here. The first is Menton's hostility toward Jews; the other is the political inexpediency of investigating within the Muslim quarter, which might have produced a good deal more complication for him and the French than he wanted, or than investigation among the Jews would produce.

142. Thus, not only in Damascus itself again in 1848 and 1890; but in Cairo in 1844, 1890, and 1901-2; in Dayr al-Qayr and Jerusalem in 1847; in Aleppo in 1850 and 1875; in Istanbul in 1870 and 1874; in Alexandria in 1870, 1882, and 1901-7; in Edirne in 1872; and in Izmir in 1872 and 1874—to name just a few.

143. *"Bordereau"* is simply a French word meaning "note" or "memorandum," but also can, and in this case does, refer more specifically to an official form or covering note for documents enclosed with it in a folder or envelope.

144. At least one other version asserts that a counter-espionage agent named Bruecker (yes, a French agent with a German surname!) snatched it from the loge of the concierge at the Embassy. For what it is worth, von Schwartzkoppen later asserted that it could not have come from a wastepaper basket in his office, because he had never received it. He speculated that it may have been intended for him and so it was in his letter box in the porter's loge—and that either Mme. Bastion or a French agent had found it there, and torn it up so that it would appear to have come from his wastepaper basket. I'm not sure why such an action would have been necessary, since the author of the *bordereau* would be equally culpable of treason in either case.

145. The French term for someone moving through such a course is *stagiaire*.

146. He would be referring to two "i"s, since in French the word is *"artillerie"*.

147. His grandfather had been a fairly impoverished merchant from a family that had resided in Alsace for generations, who built up a business into something substantial.

148. Major Armand-Auguste-Ferdinand-Maries Mercier du Paty de Clam was, as fate and Dreyfus' misfortune would have it, a profound anti-Semite whose preference was for an inquisitional style of interrogation. He had the reputation for being both erratic and bullying—the classic case of someone who is extremely dangerous in being a weak person in a position of power—and was honored to be put in charge of this "case." His favorite tactic with Dreyfus was to appear at his cell in the middle of the night, waking him up with the intent of extracting confessional information out of his victim's sleep-addled brain.

149. Maurice Barres, *Scenes et Doctrines du nationalisme*, 129ff—which is a compendium of articles written by Barres for *Le Journal* during the Dreyfus trial.

150. Paleologue was so intrigued by this case, from his witnessing of Dreyfus' degradation to the subsequent events that followed through the trial at Rennes of 1899—where the innocence of Dreyfus was clear to Paleologue, but who exactly the real perpetrator had been was not yet clear—that he wrote *An Intimate Journal of The Dreyfus Case*. It was submitted to a publisher only in 1942, with instructions that it be published four years after his death. He died in 1944, and the journal was duly published four years later. It first appeared in English translation in 1957.

151. Picquart would be dismissed from the army on February 26, 1896; would duel with Henry on March 5 of the same year; and would himself be arrested and then face a court-martial in late November, 1898. He was imprisoned as a consequence until June of the following year.

152. Esterhazy subsequently fled France, on September 1, 1898.

153. Zola ends by acknowledging that he is opening himself up to libel suits. "I expose myself to that risk voluntarily." He was indeed sued shortly after this piece appeared, was condemned to a year in prison and a stiff fine, appealed the

verdict and lost his appeal, fled temporarily to England after the trial, and had his name stricken from the rolls of the French Legion of Honor in July, 1898. He died in 1902 of carbon monoxide poisoning; it seems that his chimney had somehow been sealed—by his enemies? Was it murder?—for a chimney sweep confessed on his own death bed to having deliberately sealed it for political reasons.

154. Dreyfus applied for and was granted early retirement in 1907, but volunteered to return to service when World War I broke out. Promoted to Lieutenant-Colonel on September, 26, 1914, he served for three years. He subsequently left France, moving to New York City, for a while, but returned to France where he died in Paris in 1935.

155. Herzl's theoretical discussion of what the Jewish state would be and how it would come into being was not the beginning but the culmination of at least thirty years of that sort of abstract discussion, of which the first lengthy written articulation was Moses Hess' 1862 *Rome and Jerusalem*. In that work the author argued that a Jewish polity could rise from its past as surely as the Italians were bound on reunifying their peninsula at the center of the Mediterranean in an act of restoring some of the greatness of the Roman empire that had crumbled fourteen centuries earlier.

156. There were other reforms in the years that followed: a new judicial administration, based on the French model, in 1864 and in the same year a new penal code for the rural districts that extended by 1870 to large towns and cities, a reorganization of the army and navy in 1874, among others. On the other hand, Alexander II suppressed the growing expressions of nationalist aspiration among the non-Russian peoples encompassed by his empire.

157. See above, Chapter III, iii, where I noted that the story provided to those accusing the Jews of Norwich of the murder offered a prologue to the more extensive narrative of the Protocols. The direct inspiration for the anti-Semitic forgery seems to have been a combination of several works. An 1864 anti-Napoleon III tract, *Dialogue in Hell Between Machiavelli and Montesquieu*, by the French satirist, Maurice Joly, in which Jesuit plotters are featured, may have been one. Joly may have in turn been inspired by the popular novel by Eugene Sue, *The Mysteries of the People*, in which the Jesuits also starred as the plotters. Jews were not mentioned in either work. The German writer Hermann Goedsche's 1868 novel, *Biarritz* may also have contributed to the process of inspiring the *Protocols*. In it is a chapter in which a mysterious group of rabbis meets at midnight in the old Jewish cemetery of Prague, and the Devil appears to them to guide them as the representatives of the Twelve Tribes of Israel in their conspiracy to take over the world. Goedsche's work—he was alleged to be a spy for the Prussian Secret Police—seems to have passed into French thinking by the time of the Franco-Prussian War as historical fact. One might suppose that one of those influenced was Edouard Drumont, who figured so prominently within the anti-Semitic propaganda that accompanied the Dreyfus Affair. By 1872 the "Jewish Cemetery" chapter of Goedsche's novel had appeared in St. Petersburg in Russian as a separate pamphlet claiming its contents as historical fact. A comparison of the texts of Joly's satire and the Protocols makes it quite clear that the latter translated key aspects of the former hook, line and sinker into its own, anti-Semitic, conspiracy narrative. The implications of the Protocols into the rest of twentieth-century history are not far to find, and may be felt from Hitler's *Mein Kampf* and the text of his speeches as a Nazi leader to various printed and verbal rants against the Jews that continue to appear within contemporary Islamic literature and journalism and on a range of internet sites.

158. Moreover, Nicholas is said to have contributed over 12 million rubles

of his own funds toward mass dissemination of the Protocols and other anti-Jewish hate literature. (See Salo W. Baron's *The Russian Jews Under the Tsars and Soviets*, 61).

159. Both of these organizations were fierce defendants of the Tsarist monarchy that had been under assault by revolutionary groups since before the assassination of Alexander II, strongly reactionary and profoundly anti-Semitic.

160. The entire text will be found in Maurice Samuel, *Blood Accusation*, 17.

161. Jehuda Reinharz, *Weizmann: The Making of a Statesman*, 341 (quoted in Lindemann, 341)

162. Chaplinsky, I would imagine, was not overly concerned that Shcheglovitov would falter; his reputation as a shaper of twisted, politically opportune justice was widespread.

163. The mother claimed not to have seen the victim on the day of the murder, but to have heard that he "was most probably murdered by the Jews." The son claimed that when the victim stopped by, he invited Zhenya to come out to play and the latter refused, and Andryusha went off by himself—and that his mother was not home at the time. But it later it became clear both that she was in the house at the time of Andryusha's brief visit and that Zhenya did come out to play—for starters.

164. Quoted in Alexander B. Tager, *The Decay of Czarism: the Beiliss Trial*, 26.

165. *Ibid*.

166. Since with Mishchuk gone the authorities were no longer assuming that Cheberyak and her associates were the murderers.

167. Andryusha's father, his mother's former lover, had been drafted into the army shortly before or after the boy was born, so he was brought up by his mother and step-father—lovingly, as the trial testimony made clear. But Andryusha had a natural obsession for finding his real father, who had been sent to serve in the Far East and whom, equally naturally, the boy romanticized as he grew from childhood toward adolescence.

168. Shakhovsky recanted the only directly incriminating elements in his testimony a few days after Beiliss' arrest, when confronted by the shoemaker, Nakonechny—whose shop was in the same building as the Cheberyak apartment—with the obviousness of his having lied. Shakhovsky asserted that he had been repeatedly threatened and cajoled by detectives to help point the finger toward a Jewish villain.

169. Kiev is placed within what was still the Pale of Settlement, but as a city with particularly sacred connotations for the Russian Orthodox community it was off-limits to Jews in theory. For a Jew to reside there—in Kiev there were some 5,000 Jews, out of a population of about 506,000 in 1911—s/he required a special permit, but Beiliss was in possession of such a permit, so there was in fact no question regarding the legitimacy of his residence there.

170. Samuel, 78.

171. It was subsequently revealed that Kosorotov's cooperative testimony had been somewhat expensive: he had accepted a bribe of 4000 rubles from the Ministry of Justice for his opinion. See Samuel, 82-3.

172. Samuel, 83.

173. *Ibid*, 82.

174. *Ibid*, 85.

175. Beiliss not only had a permit to live in Kiev, but to live on the premises of the brickyard which was not in the Jewish section of the city.

176. Quoted in Samuel, 165.

177. As quoted in Samuel, 162.

178. Samuel, 250.

179. The Black Hundreds was yet another right-wing, nationalistic, strongly anti-Semitic group.

180. Stalin's words are reported in the diary of the Vice-Chairman of the Politburo, Vladimir A. Malyshev, and quoted in Gregorii Kostyrchenko, *Gosudarstvennii Antsemizm v'SSSR [State Anti-Semitism in the USSR]*, 461-62.

181. The *Pravda* text is referring to the Joint Distribution Committee (JDC) a non-profit, non-partisan American Jewish organization created in 1914 to assist Jews (it eventually became non-sectarian in its efforts) around the world in the aftermath of any and all sorts of disasters largely by acting as the distribution agent for funds and other assistance often ingathered by other organizations. Before, during and after World War II and the Holocaust the JOINT, as it is often popularly called, focused on helping over a million Jewish refugees find new homes while also (after the war) overseeing the return of property plundered by the Nazis to its Jewish owners or, in the absence of surviving owners, auctioning it off to raise funds to be used in refugee assistance.

182. The USSR broke off diplomatic relations with Israel on February 11; they were restored in July.

183. See Soza Szajkowski, "The Impact of the Beilisss Case on Central and Western Europe," *American Academy for Jewish Research, Proceedings.* vol 31 (1963), 197-218. Lindemann (175) points out that Szajkowski, however, somewhat exaggerates the Jewish role in Beiliss affair agitation, (since there was such an upsurge of non-Jewish activity): "he emphasizes that 'almost nothing was done without Jewish intercession' (216)."

Chapter Six

184. He was an equal-opportunity bigot, as we have earlier noted, who wanted nobody who was not a member of the Dutch Reformed Church to take up residence in his colony, so his ornery behavior was by no means specifically anti-Jewish.

185. The nascent republic was still a long way from exhibiting such broad-mindedness where non-European races were concerned; there were horrors aplenty still awaiting Africans and Native Americans—and even Asians and Asian-Americans—as American history unfolded. But given those still-present prejudices, Washington's sentiments, offered specifically with Jews in mind, may be taken as a rebuff to the categorizing of Jews as a non-European race apart, which categorizing would be promoted late in the following century by the likes of Wilhelm Marr and Edouard Drumont—as we have seen in the previous chapter.

186. By "theoretical" I mean two things. One, that the simplest measure of citizenship was the right—for adult males, at least until 1920 in the United States—to vote, and African Americans gained that right through two constitutional amendments shortly after the Civil War. But that did not mean that in practice they could always vote without risking injury or death, by any means. Two, that there are other measures according to which African Americans would not be fully enfranchised until at least the 1970s—such as the right to use any public water fountain or restroom or restaurant seat anywhere they choose, across the country.

187. As early as 1876, Joseph Seligman, a wealthy Jewish businessman who was also a confidant of both President Ulysses S. Grant and President Rutherford B. Hayes, had been denied a room at the Grand Union Hotel in Saratoga, which created a scandal.

188. That is: the average annual influx of immigrants from Northern and

Western Europe was 176,983—and from Southern and Eastern Europe (and other countries), 685,531—in the several decades prior to 1921; in 1921 the Northern/ Western European influx was 198,082 and that from Southern/Eastern Europe (and other) was 158,367. The change, of course, did not reflect to desire to enter, just quota-enforced success in gaining entry.

189. It should be noted that a distinct upsurge in immigration began in 1892, so the strategy of going back to 1890 as a point of departure offered a solid anti-immigrant logic. In 1924 the quota level dropped to 140,999 for Northern and Western Europe, and to 21,847 for all other countries, primarily Southern and Eastern Europe—a total annual immigration influx quota of less than 165,000. In the first decade of the century, the annual influx of Italians alone was nearly 200,000. The permissible number for Italians was now set at 3,845, and of Poles, 5,982, of Russians, 2,248, of Spaniards, 131, of Greeks, 100—to name a few of the Eastern and Southern European countries. By contrast, from Northwestern Europe, 51,227 Germans could enter, 34,007 from Great Britain and Northern Ireland, 28,567 from Ireland, 9,561 from Sweden, 3,954 from France, 1,648 from the Netherlands, 228 from the Free City of Danzig, 100 each from Iceland and Luxembourg—and so on. There were also small numbers to be allowed in annually from Egypt, Armenia, Palestine, Syria, Turkey, Australia, New Zealand and the Pacific Islands, non-Egyptian Africa, and "all others."

190. On the other hand, Jews might and did become associated with objectionable acts by their Christian neighbors, particularly as the Jewish population surged out of Eastern Europe. Thus they came to be criticized for selling alcohol and weapons to Blacks by the early part of the new century—a situation associated with the riots that broke out in Atlanta in 1906, in the aftermath of which several Jewish saloon owners lost their liquor licenses and several Christian temperance leaders focused specifically on Jews for their role in the liquor trade.

191. One might note how much easier it was in the later nineteenth and early twentieth centuries for a Jew to gain public office in the South than in the North. Certainly in Atlanta, Georgia, the city of the Leo Frank Affair, the Jewish elite was far more interwoven with the social and political (Christian) establishment than was true in the North. See Steven Hertzberg's *Strangers Within the Gate City: The Jews of Atlanta, 1845-1915*.

192. He is quoted in Salo W. Baron's *Steeled by Adversity*, 322.

193. He was writing in an article, "The Hebrew of Eastern Europe in America," in *The Century Magazine*, vol. 88, Sept 14, 787.

194. Not to be confused with the rather differently angled "remake" of 2007 by the same name.

195. I make this point by way of a response to the inclusion of this observation by Bindemann in his discussion (in *The Jew Accused*, 222-3) in a manner that seems to me intended to offer a justification of the stereotype as it was being spread in the America of Leo Frank's era. This goes hand-in-hand with what I shall shortly criticize in Lindemann's entire discussion of the Frank case. See below, 252-4.

196. See Arthur Hertzberg, *Jews in America*, 125.

197. As we shall see, Frank was not exonerated until the end of the twentieth century.

198. He was actually born in Cuero, Texas (in 1884) but his family moved to Brooklyn while he was still an infant.

199. See "Leo Frank's Letter from Prison, 1914," Morris U. Schappes, ed., in *Jewish Currents*, Vol. 37, No. 2 (404; February, 1983), 9-12.

200. Quoted in Leonard Dinnerstein. *The Leo Frank Case*, 33. Worthy in what sense? Of paying for a crime, that offered the nobility of being viewable as another symbolic iteration of the Crucifixion, by an heir to the original "perpetrator" of the Crucifixion?

201. In fact that admission arrived after police applied pressure derived from Frank's comment to a private detective that "I know he can write. I have received many notes from him asking me to loan him money."

202. "Night witch" refers to a kind of hobgoblin figure well-known in southern Black culture, a ghoulish figure best-known as a killer of children crying out in their sleep at night.

203. It must be remembered that at that time and place, the American legal system afforded the police a much wider ranger of techniques for interrogating and pressuring their captives.

204. A member of the lower house of the Georgia General Assembly later recalled how "[t]here was a thirst for the blood of Mary Phagan's murderer. So intense was this feeling that the very atmosphere in and about the courthouse was charged with the sulfurous fumes of anger. I was in the courthouse several times during the trial, and the spirit, the feeling, the thought of the crowd affected me. *Without reason I found myself prejudiced against Frank. Prejudiced not from facts or testimony, but by popular belief and hostile feeling manifested by the crowd...*" (my italics).

205. The street car on which, from her family's testimony, Mary would have been riding, arrived at its stop at the corner of Marietta and Forsyth streets no earlier than precisely 12:07, according to the testimony of its motormen, and civil engineers testified that the 1,016-foot distance to the Pencil Factory door would have been a four and a half minute walk—and on a holiday, with large crowds moving along the sidewalk, it may have taken longer, so Mary was not likely to have arrived at the factory door before 12:11 or 12:12 at the earliest.

206. The motormen on the street-car remembered her getting off at her stop at closer to 12:10, which would push her arrival at the pencil factory building to past 12:15 and shrinks the possible time for Frank to accomplish the pursuit and the murder to between 12:25 and 12:45.

207. The *Georgian* observed that "many people are arguing to themselves that the negro, no matter how hard he tried or how generously he was coached, still never could have framed up a story like the one he told unless there was some foundation in fact."

208. I have suggested that by and large the Jewish factor may have been less important than the Yankee and "rich industrialist" factor in pushing against Frank, and certainly had the trial taken place 20 or 30 years earlier one could argue this even more forcefully. But by 1913-14 anti-Semitism, be it religiously, racially, or socio-economically based, was on the rise in America. Further, at one juncture Prosecutor Dorsey asked a series of vulgar questions of one witness, at which point Frank's mother apparently jumped up and yelled at the prosecutor, calling him something like a "Gentile dog" or a "Christian dog," and that outburst is believed by some to have pushed the anti-Semitic viewpoint emphatically forward, adding a level of hostile feelings toward Frank that had been more absent theretofore.

209. This makes him seem rather Christ-like—or at least Spinoza-like!

210. Dorsey was later elected Governor, a victory felt by many to have had its origins in his successful prosecution of Leo Frank.

211. A week later, on February 24, Jim Conley was tried and convicted of being an accessory after the fact to the murder of Mary Phagan and sentenced to one

year on the chain gang. Hugh Dorsey prosecuted the case and William M. Smith served as his defense counsel. Conley was released after serving for ten months.

212. By then the *Journal* was also publishing information that it seems Dorsey had supressed at the time of the trial but was now being made known, such as the fact that a biologist's analysis of hair and blood found on the lathe in the Metal Room were not Mary Phagan's, or that key witnesses for the prosecution who had impugned Frank's personality had retracted their statements, asserting that they had been pressured by the police. The retractors included the aforementioned Nina Formby, the Madame; and George Epps, Mary's friend.

213. A writ of *habeas corpus* is a judicial mandate to prison officials ordering an inmate to be brought to—or back to—court to determine whether s/he has been imprisoned lawfully and/or should be released from custody. The petition must show that the court that ordered the imprisonment made a legal or factual error; in Leo Frank's case, the claim was that the error was made by the court due to the extenuating circumstances relative to the jury and its feeling of intimidation and pressure.

214. And what caused Holmes' turnabout? A closer look at the situation? A prick of conscience like that felt by the peasant juror in the Beiliss case?

215. The Commission makes recommendations to the governor.

216. Under the circumstances, I hope that readers won't find me overly petty in reminding them that Jesus should more properly be referred to as a Judaean! Particularly given Slaton's courage and the drama of his point, that detail would be irrelevant if not for the larger historical context of this book.

217. I am not certain of the precise genealogical relationship between John Tucker Dorsey and Prosecutor Hugh Dorsey.

218. It might also be noted that, if most Georgians (and most Georgian newspapers) followed Watson's line of thinking, there were editorials praising Slaton's decision to commute Frank's sentence not only in the *New York Times*, but in the *Atlanta Journal*, the *Georgian*, and the *Augusta Chronicle*. The *Journal* observed that "the Governor has shown wisdom and courage," and the *Georgian's* editors wrote that "Governor John M. Slaton deserves the commendation of the people of Georgia."

219. At 11 p.m. on July 17, a convicted murderer named William Creen managed to sneak up on Frank while he was in bed in the prison dormitory, stab him and slash his throat with a butcher knife. Only the swift and skilled action of three nearby doctors saved his life. Frank would write to a friend on August 11 of his near-miraculous recovery: "certainly my escape was providential, and the good Lord must surely have in store for me a brighter and happier day when that honor, justly mine, will be restored to me." Given subsequent events, Frank's words are loaded with the sort of tragic irony that one finds in the most moving of Sophoclean plays. Creen would be granted a full pardon in 1933 by Governor Eugene Talmadge.

220. At the time, at least half of them were known by anyone in Marietta and its environs; detailed discussions of the entire gang did not appear until the beginning of the new millennium, with the creation of the website www.leofranklynchers.com by Stephen J. Goldfarb, an Atlanta librarian, and Steve Oney's definitive 2003 book, *And the Dead Shall Rise: The Murder of Mary Phagan and the Lynching of Leo Frank*.

221. For example, the March 7, 1982 *Tennessean*, the March 8 Athens [Georgia] *Banner-Herald*, and the March 9 *Atlanta Constitution*.

222. The three organizations were the Anti-Defamation League of B'nai B'rith—appropriately enough—the American Jewish Committee, and the Atlanta Jewish Federation. A pardon would not, however, exonerate Frank. (See three paragraphs below).

223. *A Saint at Stake.* See above, chapter three, 99-101.

224. I am not disagreeing with the assessment of Watson as motivated by a range of non-anti-Jewish prejudices in the 1890s, when he was shaping himself as a populist, but by the time of the Frank Affair I find it difficult to deny the emphatic presence of anti-Semitism in his rhetoric.

225. Albert S. Lindemann, *The Jew Accused*, 236-7.

226. *Ibid*, 240, 242 ff.

227. *Ibid*, 244.

228. *Ibid*, 268.

229. I am referring to Leonard Dinnerstein's *The Leo Frank Case* and to Steve Oney's *And the Dead Shall Rise*.

230. I am by no means ignoring the Spanish-American War and the Teddy Roosevelt era, but I would suggest that these are the exceptions that prove the rule of a much more limited self-expression of confident imperialism than began to reveal itself after World War I—or perhaps really only after World War II.

231. A *shohet* is someone trained to slaughter all meat that traditional Jews consume according to a prescribed method that conforms to the Orthodox interpretation of the Torah (essentially, Leviticus 1:5 and 3:10 and Deuteronomy 12:21); after proper slaughter, the meat is thoroughly washed and cooked to assure that it is devoid of any blood whatsoever.

232. See Saul Friedman's classic 1978 study, *The Incident at Massena*, 128-9.

233. The AJCongress was founded in 1918 to fight for equal rights for all Americans, regardless of race or religion, or national or ethnic background. As such one might say that it pursued a more directly political means of achieving its ends than the earlier-formed Anti-Definition League which, when it was founded in the context of the Leo Frank Affair, remained a subset of the much more broadly focused B'nai B'rith organization. B'nai B'rith had cultural and social as well as political goals; it founded libraries and developed book clubs; organized disaster relief and eventually created youth organizations—and by the early 1880s its focus was already international and not merely American. One might also compare AJCongress to Marshall's American Jewish Committee, (AJCommittee), founded in 1906 with an international political agenda, as an advocacy organization to protect the rights of Jews throughout the world.

234. For the full texts of these statements, see Friedman, 158-9, 166-9. Reading through Friedman's very accessible narrative, one has a sense of McCann as not only sincere in his apology, but also uncomfortable in the first place when he brought Rabbi Brennglass in to address the Blood Libel charge. One senses that he had no idea of how otherwise to handle and ultimately defuse the mess that fell into his lap.

235. The exact words of this quote were pieced together by Friedman, 135, from reminiscences of Ben Shulkin, Jack Jacobs, Eli Friedman, Abe Kauffman, and Saul Rosenbaum.

236. See Friedman, 183.

237. *Kristallnacht*—"the Night of Broken Glass"—is the term that refers to the night of November 9-10, 1938, when, in the first organized effort orchestrated by Hitler's government, Nazi hooligans and their accomplices went on a rampage against Jewish communities across Germany, killing or injuring hundreds of Jews (perhaps as many as 1500) and destroying 1574 synagogues, some 7,000 shops and countless homes. In the aftermath of the violence, more than 30,000 Jews were sent to Concentration Camps. In part inspired by the actions of England and the Netherlands in taking in Jewish refugee children, a group of American clergymen con-

vinced Democratic New York Congressman Robert Wagner to co-sponsor a bill—together with Massachusetts Republican Congresswoman Edith Rogers, so that it is known as the Wagner-Rogers bill—in early 1939 that would have brought in the children over a two-year period, the expenses of their travel and upkeep to be born by various Jewish agencies, and returned them to their parents after the just-begun war was over. A number of individuals and organizations spoke out in favor of the bill, but many more—a coalition of 30 of them—spoke out against it. Interestingly, the following year *Pets Magazine* ran a campaign to have Americans adopt purebred English puppies, lest they be harmed by German bombs, and the magazine was flooded with thousands of offers to provide haven for the dogs; a few years later Congress did manage to pass a bill to evacuate British children to the United States endangered by Nazi bombs. Those children were not even considered refugees— nor were any of them Jewish.

238. By contrast, the Kindertransport program in Great Britain absorbed 10,000 German and Austrian (mostly Jewish) children beyond the British quota numbers, without their parents—most of whom perished at the hands of the Nazis. There was, also by contrast, a small Kindertransport-like effort to the United States that did bring in about 1400 German and Austrian children between the ages of 14 months and 16 years, between 1934 and 1945. However, these received no U.S. government visa assistance, in contrast to the British government's waiver of all incoming visa requirements for its Kinderstransport children. Interestingly, a number of these children grew up to be major figures in the British arts, legal, medical and business communities. See David S, Wyman's *The Abandonment of the Jews: America and the Holocaust 1941-45* (New York: Pantheon Books, 1984), 124-42; and Jeffrey Gurock's article, "America, American Jews, and the Holocaust," in the journal *American Jewish History,* (New York: Routledge, 1997) Volume 7, 227.

239. There were preludes, in fact. There was already a congressional committee under the leadership of North Carolina Democrat Lee Slater Overman (the Overman Committee) that operated briefly toward the end of and right after World War I (Sept, 1918-June, 1919) to investigate the German and Bolshevik presence in the United States; as the post-war threat of Germany diminished, the focus shifted fully toward Communists. The Fish Committee was established in 1930 at the behest of Congressman Hamilton Fish III to investigate Communists active in the United States. The McCormack Committee (1934-37) was installed to investigate Nazi propaganda and other "subversive propaganda [that] entered the United States and the organizations that were spreading it." It was replaced by the Dies Committee the following year.

240. The Fifth Amendment reads: "No person shall be held to answer for a capital, or otherwise infamous crime, unless on a presentment or indictment of a Grand Jury, except in cases arising in the land or naval forces, or in the Militia, when in actual service in time of War or public danger; nor shall any person be subject for the same offence to be twice put in jeopardy of life or limb; nor shall he be compelled in any criminal case to be a witness against himself, nor be deprived of life, liberty, or property, without due process of law; nor shall private property be taken for public use, without just compensation." Of course the HUAC was in any case not a court of law, much less a Grand Jury, having been mandated merely to consider legislation addressing the Communist menace—but it functioned as a court, minus the rights guaranteed to Americans in courts of law.

241. The first amendment reads: "Congress shall make no law respecting an establishment of religion, or prohibiting the free exercise thereof; or *abridging the freedom of speech,* or of the press; or *the right of people to assemble,* and to petition the

government for a redress of grievances." (my italics). Thus the refusal to cooperate with the HUAC would be based on the assertion that the subpoena to appear before it was based on an abrogation of the rights of free speech and assembly: to speak out on behalf of Communism or to attend a meeting or even a rally expressing sympathy for Communism is to exercise those rights.

242. To put it in the Roman terms discussed toward the beginning of this narrative (Introduction, 6): Capitalism as an ideology and a cognate of Democracy could be called the majority secular *religio* of the United States; competing ideologies were considered to be *superstitiones*. Thus anyone who adhered, for example, to a Communist ideology was assumed and believed to be part of a *superstitio*—politically subversive, determined to destroy Democracy and freedom and their economic cognate—as Christianity had once been perceived to be by the pagan Roman *Imperium*, and as Judaism was subsequently perceived to be by the Christian Roman *Imperium* and its heirs.

243. See Ben Kayfetz, "Britain's halt of Nazi trials disclosed," *The [Washington, DC] Jewish Week*, October 25, 1985, 7. Kayfetz' reportage was based on material newly declassified by the British in 1985 in which this matter was discussed.

244. Bentley had joined the American Communist Party while a student at Columbia University, and some time after obtaining a secretarial job in the Italian Library of Information in New York City began to gather information to pass on to the Italian Communist Party to help it in its struggle against Mussolini's Fascist government. Her work brought her into contact and then romantic involvement with Jacob Golos, a member of the ACP and an operative for the KGB—which in turn, she would assert, brought her into the spy ring that included not only Klaus Fuchs, but Whittaker Chambers as well as Harry Gold and David Greenglass.

245. In 1948, Whittaker Chambers, a government informant and former Communist Party member testified to the HUAC that Alger Hiss had secretly been a Communist while in the employ of the federal government. Hiss vehemently denied this in his own testimony before the HUAC. To make a long story short, Hiss was eventually convicted of perjury (in January, 1950) and sentenced to two concurrent five-year sentences, of which he ultimately served 44 months. But to this day there is no universal agreement on his guilt or innocence.

246. The speech was not recorded and there are disputes as to the figure that he presented—205, 57, or 81—especially since he changed that figure a number of times subsequently. But in any case he never came up with a single name that was on the alleged list. (What he apparently had in hand was a document based on summaries of State Department loyalty review files *from which all the names had been removed*! McCarthy's method—of unsubstantiated accusation and innuendo—marked the next several years of his moment in the sun (a very dark sun).

247. The Democrats were unanimous in voting to condemn him; the Republicans were divided. He continued in office for the remaining two-and-a-half years of his term, a shadow of his former self and a pariah among most of his colleagues. He died before his term was up, on May 2, 1957, in Bethesda Navy Hospital, at age 48. The listed cause of death, acute hepatitis, is by most historians taken to be a complication of the cirrhosis that was a consequence of his alcoholism.

248. So much so that the State Department's "Operation Paperclip" went into effect, in a limited fashion in 1945, but with full implementation between 1950 and 1959, which in effect made it possible for certain former Nazis—scientists likely to be of use in the quest to produce more advanced atomic weaponry and/or to carry America into outer space, both of which linked efforts were perceived to be desper-

ately needed in the evolving struggle against the Red Peril—were brought into the country with their Nazi pasts expunged from the record, bypassing the usual immigration procedures that made it difficult for ordinary would-be immigrants, even refugee-immigrants, to come through our gates.

249. Fuchs had been rabidly anti-Nazi, and fled Germany in 1933 after a violent confrontation with some Nazis, so he should in no way be confused with German physicists who were part of Operation Paperclip.

250. The possession of atomic weaponry meant that they could match the United States with destructive power, if necessary. In fact, the Soviet involvement was relatively minor by the time the real war broke out, compared with that of the Communist Chinese under Mao, whose inflicting of heavy losses on the Americans was a function of the failure of the Americans and their UN allies both to procure adequate information with regard to the numbers of Chinese and to take the ability and determination of their foe seriously enough. The Americans were supported by fifteen UN-mandated allies, ranging from Canada, Colombia and Ethiopia to South Africa, Thailand and Turkey.

251. I have used the qualifying adjective "theoretical" since obviously, if the Romanovs were eliminated by the Soviet Revolution, the chasm between the few who have so much and the many who have so little was not: whatever the underlying theory of Communism might offer as a system of equality and justice has yet to manifest itself in fact due, no doubt, to the flaw in every theoretical system: that, placed in actual human hands it is subject to all of the irrational, selfish and ugly aspects that are as much a part of the human condition as are reason, selfless idealism and beauty.

252. I am making this last point to remind us that, at that time—before and during World War II, before the subsequent Cold War—to be a Communist could mean no more than embracing its ideals as preferable to being a Democrat or a Republican or a Socialist and embracing the ideals of those parties.

253. Feklisov offered the information much later—in 1997—when, some time after the collapse of the Soviet Union and the end of the Cold War, he felt compelled to speak out on the subject, over the objections of his government, on a visit to New York City. His need derived, he asserted, from his conviction that Julius was a true hero who helped the USSR in its hour of need in World War II and was later abandoned by his Soviet spymasters. "My morality does not allow me to keep silent... Julius was a true revolutionary, who was willing to sacrifice himself for his beliefs." See the long front page *Washington Post* article by Michael Dobbs, "Julius Rosenberg Spied" from the March 16, 1997 issue. Dobbs also points out rather significantly, that "[w]ithout access to the KGB files on the Rosenberg case it is difficult to corroborate the details of Feklisov's story." The article doesn't mention that Feklisov is hoping to write a book on the subject which, without his assertions, could not hope for much success. (The book came out in 2001). The same article points out that "partial confirmation of Feklisov's relationship with Rosenberg is contained in the FBI's own files" since "...Rosenberg shared a cell with an FBI informer named Jerome Tartakow who succeeded in gaining his confidence [and a]ccording to FBI records Rosenberg told Tartakow that he had meetings with two Russians, whom he named as Henry and Alex... [which names] with hindsight.. [seem to] refer to Semenov, whose code name was Henry, and Feklisov..." But this, of course, assumes that Tartakow's testimony is to be believed (and we have seen earlier how a Tsarist government "informer" in jail with Mendel Beiliss completely fudged the information he was alleged to have gotten from Beiliss). Do we have good reasons for believing

that Rosenberg, who consistently denied his guilt, even when allegedly pushed to admit it by having Ethel's head placed on the chopping block next to his, confessed otherwise to a cellmate whom he barely knew? Tartakow might have told the truth, but we cannot truly know that, any more than we can be certain that "Henry" was Semenov and that "Alex" was Feklisov.

254. *Ibid*, A18.

255. See Walter and Miriam Schneir, *Invitation to an Inquest: Reopening the Rosenberg Atom Spy Case*, 364.

256. Schneir and Schneir, 105.

257. *Ibid*. Incidentally, the offense of such "gross magnitude" — the contents of the blueprints and all the other materials (that were rejected by the Russians) — was a proposed process of producing synthetic rubber, to which proposed process the Soviets, at the very time when Harry Gold was allegedly collecting and saving all those top-secret blueprints, *had complete access* by way of $11 Billion of Lend-lease shipments being sent from the United States as part of our wartime aid program.

258. More precisely, his trial testimony was completely different from what he had told his lawyers and the FBI in the initial series of conversations that he had with them and lengthy notes that he wrote to them — as transcripts from his lawyers, Hamilton and Ballard, show.

259. Bloch, oddly, asserted that Harry Gold's mode of testifying and the fact that he had nothing obvious to gain from it, led him to accept it as truthful. Was Bloch being muddle-headed? It is inconceivable that, had he access to Gold's pre-trial testimony and written reports and/or was seriously aware of Gold's prior "record" as a tale-spinner, he would have made such an important blunder. He later wrote of how alone he had felt in the course of all of this, and yet he apparently strenuously resisted the attempts to assist him from other attorneys, notably Fyke Farmer, (about whom more, below, 291-2, 305). Did his ego — the desire to be the heroic lone cowboy operating against the prosecution machine — get in the way of his accepting help?

260. At the Jewish celebration of the Passover Seder, there are several pieces of *matzah* that are part of the centerpiece of symbolic foods on the table. The central *matzah*, according to custom, is taken out and broken in half at a prescribed point in the service, and one half is hidden. Typically, the children — whose interest is thereby more fully maintained — try to find it, and the finder gets some reward, since the meal may not be concluded until the hidden piece has been found and matched up with its other half. The word "*afikomen*" that refers to this piece of *matzah* is an Aramaic corruption of the Greek word, "*epikoiman*," meaning "after-eat" — i.e., "dessert."

261. Schneir and Schneir, 402.

262. Yakovlev, former Soviet vice-consul in New York, was also named by Gold as a co-conspirator, but he was long gone back to the other side of the Atlantic before the Rosenberg-Sobell trial took place and therefore never figured into the picture except for the role he was reported by Gold to have played. In other words, his name could be and was invoked to further the implications both of the activities of the Rosenbergs and of the extended stretch of the web of which they were the center, and if Gold was the sole source invoking his name, there was nobody around who could challenge that invocation.

263. I am giving the tip of this iceberg. For more details, see Schneir & Schneir, 398-403.

264. At first glance, one might say that there was another exception. Gold claimed that he had spent a night in a Boarding Room House hallway in Albuquerque

while awaiting his first meeting with the Greenglasses, and then registered at the Hilton Hotel the following morning, but only for the day—June 3, 1945, the day he met the Greenglasses—leaving for New York by the evening. After Gold had left both the witness stand and the courtroom, Prosecutor Saypol announced that he was going to produce a photostat of Gold's registration card from the hotel. Bloch waived the right to demand to see the original or to examine any hotel employees (presumably he did not want to prejudice the jury against his clients by appearing obstructionist). But had he examined either, he would have noted important discrepancies between that card and one from September, when Gold was in Albuquerque again (allegedly to meet with Klaus Fuchs in Santa Fe, an hour away), that not only invalidate the card as a piece of evidence, but suggest the great likelihood that it is a forgery. And how is it that no record of the bills for both stays was brought forth?—which is a question that Bloch did not ask. For a fuller discussion of this, see Schneir & Schneir, 378-90.

265. Schneir and Schneir, 278.

266. Julius would have been justified in boasting about smuggling the proximity fuse out of Emerson Radio, given its size and bulk, the fact that all belongings were checked by the security guards on the way out, that at no time did Emerson report such an item missing—and that, according to David, Julius had smuggled it out in his lunch briefcase (where it would not have fit). According to Julius, he always brought his lunch in a paper bag.

267. *Ibid*, 344.

268. He was released in 1960 and given a new identity with which to live his life somewhere in upper New York State.

269. Schneir and Schneir, 332.

270. Regarding the VENONA transcripts, see below, 293-4 and n. 274.

271. Many of the details of his testimony offered in Schneir and Schneir, 344-62 would be amusing if the story were not so tragic.

272. Morton Sobell had also left government service by then, working first for General Electric and then also for Reeves Instruments.

273. The judges were divided: Justices Vinson, Minton, Reed, Burton, Clark and Jackson voted to vacate Douglas's stay and to proceed with the execution and Justices Douglas, Frankfurter and Black voted to stay. The primary argument for proceeding without hearing further arguments was delivered by Justice Robert Jackson. Among the three dissenting opinions, that written by Douglas in particular expressed dismay that the writ of execution was being upheld when so much doubt as to the Rosenbergs' guilt and the significance of that alleged guilt remained. The apparent desperation on the part of the six Supreme Court Justices to rush to execution and get it over with stands in stark contrast to the mentality that undergirds Tractate *Sanhedrin* which we have discussed in Chapter One.

274. VENONA—this is one of at least 13 code words used to refer to the project—gathered most of its data between 1942 and 1945, most of which was decoded beginning in 1946. Within a few years of the first breaks, the Soviets apparently knew of the project; to what extent that effected the way in which they sent messages and therefore the continued reliability of ongoing interception and decrypting remains a matter of speculation. The project had originated out of distrust of Stalin and the fear that he would sign a separate peace treaty with Hitler, allowing the Germans to focus their full military strength on Great Britain and the United States; it continued in operation until 1980. By the time of the cancellation of the project somewhat under 3,000 messages out of a total of several hundred thousand had been partially or wholly decrypted.

275. And Greenglass, to repeat, recanted in 1996, asserting that he had committed perjury when he testified regarding the typing activity of his sister.

276. There are those, of course, who, like Judge Irving Kaufman in the 1950s, today in the early 21st century have no doubt as to the intense level of threat posed at that time and since that time to America by Communists inside and outside the country—whose view is that Joe McCarthy was a hero. These are most strenuously exercised by post-9/11 convictions regarding terrorists as well. Among these is the commentator Ann Coulter, whose book, *Treason: Liberal Treachery from the Cold War to the War on Terrorism*, I cannot in fairness fail to mention, although I do not agree with its rendition or interpretation of the facts—to say nothing of its consistent misstatement of facts—or with its hysterical tone.

277. Among the continuous outpouring of literature that considers this subject, compare, for instance, Walter and Miriam Schneir's 1965 *Invitation to an Inquest* and Joyce Milton's 1983 *The Rosenberg File*—but in the more than two decades since the second of these volumes appeared, various others have appeared, such as Joseph H. Sharlitt's 1989 *Fatal Error: The Miscarriage of Justice that Sealed the Rosenbergs' Fate*, or the 2001 book co-authored by Alexandre Feklisov and Sergei Kostin, *The Man Behind the Rosenbergs*, or Robert Meeropol's 2003 *An Execution in the Family*, which is in a sense an update and supplement to the 1986 volume co-authored with his brother Michael, *We Are Your Sons: The Legacy of Ethel and Julius Rosenberg*, to name a few. And then there is the matter, to repeat, of making public the VENONA transcripts and interviews with individuals such as Feklisov.

278. His claim that he wanted to set the record straight because Julius *had been such a hero, "who helped the Soviet Union in its hour of need during World War II,* and was then abandoned by his Soviet spy masters" [my italics]—as he stated in the previously mentioned *Washington Post* article—rings a little bit odd to me, given the paucity of evidence (perhaps only the brief passage in Kruschev's autobiography) that what Julius transmitted was anything close to critically important. Why was he so particularly a hero to the USSR? For what it is worth, in my own five trips to collapsing and post-Soviet Russia (and eight or nine trips to non-Russian post-Soviet states), nobody whom I encountered and queried offered the opinion that Julius had been a hero to the USSR.

279. Schneir and Schneir, 264-78.

280. This will in turn raise a question to be addressed in a moment, as to why the executions of the Rosenbergs could be construed as a sacrifice that would turn the tide, the answer to which will yield still further questions.

281. Is it conceivable that the American legal system is so much less concerned about the value of human life than that expressed in Tractate *Sanhedrin*—conceived, as we recall, more than two millennia ago in Judaea—where every effort was to be made to avoid mistakenly executing someone who was innocent of the capital crime for which s/he was charged?

282. Fuchs apparently transmitted a range of specific information on everything from details pertaining to nuclear physics and the production of uranium enrichment plants to precise details regarding the design and manufacture of the atomic bomb.

283. See, for example, Joseph H. Sharlitt's *Fatal Error*.

284. This was the argument, in fact, articulated by Supreme Court Justice William O. Douglas when he granted a stay of execution on June 17. But he was overruled by six of his eight colleagues within two days—and the Rosenbergs were put to death within a few hours of their rejection of that argument. Douglas would

write in his memoir, *The Court Years*, that his fellow-justices were driven by the anti-Communist hysteria that prevailed, and so "ran pell-mell with the mob in the Rosenberg case."

285. Again, compare this with the pains to which Tractate *Sanhedrin*, contrived as we have seen nearly two millennia earlier, goes to assure that the selection of both judges and witnesses is done in a manner not to prejudice the case of the defendant, especially in a capital trial.

286. Schneir and Schneir, 271. Both Koski and Derry were called to the stand by the prosecution. Koski was employed in the Explosion Division's Implosion Research group, whose job it was to obtain shadow photographs of imploding cylinders, and Derry was an electrical engineer. The Schneirs subsequently interviewed Derry, who expressed surprise that he had even been called to the stand to make an evaluation of Greenglass's sketches, since he (Derry) was a construction man, not a scientist, certainly not a physicist.

287. *Ibid*, 277.

288. One is reminded in this of the Dreyfus and even more so the Frank case, where what happened in the courtroom was affected by the words and actions of the press and the crowd outside—but in this case there seems to have been deliberate manipulation of both by the U.S. District Attorney and his office.

289. This strikes me as somewhat reminiscent of McCarthy's infamous claim to have a list of government Communists: he held up a piece of paper that nobody thought to examine, on which there was no such list. See above, 246 and 272.

290. His words, quoted in a March 16, 1997 *Washington Post* article are that "[t]he debate is closed. It's all over. There is no longer any debate among serious people that Julius Rosenberg was a spy for the Soviet Union."

291. His words are in the same *Washington Post* article. The 1983 book was co-authored with Joyce Milton. At the time of its appearance (coinciding with the thirtieth anniversary of the executions) a number of individuals questioned the validity of its absolute assertion that "the evidence is compelling that Julius Rosenberg... [was] the coordinator of an extensive espionage operation... to pass on information on top secret military projects." The questioning, not surprisingly, is based on doubts regarding the validity of certain documents to which Radosh and Milton refer in their book and of a number of human sources, notably the jailhouse informer, Jerome Eugene Tartakow—to whom Julius is alleged to have spilled all the beans regarding the espionage activities that he was otherwise denying to the last moment of his life. At the very least, one does wonder why Tartakow would be privileged by Julius with such phenomenal information, offered casually over jailhouse chess games. See the letter exchange in the October 24, 1983 issue of *New York* magazine, among other places where some of these questions are raised.

292. If it may be legitimately noted that for their sons and historians like the Schneirs, it is essential to continue to believe the Rosenbergs innocent, it must also be noted that to many of those writers and historians who write enthusiastically about their guilt, it is essential to them to believe the Rosenbergs guilty. This issue is certainly a classic example of the distinction between history and historiography about which I was so insistent at the outset of this entire narrative. And at any rate, my point has less to do with the guilt or innocence of the Rosenbergs than with how their case was handled.

293. See, for example, Shneir and Schneir, 245.

294. See above, 301, and Schneir and Schneir, 277.

295. See above, 248 and the reference to Operation Paperclip.

296. In their 1983 *The Rosenberg File*. See above, 303.

297. See above, 241-242.

298. Among the ironies of this, of course, is the fact that, as the Communist world developed and solidified, particularly in the Soviet Union of Joseph Stalin, Jews were so often seen as part of a *superstitio*, overly connected to Capitalist ideas and therefore a threat to the Communist state. This would have implications for Soviet Jewry from the time of Stalin's "Doctor trials" (See above, 212-213)—that coincided with the time of the executions of the Rosenbergs—to the era of Brezhnev.

299. An additional note might be offered on the matter of finding guilty and/ or executing an innocent person to serve political ends, as may or may not have happened in the first instance (found guilty) in the Dreyfus case in France, which, because he was not executed, ultimately had time to be reversed; and as happened in the second instance (executed) in the Rosenberg case in the United States. Thus, not that long ago it emerged that perhaps the most notorious spy of at least the first half of the twentieth century—Margaretha Geertruida Zelle, better known as Mata Hari—was not guilty as charged, but was executed because it served the political needs of both German and French intelligence. Neither religion nor nationality was the issue, but pure politics. See the article by Russell Warren Howe, "Mournful fate of Mata Hari, the spy who wasn't guilty," in *Smithsonian Magazine*, (May, 1986), 132-59.

300. Sam Roberts, "57 Years Later, Figure in Rosenberg Case Says He Spied for Soviets," *The New York Times*, Friday, September 12, 2008, A1 and A14.

301. *Ibid*, A14, column 2.

Chapter Seven

302. See, for example, Richard Rubenstein, *After Auschwitz*; Eliezer Berkovits, *Faith after the Holocaust*; and Emile Fackenheim, *God's Presence in History*; as well the collection of essays edited by Eva Fleischner based on a conference held at the Church of St. John the Divine in New York City, *Auschwitz: Beginning of a new Era?*

303. See the importance of that distinction as it is discussed above in the Introduction, 2-7, 9-11.

304. The World Center of the Baha'i Faith is located in Haifa and Akko, Israel.

305. In theory, if not always entirely in fact. Think, for example, of Blue Laws that limit what one can do and buy on Sundays ("the Lord's Day" in most of the Christian tradition) but not on days sacred to other faiths, including Judaism.

306. Of course, carried to its logical extreme, one can always ask that question, in any trial—absolute objectivity in the courtroom may be as difficult to assure as absolute objectivity in historiography. Since we all bring our subjective viewpoints and prejudices to every situation in which we find ourslves, then there are surely trial contexts in which, serving in whatever capacity, we might not be capable of objectivity. Tractate *Sanhedrin*, as we have seen, tried to limit the potentially dangerous consequences of this verity by automatically ruling out certain individuals from serving as witnesses or judges/jury, especially in a capital case. Similarly, the Anglo-American system by which a jury is chosen seeks to minimize that danger by vetting all those who would serve on a jury to root out those whose prejudices or inclinations might push them too automatically in a given direction. It is precisely these issues that raise red flags in the Rosenberg-Sobell trial with respect to both the judge and the jury, as we have seen in the previous chapter.

307. Klaus Barbie was a Gestapo officer whose center of operations was Lyon, France. His personal involvement in torturing men, women and children among the 14,000 individuals for whose deaths he was directly responsible led to his being

known as the Butcher of Lyon. After the war he worked for the US Army and was helped to move on to Bolivia, where he was active, under a pseudonym, as a drug and arms dealer—and may have helped bring about the capture and death of Che Guevara in 1967. He was eventually identified in 1971, deported to France in 1983 and finally brought to trial in Lyon on 11 May, 1987. He was found guilty of crimes against humanity on July 4, sentenced to life imprisonment—and died in prison of leukemia four years later. Demjanjuk will be the subject of the next section of this narrative.

308. See Malkin's *Eichmann in My Hands* for a page-turning account of both who he was and the process by which Eichmann was removed to Israel, which process I am merely summarizing here.

309. As a matter of historical fact, several important writers have put the lie to that generalization, none more stridently and eloquently then Eliezer Berkovits, in his *Faith after the Holocaust*, 27-36. Berkovits points out not only why that generalization when it did apply, did so under circumstances in which there was no logical or reasonable way in which Jews could have acted otherwise; how there were so many times and places when and where it was not true, about which one rarely hears; and why the world had such a psychological and political stake in repeating as a mantra that it was invariably true. Israeli Jews had their own psychological need for embracing the idea, but their perspective largely changed after the Eichmann trial.

310. One thinks, for example of the Vatican's continued failure to acknowledge the legitimacy of the state, at that time, by failing, like Argentina did, to accede to diplomatic relations with Israel.

311. See Gideon Hausner, *Justice in Jerusalem*, 278.

312. Joche Von Lang, ed., *Eichmann Interrogated: Transcripts from the Archives of the Israeli Police*, xxi.

313. This had a literal turn, for Malkin, as an artist, filled notebooks and Argentine travel guides with sketches and drawings—of family members, of Eichmann, of Hitler, of quasi-religious iconography, among other subjects—while awaiting the moment to capture Eichmann and subsequently while guarding him until the time of his removal to Israel.

314. See Malkin, 214.

315. Hausner, 280.

316. *Ibid*, 282.

317. One thinks, perhaps again with a sense of irony, of how that principle—of proving that a copy of some document is ineluctably valid and tells the story it is purported by the prosecution to tell—was ignored at crucial moments in the Rosenberg-Sobell trial, specifically with regard to Harry Gold's registration cards at the Albuquerque Hilton Hotel. See above, 283 and n 264.

318. An American journalist dubbed the Israeli statute "jungle law"—as if such statutes had not been adopted by a dozen other countries for the same purpose, and as if the unprecedented nature of the Nazi Holocaust did not inherently require unprecedented legal thinking in order to deal with its perpetrators.

319. Yet again I find irony in this last notion, when the Eichmann trial is juxtaposed with that of the Rosenbergs and Morton Sobell—in which the evidence, beginning with the Brownell memo, is fairly clear that the intention was to create a show trial, and in which the non-impartial prejudices of prosecution and judge so profoundly inflated the role of the accused within the Soviet espionage machinery in order to justify both the procedures in and out of the courtroom and the punishments meted out to them.

320. Hausner, 291.

321. For an interesting if flawed discussion of Grueber and perhaps the key theological question provoked by the Holocaust—why do the innocent suffer in a world created by a God deemed both all-powerful and all-good (is God not all-powerful, or not all-good, or are the sufferers somehow in some way not as innocent as one supposes)?—see the first chapter of Richard Rubenstein's *After Auschwitz* (Second Edition).

322. Hausner, 299.

323. *Ibid*, 300.

324. *Ibid*, 300-301. The fifteen counts of the indictment all fall under Sections 1 and 3 of that 1950 Law.

325. In Israel itself there was no television yet. The proceedings were widely covered by radio and print media, and the entire country became, as it were, one large courtroom in which discussion and debate continued unabated for months.

326. See above, chapter one, 33-6. Of course, a capital case such as this would actually have required a Sanhedrin of 23 or even 71—but the point is that "professionals" adjudicated the case, not a "jury of one's [untutored] peers."

327. The texts of final taped and written transcripts were vetted by the court itself.

328. Hausner, 312.

329. Hausner, 314.

330. Even the implied temporal argument that might have been adduced—that at the time of Eichmann's crimes Israel didn't exist—was provided with a response. For the presence of a Jewish community in Palestine had not only been internationally recognized since the Balfour Declaration of 1917 and the peace treaties following World War I, but more importantly, Palestinian Jews had fought under their own flag, as allies with the British, French and Americans, during World War II.

331. Hausner, 316.

332. It might also be noted that Eichmann himself, when he was captured, recognizing that his captors were Israelis, initially stated to them that he wished to be tried in Argentina or Germany. But a few hours later he relented and said that he was "prepared to proceed to Israel to stand trial" and signed a document asserting "....of my own free will that, since my true identity has been discovered, I realize that it is futile for me to attempt to go on evading justice. I state that I am prepared to travel to Israel to stand trial in that country before a competent court..." See Hausner, 275; and Malkin, 230-31.

333. This was part of the comment of the Earl of Birkenhead, as quoted in Hausner, 321.

334. Or many millions more, if one does not limit Eichmann to crimes against the Jews—as the prosecution did not.

335. Hausner, 323-4.

336. It might not be out of place to offer the argument with regard to Cain's guilt that there was no precedent for his act—no prior human deaths of any sort—and, as siblings, he and his brother must have scuffled a thousand times before, as they grew up. So there was no necessary reason for Cain to suppose that this time Abel would not get up again after Cain pummelled him. And thus, Cain's guilt was not in killing his brother, but, once recognizing what he had done, in denying it. When God asks him about it, Cain replies that he knows nothing about it, doesn't know where his brother is, for "Am I my brother's keeper?" he asks rhetorically. It is only at that moment, after his denial of responsibility, and his shame-free statement of abdication of his role as his (younger) brother's keeper, that God roars back at him

that "The blood of your brother cries out from the earth" and with a statement of Cain's punishment. See Genesis 4:9-15.

337. Hausner, 325.

338. For example, it ruled as inadmissable most of the evidence pertaining to the Jewish resistance. The prosecution's conviction was that part of framing the scope of Eichmann's crimes was to understand the behavior of his victims, but were most often overruled on this matter. The judges also rejected as inadmissable evidence of his guilt the 62 transcripts annotated by Eichmann—a handwriting expert verified that these were his annotations—presented by the prosecution, of talks conducted in Argentina between Eichmann and the Dutch Nazi journalist, Willem Sassen, over a five-month period in 1957. These talks were to be the basis of a book that would both detail the Final Solution and argue, in effect, that it was the Jews themselves who were ultimately responsible for it. In the transcripts, Eichmann would also observe that "There was nothing personal in it... Personally I never had any bad experience with a Jew... The enemy was not persecuted individually. It was a matter of a political solution [to the problem that Germany—and then Europe, presumably—was not big enough for 'both Germans and Jews']." The Israeli judges argued, 2-1, that the prosecution had not established a sufficiently incontrovertible tie between Eichmann and the document. See Hausner, 9-11 and 348-50. Compare this reluctance with the eagerness with which Judge Kaufman embraced questionable "documentary evidence" of the Rosenbergs' guilt.

339. Hausner, 350f.

340. *Ibid*, 352.

341. *Ibid*, 353.

342. Hausner, 355. *Kristallnacht*, ("The Night of Broken Glass"), the night of November 9-10, 1938, was the first somewhat systematic action against the Jews of Germany undertaken by the Nazis, in which scores of synagogues and hundreds of Jewish shops and homes were seriously damaged or destroyed, and thousands of Jews were either injured or murdered. Ironically, on the other hand, it marked the end of a five-year period of constant, random, street violence against German Jews; thereafter, the streets were safer for them than they had been theretofore—but that was because the details of a calmer, cleaner, more systematic program of destruction were being worked out by the Nazi brass.

343. In the context of our narrative, one cannot help wondering how Harry Gold or David Greenglass would have fared in this courtroom, or how Eichmann would have fared in Judge Kaufman's courtroom. There are certainly parallels, at least in theory, regarding the two situations and the question that they raised with regard to how far an individual will go verbally to save himself and/or to protect certain other loved ones, and with regard to how convincing s/he can or cannot seem to whom.

To clarify Eichmann's relationship to the liquidation of Hungarian Jewry: Hungary became a puppet state of Nazi Germany only in spring, 1944, by which time the war was clearly moving to an unsuccessful conclusion for Hitler. Eichmann came to Budapest to take personal charge of a process that was awesomely efficient—all the exterminationist experiments in other countries during the previous four years paid off—and managed, for example, to deport half of Hungary's 750,000 Jews in a mere 46 days. Equally to the point: Hungary's Jews were the only Jewish population whose destroyers proceeded with the annihilation with full knowledge that the war was lost before they began the process of annhiliation. (See Raoul Hilberg, *Destruction of the European Jews*, 510).

344. Hausner, 361. The Madagascar plan was an idea that had been floated by various individuals (and not only German Nazis) for removing all of European Jewry to the island of Madagascar, off the east coast of Africa. In the summer of 1940 such a plan had started to gain traction, and it fell to Eichmann to come up with the details of a refined plan, which he did by August 15. The Eichmann plan called for the deportation of 1 million Jews per year over a four-year period to the territory, using British naval ships (the Nazis anticipated an immanent collapse of British resistance to them), to remove Jews to what had formerly been French colonial territory (since France was on the verge of falling). To many among the Nazi brass this plan seemed superior to the relatively piecemeal effort of deportations to Poland. Eventually—Britain didn't fall and the war was clearly going to continue for some time—the Madagascar Plan was dropped in favor of the Final Solution articulated at Wannsee.

345. *Ibid*, 368-9.

346. Theresienstadt, near Prague (and called "Terezin" in Czech) was designed as a source of propaganda; a waystation to Auschwitz for nearly all of its temporary inhabitants, it was designed to afford the impression that the Jews incarcerated there were enjoying a wonderful life—given the reality of war around them—with music and culture and the movie-set trappings of a comfortable cafe life.

347. Joseph Kessel, writing in *France-Soir*, July 7, 1961; quoted in Hausner, 368.

348. The Nuremberg Laws were enacted in 1935 to denaturalize German Jews; thereafter they were not considered citizens of the Reich and therefore not protected by its laws on the one hand and on the other were prevented from participation in a number of Reich activities. Both sides of this equation expanded over the next several years.

349. Sixteen witnesses were deposed on behalf of the defense, including several who were in prison on criminal charges, primarily war crimes, including Franz Slavik and Franz Novick in Austria; Hermann Krumey, Erich von dem Bach-Zelewski and Richard Baer in Germany; and Herbert Kappler in Italy.

350. For details, see Hausner, 374-87.

351. *Ibid*, 390. While the tapes could not be procured for the trial, and the judges could express certain doubts about the absolute reliability of the written Sassen texts, their impact could still be felt in the context of other written documentary and oral testimony.

352. Hitler had been willing to allow a certain number of Jews to be deported elsewhere than to the death camps to which Eichmann was sending them, in exchange for the 300,000 Jews of Budapest.

353. Hausner, 401.

354. *Ibid*, 402.

355. There was a small series of exceptions to this: Servatius passed over without mention the strongly incriminating testimony of Professor Six and the affidavits of Mildner, Hoffman and Morgen that the defense itself had submitted.

356. Hausner, 406-7. To our ears, this last assertion may have a familiar ring—in a reversed direction. For we may recall how the prosecution in the Rosenberg-Sobell case used the same sort of imagery, as it sought to identify a series of links that added up to an incontrovertible chain of guilt for them. Here the chain of guilt is said to be lacking a number of crucial links.

357. *Ibid*, 408.

358. *Ibid*, 423.

359. *Ibid*, 426.

360. The President of the Supreme Court, Justice Yitzhak Olshan, presided. On the bench with him were Relieving President, Dr. Simon Agranat, and Justices Dr. Moshe Silberg, Dr. Yoel Sussman and Dr. Alfred Vitkon.

361. Hausner, 453.

362. By interesting coincidence for our narrative, Jackson would soon thereafter become a justice of the United States Supreme Court, where he would end up writing the primary and most emphatic opinion vacating Justice Douglas' stay of execution of the Rosenbergs and justifying the rush to execute them imediately. See above, Chapter Six, 291-2 and n 273.

363. Hausner, 453.

364. Among the myriad publications that grew out of the affair is that by Akiva W. Deutsch, *The Eichmann Trial in the Eyes of Israeli Youngsters*, which focusses on the diverse aspects of this issue.

365. I am quoting from Miriam Bernstein-Benschlomo's translation of the article as it appears in the volume of essays by Scholem, *On Jews and Judaism in Crisis*, 298 ff.

366. The review article was in the October 13, 1963 issue of *The Observer*.

367. The articles appeared in February and March, 1963 issues of the magazine, and the book, *Eichmann in Jerusalem: A Report on the Banality of Evil*, also in 1963.

368. Arendt, 267.

369. *Ibid*, 6.

370. It is interesting—remarkable and inexplicable, really, unless we simply assume anti-Semitism as a motive—that *The New Yorker* refused to print any of the numerous letters and essays addressed to the magazine in response to and in the wake of her five-part article.

371. The full title is *And the Crooked Shall Be Made Straight: The Jewish Catastrophe and Hannah Arendt's Narrative*. Walter Laqueur wrote a review of Robinson's book to which Arendt then responded in her chapter "The Formidable Dr. Robinson" in her 1978 book, *The Jew as Pariah*. A more recent and also important discussion—and more sympathetic to Arendt—will be found in chapter two, "Banality" of Gerald E. Markle's 1995 book, *Meditations of a Holocaust Traveler*. There are many more books and articles on Arendt's book, of course.

372. "Fuehrer" is merely the German word for "leader," but after the Nazi era, when the word had been so repeatedly and exclusively used by Nazi Germans to refer to or address Hitler, it acquired a distinct and quite negative nuance. Particularly when used in English-language contexts—and she was writing in English—the term has had a specifically Hitlerian connotation since World War II, and would hardly be used except in reference to Hitler. It is this nuance to which Scholem refers and which he finds so offensive in Arendt's phraseology.

373. Of particular note among the many critics, because her words are succinct and because they are part of her introduction to Gideon Hausner's book, is the prominent Jewish American historian, Barbara Tuchman, who notes that "to have been so taken in by Eichmann's version of himself is one of the puzzles of modern journalism. From a presumed historian it is inexplicable." See Hausner, xix-xx.

374. "Arendt and the Eichmann Controversy," in *Modern Judaism*, vol 13, No. 1 (February, 1983), 75-94.

375. Barnouw, 80-81.

376. *Ibid*, 81.

377. I do not at all mean, by this last pair of words to exclude other than Jewish victims from the tragedy and its dignity, but in the context of this narrative and

specifically the article by Barnouw, I cannot avoid the feeling that the Jewishness of the victims discussed by Arendt and by Barnouw and which were the primary focus, as victims, of the Eichmann trial, is a factor in what Barnouw writes in her article and how she writes it.

Chapter Eight

378. See below, 400-1 and nn 454 and 455. Between the time of writing and final editing for publication, Demjanjuk was actually extradited to Germany, at age 89, to face trial and was found guilty two years later. He died shortly thereafter, at age 91, while his case was on appeal.

379. Allan A. Ryan, *Quiet Neighbors: Prosecuting Nazi War Criminals in America*, 30-31. Ryan's quotes, as he points out, come from Joseph C. Goulden, *The Best Years*, 308.

380. *Ibid*, 31.

381. *Ibid*, 32. The details follow on 32-35.

382. *Ibid*, 42.

383. "John" is merely the English-language equivalent of "Ivan."

384. Ryan, 99.

385. The allusion, incidently, is to the notorious Russian Tsar Ivan III whose excesses of cruelty earned him that epithet.

386. This raises an interesting question: how, then, did Hanusiak gain access to those archives? If the answer is that, because, unlike many Ukrainian-Americans, he was not anti-Soviet, but even, as the nature of his publication would suggest, pro-Soviet, then could his assertions, or the "evidence" that he passed along to INS, indeed be part of a "Soviet conspiracy" to avenge the USSR against "traitors" such as Ukrainians who left the USSR and gained refuge in the United States—which would be part of Demjanjuk's defense, for example? Based on the discussion thus far, we cannot be certain, but we certainly cannot rule out the possibility. On the other hand, of the 73 people listed by Hanusiak, only seven were charged by INS, and only after further research. Of those seven, two confessed that the charges were true, two committed suicide shortly after the charges were filed, and three—including Demjanjuk—contested the charges.

387. There is, of course, some irony (yet again in this two-thousand-year-long narrative) in all of this, particularly if it is laid side-by-side with aspects of the Rosenberg-Sobell trial of nearly 30 years earlier. One of the points that Ryan makes in his account of these negotiations is the importance to the American judicial system of assuring the rights of the defendants. "Recognition of an individual's rights against the government is the keystone of the American legal system." My discussion of the Rosenberg-Sobell affair makes it clear that I have serious doubts as to the degree to which this verity was fufilled in their case—and the idea that, as Ryan notes, he was pointing out this judicial nicety of the American system to the representatives of the Soviet regime, given the fact that it was that very regime for whom the Rosenbergs and Sobell were accused of committing espionage, is ironic indeed.

388. Federenko confessed to having been a Camp guard and to having lied on his immigration application and was extradited to Ukraine. In the photo spread the INS people added various and sundry head shots, with the intention, of course, of seeing whether or not the survivors consistently picked out Federenko. Among those photos they happened to include Demjanjuk's 1951 visa application photo—and a number of survivors also pointed to his image, unsolicited, as that of Ivan *Grozny*.

389. Ryan, 106-7.

390. Such proceedings are treated with the intensity of a criminal proceeding, not a civil proceeding; the case against a defendant, to succeed, must be airtight—and it is judged not by a jury but by a judge.

391. The prosecuting attorneys who served under the direction of Ryan and his assistant, Neil Sher, were Norman Moscowits and Jack Horrigan.

392. Ryan, 118.

393. *Ibid*, 130.

394. For the prosecution, forensic expert Gideon Epstein of the INS extracted pinprick ink samples and a tiny corner of the paper for microscopic testing to determine the age of the document; photographed and studied the signatures, analyzing stroke, pressure and other features; examined the card for signs of erasures that might indicate a name substitution. In the end he saw nothing that could suggest a forgery. The same conclusion was arrived at by the defense's expert.

395. Ryan, 134.

396. *Ibid*, 134-5.

397. Presumably either his eye color slightly changed, or his own self-descriptive perception of exactly how to describe the color of his grey-blue eyes changed.

398. *Ibid*, 138.

399. We are reminded both that the revival of the Klan in the south was due in large part to the Leo Frank trial before World War I—and that the pressure on the court at that time and place from the crowds outside the courtroom was intense—and that that revival also included a spread northward, of which we have earlier seen evidence in Massena, New York in the late 1920s. In this last regard, we have also noted, albeit obliquely, the presence of Klan activity in northern Ohio in the context of the McCarthy-era atmosphere that informed the Rosenberg-Sobell trial, in the early 1950s—I am referring to Clarence Brandenberg and the 1969 Klan rally. That spread obviously still encompassed northern Ohio in the early 1980s.

400. *Ryan*, 113.

401. *Ibid*, 114.

402. The most famous "Jewish trial" involving Holocaust denial—which I am not discussing in the course of this book, in the interests of space—was that which took place in England in 1998. The defendant was the Jewish American historian, Deborah Lipstadt, who, in her seminal book on the subject of Holocaust denial, *Denying the Holocaust: The Growing Assault on Truth and Memory*, mentioned, among others, the Englishman David Irving as a key figure in the denial "movement." Irving sued her and her publisher for defamation, but the British court—in the person of Justice Gray—not only ruled decisively in her favor, but took the opportunity to excoriate Irving as a "right-wing pro-Nazi polemicist." The most vocal and well-publicized contemporary denier is President Ahmadinejad of Iran, who frequently peppers his speeches with references to—and in December, 2006 organized an entire conference to focus on—the Holocaust as a Jewish fabrication.

403. O'Connor had been recommended to the family by his father, Edward M. O'Connor. O'Connor père had served four decades earlier as one of the commissioners adminstering the DP Act passed by Congress in 1948, in which capacity "he approved the admission of members of Waffen SS units and was criticized for favoring admission for Hitler's supporters over his victims." (Tom Teicholz, *The Trial of Ivan the Terrible: State of Israel vs. John Demjanjuk*, 42.) The elder O'Connor had recommended his son after his advice had been sought by an old friend, Jerome Brentar, a Cleveland Travel Agent and an important Demjanjuk supporter—and an individual affiliated with Holocaust revisionist groups.

404. Teicholz, 71, quoting INS attorney and OSI Deputy Director Martin Mendelsshon.

405. *Ibid*, 81.

406. I have not myself seen the transcripts of the remarks, but am reporting them based on a statement of a colleague, Marc Masurovsky, who, while he was working for Allan Ryan's OSI office in the mid-1980s, saw them.

407. He is quoted thusly in the front-page article of the September 30, 1986 issue of Cleveland's *The Plain Dealer*. His confidence was interestingly expressed, in such terms. For his words suggest somewhat of an idealized and therefore mythologized view of Israel and/or of Jews that is the opposite side of the coin of the Nazi and other negative, demonizing views of Jews. Both views share in common an inability to see Jews simply as people, good and bad, with virtues and flaws. Both views deny the possibility of normalcy to Jews and to Jewish-Christian relations.

408. *Ibid*, 2-A. Interestingly, where the Eichmann case was seen as important primarily in bringing the reality of the Holocaust before Israeli youth (and the world), the Demjanjuk case, a generation later—and in the wake of three more Arab-Israeli Wars—was seen more as important in validating the existential significance of the State of Israel and in helping Israeli youth (and the world) not to take it for granted.

409. In fact, Defense counselor John Martin had at the time asked for and received a five-day recess from Judge Battisti in order to have sufficient time to consult his documents expert regarding the Trawniki card. His expert, Joseph Tholl, was never called upon to render an opinion—although, having announced that he would not challenge the authenticity of the card, Martin would later assert that he had not been given sufficient time to examine it!

410. About this, one might make two comments: that we don't know where Buchanan acquired that information, so that we cannot judge its truth value; that if it is accurate it could either mean that Rosenberg was lying at the time of his trial testimony or it could mean that, back in 1947, he believed that Ivan had been killed. If we remember that he was among the few who managed ultimately to escape in the heat of the uprising, it is also possible that he was simply mistaken and subsequently—35 years later—shocked and surprised to see Ivan's image in the Federenko photo spread and then still later to find out that Ivan was still alive.

411. Jankel Wiernik was a survivor who escaped Treblinka after the 1943 uprising. He referred to Ivan the gas chamber operator in the memoir he wrote, *A Year in Treblinka*, and died in 1972, well before the Demjanjuk affair surfaced.

412. Patrick Buchanan, "Leaks found in Ryan's 'airtight' case on Demjanjuk," *The Plain Dealer*, January 4, 1987, 1-2D

413. Michele Lesie, "Judgment in Jerusalem: Was Demjanjuk 'Ivan the Terrible'?," *The Plain Dealer*, February 8, 1987, 18-A.

414. *Ibid.*

415. To repeat and further the argument: the prosecution would echo earlier American charges that he was a captured Red Army soldier eager to escape the horrific condition that characterized German POW camps; and that he was a Ukrainian who had sufferred under Stalin in the 1930s to a sufficient extent that he would be willing to join the German side against Russia; and added to those assertions the claim that he possessed a skill that the Germans could use in a place like Treblinka: he could drive. The idea that he already possessed that skill before the war would be argued in further enumerating the ways in which Demjanjuk had lied about his past when he sought immigration ot the United States: he had at one point claimed that he took a driving course and received a driver's license several years after the war, while in an allied DP camp.

416. Number 1393 apears both on the photograph and on the card.

417. Interestingly, neither side called attention to the disparity in eye color, which had been raised by the defense in Cleveland. That strategy had backfired when the prosecution pointed out that Demjanjuk had identified his eye color on his American visa and immigration forms not as it was indicated on the Trawniki card—blue—but as all of the witnesses had identified it: grey. So the card offered an error, by his own self-description, rather than the witnesses being wrong.

418. More to the point, perhaps, prosecution attorney Shaked dismantled the claim to expertise of Robertson altogether, first by pointing out that the organization of which she was a member, the World Association of Documents Examiners (WADE) did not require forensic document experience as an admission criterion, and the U.S. courts did not find their members qualified as experts; then by noting that she had no knowledge of chemistry by which she could analyze the elements of the card she claimed to have analyzed.

419. I am quoting Blattman from the Friday, February 5, 1988 article, "Prosecution sums up '3-river' case against Demjanjuk" in the *Cleveland Jewish News*, 25.

420. Teicholz, 270-1.

421. *Ibid*, 271.

422. *Ibid*, 273.

423. *Ibid*, 273.

424. Or perhaps he was aware—but in that case he miscalculated the nature of that evocative weight on the court.

425. *Ibid*, 274-5

426. This was the very Danylchenko who was referenced in the original Husniak and subsequent articles in *News from Ukraine*. Treblinka was divided, essentially, into an upper camp (Camp One) and a lower camp (Camp Two). The gas chamber was located in the upper part of Camp Two.

427. Teicholz, 295.

428. This rather lengthy chapter from the last book of the Pentateuch offers a strong statement to the Israelites from Moses of the consequences of obeying and/ or disobeying the word of God (in a nutshell: extremes of reward and punishment). By "interesting" in the context of our discussion I mean the fact that a twentieth-century Israeli justice would quote from "God's word" in offering a legal decision; this implies a sense of interweave between law and religion such as was discussed in the introduction to this volume. For the record, I believe that Judge Levin was either misremembering or misinterpreting the meaning of that biblical chapter with regard to its applicability to his point regarding witness identifications of Ivan—but that is beside the point that I am making.

429. Teicholz, 299-300. A reminder that the only legal condition in which the death penalty is stipulated by Israeli law is that pertaining to Nazi crimes.

430. See Susan Adams, "Ivan the Terrible's Terrible Defense," *The American Lawyer*, October, 1988, 148-157.

431. *Ibid*, 149.

432. The overturning of that verdict under appeal had little to do with the expertise of O'Connor and Gill. Their handling of it in the first place had produced the guilty verdict that was subsequently overturned.

433. Adams, 152.

434. It still would have meant that he had collaborated with the Nazis and that he had lied on his immigration forms, but it might have saved his life (assuming that his appeal were to be turned down).

435. Incidentally, it is not clear what drew Eitan to the Demjanjuk case or to offer his services to Sheftel any more than what prompted his apparent suicide. With respect to the latter event, there was no suicide note and none of his family or friends had perceived him as depressed in any way. Could he have been pushed?

436. Teicholz, 303. The thrower of the acid, Yisrael Yehezkeli—who had lost many family members at Treblinka, and was, according to friends, very upset at Eitan's death—was arrested and convicted of aggravated assault and given a five-year jail sentence (two of which were suspended) and ordered to pay a series of fines to cover Sheftel's medical expenses and to compensate him for his suffering.

437. He was writing to Pier Arrigo Carnier, who was writing a book, *Lo Sterminio Mancato* (*The Missing Exterminator*), which deals with the fate of Italian Jews. In his discussion he writes about the transfer of 150 members of the *Aktion Reinhard* execution squads to Trieste, in Northern Italy, when the *Aktion* was concluded in Poland.

438. He is quoted in Gitta Sereny's article, "New data good, bad to Demjanjuk," in Cleveland's *The Plain Dealer*, Saturday, January 14, 1989, 5-B.

439. See above, 364. Danylchenko's testimony was brought out, by way of Hanusiak's original article and "file" on Ukrainian-American Nazi collaborators, at the time of the Demjanjuk denaturalization hearings, but the Americans were not given permission at that time to question him, nor, apparently, did the Soviets reinterrogate him. Danylchenko had named Ivan as a fellow guard at Sobibor; he claimed to have worked together with Ivan until "March or April, 1944." But the camp was dismantled in October, 1943, and more to the point, survivor witnesses from Treblinka placed him there.

440. Danylchenko had died in 1985. Sereny did interview his wife, who apparently knew little about his wartime activities; she also spoke with the Soviet war-crimes procurator, Natalya Kolesnikova, among others.

441. Associated Press article, "Demjanjuk kin seeks acquittal: Ivan Marchenko was 'Ivan,' says son-in-law," *The Plain Dealer*, Saturday, June 16, 1990, 2-A.

442. *Ibid.*

443. The name is transliterated into Latin letters as both Marchenko and Marczenko; I have opted for whichever spelling is used by the source I am quoting; otherwise I prefer "Marczenko."

444. Sharon LaFraniere, "U.S. Court to Review Extradition of 'Ivan': New Evidence Shakes Israeli War Crime Case," *The Plain Dealer*, Saturday, June 6, 1992, A-3.

445. Michele Lesie, "The Last Word: Israeli court to decide John Demjanjuk's fate," *The Plain Dealer*, Sunday, July 25, 1993, 1-C, 4-C.

446. Danylchenko had testified that Demjanjuk was "repeatedly assigned by the Germans to get Jews in surrounding ghettos and deliver them in trucks to the [Sobibor] camp to be killed."

447. Cynthia Mann, "Court delays deportation of Demjanjuk: Holocaust survivors hope for new trial," *Washington Jewish Week*, August 26, 1993, 25.

448. *Ibid.*

449. *Washington Jewish Week* editorial, August 26, 1993, 26.

450. The court echoed Harish's comment, stating that "on the basis of the evidence available, it is unlikely that Demjanjuk would be convicted of the alternative charges, and risking a further acquittal is not in the public interest."

451. The court argued, in part, moreover, that the assumptions made regarding Demjanjuk's role as Ivan the Terrible had driven the earlier citizenship/deportation trial, and since those assumptions had been overturned by the Israeli Supreme Court, the very basis for that earlier verdict was compromised.

452. "U.S. 'Nazi Guard' faces deportation," *BBC News*, 22 December 2006.

453. In fact, as I was reviewing this manuscript for final pre-publication edits, I came across a brief statement in the March 16, 2009 internet newswire service, *Guysen International News*, (submitted at 12:21 PM), noting that "[a] German court has finally issued an international arrest warrant for John Demjanjuk for participating in the killing of 29,000 Jews when he was a prison guard at the Sobibor concentration camp." A month later, I heard a radio news report mentioning that he had been brought from his home to the Cleveland Seventh District Court in a wheel chair, apparently in the context of addressing the German warrant. He was sent home either later the same day or the following day and it was not clear as to the resolution of this latest legal gambit. By Monday, May 11 it became clear: on that day, according to an Associated Press report from Cleveland, "Federal agents carrying John Demjanuk in a wheelchair put him on a small jet Monday to be deported to Germany... The deportation came four days after the U.S. Supreme Court refused to consider Demjanjuk's request to block deportation and about 31/2 years after he was last ordered deported... Earlier Monday, his son, John Demjanjuk, Jr., said an appeal in a U.S. court would go ahead even if his father isn't in the country... Also Monday, a Berlin court rejected an appeal aimed at preventing deportation." See the following footnote. (The AP story was based on reporting by Melissa Eddy in Berlin, Thomas J. Sheeran in Cleveland, and Kantele Franko in Columbus, OH.)

454. I have left these last two sentences essentially intact, in spite of the most recent developments reported in the previous footnote: he still could have ended up back in America as a stateless alien, or even with his citizenship rights restored. As it subsequently turned out, he *was* deported—for trial to Germany—and, on May 12, 2011, found guilty of 28,060 counts (one source says 27,900, but I believe it is mistaken) of accessory to murder—one each for the deaths of that number of individuals killed at Sobibor in which he is said to have had a role. He was sentenced to a five-year jail term, which took into consideration his age and frail condition. German Judge Ralph Alt asserted that the trail of documents tying him to Sobibor is incontrovertible, but allowed him to remain out of prison—he was placed in a German nursing home, while the appeal process moved forward. See fn 467

455. See above, nn 378, 453 and 454. My use of "s/he" is not simply an attempt at political correctness. While the lion's share of the cases of accused former war criminals in America have been men, a few have been women. The most notorious, perhaps, is Hermine Braunsteiner, a Queens, NY housewife against whom INS began deportation proccedings in 1972, the first public case involving Nazi war-crimes in the United States in fifteen years. She was accused of having been a sadistic guard at the Maidanek death camp—the "Mare of Maidanek"—who typically beat women, often to death, with a whip whose straps were studded with lead bullets. She ended up extradited to Germany where she was tried in the Duesseldorf proceedings of 1975-81. She was found guilty of committing multiple murders and sentenced to a life sentence in a German prison. See Ryan, 46-52 and 333-4.

456. Ryan, 215.

457. *Ibid*, 148. Ryan quotes both numbers from different scholarly sources.

458. *Ibid*, 152.

459. *Ibid*, 153.

460. *Ibid*, 155-6.

461. *Ibid*, 174.

462. The government's extradition case had in part rested on its view that the 1901 Serbian treaty applied to 1951 Yugoslavia as a direct descendant of the

Serbian state, but Hall argued that such an evaluation resides in the hands of a judge, as a representative of the judiciary, and not the executive (or legislative) branch(es) of government.

463. Ryan, 169.

464. He had actually never been granted citizenship, and his visitor's visa had, of course, expired.

465. Quoted in Ryan, 185.

466. If on the one hand I need not remind the reader of the earlier-mentioned importance of the Cold War and policies such as Operation Paperclip in helping to push forward the relative disinterest in former Nazis, on the other it should be remembered that the upsurge in interest in various aspects of the Holocaust, which began with the capture and trial of Eichmann, reached a new level with the opening of the U.S. Holocaust Memorial Museum in 1991. That the OSI's offices should have become increasingly active in the 1990s makes perfect sense. See the article by Michael Isikoff, "Nazi-Hunting Office Is Busier Than Ever" in the May 3, 1993 issue of *The Washington Post*, A17. There remained critics at that time, like Patrick Buchanan and Rep. James A. Traficant, Jr., (D-Ohio), who maintained that the OSI consistently distorted evidence in a "persecution" campaign against aging Eastern European-Americans—an echo of the earlier assertion that the deportation cases depended on fake evidence ginned up by the USSR in its "persecution campaign" against the same group of people. Such assertions persist to this day—and for what it is worth, Traficant was expelled from Congress in 2002 in a bribe-taking and racketeering scandal and sentenced to an eight-year prison term which he is still serving. This rather undercut the effectiveness of his championing such "victims" of OSI persecution.

467. But see above, n 453 and 454 for the 2009 and 2011 installments for Demjanjuk's legal saga. By the time of this footnote's last iteration (Spring, 2012) the case was virtually resolved: the German court to which he was extradited found him guilty, and he died at age 91, on March 17, 2012, while awaiting the response to the appeal put forth by his lawyers. Since his conviction was still under appeal, he died without having been found guilty according to German law.

Chapter Nine

468. I mention these particular three because they all begin either in the United States or elsewhere in the Americas and end up back in Europe. Schellong is of interest because he is an exception to the rule regarding most former Nazis with whom, over the years, the OSI has dealt, who have come from countries other than Germany—Poland, Lithuania, Hungary, Croatia, Ukraine and the like. In other words, they operated under the authority of the German Nazis. Most of the German Nazis had an easier time, it seems, getting to South America, thanks to a number of "assistance" programs, than to the U.S.—with the exception of high-level German scientists, who were wont to enter the United States under the "Operation Paperclip" program, as we have earlier noted. But among the exceptions to this "rule" was Schellong, who had been a Captain in the SS, and served as a concentration camp guard in a number of places, including Sachsenburg and Dachau. He entered the United States under the Immigration and Nationality Act of 1952, in 1957, obtaining American citizenship five years later. His immigration claim—that he had been merely a soldier in the German army, fighting the Russians, and had had nothing to do with the camps—was uncovered as false in the late 1970s and he was ordered denaturalized and deported in 1982 after a Federal court ruled that he had lied on his

immigration and citizenship applications. In 1987 the U.S. Supreme Court refused to hear a final appeal and he was deported the folowing year to West Germany.

469. Barbie, "The Butcher of Lyon," known for his personally torturing and killing some 4,000 people as head of the Gestapo in Lyon, and for masterminding the round-up and deportation to Auschwitz of 44 Jewish children from an orphanage at Izieu in 1944, was tried and sentenced to death in absentia by French courts in 1952 and 1954. He was discovered in Bolivia 1971 by Serge and Beate Klarsfeld, handed over to French authorities finally in 1983 and put on trial in May, 1987. In his trial he showed not a scintilla of remorse, and argued that he was being illegally tried, since he had been brought by force from his refuge in Bolivia (with the cooperation of the Bolivian government at that time). He was found guilty of crimes against humanity in July, and sentenced to life imprisonment, (which in France, in effect, means 20 years), but died in prison four years later, of leukemia. One of the ironies of his sentence is that he was spared the guillotine because the son of one of his victims had been instrumental in causing the death penalty to be abolished in France. An interesting aspect of his case is that his alias, Klaus Altmann, was apparently given to him by American intelligence officers who secretly took him on as an agent in 1947 while telling French post-war authorities that they had no idea of his whereabouts.

470. Linnas was an Estonian who had entered the United States in 1952 by way of a "displaced persons" status claim akin to that asserted by John Demjanjuk. He had, it turns out, operated a Nazi-run concentration camp in Tartu, Estonia, where he allegedly directed and personally participated in the murder of thousands of men, women and children who were herded into anti-tank ditches where they were shot. He was stripped of his American citizenship by the Federal District Court in Westbury, NY in 1981, a 1986 federal appeals court upheld his conviction, (ruling that the evidence was "overwhelming and largely uncontroverted"), and on April 20, 1987 the U.S. Supreme Court refused to hear a final appeal. That same day he was flown to the Soviet Union on a Czech jet—a number of emigre groups, as in the Demjanjuk case, asserted that he had been framed by the USSR, in this case as part of an anti-Baltic States, as opposed to anti-Ukraine, campaign—to be tried for war crimes. Linnas had in fact been tried in absentia in Estonia back in 1962, at which time the USSR had asked that he be extradited from the United States, but that request was turned down for 25 years. He died in a prison hospital three months after arriving back into the Soviet Union. Interestingly, his legal counsel in the U.S. was former U.S Attorney General Ramsey Clark—who also represented the PLO in the Leon Klinghoffer lawsuit.

471. See above, Chapter Five, 212-13

472. "*Samizdat*" is the Russian term used to refer to literature that the Soviet authorities regarded as subversive and therefore had to be produced and distributed in a clandestine manner. The coinage means "self (*sam*)-published (*izdat*)" —referring to the fact that all such materials were printed privately (in secret); typically, a person would print up a few copies of some text, and pass them on to a few people, each of whom was expected to make a few more and pass them along, and so on. The system moved too quickly and exponentially for the authorities to keep up with it in their attempts to destroy such subversive materials.

473. *Aliyah* literally means "going up" and derives as a concept from the original sense of going up to Jerusalem both literally, (since the city is located on a series of hills) and metaphorically, since within the Jewish tradition, Jerusalem is closer to heaven, spiritually speaking, and thus to God, than any other place on earth. The term continues to be used in the modern, secular reality of contemporary Israel to

refer to immigrating to what is still very much conceived of—in the Hebrew-language vocabulary of even secular Israelis (and sometimes, therefore, unconsciously) as a Sacred Land.

474. I hope I may be forgiven, in the interests of the particular direction of my discussion, for not spending the necessary time in the main body of this text to review the complications that Butman and others recognized were inherent in the plan that they were devising. Not the logistical difficulties that would be obvious to any reader without spelling them out—but the difficulties of conscience. Assuming that they would be successful, and escape the country, whom would they leave behind and how would those friends and loved ones be affected by having had contact with them? What would the KGB do by way of searches, arrests, the shutting down of even the semblance of programs that addressed Jewish life? But if they did not attempt to leave and didn't thereby make a statement that the world would hear, what hope could they have that either those whom they would be leaving behind if they did leave or they who would be leaving could or would ever have the opportunity to lead the sort of Jewish lives that they sought? See Butman, *From Leningrad to Jerusalem: The Gulag Way. Hijacking Plot and Trial*, 112-15.

475. *Ibid*, XIV.

476. *Ibid*, 163

477. *Ibid*, 171.

478. *Ibid*, 178.

479. *Ibid*, 179.

480. *Ibid*, 208-9.

481. *Ibid*, 210-11.

482. *Ibid*, 232-3.

483. *Ibid*, 235. Specific reference would be made by the defense lawyers to the Tokyo Convention of 1969, which would have obligated the Swedes to return the plane.

484. *Ibid*, 225.

485. For reasons known only to him, Butman never names his lawyer, which is why I have failed to do so.

486. Butman, 244.

487. For the purposes of this book, I need to make that distinction (between Jewish and non-Jewish)—in general and in order to justify not including a discussion of Sakharov—but needless to say there are both conceptual overlap and parallels on all fronts between the broader movement and the specifically Jewish/Zionist movement. Both grew out of frustration with the Soviet regime's suppression of human rights; the Jewish/Zionist movement had a specific identity focus and the persecution of its members was based on that—Jewish—identity. Sakharov, it should be noted, in another instance of historical irony relevant to this book, played two major scientific roles in Soviet and world history before his political convictions and activities led to his being stripped of the right to function as a scientist. One was as a cosmologist. The other was as a major player in the developing Soviet atomic bomb program under Igor Kurchatov, between mid-1948 and late 1953; he was part of the successful "Joe-1" blast. It was the success of that program, we might recall, that was alleged to have been facilitated by the espionage efforts of the Rosenbergs and their associates, with dire consequences for the United States and humanity. (**See above, 270**). To read Sakharov's biography is, incidentally, to find yet another proof of the lie to that double assertion.

488. Butman, 102 ff.

489. The goal of the Basques was to force the Spanish government to yield independence to the Basque areas of northeastern Spain; their method was and has usually been, violent: typically, judiciously placed bombs.

490. Soviet law permitted the filing of an appeal by a prisoner within seven days of being sentenced, although the specifics of such a time frame would in any event be set aside in this case, given the world-wide response to the situation.

491. The day before, on December 30, Franco had also commuted the death sentences of the Basque separatists.

492. Butman, 248.

493. *Ibid*, 251-2. A bit more about Sharansky follows below. At the risk of sounding pompous, I note for those concerned about transliteration propriety that the proper transliteration is "Shcharansky," but—presumably because the consonantal cluster "shch" is difficult for many English-speakers, the name is most often transliterated as it is in the English translation of Butman's book. I will conform to that convention and (in spite of yearning for phonemic purity) spell "Sharansky."

494. *Ibid*, 265.

495. *Ibid*, 269.

496. *Ibid*, 268.

497. *Ibid*, 271-3.

498. *Ibid*, 273.

499. *Ibid*, 279.

500. *Ibid*, XIV.

501. By then, Sakharov himself had been long engaged in the human rights struggle—he received the Nobel Peace Prize in 1973—although he would not be arrested and confined to house arrest in Gorky until 1980. He must have had a profound influence on Sharansky.

502. Note my use of the phrase "Jewish Israelis," to underscore the fact that, although commonly referred to as "the Jewish State," Israel's citizenry includes, among others, a substantial number of Christians, Muslims and members of other faiths. Jews are citizens of England and France, which are decidedly Anglican and Catholic, respectively, in many respects. These are at the same time secular democracies—as Israel is—and few people would refer to the two of them as "an Anglican state" and "a Catholic state."

503. In his book, *The Case for Democracy: The Power of Freedom to Overcome Tyranny and Terror* (co-written with Ron Dermer), Sharansky by no means discounts the Palestinian desire for an independent state. He asserts that, within the context of human rights, safety and stability for all the inhabitants of the area, he "outlines [a] plan to help the Palestinians build a free society and help Israelis and Palestinians forge a lasting peace" but "not at the expense of the State of Israel." Not all would agree with his "outline." For a concise discussion of the Israeli-Palestinian issue within the larger context of Israeli democratic and/or humanistic aims (but without specific reference to Sharansky) see Ori Z. Soltes, *Untangling the Web*.

504. I am thinking, in the latter case, of an individual such as Baruch Goldstein, and his gunning down of 29 Palestinian Arabs in the Mosque within the Hebron Cave of the Patriarchs. In his case, the subsequent legal question did not involve him—he was ultimately disarmed by Palestinian Arabs and beaten to death at the site—but did involve the decision by the army not to institute a court proceeding to try those who beat him to death, treating his death simply as an unsolved murder. But there have been other, less extreme cases of Goldstein-like actions where the perpetrator has survived and had to face the court.

505. Interestingly, Gideon Hausner already alluded to this general situation, of a Jewish state putting its own or others on trial—already, therefore, as an issue on the Israeli legal mind well before the changed conditions of Israeli life after 1967—in his summing up of the case against Eichmann, when he referred to the trial of the soldiers who had killed Arab civilians back in October, 1956. See Hausner, 396.

506. Dr. Daniel Elazar, then professor of political science and director of the Center for the Study of Federalism at Temple University and also a professor at Bar Ilan University in Israel, as quoted in Gloria Ulmer's article in *The Cleveland Jewish News*, Friday, February 18, 1983, 6.

507. The very title of the article says it clearly: "Trial of Palestinian Leader Focuses Attention on Israeli Courts." The Israeli courts are on trial as much as Barghouti. The article appeared on page A11 of the Monday, May 5, 2003 International Edition.

508. This view was expressed and quoted at some length in the article by Lior Yavne, a spokesman for the Israeli human rights organization, B'tselem.

509. Myre, *op citum.*

510. Of course, those who believe the court's decision was wrong might also feel that the entire legal process was a sham.

511. Thus, for example, between the time of the construction of the first phases of the fence in 2002 and the end of 2007, suicide-bomber attacks in Israel were reduced by 90%. A court that demands the removal of a given part of the fence in the face of security claims by the government or the military—should something terroristic transpire, resulting in civilian injuries and/or death, after it rules that the shift be made—would face the charge that it had been morally negligent even if it had been legally above board.

512. That double standard can have a benign face. When Dean Heinrich Grueber, the German pastor who opposed Eichmann, risked his life to save Jews and survived to testify against Eichmann in Jerusalem (see above, 336), was interviewed regarding why God permitted the Holocaust, his view was that God was angry at His "Chosen People" and that Hitler was a chastising rod of that anger. He went on to note his concern that today (he was speaking in the mid-1960s) too many Jews are again involved in activities such as banks and brothels and the press—that are presumably okay for Christians— that leave them open to the kind of hostility used by Hitler in the 1920s. The problem is that Grueber's view of Jews as angels who should not do certain things ends up with consequences as dangerous as those derived from viewing Jews as demons—since disappointment at the Jewish failure to be angels and not mere humans can and usually will eventually lead to their being demonized. See chapter one of Richard Rubenstein's *After Auschwitz* (Second Edition).

513. "Teaching of Contempt" is the phrase commonly used in the last forty years or so to refer to the centuries' long demonization of Jews and Judaism by the Church. The break-throughs to which I allude include the Second Vatican Council of the early 1960s and the arrival of the Vatican to recognizing the legitimacy of the State of Israel's existence in the early 1990s, as well as the decision made by the majority of American Lutherans late in that decade to reject Luther's often viciously anti-Jewish late writings while not feeling that they are thereby rejecting Luther. See especially the essays by Gregory Baum, Eva Fleischner, Johannes Christiaan Hoek-endijk, and Aarne Siirala in Fleischner's *Auschwitz: Beginning of a New Era?*

514. The precise charge was one count of conspiracy to deliver national defense information to a foreign government, which falls under US Code 18/794(c): "gathering or delivering defense information to aid a foreign government."

515. President Reagan had signed an Executive Agreement with Israel in 1983

in which the United States promised to relay any intelligence information necessary to Israel's survival.

516. The uncharacteristic Israeli decision not to respond militarily was due to an American request to stand down in order not to further complicate the Persian Gulf War, (aka Operation Desert Storm), in which the U.S. was allied with many Arab states in its first invasion of Iraq.

517. The "they" to whom he refers is the majority of American Jewry and its leaders who, out of fear, did not speak up loudly enough to galvanize the American government to act against the Holocaust of European Jews.

518. Quoted in the spring 1993 issue of *Viewpoint Magazine*, 31.

519. The discussion of American apathy and the Jewish American fear of speaking up was first discussed at length in Arthur Morse's *While Six Million Died*, which first appeared in 1967—just prior to the time when America and other Israeli allies were shrugging their shoulders as if there was nothing they could do when, on the eve of the Six-Day War of June 1967, it appeared that Israel would be annihilated. The blurb on the front cover of Morse's book refers to his narrative as "[t]he breathtaking story of how America ducked chance after chance to save the Jews." A small number of subsequent books have furthered the discussion initiated by Morse. One might suppose that Pollard was familiar with some of this literature, or at least the history upon which it is based. One might add that not only were Israel's allies silent on the eve of the Six-Day War, but with the outbreak of the Yom Kippur War of October, 1973, when initially the Israelis, who deliberately avoided the pre-emptive strike strategy of 1967, were being bombarded and pushed back, the Nixon administration and its Secretary of State, Henry Kissinger, both denied additional arms to the beleaguered Israelis until the eleventh hour—although a substantial arms airlift did eventuate—and presented themselves as unable to push toward a negotiated ceasefire until the eventual Israeli counter-attack had encircled the Egyptian fifth army and the Israelis were on the roads to both Cairo and Damascus. Within this historical context, Pollard's paranoia on behalf of Israel is not entirely far-fetched—which is a separate matter from the (il)legality of his actions.

520. See Primo Levi, *The Drowned and the Saved*, (New York: Summit Books, 1989), chapter one. Moreover, if he is the psychopath with an 007 complex that Ronald Olive—a retired Naval officer, where he led the Pollard investigation—accuses him of being in his book, *Capturing Jonathan Pollard: How One of the Most Notorious Spies in American History was Brought to Justice* (Annapolis, MD: Naval Institute Press, 2006), then nothing Pollard says or writes may be taken at face-value. So do we take Olive at face value regarding Pollard? The "dialogue" between them is for the most part a disputation with only one side speaking—but that does not negate the Levian possibility regarding Pollard's words. See below, 449-450.

521. Olive asserts that he was paid about $2500 per month and that he and his wife, Anne, were provided with several first class trips to Europe and Israel.

522. Olive asserts that "Pollard passed more secrets to a foreign power (360-plus cubic feet of paper), in the shortest amount of time, than any spy before or after him." So if we do not know exactly what he passed along, we do have an (unverifiable) assertion regarding the volume of documents concerned.

523. This is, of course, how the Trial of Alfred Ducytus was handled, for the same theoretical reason.

524. In a conversation in October, 2012 with one of Pollard's lead attorneys I was informed that eventually they did see the memorandum.

525. In terms of disputational and definitional issues within this context, it

might be noted that in John A. Walker, Jr.'s foreword to the book by George P. Morse, *America Twice Betrayed: Reversing 50 Years of Government Security Failure*, the convicted spy, writing from his jail cell, asserts at the end of the second paragraph that "I disagree with Mr. Morse when he refers to espionage as treason, [which is] an entirely different matter." On Walker, see 441ff.

526. The source is quoted, albeit anonymously, in the June 16, 1986 issue of *Time*, 14-15.

527. As with the Rosenberg case, there have been and will continue to be articles and books arguing different points of view. The most damning work indicting Pollard is the aforementioned book by Ron Olive, *Capturing Jonathan Pollard*—but Pollard's wife, Esther (he married her from prison some time after his divorce from Anne; see fn 529) noted in a November 19, 2006 Op Ed piece in *The Jerusalem Post* that "Olive's assertions are "old lies...repackaged..., an exercise in "speculation, rumor, myths and lies." An Op Ed piece a week later (also in *The Jerusalem Post*) by Pollard's pro bono lawyers since 2000, Eliot Lauer and Jacques Semmelman tears Olive's assertions apart on the well-argued and detailed grounds that Olive makes claims that are impossible unless he had access to classified documents which he claims not to have had and which, legally, he cannot have had.

528. This is purely speculative on my part, but the fact that the Iran-Contra scandal blew up in the face of the Reagan administration in the midst of this affair—November, 1986—suggests the possibility that one motive for wanting more rather than less darkness attached to the Pollard narrative may have been to distract from that scandal. See below, the American public regarding Weinberger's role in the Iran-Contra scandal.

529. His wife received two concurrent five-year sentences, and she ended up serving only the forty months required as a maximum pre-parole sentence. She moved subsequently to Israel where her medical and other basic needs were largely met by "The Public Committee for Jonathan Pollard in Israel." She eventually moved back to the United States, settling in California. Anne and Jonathan were also divorced soon after her release from prison, (allegedly because he did not wish to keep her tied down to someone in prison for life) although she continued and continues to be active with those groups seeking his freedom from prison.

530. Shortly before his death of pneumonia in 2006, Weinberger made the statement that Pollard's punishment was unduly harsh—not that that statement has made a difference.

531. Named for Massachusetts Democratic Congressman, Edward Patrick Boland, who proposed it, the Boland Amendment was the name given to three U.S. legislative amendments passed between December, 1982 and December, 1984 that were all designed to limit American government assistance to the Contras in their struggle against the Sandinista government of Nicaragua.

532. Pollard's accusers and detractors assert that his efforts inherently undermined the U.S.-Israeli relationship, but they further claim that relations between the U.S. and the Arabo-Islamic world were harmed due to the perception in that world that the balance of power has shifted unfairly to Israel though the American Pollard's intervention—and that, moreover, if the Israelis, in possession of sensitive American security information through Pollard were to end up selling it to the Soviets, American security would be compromised. Few rational analysts embraced the second and even fewer the third of these assertions, however.

533. I referenced his foreword to George P. Morse's book, *America Twice Betrayed*, above, n 525.

534. And/or after having been compromised by an FBI spy named Martynov, who overheard a conversation by chance in Moscow and subsequently played a key role in compromising Walker's cover—which is the spin offered by former FBI agent Victor Cherkashin in his book, *Spy Handler*, rather than the more prevalent story that credits Barbara with primary responsibility for Walker's fall.

535. In the affidavits from Rear Admiral William Studeman, Director of Naval intelligence, aside from his assertions that pointed to the spy ring in general, he noted, for example that "Whitworth compromised detailed plans for primary, secondary and emergency communications circuits, which are used by the National Command Authority [i.e., President Reagan] to maintain contact with operational units," and that, as a consequence of his efforts the Soviets can now gauge the "true capabilities and vulnerabilities of the U.S. Navy [and] identify the specific steps which could achieve the greatest gains" with regard to the efficient operation of their fleet. But it is not clear to me how and why Whitworth would, as the subordinate of Walker, be singled out as having been more nefarious and therefore worthy of more profound punishment than Walker, unless, perhaps, we take into account the plea-bargain process.

536. Statements by Walker are from P. Earley, *Family of Spies: Inside the John Walker Spy Ring.* (New York: Bantam Books, 1988).

537. In fact the headline in the brief February 17, 2000 AP (Boston) article that provoked the blog comment reads "Soviet Spy Michael Walker Goes Free—No Protest from CIA or Congress."

538. See, for example, the discussions in the articles by Larry Yudelson, "Next Stage in Pollard Case: Parole Push Gains Momentum, in the April 1-7, 1994 issue of the *South Florida Jewish Tribune*, 8—in which President Clinton is quoted, thusly informed by the Justice Department and his advisors, as referring to Pollard as having committed "one of the most serious crimes against our country," and also to "the considerable damage that his actions caused our nation"—and by Sam Skolnik, "New flap erupts over Pollard: CIA charges that prisoner is 'continuing security risk'," in the December 1, 1994 issue of the *Washington Jewish Week*, 3.

539. In the aforementioned Skolnik article, Seymour Reich, former President of B'nai B'rith International and then-President of the Zionist Organization of America, is quoted as asserting that "once again, anonymous sources in the American intelligence community have repeated the ludicrous and unfounded charge that Jonathan Pollard has sought to reveal classified information from behind prison bars. As in the past, this charge has been curiously timed to coincide with a high-level U.S.-Israel meeting at which the Pollard case may be raised... [T]here are those in the intelligence community who want to keep Jonathan in jail for life." Is Reich being paranoid? Perhaps—but the assertion by the CIA official, Colin Jellish, to the Intelligence Committee, that, thanks to a prodigious memory Pollard was still in possession of piles of classified intelligence information which he was attempting to forward to the Israelis from behind bars in his outgoing correspondence (all of which is passed through hyper-focused scrutiny by prison and naval intelligence authorities) could hardly be more absurd. So who is paranoid of whom?

540. See Lynn Fischer, ed., *Security Awareness in the 1980s: Feature Articles from Security Awareness Bulletin, 1981-89*, 61-9. Several other cases mentioned in my discussion, as well as many more that I don't mention, are discussed in other parts of that book.

541. His lawyers have argued that he should be eligible for parole after 17 years. The charges to which he pleaded guilty resulted from a plea bargain that

reduced them from a ten-fold charge that, had he been found guilty, could have led to a sentence of three life-terms.

542. Eric Lichtblau, "Jailed C.I.A. Mole Kept Spying For Russia, via Son, U.S. Says," *New York Times*, Friday, January 20, 2009, A1 and A14.

543. He pleaded guilty to and was convicted of selling the identities of fellow C.I.A. officers to the Russians—with a range of possible consequences, from compromising their ability to transmit useful information to the United States to their deaths.

544. See above, nn 520-22.

545. *Capturing Jonathan Pollard*, IX.

546. Robert Eringer, "Poor Jonathan Pollard," *The Investigator*, January 24, 2009.

547. *Capturing Jonathan Pollard*, X.

548. Ibid, XII.

549. "Poor Jonathan Pollard," 1.

550. Those judged by the Inquisition were either innocent of being crypto-Jews or guilty, having been forced, however, by an anti-Jewish, Church-led monarchy to hide their Judaism in order to survive. Dreyfus was innocent of betraying France to its Prussian enemy. Pollard was guilty of transmitting military information of some sort to the United States' ally, Israel. So I don't mean to equate the three situations, except in terms of how we judge the sources of information available to us regarding them.

551. *Capturing Jonathan Pollard*, 89.

552. *Ibid*, XII.

553. The article, on page 40, is actually the write-up of a speech he had delivered on December 20, 1992 to a Pollard rally.

554. By the early 1990s and the time of the Clinton administration that distancing became much more minimal (but not by any means non-existent) in the American Jewish community.

555. *Jerusalem Post*, (Foreign Service), March 10, 1987.

556. Avineri's perspective may be that of an Israeli eager to affirm the greater psychological comfort of Israeli than American Jews—which is another issue altogether. Since the founding of the State of Israel there has always been an undercurrent of debate between the two communities regarding their relative existential difficulties—the trials that the one points out that the other is compelled by its circumstances to endure. In any case, it might be noted that the fear that Avineri perceived, to whatever extent it was there at the time of his writing, explicitly dissipated somewhat—perhaps a good deal—a few years later. See the uncredited JTA news service article, "U.S. Jewish community less wary about reaching out to Pollard," that appeared, among other places, in the November 3, 1989 issue of the *Cleveland Jewish News*, 53.

557. The article appears on page 10.

558. The book, *Legend or History (Fabia o Storia): San Domenicino de Val*, was being distributed every August to parishioners of and visitors to the San Domenichino Church of Marina di Massa in its commemoration of the alleged crucifixion and bleeding to death, for ritual purposes, of five-year-old Domenicino de Val, in 1250, by the Jews of Saragossa, Spain.

559. See above, 65-6.

560. See above, Chapter Two,41-52.

561. Now, that would be *superstitio*, wouldn't it?

562. As recently as in an April, 2009, article by Jeff Stein in *Congressional*

Quarterly, Rep. Jane Harman, a California Democrat with a longtime involvement in intelligence issues was subject to an NSA wiretap the result of which was an assertion—which she vigorously denied as "an outrageous and recycled canard" about which "those who are peddling these false accusations should be ashamed of themselves"—that she offered to "a suspected Israeli agent" to intervene in an espionage-related case against two AIPAC officials (the primary pro-Israel lobby on Capitol Hill), back in 2005, in exchange for support in a campaign to chair the Congressional Intelligence Committee. Interestingly, the transcripts are apparently not available—and the Harman investigation was "dropped for 'lack of evidence' "—but that did not prevent the article's author from quoting an anonymous source as asserting that the transcripts were damning, nor from offering a headline "Sources: Wiretap Recorded Rep. Harman Promising to Intervene for AIPAC" as if it were both a proven fact and a current event. One could just as easily argue from the bits of the alleged conversation provided in the article that Harman emphatically rejected the idea of such an "exchange" and therefore abruptly terminated the conversation. Perhaps the more interesting question is why the phone of a US Congresswoman was being tapped by the NSA in the first place. Was it because she was both involved in intelligence issues and part of a particular—Jewish—"ethnicity" and therefore inherently suspect of such questionable behavior and loyalty where the U.S. and Israel are concerned? That is impossible to determine with any certainty, of course. But a subsequent spate of articles (eg, *New York Times*, April 5, 22, and 29, 2009) suggest that it was the unnamed person with whom she was speaking who was being wiretapped, and she just happened to be the one on the other end of that person's conversation. Harman has demanded that the transcripts of that conversation be released; the Justice Department has said they cannot, for security reasons. So on the one hand, she is being subject, Spanish Inquisition-style, minimally to innuendo and maximally to accusation—and the report of the wire-tapped conversation may (or may not) have lost Harman the chairmanship of the Intelligence Committee—and on the other, we citizens of this democracy are not in a position to be able to judge whether that style is necessary for our own protection. Whom do we believe? The beat goes on.

563. I say "almost" since the Japanese American population was certainly subject to such suspicion during World War II—although that was during war time and we were at war with Japan (which does not make the incarceration of Japanese Americans at that time any less despicable or unjust, particularly in comparison to the non-incarceration of German Americans or Italian Americans). And of course, Catholic Americans have periodically been suspected of greater loyalty to the Pope than to the United States by some Protestant Americans—a factor in presidential politics from the time of Al Smith (see above, Massena, 258) to that of JFK.

564. At least two sources carried this story in 1993: an unsigned article in the *Los Angeles Times*, from June 6, 1993, A6; and a longish article by Yossi Melman in the October, 1993 issue of *Moment Magazine*. The Israeli military had successfully imposed absolute media silence regarding the case between the time of Amit's arrest on March 24, 1986 and 1993.

565. Interestingly, the January 12, 2009 issue of *Newsweek* offered a small article on page 10 by Dan Ephron, in which the author writes that for the first time Pollard himself was asking outgoing President Bush for a commutation of his sentence—with the intention of getting back into the world in order "to work on helping develop alternative sources of energy so that the U.S. can reduce its independence on foreign oil." At the time, former CIA Director James Woolsey said he would support the request if Pollard both showed contrition and agreed to "re-

nounce any profits from books or other projects linked to the case." Woolsey had advised President Clinton to resist the requests on Pollard's behalf by Israeli officials in the 1990s—and apparently whoever advised President Bush convinced him to resist Pollard's own request. He remains behind bars. The unresolved nature of the situation is reflected further in a September 19, 2009 article in the *Washington Jewish Week* that transmits an article from the *Jerusalem Post*, in which a retired Israeli judge, Israel's State Comptroller, Micha Lindenstrauss—in defending Israel against the accusation of not having done enough to help secure Pollard's release—suggests, based on the view of "professor Kenneth Mann, a well-known expert in U.S. and criminal law," that "Pollard apparently did not enjoy his constitutional right of due legal process. He cites the U.S. Constitution's Fifth Amendment…" The quoted response of Pollard's wife, Esther, ignores this issue, focusing her rancor, rather, on the Israeli government, for attempting "to whitewash the betrayal and abandonment of an Israeli agent in peril by successive governments of Israel," by means of Lindenstrauss's report.

566. In yet another twist to this narrative, Ariel Toaff, a professor of history at Bar-Ilan University, and the son of Elio Toaff, referred to as Italy's most beloved rabbi, came out with a book, *Pasque di Sangue: Ebrei d'Europa e omicidi rituali (Passover of Blood: The Jews of Europe and Ritual Murder)*—in 2007—in which he asserts that in some Ashkenazi (Central European Jewish) communities in the fifteenth century, the ritual slaughter of Christians, for the purposes of drinking their blood, was practiced in secret. The basis for Toaff's assertion—which will be familiar to the reader of this text—is a number of confessions by torture extracted from some Jews in Central Europe at that time. Not surprisingly, Toaff's book has created something of a scandal and his academic colleagues have lambasted him for the methodological flaw they see in it: that he takes words uttered under torture at face value. Given the strict prohibitions against even eating animal meat that still shows traces of blood on or in it, the notion, as we have seen, is preposterous. That does not mean that an academic—even a Jewish academic (pace Hannah Arendt!)—interested in acquiring notoriety won't promote the notion.

Index